for

Martin P. Levine
(1950–1993)

colleague, coauthor, friend

CONTENTS

PART FIVE
MEN AND HEALTH: BODY AND MIND   235

PREFACE

Over the past ten years, we have been teaching courses on the male experience, or "men's lives." Our courses have reflected both our own education and recent research by feminist scholars and profeminist men in U.S. society. (By profeminist men, we mean active supporters of women's efforts against male violence and claims for equal opportunity, political participation, sexual autonomy, family reform, and equal education.) Gender, scholars have demonstrated, is a central feature of social life—one of the chief organizing principles around which our lives revolve. Gender shapes our identities and the institutions in which we find ourselves. In the university, women's studies programs and courses about women in traditional disciplines have explored the meaning of gender in women's lives. But what does it mean to be a man in contemporary U.S. society?

This anthology is organized around specific themes that define masculinity and the issues men confront over the course of their lives. In addition, a social-constructionist perspective has been included that examines how men actively construct masculinity within a social and historical context. Related to this construction and integrated in our examination are the variations that exist among men in relation to class, race, and sexuality.

We begin Part One with issues and questions that unravel the "masculine mystique" and reveal various dimensions of men's position in society and their relationships with women and with other men. Parts Two through Nine examine the different issues that emerge for men at different times of their lives and the ways in which their lives change over time. We touch on central moments related to boyhood, adolescence, sports, occupations, marriage, and fatherhood, and explore men's emotional and sexual relationships with women and with other men. The final part, "Men and the Future," explores some of the ways in which men are changing and some possible directions by which they might continue to change.

Although a major component of the traditional, normative definition of masculinity is independence, we are pleased to acknowledge those colleagues and friends whose criticism and support have been a constant help throughout our work on this project. Karen Hanson, our editor at Allyn and Bacon, inherited this project and has embraced it as her own, facilitating our work at every turn. Chris Cardone and Bruce Nichols, our original editors, were supportive from the start and helped get the project going. Many other scholars who work on issues of masculinity, such as Bob Blauner, Robert Brannon, Harry Brod, Rocco Capraro, Bob Connell, James Harrison, Jeff Hearn, Martin Levine, Joe Pleck, Tony Rotundo, Don Sabo, and Peter Stein, have contributed to a supportive intellectual community in which to work.

We also thank the following reviewers for their helpful comments and suggestions: Margaret Anderson, University of Delaware; Judith Barker, Ithaca College; Nicola Beisel, Northwestern University; Bob Blauner, University of California, Berkeley; Chip Capraro, Hobart and William Smith Colleges; Douglas Gertner, Colorado State University; Christopher Kilmartin, Mary Washington College; Dr. H. Elaine Lindgren, North Dakota State University; Ron Matson, The Wichita State University; Michael

Messina-Yauchzy, Syracuse University; Joyce M. Nielsen, University of Colorado at Boulder; Beth Rushing, Kent State University; Don Sabo, D'Youville College; Kathleen Tiemann, University of North Dakota; Diane Villwock, Morehead State University; Tim Wernette, University of Arizona; and Carol S. Wharton, University of Richmond. Colleagues at the State University of New York at Stony Brook and the University of Southern California have also been supportive of this project. We are especially grateful to Diane Barthel, Ruth Schwartz Cowan, John Gagnon, Barry Glassner, Norman Goodman, Nilufer Isvan, Carol Jacklin, and Barrie Thorne. A fellowship from the Lilly Foundation has generously supported Kimmel's work on pedagogical issues of teaching about men and masculinity.

This book is the product of the profeminist men's movement as well—a loose network of men who support a feminist critique of traditional masculinity and women's struggles to enlarge the scope of their personal autonomy and public power. These men are engaged in a variety of efforts to transform masculinity in ways that allow men to live fuller, richer, and healthier lives. The editors of *Changing Men* (with whom we work as Book Review Editor and Sports Editor), Mike Biernbaum and Rick Cote, have labored for more than a decade to provide a forum for antisexist men. We acknowledge their efforts with gratitude and respect.

Our families, friends, and colleagues have provided a rare atmosphere that combines intellectual challenge and emotional support. We are grateful to Judith Brisman, Martin Duberman, and Eli Zal, Kate Ellis, Frances Goldin, Cathy Greenblat, Pam Hatchfield, Sandi Kimmel, David Levin, Mary Morris and Larry O'Connor, Lillian and Hank Rubin, and Mitchell Tunick. We want especially to acknowledge our fathers and mothers for providing such important models—not of being women or men, but of being adults capable of career competence, emotional warmth, and nurturance (these are not masculine or feminine traits). Finally, we thank Pierrette Hondagneu and Iona Mara-Drita, who have lived with this project since its beginning. We are grateful that they share these men's lives.

In our last edition, we welcomed Miles Hondagneu-Messner, who is probably now almost ready to read these words. We now welcome his brother Sasha with the same hopes for a new masculinity based on compassion, caring, and the ability to penetrate a zone defense.

We dedicate this edition of *Men's Lives* to Martin P. Levine with aching sadness at the loss of a dear friend and with deep gratitude that such a fine man touched our lives. As the founder of the Gay and Lesbian Caucus of the American Sociological Association as well as the Sociologist AIDS Network, Marty was a central figure in bringing the concerns of the gay and lesbian communities to the mainstream of our discipline. We have been pleased to publish his work in each edition of *Men's Lives* and dedicate ourselves to help end AIDS and the prejudices accompanying it that together took his life.

M.S.K.
M.A.M.

INTRODUCTION

This is a book about men. But, unlike other books about men, which line countless library shelves, this is a book about men *as men*. It is a book in which men's experiences are not taken for granted as we explore the "real" and significant accomplishments of men, but a book in which those experiences are treated as significant and important in themselves.

MEN AS "GENDERED BEINGS"

But what does it mean to examine men "as men"? Most courses in a college curriculum are about men, aren't they? But these courses routinely deal with men only in their public roles, so we come to know and understand men as scientists, politicians, military figures, writers, and philosophers. Rarely, if ever, are men understood through the prism of gender.

But listen to some male voices from some of these "ungendered" courses. Take, for example, composer Charles Ives, debunking "sissy" types of music; he said he used traditional tough guy themes and concerns in his drive to build new sounds and structures out of the popular musical idiom (cf. Wilkinson, 1986: 103). Or architect Louis Sullivan, describing his ambition to create "masculine forms": strong, solid, commanding respect. Or novelist Ernest Hemingway, retaliating against literary enemies by portraying them as impotent or homosexual.

Consider also political figures, such as Cardinal Richelieu, the seventeenth-century French First Minister to Louis XIII, who insisted that it was "necessary to have masculine virtue and do everything by reason" (cited in Elliott, 1984: 20). Closer to home, recall President Lyndon Baines Johnson's dismissal of a political adversary: "Oh him. He has to squat to piss!" Or his boast that during the Tet offensive in the Vietnam War, he "didn't just screw Ho Chi Minh. I cut his pecker off!"

Democrats have no monopoly on unexamined gender coloring their political rhetoric. Richard Nixon was "afraid of being acted upon, of being inactive, of being soft, or being thought impotent, of being dependent upon anyone else," according to his biographer, Bruce Mazlish. And don't forget Vice-President George Bush's revealing claim that in his television debate with Democratic challenger Geraldine Ferraro he had "kicked ass." (That few political pundits criticized such unapologetic glee concerning violence against women is again indicative of how invisible gender issues are in our culture.) Indeed, recent political campaigns have revolved, in part, around gender issues, as each candidate attempted to demonstrate that he was not a "wimp" but was a "real man." (Of course, the few successful female politicians face the double task of convincing the electorate that they are not the "weak-willed wimps" that their gender implies in the public mind while *at the same time* demonstrating that they are "real women.")

These are just a few examples of what we might call gendered speech, language that uses gender terms to make its case. And these are just a few of the thousands of examples one could find in every academic discipline of how men's lives are organized around gender issues, and how gender remains one of the organizing principles of social life. We come to know ourselves and our world through the prism of gender. Only we act as if we didn't know it.

Fortunately, in recent years, the pioneering work of feminist scholars, both in traditional disciplines and in women's studies, and of feminist women in the political arena has made us aware of the centrality of gender in our lives. Gender, these scholars have demonstrated, is a central feature of social life, one of the central organizing principles around which our lives revolve. In the social sciences, gender has now taken its place alongside class and race as the three central mechanisms by which power and resources are distributed in our society, and the three central themes out of which we fashion the meanings of our lives.

We certainly understand how this works for women. Through women's studies courses and also in courses about women in traditional disciplines, students have explored the complexity of women's lives, the hidden history of exemplary women, and the daily experiences of women in the routines of their lives. For women, we know how gender works as one of the formative elements out of which social life is organized.

THE INVISIBILITY OF GENDER: A SOCIOLOGICAL EXPLANATION

Too often, though, we treat men as if they had no gender, as if only their public personae were of interest to us as students and scholars, as if their interior experience of gender was of no significance. This became evident when one of us was in a graduate seminar on Feminist Theory several years ago. A discussion between a white woman and a black woman revolved around the question of whether their similarities as women were greater than their racial differences as black and white. The white woman asserted that the fact that they were both women bonded them, in spite of their racial differences. The black woman disagreed.

"When you wake up in the morning and look in the mirror, what do you see?" she asked.

"I see a woman," replied the white woman.

"That's precisely the issue," replied the black woman. "I see a black woman. For me, race is visible every day, because it is how I am not privileged in this culture. Race is invisible to you, which is why our alliance will always seem somewhat false to me."

Witnessing this exchange, Michael Kimmel was startled. When he looked in the mirror in the morning, he saw, as he put it, "a human being: universally generalizable. The generic person." What had been concealed—that he possessed both race and gender—had become strikingly visible. As a white man, he was able not to think about the ways in which gender and race had affected his experiences.

There is a sociological explanation for this blind spot in our thinking: the mechanisms that afford us privilege are very often invisible to us. What makes us marginal (unempowered, oppressed) are the mechanisms that we understand, because those are the ones that are most painful in daily life. Thus, white people rarely think of themselves as "raced" people, rarely think of race as a central element in their experience. But people of color are marginalized by race, and so the centrality of race is both painfully obvious and urgently needs study. Similarly, middle-class people do not acknowledge the importance of social class as an organizing principle of social life, largely because for them class is an invisible force that makes everyone look pretty much the same. Working-class people, on the other hand, are often painfully aware of the centrality of class in their lives. (Interestingly, upper-class people are often more aware of class dynamics than are middle-class people. In part, this may be the result of the emphasis on status within the upper class, as lineage, breeding, and family honor take center stage. In part, it may also be the result of a peculiar marginalization of the upper class in our society, as in the overwhelming number of television shows and movies that are ostensibly about just plain [i.e., middle-class] folks.)

In this same way, men often think of themselves as genderless, as if gender did not matter in the daily experiences of our lives. Certainly, we can see the biological sex of individuals, but we rarely understand the ways in which *gender*—that complex of social meanings that is attached to biological sex—is enacted in our daily lives. For example, we treat male scientists as if their being men had nothing to do with the organization of their experiments, the logic of scientific inquiry, or the questions posed by science itself. We treat male political figures as if masculinity were not even remotely in their consciousness as they do battle in the political arena.

This book takes a position directly opposed to such genderlessness for men. We believe that men are also "gendered," and that this gendering process, the transformation of biological males into socially interacting men, is a central experience for men. That we are unaware of it only helps to perpetuate the inequalities based on gender in our society.

In this book, we will examine the various ways in which men are gendered. We have gathered together some of the most interesting, engaging, and convincing materials from the past decade that have been written about men. We believe that *Men's Lives* will allow readers to explore the meanings of masculinity in contemporary U.S. culture in a new way.

EARLIER EFFORTS TO STUDY MEN

Certainly, researchers have been examining masculinity for a long time. Historically, there have been three general models that have governed social scientific research on men and masculinity. *Biological models* have focused on the ways in which innate biological differences between males and females programmed different social behaviors. *Anthropological models* have examined masculinity cross-culturally, stressing the variations in the behaviors and attributes associated with being a man. And, until recently, *sociological models* have stressed how socialization of boys and girls included accommodation to a "sex role" specific to one's biological sex. Although each of these perspectives helps to understand the meaning of masculinity and femininity, each is also limited in its ability to fully explain how gender operates in any culture.

Relying on differences in reproductive biology, some scholars have argued that the physiological organization of males and females makes the differences we observe in psychological temperament and social behaviors inevitable. One perspective holds that differences in endocrine functioning are the cause of gender difference, that testosterone predisposes males toward aggression, competition, and violence, whereas estrogen predisposes females toward passivity, tenderness, and exaggerated emotionality. Others insist that these observed behavioral differences derive from the differences between the size or number of sperm and eggs. Since a male can produce 100 million sperm with each ejaculation, whereas a female can produce fewer than 20 eggs capable of producing healthy offspring over the course of her life, these authors suggest that men's "investment" in their offspring is significantly less than women's investment. Other authors arrive at the same conclusion by suggesting that the different size of egg and sperm, and the fact that the egg is the source of the food supply, impels temperamental differences. Reproductive "success" to males means the insemination of as many females as possible; to females, reproductive success means carefully choosing one male to mate with and insisting that he remain present to care for and support their offspring. Still other authors argue that male and female behavior is governed by different halves of the brain; males are ruled by the left hemisphere, which controls rationality and abstract thought, whereas females are governed by the right hemisphere, which controls emotional affect and creativity. (For examples of these works, see Wilson, 1976; Trivers, 1972; Goldberg, 1975; and Goldberg, 1986.)

Observed normative temperamental differences between women and men that are assumed to be of biological origin are easily translated into political prescriptions. In this ideological sleight of hand, what is *normative* (i.e., what is prescribed) is translated into what is *normal*, and the mechanisms of this transformation are the assumed biological imperative. George Gilder, for example, assembles the putative biological differences between women and men into a call for a return to traditional gender roles. Gilder believes that male sexuality is, by nature, wild and lusty, "insistent" and "incessant," careening out of control and threatening anarchic disorder, unless it can be controlled and constrained. This is the task of women. When women refuse to apply the brakes to male sexuality—by asserting their own or by choosing to pursue a life outside the domestic sphere—they abandon their "natural" function for illusory social gains. Sex education, abortion, and birth control are all condemned as facilitating women's escape from biological necessity. Similarly, he argues against women's employment, since the "unemployed man can contribute little to the community and will often disrupt it, but the woman may even do more good without a job than with one" (Gilder, 1986: 86).

The biological argument has been challenged by many scholars on several grounds. The implied causation between two observed sets of differences (biological differences and different behaviors) is misleading, since there is no logical reason to assume that one caused the other, or that the line of causation moves only from the biological to the social. The selection of biological evidence is partial, and generalizations from "lower" animal species to human beings are always suspect. One sociologist asks if these differences are "natural," why their enforcement must be coercive, why males and females have to be forced to assume the rules that they are naturally supposed to play (see Epstein, 1986:8). And one primatologist argues that the evidence adduced to support the current status quo might also lead to precisely the opposite conclusions, that biological differences would impel female promiscuity and male fragility (see Hrdy, 1981). Biological differences between males and females would appear to set some parameters for differences in social behavior, but would not dictate the temperaments of men and women in any one culture. These psychological and social differences would appear to be the result far more of the ways in which cultures interpret, shape, and modify these biological inheritances. We may be born males or females, but we become men and women in a cultural context.

Anthropologists have entered the debate at this point, but with different positions. For example, some anthropologists have suggested that the universality of gender differences comes from specific cultural adaptations to the environment, whereas others describe the cultural variations of gender roles, seeking to demonstrate the fluidity of gender and the primacy of cultural organization. Lionel Tiger and Robin Fox argue that the sexual division of labor is universal because of the different nature of bonding for males and females. "Nature," they argue, "intended mother and child to be together" because she is the source of emotional security and food; thus, cultures have prescribed various behaviors for women that emphasize nurturance and emotional connection (Tiger and Fox, 1984: 304). The bond between men is forged through the necessity of "competitive cooperation" in hunting; men must cooperate with members of their own tribe in the hunt and yet compete for scarce resources with men in other tribes. Such bonds predispose men toward the organization of the modern corporation or governmental bureaucracy.

Such anthropological arguments omit as much as they include, and many scholars have pointed out problems with the model. Why did not intelligence become sex linked, as this model (and the biological model) would imply? Such positions also reveal a marked conservatism: the differences between women and men are the differences that nature or cultural evolution intended, and are therefore not to be tampered with.

Perhaps the best known challenge to this anthropological argument is the work of Margaret Mead. Mead insisted that the variations among cultures in their prescriptions of gender roles required the conclusion that culture was the more decisive cause of these differences. In her classic study, *Sex and Temperament in Three Primitive Societies* (1935), Mead observed such wide variability among gender role prescriptions—and such marked differences from our own—that any universality implied by biological or anthropological models had to be rejected. And although the empirical accuracy of Mead's work has been challenged in its specific arguments, the general theoretical arguments remain convincing.

Psychological theories have also contributed to the discussion of gender roles, as psychologists have specified the specific developmental sequences for both males and females. Earlier theorists observed psychological distancing from the mother as the precondition for independence and autonomy, or suggested a sequence that placed the capacity for abstract reason as the developmental stage beyond relational reasoning. Since it is normative for males to exhibit independence and the capacity for abstract reason, it was argued that males are more successful at negotiating these psychological passages, and implied that women somehow lagged behind men on the ladder of developmental success. (Such arguments may be found in Freud, Erikson, and Kohlberg.)

But these models, too, have been challenged, most recently by sociologist Nancy Chodorow, who argued that women's ability to connect contains a more fundamentally human trait than the male's need to distance, and by psychologist Carol Gilligan, who claimed that women's predisposition toward relational reasoning may contain a more humane strategy of thought than recourse to abstract principles. Regardless of our assessment of these arguments, Chodorow and Gilligan rightly point out that the highly ideological assumptions that make masculinity the normative standard against which the psychological development of *both* males and females was measured would inevitably make femininity problematic and less fully developed. Moreover, Chodorow explicitly insists that these "essential" differences between women and men are socially constructed and thus subject to change.

Finally, sociologists have attempted to synthesize these three perspectives into a systematic explanation of "sex roles." These are the collection of attitudes, attributes, and behaviors that is seen as appropriate for males and appropriate for females. Thus, masculinity is associated with technical mastery, aggression, competitiveness, and cognitive abstraction, whereas femininity is associated with emotional nurturance, connectedness, and passivity. Sex role theory informed a wide variety of prescriptive literature (self-help books) that instructed parents on what to do if they wanted their child to grow up as a healthy boy or girl.

The strongest challenge to all these perspectives, as we have seen, came from feminist scholars, who have specified the ways in which the assumptions about maturity, development, and health all made masculinity the norm against which both genders were measured. In all the social sciences, these feminist scholars have stripped these early studies of their academic facades to reveal the unexamined ideological assumptions contained within them. By the early 1970s, women's studies programs began to articulate a new paradigm for the study of gender, one that assumed nothing about men or women beforehand, and that made no assumptions about which gender was more highly developed. And by the mid 1970s, the first group of texts about men appeared that had been inspired by these pioneering efforts by feminist scholars.

THINKING ABOUT MEN: THE FIRST GENERATION

In the mid 1970s, the first group of works on men and masculinity appeared that was directly influenced by these feminist critiques of the traditional explanations for gender differences. Some books underscored the costs to men of traditional gender role prescriptions, exploring how some aspects of men's lives and experiences are constrained and underdeveloped by the relentless pressure to exhibit other behaviors associated with masculinity. Books such as Marc Feigen-Fasteau's *The Male Machine* (1974) and Warren Farrell's *The Liberated Man* (1975) discussed the costs to men's health—both physical and psychological—and the quality of relationships with women, other men, and their children of the traditional male sex role.

Several anthologies explored the meanings of masculinity in the United States by adopting a feminist-inspired prism through which to view men and masculinity. For example, Deborah David and Robert Brannon's *The Forty-Nine Percent Majority* (1976) and Joseph Pleck and Jack Sawyer's *Men and Masculinity* (1974) presented panoramic views of men's lives, from within a framework that accepted the feminist critique of traditional gender arrangements. Elizabeth Pleck and Joseph Pleck's *The American Man* (1980) suggested an historical evolution of contemporary themes. These works explored both the "costs" and the privileges of being a man in modern U.S. society.

Perhaps the single most important book to criticize the normative organization of the male sex role was Joseph Pleck's *The Myth of Masculinity* (1981). Pleck carefully deconstructed the constituent elements of the male sex role, and reviewed the empirical literature for each component part. After demonstrating that the empirical literature did not support these normative features, Pleck argued that the male sex role model was incapable of describing men's experiences. In its place, he posited a male "sex role strain" model that specified the contemporary sex role as problematic, historically specific, and also an unattainable ideal.

Building on Pleck's work, a critique of the sex role model began to emerge. Sex roles had been cast as the static containers of behaviors and attitudes, and biological males and females were required to fit themselves into these containers, regardless of how ill-fitting these clusters of behaviors and attitudes felt. Such a model was ahistorical and suggested a false cultural universalism, and was therefore ill equipped to understand the ways in which sex roles change, and the ways in which individuals modify those roles through the enactments of gender expectations. Most telling, however, was the way in which the sex role model ignored the ways in which definitions of masculinity and femininity were based on, and reproduced, relationships of power. Not only do men as a group exert power over women as a group, but the definitions of masculinity and femininity reproduce those power relations. Power dynamics are an essential element in both the definition and the enactments of gender.

This first generation of research on masculinity was extremely valuable, particularly since it challenged the unexamined ideology that made masculinity the gender norm against which both men and women were measured. The old models of sex roles had reproduced the domination of men over women by insisting on the dominance of masculine traits over feminine traits. These new studies argued against both the definitions of either sex, and the social institutions in which those differences were embedded. A new model looked at "gender relations" and understood how the definition of either masculinity or femininity was relational, that is, how the definition of one gender depended, in part, on the understanding of the definition of the other.

In the early 1980s, the research on women again surged ahead of the research on men and masculinity. This time, however, the focus was not on the ways in which sex roles reproduce the power relations in society, but rather on the ways in which femininity is experienced differently by women in various social groups. Gradually, the notion of a single femininity—which was based on the white middle-class Victorian notion of female passivity, langorous beauty, and emotional responsiveness—was replaced by an examination of the ways in which women differ in their gender role expectations by race, class, age, sexual orientation, ethnicity, region, and nationality.

The research of men and masculinity is now entering a new stage, in which the variations among men are seen as central to the understanding of men's lives. The unexamined assumption in earlier studies had been that one version of masculinity—white, middle-age, middle-class, heterosexual—was the sex role into which all men were struggling to fit in our society. Thus, working-class men, men of color, gay men, and younger and older men were all observed as departing in significant ways from the traditional definitions of masculinity. Therefore, it was easy to see these men as enacting "problematic" or "deviant" versions of masculinity. Such theoretical assertions, however, reproduce precisely the power relationships that keep these men in subordinate positions in our society. It is not only that middle-class, middle-aged, heterosexual white masculinity becomes the standard against which all men are measured, but that this definition, itself, is used against those who do not fit as a way to keep them down. The normative definition of masculinity is not the "right" one, but it is the one that is dominant.

The challenge to the hegemonic definition of masculinity came from men whose masculinity was cast as deviant: men of color, gay men, and ethnic men. We understand now that we cannot speak of "masculinity" as a singular term, but must examine *masculinities*: the ways in which different men construct different versions of masculinity. Such a perspective can be seen in several recent works, such as Harry Brod's *The Making of Masculinities* (1987), Michael Kimmel's *Changing Men: New Directions in Research on Men and Masculinity* (1987), and Tim Carrigan, Bob Connell, and John Lee's "Toward a New Sociology of Masculinity" (1985). Bob Connell's *Gender and Power* (1987) and Jeff Hearn's *The Gender of Oppression* (1987) represent the most sophisticated theoretical statements of this perspective. Connell argues that the oppression of women is a chief mechanism that links the various masculinities, and that the marginalization of certain masculinities is an important component of the reproduction of male power over women. This critique of the hegemonic definition of masculinity as a perspective on men's lives is one of the organizing principles of our book, which is the first college-level text in this second generation of work on men and masculinities.

Now that we have reviewed some of the traditional explanations for gender relations, and have situated this book within the research on gender in general, and men in particular, let us briefly outline exactly the theoretical perspective we have employed in the book. Not only does our theoretical framework provide the organizing principle of the book as a whole, it also provided some of the criteria for the selection of the articles that are included.

THE SOCIAL CONSTRUCTION OF MASCULINITIES

Men are not born, growing from infants through boyhood to manhood, to follow a predetermined biological imperative, encoded in their physical organization. To be a man is to participate in social life as a man, as a gendered being. Men are not born; they are made. And men make themselves, actively constructing their masculinities within a social and historical context.

This book is about how men are made and how men make themselves in contemporary U.S. society. It is about what masculinity means, about how masculinity is organized, and about the social institutions that sustain and elaborate it. It is a book in which we will trace what it means to be a man over the course of men's lives.

Men's Lives revolves around three important themes that are part of a social scientific perspective. First, we have adopted a *social contructionist* perspective. By this we mean that the important fact of men's lives is not that they are biological males, but that they become men. Our sex may be male, but our identity as men is developed through a complex process of interaction with the culture in which we both learn the gender scripts appropriate to our culture, and attempt to modify those scripts to make them more palatable. The second axis around which the book is organized follows from our social constructionist perspective. As we have argued, the experience of masculinity is not uniform and universally generalizable to all men in our society. Masculinity differs dramatically in our society, and we have organized the book to illustrate the *variations* among men in the construction of masculinity. Third, we have adopted a *life course* perspective, to chart the construction of these various masculinities in men's lives, and to examine pivotal developmental moments or institutional locations during a man's life in which the meanings of masculinity are articulated. These three per-spectives—social constructionism, variations among men, and the life course per-spective—will define the organization of this book and the criteria we have used to select the articles included.

The Social Constructionist Model

The social constructionist perspective argues that the meaning of masculinity is nei-ther transhistorical nor culturally universal, but rather varies from culture to culture and within any one culture over time. Thus, males become men in the United States in the late twentieth century in a way that is very different from men in Southeast Asia, or Kenya, or Sri Lanka. The meaning of masculinity varies from culture to culture.

Men's lives also vary within any one culture over time. The experience of mas-culinity in the contemporary United States is very different from that experience 150 years ago. Who would argue that what it meant to be a "real man" in seventeenth-century France (at least among the upper classes)—high-heeled patent leather shoes, red velvet jackets covering frilly white lace shirts, lots of rouge and white powder makeup, and a taste for the elegant refinement of ornate furniture—bears much re-semblance to the meaning of masculinity among a similar class of French men today?

A perspective that emphasizes the social construction of gender is, therefore, both *historical* and *comparative*. It allows us to explore the ways in which the meanings of gender vary from culture to culture, and how they change within any one culture over historical time.

Variations Among Men

Masculinity also varies *within* any one society by the various types of cultural groups that compose it. Subcultures are organized around other poles, which are the primary way in which people organize themselves and by which resources are distributed. And men's experiences differ from one another in the ways in which social scientists have identified as the chief structural mechanisms along which power and resources are dis-tributed. We cannot speak of masculinity in the United States as if it were a single, eas-ily identifiable commodity. To do so is to risk positing one version of masculinity as normative, and making all other masculinities problematic.

In the contemporary United States, masculinity is constructed differently by class culture, by race and ethnicity, and by age. And each of these axes of masculinity mod-ifies the others. Black masculinity differs from white masculinity, yet each of them is also further modified by class and age. A 30-year-old middle-class black man will have some things in common with a 30-year-old middle-class white man that he might not share with a 60-year-old working-class black man, although he will share with him elements of masculinity that are different from the white man of his class and age. The resulting matrix of *masculinities* is complicated and often the elements are cross-cutting, but without understanding this, we risk collapsing all masculinities into one hegemonic version.

The challenge to a singular definition of masculinity as the normative definition is the second axis around which the readings in this book revolve.

③ The Life Course Perspective

The meaning of masculinity is not constant over the course of any man's life, but will change as he grows and matures. The issues confronting a man about proving himself, feeling successful, and the social institutions in which he will attempt to enact his definitions of masculinity will change throughout his life. Thus, we have adopted a *life course perspective* to discuss the ways in which different issues will emerge for men at different times of their lives, and the ways in which men's lives, themselves, change over time. The life course perspective we have employed will examine men's lives at various pivotal moments in their development from young boys to adults. Like a slide show, these points will freeze the action for a short while, to afford us the opportunity to examine in more detail the ways in which different men in our culture experience masculinity at any one time.

The book's organization reflects these three concerns. The first two parts set the context through which we shall examine men's lives. Parts Three through Nine follow those lives through their full course, examining central moments experienced by men in the United States today. Specifically, Parts Two and Three touch on boyhood and adolescence, discussing some of the institutions organized to embody and reproduce masculinities in the United States, such as fraternities, the Boy Scouts, and sports groups. Part Four, "Men and Work," explores the ways in which masculinities are constructed in relation to men's occupations. Part Five, "Men and Health: Body and Mind," deals with heart attacks, stress, AIDS, and other health problems among men. Part Six, "Men with Women: Intimacy and Power," describes men's emotional and sexual relationships. We deal with heterosexuality and homosexuality, mindful of the ways in which variations are based on specific lines (class, race, ethnicity). Part Seven, "Men with Men: Friendships and Fears," describes emotional and physical (but not necessarily sexual) relationships that men develop through their lives. Part Eight, "Male Sexualities," studies the normative elements of heterosexuality and probes the controversial political implications of pornography as a source of both straight and gay men's sexual information. Part Nine, "Men in Families," concentrates on masculinities within the family and the role of men as husbands, fathers, and senior citizens. Part Ten, "Men and the Future," examines some of the ways in which men are changing and points to some directions in which men might continue to change.

Our perspective, stressing the social construction of masculinities over the life course, will, we believe, allow a more comprehensive understanding of men's lives in the United States today.

REFERENCES

Brod, Harry, ed. *The Making of Masculinities.* Boston: Unwin, Hyman, 1987.

Carrigan, Tim, Bob Connell, and John Lee. "Toward a New Sociology of Masculinity" in *Theory and Society,* 1985, 5(14).

Chodorow, Nancy. *The Reproduction of Mothering.* Berkeley: University of California Press, 1978.

Connell, R. W. *Gender and Power.* Stanford, CA: Stanford University Press, 1987.

David, Deborah and Robert Brannon, eds. *The Forty-Nine Percent Majority.* Reading, MA: Addison-Wesley, 1976.

Elliott, J. H. *Richelieu and Olivares.* New York: Cambridge University Press, 1984.

Epstein, Cynthia Fuchs. "Inevitability of Prejudice" in *Society,* Sept. /Oct., 1986.

Farrell, Warren. *The Liberated Man.* New York: Random House, 1975.

Feigen-Fasteau, Marc. *The Male Machine.* New York: McGraw-Hill, 1974.

Gilligan, Carol. *In a Different Voice.* Cambridge, MA: Harvard University Press, 1982.

Gilder, George. *Men and Marriage.* Gretna, LA: Pelican Publishers, 1986.

Goldberg, Steven. *The Inevitability of Patriarchy.* New York: William Morrow & Co., 1975.

———. 1986. "Reaffirming the Obvious" in *Society*, Sept./Oct., 1986.

Hearn, Jeff. *The Gender of Oppression.* New York: St. Martin's Press, 1987.

Hrdy, Sandra Blaffer. *The Woman That Never Evolved.* Cambridge, MA: Harvard University Press, 1981.

Kimmel, Michael S., ed. *Changing Men: New Directions in Research on Men and Masculinity.* Newbury Park, CA: Sage Publications, 1987.

Mead, Margaret. *Sex and Temperament in Three Primitive Societies.* New York: McGraw-Hill, 1935.

Elizabeth Pleck and Joseph Pleck, eds. *The American Man.* Englewood Cliffs, NJ: Prentice-Hall, 1980.

Pleck, Joseph. *The Myth of Masculinity.* Cambridge, MA: M.I.T. Press, 1981.

——— and Jack Sawyer, eds. *Men and Masculinity.* Englewood Cliffs, NJ: Prentice-Hall, 1974.

Tiger, Lionel and Robin Fox. *The Imperial Animal.* New York: Holt, Rinehart & Winston, 1984.

Trivers, Robert. "Parental Investment and Sexual Selection" in *Sexual Selection and the Descent of Man* (B. Campbell, ed.). Chicago: Aldine Publishers, 1972.

Wilkinson, Rupert. *American Tough: The Tough Guy Tradition and American Character.* New York: Harper & Row, 1986.

Wilson, E. O. *Sociobiology: The New Synthesis.* Cambridge, MA: Harvard University Press, 1976.

PART ONE

PERSPECTIVES ON MASCULINITIES

A quick glance at any magazine rack or television talk-show is enough to make you aware that these days, men are confused. What does it mean to be a "real man"? How are men supposed to behave? What are men supposed to feel? How are men to express their feelings? Who are we supposed to be like: Tootsie or Rambo? Clint Eastwood or Phil Donahue? Rhett Butler or Ashley Wilkes?

We are daily bombarded with images and handy rules to help us negotiate our way through a world in which all the rules seem to have suddenly vanished or changed. Some tell us to reassert traditional masculinity against all contemporary challenges. But a strength built only on the weakness of others hardly feels like strength at all. Others tell us that men are in power, the oppressor. But if men are in power as a group, why do individual men often feel so powerless? Can men change?

These questions will return throughout this book. In this section, several authors begin to examine some of the issues that define the depth of the question about men and masculinity. These articles begin to unravel the "masculine mystique" and suggest various dimensions of men's position in society, their power, their powerlessness, and their confusion. Joseph Pleck, for example, explores contemporary definitions of masculinity, and the ways in which these definitions shape men's relations with women, with other men, and in society in general. Michael Kaufman takes men's problematic relationship to violence as a core theme in men's experience in society.

But we cannot speak of "men" as some universal category that is experienced in the same ways by each man. "All men are alike," runs a popular wisdom. But are they really? Are gay men's experiences with work, relationships, love, and politics similar to those of straight men? Do black and Chicano men face the same problems and conflicts in their daily lives that white men face? Do middle class men have the same political interests as blue-collar men? The answers to these questions, as the articles in this part suggest, are not simple.

Although earlier studies of men and masculinity focused on the apparently universal norms of masculinity, recent work has attempted to demonstrate how different the worlds of various men are. Men are divided along the same lines that divide any other group: race, class, sexual orientation, ethnicity, age, and geographic region. Men's lives

vary in crucial ways, and understanding these variations will take us a long way toward understanding men's experiences.

Earlier studies that suggested a single universal norm of masculinity reproduced some of the problems they were trying to solve. To be sure, *all* benefit from the inequality between women and men; for example, think of how rape jokes or male-exclusive sports culture provide contexts for the bonding of men across class, race, and ethnic lines while denying full participation to women. But the single, seemingly universal masculinity obscured ways in which some men hold and maintain power over other men in our society, hiding the fact that all men do not share equally in the fruits of gender inequality.

Here is how sociologist Erving Goffman put it in his important book, *Stigma* (New York: Doubleday, 1963, p. 128):

> *In an important sense there is only one complete unblushing male in America: a young, married, white, urban, northern, heterosexual Protestant father of college education, fully employed, of good complexion, weight, and height, and a recent record in sports. Every American male tends to look out upon the world from this perspective, this constituting one sense in which one can speak of a common value system in America. Any male who fails to qualify in any one of these ways is likely to view himself—during moments at least—as unworthy, incomplete, and inferior.*

As Goffman suggests, the middle-class, white, heterosexual masculinity is used as the marker against which other masculinities are measured, and by which standard they may be found wanting. What is *normative* (prescribed) becomes translated into what is *normal*. In this way, heterosexual men maintain their status by the oppression of gay men; middle-aged men can maintain their dominance over older and younger men; upper-class men can exploit working-class men; and white men can enjoy privileges at the expense of men of color.

The articles by Manning Marable and Maxine Baca Zinn challenge popularly held negative stereotypes of black and Chicano males as pathologically "macho." Instead, they suggest that an understanding of ethnic minority men must begin with a critical examination of how institutionalized racism, particularly (but not exclusively) in the economy, shapes and constrains the possibilities, choices, and personal life-styles of black and Chicano men. Calls for "changing masculinities," these articles suggest, must involve an emphasis on *institutional* transformation, to which Marable's argument gives a special political urgency.

Michael Kimmel's article gives an illuminating glimpse into how ethnic identity informs our conceptions of masculinity in feminist politics. And Seymour Kleinberg's discussion of gay politics highlights the dangers in assuming a universal "natural" heterosexuality when thinking about the politics of masculinities. Together, the articles in this section reveal that men's experiences vary enormously; students of men's lives must pay special attention to the richness of that diversity.

MEN'S POWER WITH WOMEN, OTHER MEN, AND SOCIETY:
A MEN'S MOVEMENT ANALYSIS

JOSEPH H. PLECK

My aim in this paper is to analyze men's power from the perspective afforded by the emerging antisexist men's movement. In the last several years, an antisexist men's movement has appeared in North America and in the Western European countries. While it is not so widely known as the women's movement, the men's movement has generated a variety of books, publications, and organizations,[1] and is now an established presence on the sex role scene. The present and future political relationship between the women's movement and the men's movement raises complex questions which I do not deal with here, though they are clearly important ones. Instead, here I present my own view of the contribution which the men's movement and the men's analysis make to a feminist understanding of men and power, and of power relations between the sexes. First, I will analyze men's power over women, particularly in relation to the power that men often perceive women have over them. Then I will analyze two other power relationships men are implicated in—men's power with other men, and men's power in society more generally—and suggest how these two other power relationships interact with men's power over women.

MEN'S POWER OVER WOMEN, AND WOMEN'S POWER OVER MEN

It is becoming increasingly recognized that one of the most fundamental questions raised by the women's movement is not a question about women at all, but rather a question about men: Why do men oppress women? There are two general kinds of answers to this question. The first is that men want power over women because it is in their rational self-interest to do so, to have the concrete benefits and privileges that power over women provides them. Having power, it is rational to want to keep it. The second kind of answer is that men want to have power over women because of deep-lying psychological needs in male personality. These two views are not mutually exclusive, and there is certainly ample evidence for both. The final analysis of men's

[1]. See, for example, Deborah David and Robert Brannon, eds., *The Forty-Nine Percent Majority: Readings on the Male Role* (Reading, Mass.: Addison-Wesley, 1975); Warren Farrell, *The Liberated Man* (New York: Bantam Books, 1975); Marc Feigen-Fasteau, *The Male Machine* (New York: McGraw-Hill, 1974); Jack Nichols, *Men's Liberation: A New Definition of Masculinity* (Baltimore: Penguin, 1975); John Petras, eds., *Sex: Male/Gender: Masculine* (Port Washington, N.J.: Alfred, 1975); Joseph H. Pleck and Jack Sawyer, eds., *Men and Masculinity* (Englewood Cliffs, N.J.: Prentice-Hall, 1974). See also the *Man's Awareness Network (M.A.N.) Newsletter*, a regularly updated directory of men's movement activities, organizations, and publications, prepared by a rotating group of men's centers (c/o Knoxville Men's Resource Center, P.O. Box 8060, U.T. Station, Knoxville, Tenn. 37916); the Men's Studies Collection, Charles Hayden Humanities Library, Massachusetts Institute of Technology, Cambridge, Mass. 02139.

oppression of women will have to give attention equally to its rational and irrational sources.

I will concentrate my attention here on the psychological sources of men's needs for power over women. Let us consider first the most common and commonsense psychological analysis of men's need to dominate women, which takes as its starting point the male child's early experience with women. The male child, the argument goes, perceives his mother and his predominantly female elementary school teachers as dominating and controlling. These relationships *do* in reality contain elements of domination and control, probably exacerbated by the restriction of women's opportunities to exercise power in most other areas. As a result, men feel a lifelong psychological need to free themselves from or prevent their domination by women. The argument is, in effect, that men oppress women as adults because they experienced women as oppressing them as children.

According to this analysis, the process operates in a vicious circle. In each generation, adult men restrict women from having power in almost all domains of social life except child rearing. As a result, male children feel powerless and dominated, grow up needing to restrict women's power, and thus the cycle repeats itself. It follows from this analysis that the way to break the vicious circle is to make it possible for women to exercise power outside of parenting and parentlike roles and to get men to do their half share of parenting.

There may be a kernel of truth in this "mother domination" theory of sexism for some men, and the social changes in the organization of child care that this theory suggests are certainly desirable. As a general explanation of men's needs to dominate women, however, this theory has been quite overworked. This theory holds women themselves rather than men ultimately responsible for the oppression of women—in William Ryan's phrase, "blaming the victim" of oppression for her own oppression.[2] The recent film

One Flew over the Cuckoo's Nest presents an extreme example of how women's supposed domination of men is used to justify sexism. This film portrays the archetypal struggle between a female figure depicted as domineering and castrating and a rebellious male hero (played by Jack Nicholson) who refuses to be emasculated by her. This struggle escalates to a climactic scene in which Nicholson throws her on the floor and nearly strangles her to death—a scene that was accompanied by wild cheering from the audience when I saw the film. For this performance, Jack Nicholson won the Academy Award as the best actor of the year, an indication of how successful the film is in seducing its audience to accept this act of sexual violence as legitimate and even heroic. The hidden moral message of the film is that because women dominate men, the most extreme forms of sexual violence are not only permissible for men, but indeed are morally obligatory.

To account for men's needs for power over women, it is ultimately more useful to examine some other ways that men feel women have power over them than fear of maternal domination.[3] There are two forms of power that men

2. William Ryan, *Blaming the Victim* (New York: Pantheon, 1970).

3. In addition to the mother domination theory, there are two other psychological theories relating aspects of the early mother–child relationship in men's sexism. The first can be called the "mother identification" theory, which holds that men develop a "feminine" psychological identification because of their early attachment to their mothers and that men fear this internal feminine part of themselves, seeking to control it by controlling those who actually are feminine, i.e., women. The second can be called the "mother socialization" theory, holding that since boys' fathers are relatively absent as sex-role models, the major route by which boys learn masculinity is through their mothers' rewarding masculine behavior, and especially through their mothers' punishing feminine behavior. Thus, males associate women with punishment and pressure to be masculine. Interestingly, these two theories are in direct contradiction, since the former holds that men fear women because women make men feminine, and the latter holds that men fear women because women make men masculine. These theories are discussed at greater length in Joseph H. Pleck's "Men's Traditional Attitudes toward Women: Conceptual Issues in Research" in *The Psychology of Women: New Directions in Research*, ed. Julia Sherman and Florence Denmark (New York: Psychological Dimensions, 1978).

perceive women as holding over them which derive more directly from traditional definitions of adult male and female roles, and have implications which are far more compatible with a feminist perspective.

The first power that men perceive women having over them is *expressive power*, the power to express emotions. It is well known that in traditional male–female relationships, women are supposed to express their needs for achievement only vicariously through the achievements of men. It is not so widely recognized, however, that this dependency of women on men's achievement has a converse. In traditional male–female relationships, men experience their emotions vicariously through women. Many men have learned to depend on women to help them express their emotions, indeed, to express their emotions for them. At an ultimate level, many men are unable to feel emotionally alive except through relationships with women. A particularly dramatic example occurs in an earlier Jack Nicholson film, *Carnal Knowledge*. Art Garfunkel, at one point early in his romance with Candice Bergen, tells Nicholson that she makes him aware of thoughts he "never even knew he had." Although Nicholson is sleeping with Bergen and Garfunkel is not, Nicholson feels tremendously deprived in comparison when he hears this. In a dramatic scene, Nicholson then goes to her and angrily demands: "You tell him his thoughts, now you tell me *my* thoughts!" When women withhold and refuse to exercise this expressive power for men's benefit, many men, like Nicholson, feel abject and try all the harder to get women to play their traditional expressive role.

A second form of power that men attribute to women is *masculinity-validating* power. In traditional masculinity, to experience oneself as masculine requires that women play their prescribed role of doing the things that make men feel masculine. Another scene from *Carnal Knowledge* provides a pointed illustration. In the closing scene of the movie, Nicholson has hired a call girl whom he has rehearsed and coached in a script telling him how strong and manly he is, in order to get him sexually aroused. Nicholson seems to be in control, but when she makes a mistake in her role, his desperate reprimands show just how dependent he is on her playing out the masculinity-validating script he has created. It is clear that what he is looking for in this encounter is not so much sexual gratification as it is validation of himself as a man—which only women can give him. As with women's expressive power, when women refuse to exercise their masculinity-validating power for men, many men feel lost and bereft and frantically attempt to force women back into their accustomed role.

As I suggested before, men's need for power over women derives both from men's pragmatic self-interest and from men's psychological needs. It would be a mistake to overemphasize men's psychological needs as the sources of their needs to control women, in comparison with simple rational self-interest. But if we are looking for the psychological sources of men's needs for power over women, their perception that women have expressive power and masculinity-validating power over them is critical to analyze. These are the two powers men perceive women as having, which they fear women will no longer exercise in their favor. These are the two resources women possess which men fear women will withhold, and whose threatened or actual loss leads men to such frantic attempts to reassert power over women.

Men's dependence on women's power to express men's emotions and to validate men's masculinity has placed heavy burdens on women. By and large, these are not powers over men that women have wanted to hold. These are powers that men have themselves handed over to women, by defining the male role as being emotionally cool and inexpressive, and as being ultimately validated by heterosexual success.

There is reason to think that over the course of recent history—as male–male friendship has declined, and as dating and marriage have occurred more universally and at younger ages—the demands on men to be emotionally inexpressive and to prove masculinity through relating to women have become stronger. As a result, men have given women increasingly more expressive power and more masculinity-validating power over them, and have become increasingly dependent on women for emotional and sex-role validation. In the context of this increased dependency on women's power, the emergence of the women's movement now, with women asserting their right not to play these roles for men, has hit with a special force.

It is in this context that the men's movement and men's groups place so much emphasis on men learning to express and experience their emotions with each other, and learning how to validate themselves and each other as persons, instead of needing women to validate them emotionally and as men. When men realize that they can develop in themselves the power to experience themselves emotionally and to validate themselves as persons, they will not feel the dependency on women for these essential needs which has led in the past to so much male fear, resentment, and need to control women. Then men will be emotionally more free to negotiate the pragmatic realignment of power between the sexes that is underway in our society.

MEN'S POWER WITH OTHER MEN

After considering men's power over women in relation to the power men perceive women having over them, let us consider men's power over women in a second context: the context of men's power relationships with other men. In recent years, we have come to understand that relations between men and women are governed by a sexual politics that exists outside individual men's and women's needs and choices. It has taken us much longer to recognize that there is a systematic sexual politics of male–male relationships as well. Under patriarchy, men's relationships with other men cannot help but be shaped and patterned by patriarchal norms, though they are less obvious than the norms governing male–female relationships. A society could not have the kinds

of power dynamics that exist between women and men in our society without certain kinds of systematic power dynamics operating among men as well.

One dramatic example illustrating this connection occurs in Marge Piercy's recent novel *Small Changes*. In a flashback scene, a male character goes along with several friends to gang rape a woman. When his turn comes, he is impotent; whereupon the other men grab him, pulling his pants down to rape *him*. This scene powerfully conveys one form of the relationship between male–female and male–male sexual politics. The point is that men do not just happily bond together to oppress women. In addition to hierarchy over women, men create hierarchies and rankings among themselves according to criteria of "masculinity." Men at each rank of masculinity compete with each other, with whatever resources they have, for the differential payoffs that patriarchy allows men.

Men in different societies choose different grounds on which to rank each other. Many societies use the simple facts of age and physical strength to stratify men. The most bizarre and extreme form of patriarchal stratification occurs in those societies which have literally created a class of eunuchs. Our society, reflecting its own particular preoccupations, stratifies men according to physical strength and athletic ability in the early years, but later in life focuses on success with women and ability to make money.

In our society, one of the most critical rankings among men deriving from patriarchal sexual politics is the division between gay and straight men. This division has powerful negative consequences for gay men and gives straight men privilege. But in addition, this division has a larger symbolic meaning. Our society uses the male heterosexual–homosexual dichotomy as a central symbol for *all* the rankings for masculinity, for the division on *any* grounds between males who are "real men" and have power and males who are not. Any kind of powerlessness or refusal to compete becomes imbued with the imagery of homosexuality. In the men's movement documentary film *Men's Lives*,[4] a high school male who studies modern dance says that others often think he is gay because he is a dancer. When asked why, he gives three reasons: because dancers are "free and loose," because they are "not big like football players," and because "you're not trying to kill anybody." The patriarchal connection: if you are not trying to kill other men, you must be gay.

Another dramatic example of men's use of homosexual derogations as weapons in their power struggle with each other comes from a document which provides one of the richest case studies of the politics of male–male relationships to yet appear: Woodward and Bernstein's *The Final Days*. Ehrlichman jokes that Kissinger is "queer," Kissinger calls an unnamed colleague a psychopathic homosexual, and Haig jokes that Nixon and Rebozo are having a homosexual relationship. From the highest ranks of male power to the lowest, the gay–straight division is a central symbol of all the forms of ranking and power relationships which men put on each other.

The relationships between the patriarchal stratification and competition which men experience with each other and men's patriarchal domination of women are complex. Let us briefly consider several points of interconnection between them. First, women are used as *symbols of success* in men's competition with each other. It is sometimes thought that competition for women is the ultimate source of men's competition with each other. For example, in *Totem and Taboo* Freud presented a mythical reconstruction of the origin of society based on sons' sexual competition with the father, leading to their murdering the father. In this view, if women did not exist, men would not have anything to compete for with each other. There is considerable reason, however, to see women not as the ultimate source of male–male competition, but rather as only symbols in a male contest where real roots lie much deeper.

The recent film *Paper Chase* provides an interesting example. This film combines the story of a small group of male law students in their first year of law school with a heterosexual love story between one of the students (played by Timothy Bottoms) and the professor's daughter. As the film develops, it becomes clear that the real business is the struggle within the group of male law students for survival, success, and the professor's blessing—a patriarchal struggle in which several of the less successful are driven out of school and one even attempts suicide. When Timothy Bottoms gets the professor's daughter at the end, she is simply another one of the rewards he has won by doing better than the other males in her father's class. Indeed, she appears to be a direct part of the patriarchal blessing her father has bestowed on Bottoms.

Second, women often play a *mediating* role in the patriarchal struggle among men. Women get men together with each other and provide the social lubrication necessary to smooth over men's inability to relate to each other noncompetitively. This function has been expressed in many myths, for example, the folk tales included in the Grimms' collection about groups of brothers whose younger sister reunites and reconciles them with their kingfather, who has previously banished and tried to kill them. A more modern myth, James Dickey's *Deliverance*, portrays what happens when men's relationships with each other are not mediated by women. According to Carolyn Heilbrun,[5] the central message of *Deliverance* is that when men get beyond the bounds of civilization, which really means beyond the bounds of the civilizing effects of women, men rape and murder each other.

A third function women play in male–male sexual politics is that relationships with women provide men a *refuge* for the dangers and stresses of relating to other males. Traditional relationships with women have provided men a safe

4. Available from New Day Films, P.O. Box 615, Franklin Lakes, N.J. 07417.

5. Carolyn G. Heilbrun, "The Masculine Wilderness of the American Novel," *Saturday Review* 41 (January 29, 1972), pp. 41–44.

place in which they can recuperate from the stresses they have absorbed in their daily struggle with other men, and in which they can express their needs without fearing that these needs will be used against them. If women begin to compete with men and have power in their own right, men are threatened by the loss of this refuge.

Finally, a fourth function of women in males' patriarchal competition with each other is to reduce the stress of competition by serving as an *underclass*. As Elizabeth Janeway has written in *Between Myth and Morning*,[6] under patriarchy women represent the lowest status, a status to which men can fall only under the most exceptional circumstances, if at all. Competition among men is serious, but its intensity is mitigated by the fact that there is a lowest possible level to which men cannot fall. One reason men fear women's liberation, writes Janeway, is that the liberation of women will take away this unique underclass status of women. Men will now risk falling lower than ever before, into a new underclass composed of the weak of both sexes. Thus, women's liberation means that the stakes of patriarchal failure for men are higher than they have been before, and that it is even more important for men not to lose.

Thus, men's patriarchal competition with each other makes use of women as symbols of success, as mediators, as refuges, and as an underclass. In each of these roles, women are dominated by men in ways that derived directly from men's struggle with each other. Men need to deal with the sexual politics of their relationships with each other if they are to deal fully with the sexual politics of their relationships with women.

Ultimately, we have to understand that patriarchy has two halves which are intimately related to each other. Patriarchy is a *dual* system, a system in which men oppress women, and in which men oppress themselves and each other. At one

level, challenging one part of patriarchy inherently leads to challenging the other. This is one way to interpret why the idea of women's liberation so soon led to the idea of men's liberation, which in my view ultimately means freeing men from the patriarchal sexual dynamics they now experience with each other. But because the patriarchal sexual dynamics of male–male relationships are less obvious than those of male–female relationships, men face a real danger: while the patriarchal oppression of women may be lessened as a result of the women's movement, the patriarchal oppression of men may be untouched. The real danger for men posed by the attack that the women's movement is making on patriarchy is not that this attack will go too far, but that it will not go far enough. Ultimately, men cannot go any further in relating to women as equals than they have been able to go in relating to other men as equals—an equality which has been so deeply disturbing, which has generated so many psychological as well as literal casualties, and which has left so many unresolved issues of competition and frustrated love.

MEN'S POWER IN SOCIETY

Let us now consider men's power over women in a third and final context, the context of men's power in the larger society. At one level, men's social identity is defined by the power they have over women and the power they can compete for against other men. But at another level, most men have very little power over their own lives. How can we understand this paradox?

The major demand to which men must accede in contemporary society is that they play their required role in the economy. But this role is not intrinsically satisfying. The social researcher Daniel Yankelovich[7] has suggested that about 80 percent of U.S. male workers experience their jobs as intrinsically meaningless and onerous.

---

6. Elizabeth Janeway, *Between Myth and Morning* (Boston: Little, Brown, 1975); see also Elizabeth Janeway, "The Weak are the Second Sex," *Atlantic Monthly* (December 1973), pp. 91–104.

7. Daniel Yankelovich, "The Meaning of Work," in *The Worker and the Job*, ed. Jerome Rosow (Englewood Cliffs, N.J.: Prentice-Hall, 1974).

They experience their jobs and themselves as worthwhile only through priding themselves on the hard work and personal sacrifice they are making to be breadwinners for their families. Accepting these hardships reaffirms their role as family providers and therefore as true men.

Linking the breadwinner role to masculinity in this way has several consequences for men. Men can get psychological payoffs from their jobs which these jobs never provide in themselves. By training men to accept payment for their work in feelings of masculinity rather than in feelings of satisfaction, men will not demand that their jobs be made more meaningful, and as a result jobs can be designed for the more important goal of generating profits. Further, the connection between work and masculinity makes men accept unemployment as their personal failing as males, rather than analyze and change the profit-based economy whose inevitable dislocations make them unemployed or unemployable.

Most critical for our analysis here, men's role in the economy and the ways men are motivated to play it have at least two negative effects on women. First, the husband's job makes many direct and indirect demands on wives. In fact, it is often hard to distinguish whether the wife is dominated more by the husband or by the husband's job. Sociologist Ralph Turner writes: "Because the husband must adjust to the demands of his occupation and the family in turn must accommodate to his demands on behalf of his occupational obligations, the husband appears to dominate his wife and children. But as an agent of economic institutions, he perceives himself as controlled rather than as controlling."[8]

Second, linking the breadwinner role to masculinity in order to motivate men to work means that women must not be allowed to hold paid work. For the large majority of men who accept dehumanizing jobs only because having a job validates their role as family breadwinner, their

wives' taking paid work takes away from them the major and often only way they have of experiencing themselves as having worth. Yankelovich suggests that the frustration and discontent of this group of men, whose wives are increasingly joining the paid labor force, is emerging as a major social problem. What these men do to sabotage women's paid work is deplorable, but I believe that it is quite within the bounds of a feminist analysis of contemporary society to see these men as victims as well as victimizers.

One long-range perspective on the historical evolution of the family is that from an earlier stage in which both wife and husband were directly economically productive in the household economic unit, the husband's economic role has evolved so that now it is under the control of forces entirely outside the family. In order to increase productivity, the goal in the design of this new male work role is to increase men's commitment and loyalty to work and to reduce those ties to the family that might compete with it. Men's jobs are increasingly structured as if men had no direct roles or responsibilities in the family—indeed, as if they did not have families at all. But paradoxically, at the same time that men's responsibilities in the family are reduced to facilitate more efficient performance of their work role, the increasing dehumanization of work means that the satisfaction which jobs give men is, to an increasing degree, *only* the satisfaction of fulfilling the family breadwinner role. That is, on the one hand, men's ties to the family have to be broken down to facilitate industrial work discipline; but on the other hand, men's sense of responsibility to the family has to be increased, but shaped into a purely economic form, to provide the motivation for men to work at all. Essential to this process is the transformation of the wife's economic role to providing supportive services, both physical and psychological, to keep him on the job, and to take over the family responsibilities which his expanded work role will no longer allow him to fulfill himself. The wife is then bound to her husband by her economic dependency on him, and the husband in turn is bound

8. Ralph Turner, *Family Interaction* (New York: Wiley, 1968), p. 282.

to his job by his family's economic dependence on him.

A final example from the film *Men's Lives* illustrates some of these points. In one of the most powerful scenes in the film, a worker in a rubber plant resignedly describes how his bosses are concerned, in his words, with "pacifying" him to get the maximum output from him, not with satisfying his needs. He then takes back this analysis, saying that he is only a worker and therefore cannot really understand what is happening to him. Next, he is asked whether he wants his wife to take a paid job to reduce the pressure he feels in trying to support his family. In marked contrast to his earlier passive resignation, he proudly asserts that he will never allow her to work, and that in particular he will never scrub the floors after he comes home from his own job. (He correctly perceives that if his wife did take a paid job, he would be under pressure to do some housework.) In this scene, the man expresses and then denies an awareness of his exploitation as a worker. Central to his coping with repressing his incipient awareness of his exploitation is his false consciousness of his superiority and privilege over women. Not scrubbing floors is a real privilege, and deciding whether or not his wife will have

paid work is a real power, but the consciousness of power over his own life that such privilege and power give this man is false. The relative privilege that men get from sexism and, more importantly, the false consciousness of privilege men get from sexism plays a critical role in reconciling men to their subordination in the larger political economy. This analysis does not imply that men's sexism will go away if they gain control over their own lives, or that men do not have to deal with their sexism until they gain this control. I disagree with both. Rather, my point is that we cannot fully understand men's sexism or men's subordination in the larger society unless we understand how deeply they are related.

To summarize, a feminist understanding of men's power over women, why men have needed it, and what is involved in changing it, is enriched by examining men's power in a broader context. To understand men's power over women, we have to understand the ways in which men feel women have power over them, men's power relationships with other men, and the powerlessness of most men in the larger society. Rectifying men's power relationship with women will inevitably both stimulate and benefit from the rectification of these other power relationships.

THE CONSTRUCTION OF MASCULINITY AND THE TRIAD OF MEN'S VIOLENCE

MICHAEL KAUFMAN

The all too familiar story: a woman raped, a wife battered, a lover abused. With a sense of immediacy and anger, the women's liberation movement has pushed the many forms of men's violence against women—from the most overt to the most subtle in form—into popular consciousness and public debate. These forms of violence are one aspect of our society's domination by men that, in outcome, if not always in design, reinforce that domination. The act of violence is many things at once. At the same instant it is the individual man acting out relations of sexual power; it is the violence of a society—a hierarchical, authoritarian, sexist, class-divided, militarist, racist, impersonal, crazy society—being focused through an individual man onto an individual woman. In the psyche of the individual man it might be his denial of social powerlessness through an act of aggression. In total these acts of violence are like a ritualized acting out of our social relations of power: the dominant and the weaker, the powerful and the powerless, the active and the passive . . . the masculine and the feminine.

For men, listening to the experience of women as the objects of men's violence is to shatter any complacency about the sex-based status quo. The power and anger of women's responses forces us to rethink the things we discovered when we were very young. When I was eleven or twelve years old a friend told me the difference between fuck-ing and raping. It was simple: with rape you tied the woman to a tree. At the time the anatomical details were still a little vague, but in either case it was something "we" supposedly did. This knowledge was just one part of an education, started years before, about the relative power and privileges of men and women. I remember laughing when my friend explained all that to me. Now I shudder. The difference in my responses is partially that, at twelve, it was part of the posturing and pretense that accompanied my passage into adolescence. Now, of course, I have a different vantage point on the issue. It is the vantage point of an adult, but more importantly my view of the world is being reconstructed by the intervention of that majority whose voice has been suppressed: the women.

This relearning of the reality of men's violence against women evokes many deep feelings and memories for men. As memories are recalled and recast, a new connection becomes clear: violence by men against women is only one corner of a triad of men's violence. The other two corners are violence against other men and violence against oneself.

On a psychological level the pervasiveness of violence is the result of what Herbert Marcuse called the "surplus repression" of our sexual and emotional desires.[1] The substitution of violence for desire (more precisely, the transmutation of

Reprinted from *Beyond Patriarchy: Essays on Pleasure, Power, and Change*, edited by Michael Kaufman. Toronto: Oxford University Press, 1987. Reprinted by permission.

violence into a form of emotionally gratifying activity) happens unequally in men and women. The construction of masculinity involves the construction of "surplus aggressiveness." The social context of this triad of violence is the institutionalization of violence in the operation of most aspects of social, economic, and political life.

The three corners of the triad reinforce one another. The first corner—violence against women—cannot be confronted successfully without simultaneously challenging the other two corners of the triad. And all this requires a dismantling of the social feeding ground of violence: patriarchal, heterosexist, authoritarian, class societies. These three corners and the societies in which they blossom feed on each other. And together, we surmise, they will fall.

THE SOCIAL CONTEXT

In spite of proclamations from the skewed research of sociobiologists, there is no good evidence that men's violence is the inevitable and natural result of male genes or hormones. To the contrary, anthropology tells us of many early societies with little or no violence against women, against children, or among men. However, given the complexity of the issues concerning the roots of violence, the essential question for us is not whether men are predisposed to violence but what society does with this violence. Why has the linchpin of so many societies been the manifold expression of violence perpetrated disproportionately by men? Why are so many forms of violence sanctioned or even encouraged? Exactly what is the nature of violence? And how are patterns of violence and the quest for domination built up and reinforced?

In other words, the key questions having to do with men's violence are not biological but are related to gender and society—which is why I speak not of "male violence" (a biological category) but rather of "men's violence" (the gender category).

For every apparently individual act of violence there is a social context. This is not to say there are no pathological acts of violence; but even in that case the "language" of the violent act, the way the violence manifests itself, can only be understood within a certain social experience. We are interested here in the manifestations of violence that are accepted as more or less normal, even if reprehensible: fighting, war, rape, assault, psychological abuse, and so forth. What is the context of men's violence in the prevalent social orders of today?

Violence has long been institutionalized as an acceptable means of solving conflicts. But now the vast apparati of policing and war making maintained by countries the world over pose a threat to the future of life itself.

"Civilized" societies have been built and shaped through the decimation, containment, and exploitation of other peoples: extermination of native populations, colonialism, and slavery. Our relationship with the natural environment has often been described with the metaphor of rape. An attitude of conquering nature, of mastering an environment waiting to be exploited for profit, has great consequences when we possess a technology capable of permanently disrupting an ecological balance shaped over hundreds of millions of years.

The daily work life of industrial, class societies is one of violence. Violence poses as economic rationality as some of us are turned into extensions of machines, while others become brains detached from bodies. Our industrial process becomes the modern-day rack of torture where we are stretched out of shape and ripped limb from limb. It is violence that exposes workers to the danger of chemicals, radiation, machinery, speedup, and muscle strain.

The racism, sexism, and heterosexism that have been institutionalized in our societies are socially regulated acts of violence. Our cities, our social structure, our work life, our relation with nature, our history, are more than a backdrop to the prevalence of violence. They are violence; violence in an institutionalized form encoded into physical structures and socioeconomic relations. Much of the sociological analysis of violence in our societies implies simply that violence is learned by witnessing and experiencing social violence: man kicks boy, boy kicks dog.[2] Such experiences of transmitted violence are a reality, as the analysis of wife battering indicates, for many batterers were themselves abused as children. But more essential is that our personalities and sexuality, our needs and fears, our strengths and weaknesses, our selves are created—not simply learned—through our lived reality. The violence of our social order nurtures a psychology of violence, which in turn reinforces the social, economic and political structures of violence. The ever-increasing demands of civilization and the constant building upon inherited structures of violence suggest that the development of civilization has been inseparable from a continuous increase in violence against humans and our natural environment.

It would be easy, yet ultimately not very useful, to slip into a use of the term "violence" as a metaphor for all our society's antagonisms, contradictions, and ills. For now, let us leave aside the social terrain and begin to unravel the nature of so-called individual violence.

THE TRIAD OF MEN'S VIOLENCE

The longevity of the oppression of women must be based on something more than conspiracy, something more complicated than biological handicap and more durable than economic exploitation (although in differing degrees all these may feature).

—Juliet Mitchell[3]

It seems impossible to believe that mere greed could hold men to such a steadfastness of purpose.

—Joseph Conrad[4]

The field in which the triad of men's violence is situated is a society, or societies, grounded in structures of domination and control. Although at times this control is symbolized and embodied in the individual father—patriarchy, by definition—it is more important to emphasize that patriarchal structures of authority, domination, and control

are diffused throughout social, economic, political, and ideological activities and in our relations to the natural environment. Perhaps more than in any previous time during the long epoch of patriarchy, authority does *not* rest with the father, at least in much of the advanced capitalist and noncapitalist world. This has led more than one author to question the applicability of the term patriarchy.[5] But I think it still remains useful as a broad, descriptive category. In this sense Jessica Benjamin speaks of the current reign of patriarchy without the father. "The form of domination peculiar to this epoch expresses itself not directly as authority but indirectly as the transformation of all relationships and activity into objective, instrumental, depersonalized forms."[6]

The structures of domination and control form not simply the background to the triad of violence, but generate, and in turn are nurtured by, this violence. These structures refer both to our social relations and to our interaction with our natural environment. The relation between these two levels is obviously extremely complex. It appears that violence against nature—that is, the impossible and disastrous drive to dominate and conquer the natural world—is integrally connected with domination among humans. Some of these connections are quite obvious. One thinks of the bulldozing of the planet for profit in capitalist societies, societies characterized by the dominance of one class over others. But the link between the domination of nature and structures of domination of humans go beyond this.

THE INDIVIDUAL REPRODUCTION OF MALE DOMINATION

No man is born a butcher.

—Bertolt Brecht[7]

In a male-dominated society men have a number of privileges. Compared to women we are free to walk the streets at night, we have traditionally escaped domestic labor, and on average we have higher wages, better jobs, and more power. But these advantages in themselves cannot explain the individual reproduction of the relations of male domination, that is, why the individual male from a very early age embraces masculinity. The embracing of masculinity is not only a "socialization" into a certain gender role, as if there is a preformed human being who learns a role that he then plays for the rest of his life. Rather, through his psychological development he embraces and takes into himself a set of gender-based social relations: the person that is created through the process of maturation becomes the personal embodiment of those relations. By the time the child is five or six years old, the basis for lifelong masculinity has already been established.

The basis for the individual's acquisition of gender is that the prolonged period of human childhood results in powerful attachments to parental figures. (Through a very complex process, by the time a boy is five or six he claims for himself the power and activity society associates with masculinity.) He embraces the project of controlling himself and controlling the world. He comes to personify activity. Masculinity is a reaction against passivity and powerlessness, and with it comes a repression of a vast range of human desires and possibilities: those that are associated with femininity.

Masculinity is unconsciously rooted before the age of six, is reinforced as the child develops, and then positively explodes at adolescence, obtaining its definitive shape for the individual. The masculine norm has its own particular nuances and traits dependent on class, nation, race, religion, and ethnicity. And within each group it has its own personal expression. In adolescence the pain and fear involved in repressing "femininity" and passivity, start to become evident. For most of us, the response to this inner pain is to reinforce the bulwarks of masculinity. The emotional pain created by obsessive masculinity is stifled by reinforcing masculinity itself.

THE FRAGILITY OF MASCULINITY

Masculinity is power. But masculinity is terrifyingly fragile because it does not really exist in the sense we are led to think it exists; that is, as a biological reality—something real that we have inside ourselves. It exists as ideology; it exists as scripted behavior; it exists within "gendered" relationships. But in the end it is just a social institution with a tenuous relationship to that with which it is supposed to be synonymous: our maleness, our biological sex. The young child does not know that sex does not equal gender. For him to be male is to be what he perceives as being masculine. The child is father to the man. Therefore, to be unmasculine is to be desexed— "castrated."

The tension between maleness and masculinity is intense because masculinity requires a suppression of a whole range of human needs, aims, feelings, and forms of expression. Masculinity is one-half of the narrow, surplus-repressive shape of the adult human psyche. Even when we are intellectually aware of the difference between biological maleness and masculinity, the masculine ideal is so embedded within ourselves that it is hard to untangle the person we might want to become (more "fully human," less sexist, less surplus-repressed, and so on) from the person we actually are.

But as children and adolescents (and often as adults), we are not aware of the difference between maleness and masculinity. With the exception of a tiny proportion of the population born as hermaphrodites, there can be no biological struggle to be male. The presence of a penis and testicles is all it takes. Yet boys and men harbor great insecurity about their male credentials. This insecurity exists because maleness is equated with masculinity; but the latter is a figment of our collective, patriarchal, surplus-repressive imaginations.

In a patriarchal society being male is highly valued, and men value their masculinity. But everywhere there are ambivalent feelings. That the initial internalization of masculinity is at the father's knee has lasting significance. Andrew Tolson states that "to the boy, masculinity is both mysterious and attractive (in its promise of a world of work and power), and yet, at the same time, threatening (in its strangeness, and emotional distance). . . . It works both ways; attracts and repels in dynamic contradiction. This simultaneous distance and attraction is internalized as a permanent emotional tension that the individual must, in some way, strive to overcome."[8]

Although maleness and masculinity are highly valued, men are everywhere unsure of their own masculinity and maleness, whether consciously or not. When men are encouraged to be open, as in men's support and counseling groups, it becomes apparent that there exists, often under the surface, an internal dialogue of doubt about one's male and masculine credentials.

MEN'S VIOLENCE AGAINST WOMEN

In spite of the inferior role which men assign to them, women are the privileged objects of their aggression.

—Simone de Beauvoir[9]

Men's violence against women is the most common form of direct, personalized violence in the lives of most adults. From sexual harassment to rape, from incest to wife battering to the sight of violent pornographic images, few women escape some form of men's aggression.

My purpose here is not to list and evaluate the various forms of violence against women, nor to try to assess what can be classed as violence per se.[10] It is to understand this violence as an expression of the fragility of masculinity combined with men's power. I am interested in its place in the perpetuation of masculinity and male domination.

In the first place, men's violence against women is probably the clearest, most straightforward expression of relative male and female power. That the relative social, economic, and political power can be expressed in this manner is, to a large part, because of differences in physical strength and in a lifelong training (or lack of training) in fighting. But it is also expressed this way because of the active/passive split. Activity as aggression is part of the masculine gender definition. That is not to say this definition al-

ways includes rape or battering, but it is one of the possibilities within a definition of activity that is ultimately grounded in the body.

Rape is a good example of the acting out of these relations of power and of the outcome of fragile masculinity in a surplus-repressive society. In the testimonies of rapists one hears over and over again expressions of inferiority, powerlessness, anger. But who can these men feel superior to? Rape is a crime that not only demonstrates physical power, but that does so in the language of male–female sex-gender relations. The testimonies of convicted rapists collected by Douglas Jackson in the late 1970s are chilling and revealing.[11] Hal: "I feel very inferior to others. . . . I felt rotten about myself and by committing rape I took this out on someone I thought was weaker than me, someone I could control." Len: "I feel a lot of what rape is isn't so much sexual desire as a person's feelings about themselves and how that relates to sex. My fear of relating to people turned to sex because . . . it just happens to be the fullest area to let your anger out on, to let your feelings out on."

Sometimes this anger and pain are experienced in relation to women but just as often not. In either case they are addressed to women who, as the Other in a phallocentric society, are objects of mystification to men, the objects to whom men from birth have learned to express and vent their feelings, or simply objects with less social power and weaker muscles. It is the crime against women par excellence because, through it, the full weight of a sexually based differentiation among humans is played out.

Within relationships, forms of men's violence such as rape, battering, and what Meg Luxton calls the "petty tyranny" of male domination in the household[12] must be understood both "in terms of violence directed against women as women and against women as wives."[13] The family provides an arena for the expression of needs and emotions not considered legitimate elsewhere.[14] It is the one of the only places where men feel safe enough to express emotions. As the dams break, the flood pours out on women and children.[15] The family also becomes the place where the violence suffered by individuals in their work lives is discharged. "At work men are powerless, so in their leisure time they want to have a feeling that they control their lives."[16]

While this violence can be discussed in terms of male aggression, it operates within the dualism of activity and passivity, masculinity and femininity. Neither can exist without the other. This is not to blame women for being beaten, nor to excuse men who beat. It is but an indication that the various forms of men's violence against women are a dynamic affirmation of a masculinity that can only exist as distinguished from femininity. It is my argument that masculinity needs constant nurturing and affirmation. This affirmation takes many different forms. The majority of men are not rapists or batterers, although it is probable that the majority of men have used superior physical strength or some sort of physical force or threat of force against a woman at least once as a teenager or an adult. But in those who harbor great personal doubts or strongly negative self-images, or who cannot cope with a daily feeling of powerlessness, violence against women can become a means of trying to affirm their personal power in the language of our sex-gender system. That these forms of violence only reconfirm the negative self-image and the feelings of powerlessness shows the fragility, artificiality, the precariousness of masculinity.

VIOLENCE AGAINST OTHER MEN

At a behavioral level, men's violence against other men is visible throughout society. Some forms, such as fighting, the ritualized display violence of teenagers and some groups of adult men, institutionalized rape in prisons, and attacks on gays or racial minorities, are very direct expressions of this violence. In many sports, violence is incorporated into exercise and entertainment. More subtle forms are the verbal put-down or, combined with economic and other factors, the competition in the business, political, or academic world. In its most frightening form, violence has long been an acceptable and even preferred method of addressing differences and conflicts among different groups and states. In the case of war, as in many other manifestations of violence, violence against other men (and civilian women) combines with autonomous economic, ideological, and political factors.

But men's violence against other men is more than the sum of various activities and types of behavior. In this form of violence a number of things are happening at once, in addition to the autonomous factors involved. Sometimes mutual, sometimes one-sided, there is a discharge of aggression and hostility. But at the same time as discharging aggression, these acts of violence and the ever-present potential for men's violence against other men reinforce the reality that relations between men, whether at the individual or state level, are relations of power.[17]

Most men feel the presence of violence in their lives. Some of us had fathers who were domineering, rough, or even brutal. Some of us had fathers who simply were not there enough; most of us had fathers who either consciously or unconsciously were repelled by our need for touch and affection once we had passed a certain age. All of us had experiences of being beaten up or picked on when we were young. We learned to fight, or we learned to run; we learned to pick on others, or we learned how to talk or joke our way out of a confrontation. But either way these early experiences of violence caused an incredible amount of anxiety and required a huge expenditure of energy to resolve. That anxiety is crystallized in an unspoken fear (particularly among heterosexual men): all other men are my potential humiliators, my enemies, my competitors.

But this mutual hostility is not always expressed. Men have formed elaborate institutions of male bonding and buddying: clubs, gangs, teams, fishing trips, card games, bars, and gyms, not to mention that great fraternity of Man. Certainly, as many feminists have pointed out, straight male clubs are a subculture of male privilege. But they are also havens where men, by common consent, can find safety and security among other men. They are safe houses where our love and affection for other men can be expressed.

Freud suggested that great amounts of passivity are required for the establishment of social relations among men but also that this very passivity arouses a fear of losing one's power. (This fear takes the form, in a phallocentric, male-dominated society, of what Freud called "castration anxiety.") There is a constant tension of activity and passivity. Among their many functions and reasons for existence, male institutions mediate this tension between activity and passivity among men.

My thoughts take me back to grade six and the constant acting out of this drama. There was the challenge to fight and a punch in the stomach that knocked my wind out. There was our customary greeting with a slug in the shoulder. Before school, after school, during class change, at recess, whenever you saw another one of the boys whom you hadn't hit or been with in the past few minutes, you'd punch each other on the shoulder. I remember walking from class to class in terror of meeting Ed Skagle in the hall. Ed, a hefty young football player a grade ahead of me, would leave a big bruise with one of his friendly hellos. And this was the interesting thing about the whole business; most of the time it was friendly and affectionate. Long after the bruises have faded, I remember Ed's smile and the protective way he had of saying hello to me. But we couldn't express this affection without maintaining the active/passive equilibrium. More precisely, within the masculine psychology of surplus aggression, expressions of affection and of the need for other boys had to be balanced by an active assault.

But the traditional definition of masculinity is not only surplus aggression. It is also exclusive heterosexuality, for the maintenance of masculinity requires the repression of homosexuality.[18] Repression of homosexuality is one thing, but how do we explain the intense fear of homosexuality, the homophobia, that pervades so much male interaction? It isn't simply that many men may choose not to have sexual relations

with other men; it is rather that they will find this possibility frightening or abhorrent.

Freud showed that the boy's renunciation of the father—and thus men—as an object of sexual love is a renunciation of what are felt to be passive sexual desires. For the boy to deviate from this norm is to experience severe anxiety, for what appears to be at stake is his ability to be active. Erotic attraction to other men is sacrificed because there is no model central to our society of active, erotic love for other males. The emotionally charged physical attachments of childhood with father and friends eventually breed feelings of passivity and danger and are sacrificed. The anxiety caused by the threat of losing power and activity is "the motive power behind the 'normal' boy's social learning of his sex and gender roles." Boys internalize "our culture's definition of 'normal' or 'real' man: the possessor of a penis, therefore loving only females and that actively; the possessor of a penis, therefore 'strong' and 'hard,' not 'soft,' 'weak,' 'yielding,' 'sentimental,' 'effeminate,' passive. To deviate from this definition is not to be a real man. To deviate is to arouse [what Freud called] castration anxiety."[19]

Putting this in different terms, the young boy learns of the sexual hierarchy of society. This learning process is partly conscious and partly unconscious. For a boy, being a girl is a threat because it raises anxiety by representing a loss of power. Until real power is attained, the young boy courts power in the world of the imagination (with superheroes, guns, magic, and pretending to be grown-up). But the continued pull of passive aims, the attraction to girls and to mother, the fascination with the origin of babies ensure that a tension continues to exist. In this world, the only thing that is as bad as being a girl is being a sissy, that is, being like a girl.[20] Although the boy doesn't consciously equate being a girl or sissy with homosexual genital activity, at the time of puberty these feelings, thoughts, and anxieties are transferred onto homosexuality per se.

For the majority of men, the establishment of the masculine norm and the strong social prohibitions against homosexuality are enough to bury the erotic desire for other men. The repression of our bisexuality is not adequate, however, to keep this desire at bay. Some of the energy is transformed into derivative pleasures—muscle building, male comradeship, hero worship, religious rituals, war, sports—where our enjoyment of being with other men or admiring other men can be expressed. These forms of activity are not enough to neutralize our constitutional bisexuality, our organic fusion of passivity and activity, and our love for our fathers and our friends. The great majority of men, in addition to those men whose sexual preference is clearly homosexual, have, at some time in their childhood, adolescence, or adult life, had sexual or quasi-sexual relations with other males, or have fantasized or dreamed about such relationships. Those who don't (or don't recall that they have), invest a lot of energy in repressing and denying these thoughts and feelings. And to make things worse, all those highly charged male activities in the sportsfield, the meeting room, or the locker room do not dispel eroticized relations with other men. They can only reawaken those feelings. It is, as Freud would have said, the return of the repressed.

Nowhere has this been more stunningly captured than in the wrestling scene in the perhaps mistitled book, *Women in Love*, by D. H. Lawrence. It was late at night. Birkin had just come to Gerald's house after being put off following a marriage proposal. They talked of working, of loving, and fighting, and in the end stripped off their clothes and began to wrestle in front of the burning fire. As they wrestled, "they seemed to drive their white flesh deeper and deeper against each other, as if they would break into a oneness." They entwined, they wrestled, they pressed nearer and nearer. "A tense white knot of flesh [was] gripped in silence." The thin Birkin "seemed to penetrate into Gerald's more solid, more diffuse bulk, to interfuse his body through the body of the other, as if to bring it subtly into subjection, always seizing with some rapid necromantic foreknowledge every motion of the other flesh, converting and counteracting

it, playing upon the limbs and trunk of Gerald like some hard wind. . . . Now and again came a sharp gasp of breath, or a sound like a sigh, then the rapid thudding of movement on the thickly-carpeted floor, then the strange sound of flesh escaping under flesh."[21]

The very institutions of male bonding and patriarchal power force men to constantly reexperience their closeness and attraction to other men, that is, the very thing so many men are afraid of. Our very attraction to ourselves, ambivalent as it may be, can only be generalized as an attraction to men in general.

A phobia is one means by which the ego tries to cope with anxiety. Homophobia is a means of trying to cope, not simply with our unsuccessfully repressed, eroticized attraction to other men, but with our whole anxiety over the unsuccessfully repressed passive sexual aims, whether directed toward males or females. Homophobia is not merely an individual phobia, although the strength of homophobia varies from individual to individual. It is a socially constructed phobia that is essential for the imposition and maintenance of masculinity. A key expression of homophobia is the obsessive denial of homosexual attraction; this denial is expressed as violence against other men. Or to put it differently, men's violence against other men is one of the chief means through which patriarchal society simultaneously expresses and discharges the attraction of men to other men.[22]

The specific ways that homophobia and men's violence toward other men are acted out varies from man to man, society to society, and class to class. The great amount of *directly expressed* violence and violent homophobia among some groups of working class youth would be well worth analyzing to give clues to the relation of class and gender.

This corner of the triad of men's violence interacts with and reinforces violence against women. This corner contains part of the logic of surplus aggression. Here we begin to explain the tendency of many men to use force as a means of simultaneously hiding and expressing their feelings. At the same time the fear of other men, in particular the fear of weakness and passivity in relation to other men, helps create our strong dependence on women for meeting our emotional needs and for emotional discharge. In a surplus-repressive patriarchal and class society, large amounts of anxiety and hostility are built up, ready to be discharged. But the fear of one's emotions and the fear of losing control mean that discharge only takes place in a safe situation. For many men that safety is provided by a relationship with a woman where the commitment of one's friend or lover creates the sense of security. What is more, because it is a relationship with a woman, it unconsciously resonates with that first great passive relation of the boy with his mother. But in this situation and in other acts of men's violence against women, there is also the security of interaction with someone who does not represent a psychic threat, who is less socially powerful, probably less physically powerful, and who is herself operating within a pattern of surplus passivity. And finally, given the fragility of masculine identity and the inner tension of what it means to be masculine, the ultimate acknowledgement of one's masculinity is in our power over women. This power can be expressed in many ways. Violence is one of them.

When I speak of a man's violence against himself I am thinking of the very structure of the masculine ego. The formation of an ego on an edifice of what Herbert Marcuse called surplus repression and surplus aggression is the building of a precarious structure of internalized violence. The continual conscious and unconscious blocking and denial of passivity and all the emotions and feelings men associate with passivity—fear, pain, sadness, embarrassment—is a denial of part of what we are. The constant psychological and behavioral vigilance against passivity and its derivatives is a perpetual act of violence against oneself.

The denial and blocking of a whole range of human emotions and capacities are compounded by the blocking of avenues of discharge. The discharge of fear, hurt, and sadness, for example (through crying or trembling), is necessary be-

cause these painful emotions linger on even if they are not consciously felt. Men become pressure cookers. The failure to find safe avenues of emotional expression and discharge means that a whole range of emotions are transformed into anger and hostility. Part of the anger is directed at oneself in the form of guilt, self-hate, and various physiological and psychological symptoms. Part is directed at other men. Part of it is directed at women.

By the end of this process, our distance from ourselves is so great that the very symbol of maleness is turned into an object, a thing. Men's preoccupation with genital power and pleasure combines with a desensitization of the penis. As best he can, writes Emmanuel Reynaud, a man gives it "the coldness and the hardness of metal." It becomes his tool, his weapon, his thing. "What he loses in enjoyment he hopes to compensate for in power; but if he gains an undeniable power symbol, what pleasure can he really feel with a weapon between his legs?"[23]

BEYOND MEN'S VIOLENCE

Throughout Gabriel Garcia Marquez's *Autumn of the Patriarch*, the ageless dictator stalked his palace, his elephantine feet dragging forever on endless corridors that reeked of corruption. There was no escape from the world of terror, misery, and decay that he himself had created. His tragedy was that he was "condemned forever to live breathing the same air which asphyxiated him."[24] As men, are we similarly condemned; or is there a road of escape from the triad of men's violence and the precarious structures of masculinity that we ourselves recreate at our peril and that of women, children, and the world?

Prescribing a set of behavioral or legal changes to combat men's violence against women is obviously not enough. Even as more and more are convinced there is a problem, this realization does not touch the unconscious structures of masculinity. Any man who is sympathetic to feminism is aware of the painful contradiction between his conscious views and his deeper emotions and feelings.

The analysis in this article suggests that men and women must address each corner of the triad of men's violence and the socioeconomic, psychosexual orders on which they stand. Or to put it more strongly, it is impossible to deal successfully with any one corner of this triad in isolation from the others.

The social context that nurtures men's violence and the relation between socioeconomic transformation and the end of patriarchy have been major themes of socialist feminist thought. This framework, though it is not without controversy and unresolved problems, is one I accept. Patriarchy and systems of authoritarianism and class domination feed on each other. Radical socioeconomic and political change is a requirement for the end of men's violence. But organizing for macrosocial change is not enough to solve the problem of men's violence, not only because the problem is so pressing here and now, but because the continued existence of masculinity and surplus aggressiveness works against the fundamental macrosocial change we desire.

The many manifestations of violence against women have been an important focus of feminists. Women's campaigns and public education against rape, battering, sexual harassment, and more generally for control by women of their bodies are a key to challenging men's violence. Support by men, not only for the struggles waged by women, but in our own workplaces and among our friends is an important part of the struggle. There are many possible avenues for work by men among men. These include: forming counselling groups and support services for battering men (as is now happening in different cities in North America); championing the inclusion of clauses on sexual harassment in collective agreements and in the constitutions or bylaws of our trade unions, associations, schools, and political parties; raising money, campaigning for government funding, and finding other means of support for rape crisis centers and shelters for battered women; speaking out against violent and sexist pornography; building neighborhood campaigns of wife and child abuse; and

personally refusing to collude with the sexism of our workmates, colleagues, and friends. The latter is perhaps the most difficult of all and requires patience, humor, and support from other men who are challenging sexism.

But because men's violence against women is inseparable from the other two corners of the triad of men's violence, solutions are very complex and difficult. Ideological changes and an awareness of problems are important but insufficient. While we can envisage changes in our child-rearing arrangements (which in turn would require radical economic changes) lasting solutions have to go far deeper. Only the development of non–surplus-repressive societies (whatever these might look like) will allow for the greater expression of human needs and, along with attacks on patriarchy per se, will reduce the split between active and passive psychological aims.[25]

The process of achieving these long-term goals contains many elements of economic, social, political, and psychological change each of which requires a fundamental transformation of society. Such a transformation will not be created by an amalgam of changed individuals; but there *is* a relationship between personal change and our ability to construct organizational, political, and economic alternatives that will be able to mount a successful challenge to the status quo.

One avenue of personal struggle that is being engaged in by an increasing number of men has been the formation of men's support groups. Some groups focus on consciousness raising, but most groups stress the importance of men talking about their feelings, their relations with other men and with women, and any number of problems in their lives. At times these groups have been criticized by some antisexist men as yet another place for men to collude against women. The alternatives put forward are groups whose primary focus is either support for struggles led by women or the organization of direct, antisexist campaigns among men. These activities are very important, but so too is the development of new support structures among men. And these structures must go beyond the traditional form of consciousness raising.

Consciousness raising usually focuses on manifestations of the oppression of women and on the oppressive behavior of men. But as we have seen, masculinity is more than the sum total of oppressive forms of behavior. It is deeply and unconsciously embedded in the structure of our egos and superegos; it is what we have become. An awareness of oppressive behavior is important, but too often it only leads to guilt about being a man. Guilt is a profoundly conservative emotion and as such is not particularly useful for bringing about change. From a position of insecurity and guilt, people do not change or inspire others to change. After all, insecurity about one's male credentials played an important part in the individual acquisition of masculinity and men's violence in the first place.

There is a need to promote the personal strength and security necessary to allow men to make more fundamental personal changes and to confront sexism and heterosexism in our society at large. Support groups usually allow men to talk about our feelings, how we too have been hurt growing up in a surplus-repressive society, and how we, in turn, act at times in an oppressive manner. We begin to see the connections between painful and frustrating experiences in our own lives and related forms of oppressive behavior. As Sheila Rowbotham notes, "the exploration of the internal areas of consciousness is a political necessity for us."[26]

Talking among men is a major step, but it is still operating within the acceptable limits of what men like to think of as rational behavior. Deep barriers and fears remain even when we can begin to recognize them. As well as talking, men need to encourage direct expression of emotions—grief, anger, rage, hurt, love—within these groups and the physical closeness that has been blocked by the repression of passive aims, by social prohibition, and by our own superegos and sense of what is right. This discharge of emotions has many functions and outcomes: like all forms of emotional and physical discharge it lowers the tension within the human system and reduces the likelihood of a spontaneous discharge of emotions through outer- or inner-directed violence.

But the expression of emotions is not an end in itself; in this context it is a means to an end. Stifling the emotions connected with feelings of hurt and pain acts as a sort of glue that allows the original repression to remain. Emotional discharge, in a situation of support and encouragement, helps unglue the ego structures that require us to operate in patterned, phobic, oppressive, and surplus-aggressive forms. In a sense it loosens up the repressive structures and allows us fresh insight into ourselves and our past. But if this emotional discharge happens in isolation or against an unwitting victim, it only reinforces the feelings of being powerless, out of control, or a person who must obsessively control others. Only in situations that contradict these feelings—that is, with the support, affection, encouragement, and backing of other men who experience similar feelings—does the basis for change exist.[27]

The encouragement of emotional discharge and open dialogue among men also enhances the safety we begin to feel among each other and in turn helps us to tackle obsessive, even if unconscious, fear of other men. This unconscious fear and lack of safety are the experience of most heterosexual men throughout their lives. The pattern for homosexual men differs, but growing up and living in a heterosexist, patriarchal culture implants similar fears, even if one's adult reality is different.

Receiving emotional support and attention from a group of men is a major contradiction to experiences of distance, caution, fear, and neglect from other men. This contradiction is the mechanism that allows further discharge, emotional change, and more safety. Safety among even a small group of our brothers gives us greater safety and strength among men as a whole. This gives us the confidence and sense of personal power to confront sexism and homophobia in all its various manifestations. In a sense, this allows us each to be a model of a strong, powerful man who does not need to operate in an oppressive and violent fashion in relation to women, to other men, or to himself. And that, I hope, will play some small part in the challenge to the oppressive reality of patriarchal, authoritarian, and class societies. It will be changes in our own lives inseparably intertwined with changes in society as a whole that will sever the links in the triad of men's violence.

NOTES

My thanks to those who have given me comments on earlier drafts of this paper, in particular my father, Nathan Kaufman, and to Gad Horowitz. As well, I extend my appreciation to the men I have worked with in various counseling situations who have helped me develop insights into the individual acquisition of violence and masculinity.

1. Herbert Marcuse, *Eros and Civilization* (Boston: Beacon Press, 1975; New York: Vintage, 1962): Gad Horowitz, *Repression* (Toronto: University of Toronto Press, 1977).
2. This is the approach, for example, of Suzanne Steinmetz. She says that macrolevel social and economic conditions (such as poverty, unemployment, inadequate housing, and the glorification and acceptance of violence) lead to high crime rates and a tolerance of violence that in turn leads to family aggression. See her *Cycle of Violence* (New York: Praeger, 1977), 30.
3. Juliet Mitchell, *Psychoanalysis and Feminism* (New York: Vintage, 1975), 362.
4. Joseph Conrad, *Lord Jim* (New York: Bantam Books, 1981), 146; first published 1900.
5. See for example Michele Barrett's thought-provoking book, *Women's Oppression Today* (London: Verso/New Left Books, 1980), 10–19, 250–1.
6. Jessica Benjamin, "Authority and the Family Revisited: or, A World Without Fathers?" *New German Critique* (Winter 1978), 35.
7. Bertolt Brecht, *Three Penny Novel*, trans. Desmond I. Vesey (Harmondsworth: Penguin, 1965), 282.
8. Andrew Tolson, *The Limits of Masculinity* (London: Tavistock, 1977), 25.
9. Simone de Beauvoir, in the *Nouvel Observateur*, Mar. 1, 1976. Quoted in Diana E. H. Russell and Nicole Van de Ven, eds., *Crimes Against Women* (Millbrae, Calif.: Les Femmes, 1976), xiv.
10. Among the sources on male violence that are useful, even if sometimes problematic, see Leonore E. Walker, *The Battered Woman* (New York: Harper Colophon, 1980); Russell and Van de Ven, *op. cit.*; Judith Lewis Herman, *Father-Daughter Incest* (Cambridge, Mass.: Harvard University Press, 1981); Suzanne K. Steinmetz, *The Cycle of Violence* (New York: Praeger, 1977); Sylvia Levine and Joseph Koenig, *Why Men Rape* (Toronto: Macmillan, 1980); Susan Brownmiller, *op. cit.*, and Connie Guberman and Margie Wolfe, eds., *No Safe Place* (Toronto: Women's Press, 1985).
11. Levine and Koenig, *op. cit.*, pp. 28, 42, 56, 72.
12. Meg Luxton, *More Than a Labour of Love* (Toronto: Women's Press, 1980), 66.
13. Margaret M. Killoran, "The Sound of Silence Breaking: Toward a Metatheory of Wife Abuse" (M.A. thesis, McMaster University, 1981), 148.
14. Barrett and MacIntosh, *op. cit.*, 23.
15. Of course, household violence is not monopolized by men. In the United States roughly the same number of domestic homicides are committed by each sex. In 1975, 8.0% of homicides were committed by husbands against wives and 7.8% by wives against husbands. These figures, however, do not indicate the chain of violence, that is, the fact that most of these women were reacting to battering by their husbands. (See Steinmetz, *op. cit.*, p. 90.) Similarly, verbal and physical abuse of children appears to be committed by men and women equally. Only in the case of incest is there a near monopoly by men. Estimates vary greatly, but between one-fifth and one-third of all girls experience some sort of sexual contact with an adult male, in most cases with a father, stepfather, other relative, or teacher. (See Herman, *op. cit.*, 12 and *passim*.)
16. Luxton, *op. cit.*, p. 65.
17. This was pointed out by I. F. Stone in a 1972 article on the Vietnam war. At a briefing about the U.S. escalation of bombing in the North, the Pentagon official described U.S. strategy as two boys fighting: "If one boy gets the other in an arm lock, he can probably get his adversary to say 'uncle' if he increases the

pressure in sharp, painful jolts and gives every indication of willingness to break the boy's arm"
("Machismo in Washington," reprinted in Pleck and
Sawyer, *op. cit.*, 131). Although women are also
among the victims of war, I include war in the category of violence against men because I am here referring to the causality of war.

18. This is true both of masculinity as an institution
and masculinity for the individual. Gay men keep certain parts of the self-oppressive masculine norm intact
simply because they have grown up and live in a predominantly heterosexual, male-dominated society.

19. Horowitz, *op. cit.*, 99.

20. This formulation was first suggested to me by
Charlie Kreiner at a men's counseling workshop in
1982.

21. D. H. Lawrence, *Women in Love* (Harmondsworth: Penguin, 1960), 304–5; first published 1921.

22. See Robin Wood's analysis of the film *Raging
Bull*. M. Kaufman, ed. *Beyond Patriarchy*. Toronto:
Oxford University Press, 1987.

23. Emmanuel Reynaud, *Holy Virility*, translated by
Ros Schwartz (London: Plato Press, 1983), 41–2.

24. Gabriel Garcia Marquez, *Autumn of the Patriarch*, trans. Gregory Rabassa (Harmondsworth: Penguin, 1972), 111; first published 1967.

25. For a discussion on non–surplus-repressive societies, particularly in the sense of being complementary with Marx's notion of communism, see Horowitz,
op. cit., particularly chapter 7, and also Marcuse, *op.
cit.*, especially chaps. 7, 10, and 11.

26. Rowbotham, *op. cit.*, 36.

27. As is apparent, although I have adopted a
Freudian analysis of the unconscious and the mechanisms of repression, these observations on the therapeutic process—especially the importance of a
supportive counseling environment, peer-counseling
relations, emotional discharge, and the concept of
contradiction—are those developed by forms of co-
counseling, in particular, reevaluation counseling.
But unlike the latter, I do not suppose that any of us
can discharge all of our hurt, grief, and anger and uncover an essential self simply because our "self" is
created.

THE BLACK MALE:
SEARCHING BEYOND STEREOTYPES

MANNING MARABLE

What is a Black man? Husband and father. Son and brother. Lover and boyfriend. Uncle and grandfather. Construction worker and sharecropper. Minister and ghetto hustler. Doctor and mineworker. Auto mechanic and presidential candidate.

What is a Black man in an institutionally racist society, in the social system of modern capitalist America? The essential tragedy of being Black and male is our inability, as men and as people of African descent, to define ourselves without the stereotypes the larger society imposes upon us, and through various institutional means perpetuates and permeates within our entire culture. Our relations with our sisters, our parents and children, and indeed across the entire spectrum of human relations are imprisoned by images of the past, false distortions that seldom if ever capture the essence of our being. We cannot come to terms with Black women until we understand the half-hidden stereotypes that have crippled our development and social consciousness. We cannot challenge racial and sexual inequality, both within the Black community and across the larger American society, unless we comprehend the critical difference between the myths about ourselves and the harsh reality of being Black men.

CONFRONTATION WITH WHITE HISTORY

The conflicts between Black and white men in contemporary American culture can be traced directly through history to the earliest days of chat-

tel slavery. White males entering the New World were ill adapted to make the difficult transition from Europe to the American frontier. As recent historical research indicates, the development of what was to become the United States was accomplished largely, if not primarily, by African slaves, men and women alike. Africans were the first to cultivate wheat on the continent; they showed their illiterate masters how to grow indigo, rice, and cotton; their extensive knowledge of herbs and roots provided colonists with medicines and preservatives for food supplies. It was the Black man, wielding his sturdy axe, who cut down most of the virgin forest across the southern colonies. And in times of war, the white man reluctantly looked to his Black slave to protect him and his property. As early as 1715, during the Yemassee Indian war, Black troops led British regulars in a campaign to exterminate Indian tribes. After another such campaign in 1747, the all-white South Carolina legislature issued a public vote of gratitude to Black men, who "in times of war, behaved themselves with great faithfulness and courage, in repelling the attacks of his Majesty's enemies." During the American Revolution, over two thousand Black men volunteered to join the beleaguered Continental Army of George Washington, a slaveholder. A generation later, two thousand Blacks from New York joined the state militia's segregated units during the War of 1812, and Blacks fought bravely under Andrew Jackson at the Battle of New Orleans. From

Manning Marable, "The Black Male: Searching Beyond Stereotypes," in R. Majors and J. Gordon, eds., *The American Black Male* (Chicago: Nelson-Hall, 1993).

Crispus Attucks to the 180,000 Blacks who fought in the Union Army during the Civil War, Black men gave their lives to preserve the liberties of their white male masters.

The response of white men to the many sacrifices of their sable counterparts was, in a word, contemptuous. Their point of view of Black males was conditioned by three basic beliefs. Black men were only a step above the animals—possessing awesome physical power but lacking in intellectual ability. As such, their proper role in white society was as laborers, not as the managers of labor. Second, the Black male represented a potential political threat to the entire system of slavery. And third, but by no means last, the Black male symbolized a lusty sexual potency that threatened white women. This uneven mixture of political fears and sexual anxieties was reinforced by the white males' crimes committed against Black women, the routine rape and sexual abuse that all slave societies permit between the oppressed and the oppressor. Another dilemma seldom discussed publicly, was the historical fact that some white women of social classes were not reluctant to request the sexual favors of their male slaves. These inherent tensions produced a racial model of conduct and social context that survived the colonial period and continued into the twentieth century. The white male–dominated system dictated that the only acceptable social behavior of any Black male was that of subservience—the loyal slave, the proverbial Uncle Tom, the ever-cheerful and infantile Sambo. It was not enough that Black men must cringe before their white masters; they must express open devotion to the system of slavery itself. Politically, the Black male was unfit to play even a minor role in the development of democracy. Supreme Court Chief Justice Roger B. Tawney spoke for his entire class in 1857: "Negroes [are] beings of an inferior order, and altogether unfit to associate with the white race, either by social or political relations; and so far inferior that they have no rights which the white man was bound to respect." Finally, black males disciplined for various crimes against

white supremacy—such as escaping from the plantation, or murdering their masters—were often punished in a sexual manner. On this point, the historical record is clear. In the colonial era, castration of Black males was required by the legislatures of North and South Carolina, Virginia, Pennsylvania, and New Jersey. Black men were castrated simply for striking a white man or for attempting to learn to read and write. In the late nineteenth century, hundreds of Black male victims of lynching were first sexually mutilated before being executed. The impulse to castrate Black males was popularized in white literature and folklore, and even today, instances of such crimes are not entirely unknown in the rural South.

The relations between Black males and white women were infinitely more complex. Generally, the vast majority of white females viewed Black men through the eyes of their fathers and husbands. The Black man was simply a beast of burden, a worker who gave his life to create a more comfortable environment for her and her children. And yet, in truth, he was still a man. Instances of interracial marriage were few, and were prohibited by law even as late as the 1960s. But the fear of sexual union did not prohibit many white females, particularly indentured servants and working-class women from soliciting favors from Black men. In the 1840s, however, a small group of white middle-class women became actively involved in the campaign to abolish slavery. The founders of modern American feminism—Susan B. Anthony, Elizabeth Cady Stanton, and Lucretia Mott—championed the cause of emancipation and defended Blacks' civil rights. In gratitude for their devotion to Black freedom, the leading Black abolitionist of the period, Frederick Douglass, actively promoted the rights of white women against the white male power structure. In 1848, at the Seneca Falls, New York, women's rights convention, Douglass was the only man, Black or white, to support the extension of voting rights to all women. White women looked to Douglass for leadership in the battle against sexual and racial discrimination. Yet curiously, they were frequently hostile to the continued contributions of Black women to the cause of freedom. When the brilliant orator Sojourner Truth, second only to Douglass as a leading figure in the abolitionist movement, rose to lecture before an 1851 women's convention in Akron, Ohio, white women cried out, "Don't let her speak!" For these white liberals, the destruction of slavery was simply a means to expand democratic rights to white women: the goal was defined in racist terms. Black men like Douglass were useful allies only so far as they promoted white middle-class women's political interests.

The moment of truth came immediately following the Civil War, when Congress passed the Fifteenth Amendment, which gave Black males the right to vote. For Douglass and most Black leaders, both men and women, suffrage was absolutely essential to preserve their new freedoms. While the Fifteenth Amendment excluded females from the electoral franchise, it nevertheless represented a great democratic victory for all oppressed groups.

For most white suffragists, however, it symbolized the political advancement of the Black male over white middle-class women. Quickly their liberal rhetoric gave way to racist diatribes. "So long as the Negro was lowest in the scale of being, we were willing to press his claims," wrote Elizabeth Cady Stanton in 1865. "But now, as the celestial gate to civil rights is slowly moving on its hinges, it becomes a serious question whether we had better stand aside and see 'Sambo' walk into the kingdom first." Most white women reformists concluded that "it is better to be the slave of an educated white man than of a degraded, ignorant black one." They warned whites that giving the vote to the Black male would lead to widespread rape and sexual assaults against white women of the upper classes. Susan B. Anthony vowed, "I will cut off this right arm of mine before I will ever work for or demand the ballot for the Negro and not the [white] woman." In contrast, Black women leaders like Sojourner Truth and Frances E. Watkins

Harper understood that the enfranchisement of Black men was an essential step for the democratic rights of all people.

The division between white middle-class feminists and the civil rights movement of Blacks, beginning over a century ago, has continued today in debates over affirmative action and job quotas. White liberal feminists frequently use the rhetoric of racial equality but often find it difficult to support public policies that will advance Black males over their own social group. Even in the 1970s, such liberal women writers as Susan Brownmiller continued to resurrect the myth of the "Black male-as-rapist" and sought to define white women in crudely racist terms. The weight of white history, from white women and men alike, has been an endless series of stereotypes used to frustrate the Black man's images of himself and to blunt his constant quest for freedom.

CONFRONTING THE BLACK WOMAN

Images of our suffering—as slaves, sharecroppers, industrial workers, and standing in unemployment lines—have been intermingled in our relationship with the Black woman. We have seen her straining under the hot southern sun, chopping cotton row upon row and nursing our children on the side. We have witnessed her come home, tired and weary after working as a nurse, cook, or maid in white men's houses. We have seen her love of her children, her commitment to the church, her beauty and dignity in the face of political and economic exploitation. And yet, so much is left unsaid. All too often the Black male, in his own silent suffering, fails to communicate his love and deep respect for the mother, sister, grandmother, and wife who gave him the courage and commitment to strive for freedom. The veils of oppression, and the illusions of racial stereotypes, limit our ability to speak the inner truths about ourselves and our relationships to Black women.

The Black man's image of the past is, in most respects, a distortion of social reality. All of us can feel the anguish of our great-grandfathers as they witnessed their wives and daughters being raped by their white masters, or as they wept when their families were sold apart. But do we feel the double bondage of the Black woman, trying desperately to keep her family together and yet at times distrusted by her own Black man? Less than a generation ago, most Black male social scientists argued that the Black family was effectively destroyed by slavery; that the Black man was much less than a husband or father; and that the result was a "Black matriarchy" that crippled the economic, social, and political development of the Black community. Back in 1965, Black scholar C. Eric Lincoln declared that the slavery experience had "stripped the Negro male of his masculinity" and "condemned him to a eunuch-like existence in a culture that venerates masculine primacy." The rigid rules of Jim Crow applied more to Black men than to their women, according to Lincoln: "Because she was frequently the white man's mistress, the Negro woman occasionally flaunted the rules of segregation. . . . The Negro [male] did not earn rewards for being manly, courageous, or assertive, but for being accommodating—for fulfilling the stereotype of what he has been forced to be." The social by-product of Black demasculinization, concluded Lincoln, was the rise of Black matriarchs, who psychologically castrated their husbands and sons. "The Negro female has had the responsibility of the Negro family for so many generations that she accepts it, or assumes it, as second nature. Many older women have forgotten why the responsibility developed upon the Negro woman in the first place, or why it later became institutionalized," Lincoln argues. "And young Negro women do not think it absurd to reduce the relationship to a matter of money, since many of them probably grew up in families where the only income was earned by the mothers: the fathers may not have been in evidence at all." Other Black sociologists perpetuated these stereotypes, which only served to turn Black women and men against each other instead of focusing their energies and talents in the struggle for freedom.

Today's social science research on Black female–male relations tells us what our common sense should have indicated long ago—that the essence of Black family and community life has been a positive, constructive, and even heroic experience. Andrew Billingsley's *Black Families in White America* illustrates that the Black "extended family" is part of our African heritage that was never eradicated by slavery or segregation. The Black tradition of racial cooperation, the collectivist rather than individualistic ethos, is an outgrowth of the unique African heritage that we still maintain. It is clear that the Black woman was the primary transmitter and repositor of the cultural heritage of our people and played a central role in the socialization and guidance of Black male and female children. But this fact does not by any way justify the myth of a "Black matriarchy." Black women suffered from the economic exploitation and racism Black males experienced—but they also were trapped by institutional sexism and all of the various means of violence that have been used to oppress all women, such as rape, "wife beating," and sterilization. The majority of the Black poor throughout history have been overwhelmingly female; the lowest paid major group within the labor force in America is black women, not men.

In politics, the sense of the Black man's relations with Black women are again distorted by stereotypes. Most of us can cite the achievement of the great Black men who contributed to the freedom of our people: Frederick Douglass, W. E. B. DuBois, Marcus Garvey, Martin Luther King, Jr., Malcolm X, Paul Robeson, Medgar Evers, A. Philip Randolph. Why then are we often forgetful of Harriet Tubman, the fearless conductor on the Underground Railroad, who spirited over 350 slaves into the North? What of Ida B. Wells, newspaper editor and antilynching activist; Mary Church Terrell, educator, member of the Washington, D.C., Board of Education from 1895 to 1906, and civil rights leader; Mary McLeod Bethune, college president and director of the Division of Negro Affairs for the National Youth Administration; and Fannie Lou Hamer, courageous desegregation leader in the South during the 1960s? In simple truth, the cause of Black freedom has been pursued by Black women and men equally. In Black literature, the eloquent appeals to racial equality penned by Richard Wright, James Baldwin, and Du Bois are paralleled in the works of Zora Neale Hurston, Alice Walker, and Toni Morrison. Martin Luther King, Jr., may have expressed for all of us our collective vision of equality in his "I Have a Dream" speech at the 1963 March on Washington—but it was the solitary act of defiance by the Black woman, Rosa Parks, that initiated the great Montgomery bus boycott in 1955 and gave birth to the modern civil rights movement. The struggle of our foremothers and forefathers transcends the barrier of gender, as Black women have tried to tell their men for generations. Beyond the stereotypes, we find a common heritage of suffering, and a common will to be free.

THE BLACK MAN CONFRONTS HIMSELF

The search for reality begins and ends with an assessment of the actual socioeconomic condition of Black males within the general context of the larger society. Beginning in the economic sphere, one finds that the illusion of Black male achievement in the marketplace is undermined by statistical evidence. Of the thousands of small businesses initiated by Black entrepreneurs each year, over 90 percent go bankrupt within thirty-six months. The Black businessman suffers from redlining policies of banks, which keep capital outside his hands. Only one out of two hundred Black businessmen have more than twenty paid employees, and over 80 percent of all Black men who start their own firms must hold a second job, working sixteen hours and more each day to provide greater opportunities for their families and communities. In terms of actual income, the gap between the Black man and the white man has increased in the past decade. According to the Bureau of Labor Statistics, in 1979 only forty-six thousand Black men earned salaries between $35,000 and $50,000 annually. Fourteen thousand Black men (and only two thousand Black women) earned $50,000 to $75,000 that year. And in the highest income level, $75,000 and above, there were four thousand Black males compared to five hundred and forty-eight thousand white males. This racial stratification is even sharper at the lower end of the income scale. Using 1978 poverty statistics, only 11.3 percent of all white males under fourteen years old live in poverty, while the figure for young Black males is 42 percent. Between the ages of fourteen and seventeen, 9.6 percent of white males and 38.6 percent of Black males are poor. In the age group eighteen to twenty-one years, 7.5 percent of white males and 26.1 percent of all Black males are poor. In virtually every occupational category, Black men with identical or superior qualifications earn less than their white male counterparts. Black male furniture workers, for example, earn only 69 percent of white males' average wages; in printing and publishing, 68 percent; in all nonunion jobs, 62 percent.

Advances in high-technology leave Black males particularly vulnerable to even higher unemployment rates over the next decades. Millions of Black men are located either in the "old line" industries such as steel, automobiles, rubber, and textiles, or in the public sector—both of which have experienced severe job contractions. In agriculture, to cite one typical instance, the disappearance of Black male workers is striking. As late as forty years ago, two out of every five Black men were either farmers or farm workers. In 1960, roughly 5 percent of all Black men were still employed in agriculture, and another 3 percent owned their own farms. By 1983, however, less than 130,000 Black men worked in agriculture. From 1959 to 1974, the number of Black-operated cotton farms in the South dropped from 87,074 to 1,569. Black tobacco farmers declined in number from 40,670 to barely 7,000 during the same period. About three out of four black men involved in farming today are not self-employed.

From both rural and urban environments, the numbers of jobless Black adult males have soared since the late 1960s. In 1969, for example, only 2.5 percent of all Black married males with families were unemployed. This percentage increased to about 10 percent in the mid-1970s, and with the recession of 1982–1984 exceeded 15 percent. The total percentage of all Black families without a single income earner jumped from 10 percent in 1968 to 18.5 percent in 1977—and continued to climb into the 1990s.

These statistics fail to convey the human dimensions of the economic chaos of Black male joblessness. Thousands of jobless men are driven into petty crime annually, just to feed their families; others find temporary solace in drugs or alcohol. The collapse of thousands of black households and the steady proliferation of female-headed, single-parent households is a social consequence of the systematic economic injustice inflicted upon Black males.

Racism also underscores the plight of Black males within the criminal justice system. Every year in this country there are over 2 million arrests of Black males. About three hundred thousand Black men are currently incarcerated in federal and state prisons or other penal institutions. At least half of the Black prisoners are less than thirty years of age, and over one thousand are not even old enough to vote. Most Black male prisoners were unemployed at the time of their arrests; the others averaged less than $8,000 annual incomes during the year before they were jailed. And about 45 percent of the thirteen hundred men currently awaiting capital punishment on death row are Afro-Americans. As Lennox S. Hinds, former National Director of the National Conference of Black Lawyers has stated, "Someone black and poor tried for stealing a few hundred dollars has a 90 percent likelihood of being convicted of robbery with a sentence averaging between 94 to 138 months. A white business executive who embezzled hundreds of thousands of dollars has only a 20 percent likelihood of conviction with a sentence averaging about 20 to 48 months." Justice is not "color blind" when Black males are the accused.

What does the economic and social destruction of Black males mean for the Black commu-

nity as a whole? Dr. Robert Staples, associate professor of sociology at the University of California–San Francisco, cites some devastating statistics of the current plight of younger Black males:

Less than twenty percent of all black college graduates in the early 1980s are males. The vast majority of young black men who enter college drop out within two years.

At least one-fourth of all black male teenagers never complete high school.

Since 1960, black males between the ages of 15 to 20 have committed suicide at rates higher than that of the general white population. Suicide is currently the third leading cause of death, after homicides, and accidents, for black males aged 15 to 24.

About half of all black men over age 18 have never been married [or are] separated, divorced or widowed.

Despite the fact that several million black male youths identify a career in professional athletics as a desirable career, the statistical probability of any black man making it to the pros exceeds 20,000 to one.

One half of all homicides in America today are committed by black men—whose victims are other black men.

The typical black adult male dies almost three years before he can even begin to collect Social Security.

Fred Clark, a staff psychologist for the California Youth Authority, states that the social devastation of an entire generation of Black males has made it extremely difficult for eligible Black women to locate partners. "In Washington, D.C., it is estimated that there is a one to twelve ratio of black [single] males to eligible females," Clark observes. "Some research indicates that the female is better suited for surviving alone than the male. There are more widowed and single black females than males. Males die earlier and more quickly than females when single. Single black welfare mothers seem to live longer than single unemployed black males."

Every socioeconomic and political indicator illustrates that the Black male in America is facing an unprecedented crisis. Despite singular examples of successful males in electoral politics, business, labor unions, and the professions, the overwhelming majority of Black men find it difficult to acquire self-confidence and self-esteem within the chaos of modern economic and social life. The stereotypes imposed by white history and by the lack of knowledge of our own past often convince many younger Black males that their struggle is too overwhelming. Black women have a responsibility to comprehend the forces that destroy the lives of thousands of their brothers, sons, and husbands. But Black men must understand that they, too, must overcome their own inherent and deeply ingrained sexism, recognizing that Black women must be equal partners in the battle to uproot injustice at every level of the society. The strongest ally Black men have in their battle to achieve Black freedom is the Black woman. Together, without illusions and false accusations, without racist and sexist stereotypes, they can achieve far more than they can ever accomplish alone.

REFERENCES

Davis, A. Y. 1981. *Women, Race and Class*. New York: Random House.

Billingsley, A. 1968. *Black Families in White America*. Englewood Cliffs, NJ: Prentice-Hall.

Lincoln, C. E. 1965. "The Absent Father Haunts the Negro Family." *New York Times Magazine*, Nov. 28.

Clark, K. 1965. *Dark Ghetto*. New York: Harper and Row.

Marable, M. 1983. *How Capitalism Underdeveloped Black America*. Boston: South End Press.

CHICANO MEN AND MASCULINITY

MAXINE BACA ZINN

Only recently have social scientists begun to systematically study the male role. Although men and their behavior had been assiduously studied (Pleck and Brannon, 1978), masculinity as a specific topic had been ignored. The scholar's disregard of male gender in the general population stands in contrast to the preoccupation with masculinity that has long been exhibited in the literature on minority groups. The social science literature on Blacks and Chicanos specifically reveals a long-standing interest in masculinity. A common assumption is that gender roles among Blacks are less dichotomous than among Whites, and more dichotomous among Chicanos. Furthermore, these differences are assumed to be a function of the distinctive historical and cultural heritage of these groups. Gender segregation and stratification, long considered to be a definitive characteristic of Chicanos, is illustrated in Miller's descriptive summary of the literature:

> *Sex roles are rigidly dichotomized with the male conforming to the dominant-aggressive archetype, and the female being the polar opposite—subordinate and passive. The father is the unquestioned patriarch—the family provider, protector and judge. His word is law and demands strict obedience. Presumably, he is perpetually obsessed with the need to prove his manhood, oftentimes through excessive drinking, fighting, and/or extramarital conquests (1979:217).*

The social science image of the Chicano male is rooted in three interrelated propositions: (1) That a distinctive cultural heritage has created a rigid cult of masculinity, (2) That the masculinity cult generates distinctive familial and socialization patterns, and (3) That these distinctive patterns ill-equip Chicanos (both males and females) to adapt successfully to the demands of modern society.

The machismo concept constitutes a primary explanatory variable for both family structure and overall subordination. Mirandé critically outlines the reasoning in this interpretation:

> *The macho male demands complete deference, respect and obedience not only from the wife but from the children as well. In fact, social scientists maintain that this rigid male-dominated family structure has negative consequences for the personality development of Mexican American children. It fails to engender achievement, independence, self-reliance or self worth—values which are highly esteemed in American society. . . . The authoritarian Mexican American family constellation then produces dependence and subordination and reinforces a present time orientation which impedes achievement (1977:749).*

In spite of the widely held interpretation associated with male dominance among Chicanos, there is a growing body of literature which refutes past images created by social scientists. My purpose is to examine empirical challenges to machismo, to explore theoretical developments in the general literature on gender, and to apply both of these to alternative directions for studying and understanding Chicano men and masculinity. My central theme is that while ethnic

M. Baca Zinn, "Chicano Family Research: Conceptual distortions and alternative directions" appeared in *The Journal of Ethnic Studies* 10:2, pp. 29–44. Reprinted with permission.

status may be associated with differences in masculinity, those differences can be explained by structural variables rather than by references to common cultural heritage.

THEORETICAL CHALLENGES TO CULTURAL INTERPRETATIONS: THE UNIVERSALITY OF MALE DOMINANCE

The generalization that culture is a major determinant of gender is widely accepted in the social sciences. In the common portrayal of Chicanos, exaggerated male behavior is assumed to stem from inadequate masculine identity.

The social science literature views machismo as a compensation for feelings of inadequacy and worthlessness. This interpretation is rooted in the application of psychoanalytic concepts to explain both Mexican and Chicano gender roles. The widely accepted interpretation is that machismo is the male attempt to compensate for feelings of internalized inferiority by exaggerated masculinity. "At the same time that machismo is an expression of power, its origin is ironically linked to powerlessness and subordination." The common origins of inferiority and machismo are said to lie in the historical conquest of Mexico by Spain involving the exploitation of Indian women by Spanish men thus producing the hybrid Mexican people having an inferiority complex based on the mentality of a conquered people (Baca Zinn, 1980b:20).

The assumption that male dominance among Chicanos is rooted in their history and embedded in their culture needs to be critically assessed against recent discussions concerning the universality of male dominance. Many anthropologists consider all known societies to be male dominant to a degree (Stockard and Johnson 1980:4). It has been argued that in all known societies male activities are more highly valued than female activities, and that this can be explained in terms of the division of labor between domestic and public spheres of society (Rosaldo, 1973). Women's child-bearing abilities limit their participation in public sphere activities and allow men the freedom to participate in and control the

public sphere. Thus in the power relations between the sexes, men have been found to be dominant over women and to control economic resources (Spence 1978:4).

While differing explanations of the cause of male dominance have been advanced, recent literature places emphasis on networks of social relations between men and women and the status structures within which their interactions occur. This emphasis is crucial because it alerts us to the importance of structural variables in understanding sex stratification. Furthermore, it casts doubt on interpretations which treat culture (the systems of shared beliefs and orientations unique to groups) as the cause of male dominance. If male dominance is universal, then it cannot be reduced to the culture of a particular category of people.

CHALLENGES TO MACHISMO

Early challenges to machismo emerged in the protest literature of the 1960s and 1970s and have continued unabated. Challenges are theoretical, empirical, and impressionistic. Montiel, in the first critique of machismo, set the stage for later refutations by charging that psychoanalytic constructs resulted in indiscriminate use of machismo, and that this made findings and interpretations highly suspect (1970). Baca Zinn (1975:25) argued that viewing machismo as a compensation for inferiority (whether its ultimate cause is seen as external or internal to the oppressed), in effect blames Chicanos for their own subordination. Sosa Riddell proposed that the machismo myth is exploited by an oppressive society which encourages a defensive stance on the part of Chicano men (1974). Delgado (1974:6) in similar fashion, wrote that stereotyping acts which have nothing to do with machismo and labeling them as such was a form of societal control.

Recent social science literature on Chicanos has witnessed an ongoing series of empirical challenges to the notion that machismo is the norm in marital relationships (Grebler, Moore and Guzman, 1970; Hawkes and Taylor, 1975;

Ybarra, 1977; Cromwell and Cromwell, 1978; Cromwell and Ruiz, 1979; Baca Zinn, 1980a). The evidence presented in this research suggests that in the realm of marital decision making, egalitarianism is far more prevalent than macho dominance.

Cromwell and Ruiz find that the macho characterization prevalent in the social science literature is "very compatible with the social deficit model of Hispanic life and culture" (1979:355). Their re-analysis of four major studies on marital decision making (Cromwell, Corrales and Torsellio, 1973; Delchereo, 1969; Hawkes and Taylor, 1975; and Cromwell and Cromwell, 1978) concludes that "the studies suggest that while wives make the fewest unilateral decisions and husbands make more, joint decisions are by far the most common in these samples . . ." (1979:370).

Other studies also confirm the existence of joint decision making in Chicano families and furthermore they provide insights as to factors associated with joint decision making, most importantly that of wives' employment. For example, Ybarra's survey of 100 married Chicano couples in Fresno, California found a range of conjugal role patterns with the majority of married Chicano couples sharing decision making. Baca Zinn (1980a) examined the effects of wives' employment outside of the home and level of education through interviews and participation in an urban New Mexico setting. The study revealed differences in marital roles and marital power between families with employed wives and nonemployed wives. "In all families where women were not employed, tasks and decision making were typically sex segregated. However, in families with employed wives, tasks and decision making were shared" (1980a:51).

Studies of the father role in Chicano families also called into question the authoritative unfeeling masculinized male figure (Mejia, 1976; Luzod and Arce, 1979). These studies are broadly supportive of the marital role research which points to a more democratic egalitarian approach to family roles. Luzod and Arce conclude:

It is not our contention to say that no sex role differences occur within Chicano families, but rather demonstrate the level of importance which both the father and mother give to respective duties as parents as well as the common hopes and desires they appear to share equally for their progeny than was commonly thought. It therefore appears erroneous to focus only on maternal influences in the Chicano family since Chicano fathers are seen as being important to the children and moreover may provide significant positive influences on the development of their children (1979:19).

Recent empirical refutations of super-masculinity in Chicano families have provided the basis of discussions of the Chicano male role (Valdez, 1980; Mirandé, 1979, 1981). While these works bring together in clear fashion impressionistic and empirical refutations of machismo, they should be considered critical reviews rather than conceptual refutations. In an important essay entitled, "Machismo: Rucas, Chingasos, y Chingaderas" (1981), Mirandé critically assesses the stereotypic components of machismo, yet he asserts that it also has authentic components having to do with the resistance of oppression. While this is a significant advance, it requires conceptual focus and analysis.

UNANSWERED QUESTIONS, UNRESOLVED ISSUES AND UNRECOGNIZED PROBLEMS

The works discussed above provide a refutation of the simplistic, one-dimensional model of Chicano masculinity. As such they constitute important contributions to the literature. My own argument does not contradict the general conclusion that machismo is a stereotype, but attempts to expand it by posing some theoretical considerations.

In their eagerness to dispute machismo and the negative characteristics associated with the trait, critics have tended to neglect the phenomenon of male dominance at societal, institutional, and interpersonal levels. While the cultural stereotype of machismo has been in need of critical analysis, male dominance does exist among

Chicanos. Assertions such as the following require careful examination:

> *There is sufficient evidence to seriously question the traditional male dominant view (Mirandé, 1979:47).*

Although male dominance may not typify marital decision making in Chicano families, it should not be assumed that it is nonexistent either in families or in other realms of interaction and organization.

Research by Ybarra (1977) and Baca Zinn (1980) found both egalitarian and male-dominant patterns of interaction in Chicano families. They found these patterns to be associated with distinct social conditions of families, most notably wives' employment. The finding that male dominance can be present in some families but not in others, depending on specific social characteristics of family members, is common in family research.

The important point is that we need to know far more than we do about which social conditions affecting Chicanos are associated with egalitarianism and male dominance at both micro and macro levels of organization. Placing the question within this framework should provide significant insights by enlarging the inquiry beyond that of the culture stereotype of machismo. It is necessary to guard against measuring and evaluating empirical reality against this stereotype. The dangers of using a negative ideal as a normative guide are raised by Eichler (1980). In a provocative work, she raises the possibility that the literature challenging gender stereotypes, while explicitly attempting to overcome past limitations of the gender roles research may operate to reinforce the stereotype. Thus, it could be argued that energy expended in refuting machismo may devote too much attention to the concept, and overlook whole areas of inquiry. We have tended to assume that ethnic groups vary in the demands imposed on men and women. "Ethnic differences in sex roles have been discussed by large numbers of social scientists" (Romer and Cherry, 1980:246). However, these discussions have treated differences as cultural or subcultural in nature. Davidson and Gordon are critical of subcultural explanations of differences in gender roles because they "fail to investigate the larger political and economic situations that affect groups and individuals. They also fail to explain how definition of the roles of women and men, as well as those associated with ethnicity, vary over time and from place to place" (1979:124).

1. What specific social conditions are associated with variation in general roles among Chicanos?
2. If there are ethnic differences in gender roles, to what extent are these a function of shared beliefs and orientations (culture) and to what extent are they a function of men's and women's place in the network of social relationships (structure)?
3. To what extent are gender roles among Chicanos more segregated and male dominated than among other social groups?
4. How does ethnicity contribute to the subjective meaning of masculinity (and femininity)?

STRUCTURAL INTERPRETATIONS OF GENDER ROLES

There is a good deal of theoretical support for the contention that masculine roles and masculine identity may be shaped by a wide range of variables having less to do with culture than with common structural position. Chafetz calls into question the cultural stereotype of machismo by proposing that it is a socioeconomic characteristic:

> *. . . more than most other Americans, the various Spanish speaking groups in this country (Mexican American, Puerto Rican, Cuban), . . . stress dominance, aggressiveness, physical prowess and other stereotypical masculine traits. Indeed the masculine sex role for this group is generally described by reference to the highly stereotyped notion of machismo. In fact, a strong emphasis on masculine aggressiveness and dominance may be characteristic of most groups in the lower ranges of the socioeconomic ladder (1979:54).*

Without discounting the possibility that cultural differences in male roles exist, it makes good conceptual sense to explain these differences in terms of sociostructural factors. Davidson and Gordon suggest that the following social conditions affect the development of gender roles in ethnic groups: (1) the position of the group in the stratification system, (2) the existence of an ethnic community, (3) the degree of self identification with the minority group (1979:120). Romer and Cherry more specifically propose that ethnic or subcultural sex role definitions can be viewed as functions of the specific and multiple role demands made on a given subgroup such as skilled or unskilled workers, consumers, etc., and the cultural prism through which these role expectations are viewed (1980:246). Both of these discussions underscore the importance of the societal placement of ethnics in the shaping of gender roles. This line of reasoning should not be confused with "culture of poverty" models which posit distinctive subcultural traits among the lower class. However, it can be argued that class position affects both normative and behavioral dimensions of masculinity.

The assumption that Chicanos are more strongly sex typed in terms of masculine identity is called into question by a recent study. Senour and Warren conducted research to question whether ethnic identity is related to masculine and feminine sex role orientation among Blacks, Anglos and Chicanos. While significant sex differences were found in all categories, Senour and Warren concluded that Mexican American males did not emerge as super masculine in comparison to Black and Anglo males (1976:2).

There is some support for this interpretation. In roles dealing with masculinity among Black males, Parker and Kleiner (1977) and Staples (1978) find that role performance must be seen in light of the structurally generated inequality in employment, housing, and general social conditions. Staples writes:

. . . men often define their masculinity in terms of the ability to impregnate women and to reproduce prolifically children who are extensions of themselves, especially sons. For many lower income black males there is an inseparable link between their self image as men and their ability to have sexual relations with women and the subsequent birth of children from those sexual acts. At the root of this virility cult is the lack of role fulfillment available to men of the underclass. The class factor is most evident here, if we note that middle class black males sire fewer children than any other group in this society (1978:178).

What is most enlightening about Staples' discussion of masculinity is that it treats male behavior and male identity not as a subcultural phenomenon, but as a consequence of social structural factors associated with race and class.

A thoughtful discussion of inequality, race, and gender is provided by Lewis (1977). Her analysis enlarges upon Rosaldo's model of the domestic public split as the source of female subordination and male dominance discussed earlier. It has pertinent structural considerations. Lewis acknowledges the notion of a structural opposition between the domestic and public spheres which offers useful insights in understanding differential participation and evaluation of men and women. Nevertheless, she argues that its applicability to racial minority men and women may be questionable since historically Black men (like Black women) have been excluded from participation in public sphere institutions. Lewis asserts:

What the black experience suggests is that differential participation in the public sphere is a symptom rather than a cause of structural inequality. While inequality is manifested in the exclusion of a group from public life, it is actually generated in the groups' unequal access to power and resources in a hierarchically arranged social order. Relationships of dominance and subordination, therefore, emerge from a basic structural opposition between groups which is reflected in exclusion of the subordinate group from public life (1977:342).

Lewis then argues that among racially oppressed groups, it is important to distinguish between the public life of the dominant and the dominated societies. Using this framework we recognize a range of male participation from token admittance to the public life of the dominant group to its attempts to destroy the public life within a dominated society. She points to the fact that Mexican American men have played strong public roles in their own dominated society, and as Mexican Americans have become more assimilated to the dominating society, sex roles have become less hierarchical. The significant feature of this argument has to do with the way in which attention is brought to shifts in power relationships between the dominant society and racial minorities, and how these shifts effect changes in relationships between the sexes. Lewis' analysis makes it abundantly clear that minority males' exclusion from the public sphere requires further attention.

CHICANO MASCULINITY AS A RESPONSE TO STRATIFICATION AND EXCLUSION

There are no works, either theoretical or empirical, specifically devoted to the impact of structural exclusion on male roles and male identity. However, there are suggestions that the emphasis on masculinity might stem from the fact that alternative roles and identity sources are systematically blocked from men in certain social categories. Lillian Rubin, for example, described the martial role egalitarianism of middle-class professional husbands as opposed to the more traditional authoritarian role of working class husbands in the following manner:

> . . . the professional male is more secure, has more status and prestige than the working class man, factors which enable him to assume a less overtly authoritarian role within the family. There are, after all, other places, other situations where his authority and power are tested and accorded legitimacy. At the same time, the demands of his work role for a satellite wife require that he risk the consequences of a more egalitarian family ideology. In contrast, for the working class men, there are few such rewards in the world outside the home. The family is usually the only place where

> he can exercise power, demand obedience to his authority. Since his work role makes no demands for wifely participation, he is under fewer and less immediate external pressures to accept the egalitarian ideology (Rubin, 1976:99).

Of course, Rubin is contrasting behaviors of men in different social classes, but the same line of thinking is paralleled in Ramos' speculation that for some Chicanos what has been called "machismo" may be a "way of feeling capable in a world that makes it difficult for Chicanos to demonstrate their capabilities" (Ramos, 1979:61).

We must understand that while maleness is highly valued in our society, it interacts with other categorical distinctions in both manifestation and meaning. As Stoll (1974:124) presents this idea, our society is structured to reward some categories in preference to others (e. g., men over women) but the system is not perfectly rational. First the rewards are scarce, second, other categories such as race, ethnicity and other statuses are included in the formula. Furthermore, the interaction of different categories with masculinity contributes to multiple societal meanings of masculinity, so that "one can never be sure this aspect of one's self will not be called into dispute. One is left having to account for oneself, thus to be on the defensive" (Stoll, 1974:124). It is in light of the societal importance attributed to masculinity that we must assess Stoll's contention that "gender identity is a more profound personal concern for the male in our society than it is for women, because women can take it for granted that they are female" (Stoll, 1974:105). This speculation may have implications for Chicanos as well. Perhaps it will be found that ethnic differences in the salience of gender are not only one of degree but that their relative significance has different meanings. In other words, gender may not be a problematic identifier for women if they can take if for granted, though it may be primary because many still participate in society through their gender roles. On the other hand, men in certain social categories have had more roles and sources of identity open to them. However, this has not been the case for Chicanos or other men of color. Perhaps manhood takes on greater importance for those who do not have access to socially valued roles. Being male is one sure way to acquire status when other roles are systematically denied by the workings of society. This suggests that an emphasis on masculinity is not due to a collective internalized inferiority, rooted in a subcultural orientation. To be "hombre" may be a reflection of both ethnic and gender components and may take on greater significance when other roles and sources of masculine identity are structurally blocked. Chicanos have been excluded from participation in the dominant society's political–economic system. Therefore, they have been denied resources and the accompanying authority accorded men in other social categories. My point that gender may take on a unique and greater significance for men of color is not to justify traditional masculinity, but to point to the need for understanding societal conditions that might contribute to the meaning of gender among different social categories. It may be worthwhile to consider some expressions of masculinity as attempts to gain some measure of control in a society that categorically denies or grants people control over significant realms of their lives.

Turner makes this point about the male posturing of Black men: "Boastful, or meek, these performances are attempts by black men to actualize control in some situation" (Turner, 1977:128). Much the same point is made in discussions of Chicanos. The possibility has been raised that certain aggressive behaviors on the part of Chicano men were "a calculated response to hostility, exclusion, and racial domination," and a "conscious rejection of the dominant society's definition of Mexicans as passive, lazy, and indifferent" (Baca Zinn, 1975:23). Mirandé (1981:35) also treats machismo as an adaptive characteristic, associated with visible and manifest resistance of Chicano men to racial oppression. To view Chicano male behavior in this light is not to disregard possible maladaptive consequences of overcompensatory masculinity, but rather to recast masculinity in terms of responses to structural conditions.

Differences in normative and behavioral dimensions of masculinity would be well worth exploring. Though numerous recent studies have challenged macho male dominance in the realm of family decision making, there is also evidence that patriarchal *ideology* can be manifested even in Chicano families where decision making is not male dominant. Baca Zinn's findings of *both* male dominant and egalitarian families revealed also that the ideology of patriarchy was expressed in all families studied:

> *Patriarchal ideology was expressed in statements referring to the father as the "head" of the family, as the "boss," as the one "in charge." Informants continually expressed their beliefs that it "should be so." Findings confirmed that while male dominance was a cultural ideal, employed wives openly challenged that dominance on a behavioral level (1975:15).*

It is possible that such an ideology is somehow associated with family solidarity. This insight is derived from Michel's analysis of family values (cited in Goode, 1963:57). Drawing on cross cultural studies, she reports:

> *. . . the concept of the strength or solidarity of the family is viewed as being identical with the father . . . the unity of the family is identified with the prerogatives of the father.*

If this is the case, it is reasonable to suggest that the father's authority is strongly upheld because family solidarity is important in a society that excludes and subordinates Chicanos. The tenacity of patriarchy may be more than a holdover from past tradition. It may also represent a contemporary cultural adaptation to the minority condition of structural discrimination.

CONCLUSION

The assumption that male dominance among Chicanos is exclusively a cultural phenomenon is contradicted by much evidence. While many of the concerns raised in this paper are speculative in nature, they are nevertheless informed by current conceptualization in relevant bodies of literature. They raise the important point that we need further understanding of larger societal conditions in which masculinity is embedded and expressed. This forces us to recognize the disturbing relationship between the stratification axes of race, class and sex. To the extent that systems of social inequality limit men's access to societally valued resources, they also contribute to sexual stratification. Men in some social categories will continue to draw upon and accentuate their masculinity as a socially valued resource. This in turn poses serious threats to sexual equality. We are compelled to move the study of masculinity beyond narrow confines of subcultural roles, and to make the necessary theoretical and empirical connections between the contingencies of sex and gender and the social order.

REFERENCES

Baca Zinn, Maxine.
1975 "Political Familism: Toward Sex Role Equality in Chicano Families," *International Journal of Chicano Studies Research* 6:13–26.
1980a "Employment and Education of Mexican American Women: The Interplay of Modernity and Ethnicity in Eight Families." *Harvard Educational Review* 50:47–62.
1980b "Gender and Ethnic Identity Among Chicanos." *Frontiers*: V(2)18–24.
Chafetz, Janet Saltzman.
1974 *Masculine/Feminine or Human*. E. E. Ithica. Ill.: Peacock Publishers, Inc.
Cromwell, Vicky L. and Ronald E. Cromwell.
1978 "Perceived Dominance in Decision-Making and Conflict Resolution Among Anglo, Black and Chicano Couples." *Journal of Marriage and the Family*. 40(Nov.):749–759.
Cromwell, Ronald E. and Rene E. Ruiz.
1979 "The Myth of Macho Dominance in Decision Making Within Mexican and Chicano Families." *Hispanic Journal of Behavioral Sciences*. 1:355–373.
Davidson, Laurie and Laura Kramer Gordon.
1979 *The Sociology of Gender*. Rand McNally College Publishing Co.
Delgado, Abelardo.
1974 "Machismo." *La Luz*. (Dec.):6.
Eichler, Margrit.
1980 *The Double Standard: A Feminist Critique of Feminist Social Science*. St. Martin's Press.
Grebler, Leo, Joan W. Moore and Ralph C. Guzman.
1970 *The Mexican American People: The Nation's Second Largest Minority*. The Free Press.
Hawkes, Glenn R. and Minna Taylor.

1975 "Power Structure in Mexican and Mexican-American Farm Labor Families." *Journal of Marriage and the Family*. 37:807-811.
Hyde, Janet Shibley and B. G. Rosenberg.
1976 Half the Human Experience. *The Psychology of Women*. D. C. Heath and Company.
Lewis, Diane K.
1977 "A Response to Inequality: Black Women, Racism, and Sexism" *SIGNS: Journal of Women in Culture and Society*. 3:339–361
Luzod, Jimmy A. and Carlos H. Arce.
1979 "An Exploration of the Father Role in the Chicano Family." Paper presented at the National Symposium on the Mexican American Child. Santa Barbara, California.
Mejia, Daniel P.
1976 Cross-Ethnic Father Role: Perceptions of Middle Class Anglo American Parents, Doctoral Dissertation, University of California, Irvine.
Miller, Michael V.
1975 "Variations in Mexican-American Family Life: A Review Synthesis." Paper presented at Rural Sociological Society, San Francisco, California.
Mirandé, Alfredo.
1977 "The Chicano Family: A Reanalysis of Conflicting Views." *Journal of Marriage and the Family*. 39:747–756.
1979 "A Reinterpretation of Male Dominance in the Chicano Family." *Family Coordinator* 28(4): 473–497.
1981 "Machismo: Rucas, Chingasos, y Chingaderas." *De Colores*, Forthcoming.
Montiel, Miguel.
1970 "The Social Science Myth of the Mexican American Family." *El Grito*. 3:56–63.
Parker, Seymour and Robert J. Kleiner.

1977 "Social and Psychological Dimensions of the Family Role Performance of the Negro Male." Pp. 102–117 in Doris Y. Wilkinson and Ronald L. Taylor (editors), *The Black Male in America*. Nelson-Hall.

Pleck, Joseph H. and Robert Brannon.
1978 "Male Roles and the Male Experience: Introduction." *Journal of Social Issues*. 34:1–4.

Ramos, Reyes.
1979 "The Mexican American: Am 1 Who They Say I Am?" Pp. 49–66 in Arnulfo D. Trejo (editor), *The Chicanos as We See Ourselves*. The University of Arizona Press.

Riddell, Adaljisa Sosa.
1974 "Chicanas and El Movimiento." *Aztlan*. 5(1 and 2):155–165.

Romer, Nancy and Debra Cherry.
1980 "Ethnic and Social Class Differences in Children's Sex-Role Concepts." *Sex Roles*. 6:245–263.

Rosaldo, Michelle and Louise Lamphere.
1974 *Woman, Culture, and Society*. Stanford: Stanford University Press.

Rubin, Lillian
1976 *Worlds of Pain*. Basic Books.

Senour, Maria Neito and Lynda Warren.
1976 "Sex and Ethnic Differences in Masculinity, Femininity and Anthropology." Paper presented at the meeting of the Western Psychological Association, Los Angeles, California.

Spence, Janet T. and Robert L. Helmreich.
1978 *Masculinity and Femininity: The Psychological Dimensions, Correlates and Antecedents*. University of Austin Press.

Staples, Robert.
1978 "Masculinity and Race: The Dual Dilemma of Black Men." *Journal of Social Issues*. 34:169–183.

Stockard, Jean and Miriam M. Johnson.
1980 *Sex Roles*. Englewood Cliffs, New Jersey: Prentice-Hall

Stoll, Clarice Stasz.
1974 *Male and Female: Socialization, Social Roles, and Social Structure*. William C. Brown Publishers.

Turner, William H.
1977 "Myths and Stereotypes: The African Man in America." Pp. 122–144 in Doris Y. Wilkinson and Ronald L. Taylor (editors), *The Black Male in America*. Nelson-Hall.

Valdez, Ramiro.
1980 "The Mexican American Male: A Brief Review of the Literature." *Newsletter of the Mental Health Research Project*, I.D.R.A. San Antonio: 4–5.

Ybarra-Soriano, Lea.
1977 *Conjugal Role Relationships in the Chicano Family*. Ph.D. diss. University of California at Berkeley.

JUDAISM, MASCULINITY
AND FEMINISM

MICHAEL S. KIMMEL

In the late 1960s, I organized and participated in several large demonstrations against the war in Vietnam. Early on—it must have been 1967 or so—over 10,000 of us were marching down Fifth Avenue in New York urging the withdrawal of all U.S. troops. As we approached one corner, I noticed a small but vocal group of counter-demonstrators, waving American flags and shouting patriotic slogans. "Go back to Russia!" one yelled. Never being particularly shy, I tried to engage him. "It's my duty as an American to oppose policies I disagree with. This is patriotism!" I answered. "Drop dead, you commie Jew fag!" was his reply.

Although I tried not to show it, I was shaken by his accusation, perplexed and disturbed by the glib association of communism, Judaism, and homosexuality. "Only one out of three," I can say to myself now, "is not especially perceptive." But yet something disturbing remains about that linking of political, religious, and sexual orientations. What links them, I think, is a popular perception that each is not quite a man, that each is less than a man. And while recent developments may belie this simplistic formulation, there is, I believe, a kernel of truth to the epithet, a small piece I want to claim, not as vicious smear, but proudly. I believe that my Judaism did directly contribute to my activism against that terrible war, just as it currently provides the foundation for my participation in the struggle against sexism.

What I want to explore here are some of the ways in which my Jewishness has contributed to becoming an anti-sexist man, working to make this world a safe environment for women (and men) to fully express their humanness. Let me be clear that I speak from a cultural heritage of Eastern European Jewry, transmuted by three generations of life in the United States. I speak of the culture of Judaism's effect on me as an American Jew, not from either doctrinal considerations—we all know the theological contradictions of a biblical reverence for women, and prayers that thank God for not being born one—nor from an analysis of the politics of nation states. My perspective says nothing of Middle-Eastern machismo; I speak of Jewish culture in the diaspora, not of Israeli politics.

The historical experience of Jews has three elements that I believe have contributed to this participation in feminist politics. First, historically, the Jew is an *outsider*. Wherever the Jew has gone, he or she has been outside the seat of power, excluded from privilege. The Jew is the symbolic "other," not unlike the symbolic "otherness" of women, gays, racial and ethnic minorities, the elderly and the physically challenged. To be marginalized allows one to see the center more clearly than those who are in it, and

Reprinted from *Changing Men*, Summer/Fall 1987.

This essay was originally prepared as a lecture on "Changing Roles for the American Man" at the 92nd Street Y in November, 1983. I am grateful to Bob Brannon and Harry Brod for comments and criticisms of an earlier draft.

42

presents grounds for alliances among marginal groups.

But the American Jew, the former immigrant, is "other" in another way, one common to many ethnic immigrants to the United States. Jewish culture is, after all, seen as an ethnic culture, which allows it to be more oppressive and emotionally rich than the bland norm. Like other ethnic subgroups, Jews have been characterized as emotional, nurturing, caring. Jewish men hug and kiss, cry and laugh. A little too much. A little too loudly. Like ethnics.

Historically, the Jewish man has been seen as less than masculine, often as a direct outgrowth of this emotional "respond-ability." The historical consequences of centuries of laws against Jews, of anti-Semitic oppression, are a cultural identity and even a self-perception as "less than men," who are too weak, too fragile, too frightened to care for our own. The cruel irony of ethnic oppression is that our rich heritage is stolen from us, and then we are blamed for having no rich heritage. In this, again, the Jew shares this self-perception with other oppressed groups who, rendered virtually helpless by an infantilizing oppression, are further victimized by the accusation that they are, in fact, infants and require the beneficence of the oppressor. One example of this cultural self-hatred can be found in the comments of Freud's colleague and friend Weininger (a Jew) who argued that "the Jew is saturated with femininity. The most feminine Aryan is more masculine than the most manly Jew. The Jew lacks the good breeding that is based upon respect for one's own individuality as well as the individuality of others."

But, again, Jews are also "less than men" for a specific reason as well. The traditional emphasis on literacy in Jewish culture contributes in a very special way. In my family, at least, to be learned, literate, a rabbi, was the highest aspiration one could possibly have. In a culture characterized by love of learning, literacy may be a mark of dignity. But currently in the United States literacy is a cultural liability. Americans contrast egghead intellectuals, divorced from the real world, with men of action—instinctual, passionate, fierce, and masculine. Senator Albert Beveridge of Indiana counseled in his 1906 volume *Young Man and the World* (a turn of the century version of *Real Men Don't Eat Quiche*) to "avoid books, in fact, avoid all artificial learning, for the forefathers put America on the right path by learning from completely natural experience." Family, church and synagogue, and schoolroom were cast as the enervating domains of women, sapping masculine vigor.

Now don't get me wrong. The Jewish emphasis on literacy, on mind over body, does not exempt Jewish men from sexist behavior. Far from it. While many Jewish men avoid the Scylla of a boisterous and physically harassing misogyny, we can often dash ourselves against the Charybdis of a male intellectual intimidation of others. "Men with the properly sanctioned educational credentials in our society," writes Harry Brod, "are trained to impose our opinions on others, whether asked for or not, with an air of supreme self-confidence and aggressive self-assurance." It's as if the world were only waiting for our word. In fact, Brod notes, "many of us have developed mannerisms that function to intimidate those customarily denied access to higher educational institutions, especially women."[1] And yet, despite this, the Jewish emphasis on literacy has branded us, in the eyes of the world, less than "real" men.

Finally, the historical experience of Jews centers around, hinges upon our sense of morality, our ethical imperatives. The preservation of a moral code, the commandment to live ethically, is the primary responsibility of each Jew, male or female. Here, let me relate another personal story. Like many other Jews, I grew up with the words "Never Again" ringing in my ears, branded indelibly in my consciousness. For me they implied a certain moral responsibility to bear witness, to remember—to place my body, visibly, on the side of justice. This moral responsibility inspired my participation in the anti-war movement, and my active resistance of the draft *as a Jew*. I remember family dinners in front of the CBS Evening News, watching Walter Cronkite recite the daily tragedy of the war in Vietnam. "Never again," I said to myself, crying myself to sleep after watching napalm fall on Vietnamese villagers. Isn't this the brutal terror we have sworn ourselves to preventing when we utter those two words? When I allowed myself to feel the pain of those people, there was no longer a choice; there was, instead, a moral imperative to speak out, to attempt to end that war as quickly as possible.

In the past few years, I've become aware of another war. I met and spoke with women who had been raped, raped by their lovers, husbands, and fathers, women who had been beaten by those husbands and lovers. Some were even Jewish women. All those same words—Never Again—flashed across my mind like a neon meteor lighting up the darkened consciousness.

Hearing that pain and that anger prompted the same moral imperative. We Jews say "Never Again" to the systematic horror of the Holocaust, to the cruel war against the Vietnamese, to Central American death squads. And we must say it against this war waged against women in our society, against rape and battery.

So in a sense, I see my Judaism as reminding me every day of that moral responsibility, the *special* ethical imperative that my life, as a Jew, gives to me. Our history indicates how we have been excluded from power, but also, as men, we have been privileged by another power. Our Judaism impels us to stand against any power that is illegitimately constituted because we know only too well the consequences of that power. Our ethical vision demands equality and justice, and its achievement is our historical mission.

NOTE

1. Harry Brod, "Justice and a Male Feminist" in *The Jewish Newspaper* (Los Angeles) June 6, 1985, p. 6.

THE NEW MASCULINITY OF GAY MEN, AND BEYOND

SEYMOUR KLEINBERG

WHERE HAVE ALL THE SISSIES GONE: A VIEW FROM THE 1970S

One week after Labor Day 1977, I made a trip to the Anvil Bar, a gay club in New York City. For a long time I had wanted to know whether the legends of debauchery one heard with some skepticism were accurate. No one I knew was a member, and I had been told by those who claimed to be informed that I was not a likely type to crash successfully. I presumed they meant that my only leather jacket, tailored like a blazer, would not pass muster. Then a close friend became enamored of a go-go boy who danced there, joined the Anvil, and took me along to meet Daniel.

The bar nearly lived up to its fame. The boys do dance continually on top of the four-sided bar, they do strip naked, not counting construction shoes or cock rings. There is a back room where no-nonsense, hard-core porno films silently and continually flicker, shown by a mesmerized projectionist wearily perched on the ledge of the back wall. A small pitch-dark cubicle called the fuck room opens off the rear wall. In the middle of the front-room bar is a stage raised five feet where fist-fucking demonstrations used to be held at 3 a.m. if the crowd was enthusiastic, but those spontaneous shows were stopped when they began to draw tourists from the uptown discos. Now it is used by the dancers, who take turns exhibiting their specialties in the limelight. The boys range from extraordinary to middling, from high-schoolers to forty-year-olds, from professionals (everything) to amateurs who move awkwardly but who are graceful and stunning when they don't move at all. There are types for every taste and some for none. Hispanic and black, WASP and Italian, the boys dance three hours of a six-hour stint for $25 a night, three or four times a week. There are always new faces, and the management is liberal about letting anyone with a good body try out. Usually, there is one dancer who has had some ballet training and is naive enough to make that clear; he is invariably the least favored by the clientele.

My friend's Daniel is unusual. He is one of the few boys who can use the trapeze bars bolted to the ceiling with real expertise. Without breaking the rhythm of his dance, he leaps for a trapeze and spends four or five minutes on or swinging from one bar to another in the most daring manner. When he alights, it is with a sure flip back onto the bar, where he continues to dance with an unbroken stride. Daniel has never fallen, as some of the boys have (a broken nose or a fractured arm is not unheard of), nor has he crashed into a customer since he holds his drugs well.

"The New Masculinity of Gay Men," written in 1978, was originally published as a chapter of Kleinberg's book *Alienated Affections* (New York: St. Martin's Press, 1980). "Life After Death: A View from the Late 1980s" is excerpted from an article in the *New Republic*, 11 and 18 Aug., 1986.

His other specialty is his ability to grab with his buttocks the folded one-dollar or five-dollar tips the men at the bar hold between their teeth, a variation on the skill of the Cotton Club girls of Harlem in the twenties and thirties. His perfect behind descends in time to the music over the customer's uplifted face, and there is a round of applause when the money disappears into those constricted rosy cheeks.

Like most of the clientele, Daniel looks like a college athlete or construction worker, two favored images these recent seasons. Clothed, he wears the uniform of the moment: cheap plaid flannel shirts and jeans, or if it is really warm just overalls, and boots or construction worker's shoes no matter what the weather is. With the first signs of frost, boots and heavy leather bomber jackets are *de rigueur*.

Daniel is also typical of one type of club client in that he is a masochist, a "slave" who sleeps with other men with the permission of his master (who instructs him to charge a hefty fee). While Daniel's masochism has taken a pecuniary turn, he is not really a whore, for he is indifferent to money, keeping only what he needs for his uppers and poppers, his grass and coke. He dances frenetically four nights a week and does what he is told because he finds that exciting. There is little that he has not experienced sexually, and at twenty-two, his tastes are now as perverse as any possibilities Western civilization has devised.

To look at him, one would hardly suspect that this Irish kid from Queens with his thatch of reddish hair, cowlick and all, this sweet-faced boy built like a swimmer in his blue-collar uniform, lives a life more sexually extreme than anything described by the Marquis de Sade. When he discusses his life, it appears to be an endless dirty movie, but the anecdotes tend to leave his listeners in a moral vacuum. While it is possible to become erotically excited hearing his adventures, it is difficult to judge them without feeling prudish. Conventional moral standards are tangential, psychological ones almost as irrelevant. One is not really shocked; rather, one feels adrift, puzzled, perhaps bemused. Most of all, this nice boy seems very remote.

The values of his generation, acted out as theater of the absurd, are even more histrionic in Daniel's life. Just as one does not expect experimental theater or avant-garde art to live up to the standards of naturalism, one does not try to understand Daniel's life from the lessons of one's own experience: the collective sanity of the past is momentarily dumb.

What one struggled to learn and call "adult" as the final approbation now looks somewhat priggish. If one wanted to use such standards, why go to the Anvil at all? But once one *is* there or at the Mine Shaft or any of half a dozen bars just like them, what does one use to understand this spectacle of men? Some, like me, are clearly audience at a drama where only the actors understand the play. Intuition is not trustworthy, and easy judgments make one feel like a tourist. But whether or not one wishes to refrain from judgment, one thing is clear, if not glaring. The universal stance is a studied masculinity. There are no limp wrists, no giggles, no indiscreet hips swiveling. Walk, talk, voice, costume, grooming are just right: this is macho country. It is a rigorous place where one destroys oneself in drugs and sexual humiliation.

The same impulses are evident in other scenes. Fire Island Pines is as besotted and extreme as the leather and Levis world, and often they overlap, but the Pines is playful. Like its shabbier neighbor, Cherry Grove, the Pines enjoys the long legacy of camp. It loves to dictate next year's chic to café society, for novelty, flair, and sophistication are as paramount in this scene as they are in the world of women's fashion. For a time, the place seemed to veer toward egalitarianism: only youthful beauty was required if one were not rich. But with inflation, the freeloading beauty has to be spectacular indeed. The dance halls of the Pines and the Grove, like the waterfront bars, are filled with handsome men posing in careful costumes, and no matter how elegant or expensive, they are all butch.

As a matter of fact, young gay men seem to have abjured effeminacy with universal success. Muscular bodies laboriously cultivated all year round are standard; youthful athletic agility is everyone's style. The volleyball game on the beach is no longer a camp classic; now it takes itself as seriously as the San Francisco gay softball team. Hardness is in.

But talk to these men, sleep with them, befriend them, and the problems are the old familiar ones: misery when they are in love, loneliness when they are not, frustration and ambitiousness at work, and a monumental self-centeredness that exacerbates the rest. These have been the archetypes of unhappiness in homosexual America for as long as I can remember.

What is different from anything else I remember, however, is the relentless pursuit of masculinity. There are no limits; the most oppressive images of sexual violence and dominance are adopted unhesitatingly. Though the neo-Nazi adorations—fascinating fascism as Susan Sontag terms them—are more sinister than the innocuous ideals of the weight-lifting room, they are equally mindless. The offense is not aesthetic; it is entirely political. The homosexuals who adopt images of masculinity, conveying their desire for power and their belief in its beauty, are in fact eroticizing the very values of straight society that have tyrannized their own lives. It is the tension between this style and the content of their lives that demands the oblivion of drugs and sexual libertinism. In the past, the duplicity of closeted lives found relief in effeminate camping; now the suppression of denial of the moral issue in their choice is far more damaging. The perversity of imitating their oppressors guarantees that such blindness will work itself out as self-contempt.

Sex and Sexual Politics

This is the central message of the macho bar world: manliness is the only real virtue; other values are contemptible. And manliness is not some philosophical notion or psychological state; it is not even morally related to behavior. It lies exclusively in the glamorization of physical strength.

This idea of masculinity is so conservative it is almost primitive. That homosexuals are attracted to it and find it gratifying is not a total surprise. Gay male sexual preference has always favored a butch boyish beauty and only in artistic or intellectual circles has beauty been allowed a certain feyness. Butchness is always relative; the least swishy man in the room is the most butch. It usually meant one looked straight, one could pass. In the past, an over-enthusiasm for butchness translated itself into a taste for rough trade. Those who were too frightened or sane to pursue that particular quarry could always find a gay partner who would accommodatingly act the part.

There is a special eroticism in the experience of pretending to be degraded that is by no means rare in adult sexual behavior of whatever persuasion. The homosexual whose erotic feelings are enhanced by the illusion that his partner holds him in contempt, who is thrilled when told his ass or mouth is just like a cunt, is involved in a complicated self-deception. What appears to be happening is a homosexual variation of masochism: the contempt of the "straight" partner emblazes gay self-contempt, which in turn is exploited as an aphrodisiac. Why this process works is less clear than how it does.

The complex tie between the need for degradation and sexual excitement has never been satisfactorily explored, though Freud began the effort over eighty years ago and writers and artists have always intuitively understood it. It seems to be prominent in societies that are advanced, where sexual mores are liberal or ambivalent, and where intellectual life is very sophisticated. In times like ours, when women are redefining their roles and images, men must also redefine theirs. As women forgo in dress and appearance the *style* of their oppression (it is the easiest to abandon and thus one of the first aspects to go), and as glamor falls under a suspicious light, men, increasingly accused of being the symbol of sexism, are forced to confront their own ideas of masculinity.

While straight men define their ideas from a variety of sources (strength, achievement, success, money), two of those sources are always their attitudes toward women and toward paternity. It is no coincidence that the same decade that popularized liberation for women and announced that the nuclear family was a failure also saw men return to a long-haired, androgynous style. If straight men are confused about their maleness, what is the dilemma for gay men, who rarely did more than imitate these ideas?

It is no accident that the macho gesture is always prominent in those gay bars and resorts where women are entirely absent. Certain gay locales have always catered exclusively to one sex: porno movie houses and bookstores, baths, public toilets. The new bars are often private clubs as much for the sake of legally barring women as for screening male customers. Their atmosphere is eerily reminiscent of the locker room. And, of course, while they are there, the men live as if there were no women in the world. This is a useful illusion. It allows some of them to get gang-banged in the back rooms and still evade the self-reproach that derives from the world's contempt for homosexual men who behave sexually like women. If there are no women in the world, some men simply must replace them. With women absent, whether one is sexually active or passive is no longer the great dividing issue.

In fact, some of the men who look most butch are the most liberated in bed, the least role-oriented. While there is still much role preference for passivity, it no longer has the clear quality it had in the past. Then, gay men made unmistakable announcements: those who liked to be fucked adopted effeminate mannerisms; those who were active tried to look respectable.

Quentin Crisp in his autobiography, *The Naked Civil Servant*, epitomized these attitudes. He documents the anger of an acquaintance railing at the misfortune of having picked up a young soldier who wanted to be fucked: "All of a sudden, he turned over. After all I'd done—flitting

about the room in my wrap . . . camping myself silly. My dear, I was disgusted."[1] Today, to replace the usually reliable information that straight or campy behavior conveyed in the past, gay men at the leather bars have taken to elaborate clothing signals: key chains or handkerchiefs drooping from left or right pocket in blue or yellow or red all have coded meanings. Occasionally, some of the *cognoscenti* lie and misalliances occur. Of course, one could ask a prospective partner what his preferences are, but that is the least likely behavior between strangers.

If I am critical of the present style, it is not because I advocate a return to the denigrations of the past. Quentin Crisp's rebelliousness testifies to the hourly misery of gay life when all the sexual roles are petrified. He considered all his friends "pseudo men in search of pseudo women." That is not an improvement on pseudo men in search of nothing. Nor is his sense of inferiority: "I regard all heterosexuals, however low, as superior to any homosexual, however noble." Such estimates were commonplace for men subjected to lifelong ridicule because they could not or would not disguise their effeminacy.

But camping for Crisp and for the entire homosexual world until the end of the 1950s was not just the expression of self-contempt by men pretending to be women and feeling pseudo as both. Camping also gave homosexual men an *exclusive* form of behavior that neither women nor straight men could adopt. Some women and straight men are camp, but that is another story.

Camping in the gay world did not mean simply behaving in a blatantly effeminate manner; that was camp only when performed in the presence of those it irritated or threatened or delighted. Swishing is effective only if someone else notices, preferably registering a sense of shock, or ideally, outrage. In discreet bars like the Blue Parrot in 1950, men impeccably Brooks Brothers and as apparently WASP as one's banker could, in a flicker, slide into limpness. They had available a persona that mixed ironic distance, close observation, and wit, all allies of sanity.

Camping did express self-denigration, but it was a complex criticism. For example, the women whom these men imitated were themselves extraordinary; androgynous idols like Garbo or Dietrich symbolized an ambiguous and amoral sexuality. But more important, in their campy behavior, gay men revealed an empathic observation of women and feminine interests.

When camping also released for gay men some of their anger at their closeted lives, it became a weapon as well as a comment. The behavior chosen for imitation or ridicule was usually evidence of sexist attitudes, of positions women had taken or were forced to take that had effeminized them out of their humanity. It is for this reason that feminists object to drag queens who still try to resemble the slavish emblems of the past, and their criticism would be valid if the imitations were sincere. But men in drag are not swept up in the delusion that they are women; only insane men in drag believe that. The rest are committed to ambiguity; they are neither men nor women and are only rarely androgynous— the aura of the drag is neuter.

When a gay man said, "Oh, Mary, come off it," he was sneering at pretension, self-deceit, or prudery. That it took the form of reminding one's fellow faggot that he was in reality no better than a woman, and often not as good with his "pseudo" sexual equipment, is not politically commendable, but why should gay men have had a special consciousness about sexism? At least they had a sure recognition of it: they imitated women because they understood that they were victims in sisterhood of the same masculine ideas about sexuality. Generations of women defined themselves entirely in men's terms, and homosexual men often seemed to accept the same values.

But there was also a chagrined recognition that they just could not live up to expectations. They could not be men as heterosexuals defined manhood; most of all they could not be men because they did not sleep with women or beget children. No amount of manliness could counterbalance that. Between the values of virility that

they did not question and their rage at having no apparent alternatives, gay men would camp out their frustration. It was not a particularly effective means of ending oppression, but it was a covert defiance of a society that humiliated them.

With the political and social changes of the sixties, a new androgyny seemed to be on the verge of life. Heterosexual and homosexual suddenly became less interesting than just sexual. Getting out of the closet was more than announcing one was gay; it was a pronouncement that one was free of sexual shame. The new mood fostered this; even straight boys looked prettier than girls. The relief at seeing male vanity in the open, surrendered to and accepted, made it possible for homosexuals to reconsider some of their attitudes toward themselves. It was no longer extraordinary to look effeminate in a world where most sexual men looked feminine and where sexually liberated women were the antithesis of the glamorous and fragile.

Sexual style had become a clear political issue. Conventional manliness was properly identified with reaction and repression. The enemy had a crewcut, was still posturing in outmoded chivalric stances, while his wife and daughter and son embraced the revolutionary notion of rolelessness. To some extent, this is where American society still is: searching for a sense of what roles, if any, are appropriate for adult men and women. Only the betrayed patriarch still refuses to acknowledge the permanence of these changes, since for him they are pure deprivations, erosions of his long, long, privilege.

Homosexuality and Masculinity

"Feminist" is a term that increasing numbers of gay men apply to themselves as they come to recognize the common oppression of homosexuals and women. The empathy of gay men in the past is the foundation for this newer understanding, and it is heartening to discover that a mutual sense of victimization need not always lead to self-denigration. If in the past women were less likely to feel self-contempt at being women than gay men felt at being homosexual, it was partly because women were rewarded for their acquiescence and partly because they did not have to experience the sense of having betrayed their birthright. Homosexual men usually gave up paternity as well as other prerogatives for their gayness and too often felt gypped for what they got. They exchanged the simplicity of being phallic oppressors for advantages much more dubious, and the sense that they had betrayed their best interests was haunting. As more gays come to realize the bankruptcy of conventional ideas of masculinity, it is easier for them to forgo the sexism they shared with heterosexual men.

Unfortunately, heterosexuals cling to their sexual definitions with even greater tenacity. For example, the Save Our Children slogan is not as banal as it sounds; the phobic hostility behind it expresses a genuine fear that some children will be lost, lost to patriarchy, to the values of the past, to the perpetuation of conventional ideas of men and women. There is a fear of homosexuality that is far beyond what the surface can explain.

Many gays, especially apolitical ones, are dismissive of Anita Bryant and what she represents. Remarks like "Straights will just have to hope that heterosexuality can hold its own on the open market" express a contempt for the fears, but not much understanding of them. It *is* puzzling: where does this idea of the frailty of heterosexuality come from, the assumption that a mere knowledge that teachers or ordinary people are gay will automatically seduce children? It comes from the panic about new sexual ideas, but most of all, about the identity of women.

It often sounds absurd when conservatives accuse feminist women of attempting to destroy the family, though it does not stop them from making the accusation. It is easier to appear sensible talking about the seduction of children by homosexuals. I suggest that much of the recent vehemence about the children is deflected from a much more central rage against women who are redefining their ideas about child rearing. The

political issue is always hottest when women's connection with motherhood is raised. Thus, the issues of child rearing and anti-abortion gather a conservative support that puzzles liberal America. What these issues have in common is the attempt of women to free themselves from conventional roles, crucially their roles as mothers. That liberation is the first wave; the secondary one, far more perilous, lies beneath the surface: it demands that men liberate themselves from their notions as well, since the central ideas about masculinity have always been related to the unquestioned responsibilities of men as husbands and fathers.

It is curious that lesbians are never mentioned when child molestation is raised as an issue, and when lesbians are attacked, as they were at Houston, it is in relation to their militant feminism, not in relation to their being school teachers. Lesbians have usually been exempt from heterosexual fears about seduction, partly because they are women and, like all women, traditionally powerless. When they are attacked, when the press notices lesbian issues, it is often in connection with custody cases. There the issue of saving the children for heterosexuality and precisely for patriarchy is clear. These lesbians who once lived as straight women, who married and had children, are objects of the most extreme wrath, and one that has used the judicial system as its instrument to punish them.

But most lesbians are not mothers, and most lesbian mothers do not end up, fortunately, as victims in custody hearings. Lesbians are usually dismissed as unimportant, as nuisances. It is the lowest rung on the ladder of social contempt. But gay men who have abdicated their privileges, who have made sexual desire a higher priority than power over women, are indeed not men at all.

Bryant's keynote is that homosexuals should return to the closet. That would solve the problem for straights, since it is *visibility* that is terrifying. To be openly gay without contrition or guilt or shame is to testify that there are viable alternative sexual styles. But the real alternative for the children is not necessarily homosexuality; it is to reject the old verities of masculine and feminine.

Ironically, the men at the Anvil have not rejected those verities at all. Their new pseudomasculinity is a precise response to the confusions of a society venturing toward sexual redefinition. But it is in its way as reactionary as the hysteria that Anita Bryant's campaign consolidated.

The men of the macho bars will not buy Quentin Crisp's book, or if they do, they will not read it sympathetically, whereas they *are* part of the audience that made the story of football player David Kopay a best seller.[2] I do not want to belittle Kopay's modest effort, but its success depends more on his image than on his courage. Effeminate men like Crisp who have the courage to defy society are eccentric; butch men are heroic. Of course, what is left unsaid is that Kopay could have passed: no one would have known if he hadn't told them, and having once announced it, he can still pass. What could sissies like Crisp do even if they didn't flaunt it? Crisp's *life* is an act of courage.

Ex-soldier Leonard Matlovich is also a respectable image.[3] When media reporters treat him and Kopay just like the mainstream Americans they have always been, they make a point many gays approve of: homosexual men are really like everyone else. If beneath Matlovich's conservative, bemedalled chest beat aberrant yearnings, the public, if not the army, can accommodate them. What makes Kopay and Matlovich seem acceptable to gays and straights alike, while the Quentin Crisps remain pitiful?

Crisp was defiant and miserable, an acknowledged victim, and unrepentant: it was all agony, but it couldn't have been any other way. Even more, Crisp made his sexuality the obsession of his life. His whole existence was devoted to proclaiming his homosexuality; it is the meaning of his life. Today, his heir is Daniel, who is as absorbed in the same singular definition of himself. Daniel's life seems consecrated to pleasure while Crisp's was miserable, and that is an enormous difference. But the source of his pleasure in sexuality is as extreme, as dangerous and defiant as the quest for pleasure in Crisp's life. I may feel that Crisp is morally superior because he has suffered and Daniel refuses to, but that is only a sentimental notion. What is stunning in both their lives is the exclusivity of sexuality, and while Daniel is not heroic, his life demands that one refrain from easy judgment. The drama of such displays is filled with meaning for them and us. These lives are not like others'.

Kopay and Matlovich are fighting to be like everyone else. They claim that they are just like other football players or professional soldiers, and I do not dispute them. Compared to their conventionality, their homosexuality is almost incidental. Neither of them has gotten off quite free, nor have they seemed to expect to. For reasons they articulate with unquestionable credibility, they could not tolerate the duplicity of being conservative, rather ordinary men and secret homosexuals. Ironically, to some extent they have now become extraordinary men if somewhat commonplace homosexuals.

The men in leather watching naked go-go boys and having sex in back-room bars are not like Crisp or Daniel whom they regard as a kind of erotic theater; they are much closer to Kopay and Matlovich with whom they can identify. The rock-bottom premise of such sympathy is that all forms of traditional masculinity are respectable; all symptoms of effeminacy are contemptible. Real sexual extremism, like Daniel's, belongs to a netherworld; it is not regarded as liberated but as libertine. Daniel is the complete sexual object, and his presence makes the bar world the psychological equivalent of the brothel for the men who watch him. He turns them on, and then they can play whore or client or both.

Most men who are ardent for leather defend it as play. Dressing butch is another version of the gay uniform. What is the harm of walking through the world dressed like a construction worker? What does it matter what costume you wear to the ball? Go as Cinderella's fairy godmother, and you may break the law. But go as

Hell's Angels, and you risk breaking your own spirit.

It is no coincidence that in the macho bar world and the libertine baths the incidence of impotence is so high that it is barely worth remarking, or that gay men increasingly rely on the toys and trappings of sadomasochism. It is not irrelevant that the new gay image of virility is most often illustrated in pornography.

Manly means hot, and hot is everything. Why then isn't it working better? Men tell me that I do not appreciate this new celebration of masculinity, that I am overlooking the important "fact": "We fell for masculinity when we were twelve; there must be something to it because it made us gay. Most of us didn't become gay because we fell in love with sissies; we became sissies because we fell in love with men, usually jocks."

It sounds familiar. And so what if one chooses to make one's life pornographic? Isn't that only the most recent version of sexual devotion, of incarnating Eros in one's life? Besides, it's too late to be a dogooder. Obviously, as soon as one sets up notions of propriety, no matter how well intended, they will be preempted by the worst, most coercive forces in our society. One is then forced to accept all choices of style; the alternative is to find oneself allied with oppression. In the arena of sexual politics, there is the left and the right. Those who think they are in the middle will ultimately discover that the center is the right.

But my feelings tell me that there is another version; that macho is somehow another closet, and not a new one—many have suspected that it's the oldest closet in the house. Macho cultures have always had more covert homosexuality. Without belaboring the analogy, there is one consistency. In those cultures, homosexuality is not a sexual identity; it is defined as role. Only the passive partner, which means anally passive or orally active, is homosexual; the other role is reserved for men, because one either is a man or one is not; that is, one is a woman, and a woman who cannot bear a child and attest to a man's virility is beneath contempt, at best a whore.

The men in the macho bars are not like this. They have adopted a style and abandoned its psychic origin in sexual role playing. Apparently they have rescued the best and discarded the worst. But it is an appearance that resonates with unexamined yearnings. It says I am strong and I am free, that gay no longer means the contemptibleness of being nelly, which is the old powerless *reactiveness* to oppression. Insofar as it does that—strong is better than weak, free is always good—it is an improvement on the past. But it claims more: it says that this is a choice, a proper fulfillment of those initial desires that led us to love men, and even at its oddest, it is only playful.

But it is not free, not strong, and it is dangerous play. It is dangerous to dress up like one's enemy, and worse, it can tie one to him as helplessly as ever. It still says that he, the powerful brute, is the definer, to which we then react. It is the other side of nelly, and more helpless because it denies that one is helpless at all. Effeminacy acknowledged the rage of being oppressed in defiance; macho denies that there *is* rage and oppression. The strength of those new bodies is a costume designed for sexual allure and for the discotheque. Passing for the enemy does not exempt one from the wrath. Men in leather are already the easiest marks for violent teenagers on a drunken rampage in Greenwich Village or on Mission Street on a Saturday night. Macho is another illusion. The lessons of Negroes who disliked blackness, or Jews who insisted they were assimilated, really *German*, are ignored. To some whites, everything not white is black; to Nazis, Jews are Jews, sidelocks or no. Telling the enemy one is as good as he is because one is like him does not appease him; often it makes him more vicious, furious because somehow his victim seems to approve his scorn. And the freedom—that too is illusory except as sexual taste. In that area alone, there has been real change. Compared to their counterparts in the past gay men today have found a freedom to act out their erotic tastes. But taste is not a choice; usually, it is a tyrant.

Homosexuals at their most oppressed have not been in love with men; they have been in love with masculinity. The politics of the New Left and the sexual aesthetics of androgyny have not lasted, but they seemed to be offering alternatives that were authentic, better choices than the ones we had. The new style seems both inauthentic and barely better than the old options. Sometimes it seems worse.

That is what is disturbing and enraging: to find it the growing choice in the 1980s. Does it seriously matter that some men choose to imitate their worst enemies? What is remarkable about such an old story? For one, it is so unnecessary. For the first time in modern history, there are real options for gays. The sissies in the Blue Parrot had little choice other than to stay home. They could only pretend their lives were ordinary. That pretense was survival, but one that led fatally to rage and self-contempt. The theatricality of camping helped to keep some sanity and humanity because it was an awareness of one's helplessness. Macho values are the architects of closeted lives, and adopting that style is the opposite of awareness. Whatever its ironies, they are not critical ones.

Fortunately, gay men are less helpless than they have ever been before, and because of that they are more threatened. What is worth affirming is not bravura, but political alliance with women and with a whole liberal America that is dedicated to freedom of personal choice. *That* is worth celebrating.

**LIFE AFTER DEATH:
A VIEW FROM THE LATE 1980s**

These days the mood of the gay community ranges from cloudy optimism to crystal-clear despair, depending on whom you talk to. I've been talking to gay activists, journalists, academics, therapists and medical doctors, businessmen, poets and painters, working-class men, and men who don't work, either because they don't need to or because they can't find a job. Some are Marxists, some lesbian feminists, and some have no politics but sexual politics. the term "gay community" refers partly to a discernible group of homosexual men and lesbians in large cities, and partly to a political idea. The media made it a term to reckon with long before anyone could say what it was. In 1969 "gay community" was largely a political idea and a myth. Even then there was a community in the simplest sense of the word, but what it looked like, as in the case of the blind men describing the elephant, depended on what you touched.

Seventeen years later, there are listings in the Yellow Pages. Coherent and representative groups have emerged, particularly in San Francisco, Los Angeles, and New York. They differ enough to be unable to provide a national leadership, and persistent closetry makes estimates of their numbers and their members rough at best, but a gay man or woman would likely feel at home in any of those three cities. The real differences are geographical, not political or social, and there is no single lifestyle or even a dominant one. The promiscuous one that became the hallmark of urban gay life in the early seventies—newsworthy because it was commercial and outrageous and because it gradually became the self-defining image of so many gay men—no longer prevails as it once did.

Today the general mood is grim. Everyone is either melancholy or anxious, afraid not only of AIDS but of the growing signs of hostility toward gay men and women. It is chilling when the *New York Times*, purportedly in the interests of balanced journalism, publishes William F. Buckley in support of tattooing homosexual men and intravenous-drug users, while the word "quarantine" quivers between the lines of the article. (I naively waited for letters of protest from both the Jewish and gay communities. Wouldn't Jews be disgusted by the parodic horror of the suggestion?) Though Buckley is absurd, the fears he touches are not.

Helplessness about AIDS and uncertainty about the social future are exacerbated for gay men and women by their memories of the past.

This is one reason so many are eager to be involved with gay organizations, to be tangibly connected to a real, not an ideological community. To be passive again is to stress one's helplessness, to be waiting for the next blow and wondering if the humiliation will be bearable.

Most of society is less concerned about who is responsible for the AIDS epidemic than with how gay men are going to behave in order to inhibit its spread. That issue, it should be said at once, arose in the gay community almost as soon as it was clear that AIDS was regarded as a gay disease. The closing of the bathhouses in San Francisco and New York was the occasion for raising the question in public. Publicly and privately it was admitted that the issue of accountability and social responsibility would have to be addressed. Obviously, this meant altering sexual behavior and style of life. Efforts were made in every large North American city with a gay community to inform and educate gay men about "safe sex," hoping that would be enough to halt the spread of AIDS. It is not yet clear how much deprivation this entails or how successful the educational campaign has been. History does not offer much ground for optimism: venereal epidemics of the past ended not with altered sexual behavior but with the discovery of penicillin.

But another issue, internal and not yet explored in any public way, has now arisen and needs attention, an issue that the symptoms of the crisis sometimes hint at: what does it mean to be homosexual in the modern world? This question is not about grievances and injustices, and it cannot be answered on the barricades, especially the barricade of rhetoric. As long as the subject of gay identity is argued in terms of whether it is good or bad, legitimate or illegitimate, there is no energy left to address the question of what it is. The new activism cannot address the more important internal questions the crisis has raised. The sources of change are elsewhere, in behavior and in thought about the homosexual condition that most men and women are reluctant to embrace.

Promiscuity and Liberation

Some have refused to change; they search for safe places to practice old pleasures. Latin America and the Caribbean have long accommodated homosexual men with their informal bordellos, their "muchachos" who are partners to passive men but who do not think of themselves as homosexual. It is only a question of time before these gay men spread AIDS to other islands near Haiti, from which they probably first brought it to the mainland. It is hard to gauge the state of mind of such men. They may be filled with rage and seeking revenge. They may fatalistically believe that their behavior doesn't matter. They don't feel they are doing anything wrong, or they don't care. They have no moral sense, or they are immoral. It's bad enough to live in dread of dying an awful premature death. Yet to be filled with desire for revenge, or to be without desire at all, even for ordinary dignity, is a terrible way to live or die. I assume that such men act less from conscious indecency than from pure evasion. To emphasize sexual desire and desirability is a very effective way to mask anxiety. The habit of promiscuity doesn't allow much room for introspection.

Promiscuity is a broad term. For some men, it means serial affairs or brief erotic relationships. For others, there are no relationships at all; sexual encounters begin and end with momentary arousal. And for some men, promiscuity is all of these—having a lover, and having someone else, and having anyone else. Promiscuity is time consuming and repetitive. Still, it also has another history and meaning for gay men; and it is that history, and that meaning, with which gay men in the shadow of AIDS must grapple.

In the last fifteen years or so, until AIDS appeared, promiscuity had been a rich if not invaluable experience for gay men, uniting a sense of liberation with a politics of resentment, a feeling of living at the modern edge with an outlet for aggressions created by long-held grievances. Such a combination is explosive, of course, and antiintellectual. But gay men did not invent sexual liberation. They merely stamped it with their hallmark of aggressive display. Casual sex, freed from commercialism, seemed a glamorous portent of a society free from sexism. After "Stonewall," the riot at a New York bar in which gay men successfully resisted arrest and inadvertently inaugurated gay liberation, gay activists felt they were going to redefine the old terms, junk the guilt and the remorse. They were already discarding with contempt the shrinks and the moralists, paying some of them back for the years of misery they had helped to create, the self-dislike they had urged gays to internalize for the sake of what now seemed merely propriety. Out the window went "sick" and "bad." Many could hardly believe they were jettisoning that dismal baggage.

Those years of sexual opportunism were a time of indifference to psychological inquiry. Description was a higher priority. After so much silence, the need to explain and the desire to shock were first on the agenda of gay writers and intellectuals, while the majority of gay men were exploring an exhilarating sense of relief in discos, bars with back rooms, and the baths. The politics of that eroticism had as much to do with ego as with eros: gay men said that sexuality did not diminish social status, to say nothing of intellectual or professional stature—no matter how vividly it was practiced.

In the early seventies, when movement politics was at the zenith of its popularity, the values it promoted were very seductive. It said the old romantic pieties were a slavish imitation of straight society, where they were already undergoing vigorous scrutiny from feminists. If women and blacks could use politics to demand that society acknowledge they had been unjustly treated, why not gay men? If the acknowledgment of that injustice took the form of striking down old laws and replacing them with better ones, then that, obviously, was the agenda. But for the most part, neither the victories nor the defeats changed the daily lives of gay men and women very much. With or without sodomy laws, most lived without concern

for legality. It was understood that the principal struggle was psychological, a demand first for recognition, then for acceptance; the bold terms in which that demand was couched guaranteed the right to pursue a sexual lifestyle of their own choosing. After Stonewall, gays chose to be very visible.

Before Stonewall, promiscuous sex was illegal, but it was no particular threat to health. If the heart and heat of gay politics has been to ensure the right to fuck who, when, and where one pleases, then the consequences now for the movement have a rough poetic justice. The more that sex dominated the style of life, from discos to parades, with rights secured or not, the less need most men felt they had for politics—and the less others, such as lesbians, feminists, and minorities, felt the gay movement offered them. For gay men sexual politics became something oddly literal. Both before and after the movement, promiscuity was honored as the sign of an individual's aggressiveness (no matter how passive he was in bed). To fuck was to defy, as bad girls of the past did, dismantling some of society's dearest notions about virtue. But most homosexuals want to be conventional. They are no more imaginative, courageous, or innovative than their neighbors. They want a good life on the easiest terms they can get. Many regard as uninteresting the activism that a handful of men and women are devoted to.

By the late seventies, movement politics displaced flamboyant effeminacy. The piece of trade (a man who is fellated by another but pretends to be heterosexual) whose very pose of masculinity ensured his contempt for his homosexual partner, had been replaced by that formerly groveling queen himself, now looking more virile than his proletarian idol. The dominant image of rebellion was no longer the defiant queens with their merciless ironies but powerful, strong bodies modeled on working-class youth. This new image exposed the erotic ideal of gay male life more clearly and responsively than anything since classical Greece. It was a vast improvement. Liberation freed gays from a lot of burdens, and one of the biggest was to end the search for masculinity among the enemy.

But paralleling the rise of the macho body has been the decline of the health of the male community—a nasty coincidence, if you believe in coincidence. The deeper truth, however, is that the very values that motivated us to look strong rather than be strong are the same values that elevated promiscuity as the foundation of a social identity. AIDS is mobilizing many to work in agencies caring for the ill, allowing them opportunities for sympathy and generosity—but that, too, is not the basis of an identity. What is killing you is not likely to give you a sense of self.

Even if AIDS were cured tomorrow, the style and identity of gay life in the seventies and mid-eighties would be as dated as the sexual mores of closeted homosexual life are now. Many men may rush back to the baths, but it can no longer be the liberating experience it once was. AIDS has nullified promiscuity as politically or even psychologically useful and has replaced one set of meaning with another. It has now become mythic as the dark side of sexuality, Thanatos to Eros. The life force that is the sexual drive has always had its counterpart, and AIDS is the most dramatic juxtaposition of the need for another and the fear of the other, of pain and pleasure, of life and death, in modern medical history. From the ancient Greeks on down, without a moment's interruption, the interpretation has been the same: unfettered sexuality means death, whether through dishonor, the wrath of the gods, or nature itself. We are the heirs of those legends. AIDS, like a blotter, has absorbed those old meanings.

Life after Death

There is much, then, that gay men must give up. The loss of sexual life, nearly as much as the grief and fear, is a deprivation for which no amount of civic work or marching to banners of Gay Pride can compensate. The most dramatic changes have occurred among those large numbers of men who have become abstinent, assuming a sense of responsibility to themselves if not to others. Not only must gay men refrain from what alone gave them a powerful enough identity to make a mark on the consciousness of society, a behavior that replaced society's contempt with the much more respectable fear and anger, but they must cease to think of themselves as unloved children. They must do both before they can have social acceptance or before their own behavior can have meaning for each other more nurturing than it has been. It is very hard to give up a sense of deprivation when little that created it has disappeared, and worse, when one is beset with fear.

One thing, however, is clear: gay men are not acting in concert. If gay men sensed they belonged to a recognized community, instead of struggling still to assert their legitimacy, the task would be simpler. If they felt the larger society was no longer so adamantly adversarial, they could give up the sense of injustice that makes talk of social responsibility seem hypocritical. And if their own experiences with each other had provided them with bonds deeper than momentary pleasure, they could trust themselves to act as a group in which members assumed responsibility for each other.

As long as the larger society continues to prefer the old homosexual invisibility, the nice couple next door to whom anyone can condescend, as long as that society fails to express its responsibilities to gay men, the harder it will be for gay men to give up their seductive sense of grievance. Those men who act irresponsibly in the midst of this crisis betray their isolation, their failure to feel they belong either to a gay community or to a larger one. They perceive the demand for accountability as a demand from strangers. Society has not acted as the surrogate family in which we all develop our loyalties and moral sense. In fact, too often it acts just like the family of gay men: filled with contempt or indifference.

Many gays are now relieved that sex is no longer a banner issue. It is not even so important that we all stand up to be counted; enough of us have stood up to satisfy the curious. Instead, much as other groups in U.S. society have done, the gay community has had to reassess more profoundly its relationship to the larger society. Customarily, that relationship has been adversarial. Now, for the first time in my memory, the gay community expects help. It hopes for sympathy from heterosexual society. It expects that those who are ordinarily silent will be uncomfortable with such neutrality when orthodox religious leaders proclaim AIDS the scourge of God upon homosexuals, or when politicians exploit and promote fear.

AIDS has made it necessary for gay men to begin questioning themselves. For too long we have lived as if we were driven, too impelled to know what we were doing and what, consequently, was happening to us. It takes perhaps half a lifetime before one is capable of the introspection (not self-absorption) necessary to make sense of the past and thus act as a morally free adult. The same is true of groups. There are moments in history when groups, too, must tell the truth about themselves.

NOTES

1. Quentin Crisp, *The Naked Civil Servant* (New York: New American Library, 1983).
2. David Kopay and Perry D. Young, *The David Kopay Story* (New York: Arbor House, 1980).

3. Leonard Matlovich was formerly a sergeant in the U.S. Army.

PART TWO

FROM BOYS TO MEN

"One is not born, but rather becomes, a woman," wrote the French feminist thinker, Simone de Beauvoir in her ground-breaking book, *The Second Sex* (NY: Vintage, 1958). The same is true for men. And the social processes by which boys become men are complex and important. How does early childhood socialization differ for boys and girls? What specific traits are emphasized for boys that mark their socialization as different? What types of institutional arrangements reinforce those traits? How do the various institutions in which boys find themselves—school, family, and friends—influence their development? What of the special institutions that promote "boy's life" or an adolescent male subculture?

During childhood and adolescence, masculinity becomes a central theme in a boy's life. *New York Times* editor A. M. Rosenthal put the dilemma this way: "So there I was, 13 years old, the smallest boy in my freshman class at DeWitt Clinton High School, smoking a White Owl cigar. I was not only little, but I did not have longies—long trousers—and was still in knickerbockers. Obviously, I had to do something to project my fierce sense of manhood" (*New York Times*, 26 April 1987). That the assertion of manhood is part of a boy's natural development is suggested by Roger Brown, in his text book, *Social Psychology* (NY: Free Press, 1965, p. 161):

In the United States, a real boy climbs trees, disdains girls, dirties his knees, plays with soldiers, and takes blue for his favorite color. When they go to school, real boys prefer manual training, gym, and arithmetic. In college the boys smoke pipes, drink beer, and major in engineering or physics. The real boy matures into a "man's man" who plays poker, goes hunting, drinks brandy, and dies in the war.

The articles in this section address the question of a boy's development. For example, Barrie Thorne discusses the consequences of separate and same-sex play for boys and girls in elementary schools. The next three articles examine some distinctly male arenas for gender identity and development. Jeffrey P. Hantover provides an historical account of the creation of the Boy Scouts of America as an attempt to develop an institution to rescue boys from the dangers of perceived "feminization"—a real "boys' liberation" movement. Richard Majors describes the black male style of "cool pose" as a strategy to counter the way racism "emasculates" black men. Finally, the contemporary collegiate fraternity, as Peter Lyman shows, continues to provide a homosocial haven for young men, an island of brotherhood, with some serious consequences for women.

For every boy aged 5 - 12 in the U.S.,
2 G.I. Joe products are sold yearly.

DEMILITARIZE THE PLAYGROUND

GIRLS AND BOYS TOGETHER . . . BUT MOSTLY APART:
GENDER ARRANGEMENTS IN ELEMENTARY SCHOOL

BARRIE THORNE

Throughout the years of elementary school, children's friendships and casual encounters are strongly separated by sex. Sex segregation among children, which starts in preschool and is well established by middle childhood, has been amply documented in studies of children's groups and friendships (e.g., Eder & Hallinan, 1978; Schofield, 1981) and is immediately visible in elementary school settings. When children choose seats in classrooms or the cafeteria, or get into line, they frequently arrange themselves in same-sex clusters. At lunchtime, they talk matter-of-factly about "girls' tables" and "boys' tables." Playgrounds have gendered turfs, with some areas and activities, such as large playing fields and basketball courts, controlled mainly by boys, and others—smaller enclaves like jungle-gym areas and concrete spaces for hopscotch or jumprope—more often controlled by girls. Sex segregation is so common in elementary schools that it is meaningful to speak of separate girls' and boys' worlds.

Studies of gender and children's social relations have mostly followed this "two worlds" model, separately describing and comparing the subcultures of girls and of boys (e.g., Lever, 1976; Maltz & Borker, 1983). In brief summary: Boys tend to interact in larger, more age-hetero-geneous groups (Lever, 1976; Waldrop & Halverson, 1975; Eder & Hallinan, 1978). They engage in more rough and tumble play and physical fighting (Maccoby & Jacklin, 1974). Organized sports are both a central activity and a major metaphor in boys' subcultures; they use the language of "teams" even when not engaged in sports, and they often construct interaction in the form of contests. The shifting hierarchies of boys' groups (Savin-Williams, 1976) are evident in their more frequent use of direct command, insults, and challenges (Goodwin, 1980).

Fewer studies have been done of girls' groups (Foot, Chapman, & Smith, 1980; McRobbie & Garber, 1975), and—perhaps because categories for description and analysis have come more from male than female experience—researchers have had difficulty seeing and analyzing girls' social relations. Recent work has begun to correct this skew. In middle childhood, girls' worlds are less public than those of boys; girls more often interact in private places and in smaller groups or friendship pairs (Eder & Hallinan, 1978; Waldrop & Halverson, 1975). Their play is more cooperative and turn-taking (Lever, 1976). Girls have more intense and exclusive friendships, which take shape around keeping and telling secrets, shifting alliances, and indi-

Reprinted from Willard W. Hartup and Zick Rubin, eds., *Relationships and Development*. Hillsdale, NJ: Lawrence Erlbaum Associates, 1986. Volume sponsored by the Social Science Research Center, Copyright © 1986 by Lawrence Erlbaum Associates, Inc.

rect ways of expressing disagreement (Goodwin, 1980; Lever, 1976; Maltz & Borker, 1983). Instead of direct commands, girls more often use directives which merge speaker and hearer, e.g., "let's" or "we gotta" (Goodwin, 1980).

Although much can be learned by comparing the social organization and subcultures of boys' and of girls' groups, the separate worlds approach has eclipsed full, contextual understanding of gender and social relations among children. The separate worlds model essentially involves a search for group sex differences, and shares the limitations of individual sex difference research. Differences tend to be exaggerated and similarities ignored, with little theoretical attention to the integration or similarity and difference (Unger, 1979). Statistical findings of difference are often portrayed as dichotomous, neglecting the considerable individual variation that exists; for example, not all boys fight, and some have intense and exclusive friendships. The sex difference approach tends to abstract gender from its social context, to assume that males and females are qualitatively and permanently different (with differences perhaps unfolding through separate developmental lines). These assumptions mask the possibility that gender arrangements and patterns of similarity and difference may vary by situation, race, social class, region, and subculture.

Sex segregation is far from total, and is a more complex and dynamic process than the portrayal of separate worlds reveals. Erving Goffman (1977) has observed that sex segregation has a "with-then-apart" structure; the sexes segregate periodically, with separate spaces, rituals, and groups, but they also come together and are, in crucial ways, part of the same world. This is certainly true in the social environment of elementary schools. Although girls and boys do interact as boundaried collectivities—an image suggested by the separate worlds approach—there are other occasions when they work or play in relaxed and integrated ways. Gender is less central to the organization and meaning of some situations than others. In short, sex segregation is not static, but is a variable and complicated process.

To gain an understanding of gender which can encompass both the "with" and the "apart" of sex segregation, analysis should start not with the individual, nor with a search for sex differences, but with social relationships. Gender should be conceptualized as a system of relationships rather than as an immutable and dichotomous given. Taking this approach, I have organized my research on gender and children's social relations around questions like the following: How and when does gender enter into group formation? In a given situation, how is gender made more or less salient or infused with particular meanings? By what rituals, processes, and forms of social organization and conflict do "with-then-apart" rhythms get enacted? How are these processes affected by the organization of institutions (e.g., different types of schools, neighborhoods, or summer camps), varied settings (e. g., the constraints and possibilities governing interaction on playgrounds vs. classrooms), and particular encounters?

METHODS AND SOURCES OF DATA

This study is based on two periods of participant observation. In 1976–1977 I observed for 8 months in a largely working-class elementary school in California, a school with 8% Black and 12% Chicana/o students. In 1980 I did fieldwork for 3 months in a Michigan elementary school in similar size (around 400 students), social class, and racial composition. I observed in several classrooms—a kindergarten, a second grade, and a combined fourth-fifth grade—and in school hallways, cafeterias, and playgrounds. I set out to follow the round of the school day as children experience it, recording their interactions with one another, and with adults, in varied settings.

Participant observation involves gaining access to everyday, "naturalistic" settings and taking systematic notes over an extended period of time. Rather than starting with preset categories for recording, or with fixed hypotheses for testing, participant-observers record detail in ways which maximize opportunities for discovery.

Through continuous interaction between observation and analysis, "grounded theory" is developed (Glaser & Strauss, 1967).

The distinctive logic and discipline of this mode of inquiry emerges from: (1) theoretical sampling—being relatively systematic in the choice of where and whom to observe in order to maximize knowledge relevant to categories and analysis which are being developed; and (2) comparing all relevant data on a given point in order to modify emerging propositions to take account of discrepant cases (Katz, 1983). Participant observation is a flexible, open-ended and inductive method, designed to understand behavior within, rather than stripped from, social context. It provides richly detailed information which is anchored in everyday meanings and experience.

DAILY PROCESSES OF SEX SEGREGATION

Sex segregation should be understood not as a given, but as the result of deliberate activity. The outcome is dramatically visible when there are separate girls' and boys' tables in school lunchrooms, or sex-separated groups on playgrounds. But in the same lunchroom one can also find tables where girls and boys eat and talk together, and in some playground activities the sexes mix. By what processes do girls and boys separate into gender-defined and relatively boundaried collectivities? And in what contexts, and through what processes, do boys and girls interact in less gender-divided ways?

In the school settings I observed, much segregation happened with no mention of gender. Gender was implicit in the contours of friendship, shared interest, and perceived risk which came into play when children chose companions—in their prior planning, invitations, seeking-of-access, saving-of-places, denials of entry, and allowing or protesting of "cuts" by those who violated the rules for lining up. Sometimes children formed mixed-sex groups for play, eating, talking, working on a classroom project, or moving through space. When adults or children explicitly invoked gender—and this was nearly always in ways which separated girls and boys—boundaries were heightened and mixed-sex interaction became an explicit arena of risk.

In the schools I studied, the physical space and curricula were not formally divided by sex, as they have been in the history of elementary schooling (a history evident in separate entrances to old school buildings, where the words "Boys" and "Girls" are permanently etched in concrete). Nevertheless, gender was a visible marker in the adult-organized school day. In both schools, when the public address system sounded, the principal inevitably opened with: "Boys and girls . . . ," and in addressing clusters of children, teachers and aides regularly used gender terms ("Heads down, girls"; "The girls are ready and the boys aren't"). These forms of address made gender visible and salient, conveying an assumption that the sexes are separate social groups.

Teachers and aides sometimes drew upon gender as a basis for sorting children and organizing activities. Gender is an embodied and visual social category which roughly divides the population in half, and the separation of girls and boys permeates the history and lore of schools and playgrounds. In both schools—although through awareness of Title IX, many teachers had changed this practice—one could see separate girls' and boys' lines moving, like caterpillars, through the school halls. In the 4th–5th grade classroom the teacher frequently pitted girls against boys for spelling and math contests. On the playground in the Michigan school, aides regarded the space close to the building as girls' territory, and the playing fields "out there" as boys' territory. They sometimes shooed children of the other sex away from those spaces, especially boys who ventured near the girls' area and seemed to have teasing in mind.

In organizing their activities, both within and apart from the surveillance of adults, children also explicitly invoked gender. During my fieldwork in the Michigan school, I kept daily records of who sat where in the lunchroom. The amount of sex segregation varied: It was least at the first grade tables and almost total among sixth graders. There was also variation from classroom to classroom within a given age, and from day to day. Actions like the following heightened the gender divide:

> In the lunchroom, when the two second grade tables were filling, a high-status boy walked by the inside table, which had a scattering of both boys and girls, and said loudly, "Oooo, too many girls," as he headed for a seat at the far table. The boys at the inside table picked up their trays and moved, and no other boys sat at the inside table, which the pronouncement had effectively made taboo.

In the end, that day (which was not the case every day), girls and boys ate at separate tables.

Eating and walking are not sex-typed activities, yet in forming groups in lunchrooms and hallways children often separated by sex. Sex segregation assumed added dimensions on the playground, where spaces, equipment, and activities were infused with gender meanings. My inventories of activities and groupings on the playground showed similar patterns in both schools: Boys controlled the large fixed spaces designated for team sports (baseball diamonds, grassy fields used for football or soccer); girls more often played closer to the building, doing tricks on the monkey bars (which, for 6th graders, became an area for sitting and talking) and using cement areas for jumprope, hopscotch, and group games like four-square. (Lever, 1976, provides a good analysis of sex-divided play.) Girls and boys most often played together in kickball, and in group (rather than team) games like four-square, dodgeball, and handball. When children used gender to exclude others from play, they often drew upon beliefs connecting boys to some activities and girls to others:

> A first grade boy avidly watched an all-female game of jump rope. When the girls began to shift positions, he recognized a means of access to the play and he offered, "I'll swing it." A girl responded, "No way, you don't know how to do it, to swing it. You gotta be a girl." He left without protest.

Although children sometimes ignored pronouncements about what each sex could or could not do, I never heard them directly challenge such claims.

When children had explicitly defined an activity or a group as gendered, those who crossed the boundary—especially boys who moved into female-marked space—risked being teased. ("Look! Mike's in the girls' line!" "That's a girl over there," a girl said loudly, pointing to a boy sitting at an otherwise all-female table in the lunchroom.") Children, and occasionally adults, used teasing—especially the tease of "liking" someone of the other sex, or of "being" that sex by virtue of being in their midst—to police gender boundaries. Much of the teasing drew upon heterosexual romantic definitions, making cross-sex interaction risky, and increasing social distance between boys and girls.

RELATIONSHIPS BETWEEN THE SEXES

Because I have emphasized the "apart" and ignored the occasions of "with," this analysis of sex segregation falsely implies that there is little contact between girls and boys in daily school life. In fact, relationships between girls and boys—which should be studied as fully as, and in connection with, same-sex relationships—are of several kinds:

1. "Borderwork," or forms of cross-sex interaction which are based upon and reaffirm boundaries and asymmetries between girls' and boys' groups;
2. Interactions which are infused with heterosexual meanings;
3. Occasions where individuals cross gender boundaries to participate in the world of the other sex; and
4. Situations where gender is muted in salience, with girls and boys interacting in more relaxed ways.

Borderwork

In elementary school settings boys' and girls' groups are sometimes spatially set apart. Same-sex groups sometimes claim fixed territories such as the basketball court, the bars, or specific lunchroom tables. However, in the crowded, multifocused, and adult-controlled environment of the school, groups form and disperse at a rapid rate and can never stay totally apart. Contact between girls and boys sometimes lessens sex segregation, but gender-defined groups also come together in ways which emphasize their boundaries.

"Borderwork" refers to interaction across, yet based upon and even strengthening gender boundaries. I have drawn this notion from Fredrik Barth's (1969) analysis of social relations which are maintained across ethnic boundaries without diminishing dichotomized ethnic status.[1] His focus is on more macro, ecological arrangements; mine is on face-to-face behavior. But the insight is similar: Groups may interact in ways which strengthen their borders, and the maintenance of ethnic (or gender) groups can best be understood by examining the boundary that defines the group, "not the cultural stuff that it encloses" (Barth, 1969, p. 15). In elementary schools there are several types of borderwork: contests or games where gender-defined teams compete; cross-sex rituals of chasing and pollution; and group invasions. These interactions are asymmetrical, challenging the separate-but-parallel model of "two worlds."

Contests

Boys and girls are sometimes pitted against each other in classroom competitions and playground games. The 4th–5th grade classroom had a boys' side and a girls' side, an arrangement that re-emerged each time the teacher asked children to choose their own desks. Although there was some within-sex shuffling, the result was always a spatial moiety system—boys on the left, girls on the right—with the exception of one girl (the "tomboy" whom I'll describe later), who twice chose a desk with the boys and once with the

girls. Drawing upon and reinforcing the children's self-segregation, the teacher often pitted the boys against the girls in spelling and math competitions, events marked by cross-sex antagonism and within-sex solidarity:

The teacher introduced a math game; she would write addition and subtraction problems on the board, and a member of each team would race to be the first to write the correct answer. She wrote two scorekeeping columns on the board: 'Beastly Boys'. . . 'Gossipy Girls.' The boys yelled out, as several girls laughed, 'Noisy girls! Gruesome girls!' The girls sat in a row on top of their desks; sometimes they moved collectively, pushing their hips or whispering 'pass it on.' The boys stood along the wall, some reclining against desks. When members of either group came back victorious from the front of the room, they would do the 'giving five' handslapping ritual with their team members.

On the playground a team of girls occasionally played against a team of boys, usually in kickball or team two-square. Sometimes these games proceeded matter-of-factly, but if gender became the explicit basis of team solidarity, the interaction changed, becoming more antagonistic and unstable:

Two fifth-grade girls against two fifth-grade boys in a team game of two-square. The game proceeded at an even pace until an argument ensued about whether the ball was out or on the line. Karen, who had hit the ball, became annoyed, flashed her middle finger at the other team, and called to a passing girl to join their side. The boys then called out to other boys, and cheered as several arrived to play. 'We got five and you got three!' Jack yelled. The game continued, with the girls yelling, 'Bratty boys! Sissy boys!' and the boys making noises— 'weee haw''ha-ha-ha'—as they played.

Chasing

Cross-sex chasing dramatically affirms boundaries between girls and boys. The basic elements of chase and elude, capture and rescue (Sutton-Smith, 1971) are found in various kinds of tag with formal rules, and in informal episodes of

1. I am grateful to Frederick Erickson for suggesting the relevance of Barth's analysis.

chasing which punctuate life on playgrounds. These episodes begin with a provocation (taunts like "You can't get me!" or "Slobber monster!"; bodily pokes or the grabbing of possessions). A provocation may be ignored, or responded to by chasing. Chaser and chased may then alternate roles. In an ethnographic study of chase sequences on a school playground, Christine Finnan (1982) observes that chases vary in number of chasers to chased (e.g., one chasing one, or five chasing two); form of provocation (a taunt or a poke); outcome (an episode may end when the chased outdistances the chaser, or with a brief touch, being wrestled to the ground, or the recapturing of a hat or a ball); and in use of space (there may or may not be safety zones).

Like Finnan (1982), and Sluckin (1981), who studied a playground in England, I found that chasing has a gendered structure. Boys frequently chase one another, an activity which often ends in wrestling and mock fights. When girls chase girls, they are usually less physically aggressive; they less often, for example, wrestle one another to the ground.

Cross-sex chasing is set apart by special names—"girls chase the boys"; "boys chase the girls"; "the chase"; "chasers"; "chase and kiss"; "kiss chase"; "kissers and chasers"; "kiss or kill"—and by children's animated talk about the activity. The names vary by region and school, but contain both gender and sexual meanings (this form of play is mentioned, but only briefly analyzed, in Finnan, 1981; Sluckin, 1981; Parrott, 1972; and Borman, 1979).

In "boys chase the girls" and "girls chase the boys" (the names most frequently used in both the California and Michigan schools) boys and girls become, by definition, separate teams. Gender terms override individual identities, especially for the other team ("Help, a girl's chasin' me!"; "C'mon Sarah, let's get that boy"; "Tony, help save me from the girls"). Individuals may call for help from, or offer help to, others of their sex. They may also grab someone of their sex and turn them over to the opposing team: "Ryan grabbed Billy from behind, wrestling him to the ground. 'Hey, girls, get 'im,' Ryan called."

Boys more often mix episodes of cross-sex with same-sex chasing. Girls more often have safety zones, places like the girls' restroom or an area by the school wall, where they retreat to rest and talk (sometimes in animated postmortems) before new episodes of cross-sex chasing begin.

Early in the fall in the Michigan school, where chasing was especially prevalent, I watched a second grade boy teach a kindergarten girl how to chase. He slowly ran backwards, beckoning her to pursue him, as he called, "Help, a girl's after me." In the early grades chasing mixes with fantasy play, e.g., a first-grade boy who played, "sea monster," his arms outflung and his voice growling, as he chased a group of girls. By third grade, stylized gestures—exaggerated stalking motions, screams (which only girls do), and karate kicks—accompany scenes of chasing.

Names like "chase and kiss" mark the sexual meanings of cross-sex chasing, a theme I return to later. The threat of kissing—most often girls threatening to kiss boys—is a ritualized form of provocation. Cross-sex chasing among sixth graders involves elaborate patterns of touch and touch avoidance, which adults see as sexual. The principal told the sixth graders in the Michigan school that they were not to play "pom-pom," a complicated chasing game, because it entailed "inappropriate touch."

Rituals of Pollution

Cross-sex chasing is sometimes entwined with rituals of pollution, as in "cooties," where specific individuals or groups are treated as contaminating or carrying "germs." Children have rituals for transferring cooties (usually touching someone else and shouting "You've got cooties!"), for immunization (e.g., writing "CV" for "cootie vaccination" on their arms), and for eliminating cooties (e.g., saying "no gives" or using "cootie catchers" made of folded paper described in Knapp & Knapp, 1976). While girls may give cooties to girls, boys do not generally give cooties to one another (Samuelson, 1980).

In cross-sex play, either girls or boys may be defined as having cooties, which they transfer through chasing and touching. Girls give cooties to boys more often than vice versa. In Michigan, one version of cooties is called "girl stain"; the fourth-graders whom Karkau, 1973, describes, used the phrase "girl touch." "Cootie queens, "or "cootie girls" (there are no "kings" or "boys") are female pariahs, the ultimate school untouchables, seen as contaminating not only by virtue of gender, but also through some added stigma such as being overweight or poor.[2] That girls are seen as more polluting than boys is a significant asymmetry, which echoes cross-cultural patterns, although in other cultures female pollution is generally connected to menstruation, and not applied to prepubertal girls.

Invasions

Playground invasions are another asymmetric form of borderwork. On a few occasions I saw girls invade and disrupt an all-male game, most memorably a group of tall sixth-grade girls who ran onto the playing field and grabbed a football which was in play. The boys were surprised and frustrated, and, unusual for boys this old, finally tattled to the aide. But in the majority of cases, boys disrupt girls' activities rather than vice versa. Boys grab the ball from girls playing four-square, stick feet into a jumprope and stop an on-going game, and dash through the area of the bars, where girls are taking turns performing, sending the rings flying. Sometimes boys ask to join a girls' game and then, after a short period of seemingly earnest play, disrupt the game:

> Two second-grade boys begged to "twirl" the jumprope for a group of second-grade girls who had been jumping for some time. The girls agreed, and the boys began to twirl. Soon, without announcement, the boys changed from "seashells, cockle bells' to "hot peppers" (spinning the rope

very fast), and tangled the jumper in the rope. The boys ran away laughing.

Boys disrupt girls' play so often that girls have developed almost ritualized responses: They guard their ongoing play, chase boys away, and tattle to the aides. In a playground cycle which enhances sex segregation, aids who try to spot potential trouble before it occurs sometimes shoo boys away from areas where girls are playing. Aides do not anticipate trouble from girls who seek to join groups of boys, with the exception of girls intent on provoking a chase sequence. And indeed, if they seek access to a boys' game, girls usually play with boys in earnest rather than breaking up the game.

A close look at the organization of borderwork—or boundaried interactions between the sexes—shows that the worlds of boys and girls may be separate but they are not parallel, nor are they equal. The worlds of girls and boys articulate in several asymmetric ways:

1. On the playground, boys control as much as ten times more space than girls, when one adds up the area of large playing fields and compares it, with the much smaller areas where girls predominate. Girls, who play closer to the building, are more often watched over and protected by the adult aides.

2. Boys invade all-female games and scenes of play much more than girls invade boys. This, and boys' greater control of space, correspond with other findings about the organization of gender, and inequality, in our society: compared with men and boys, women and girls take up less space, and their space, and talk, are more often violated and interrupted (Greif, 1982; Henley, 1977; West & Zimmerman, 1983).

3. Although individual boys are occasionally treated as contaminating (e.g., a third grade boy who [to] both boys and girls was "stinky" and "smelled like pee"), girls are more often defined as polluting. This pattern ties to themes that I discuss later: It is more taboo for a boy to play with (as opposed to invade) girls, and girls are more sexually defined than boys.

---

2. Sue Samuelson (1980) reports that in a racially mixed playground in Fresno, California, Mexican-American, but not Anglo children gave cooties. Racial, as well as sexual inequality may be expressed through these forms.

A look at the boundaries between the separated worlds of girls and boys illuminates within-sex hierarchies of status and control. For example, in the sex-divided seating in the 4th–5th grade classroom, several boys recurringly sat near "female space": their desks were at the gender divide in the classroom, and they were more likely than other boys to sit at a predominantly female table in the lunchroom. These boys—two non-bilingual Chicanos and an overweight "loner" boy who was afraid of sports—were at the bottom of the male hierarchy. Gender is sometimes used as a metaphor for male hierarchies; the inferior status of boys at the bottom is conveyed by calling them "girls":

Seven boys and one girl were playing basketball. Two younger boys came over and asked to play. While the girl silently stood, fully accepted in the company of players, one of the older boys disparagingly said to the younger boys, 'You girls can't play.'[3]

In contrast, the girls who more often travel in the boys' world, sitting with groups of boys in the lunchroom or playing basketball, soccer, and baseball with them, are not stigmatized. Some have fairly high status with other girls. The worlds of girls and boys are asymmetrically arranged, and spatial patterns map out interacting forms of inequality.

Heterosexual Meanings

The organization and meanings of gender (the social categories "woman/man," "girl/boy") and of sexuality vary cross-culturally (Ortner & Whitehead, 1981)—and, in our society, across the life course. Harriet Whitehead (1981) observed that in our (Western) gender system, and that of many traditional North American Indian cultures, one's choice of a sexual object, occupation, and one's

dress and demeanor are closely associated with gender. However, the "center of gravity" differs in the two gender systems. For Indians, occupational pursuits provide the primary imagery of gender; dress and demeanor are secondary, and sexuality is least important. In our system, at least for adults, the order is reversed: heterosexuality is central to our definitions of "man" and "woman" ("masculinity"/"femininity"), and the relationships that obtain between them, whereas occupation and dress/demeanor are secondary.

Whereas erotic orientation and gender are closely linked in our definitions of adults, we define children as relatively asexual. Activities and dress/demeanor are more important than sexuality in the cultural meanings of "girl" and "boy." Children are less heterosexually defined than adults, and we have nonsexual imagery for relations between girls and boys. However, both children and adults sometimes use heterosexual language—"crushes," "like," "goin' with," "girlfriends," and "boyfriends"—to define cross-sex relationships. This language increases through the years of elementary school; the shift to adolescence consolidates a gender system organized around the institution of heterosexuality.

In everyday life in the schools, heterosexual and romantic meanings infuse some ritualized forms of interaction between groups of boys and girls (e.g., "chase and kiss") and help maintain sex segregation, "Jimmy likes Beth" or "Beth likes Jimmy" is a major form of teasing, which a child risks in choosing to sit by or walk with someone of the other sex. The structure of teasing, and children's sparse vocabulary for relationships between girls and boys, are evident in the following conversation which I had with a group of third-grade girls in the lunchroom:

Susan asked me what I was doing, and I said I was observing the things children do and play. Nicole volunteered, 'I like running, boys chase all the girls. See Tim over there? Judy chases him all around the school. She likes him.' Judy, sitting across the table, quickly responded, 'I hate him. I like him for a friend.' 'Tim loves Judy,' Nicole said in a loud, sing-song voice.

---

3. This incident was recorded by Margaret Blume, who, for an undergraduate research project in 1982, observed in the California school where I earlier did fieldwork. Her observations and insights enhanced my own, and 1 would like to thank her for letting me cite this excerpt.

In the younger grades, the culture and lore of girls contain more heterosexual romantic themes than that of boys. In Michigan, the first-grade girls often jumped rope to a rhyme which began: "Down in the valley where the green grass grows, there sat Cindy (name of jumper), as sweet as a rose. She sat, she sat, she sat so sweet. Along came Jason, and kissed her on the cheek . . . first comes love, then comes marriage, then along comes Cindy with a baby carriage . . ." Before a girl took her turn at jumping, the chanters asked her "Who do you want to be your boyfriend?" The jumper always proffered a name, which was accepted matter-of-factly. In chasing, a girl's kiss carried greater threat than a boy's kiss; "girl touch," when defined as contaminating, had sexual connotations. In short, starting at an early age, girls are more sexually defined than boys.

Through the years of elementary school, and increasing with age, the idiom of heterosexuality helps maintain the gender divide. Cross-sex interactions, especially when children initiate them, are fraught with the risk of being teased about "liking" someone of the other sex. I learned of several close cross-sex friendships, formed and maintained in neighborhoods and church, which went underground during the school day.

By the fifth grade a few children began to affirm, rather than avoid, the charge of having a girlfriend or a boyfriend; they introduced the heterosexual courtship rituals of adolescence:

> In the lunchroom in the Michigan school, as the tables were forming, a high-status fifth-grade boy called out from his seat at the table: 'I want Trish to sit by me.' Trish came over, and almost like a king and queen, they sat at the gender divide—a row of girls down the table on her side, a row of boys on his.

In this situation, which inverted earlier forms, it was not a loss, but a gain in status to publicly choose a companion of the other sex. By affirming his choice, the boy became unteasable (note the familiar asymmetry of heterosexual courtship rituals: the male initiated). This incident signals a temporal shift in arrangements of sex and gender.

Traveling in the World of the Other Sex

Contests, invasions, chasing, and heterosexually-defined encounters are based upon and reaffirm boundaries between girls and boys. In another type of cross-sex interaction, individuals (or sometimes pairs) cross gender boundaries, seeking acceptance in a group of the other sex. Nearly all the cases I saw of this were tomboys—girls who played organized sports and frequently sat with boys in the cafeteria or classroom. If these girls were skilled at activities central in the boys' world, especially games like soccer, baseball, and basketball, they were pretty much accepted as participants.

Being a tomboy is a matter of degree. Some girls seek access to boys' groups but are excluded; other girls limit their "crossing" to specific sports. Only a few—such as the tomboy I mentioned earlier, who chose a seat with the boys in the sex-divided fourth–fifth grade—participate fully in the boys' world. That particular girl was skilled at the various organized sports which boys played in different seasons of the year. She was also adept at physical fighting and at using the forms of arguing, insult, teasing, naming, and sports-talk of the boys' subculture. She was the only Black child in her classroom, in a school with only 8% Black students; overall that token status, along with unusual athletic and verbal skills, may have contributed to her ability to move back and forth across the gender divide. Her unique position in the children's world was widely recognized in the school. Several times, the teacher said to me, "She thinks she's a boy."

I observed only one boy in the upper grades (a fourth grader) who regularly played with all-female groups, as opposed to "playing at" girls games and seeking to disrupt them. He frequently played jumprope and took turns with girls doing tricks on the bars, using the small gestures—for example, a helpful push on the heel of a girl who needed momentum to turn her body around the bar—which mark skillful and earnest participation. Although I never saw him play in other than an earnest spirit, the girls often chased him away from their games, and both girls and boys teased him. The fact that girls seek, and have more access to boys' worlds than vice versa, and the fact that girls who travel with the other sex are less stigmatized for it, are obvious asymmetries, tied to the asymmetries previously discussed.

Relaxed Cross-Sex Interactions

Relationships between boys and girls are not always marked by strong boundaries, heterosexual definitions, or by interacting on the terms and turfs of the other sex. On some occasions girls and boys interact in relatively comfortable ways. Gender is not strongly salient nor explicitly invoked, and girls and boys are not organized into boundaries collectively. These "with" occasions have been neglected by those studying gender and children's relationships, who have emphasized either the model of separate worlds (with little attention to their articulation) or heterosexual forms of contact.

Occasions where boys and girls interact without strain, where gender wanes, rather than waxes in importance, frequently have one or more of the following characteristics:

1. The situations are organized around an absorbing task, such as a group art project or creating a radio show, which encourages cooperation and lessens attention to gender. This pattern accords with other studies finding that cooperative activities reduce group antagonism (e.g., Sherif & Sherif, 1953, who studied divisions between boys in a summer camp; and Aronson et al., 1978, who used cooperative activities to lessen racial divisions in a classroom).
2. Gender is less prominent when children are not responsible for the formation of the group. Mixed-sex play is less frequent in games like football, which require the choosing of teams, and more frequent in games like handball or dodgeball which individuals can join simply by getting into a line or a circle. When adults organize mixed-sex encounters—which they frequently do in the classroom and in physical education periods on the playground—they legitimize cross-sex contact. This removes the risk of being teased for choosing to be with the other sex.
3. There is more extensive and relaxed cross-sex interaction when principles of grouping other than gender are explicitly involved—for example, counting off to form teams for spelling or kickball, dividing lines by hot lunch or cold lunch, or organizing a work group on the basis of interests or reading ability.
4. Girls and boys may interact more readily in less public and crowded settings. Neighborhood play, depending on demography, is more often sex and age integrated than play at school, partly because with fewer numbers, one may have to resort to an array of social categories to find play partners or to constitute a game. And in less crowded environments there are fewer potential witnesses to "make something of it" if girls and boys play together.

Relaxed interactions between girls and boys often depend on adults to set up and legitimize the contact.[4] Perhaps because of this contingency—and the other, distancing patterns which permeate relations between girls and boys—the easeful moments of interaction rarely build to close friendship. Schofield (1981) makes a similar observation about gender and racial barriers to friendship in a junior high school.

IMPLICATIONS FOR DEVELOPMENT

I have located social relations within an essentially spatial framework, emphasizing the organization of children's play, work, and other activities within specific settings, and in one

---

4. Note that in daily school life, depending on the individual and the situation, teachers and aides sometimes lessened, and at other times heightened sex segregation.

type of institution, the school. In contrast, frameworks of child development rely upon temporal metaphors, using images of growth and transformation over time. Taken alone, both spatial and temporal frameworks have shortcomings; fitted together, they may be mutually correcting.

Those interested in gender and development have relied upon conceptualizations of "sex role socialization" and "sex differences." Sexuality and gender, I have argued, are more situated and fluid than these individualist and intrinsic models imply. Sex and gender are differently organized and defined across situations, even within the same institution. This situational variation (e.g., in the extent to which an encounter heightens or lessens gender boundaries, or is infused with sexual meanings) shapes and constrains individual behavior. Features which a developmental perspective might attribute to individuals, and understand as relatively internal attributes unfolding over time, may, in fact, be highly dependent on context. For example, children's avoidance of cross-sex friendship may be attributed to individual gender development in middle-childhood. But attention to varied situations may show that this avoidance is contingent on group size, activity, adult behavior, collective meanings, and the risk of being teased.

A focus on social organization and situation draws attention to children's experiences in the present. This helps correct a model like "sex role socialization" which casts the present under the shadow of the future, or presumed "endpoints" (Speier, 1976). A situated analysis of arrangements of sex and gender among those of different ages may point to crucial disjunctions in the life course. In the fourth and fifth grades, culturally defined heterosexual rituals ("goin' with") begin to suppress the presence and visibility of other types of interaction between girls and boys, such as nonsexualized and comfortable interaction, and traveling in the world of the other sex. As "boyfriend/girlfriend" definitions spread, the fifth-grade tomboy I described had to work to sustain "buddy" relationships with boys. Adult women who were tomboys often speak of early

adolescence as a painful time when they were pushed away from participation in boys' activities. Other adult women speak of the loss of intense, even erotic ties with other girls when they entered puberty and the rituals of dating, that is, when they became absorbed into the institution of heterosexuality (Rich, 1980). When Lever (1976) describes best-friend relationships among fifth-grade girls as preparation for dating, she imposes heterosexual ideologies onto a present which should be understood on its own terms.

As heterosexual encounters assume more importance, they may alter relations in same-sex groups. For example, Schofield (1981) reports that for sixth- and seventh-grade children in a middle school, the popularity of girls with other girls was affected by their popularity with boys, while boys' status with other boys did not depend on their relations with girls. This is an asymmetry familiar from the adult world; men's relationships with one another are defined through varied activities (occupations, sports), while relationships among women—and their public status—are more influenced by their connections to individual men.

A full understanding of gender and social relations should encompass cross-sex as well as within-sex interactions. "Borderwork" helps maintain separate, gender-linked subcultures, which, as those interested in development have begun to suggest, may result in different milieux for learning. Daniel Maltz and Ruth Borker (1983) for example, argue that because of different interactions within girls' and boys' groups, the sexes learn different rules for creating and interpreting friendly conversation, rules which carry into adulthood and help account for miscommunication between men and women. Carol Gilligan (1982) fits research on the different worlds of girls and boys into a theory of sex differences in moral development. Girls develop a style of reasoning, she argues, which is more personal and relational; boys develop a style which is more positional, based on separateness. Eleanor Maccoby (1982), also following the insight that because of sex segregation, girls and boys grow up in different environments, suggests implications for gender differentiated prosocial and antisocial behavior.

This separate worlds approach, as I have illustrated, also has limitations. The occasions when the sexes are together should also be studied, and understood as contexts for experience and learning. For example, asymmetries in cross-sex relationships convey a series of messages: that boys are more entitled to space and to the nonreciprocal right of interrupting or invading the activities of the other sex; that girls are more in need of adult protection, and are lower in status, more defined by sexuality, and may even be polluting. Different types of cross-sex interaction—relaxed, boundaried, sexualized, or taking place on the terms of the other sex—provide different contexts for development.

By mapping the array of relationships between and within the sexes, one adds complexity to the overly static and dichotomous imagery of separate worlds. Individual experiences vary, with implications for development. Some children prefer same-sex groupings; some are more likely to cross the gender boundary and participate in the world of the other sex; some children (e.g., girls and boys who frequently play "chase and kiss") invoke heterosexual meanings, while others avoid them,

Finally, after charting the terrain of relationships, one can trace their development over time. For example, age variation in the content and form of borderwork, or of cross and same-sex touch, may be related to differing cognitive, social, emotional, or physical capacities, as well as to age-associated cultural forms. I earlier mentioned temporal shifts in the organization of cross-sex chasing, for mixing with fantasy play in the early grades to more elaborately ritualized and sexualized forms by the sixth grade. There also appear to be temporal changes in same and cross-sex touch. In kindergarten, girls and boys touch one another more freely than in fourth grade, when children avoid relaxed cross-sex touch and instead use pokes, pushes, and other forms of mock violence, even when the touch clearly couches affection. This touch taboo is obviously related to the risk of seeming to *like* someone of the other sex. In fourth grade, same-sex touch begins to signal sexual meanings among boys, as well as between boys and girls. Younger boys touch one another freely in cuddling (arm around shoulder) as well as mock violence ways. By fourth grade, when homophobic taunts like "fag" become more common among boys, cuddling touch begins to disappear for boys, but less so for girls.

Overall, I am calling for more complexity in our conceptualization of gender and of children's social relationships. Our challenge is to retain the temporal sweep, looking at individual and group lives as they unfold over time, while also attending to social structure and context, and to the full variety of experiences in the present.

ACKNOWLEDGMENT

I would like to thank Jane Atkinson, Nancy Chodorow, Arlene Daniels, Peter Lyman, Zick Rubin, Malcolm Spector, Avril Thorne, and Margery Wolf for comments on an earlier version of this paper. Conversations with Zella Luria enriched this work.

REFERENCES

Aronson, F., et al. (1978). *The jigsaw classroom.* Beverly Hills, CA: Sage.

Barth, F. (Ed.). (1969). *Ethnic groups and boundaries.* Boston: Little, Brown.

Borman, K. M. (1979). Children's interactions in playgrounds. *Theory into Practice, 18,* 251–257.

Eder, D., & Hallinan, M. T. (1978). Sex differences in children's friendships. *American Sociological Review, 43,* 237–250.

Finnan, C. R. (1982). The ethnography of children's spontaneous play. In G. Spindler (Ed.), *Doing the ethnography of schooling* (pp. 358–380). New York: Holt, Rinehart & Winston.

Foot, H. C., Chapman, A. J., & Smith, J. R. (1980). Introduction. *Friendship and social relations in children* (pp. 1–14). New York: Wiley.

Gilligan, C. (1982) *In a different voice: Psychological theory and women's development*. Cambridge, MA: Harvard University Press.

Glaser, B. G., & Strauss, A. L. (1967). *The discovery of grounded theory*. Chicago: Aldine.

Goffman, E. (1977). The arrangement between the sexes. *Theory and Society*, *4*, 301–336.

Goodwin, M. H. (1980). Directive-response sequences in girls' and boys' task activities. In S. McConnell-Ginet, R. Borker, & N. Furman (Eds.), *Women and language in literature and society* (pp. 157–173). New York: Praeger.

Grief, E. B. (1980). Sex differences in parent-child conversations. *Women's Studies International Quarterly 3*, 253–258.

Henley, N. (1977). *Body politics: Power, sex, and nonverbal communication*. Englewood Cliffs, NJ: Prentice-Hall.

Karkau, K. (1973). *Sexism in the fourth grade*. Pittsburgh: KNOW, Inc. (pamphlet)

Katz, J. (1983). A theory of qualitative methodology: The social system of analytic fieldwork. In R. M. Emerson (Ed.), *Contemporary field research* (pp. 127–148). Boston: Little, Brown.

Knapp, M., & Knapp, H. (1976). *One potato, two potato: The secret education of American children*. New York: W. W. Norton.

Lever, J. (1976). Sex differences in the games children play. *Social Problems*, *23*, 478–487.

Maccoby, E. (1982). *Social groupings in childhood: Their relationship to prosocial and antisocial behavior in boys and girls*. Paper presented at conference on The Development of Prosocial and Antisocial Behavior. Voss, Norway.

Maccoby, E., & Jacklin, C. (1974). *The psychology of sex differences*. CA: Stanford University Press.

Maltz, D. N., & Borker, R. A. (1983). A cultural approach to male-female miscommunication. In J. J. Gumperz (Ed.), *Language and social identity* (pp. 195–216). New York: Cambridge University Press.

McRobbie, A., & Garber, J. (1975). Girls and subcultures. In S. Hall and T. Jefferson (Eds.), *Resistance through rituals* (pp. 209–223). London: Hutchinson.

Ortner, S. B., & Whitehead, H. (1981). *Sexual meanings*. New York: Cambridge University Press.

Parrott, S. (1972). Games children play: Ethnography of a second-grade recess In J. P. Spradley & D. W. McCurdy (Eds.), *The cultural experience* (pp. 206–219). Chicago: Science Research Associates.

Rich, A. (1980). Compulsory heterosexuality and lesbian existence *Signs*, *5*, 631–660.

Samuelson, S. (1980) The cooties complex. *Western Folklore*, *39*, 198–210.

Savin-Williams, R. C. (1976). An ethological study of dominance formation and maintenance in a group of human adolescents. *Child Development*, *47*, 972–979.

Schofield, J. W. (1981). Complementary and conflicting identities: Images and interaction in an interracial school. In S. R. Asher & J. M. Gottman (Eds.), *The development of children's friendships* (pp. 53–90). New York: Cambridge University Press.

Sherif, M., & Sherif, C. (1953). *Groups in harmony and tension*. New York: Harper.

THE BOY SCOUTS AND THE VALIDATION OF MASCULINITY

JEFFREY P. HANTOVER

The Boy Scouts of America was formally incorporated in 1910 and by 1916 had received a federal charter, absorbed most of the organizations which had claimed the Scouting name, and was an accepted community institution. The President of the United States was the organization's honorary president, and Scouting courses were offered in major universities. At the end of its first decade, the Boy Scouts was the largest male youth organization in American history with 358,573 scouts and 15,117 scoutmasters.

The Boy Scouts' rapid national acceptance reflected turn-of-the-century concern over the perpetuation and validation of American masculinity. The widespread and unplanned adoption of the Scout program prior to 1916 suggests that Scouting's message, unadorned by organizational sophistication, spoke to major adult concerns, one of which was the future of traditional conceptions of American masculinity.

This paper will argue that the Boy Scouts served the needs of adult men as well as adolescent boys. The supporters of the Scout movement, those who gave their time, money, and public approval, believed that changes in work, the family, and adolescent life threatened the development of manliness among boys and its expression among men. They perceived and promoted Scouting as an agent for the perpetuation of manliness among adolescents; the Boy Scouts provided an environment in which boys could become "red blooded" virile men. Less explicitly, Scouting provided men an opportunity to counteract the perceived feminizing forces of their lives and to act according to the traditional masculine script.

THE OPPORTUNITY TO BE A MAN: RESTRICTION AND ITS CONSEQUENCES

Masculinity is a cultural construct and adult men need the opportunity to perform normatively appropriate male behaviors. Masculinity is not affirmed once and for all by somatic change; physical development is but a means for the performance of culturally ascribed behaviors. American masculinity is continually affirmed through ongoing action. What acts a man performs and how well he does them truly make a male a man.

However, the availability of opportunities is not constant. Anxiety about the integrity and persistence of the male role can result from a restriction of opportunities experienced by the individual and the groups with which he identifies. Adult experiences produce adult anxieties. Masculine anxiety can arise when adult men know the script and wish to perform according to cultural directions but are denied the opportunity to act: The fault lies in social structuring of opportunities and not in individual capabilities and motivations.

Reprinted from *Journal of Social Issues* Volume 34, Number 1, 1978.

The author wishes to thank Joseph Pleck and Mayer Zald for their constructive comments.

The anxiety men increasingly exhibited about the naturalness and substance of manliness in the period 1880 to World War I flowed from changes in institutional spheres traditionally supportive of masculine definitional affirmation. Feminism as a political movement did raise fears of feminization but, as Filene (1975) suggests, in relation to preexistent anxiety about the meaning of manliness. Changes in the sphere of work, the central institutional anchorage of masculinity, undercut essential elements in the definition of manliness. Men believed they faced diminishing opportunities for masculine validation and that adolescents faced barriers to the very development of masculinity.

Masculine anxiety at the turn of the century was expressed in the accentuation of the physical and assertive side of the male ideal and in the enhanced salience of gender in social life. The enthronement of "muscularity" is evident in leisure activities, literary tastes, and cultural heroes. In the early nineteenth century, running and jumping were not exercises befitting a gentleman (Rudolph, 1962), but now men took to the playing fields, gyms, and wilderness in increasing numbers. Football, baseball, hiking, and camping became popular and were defended for their contribution to the development of traditional masculine character. Popular magazine biographies of male heroes in the period 1894 to 1913 shifted from an earlier idealization of passive traits such as piety, thrift, and industry to an emphasis on vigor, forcefulness, and mastery (Greene, 1970). Literary masculinization extended beyond mortals like Teddy Roosevelt to Christ who was portrayed as "the supremely manly man": attractive to women, individualistic, athletic, self-controlled, and aggressive when need be—"he was no Prince of Peace-at-any-price" (Conant, 1915, p. 117).

Sex-role distinctions became increasingly salient and rigid. The birth control issue became enmeshed in the debate over women's proper role; diatribes against expanded roles for women accompanied attacks on family limitation. The increased insistence on sexual purity in fiction

and real life was a demand for women to accept the traditional attributes of purity, passivity, and domesticity. The emphasis on the chivalric motif in turn-of-the-century youth organizations (Knights of King Arthur, Order of Sir Galahad, Knights of the Holy Grail) can be interpreted as an expression of the desire to preserve male superordination in gender relations.

PERCEIVED FORCES OF FEMINIZATION

Men in the period 1880 to World War I believed that opportunities for the development and expression of masculinity were being limited. They say forces of feminization in the worlds of adults and adolescents. I will concentrate on changes in the adult opportunity structure. However, the forces of feminization that adolescents were thought to face at home and school should be mentioned, for they contributed to the anxiety of men worried about the present and wary of the future.

For the expanding urban middle class, the professionalization and sanctification of motherhood, the smaller family size, the decline in the number of servants who could serve as buffers between mother and son, and the absence of busy fathers from the home made the mother–son relationship appear threatening to proper masculine socialization. The expansion of the public high school took sons out of the home but did not allay fears of feminization. Female students outnumbered males, the percentage of female staff rose steadily between 1880 and World War I, and the requirements of learning demanded "feminine" passivity and sedentariness. Education would weaken a boy's body and direct his mind along the "psychic lines" of his female instructors. Finally, let me suggest that G. Stanley Hall's concept of adolescence may have generated sexrole anxiety by extending and legitimating dependency as a natural stage in the developmental cycle. A cohort of men who had reached social maturity before the use and public acceptance of adolescence as an age category, who had experienced the rural transition to manhood at an early age, and who had fought as teenagers in the Civil War or knew those who had were confronted with a generation of boys whose major characteristics were dependency and inactivity.

Changes in the nature of work and in the composition of the labor force from 1880 to World War I profoundly affected masculine self-identity. From 1870 to 1910 the number of clerical workers, salespeople, government employees, technicians, and salaried professionals increased from 756 thousand to 5.6 million (Hays, 1957). The dependency, sedentariness, and even security of these middle-class positions clashed with the active mastery, independence, self-reliance, competitiveness, creativity, and risk-taking central to the traditional male ideal (Mills, 1951). In pre-Civil War America, there were opportunities to approach that ideal: It is estimated that over 80% of Americans were farmers or self-employed businessmen (Mills, 1951). They owned the property they worked; they produced tangible goods; and they were not enmeshed in hierarchical systems of "command and obedience."

Industrialization and bureaucratization reduced opportunities to own one's business, to take risks, exercise independence, compete, and master men and nature. The new expanded middle class depended on others for time, place, and often pace of work. The growth of chain stores crowded out independent proprietors, made small business ventures short lived, and reduced the income of merchants frequently below the level of day laborers (Anderson & Davidson, 1940). Clerical positions were no longer certain stepping stones to ownership; and clerical wages were neither high enough to meet standards of male success nor appreciably greater than those of less prestigious occupations (Filene, 1975; Douglas, 1930).

This changed occupational landscape did not go unnoticed. College graduates were told not to expect a challenging future:

The world is steadily moving toward the position in which the individual is to contribute faithfully

and duly his quota of productive or protective social effort, and to receive in return a modest, certain, not greatly variable stipend. He will adjust his needs and expenses to his income, guard the future by insurance or some analogous method, and find margin of leisure and opportunity sufficient to give large, play to individual tastes and preferences. (Shaw, 1907, p. 3)

Interestingly for this paper's thesis, graduates were to seek fulfillment in activities outside work.

The increased entry of women into the labor force raised the specter of feminization as did the changed character of work. In terms of masculine anxiety, the impact was two-fold: the mere fact of women working outside the home in larger numbers and their increased participation in jobs which demanded nonmasculine attributes. From 1870 to 1920, there was a substantial increase in the percentage of women aged 16 and over in nonagricultural occupations—from 11.8% to 21.3% (Hill, 1929). Men expressed concern over the entrance of women into a previously exclusive domain of masculine affirmation. (Women's occupations were not enumerated in the federal census until 1860.) Magazine and newspaper cartoons showed women in suits, smoking cigars, and talking business while aproned men were washing dishes, sweeping floors, and feeding babies (Smuts, 1959). Sex-role definition, not simple income, was at stake. Only one-third of employed men in 1910 worked in occupations where women constituted more than 5% of the work force (Hill, 1929). The actual threat posed by working women was more cultural than economic. Women doing what men did disconfirmed the naturalness and facticity of sex-role dichotomization.

Imposed on this general concern was the anxiety of men in white-collar positions. It was into these "nonmasculine" jobs that women entered in large numbers. Women were only 3% of the clerical work force in 1870, but 35% in 1910 (U.S. Department of Commerce, 1870; Hill, 1929). The increase for specific occupations between 1910 and 1920 is even more dramatic, especially for native white women of native parentage: female clerks increased 318%; bookkeepers, accountants, and cashiers, 257%; stenographers and typists, 121%; and sales personnel, 66% (Hill, 1929). It is to be argued that men in these occupations, feminine in character and composition, sought nonoccupational means of masculine validation, one of which was being a scoutmaster.

SCOUTING AND THE CONSTRUCTION OF MANLINESS

The Boy Scouts of America responded explicitly to adult sex-role concerns. It provided concerned men the opportunity to support "an organized effort to make big men of little boys . . . to aid in the development of that master creation, high principled, clean and clear thinking, independent manhood" (Burgess, 1914, p. 12). At the turn of the century, manliness was no longer considered the inevitable product of daily life; urbanization appeared to have removed the conditions for the natural production of manliness. Scouting advertised itself as an environmental surrogate for the farm and frontier:

> The Wilderness is gone, the Buckskin Man is gone, the painted Indian has hit the trail over the Great Divide, the hardships and privations of pioneer life which did so much to develop sterling manhood are now but a legend in history, and we must depend upon the Boy Scout Movement to produce the MEN of the future. (Daniel Carter Beard in Boy Scouts of America, 1914, p. 109)

Scouting's program and structure would counter the forces of feminization and maintain traditional manhood. Following the dictates of Hall's genetic psychology, boys were sexually segregated in a primary group under the leadership of an adult male. The gang instinct, like all adolescent instincts, was not to be repressed but constructively channeled in the service of manhood. By nature boys would form gangs, and the Boy Scouts turned the gang into a Scout patrol. The gang bred virility, did not tolerate sissies,

and would make a boy good but not a goody-goody; in short, he would "be a real boy, not too much like his sister" (Puffer, 1912, p. 157; also see Page, 1919).

The rhetoric and content of Scouting spoke to masculine fears of passivity and dependence. Action was the warp and woof of Scouting, as it was the foundation of traditional American masculinity. After-school and summer idleness led to and was itself a moral danger, and scouts were urged to do "anything rather than continue in dependent, and enfeebling, and demoralizing idleness" (Russell, 1914, p. 163). "Spectatoritis" was turning "robust, manly, self-reliant boyhood into a lot of flat-chested cigarette smokers with shaky nerves and doubtful vitality" (Seton, 1910, p. xi). So Scout activities involved all members, and advancement required each boy to compete against himself and nature. Scouting stands apart from most nineteenth-century youth organizations by its level of support for play and its full acceptance of outdoor activities as healthy for boys.

The Scout code, embodied in the Scout Oath, Law, Motto, and requirements for advancement, was a code for conduct, not moral contemplation. It was "the code of red blooded, moral manly men" (Beard, Note 1, p. 9). The action required by the code, not one's uniform or badges, made a boy a scout and differentiated a scout from a non-scout. The British made a promise to act, but the Americans made a more definite commitment to action: they took an oath. More than the British, Americans emphasized that theirs was a "definite code of personal purposes," whose principles would shape the boy's total character and behavior.

The Scout code would produce that ideal man who was master of himself and nature. The American addition to the Scout oath, "To keep myself physically strong, mentally awake, and morally straight," was a condition for such mastery. In pre-Civil War America, "be prepared" meant being prepared to die, having one's moral house in order (Crandall, 1957). The Scout motto meant being prepared to meet and master dangers, from runaway horses to theater fires and factory explosions. In emergencies, it was the scout who "stood firm, quieted those who were panic stricken and unobtrusively and efficiently helped to control the crowds" (Murray, 1937, p. 492). American Scouting added the tenth law: "A Scout is Brave." Bravery meant self-mastery and inner direction, having the courage "to stand up for the right against the coaxing of friends or the jeers or threats of enemies."

The linchpin of the Scout code was the good deed. Boys active in community service reassured males that the younger generation would become manly men. To Scout supporters the movement provided a character building "moral equivalent to war." The phrase was used by William James in 1910 to suggest a kind of Job Corps for gilded youths. They would wash windows, build roads, work on fishing boats, and engage in all types of manual labor. This work would knock the childishness out of the youth of the luxurious classes and would produce the hardiness, discipline, and manliness that previously only war had done (James, 1971). As a result, young men would walk with their heads higher, would be esteemed by women, and be better fathers and teachers of the next generation. Scouts would not accept payment for their good deeds. To take a tip was un-American, un-masculine, and made one a "bit of a boot lick" (Eaton, 1918, p. 38). Adherence to the Scout code would produce traditional manliness in boy's clothing:

The REAL Boy Scout is not a "sissy." He is not a hothouse plant, like little Lord Fauntleroy. There is nothing "milk and water" about him; he is not afraid of the dark. He does not do bad things because he is afraid of being decent. Instead of being a puny, dull, or bookish lad, who dreams and does nothing, he is full of life, energy, enthusiasm, bubbling over with fun, full of ideas as to what he wants to do and knows how he wants to do it. He has many ideals and many heroes. He is not hitched to his mother's apronstrings. While he adores his mother, and would do anything to save her from suffering or discomfort, he is self-reliant, sturdy and full of vim. (West, 1912, p. 448)

THE SCOUTMASTER AND MASCULINE VALIDATION

Scouting assuaged adult masculine anxiety not only by training boys in the masculine virtues. The movement provided adult men a sphere of masculine validation. Given the character and composition of their occupations and the centrality of occupation to the male sex role, young men in white-collar positions were especially concerned about their masculine identity. They were receptive to an organization which provided adult men the opportunity to be men as traditionally defined.

At the core of the image of the ideal scoutmaster was assertive manliness. Scoutmasters were "manly" patriots with common sense and moral character who sacrificially served America's youth (Boy Scouts of America, 1920). Scouting wanted "REAL, live men—red blooded and righthearted men—BIG men"; "No Miss Nancy need apply" (Boy Scouts of America, n.d., p. 9). Scoutmasters by the force of their characters, not by their formal positions (as in a bureaucracy), would evoke respect. They were portrayed as men of executive ability who took decisive action over a wide range of problems and were adroit handlers of men and boys. An analysis of the social characteristics and motivation of all the Chicago scoutmasters for whom there are records—original applications—through 1919 ($N = 575$) raises questions about the veracity of this portrayal (Hantover, 1976).

The first scoutmasters were men of educational, occupational, and ethnic status, but they did not serve solely from a sense of *noblesse oblige* and a disinterested commitment to all boys. They were more concerned about saving middle-class boys from the effeminizing forces of modern society than with "civilizing" the sons of the lower classes. Only four scoutmasters singled out the lower class for special mention; just 8% of the over 700 experiences with youth listed by scoutmasters were with lower-class youth. The typical Chicago scoutmaster was white, under 30, native born, Protestant, college educated, and in a whitecollar or professional/semi-professional occupation. Scoutmasters were more Protestant, better educated, and in higher prestige occupations than the adult male population of Chicago. Many teachers, clergymen, and boys' workers were scoutmasters because Scouting was part of their job, was good training for it, or at least was congruent with their vocational ideology. If we exclude those men drawn to Scouting by the requirements of their occupations, Scouting disproportionately attracted men who had borne longer the "feminine" environment of the schools and now were in occupations whose sedentariness and dependence did not fit the traditional image of American manliness.

Though the motivational data extracted from the original scoutmaster applications are limited, there does emerge from the number and quality of responses a sense that clerical workers were concerned about the development of masculinity among adolescents and its expression by adults. Clerical workers were more concerned than other occupations unrelated to youth and service about training boys for manhood, filling a boy's time with constructive activities so he would not engage in activities detrimental to the development of manhood, and about the sexual and moral dangers of adolescence.

It is not simply chance, I believe, that clerical workers gave elaborate and individualistic responses which evinced a sense of life's restrictedness and danger. A 26-year-old stenographer, "always having lived in Chicago and working indoors," felt Scouting was a way to get outdoors for himself, not the scouts. A 21-year-old clerk, implying that his career had reached its apogee, praised Scouting for its development of initiative and resourcefulness and admitted that lack of these qualities had handicapped him greatly. A draftsman, only 27, thought "association with the boys will certainly keep one from getting that old and retired feeling." Another young clerk evokes a similar sense of life's restrictedness when he writes that Scouting "affords me an opportunity to exercise control over a set of young men. I learn to realize the value of myself as a force as a personality."

The masculine anxiety that clerical workers felt may not have been generated by their occupations alone. They brought to the job achievements and attributes which at the turn of the century could have exacerbated that anxiety. Clerical workers had the highest percentage of high school educated scoutmasters of any occupational group. They were subject to the perceived feminine forces of high school without the status compensation of a college education and a professional position. With education controlled, Protestants and native Americans were more likely to be clerical workers. It was the virility and reproductive powers of the native American stock which were being questioned after the Civil War. Women in the better classes (native and Protestant) denied men the opportunity to prove their masculinity through paternity. Albion Small complained, "In some of the best middle-class social strata in the United States a young wife becomes a subject of surprised comment among her acquaintances if she accepts the burdens of maternity! This is a commonplace" (Small, 1915, p. 661). The fecundity and alleged sexuality of the immigrants raised turn-of-the-century fears about the continued dominance of the native Protestant stock. The experiences of key reference groups as well as one's own individual experiences were factors contributing to a sense of endangered masculinity.

CONCLUSION

Adult sex-role anxiety is rooted in the social structure; and groups of men are differentially affected, depending on their location in the social system and the opportunity structure they face. Critics of men's supposed nature can be dismissed as misguided by medical and religious defenders. But when the opportunity structure underlying masculinity begins to restrict, questioning may arise from the ranks of the men themselves. When taken-for-granted constructs become the objects of examination, anxiety may arise because elements in a cultural system are defended as natural, if not transcendent, rather than convenient or utilitarian. Under the disconfirming impact of social change, men may at first be more likely to reassert the validity of traditional ends and seek new avenues for their accomplishment than to redefine their ends.

"Men not only define themselves, but they actualize these definitions in real experience—*they live them*" (Berger, Berger & Kellner, 1974, p. 92). Social identities generate the need for self-confirming action. The young men in the scoutmaster ranks were the first generation to face full force the discontinuity between the realities of the modern bureaucratic world and the image of masculine autonomy and mastery and the rhetoric of Horatio Alger. They found in the Boy Scouts of America an institutional sphere for the validation of masculinity previously generated by the flow of daily social life and affirmed in one's work.

NOTE

1. Beard, D. C. Untitled article submitted to *Youth Companion*. Unpublished manuscript, Daniel Carter Beard Collection, Library of Congress, 1914.

REFERENCES

Anderson, H. D., & Davidson, P. E. *Occupational trends in the United States*. Stanford: Stanford University Press, 1940.

Berger, P., Berger, B., & Kellner, H. *The homeless mind*. New York: Vintage Press, 1974.

Boy Scouts of America. Fourth annual report. *Scouting*, 1914, 1.

Boy Scouts of America. *Handbook for scoutmasters* (2nd ed.). New York: Boy Scouts of America, 1920.

Boy Scouts of America. *The scoutmaster and his troop*. New York: Boy Scouts of America, no date.

Burgess, T. W. Making men of them. *Good Housekeeping Magazine*, 1914, 59, 3–12.

Conant, R. W. *The virility of Christ*. Chicago: no publisher, 1915.

Crandall, J. C., Jr. *Images and ideals for young Americans: A study of American juvenile literature, 1825–1860*. Unpublished doctoral dissertation, University of Rochester, 1957.

Douglas, P. *Real wages in the United States, 1890–1926*. New York: Houghton Mifflin, 1930.

Eaton, W. P. *Boy Scouts in Glacier Park*. Boston: W. A. Wilde; 1918.

Filene, P. G. *Him, her, self: Sex roles in modern America*. New York: Harcourt Brace Jovanovich, 1975.

Greene, T. P. *America's heroes: The changing models of success in American magazines*. New York: Oxford University Press, 1970.

Hantover, J. P. *Sex role, sexuality, and social status: The early years of the Boy Scouts of America*. Unpublished doctoral dissertation, University of Chicago, 1976.

Hays, S. P. *The response to industrialism: 1885–1914*. Chicago: University of Chicago Press, 1957.

Hill, J. A. *Women in gainful occupations 1870 to 1920* (Census Monograph No. 9, U.S. Bureau of the Census). Washington, D.C.: U.S. Government Printing Office, 1929.

James, W. The moral equivalent of war. In J. K. Roth (Ed.), *The moral equivalent and other essays*. New York: Harper Torchbook, 1971.

Mills, C. W. *White collar*. New York: Oxford University Press, 1951.

Murray, W. D. *The history of the boy scouts of America*. New York: Boy Scouts of America, 1937.

Page, J. F. *Socializing for the new order of educational values of the juvenile organization*. Rock Island, Ill.: J. F. Page, 1919.

Puffer, J. A. *The boy and his gang*. Boston: Houghton Mifflin, 1912.

Rudolph, F. *The American college and university*. New York: Knopf, 1962.

Russell, T. H. (Ed.). *Stories of boy life*. No location: Fireside Edition, 1914.

Seton, E. T. *Boy Scouts of America: A handbook of woodcraft, scouting, and life craft*. New York: Doubleday, Page, 1910.

Shaw, A. *The outlook for the average man*. New York: Macmillan, 1907.

Small, A. The bonds of nationality. *American Journal of Sociology*, 1915, *10*, 629–83.

Smuts, R. W. *Women and work in America*. New York: Columbia University Press, 1959.

U.S. Department of Commerce. *Ninth census of the United States, 1870: Population and social statistics* (Vol. I). Washington, D.C.: U.S. Government Printing Office, 1870.

West, J. E. The real boy scout. *Leslie's Weekly*, 1912, 448.

COOL POSE:
THE PROUD SIGNATURE OF BLACK SURVIVAL

RICHARD MAJORS

Just when it seemed that we black males were beginning to recover from past injustices inflicted by a dominant white society, we find once again that we are being revisited in a similar vein. President Reagan's de-emphasis of civil rights, affirmative action legislation and social services programs; the rise of black neoconservatives and certain black feminist groups; harshly critical media events on television (e.g., the CBS documentary "The Vanishing Family— Crisis in Black America") and in films (e.g., *The Color Purple*); and the omnipresent problems of unemployment and inadequate health care, housing, and education—all have helped to shape a negative political and social climate toward black men. For many black men this period represents a *New Black Nadir*, or lowest point, and time of deepest depression.

Black people in general, and the black man in particular, look out on a world that does not positively reflect their image. Black men learned long ago that the classic American virtues of thrift, perseverance and hard work would not give us the tangible rewards that accrue to most members of the dominant society. We learned early that we would not be Captains of Industry or builders of engineering wonders. Instead, we channeled our creative energies into construction of a symbolic universe. Therefore we adopted unique poses and postures to offset the externally imposed "zero" image. Because black men were denied access to the dominant culture's acceptable avenues of expression, we created a form of self-expression—the "Cool Pose."[1-3]

Cool Pose is a term that represents a variety of attitudes and actions that serve the black man as mechanisms for survival, defense and social competence. These attitudes and actions are performed using characterizations and roles as facades and shields.

COOL CULTURE

Historically, coolness was central to the culture of many ancient African civilizations. The Yorubas of Western Nigeria (900 B.C. to 200 A.D.) are cited as an example of an African civilization where cool was integrated into the social fabric of the community.[4] Uses of cool ranged from the way a young man carried himself before his peers to the way he impressed his elders during the initiation ritual. Coolness helped to build character and pride for individuals in such groups and is regarded as a precolonial cultural adaptation. With the advent of the modern African slave trade, cool became detached from its indigenous cultural setting and emerged equally as a survival mechanism.

Where the European saw America as the promised land, the African saw it as the land of oppression. Today, reminders of Black America's oppressive past continue in the form of chronic underemployment, inadequate housing, inferior schools, and poor health care. Because of these conditions many black men have become frustrated, angry, confused and impatient.

To help ease the pain associated with these conditions, black men have taken to alcoholism, drug abuse, homicide, and suicide. In learning to mistrust the words and actions of dominant white people, black males have learned to make great use of "poses" and "postures" which connote control, toughness, and detachment. All these forms arise from the mistrust that the black males feel towards the dominant society.

For these black males, particular poses and postures show the white man that "although you may have tried to hurt me time and time again, I can take it (and if I am hurting or weak, I'll never let you know). They are saying loud and clear to the white establishment, "I am strong, full of pride, and a survivor." Accordingly, any failures in the real world become the black man's secret.

THE EXPRESSIVE LIFE STYLE

On the other hand, those poses and postures that have an expressive quality or nature have become known in the literature as the "expressive life style."[5] The expressive life style is a way in which the black male can act cool by actively displaying particular performances that emphasize creative expression. Thus, while black people historically have been forced into conciliatory and often demeaning positions in American culture, there is nothing conciliatory about the expressive life style.

This dynamic vitality will not be denied even in limited stereotypical roles—as demonstrated by Hattie McDaniel, the maid in *Gone With the Wind* or Bill "Bojangle" Robinson as the affable servant in the Shirley Temple movies. This abiding need for creative self-expression knows no bounds, and asserts itself whether on the basketball court or in dancing. We can see it in black athletes—with their stylish dunking of the basketball, their spontaneous dancing in the end zone, and their different styles of handshakes (e.g., "high fives")—and in black entertainers with their various choreographed "cool" dance steps. These are just a few examples of black individuals in their professions who epitomize this creative expression. The expressive life style is a dynamic—not a static—art form, and new aesthetic forms are always evolving (e.g., "rap-talking" and breakdancing). The expressive life style, then, is the passion that invigorates the demeaning life of blacks in White America. It is a dynamic vitality that transforms the mundane into the sublime and makes the routine spectacular.

A CULTURAL SIGNATURE

Cool Pose, manifested by the expressive life style, is also an aggressive assertion of masculinity. It emphatically says, "White man, this is my turf. You can't match me here." Though he may be impotent in the political and corporate world, the black man demonstrates his potency in athletic competition, entertainment and the pulpit with a verve that borders on the spectacular. Through the virtuosity of a performance, he tips the socially imbalanced scales in his favor. "See me, touch me, hear me, but, white man, you can't copy me." This is the subliminal message which black males signify in their oftentimes flamboyant performance. Cool Pose, then, becomes the cultural signature for such black males.

Being cool is a unique response to adverse social, political and economic conditions. Cool provides control, inner strength, stability and confidence. Being cool, illustrated in its various poses and postures, becomes a very powerful and necessary tool in the black man's constant fight for his soul. The poses and postures of cool guard, preserve and protect his pride, dignity and respect to such an extent that the black male is willing to risk a great deal for it. One black man said it well: "The white man may control everything about me—that is, except my pride and dignity. That he can't have. That is mine and mine alone."

THE COST

Cool Pose, however, is not without its price. Many black males fail to discriminate the appropriate uses of Cool Pose and act cool much of the time, without regard to time or space.[6] Needless to say, this can cause severe problems. In many situations a black man won't allow himself to express or show any form of weakness or fear or other feelings and emotions. He assumes a facade of strength, held at all costs, rather than "blow his fronts" and thus his cool. Perhaps black men have become so conditioned to keeping up their guard against oppression from the dominant white society that this particular attitude and behavior represent for them their best safeguard against further mental or physical abuse. However, this same behavior makes it very difficult for these males to let their guard down and show affection, even for people that they actually care about or for people that may really care about them (e.g., girlfriends, wives, mothers, fathers, "good" friends, etc.).

When the art of being cool is used to put cool behaviors ahead of emotions or needs, the result of such repression of feelings can be frustration. Such frustrations sometimes cause aggression which often is taken out on those individuals closest to such men—other black people. It is sadly ironic, then, that the same elements of cool that allow for survival in the larger society may hurt black people by contributing to one of the more complex problems facing black people today—black-on-black crime.

Further, while Cool Pose enables black males to maintain stability in the face of white power, it may through inappropriate use render many of them unable to move with the mainstream or evolve in healthy ways. When misused, cool can suppress the motivation to learn, accept or become exposed to stimuli, cultural norms, aesthetics, mannerisms, values, etiquette, informa-

tion or networks that could help them overcome problems caused by white racism. Finally, in a society which has as its credo, "A man's home is his castle," it is ironic that the masses of black men have no castle to protect. Their minds have become their psychological castle, defended by impenetrable cool. Thus, Cool Pose is the bittersweet symbol of a socially disesteemed group that shouts, "We are" in face of a hostile and indifferent world that everywhere screams, "You ain't."

COOL AND THE BLACK PSYCHE

To be fully grasped, Cool Pose must be recognized as having gained ideological consensus in the black community. It is not only a quantitatively measured "social reality" but a series of equally "real" rituals of socialization. It is a comprehensive, officially endorsed cultural myth that became entrenched in the black psyche with the beginning of the slave experience. This phenomenon has cut across all socioeconomic groups in the black community, as black men fight to preserve their dignity, pride, respect and masculinity with the attitudes and behaviors of Cool Pose. Cool Pose represents a fundamental structuring of the psyche of the black male and is manifested in some way or another in the daily activities and recreational habits of most black males. There are few other social or psychological constructs that have shaped, directed or controlled the black male to the extent that the various forms of coolness have. It is surprising, then, that for a concept that has the potential to explain problems in black male and black female relationships, black-on-black crime, and black-on-black pregnancies, there is such limited research on this subject.

In the final analysis, Cool Pose may represent the most important yet least researched area with the potential to enhance our understanding and study of black behavior today.

NOTES

1. Majors, R. G., Nikelly, A. G., "Serving the Black Minority: A New Direction for Psychotherapy." *J. for Non-white Concerns*, 11:142–151 (1983).

2. Majors, R. G., "The Effects of 'Cool Pose': What Being Cool Means." *Griot*, pp. 4–5 (Spring, 1985).

3. Nikelly, A. G. & Majors, R. G. "Techniques for Counseling Black Students," *Techniques: J. Remedial Educ. & Counseling*, 2:48–54 (1986).

4. Bascom, W., *The Yoruba of Southwestern Nigeria*. (New York: Holt, Rinehart & Winston, 1969).

SUGGESTED READINGS

Glassner, B. "Kid Society." *Urban Education* 11 (1976):5–22.

Hughes, E. "Good People and Dirty Work." *Social Problems* 10 (1962):3–11.

Knapp, M. and Knapp, H. *One Potato, Two Potato. . . . : The Secret Education of American Children*. New York: Norton, 1976.

Sutton-Smith, B. *A History of Children's Play*. Philadelphia: University of Pennsylvania Press, 1981.

THE FRATERNAL BOND AS A JOKING RELATIONSHIP
A CASE STUDY OF THE ROLE OF SEXIST JOKES IN MALE GROUP BONDING

PETER LYMAN

One evening during dinner, 45 fraternity men suddenly broke into the dining room of a nearby campus sorority, surrounded the 30 women residents, and forced them to watch while one pledge gave a speech on Freud's theory of penis envy as another demonstrated various techniques of masturbation with a rubber penis. The women sat silently, staring downward at their plates, and listened for about 10 minutes, until a woman law student who was the graduate resident in charge of the house walked in, surveyed the scene and demanded, "Please leave immediately!" As she later described that moment, "There was a mocking roar from the men, 'It's tradition.' I said, 'That's no reason to do something like this, please leave!' And they left. I was surprised. Then the women in the house started to get angry. And the guy who made the penis-envy speech came back and said to us, 'That was funny to me. If that's not funny to you I don't know what kind of sense of humor you have, but I'm sorry.'"

That night the women sat around the stairwell of their house discussing the event, some angry and others simply wanting to forget the whole thing. They finally decided to ask the university to require that the men return to discuss the event. When university officials threatened to take action, the men agreed to the meeting. I had served as a faculty resident in student housing for two years and had given several talks in the dorm about humor and gender, and was asked by both the men and the women involved to attend the discussion as a facilitator, and was given permission to take notes and interview the participants later, provided I concealed their identities.

The penis-envy ritual had been considered a successful joke in previous years by both "the guys and the girls," but this year it failed, causing great tension between two groups that historically had enjoyed a friendly joking relationship. In the women's view, the joke had not failed because of its subject; they considered sexual jokes to be a normal part of the erotic joking relationship between men and women. They thought it had failed because of its emotional structure, the mixture of sexuality with aggression and the atmosphere of physical intimidation in the room that signified that the women were the object of a joking relationship between the men. A few women argued that the failed joke exposed the latent domination in men's relation to women, but this view was labeled "feminist" because it endangered the possibility of reconstituting the erotic joking relationship with the men. Although many of the men individually regretted the damage to their relationship with women

From *Changing Men*, edited by Michael Kimmel. Newbury Park, CA: Sage Publications, 1987. Reprinted by permission.

friends in the group, they argued that the special male bond created by sexist humor is a unique form of intimacy that justified the inconvenience caused the women. In reinterpreting these stories as social constructions of gender, I will focus upon the way the joke form and joking relationships reveal the emotional currents underlying gender in this situation.

THE SOCIOLOGY OF JOKES

Although we conventionally think of jokes as a meaningless part of the dramaturgy of everyday life, this convention is part of the way that the social function of jokes is concealed and is necessary if jokes are to "work." It is when jokes fail that the social conflicts that the joke was to reconstruct or "negotiate" are uncovered, and the tensions and emotions that underlie the conventional order of everyday social relations are revealed.

Joking is a special kind of social relationship that suspends the rules of everyday life in order to preserve them. Jokes indirectly express the emotions and tensions that may disrupt everyday life by "negotiating" them (Emerson, 1969, 1970), reconstituting group solidarity by shared aggression and cathartic laughter. The ordinary consequences of forbidden words are suspended by meta-linguistic gestures (tones of voice, facial expressions catch phrases) that send the message "this is a joke," and emotions that would ordinarily endanger a social relationship can be spoken safely within the micro-world created by the "the joke form" (Bateson, 1955).

Yet jokes are not just stories, they are a theater of domination in everyday life, and the success or failure of a joke marks the boundary within which power and aggression may be used in a relationship. Nearly all jokes have an aggressive content, indeed shared aggression toward an outsider is one of the primary ways by which a group may overcome internal tension and assert its solidarity (Freud, 1960, p. 102). Jokes both require and renew social bonds; thus Radcliffe-Brown pointed out that "joking rela-

tionships" between mothers-in-law and their sons-in-law provide a release for tension for people structurally bound to each other but at the same time feeling structural conflict with each other (Radcliffe-Brown, 1959). Joking relationships in medicine, for example, are a medium for the indirect expression of latent emotions or taboo topics that if directly expressed would challenge the physician's authority or disrupt the need to treat life and death situations as ordinary work (see Coser, 1959; Emerson, 1969, 1970).

In each of the studies cited above, the primary focus of the analysis was upon the social function of the joke, not gender, yet in each case the joke either functioned through a joking relationship between men and women, such as in Freud's or Radcliffe-Brown's analysis of mother-in-law jokes, or through the joking relationship between men and women. For example, Coser describes the role of nurses as a safe target of jokes: as a surrogate for the male doctor in patient jokes challenging medical authority; or as a surrogate for the patient in the jokes with which doctors expressed anxiety. Sexist jokes, therefore, should be analyzed not only in general terms of the function of jokes as a means of defending social order, but in specific terms as the mechanism by which the order of gender domination is sustained in everyday life. From this perspective, jokes reveal the way social organizations are gendered, namely, built around the emotional rules of male bonding. In this case study, gender is not only the primary content of men's jokes, but the emotional structures of the male bond is built upon a joking relationship that "negotiates" the tension men feel about their relationship with each other, and with women.

Male bonding in everyday life frequently takes the form of a group joking relationship by which men create a serial kind of intimacy to "negotiate" the latent tension and aggression they feel toward each other. The humor of male bonding relationships generally is sexual and aggressive, and frequently consists of sexist or racist jokes. As Freud (1960, p. 99) observed, the jokes that individual men direct toward women are generally erotic, tend to clever forms (like the double entendre), and have a seductive purpose. The jokes that men tell about women in the presence of other men are sexual and aggressive rather than erotic and use hostile rather than clever verbal forms; and, this paper will argue, have the creation of male group bonding as their purpose. While Freud analyzed jokes in order to reveal the unconscious, in this article, relationships will be analyzed to uncover the emotional dynamics of male friendships.

The failed penis-envy joke reveals two kinds of joking relationships between college men and women. First, the attempted joke was part of an ongoing joking relationship between "the guys and the girls," as they called each other. The guys used the joking relationship to negotiate the tension they felt between sexual interest in the girls and fear of commitment to them. The guys contrasted their sense of independence and play in male friendships to the sense of dependence they felt in their relationships with women, and used hostile joking to negotiate their fear of the "loss of control" implied by intimacy. Second, the failure of the joke uncovered the use of sexist jokes in creating bonds between men; through their own joking relationships (which they called friendship), the guys negotiated the tension between their need for intimacy with other men and their fear of losing their autonomy as men to the authority of the work world.

THE GIRLS' STORY

The women frequently had been the target of fraternity initiation rites in the past, and generally enjoyed this joking relationship with the men, if with a certain ambivalence. "There was a naked Christmas Carol event, they were singing 'We wish you a Merry Christmas,' and 'Bring on the hasty pudding' was the big line they liked to yell out. And we had five or six pledges who had to strip in front of the house and do naked jumping jacks on the lawn, after all the women in the house were lined up on the steps to watch." The women did not think these events were hostile

because they had been invited to watch, and the men stood with them watching, suggesting that the pledges, not the women, were the targets of the joke. This made the joke sexual, not sexist, and part of the normal erotic joking relationship between the guys and girls. Still, these jokes were ritual events, not real social relationships; one woman said, "We were just supposed to watch, and the guys were watching us watch. The men set up the stage and the women are brought along to observe. They were the controlling force, then they jump into the car and take off."

At the meeting with the men, two of the women spoke for the group while 11 others sat silently in the center, surrounded by about 30 men. Each tried to explain to the men why the joke had not been funny. The first began, "I'm a feminist, but I'm not going to blame anyone for anything. I just want to talk about my feelings." When she said, "these guys pile in, I mean these huge guys," the men exploded in loud cathartic laughter, and the women joined in, releasing some of the tension of the meeting. She continued, "Your humor was pretty funny as long as it was sexual, but when it went beyond sexual to sexist, then it became painful. You were saying 'I'm better than you.' When you started using sex as a way of proving your superiority it hurt me and made me angry."

The second woman speaker criticized the imposition of the joke form itself, saying that the men's raid had the tone of a symbolic rape. "I admit we knew you were coming over, and we were whispering about it. But it went too far, and I felt afraid to say anything. Why do men always think about women in terms of violating them, in sexual imagery? You have to understand that the combination of a sexual topic with the physical threat of all of you standing around terrified me. I couldn't move. You have to realize that when men combine sexuality and force it's terrifying to women." This woman alluded to having been sexually assaulted in the past, but spoke in a nonthreatening tone that made the men listen silently.

The women spoke about feeling angry about the invasion of their space, about the coercion of being forced to listen to the speeches, and about being used as the object of a joke. But they reported their anger as a psychological fact, a statement about a past feeling, not an accusation. Many began by saying, "I'm not a feminist, but . . . ," to reassure the men that although they felt angry, they were not challenging traditional gender relations. The women were caught in a double-bind; if they spoke angrily to the men they would·violate the taboo against the expression of anger by women (Miller, 1976, p. 102). If they said nothing, they would internalize their anger, and traditional feminine culture would encourage them to feel guilty about feeling angry at all (Bernardez, 1978; Lerner, 1980). In part they resolved the issue by accepting the men's construction of the event as a joke, although a failed joke; accepting the joke form absolved the men of responsibility, and transformed a debate about gender into a debate about good and bad jokes.

To be accepted as a joke, a cue must be sent to establish a "frame" [for] the latent hostility of the joke content in a safe context; the men sent such a cue when they stood next to the women during the naked jumping jacks. If the cue "this is a joke" is ambiguous, or is not accepted, the aggressive content of the joke is revealed and generally is responded to with anger or aggression, endangering the relationship. In part the women were pointing out to the men that the cue "this is a joke" had not been given in this case, and the aggressive content of the joke hurt them. If the cue is given properly and accepted, the everyday rules of social order are suspended and the rule "this is fun" is imposed on the expression of hostility.

Verbal aggression mediated by the joke form generally will be [accepted] without later consequences in the everyday world, and will be judged in terms of the formal intention of jokes, shared play marked by laughter in the interest of social order. By complaining to the university, the women had suspended the rules of joke culture, and attempted to renegotiate them by bringing in an observer; even this turned out to be too aggressive, and the women retreated to traditional gender relationships. The men had formally accepted this shift of rules in order to avoid punishment from the university, however their defense of the joke form was tacitly a defense of traditional gender rules that would define male sexist jokes toward women as erotic, not hostile.

In accepting the construction of the event as "just a joke" the women absolved the men of responsibility for their actions by calling them "little boys." One woman said, "It's not wrong, they're just boys playing a prank. They're little boys, they don't know what they're doing. It was unpleasant, but we shouldn't make a big deal out of it." In appealing to the rules of the joke form the men were willing to sacrifice their relationship to the women to protect the rules. In calling the men "little boys" the women were bending the rules trying to preserve the relationship through a patient nurturing role (see Gilligan, 1982, p. 44).

In calling the guys "little boys," the girls had also created a kind of linguistic symmetry between "the boys and the girls." With the exception of the law student, who called the girls "women," the students called the men "guys" and the women "girls." Earlier in the year the law student had started a discussion about this naming practice. The term "women" had sexual connotations that made "the girls" feel vulnerable, and "gals," the parallel to "guys," connoted "older women" to them. While the term "girls" refers to children, it was adopted because it avoided sexual connotations. Thus the women had no term like "the guys," which is a bonding term that refers to a group of friends as equals; the women often used the term "the guys" to refer to themselves in a group. As the men's speeches were to make clear, the term "guys" refers to a bond that is exclusively male, which is founded upon the emotional structure of the joke form, and which justifies it.

THE GUYS' STORY

Aside from the roar of laughter when a woman referred to their intimidating size, the men interrupted the women only once. When a woman began to say that the men obviously intended to intimidate them, the men loudly protested that the women couldn't possibly judge their intentions, that they intended the whole event only as a joke, and the intention of a joke is, by definition, just fun.

At this point the two black men in the fraternity intervened to explain the rules of male joke culture to the women. The black men said that in a sense they understood what the women meant, it is painful being the object of aggressive jokes. In fact, they said, the collective talk of the fraternity at meals and group events was made up of nothing but jokes, including many racist jokes. One said, "I know what you mean. I've had to listen to things in the house that I'd have hit someone for saying if I'd heard them outside." There was again cathartic laughter among the guys, for the male group bond consisted almost entirely of aggressive words that were barely contained by the responsibility absolving rule of the joke form. A woman responded, "Maybe people should be hit for saying those things, maybe that's the right thing to do." But the black speaker was trying to explain the rules of male joke culture to the women, "if you'd just ignored us, it wouldn't have been any fun." To ignore a joke, even though it makes you feel hurt or angry, is to show strength or coolness, the two primary masculine ideals of the group.

Another man tried to explain the failure of the joke in terms of the difference between the degree of "crudeness" appropriate among the guys and between "guys and girls." He said, "As I was listening at the edge of the room, near the door, and when I looked at the guys I was laughing but when I looked at the girls I was embarrassed. I could see both sides at the same time. It was too crude for your sense of propriety. We have a sense of crudeness you don't have. That's a cultural aspect of the difference between girls and guys."

The other men laughed as he mentioned "how crude we are at the house," and one of the black men added, "you wouldn't believe how crude it gets." Many of the men said privately that while they individually found the jokes about women vulgar, the jokes were justified because they were necessary for the formation of the fraternal bond. These men thought the mistake had been to reveal their crudeness to the women, this was "in bad taste."

In its content, the fraternal bond was almost entirely a joking relationship. In part, the joking was a kind of "signifying" or "dozens," a ritual exchange of insults that functioned to create group solidarity. "If there's one theme that goes on, it's the emphasis on being able to take a lot of ridicule, of shit, and not getting upset about it. Most of the interaction we have is verbally abusing each other, making disgusting references to your mother's sexuality, or the women you were seen with, or your sex organ, the size of your sex organ. And you aren't cool unless you can take it without trying to get back." Being cool is an important male value in other settings as well, such as sports or work; the joke form is a kind of male pedagogy in that, in one guy's words, it teaches "how to keep in control of your emotions."

But the guys themselves would not have described their group as a joking relationship or even as a male bond; they called it friendship. One man said he had found perhaps a dozen guys in the house who were special friends, "guys I could cry in front of." Yet in interviews, no one could recall any of the guys actually crying in front of each other. One said, "I think the guys are very close, they would do nearly anything for each other, drive each other places, give each other money. I think when they have problems about school, their car, or something like that, they can talk to each other. I'm not sure they can talk to each other about problems with women though." The image of crying in front of the other guys was a moving symbol of intimacy to the guys, but in fact crying would be an admission of vulnerability, which would violate the ideals of "strength" and "being cool."

Although the fraternal bond was idealized as a unique kind of intimacy upon which genuine friendship was built, the content of the joking relationship was focused upon women, including much "signifying" talk about mothers. The women interpreted the sexist jokes as a sign of vulnerability. "The thing that struck me the most about our meeting together," one said, "was when the men said they were afraid of trusting women, afraid of being seen as jerks." According to her, this had been the women's main reaction to the meeting by the other women, "How do you tell men that they don't have to be afraid, and what do you do with women who abuse that kind of trust?" One of the men on the boundary of the group remarked that the most hostile misogynist jokes came from the men with the fewest intimate relationships with women. "I think down deep all these guys would love to have satisfying relationships with women. I think they're scared of failing, of having to break away from the group they've become comfortable with. I think being in a fraternity, having close friendships with men is a replacement for having close relationships with women. It'd be painful for them because they'd probably fail."

Joking mobilized the commitment of the men to the group by policing the individual men's commitments to women and minimized the possibility of dyadic withdrawal from the group (see Slater, 1963). "One of the guys just acquired a girlfriend a few weeks ago. He's someone I don't think has had a woman to be friends with, maybe ever, at least in a long time. Everybody has been ribbing him intensely the last few weeks. It's good natured in tone. Sitting at dinner they've invented a little song they sing to him. People yell questions about his girlfriend, the size of her vagina, does she have big breasts."

Since both the jokes and the descriptions of the parties have strong homoerotic overtones, including the exchange of women as sexual partners, jokes were also targeted at homosexuality, to draw an emotional line between the homosocial male bond and homosexual relationships. Being called "queer," however, did not require a sexual relationship with another man, but only visible signs of vulnerability or nurturing behavior.

MALE BONDING AS A JOKING RELATIONSHIP

Fraternal bonding is an intimate kind of male group friendship that suspends the ordinary rules and responsibilities of everyday life through joking relationships. To the guys, dyadic friendship with a woman implied "loss of control," namely, responsibility for work and family. In dealing with women, the group separated intimacy from sex, defining the male bond as intimate but not sexual (homosocial), and relationships with women as sexual but not intimate (heterosexual). The intimacy of group friendship was built upon shared spontaneous action, "having fun," rather than the self-disclosure that marks women's friendships (see Rubin, 1983, p. 13). One of the men had been inexpressive as he listened to the discussion, but spoke about fun in a voice filled with emotion, "The penis-envy speech was a hilarious idea, great college fun. That's what I joined the fraternity for, a good time. College is a stage in my life to do crazy and humorous things. In 10 years when I'm in the business world I won't be able to carry on like this [again cathartic laughter from the men]. The initiation was intended to be humorous. We didn't think through how sensitive you women were going to be."

This speech gives the fraternal bond a specific place in the life cycle. The joking relationship is a ritual bond that creates a male group bond in the transition between boyhood and manhood, after the separation from the family, where the authority of mothers limits fun, but before becoming subject to the authority of work. One man later commented on the transitional nature of the male bond, "I think a lot of us are really scared of losing total control over our own lives. Having to sacrifice our individuality. I think we're scared of work in the same way we're scared of women." In this sense individuality is associated with what the guys called "strength," both the emotional strength suggested by being cool, and the physical strength suggested by facing the risks of sports and the paramilitary games they liked to play.

The emotional structure of the joking relationship is built upon the guys' latent anger about the discipline that middle-class male roles imposed upon them, both marriage rules and work rules. The general relationship between organization of men's work and men's domination of women was noted by Max Weber (1958, pp. 345–346), who described "the vocational specialist" as a man mastered by the rules of organization that create an impersonal kind of dependence, and who therefore seeks to create a feeling of independence through the sexual conquest of women. In each of the epochs of Western history, Weber argues, the subordination of men at work has given rise to a male concept of freedom based upon the violation of women. Although Weber tied dependence upon rules to men's need for sexual conquest through seduction, this may also be a clue to the meaning of sexist jokes and joking relationships among men at work. Sexist jokes may not be simply a matter of recreation or a means of negotiating role stress, they may be a reflection of the emotional foundations of organizational life for men. In everyday work life, sexist jokes may function as a ritual suspension of the rules of responsibility for men, a withdrawal into a microworld in which their anger about dependence upon work and women may be safely expressed.

In analyzing the contradictions and vulnerabilities the guys felt about relationships with women and the responsibilities of work, I will focus upon three dimensions of the joking relationship: (1) the emotional content of the jokes; (2) the erotics of rule breaking created by the rules of the joke form; and (3) the image of strength and "being cool" they pitted against the dependence represented by both women and work.

The Emotional Dynamic of Sexist Jokes

When confronted by the women, the men defended the joke by asserting the formal rule that the purpose of jokes is play, then by justifying the jokes as necessary in order to create a spe-

cial male bond. The defense that jokes are play defines aggressive behavior as play. This defense was far more persuasive to the men than to the women, since many forms of male bonding play are rule-governed aggression, as in sports and games. The second defense, asserting the relation between sexist jokes and male bonds, points out the social function of sexist jokes among the guys, to control the threat that individual men might form intimate emotional bonds with women and withdraw from the group. Each defense poses a puzzle about the emotional dynamics of male group friendship, for in each case male group friendship seems more like a defense against vulnerability than a positive deal.

In each defense, intimacy is split from sexuality in order to eroticize the male bond, thereby creating an instrumental sexuality directed at women. The separation of intimacy from sexuality transforms women into "sexual objects," which both justifies aggression at women by suspending their relationships to the men and devalues sexuality itself, creating a disgust at women as the sexual "object" unworthy of intimate attention. What is the origin of this conjunction between the devaluation of sexuality and the appropriation of intimacy for the male bond?

Chodorow (1978, p. 182) argues that the sense of masculine identity is constructed by an early repression of the son's erotic bond with his mother; with this repression the son's capacity for intimacy and commitment is devalued as feminine behavior. Henceforth men feel ambivalent about intimate relationships with women, seeking to replicate the fusion of intimacy and sexuality that they had experienced in their primal relationships to their mothers, but at the same time fearing engulfment by women in heterosexual relationships, like the engulfment of their infant selves by their mothers (Chodorow, 1976). Certainly the content of the group's joke suggests this repression of the attachment to the mother, as well as hostility to her authority in the family. One man reported, "There's an awful lot of jokes about people's mothers. If any topic of conversation dominates the conversation it's 'heard your mother was with Ray [one of the guys] last night.' The guys will say incredibly vulgar things about their mothers, or they'll talk about the anatomy of a guy's girlfriends, or women they'd like to sleep with." While the guys' signifying mother jokes suggest the repression Chodorow describes, the men realized that their view of women made it unlikely that marriage would be a positive experience. One said, "I think a lot of us expect to marry someone pretty enough that other men will think we got a good catch, someone who is at least marginally interesting to chat with, but not someone we'd view as a friend. But at the same time, a woman who will make sufficient demands that we won't be able to have any friends. So we'll be stuck for the rest of our lives without friends."

While the emotional dynamic of men's "heterosexual knots" may well begin in this primordial separation of infant sons from mothers, its structure is replicated in the guys' ambivalence about their fathers, and their anger about the dependence upon rules in the work world. Yet the guys themselves described the fraternal bond as a way of creating "strength" and overcoming dependence, which suggests a positive ideal of male identity. In order to explore the guys' sense of the value of the male bond, their conception of strength and its consequences for the way they related to each other and to women has to be taken seriously.

STRENGTH

Ultimately the guys justified the penis-envy joke because it created a special kind of male intimacy, but while the male group is able to appropriate its members' needs for intimacy and commitment, it is not clear that it is able to satisfy those needs, because strength has been defined as the opposite of intimacy. "Strength" is a value that represents solidarity rather than intimacy, the solidarity of a shared risk in rule-governed aggressive competition; its value is

suggested by the cathartic laughter when the first woman speaker said, "These guys poured in, these huge guys."

The eros detached from sexuality is attached to rules, not to male friends; the male bond consists of an erotic toward rules, and yet the penis-envy joke expresses most of all the guys' ambivalence about rules. Like "the lads," the male gangs who roam the English countryside, "getting in trouble" by enforcing social mores in unsocial ways (Peters, 1972), "the guys" break the rules in rule-governed ways. The joke form itself suggests this ambivalence about rules and acts as a kind of pedagogy about the relationship between rules and aggression in male work culture. The joke form expresses emotions and tensions that might endanger the order of the organization, but that must be spoken lest they damage social order. Jokes can create group solidarity only if they allow dangerous things to be said; allow a physical catharsis of tension through laughter; or create the solidarity of an "in group" through shared aggression against an "out group." In each case there is an erotic in joke forms: an erotic of shared aggression, of shared sexual feeling, or an erotic of rule breaking itself.

It has been suggested that male groups experience a high level of excitement and sexual arousal in public acts of rule breaking (Thorne & Luria, 1986). The penis-envy speech is precisely such an act, a breaking of conventional moral rules in the interest of group arousal. In each of the versions of the joking relationship in this group there is such an erotic quality: in the sexual content of the jokes, in the need for women to witness dirty talk or naked pledges, in the eros of aggression of the raid and jokes themselves. The penis-envy speech, a required event for all members of the group, is such a collective violation of the rules, and so is the content of their talk, a collective dirty talking that violates moral rules. The cathartic laughter that greeted the words, "You wouldn't believe what we say at the house," testifies to the emotional charge invested in dirty talk.

Because the intimacy of the guys' bond is built around an erotic of rule breaking, it has the serial structure of shared risk rather than the social structure of shared intimacy. In writing about the shared experience of suffering and danger of men at war, J. Glenn Gray (1959, pp. 89–90) distinguishes two kinds of male bonding, comradeship and friendship. Comradeship is based upon an erotic of shared danger, but is based upon the loss of an individual sense of self to a group identity, while friendship is based upon an individual's intellectual and emotional affinity to another individual. In the eros of friendship one's sense of self is heightened; in the eros of comradeship a sense of self is replaced by a sense of group membership. In this sense the guys were seeking comradeship, not friendship, hence the group constructed its bond through an erotic of shared activities with an element of risk, shared danger, or rule breaking: in sports, in paramilitary games, in wild parties, in joking relations. The guys called the performance of these activities "strength," being willing to take risks as a group and remaining cool.

Thus the behavior that the women defined as aggressive was seen by the men as a contest of strength governed by the rules of the joke form, to which the proper response would have been to remain "cool." To the guys, the masculine virtue of "strength" has a positive side, to discover oneself and to discover a sense of the other person through a contest of strength that is governed by rules. To the guys, "strength" is not the same as power or aggression because it is governed by rules, not anger; it is anger that is "uncool."

"BEING COOL"

It is striking that the breaking of rules was not spontaneous, but controlled by the rules of the joke form: that aggressive talk replaces action; that talk is framed by a social form that requires the consent of others; that talk should not be taken seriously. This was the lesson that the black men tried to teach the women in the group

session: In the male world, aggression is not defined as violent if it is rule governed rather than anger governed. The fraternal bond was built upon this emotional structure, for the life of the group centered upon the mobilization of aggressive energies in rule-governed activities (in sports, games, jokes, parties), in each arena aggression was highly valued (strength) only when it was rule governed (cool). Getting angry was called "losing control" and the guys thought they were most likely to lose control when they experienced themselves as personally dependent, as in relationships with women and at work.

Rule-governed aggression is a conduct that is very useful to organizations, in that it mobilizes aggressive energies but binds them to order by rules (see Benjamin, 1980, p. 154). The male sense of order is procedural rather than substantive because the male bond is formal (rule governed), rather than personal (based upon intimacy and commitment). Male groups in this sense are shame cultures, not guilt cultures, because the male bond is a group identity that subordinates the individual to the rules, and because social control is imposed through collective judgments about self-control, such as "strength" and "cool." The sense of order within such male groups is based upon the belief that all members are equally dependent upon the rules and that no personal dependence is created within the group. This is not true of the family or of relations with women, both of which are intimate, and, from the guys' point of view, are "out of control" because they are governed by emotion.

The guys face contradictory demands from work culture about the use of aggressive behavior. Aggressive conduct is highly valued in a competitive society when it serves the interests of the organization, but men also face a strong taboo against the expression of anger at work when it is not rule governed. "Competition" imposes certain rules upon aggressive group processes: Aggression must be calculated, not angry; it must be consistent with the power hierarchy of the organization, serving authority and not challenging it; if expressed, it must be indirect, as in jokes; it must serve the needs of group solidarity, not of individual autonomy. Masculine culture separates anger from aggression when it combines the value "strength" with the value "being cool." While masculine cultures often define the expression of anger as "violent" or "loss of control," anger, properly defined, is speech, not action; angry speech is the way we can defend our sense of integrity and assert our sense of justice. Thus it is anger that challenges the authority of the rules, not aggressive behavior in itself, because anger defends the self, not the organization.

The guys' joking relationship taught them a pedagogy for the controlled use of aggression in the work world, to be able to compete aggressively without feeling angry. The guys recognized the relationship between their male bond and the work world by claiming that "high officials of the university know about the way we act and they understand what we are doing." While this might be taken as evidence that the guys were internalizing their fathers' norms and thus

inheriting the mantle of patriarchy, the guys described their fathers as slaves to work and women, not as patriarchs. The guys also asserted themselves against the authority of their fathers by acting out against the authority of rules in the performance of "strength."

The guys clearly benefited from the male authority that gave them the power to impose the penis-envy joke upon the women with essentially no consequences. Men are allowed to direct anger and aggression toward women because social norms governing the expression of anger or humor generally replicate the power order of the group. It is striking, however, that the guys would not accept the notion that men have more power than women do; to them it is not men who rule, but rules that govern men. These men had so internalized the governing of male emotions by rules that their anger itself could emerge only indirectly through rule-governed forms, such as jokes and joking relationships. In these forms their anger could serve only order, not their sense of self or justice.

REFERENCES

Bateson, G. (1972). A theory of play and fantasy, In *Steps toward an ecology of mind* (pp. 177–193). New York: Ballantine.

Benjamin, J. (1978). Authority and the family revisited, or, A world without fathers. *New German Critique*, *4*(3), 13, 35–57.

Benjamin, J. (1980) The bonds of love: Rational violence and erotic domination *Feminist Studies*, *6*(1), 144–174.

Berndardez, T. (1978) Women and anger. *Journal of the American Medical Women's Association*, *33*(5), 215–219.

Bly, R. (1982). What men really want: An interview with Keith Thompson. *New Age*, pp. 30–37, 50–5l.

Chodorow, N. (1976). Oedipal asymmetries, heterosexual knots. *Social Problems*, 23, 454–468.

Chodorow, N. (1978). *The reproduction of mothering*. Berkeley: University of California Press.

Coser, R. (1959). Some social functions of laughter: A study of humor in a hospital setting. *Human Relations*, *12*, 171–182.

Emerson, J. (1969). Negotiating the serious import of humor. *Sociometry*, *32*, 169–181.

Emerson, J. (1970). Behavior in private places. In H. P. Dreitzel (Ed.), *Recent sociology: Vol. 2. Patterns in communicative behavior*. New York: Macmillan.

Freud, S. (1960). *Jokes and their relation to the unconscious*. New York: Norton.

Gilligan, C. (1982). *In a different voice*. Cambridge, MA: Harvard University Press.

Gray, G. J. (1959). *The warriors: Reflections on men in battle*. New York: Harper & Row.

Lerner, H. E. (1980). Internal prohibitions against female anger *American Journal of Psychoanalysis*, *40*, 137–148.

Miller, J. B. (1976). *Toward a new psychology of women*. Boston: Beacon.

Peters, E. L. (1972). Aspects of the control of moral ambiguities. In M. Gluckman (Ed.), *The allocation of responsibility* (pp. 109–162). Manchester: Manchester University Press.

Radcliffe-Brown, A. (1959). *Structure and function in primitive society*. Glencoe, IL: Free Press.

Rubin, L. (1983). *Intimate strangers*. New York: Harper & Row.

Slater, P. (1963). On social regression. *American Sociological Review, 28*, 339–364.

Thorne, B., & Luria, Z. (1986). Sexuality and gender in children's daily worlds. *Social Problems*.

Weber, M. (1958). Religions of the world and their directions. In H. Gerth & C. W. Mills (Eds.), *From Max Weber*. New York: Oxford University Press.

PART THREE

SPORTS AND WAR: RITES OF PASSAGE IN MALE INSTITUTIONS

Are men naturally more competitive, aggressive, and violent than women? Why are so many cultural heroes males who have been victors on the playing fields or the battlefields? Why do men so often feel that their closest relationships with other men are those that developed "in the heat of battle?" And how do men's battles with each other connect to men's domination of women? The articles in this section shed light on these questions by focusing our attention on two very male-dominated institutions: organized sports and the military.

Recently, largely because of the women's movement, sport sociologists and historians have begun to reconceptualize the meaning of sport as a social institution. Clearly, a major role of sports in the twentieth century has been to provide an institutional context for "masculinity-validation" in a rapidly changing world. Much of the experiential and ideological prominence of sports can be attributed to the fact that it is a male-created homosocial world that provides dramatic symbolic "proof" of the "natural superiority" of men over women. But as the first few articles in this section show, there is nothing "natural" about the connection between sports and what we think of as masculinity. In fact, as the first article by Don Sabo shows, organized sports is an important institutional context in which certain types of masculinity are produced and "naturalized." Here boys learn to overvalue competition and winning, to take physical pain and control their emotions, to view aggression and violence as legitimate means to achieve one's goals, to uncritically accept authority and hierarchy, and to devalue women as well as any "feminine" qualities in males. The next article by Michael Messner suggests how the narrow definitions of masculinity that boys learn in sports connect with other forms of social domination. Finally, Brian Pronger suggests that the intense camaraderie among athletes has a highly charged erotic subtext.

Men's athletic experiences often serve as a training ground for other institutions in which male bonding is valued, especially in the construction of the soldier. R. W. Connell demonstrates that violent aggression is not *the* "natural" form of masculinity; in fact, it takes a very intense process of socialization to make killers out of most men. The articles by Carol Cohn and Richard Rodriguez examine how proving manhood on the battlefield infects the actions of both leaders and followers. To Rodriguez it is the posturing of lead-

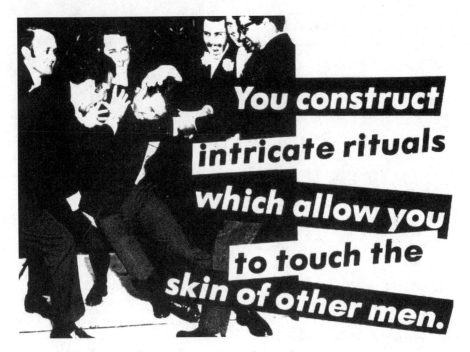

Photo courtesy of Barbara Kruger.

TANK McNAMARA®   by Jeff Millar & Bill Hinds

ers drawing "lines in the sand" that accounts for the pathos of the Gulf War; for Cohn it is the technological distancing of defense scientists that propels the development of the fascinating machinery of death and destruction that was exhibited in that, or any, war.

Together, these articles suggest that values concerning militarism have insinuated themselves deeply into the fabric of social life, and that current efforts to integrate women into the military and lift the ban against gays and lesbians—let alone challenge the disproportionate amount of human and financial resources spent on defense—will require a confrontation with some of the most deeply held assumptions about American manhood.

PIGSKIN, PATRIARCHY AND PAIN

DON SABO

I am sitting down to write as I've done thousands of times over the last decade. But today there's something very different. I'm not in pain.

A half-year ago I underwent back surgery. My physician removed two disks from the lumbar region of my spine and fused three vertebrae using bone scrapings from my right hip. The surgery is called a "spinal fusion." For seventy-two hours I was completely immobilized. On the fifth day, I took a few faltering first steps with one of those aluminum walkers that are usually associated with the elderly in nursing homes. I progressed rapidly and left the hospital after nine days completely free of pain for the first time in years.

How did I, a well-intending and reasonably gentle boy from western Pennsylvania ever get into so much pain? At a simple level, I ended up in pain because I played a sport that brutalizes men's (and now sometimes women's) bodies. *Why* I played football and bit the bullet of pain, however, is more complicated. Like a young child who learns to dance or sing for a piece of candy, I played for rewards and payoffs. Winning at sport meant winning friends and carving a place for myself within the male pecking order. Success at the "game" would make me less like myself and more like the older boys and my hero, Dick Butkus. Pictures of his hulking and snarling form filled my head and hung above my bed, beckoning me forward like a mythic Siren. If I could be like Butkus, I told myself, people would adore me as much as 1 adored him. I might even adore myself. As an adolescent I hoped sport would get me attention from girls. Later, I became more practical-minded and I worried about my future. What kind of work would I do for a living? Football became my ticket to a college scholarship which, in western Pennsylvania during the early 'sixties, meant a career instead of getting stuck in the steelmills.

THE ROAD TO SURGERY

My bout with pain and spinal "pathology" began with a decision I made in 1955 when I was eight years old. I "went out" for football. At the time, I felt uncomfortable inside my body—too fat, too short, too weak. Freckles and glasses, too! I wanted to change my image, and I felt that changing my body was one place to begin. My parents bought me a set of weights, and one of the older boys in the neighborhood was solicited to demonstrate their use. I can still remember the ease with which he lifted the barbell, the veins popping through his bulging biceps in the summer sun, and the sated look of strength and accomplishment on his face. This was to be the image of my future.

That fall I made a dinner-table announcement that I was going out for football. What followed was a rather inauspicious beginning. First, the initiation rites. Pricking the flesh with thorns until blood was drawn and having hot peppers rubbed in my eyes. Getting punched in the gut again and again. Being forced to wear a jockstrap around my nose and not knowing what was funny. Then came what was to be an endless series of proving myself: calisthenics until my arms ached; hitting hard and fast and knocking the other guy down; getting hit in the groin and not crying. I learned that pain and injury are "part of the game."

I "played" through grade school, co-captained my high school team, and went on to become an inside linebacker and defensive captain at the NCAA Division I level. I learned to be an animal. Coaches took notice of animals. Animals made first team. Being an animal meant being fanatically aggressive and ruthlessly competitive. If I saw an arm in front of me, I trampled it. Whenever blood was spilled, I nodded approval. Broken bones (not mine of course) were secretly seen as little victories within the bigger struggle. The coaches taught me to "punish the other man," but little did I suspect that I was devastating my own body at the same time. There were broken noses, ribs, fingers, toes and teeth, torn muscles and ligaments, bruises, bad knees, and busted lips, and the gradual pulverizing of my spinal column that, by the time my jock career was long over at age thirty, had resulted in seven years of near-constant pain. It was a long road to the surgeon's office.

Now surgically freed from its grip, my understanding of pain has changed. Pain had gnawed away at my insides. Pain turned my awareness inward. I blamed myself for my predicament; I thought that I was solely responsible for every twinge and sleepless night. But this view was an illusion. My pain, each individual's pain, is really an expression of a linkage to an outer world of people, events, and forces. The origins of our pain are rooted *outside*, not inside, our skins.

THE PAIN PRINCIPLE

Sport is just one of many areas in our culture where pain is more important than pleasure. Boys are taught that to endure pain is courageous, to survive pain is manly. The principle that pain is "good" and pleasure is "bad" is crudely evident in the "no pain, no gain" philosophy of so many coaches and athletes. The "pain principle" weaves its way into the lives and psyches of male athletes in two fundamental ways. It stifles men's awareness of their bodies and limits our emotional expression. We learn to ignore personal hurts and injuries because they interfere with the "efficiency" and "goals" of the "team." We become adept at taking the feelings that boil up inside us—feelings of insecurity and stress from striving so hard for success—and channeling them in a bundle of rage which is directed at opponents and enemies. This posture toward oneself and the world is not limited to "jocks." It is evident in the lives of many non-athletic men who, as "workaholics" or success-strivers or tough guys, deny their authentic physical or emotional needs and develop health problems as a result.

Today, I no longer perceive myself as an *individual* ripped off by athletic injury. Rather, I see myself as just *one more man among many men* who got swallowed up by a social system predicated on male domination. Patriarchy has two structural aspects. First, it is an hierarchical system in which men dominate women in crude and debased, slick and subtle ways. Feminists have made great progress exposing and analyzing this dimension of the edifice of sexism. But it is also a system of *intermale dominance*, in which a minority of men dominates the masses of men. This intermale dominance hierarchy exploits the majority of those it beckons to climb its heights. Patriarchy's mythos of heroism and its morality of power-worship implant visions of ecstasy and masculine excellence in the minds of the boys who ultimately will defend its inequities and ridicule its victims. It is inside this institutional framework that I have begun to explore the essence and scope of "the pain principle."

TAKING IT

Patriarchy is a form of social hierarchy. Hierarchy breeds inequity and inequity breeds pain. To remain stable, the hierarchy must either justify the pain or explain it away. In a patriarchy, women and the masses of men are fed the cultural message that pain is inevitable and that pain enhances one's character and moral worth. This principle is expressed in Judeo-Christian beliefs. The Judeo-Christian God inflicts or permits pain, yet "the Father" is still revered and loved. Likewise, as chief disciplinarian in the patriarchal family, the father has the right to inflict pain. The "pain principle" also echoes throughout traditional western sexual morality; it is better to experience the pain of *not* having sexual pleasure than it is to have sexual pleasure.

Most men learn to heed these cultural messages and take their "cues for survival" from the patriarchy. The Willie Lomans of the economy pander to the prophets of profit and the American Dream. Soldiers, young and old, salute their neo-Hun generals. Right-wing Christians genuflect before their idols of righteousness, affluence, and conformity. And male athletes adopt the visions and values that coaches are offering: to take orders, to take pain, to "take out" opponents, to take the game seriously, to take women, and to take their place on the team. And if they can't "take it," then the rewards of athletic comradery, prestige, scholarships, pro contracts, and community recognition are not forthcoming.

Becoming a football player fosters conformity to male-chauvinistic values and self-abusing lifestyles. It contributes to the legitimacy of a social structure based on patriarchal power. Male competition for prestige and status in sport and elsewhere leads to identification with the relatively few males who control resources and are able to bestow rewards and inflict punishment. Male supremacists are not born, they are made, and traditional athletic socialization is a fundamental contribution to this complex social-psychological and political process. Through sport, many males, indeed, learn to "take it"— that is, to internalize patriarchal values which, in turn, become part of their gender identity and conception of women and society.

My high school coach once evoked the pain principle during a pre-game peptalk. For what seemed an eternity, he paced frenetically and silently before us with fist clenched and head bowed. He suddenly stopped and faced us with a smile. It was as though he had approached a podium to begin a long-awaited lecture. "Boys," he began, "people who say that football is a 'contact sport' are dead wrong. Dancing is a contact sport. Football is a game of pain and violence! Now get the hell out of here and kick some ass." We practically ran through the wall leaving the locker room, surging in unison to fight the coach's war. I see now that the coach was right but for all the wrong reasons. I should have taken him at his word and never played the game!

ARTICLE 12

BOYHOOD, ORGANIZED SPORTS, AND THE CONSTRUCTION OF MASCULINITIES

MICHAEL A. MESSNER

The rapid expansion of feminist scholarship in the past two decades has led to fundamental reconceptualizations of the historical and contemporary meanings of organized sport. In the nineteenth and twentieth centuries, modernization and women's continued movement into public life created widespread "fears of social feminization," especially among middle-class men (Hantover, 1978; Kimmel, 1987). One result of these fears was the creation of organized sport as a homosocial sphere in which competition and (often violent) physicality was valued, while "the feminine" was devalued. As a result, organized support has served to bolster a sagging ideology of male superiority, and has helped to reconstitute masculine hegemony (Bryson, 1987; Hall, 1988; Messner, 1988; Theberge, 1981).

The feminist critique has spawned a number of studies of the ways that women's sport has been marginalized and trivialized in the past (Greendorfer, 1977; Oglesby, 1978; Twin, 1978), in addition to illuminating the continued existence of structural and ideological barriers to gender equality within sport (Birrell, 1987). Only recently, however, have scholars begun to use feminist insights to examine men's experiences in sport (Kidd, 1987; Messner, 1987; Sabo, 1985). This article explores the relationship between the construction of masculine identity and boyhood participation in organized sports.

I view gender identity not as a "thing" that people "have," but rather as a *process of construction* that develops, comes into crisis, and changes as a person interacts with the social world. Through this perspective, it becomes possible to speak of "gendering" identities rather than "masculinity" or "femininity" as relatively fixed identities or statuses.

There is an agency in this construction; people are not passively shaped by their social environment. As recent feminist analyses of the construction of feminine gender identity have pointed out, girls and women are implicated in the construction of their own identities and personalities, both in terms of the ways that they participate in their own subordination and the ways that they resist subordination (Benjamin, 1988; Haug, 1987). Yet this self-construction is not a fully conscious process. There are also deeply woven, unconscious motivations, fears, and anxieties at work here. So, too, in the construction of masculinity. Levinson (1978) has argued that masculine identity is neither fully "formed" by the social context, nor is it "caused" by some internal dynamic put into place during infancy. Instead, it is shaped and constructed through the interaction between the internal and the social. The internal gendering identity may set developmental "tasks," may create thresholds of anxiety and ambivalence, yet it is only through a concrete

Michael A. Messner, *Journal of Contemporary Ethnography*, Vol. 18, No. 4, January 1990, 416–444, examination of people's interactions with others within social institutions that we can begin to understand both the similarities and differences in the construction of gender identities.

In this study I explore and interpret the meanings that males themselves attribute to their boyhood participation in organized sport. In what ways do males construct masculine identities within the institution of organized sports? In what ways do class and racial differences mediate this relationship and perhaps lead to the construction of different meanings, and perhaps different masculinities? And what are some of the problems and contradictions within these constructions of masculinity?

DESCRIPTION OF RESEARCH

Between 1983 and 1985, I conducted interviews with 30 male former athletes. Most of the men I interviewed had played the (U.S.) "major sports"—football, basketball, baseball, track. At the time of the interview, each had been retired from playing organized sports for at least five years. Their ages ranged from 21 to 48, with the median, 33; 14 were black, 14 were white, and two were Hispanic; 15 of the 16 black and Hispanic men had come from poor or working-class families, while the majority (9 of 14) of the white men had come from middle-class or professional families. All had at some time in their lives based their identities largely on their roles as athletes and could therefore be said to have had "athletic careers." Twelve had played organized sports -through high school, 11 through college, and seven had been professional athletes. Though the sample was not randomly selected, an effort was made to see that the sample had a range of difference in terms of race and social class backgrounds, and that there was some variety in terms of age, types of sports played, and levels of success in athletic careers. Without exception, each man contacted agreed to be interviewed.

The tape-recorded interviews were semi-structured and took from one and one-half to six hours, with most taking about three hours. I asked each man to talk about four broad eras in his life: (1) his earliest experiences with sports in boyhood, (2) his athletic career, (3) retirement or disengagement from the athletic career, and (4) life after the athletic career. In each era, I focused the interview on the meanings of "success and failure," and on the boy's/man's relationships with family, with other males, with women, and with his own body.

In collecting what amounted to life histories of these men, my overarching purpose was to use feminist theories of masculine gender identity to explore how masculinity develops and changes as boys and men interact within the socially constructed world of organized sports. In addition to using the data to move toward some generalizations about the relationship between "masculinity and sport," I was also concerned with sorting out some of the variations among boys, based on class and racial inequalities, that led them to relate differently to athletic careers. I divided my sample into two comparison groups. The first group was made up of 10 men from higher-status backgrounds, primarily white, middle-class, and professional families. The second group was made up of 20 men from lower-status backgrounds, primarily minority, poor, and working-class families.

BOYHOOD AND THE PROMISE OF SPORTS

Zane Grey once said, "All boys love baseball. If they don't they're not real boys" (as cited in Kimmel, 1990). This is, of course, an ideological statement; In fact, some boys do *not* love baseball, or any other sports, for that matter. There are millions of males who at an early age are rejected by, become alienated from, or lose interest in organized sports. Yet all boys are, to a greater or lesser extent, judged according to their ability, or lack of ability, in competitive sports (Eitzen, 1975; Sabo, 1985). In this study I focus on those males who did become athletes—males who eventually poured thousands of hours into the development of specific physical skills. It is in boyhood that we can discover the roots of their commitment to athletic careers.

How did organized sports come to play such a central role in these boy's lives? When asked to recall how and why they initially got into playing sports, many of the men interviewed for this study seemed a bit puzzled: after all, playing sports was "just the thing to do." A 42-year-old black man who had played college basketball put it this way:

It was just what you did. It's kind of like, you went to school, you played athletics, and if you didn't, there was something wrong with you. It was just like brushing your teeth: it's just what you did. It's part of your existence.

Spending one's time playing sports with other boys seemed as natural as the cycle of the seasons: baseball in the spring and summer, football in the fall, basketball in the winter—and then it was time to get out the old baseball glove and begin again. As a black 35-year-old former professional football star said:

I'd say when I wasn't in school, 95% of the time was spent in the park playing. It was the only thing to do. It just came as natural.

And a black, 34-year-old professional basketball player explained his early experiences in sports:

My principal and teacher said, "Now if you work at this you might be pretty damned good." So it was more or less a community thing—everybody in the community said, "Boy, if you work hard and keep your nose clean, you gonna be good." 'Cause it was natural instinct.

"It was natural instinct." "I was a natural." Several athletes used words such as these to explain their early attraction to sports. But certainly there is nothing "natural" about throwing a ball through a hoop, hitting a ball with a bat, or jumping over hurdles. A boy, for instance, may have amazingly dexterous inborn hand-eye coordination, but this does not predispose him to a career of hitting baseballs any more than it predisposes him to a life as a brain surgeon. When one listens closely to what these men said about their early experiences in sports, it becomes clear that their adoption of the self-definition of "natural athlete" was the result of what Connell (1990) has called "a collective practice" that constructs masculinities. The boyhood development of masculine identity and status—truly problematic in a society that offers no official rite of passage into adulthood—results from a process of interaction with people and social institutions. Thus, in discussing early motivations in sports, men commonly talk of the importance of relationships with family members, peers, and the broader community.

FAMILY INFLUENCES

Though most of the men in this study spoke of their mothers with love, respect, even reverence, their descriptions of their earliest experiences in sports are stories of an exclusively male world. The existence of older brothers or uncles who served as teachers and athletic role models—as well as sources of competition for attention and status within the family—was very common. An older brother, uncle, or even close friend of the family who was a successful athlete appears to have acted as a sort of standard of achievement against whom to measure oneself. A 34-year-old black man who had been a three-sport star in high school said:

My uncles—my Uncle Harold went to the Detroit Tigers, played pro ball—all of 'em, everybody played sports, so I wanted to be better than anybody else. I knew that everybody in this town knew them—their names were something. I wanted my name to be just like theirs.

Similarly, a black 41-year-old former professional football player recalled:

I was the younger of three brothers and everybody played sports, so consequently I was more or less forced into it. 'Cause one brother was always better than the next brother and then I came along and had to show them that I was just as good as them. My oldest brother was an all-city ballplayer, then my other brother comes along he's all-city and all-state, and then I have to come along.

For some, attempting to emulate or surpass the athletic accomplishments of older male family members created pressures that were difficult to deal with. A 33-year-old white man explained that he was a good athlete during boyhood, but the constant awareness that his two older brothers had been better made it difficult for him to feel good about himself, or to have fun in sports;

I had this sort of reputation that I followed from the playgrounds through grade school, and through high school. I followed these guys who were all-conference and all-state.

Most of these men, however, saw their relationships with their athletic older brothers and uncles in a positive light; it was within these relationships that they gained experience and developed motivations that gave them a competitive "edge" within their same-aged peer group. As a 33-year-old black man describes his earliest athletic experiences:

My brothers were role models. I wanted to prove— especially to my brothers—that I had heart, you know, that I was a man.

When asked, "What did it mean to you to be 'a man' at that age?" he replied:

Well, it meant that I didn't want to be a so-called scaredy-cat. You want to hit a guy even though he's bigger than you to show that, you know, you've got this macho image. I remember that at that young an age, that feeling was exciting to me. And that carried over, and as I got older, I got better and I began to look around me and see, well hey! I'm competitive with these guys, even though I'm younger, you know? And then of course all the compliments come—and I began to notice a change, even in my parents—especially in my father—he was proud of that, and that was very important to me. He was extremely important . . . he showed me more affection, now that I think of it.

As this man's words suggest, if men talk of their older brothers and uncles mostly as role models, teachers, and "names" to emulate, their talk of their relationships with their fathers is more deeply layered and complex. Athletic skills and competition for status may often be learned from older brothers, but it is in boys' relationships with fathers that we find many of the keys to the emotional salience of sports in the development of masculine identity.

RELATIONSHIPS WITH FATHERS

The fact that boys' introductions to organized sports are often made by fathers who might otherwise be absent or emotionally distant adds a powerful emotional charge to these early experiences (Osherson, 1986). Although playing organized sports eventually came to feel "natural" for all of the men interviewed in this study, many needed to be "exposed" to sports, or even gently "pushed" by their fathers to become involved in activities like Little League baseball. A white, 33-year-old man explained:

I still remember it like it was yesterday—Dad and I driving up in his truck, and I had my glove and my hat and all that—and I said, "Dad, I don't want to do it." He says, "What?" I says, "I don't want to do it." I was nervous. That I might fail. And he says, "Don't be silly. Lookit: There's Joey and Petey and all your friends out there." And so Dad says, "You're gonna do it, come on." And in my memory he's never said that about anything else; he just knew I needed a little kick in the pants and I'd do it. And once you're out there and you see all the other kids making errors and stuff, and you know you're better than those guys, you know: Maybe I do belong here. As it turned out, Little League was a good experience.

Some who were similarly "pushed" by their fathers were not so successful as the aforementioned man had been in Little League baseball, and thus the experience was not altogether a joyous affair. One 34-year-old white man, for instance, said he "inherited" his interest in sports from his father, who started playing catch with him at the age of four. Once he got into Little League, he felt pressured by his father, one of the coaches, who expected him to be the star of the team:

I'd go O-for-four sometimes, strike out three times in a Little League game, and I'd dread the ride home. I'd come home and he'd say, "Go in the bathroom and swing the bat in the mirror for an hour," to get my swing level . . . It didn't help much, though, I'd go out and strike out three or four times again the next game too [laughs ironically].

When asked if he had been concerned with having his father's approval, he responded:

Failure in his eyes? Yeah, I always thought that he wanted me to get some kind of [athletic] scholarship. I guess I was afraid of him when I was a kid. He didn't hit that much, but he had a rage about him—he'd rage, and that voice would just rattle you.

Similarly, a 24-year-old black man described his awe of his father's physical power and presence, and his sense of inadequacy in attempting to emulate him:

My father had a voice that sounded like rolling thunder. Whether it was intentional on his part or not, I don't know, but my father gave me a sense, an image of him being the most powerful being on earth, and that no matter what I ever did I would never come close to him . . . There were definite feelings of physical inadequacy that I couldn't work around.

It is interesting to note how these feelings of physical inadequacy relative to the father lived on as part of this young man's permanent internalized image. He eventually became a "feared" high school football player and broke school records in weigh-lifting, yet,

As I grew older, my mother and friends told me that I had actually grown to be a larger man than my father. Even though in time I required larger clothes than he, which should have been a very concrete indication, neither my brother nor I could ever bring ourselves to say that I was bigger. We simply couldn't conceive of it.

Using sports activities as a means of identifying with and "living up to" the power and status of one's father was not always such a painful and difficult task for the men I interviewed. Most did not describe fathers who "pushed" them to become sports stars. The relationship between their athletic strivings and their identification with their fathers was more subtle. A 48-year-old black man, for instance, explained that he was not pushed into sports by his father, but was aware from an early age of the community status his father had gained through sports. He saw his own athletic accomplishments as a way to connect with and emulate his father:

I wanted to play baseball because my father had been quite a good baseball player in the Negro leagues before baseball was integrated, and so he was kind of a model for me. I remember, quite young, going to a baseball game he was in—this was before the war and all—I remember being in the stands with my mother and seeing him on first base, and being aware of the crowd . . . I was aware of people's confidence in him as a serious baseball player. I don't think my father ever said anything to me like "play sports . . . [But] I knew he would like it if I did well. His admiration was important . . . he mattered.

Similarly, a 24-year-old white man described his father as a somewhat distant "role model" whose approval mattered:

My father was more of an example . . . he definitely was very much in touch with and still had very fond memories of being an athlete and talked about it, bragged about it. . . . But he really didn't do that much to teach me skills, and he didn't always go to every game I played like some parents. But he approved and that was important, you know. That was important to get his approval. I always knew that playing sports was important to him, so I knew implicitly that it was good and there was definitely a value on it.

First experiences in sports might often come through relationships with brothers or older male relatives, and the early emotional salience of sports was often directly related to a boy's relationship with his father. The sense of commitment that these young boys eventually made to the development of athletic careers is best explained as a process of development of masculine gender identity and status in relation to same-sex peers.

MASCULINE IDENTITY AND EARLY COMMITMENT TO SPORTS

When many of the men in this study said that during childhood they played sports because "it's just what everybody did," they of course meant that it was just what *boys* did. They were introduced to organized sports by older brothers and fathers, and once involved, found themselves playing within an exclusively male world. Though the separate (and unequal) gendered worlds of boys and girls came to appear as "natural," they were in fact socially constructed. Thorne's observations of children's activities in schools indicated that rather than "naturally" constituting "separate gendered cultures," there is considerable interaction between boys and girls in classrooms and on playgrounds. When adults set up legitimate contact between boys and girls, Thorne observed, this usually results in "relaxed interactions." But when activities in the classroom or on the playground are presented to children as sex-segregated activities and gender is marked by teachers and other adults ("boys line up here, girls over there"), "gender boundaries are heightened, and mixed-sex interaction becomes an explicit arena of risk" (Thorne, 1986; 70). Thus sex-segregated activities such as organized sports as structured by adults, provide the context in which gendered identities and separate "gendered cultures" develop and come to appear natural. For the boys in this study, it became "natural" to equate masculinity with competition, physical strength, and skills. Girls simply did not (could not, it was believed) participate in these activities.

Yet it is not simply the separation of children, by adults, into separate activities that explains why many boys came to feel such a strong connection with sports activities, while so few girls did. As I listened to men recall their earliest experiences in organized sports, I heard them talk of insecurity, loneliness, and especially a need to connect with other people as a primary motivation in their early sports strivings. As a 42-year-old white man stated, "The most important thing was just being out there with the rest of the guys—being friends." Another 32-year-old interviewee was born in Mexico and moved to the United States at a fairly young age. He never knew his father, and his mother died when he was only nine years old. Suddenly he felt rootless, and threw himself into sports. His initial motivations, however, do not appear to be based on a need to compete and win:

> *Actually, what I think sports did for me is it brought me into kind of an instant family. By being on a Little League team, or even just playing with all kinds of different kids in the neighborhood, it brought what I really wanted, which was some kind of closeness. It was just being there, and being friends.*

Clearly, what these boys needed and craved was that which was most problematic for them: connection and unity with other people. But why do these young males find *organized sports* such an attractive context in which to establish "a kind of closeness" with others? Comparative observations of young boys' and girls' game-playing behaviors yield important insights into this question. Piaget (1965) and Lever (1976) both observed that girls tend to have more "pragmatic" and "flexible" orientations to the rules of games; they are more prone to make exceptions and innovations in the middle of a game in order to make the game more "fair." Boys, on the other hand, tend to have a more firm, even [in]flexible orientation to the rules of a game; to them, the rules are what protects any fairness. This difference, according to Gilligan (1982), is based on the fact that early developmental experiences have yielded deeply rooted differences between males' and females' developmental tasks, needs, and moral reasoning. Girls, who tend to define themselves primarily through connection with others, experience highly competitive situations (whether in organized sports or in other hierarchical institutions) as threats to relationships, and thus to their identities. For boys, the development of gender identity involves the construction of positional identities, where a sense of self is solidified through separation from others (Chodorow, 1978). Yet feminist psychoanalytic theory has tended to oversimplify the internal lives of men (Lichterman, 1986). Males do appear to develop positional identities, yet despite their fears of intimacy, they also retain a human need for closeness and unity with others. This ambivalence toward intimate relationships is a major thread running through masculine development throughout the life course. Here we can conceptualize what Craib (1987) calls the "elective affinity" between personality and social structure: For the boy who both seeks and fears attachment with others, the rule-bound structure of organized sports can promise to be a safe place in which to seek nonintimate attachment with others within a context that maintains clear boundaries, distance, and separation.

COMPETITIVE STRUCTURES AND CONDITIONAL SELF-WORTH

Young boys may initially find that sports gives them the opportunity to experience "some kind of closeness" with others, but the structure of sports and athletic careers often undermines the possibility of boys learning to transcend their fears of intimacy, thus becoming able to develop truly close and intimate relationships with others (Kidd, 1990; Messner, 1987). The sports world is extremely hierarchical, and an incredible amount of importance is placed on winning, on "being number one." For instance, a few years ago I observed a basketball camp put on for boys by a professional basketball coach and his staff. The youngest boys, about eight years old (who could barely reach the basket with their shots) played a brief scrimmage. Afterwards, the coaches lined them up in a row in front of the older boys who were sitting in the grandstands. One by one, the coach would stand behind each boy, put his hand on the boy's head (much in the manner of a priestly benediction), and the older boys in the stands would applaud and cheer, louder or softer, depending on how well or poorly the young boy was judged to have performed. The two or three

boys who were clearly the exceptional players looked confident that they would receive the praise they were due. Most of the boys, though, had expressions ranging from puzzlement to thinly disguised terror on their faces as they awaited the judgments of the older boys.

This kind of experience teaches boys that it is not "just being out there with the guys—being friends," that ensures the kind of attention and connection that they crave; it is being *better* than the other guys—*beating* them—that is the key to acceptance. Most of the boys in this study did have some early successes in sports, and thus their ambivalent need for connection with others was met, at least for a time. But the institution of sport tends to encourage the development of what Schafer (1975) has called "conditional self-worth" in boys. As boys become aware that acceptance by others is contingent upon being good—a "winner"—narrow definitions of success, based upon performance and winning become increasingly important to them. A 33-year-old black man said that by the time he was in his early teens:

> It was expected of me to do well in all my contests—I mean by my coaches, my peers, and my family. So I in turn expected to do well, and if I didn't do well, then I'd be very disappointed.

The man from Mexico, discussed above, who said that he had sought "some kind of closeness" in his early sports experiences began to notice in his early teens that if he played well, was a *winner*, he would get attention from others:

> It got to the point where I started realizing, noticing that people were always there for me, backing me all the time—sports got to be really fun because I always had some people there backing me. Finally my oldest brother started going to all my games, even though I had never really seen who he was [laughs]—after the game, you know, we never really saw each other, but he was at all my baseball games, and it seemed like we shared a kind of closeness there, but only in those situations. Off the field, when I wasn't in uniform, he was never around.

By high school, he said, he felt "up against the wall." Sports hadn't delivered what he had hoped it would, but he thought if he just tried harder, won one more championship trophy, he would get the attention he truly craved. Despite his efforts, this attention was not forthcoming. And, sadly, the pressures he had put on himself to excel in sports had taken most of the fun out of playing.

For many of the men in this study, throughout boyhood and into adolescence, this conscious striving for successful achievement became the primary means through which they sought connection with other people (Messner, 1987). But it is important to recognize that young males' internalized ambivalences about intimacy do not fully determine the contours and directions of their lives. Masculinity continues to develop through interaction with the social world—and because boys from different backgrounds are interacting with substantially different familial, educational, and other institutions, these differences will lead them to make different choices and define situations in different ways. Next, I examine the differences in the ways that boys from higher- and lower-status families and communities related to organized sports.

STATUS DIFFERENCES AND COMMITMENTS TO SPORTS

In discussing early attractions to sports, the experiences of boys from higher- and lower-status backgrounds are quite similar. Both groups indicate the importance of fathers and older brothers in introducing them to sports. Both groups speak of the joys of receiving attention and acceptance among family and peers for early successes in sports. Note the similarities, for instance, in the following descriptions of boyhood athletic experiences of two men. First, a man born in a white, middle-class family:

I loved playing sports so much from a very early age because of early exposure. A lot of the sports

came easy at an early age, and because they did, and because you were successful at something, I think that you're inclined to strive for that gratification. It's like, if you're good, you like it, because it's instant gratification. I'm doing something that I'm good at and I'm gonna keep doing it.

Second, a black man from a poor family:

Fortunately I had some athletic ability, and, quite naturally, once you start doing good in whatever it is—I don't care if it's jacks—you show off what you do. That's your ability, that's your blessing, so you show it off as much as you can.

For boys from both groups, early exposure to sports, the discovery that they had some "ability," shortly followed by some sort of family, peer, and community recognition, all eventually led to the commitment of hundreds and thousands of hours of playing, practicing, and dreaming of future stardom. Despite these similarities, there are also some identifiable differences that begin to explain the tendency of males from lower-status backgrounds to develop higher levels of commitment to sports careers. The most clear-cut difference was that while men from higher-status backgrounds are likely to describe their earliest athletic experiences and motivations almost exclusively in terms of immediate family, men from lower-status backgrounds more commonly describe the importance of a broader community context. For instance, a 46-year-old man who grew up in a "poor working class" black family in a small town in Arkansas explained:

In that community, at the age of third or fourth grade, if you're a male, they expect you to show some kind of inclination, some kind of skill in football or basketball. It was an expected thing, you know? My mom and my dad, they didn't push at all. It was the general environment.

A 48-year-old man describes sports activities as a survival strategy in his poor black community:

Sports protected me from having to compete in gang stuff, or having to be good with my fists. If you were an athlete and got into the fist world, that was your business, and that was okay—but you didn't have to if you didn't want to. People would generally defer to you, give you your space away from trouble.

A 35-year-old man who grew up in "a poor black ghetto" described his boyhood relationship to sports similarly:

Where I came from, either you were one of two things: you were in sports or you were out on the streets being a drug addict, or breaking into places. The guys who were in sports, we had it a little easier, because we were accepted by both groups. . . . So it worked out to my advantage, cause I didn't get into a lot of trouble—some trouble, but not alot.

The fact that boys in lower-status communities faced these kinds of realities gave salience to their developing athletic identities. In contrast, sports were important to boys from higher-status backgrounds, yet the middle-class environment seemed more secure, less threatening, and offered far more options. By the time most of these boys got into junior high or high school, many had made conscious decisions to shift their attentions away from athletic careers to educational and (nonathletic) career goals. A 32-year-old white college athletic director told me that he had seen his chance to pursue a pro baseball career as "pissing in the wind," and instead, focused on education. Similarly, a 33-year-old white dentist who was a three-sport star in high school, decided not to play sports in college, so he could focus on getting into dental school. As he put it,

I think I kind of downgraded the stardom thing. I thought it was small potatoes. And sure, that's nice in high school and all that, but on a broad scale, I didn't think it amounted to all that much.

This statement offers an important key to understanding the construction of masculine identity within a middle-class context. The status that this boy got through sports had been *very* important to him, yet he could see that "on a broad scale," this sort of status was "small

potatoes." This sort of early recognition is more than a result of the oft-noted middle-class tendency to raise "future-oriented" children (Rubin, 1976; Sennett and Cobb, 1973). Perhaps more important, it is that the *kinds* of future orientations developed by boys from higher-status backgrounds are consistent with the middle-class context. These men's descriptions of their boyhoods reveal that they grew up immersed in a wide range of institutional frameworks, of which organized sports was just one. And—importantly—they could see that the status of adult males around them was clearly linked to their positions within various professions, public institutions, and bureaucratic organizations. It was clear that access to this sort of institutional status came through educational achievement, not athletic prowess. A 32-year-old black man who grew up in a professional-class family recalled that he had idolized Wilt Chamberlain and dreamed of being a pro basketball player, yet his father discouraged his athletic strivings:

He knew I liked the game. I loved the game. But basketball was not recommended; my dad would say, "That's a stereotyped image for black youth. . . . When your basketball is gone and finished, what are you gonna do? One day, you might get injured. What are you gonna look forward to?" He stressed education.

Similarly, a 32-year-old man who was raised in a white, middle-class family, had found in sports a key means of gaining acceptance and connection in his peer group. Yet he was simultaneously developing an image of himself as a "smart student," and becoming aware of a wide range of nonsports life options:

My mother was constantly telling me how smart I was, how good I was, what a nice person I was, and giving me all sorts of positive strokes, and those positive strokes became a self-motivating kind of thing. I had this image of myself as smart, and I lived up to that image.

It is not that parents of boys in lower-status families did not also encourage their boys to work hard in school. Several reported that their parents "stressed books first, sports second." It's just that the broader social context—education, economy, and community—was more likely to *narrow* lower-status boys' perceptions of real-life options, while boys from higher-status backgrounds faced an expanding world of options. For instance, with a different socioeconomic background, one 35-year-old black man might have become a great musician instead of a star professional football running back. But he did not. When he was a child, he said, he was most interested in music:

I wanted to be a drummer. But we couldn't afford drums. My dad couldn't go out and buy me a drum set or a guitar even—it was just one of those things; he was just trying to make ends meet.

But he *could* afford, as could so many in his socioeconomic condition, to spend countless hours at the local park, where he was told by the park supervisor

that I was a natural—not only in gymnastics or baseball—whatever I did, I was a natural. He told me I shouldn't waste this talent, and so I immediately started watching the big guys then.

In retrospect, this man had potential to be a musician or any number of things, but his environment limited his options to sports, and he made the best of it. Even within sports, he, like most boys in the ghetto, was limited:

We didn't have any tennis courts in the ghetto—we used to have a lot of tennis balls, but no racquets. I wonder today how good I might be in tennis if I had gotten a racquet in my hands at an early age.

It is within this limited structure of opportunity that many lower-status young boys found sports to be *the* place, rather than *a* place, within which to construct masculine identity, status, the relationships. A 36-year-old white man explained that his father left the family when he was very young and his mother faced a very difficult struggle to make ends meet. As his words suggest, the more limited a boy's options, and the more insecure his family situation, the more likely he is to make an early commitment to an athletic career:

I used to ride my bicycle to Little League practice—if I'd waited for someone to pick me up and take me to the ball park I'd have never played. I'd get to the ball park and all the other kids would have their dad bring them to practice or games. But I'd park my bike to the side and when it was over I'd get on it and go home. Sports was the way for me to move everything to the side—family problems, just all the embarrassments—and think about one thing, and that was sports . . . In the third grade, when the teacher went around the classroom and asked everybody, "What do you want to be when you grow up?," I said, "I want to be a major league baseball player," and everybody laughed their heads off.

This man eventually did enjoy a major league baseball career. Most boys from lower-status backgrounds who make similar early commitments to athletic careers are not so successful. As stated earlier, the career structure of organized sports is highly competitive and hierarchical. In fact, the chances of attaining professional status in sports are approximately 4:100,000 for a white man, 2:100,000 for a black man, and 3:1 million for a Hispanic man in the United States (Leonard and Reyman, 1988). Nevertheless, the immediate rewards (fun, status, attention), along with the constricted (nonsports) structure of opportunity, attract disproportionately large numbers of boys from lower-status backgrounds to athletic careers as their major means of constructing a masculine identity. These are the boys who later, as young men, had to struggle with "conditional self-worth," and, more often than not, occupational dead ends. Boys from higher-status backgrounds, on the other hand, bolstered their boyhood, adolescent, and early adult status through their athletic accomplishments. Their wider range of experiences and life chances led to an early shift away from sports careers as the major basis of identity (Messner, 1989).

CONCLUSION

The conception of the masculinity-sports relationship developed here begins to illustrate the idea of an "elective affinity" between social structure and personality. Organized sports is a "gendered institution"—an institution constructed by gender relations. As such, its structure and values (rules, formal organization, sex composition, etc.), reflect dominant conceptions of masculinity and femininity. Organized sports is also a "gendering institution"—an institution that helps to construct the current gender order. Part of this construction of gender is accomplished through the "masculinizing" of male bodies and minds.

Yet boys do not come to their first experiences in organized sports as "blank slates," but arrive with already "gendering" identities due to early developmental experiences and previous socialization. I have suggested here that an important thread running through the development of masculine identity is males' ambivalence toward intimate unity with others. Those boys who experience early athletic successes find in the structure of organized sport an affinity with this masculine ambivalence toward intimacy: The rule-bound, competitive, hierarchical world of sport offers boys an attractive means of establishing an emotionally distant (and thus "safe") connection with others. Yet as boys begin to define themselves as "athletes," they learn that in order to be accepted (to have connection) through sports, they must be winners. And in order to be winners, they must construct relationships with others (and with themselves) that are consistent with the competitive and hierarchical values and structure of the sports world. As a result, they often develop a "conditional self-worth" that leads them to construct more instrumental relationships with themselves and others. This ultimately exacerbates their difficulties in constructing intimate relationships with others. In effect, the interaction between the young male's preexisting internalized ambivalence toward intimacy with the competitive hierarchical institution of sport has resulted in the construction of a masculine personality that is characterized by instrumental rationality, goal-orientation, and difficulties with intimate connection and expression (Messner, 1987).

This theoretical line of inquiry invites us not simply to examine how social institutions "socialize" boys, but also to explore the ways that boys' already-gendering identities interact with social institutions (which, like organized sport, are themselves the product of gender relations). This study has also suggested that it is not some singular "masculinity" that is being constructed through athletic careers. It may be correct, from a psychoanalytic perspective, to suggest that all males bring ambivalences toward intimacy to their interactions with the world, but "the world" is a very different place for males from different racial and socioeconomic backgrounds. Because males have substantially different interactions with the world, based on class, race, and other differences and inequalities, we might expect the construction of masculinity to take on different meanings for boys and men from differing backgrounds (Messner, 1989). Indeed, this study has suggested that boys from higher-status backgrounds face a much broader range of options than do their lower-status counterparts. As a result, athletic careers take on different meanings for these boys. Lower-status boys are likely to see athletic careers as *the* institutional context for the construction of their masculine status and identities, while higher-status males make an early shift away from athletic careers toward other institutions (usually education and nonsports careers). A key line of inquiry for future studies might begin by exploring this irony of sports careers: Despite the fact that "the athlete" is currently an example of an exemplary form of masculinity in public ideology, the vast majority of boys who become most committed to athletic careers are never well-rewarded for their efforts. The fact that class and racial dynamics lead boys from higher-status backgrounds, unlike their lower-status counterparts, to move into non-sports careers illustrates how the construction of different kinds of masculin*ties* is a key component of the overall construction of the gender order.

REFERENCES

Birrell, S. (1987) "The woman athlete's college experience: knowns and unknowns." *J. of Sport and Social Issues* 11: 82–96.

Benjamin, J. (1988) *The Bonds of Love: Psychoanalysis, Feminism. and the Problem of Domination.* New York: Pantheon.

Bryson, L. (1987) "Sport and the maintenance of masculine hegemony." Women's Studies International *Forum* 10: 349–360.

Chodorow, N. (1978) *The Reproduction of Mothering.* Berkeley: Univ. of California Press.

Connell, R. W. (1987) *Gender and Power.* Stanford, CA: Stanford Univ. Press.

Connell, R. W. (1990) "An iron man: the body and some contradictions of hegemonic masculinity," In M. A. Messner and D. F. Sabo (eds.) *Sport, Men and the Gender Order: Critical Feminist Perspectives.* Champaign, IL: Human Kinetics.

Craib, I. (1987) "Masculinity and male dominance." *Soc. Rev.* 38: 721–743.

Eitzen, D. S. (1975) "Athletics in the status system of male adolescents: a replication of Coleman's *The Adolescent Society.*" *Adolescence* 10: 268–276.

Gilligan, C. (1982) *In a Different Voice: Psychological Theory and Women's Development.* Cambridge, MA: Harvard Univ. Press.

Greendorfer, S. L. (1977) "The role of socializing agents in female sport involvement." *Research Q.* 48: 304–310.

Hall, M. A. (1988) "The discourse on gender and sport: from femininity to feminism." *Sociology of Sport J.* 5: 330–340.

Hantover, J. (1978) "The boy scouts and the validation of masculinity." *J. of Social Issues* 34: 184–195.

Haug, F. (1987) *Female Sexualization.* London: Verso.

Kidd, B. (1987) "Sports and masculinity," pp. 250–265 in M. Kaufman (ed.) *Beyond Patriarchy: Essays by Men on Pleasure, Power, and Change.* Toronto: Oxford Univ. Press.

Kidd, B. (1990) "The men's cultural centre: sports and the dynamic of women's oppression/men's repression," In M. A. Messner and D. F. Sabo (eds.) *Sport,* *Men and the Gender Order: Critical Feminist Perspectives.* Champaign, IL: Human Kinetics.

Kimmel, M. S. (1987) "Men's responses to feminism at the turn of the century." *Gender and Society* 1: 261–283.

Kimmel, M. S. (1990) "Baseball and the reconstitution of American masculinity: 1880–1920," In M. A. Messner and D. F. Sabo (eds.) *Sport, Men and the Gender Order: Critical Feminist Perspectives.* Champaign, IL: Human Kinetics.

Leonard, W. M. II and J. M. Reyman (1988) "The odds of attaining professional athlete status: refining the computations." *Sociology of Sport J.* 5: 162–169.

Lever, J. (1976) "Sex differences in the games children play." *Social Problems* 23: 478–487.

Levinson, D. J. et al. (1978) *The Seasons of a Man's Life.* New York: Ballantine.

Lichterman, P. (1986) "Chodorow's psychoanalytic sociology: a project half-completed." *California Sociologist* 9: 147–166.

Messner, M. (1987) "The meaning of success: the athletic experience and the development of male identity," pp. 193–210 in H. Brod (ed.) *The Making of Masculinities: The New Men's Studies.* Boston: Allen & Unwin.

Messner, M. (1988) "Sports and male domination: the female athlete as contested ideological terrain." *Sociology of Sport J.* 5: 197–211.

Messner, M. (1989) "Masculinities and athletic careers." *Gender and Society* 3: 71–88.

Oglesby, C. A. (Ed.) (1978) *Women and Sport: From Myth to Reality.* Philadelphia: Lea & Farber.

Osherson, S. (1986) *Finding our Fathers: How a Man's Life is Shaped by His Relationship with His Father.* New York: Fawcett Columbine.

Piaget, J. H. (1965) *The Moral Judgment of the Child.* New York: Free Press.

Rubin, L. B. (1976) *Worlds of Pain: Life in the Working Class Family.* New York: Basic Books.

Sabo, D. (1985) "Sport, patriarchy and male identity: new questions about men and sport." *Arena Rev.* 9: 2.

Schafer, W. E. (1975) "Sport and male sex role social-ization." *Sport Sociology Bull.* 4: 47–54.

Sennett, R. and J. Cobb (1973) *The Hidden Injuries of Class*. New York: Random House.

Theberge, N. (1981) "A critique of critiques: radi-cal and feminist writings on sport." *Social Forces* 60: 2.

Thorne, B. (1986) "Girls and boys together . . . but mostly apart: gender arrangements in elementary schools," pp. 167–184 in W. W. Hartup and Z. Rubin (eds.) *Relationships and Development*. Hills-dale, NJ: Lawrence Erlbaum.

Twin, S. L. [ed.] (1978) *Out of the Bleachers: Writings on Women and Sport*. Old Westbury, NY: Feminist Press.

GAY JOCKS
A PHENOMENOLOGY OF GAY MEN IN ATHLETICS[1]

BRIAN PRONGER

Imagine walking into the crowded reception area of a major athletic facility at an international swimming competition. You have spent the last year training intensively, expecting that today you are going to swim faster than ever before. The foyer is packed with athletes, all of whom are at their peak of physical fitness, ready to race. The place is exciting.

On the deck just before the race the energy is amazing. So much power and speed in one place is awe-inspiring. Everywhere you turn there are men stretching and shaking the tension out of their powerful muscles—lithe bodies being tuned for the last time before the final event. You, too, are ready to fly into action at the sound of the gun. Bang! In less than a minute the race is over. You swam your personal best—victory.

The last event in the meet is the relays, in some ways the most exciting part of any meet. Team spirit is at its height, and these guys are ready to tear up the water. As each swimmer flings himself into the pool there is a burst of energy, lane after lane. These are men pushing themselves to the limit; every fibre of every body feels itself to be the consummation of power and masculinity. The race is over. The mood is ecstatic.

Relief. You, with your teammates, hit the showers with the hundred or so other swimmers.

Everyone is exhausted and delirious from the racing. This time in the showers, overwhelming with steam and muscle, marks the end of an athletic experience. These powerful men know what it means to be men and athletes.

You exchange an ironic glance and a knowing smile with the blond swimmer from Thunder Bay next to you. The two of you, in the midst of this concentrated masculinity, also know a great deal about what it means to be athletes and men. As gay men, you and your friend from Thunder Bay have experienced many things in common with the other men at the competition, most of whom are probably straight. Other experiences, however, have been and will be different. The following is an exploration of some of those unique differences.[2]

This article uses a phenomenological perspective to shed light on those experiences that gay men have in athletics that are unlike those of nongay men. It is essential to remember that many of the experiences of men who are not gay are also open to gay men. I will argue that the experience of being gay is a matter of context, that is, of understanding oneself in the light of socially constructed sexual and gender categories. These are contexts through which one can pass through different periods of life, from day to day and from moment to moment. This fluidity of context can predispose some men to a special way of interpreting the world that is ironic. This ironic point of view can shape the experiences that gay men have in athletics.

HISTORICAL AND THEORETICAL INTRODUCTION

The first problem faced in any investigation of gay men is defining about whom we are speaking. When we discuss the anthropology or sociology of women, it is fairly clear to whom we refer. However, when we talk about gay men, we are presented with a moving target. Definitions of sexuality have changed over the years.[3] Michel Foucault and Jeffrey Weeks have suggested that the heterosexual and homosexual categories are not ahistorical and unchanging; they depend upon complex historical circumstances. The homosexual category emerged in the 18th and 19th centuries, and its creation was related to the development of capitalism and the triumph of the positive sciences.[4] Before that time there were no homosexuals, only homosexual acts. Foucault and Weeks argue that the creation of sexual categories such as *heterosexual*, *homosexual*, *pedophile*, and *transvestite* comprise a form of social control.[5] Through confinement of legitimate sexuality to heterosexuality and the family, and through the marginalization of other machinations of sexual expression, the social behaviour of individuals has, by and large, been controlled in the service of social order and economic productivity.

Most recent research on homosexuality has focused on the social historical forces that have shaped and conceptualized the lives of contemporary men and women. The concern has been with the creation of sexual categories.[6] This phenomenological investigation, as a study of the way in which athletic experience emerges for gay men, is concerned not so much with the categories themselves as with the ways that individuals interact with historically constructed sexual categories in athletic settings.[7] In conjunction with my study of gay men in athletics, I conducted in-depth interviews with 30 gay-identified men and two heterosexually identified national coaches. There was no attempt to obtain a statistically valid sample; such an approach is impossible in the study of gay men, because the meaning of being gay is highly subjective and therefore ambiguous.

Contemporary gay men, like anyone else, find themselves in a world of meaning, a world that has changed over time under the influence of a multitude of historical and cultural circumstances. The anthropologist Clifford Geertz said that "man is an animal suspended in webs of significance he himself has spun."[8] Culture, Geertz says, is such a web, and the study of it is a search for meaning. As gay men approach an athletic experience, they may confront athletic culture and find meaning in it through a special gay sensibility which has developed out of a unique web of significance drawn from the experience of being gay in a straight world. As we shall see, the world of athletics is a gymnasium of heterosexual masculinity. The unique experience that gay men can have of athletics involves the special meaning they find in masculinity.

POWER, MASCULINITY, AND ATHLETICS

In their review of the sociological literature on masculinity, Carrigan et al. write, "One of the central facts about masculinity, is that men in general are advantaged by the subordination of women."[9] One of the techniques for the subordination of women by men is a complex semiotic of masculine and feminine behaviours that communicate power. As Foucault[10] has explained, power is

- a multiplicity of force relations,
- a process that transforms, strengthens, or reverses those relations,
- the support that those force relations find in one another, and
- the strategies that these relations employ.

In patriarchal society, men have power over women; the practice of masculine behaviour by men and feminine behaviour by women is the semiotic instrument of this power.

A common understanding of the difference between masculinity and femininity can be seen if we look at the dictionary; a number of important themes emerge. Power is the distinguishing feature of masculinity, whereas lack of power is the distinguishing feature of femininity. The *Oxford English Dictionary* (OED) defines *masculine* as "having the appropriate excellences of the male sex; manly, virile, vigorous, powerful." Interestingly, whereas *masculine* is defined in terms of "excellences," the OED offers a depreciative use of *feminine*, which is "womanish, effeminate." In this depreciative use, the powerlessness that is associated with femininity is borne out. The OED defines *effeminate* as "to make unmanly; to enervate. To grow weak, languish."

One form of masculine behaviour is the development and display of physical strength, an important phenomenon in the world of athletics. The masculine development and display of physical strength by men, in conjunction with its lack in women, embody Foucault's conception of power. Power, as a multiplicity of force relations, can be seen in the dominant and subordinate positions of men and women, respectively. As a process that transforms, strengthens, or reverses those relations, the masculine development of physical strength certainly fortifies the power relations between men and women. The complementarity of masculinity and femininity, of strength and weakness, functions as a system of support that the force relations between men and women find in one another. The actual development and display of physical strength is one of the many strategies that these force relations employ.[11] Masculinity, then, is a strategy for the power relations between men and women; it is a strategy that serves the interests of patriarchal heterosexuality. Athletics, as a sign of masculinity in men, can be an instrument of those power relations.

GAY MEN AND MASCULINITY

Given the patriarchal heterosexual significance of masculinity, it can have a special meaning for gay men. In their personal lives, many urban gay

men do not benefit significantly from the hegemony that masculinity is meant to afford men; some live their lives in virtual isolation from women. Others experience their relations with women as ones of equality. Women are sensitive to the difference between men who may see them as potential lovers, sexual partners, or victims of rape and those men who have no sexual interest in women and pursue them as friends on an equal basis. All the gay men I interviewed told me their relationships with women are very good; the men feel themselves to be on equal terms with women, and women seem to trust these men more than they do other men. A rower told me:

> My involvement with women is extremely important. I would guess that a lot of my closest friendships are with women, and it's a very central thing to what I am doing, doing things with women and being close to women, very important. I would guess it would be a very even split between women friends and men friends. . . . I don't notice anything unequal any more so than with my men friends.

This ease of social intercourse makes possible personal relations with women that are not patriarchal. The patriarchal signification of the masculine/feminine spectrum of behaviors, therefore, has little meaning to gay men in their personal lives. I am not suggesting that gay men are immune to patriarchal advantage. In a patriarchal society, certain things are automatically accorded men, such as privileged professional and financial advantage over women in economic life. But here I am describing the personal experiences that gay men have with women. In gay men's personal interactions with women, masculine patriarchal semiotics are generally inappropriate and insignificant.

Although gay men are not actively involved in hegemonic relations with women, these men are not unaware of the use of the masculine/feminine spectrum of behaviours. Because gay men grow up in a predominantly heterosexual world, they have learned the standard language of masculinity. In coming out, which is a process of becoming gay-identified in some public contexts, one becomes resolved that one is not part of the mainstream of society and that, in some way, one fits the socially constructed category of the homosexual or gay man. In this often-long process, we reinterpret the predominantly heterosexual world in which we find ourselves.

One of those reinterpretations, I propose, is of the meaning of masculine and feminine behaviour. Gay men can come to see that the power relations for which the semiotics of masculinity and femininity constitute a strategy have little to do with their lives. The meaning of masculinity, consequently, begins to change. Although masculinity is often the object of sexual desire for gay men, its role in their lives is ironic. Said one of my interviewees:

> For gay men, masculinity has this kind of double edge to it; on the one side it's something they find erotically attractive to them in some ways, but on the other side it's the area which they are least able in some ways to perform correctly. For me to be masculine in my real life [like many gay men, he has developed muscles so that he can pretend to be masculine while pursuing sex] is a very difficult feat—it's something I'd have to work at constructing.

Like this man, many gay men may consciously employ masculine behaviours, yet I have also noticed that other gay men, shortly after coming out, start to show more effeminate mannerisms.[12] As one man told me, "Gay men are aware of more flexibility in these things than others." Indeed, for many gay men, masculinity and femininity cease to be experienced as what one *is*, and they become, quite consciously, ways in which one *acts*.

GAY MEN AND EFFEMINACY

Early theories of homosexuality were concerned with its aetiology.[13] Homosexuality was categorized by 19th-century medicine as a psychosocial disorder. The source of this disorder was in what was then considered to be the biological formation of gender. It was thought that homosexuality was a symptom of gender confusion. Many gay theoreticians maintain that the old conception of homosexuals as effeminate is simply fallacious. Gay men, theoreticians claim, are just as masculine as heterosexual men.[14] Any sense of incongruity, therefore, between homosexuality and athletic participation would be a misunderstanding of the true case of homosexuality. Such a reading ignores both the intrinsically heterosexual meaning of masculinity (as a semiotic instrument for the subordination of women) and the historical influences that have shaped homosexuality. My research suggests that this meaning and history cannot be so easily dismissed. Gay men are aware of the popular effeminate image of homosexuality. This image is important as a point of reference for the sense of identity and behaviour of many gay men. Furthermore, there are gay men who intentionally employ effeminate behaviour. Effeminate behaviour in men is clearly seen to signify homosexuality, and gay men who want to call attention to their sexuality can do so by behaving effeminately. Said Quentin Crisp "Blind with mascara and dumb with lipstick, I paraded the streets of Pimlico. . . . My function in life . . . was to render what was already clear, blindingly conspicuous."[15]

Gay men can employ masculine and feminine behaviours at will, depending on the social context and what they are trying to express. Most gay men have had the experience of "butching it up" when trying to hide their homosexuality. Likewise, many know what it means to, "let your hair down" and "camp it up" among friends. This variability in the use of masculine and feminine behaviours indicates an important dimension to the experience of being gay, which is the experience of fluidity.

THE FLUIDITY OF BEING GAY AND PASSING AS STRAIGHT

Whereas Foucault and others have argued that the homosexual category has come to define the entire person, I suggest that gay men experience substantial fluidity in the application of the category to themselves. Gay men contextualize their experiences. They apply culturally received categories of homosexuality at different times and under different circumstances. In a comment that was similar to those of many of the men I interviewed, one said:

> Basically, my day-to-day life is quite straight, except for lunch, the informal social occasions when I can let loose with a gay reference. Socially, maybe 2 or 3 times a week, it's getting together for dinner or going to a bar, just me and my lover; we don't live together yet. There are gay times in the week and not gay times of the week. There is a fluidity to being gay.

By the implementation of gay sensibilities (which I will describe shortly), in reference to the historically constructed category of the homosexual, gay men can create gay cultural contexts not only in gay-community settings but also in nongay settings, such as mainstream athletics. Gay culture is not limited to life in the more or less formal institutions of the gay community such as bars, sports clubs, political groups, and churches. Gay culture (keeping in mind that culture is a "web of significance") is the world in which gay people meet—socially, intellectually, artistically, emotionally, politically, sexually, spiritually, and athletically. Gay culture can be expressed wherever there are gay people.

Gay men pass in and out of gay contexts, moment to moment, day to day, and through different periods of their lives. Gay contexts are created not only by the presence of gay men but also by their decisions to interpret a situation as gay. Consequently, it is possible for a gay man to go to a gymnasium, be completely involved in the athleticism of his workout, and experience that time as being simply athletic, devoid of any gay significance as far as he is concerned. Another day, he may go to the same gymnasium and find the same men there doing much the same exercises as they were previously; this time, however, he sees the experience as a gay experience. That is, he may find the situation sexy; he

may find it ironic (as I will explain shortly); he may decide that he is with only other gay men and experience a sense of gay fraternity. The gay context depends on the man's interpretation. Self-concept also depends upon personal interpretation. A man who is a runner may enter the Boston Marathon, an event that he considers to be very important to himself athletically. His concerns are whether he will finish, what his time might be, or how painful the experience will be. Here, his concept of himself is overwhelmingly that of a runner. The same man could enter the same marathon another year, and having decided to wear a singlet with a large pink triangle emblazoned with the word *gay*, he sees himself as a gay runner and his participation in this race as an expression of his pride in being gay.

The fluidity of homosexuality is enhanced by the fact that gay men can and often do pass as straight men. In a society that assumes that everyone is heterosexual, it is relatively easy for homosexual men to "pass." This ability is a distinguishing feature of the homosexual minority; people of colour cannot easily pass as white, and women have a difficult time passing as men. Passing is particularly important in mainstream athletic culture where heterosexuality is expected.[16] Certainly, it is usually necessary for gay men to pass as straight in the potentially sexual situations of men's locker rooms and showers.

Afraid of losing their positions on teams, as a result of the compulsory heterosexuality of sport, many gay athletes find it necessary to hide their homosexuality by passing as straight. I interviewed an international competitive rower who said it was essential to seem to be heterosexual:

> You did everything you could to hang on to your seat, to make the crew, that you would never jeopardize—you wouldn't even tell the coach you had a cold. You could be crippled and you'd hide it from the coach, because if there's any perceived weakness, they'll put somebody else in the boat. So to hint that I was gay was to kiss rowing goodbye.

THE IRONIC GAY SENSIBILITY

The experiences of fluidity and passing can dispose gay men to a special way of understanding the world. This can lead one to a special knowledge that is uniquely gay. Schutz[17] argues that a phenomenological account of knowledge reveals that it is basically social. This, he says, leads to the notion of the "social distribution of knowledge," which is demonstrated in the different knowledge that men and women have in our society. I argue that just as gender in sexist society affords people special knowledge that emerges from their positions in society, so too sexual orientation, in a society that is divided along those lines, privileges people with characteristic knowledge. Gay irony is a unique way of knowing that has it origins in the social construction of heterosexist society. The ways that gay men think are very much the results of having to deal with homophobia. To avoid suffering in potentially homophobic settings like athletic teams and locker rooms, gay men learn to pass as straight. Passing predisposes gay men to a sense of irony.

From an early age, gay men are aware of this important irony—they seem to be heterosexual when in fact they are not. Most social relations are organized around heterosexuality. For boys, the social side of sports is heterosexual. One's teammates form a "boys-wanting-girls club." When a young male athlete socializes with his teammates, inside or outside the locker room, talk is often about sex with girls and the problems of dating. Bars, clubs, or athletic dances held to mark the end of a sporting season or a school victory are always heterosexual functions. In their early years, most young gay people follow this social pattern.

A gay man may follow these patterns, but because he is not really part of the heterosexual action, the budding gay man is aware of himself as an outsider, an observer. The position of the observer is an ironic stance.[18] A young homosexual person can be aware of himself as an outsider without having understood himself as homosexual. In fact, this sense of being an outsider may lead to one's self-identification as homosexual. During this time the foundation for a young gay person's sense of irony develops. In his position as an observer, the young gay man, probably unconsciously, masters some of the basic skills of the ironist. As he grows older he becomes increasingly aware of himself as the observer who seems to be part of the action. Although he may never define his world as ironic, the gay man may, nevertheless, employ irony unwittingly. (One need not analyze and define the formal structure of a way of thinking or being in order to use that structure in day-to-day life.) Growing up in a world in which heterosexuality is taken for granted, then, gay people may be introduced to the rudiments of irony. By developing this sense and seeing his world as ironic, the gay man can manipulate the socially constructed incompatibility of the appearance and the reality of his sexuality.

Wayne Booth[19] says that fundamental to irony is its invitation to reconstruct something deeper than what is apparent on the surface. While inviting one to see deeper than the superficial appearance and thereby understand what is actually meant, irony preserves the appearance. The total truth includes both appearance and reality. This technique for understanding reality while maintaining a cosmetic appearance is very useful to gay men while passing as straight. It is a technique that many of us learn to use at very young ages simply in order to survive. Because gay men feel at home with irony, even when "the closet" is not an issue, they continue to interpret their worlds ironically. Because irony brings with it a sense of superiority, a sense of looking at the world from a higher place, each gay ironic experience is a sublime reaffirmation of a gay worldview.

Gay irony is a way of thinking, communicating, and being that emerges out of the experience of being gay in a society in which people tend to believe that everyone is straight. It is a sensibility that is essentially fluid both through the lives of individuals and throughout society.

The phenomenon of being gay is a matter of context; so too is the invocation of gay irony. Not all homosexual people see themselves as "gay," and not all gay people use irony. Being gay and the use of irony are conceptual dispositions and techniques that people use to think about themselves and interpret their worlds. Irony is a form of interpretation, a way of understanding that develops out of the experience of individuals' interactions with sexual and gender categories. Gay irony, therefore, is best understood as a tendency to interpret experience ironically rather than a consistent standpoint shared by all gay men.

THE IRONIC EXPERIENCE OF GAY MEN IN ATHLETICS

In our society, which places great importance on sex and restricts "legitimate" sexuality to heterosexuality and the family, the assumption is that virtually everyone is heterosexual. This is almost universally the case in athletics, where, for example, men and women's locker rooms are always segregated. The assumption is that the heterosexual desires of men and women may be stimulated if male and female athletes were to see each other naked. The fact that men may find it sexually stimulating to be in a locker room full of other naked male athletes is either ignored or sublimated through aggressive, homophobic, and sexist humor.

The popular images of the athlete and the gay man are virtually antithetical. The history of homosexuality has constructed a less than positive and healthy conception of the homosexual man, whereas the popular image of the athlete is quintessentially healthy and positive. Many writers have suggested that athletics and healthy heterosexual masculinity are popularly equated: Bob Connell, David Kopay, and Don Sabo, to name only a few. Certainly, the popular image of the athlete as a healthy model citizen is unlike the judicial, medical, and religious models that have categorized the homosexual man as a criminal, pathological, degenerate sinner.[20] Being

both athletic and gay presents a seeming contradiction, one of which many gay athletes are aware. Many of the gay athletes to whom I spoke said that when they were younger, they thought it was impossible to be both athletic and gay. This juxtaposition of the popular models of athletics and homosexuality, of appearance and reality, in the lives of gay athletes is a significant contribution to the ironic experience of gay men in athletics.

Anagnorisis

Gay men subtly communicate their shared worldview by using irony. This subtlety has important implications for gay men; it allows them to remain undiscovered by the uninitiated, thereby affording them some protection from the expressions of homophobia that frequently accompany detection. Especially important in gay irony is *anagnorisis*, which is the observer's recognition of the ironist as an ironist with a deeper intent than that which is immediately apparent on the surface. Anagnorisis occurs when the interpreter of the irony realizes the irony in the situation. In anagnorisis, the gay ironist not only reveals meanings that have been concealed by appearances, he also reveals himself. Eye contact is the way gay men usually recognize each other in nongay settings. One manifestation of this eye contact can be a subtle, knowing look, which can be the clue for mutual anagnorisis. One man told me about being in a university weight room and watching an athlete to whom he was attracted lifting a weight. To most observers, the scenario would appear to be quite straight. A man whom he didn't know was standing nearby and watching the same athlete. Moving from the athlete to each other, their admiring eyes met, and with no more obvious gesture than a slight pause in their gazes, they became aware of their secret fraternity. In their sententious exchange of glances, having as novelist John Fowles said, "the undeclared knowledge of a shared imagination," their worlds touched. They uttered not a word.

Acting Versus Being

As a result of coming out in some contexts, gay men become more consciously aware of passing in others; gay men can start to see others' uses of masculinity as a technique for passing. This insight can bring them to a heightened awareness of their uses of masculinity as an ironic form. Rather than thinking of themselves as being masculine, gay men can come to think of themselves as acting masculine. In the 1970s, the disco group "The Village People" epitomized this masculine (and I think intensely ironic) act. Their outfits were ironic caricatures of masculinity: construction worker, policeman, Indian, and a hypermasculine-looking man with a moustache (a style known as the "clone"). One of their hit songs bad the lyrics, "Macho, macho, man; I wanna be a macho man." The clue to their irony lies in the fact that they don't say they are macho men; rather, they "wanna be" macho men. That is, they look like macho men when in fact they are not. The macho look, especially that of the clone, became very popular in gay ghettos across North America and parts of Europe. The deep and sometimes subliminal irony of the gay masculine clone style[21] may best be appreciated in the light of Wallace Stevens: "The final belief is to believe in a fiction, which you know to be a fiction, there being nothing else. The exquisite truth is to know that it is a fiction and that you believe in it willingly."[22]

Two Ironies of Muscular Bodies

The attraction that many gay men have for masculine men presents a uniquely gay male interpretation of masculinity. Athletic, muscular bodies are masculine bodies. The popularity of muscles among gay men is evidenced by the predominance of muscular iconography in gay liberation magazines, erotica, and soft-core and hard-core pornography. Over the last 15 years or so, there has been a substantial migration of gay men to gymnasiums, so much so that some major cities have gymnasiums where the majority of members are gay men. The development

of muscular bodies by gay men presents two important ironies. In the *Leviathan*, Hobbes says that "Forme is Power, because being a promise of Good, it recommendeth men to the favour of women and strangers."[23] The well-defined muscular body is a sign of strength, an indication of the power that has historically been given to men. The armour of Roman centurions was an exaggerated sculpture of a muscular male torso. The intention, no doubt, was to create the appearance of considerable strength, which would inhibit those who wished to usurp the officer's power. The truly masculine man with his muscular body asserts his authority over women and inhibits other men; his muscular appearance is meant to deter other men. This signification of muscular bodies is commonly understood. A gay man with a muscular body, however, has little intention of asserting his authority over women and may well have every intention of attracting other men. The significance that gay men give to the athletic body is ironic in that the masculine appearance that normally is meant to inhibit men emerges as an invitation to men.

The second irony of gay muscular bodies involves a dualism of mind and body. The muscled athletic male body is an expression of a powerful masculine mental disposition. John Hoberman points out that many prominent fascist leaders have exploited the athletic body (not necessarily their own bodies; i.e., they surround themselves with athletes) to express their power. Idi Amin, 6 feet and 4 inches, who before ascending to power in Uganda was the Ugandan heavyweight boxing champion, used his considerable athletic build to dramatize his political power.[24] Someone who has developed a powerful body is perceived as also having the mental resolve to mobilize his body into masculine action. By masculine action, I mean seizing patriarchal opportunities as they are presented and inhibiting other men. Some muscular gay men can be effeminate; here we have the irony of an effeminate mind in a masculine body. One man I interviewed did weight lifting exclusively as a masculine sexual lure. Pinpointing the fluidity, superficiality, and therefore irony of this masculinity, he said he used it

> *as a tool to pick up men. I think I tend to exempt myself from, well, as I think a lot of gay people do, from the standard deviation [of] male and female, masculine and feminine. That we can make up our own rules and borrow from one and the other equally, according to what you find palatable or useful or stimulating or interesting.*

This gay ironic play with masculinity is highlighted in radical drag. A man with bulging biceps and thunderous thighs wearing a slinky dress and a tiara is, through the juxtaposition of a masculine body and feminine clothes, expressing the overt irony of seeming to be "masculine" when he is also "feminine."

CONCLUSION

In conclusion, because being gay is a fluid experience and because gay men are in the unique position of being able to pass as straight in a society that assumes that everyone is heterosexual, some gay men have developed a special way of interpreting the world that is based on the manipulation of appearance and reality (i.e., the ironic gay sensibility). This is a view of the world that many gay men can apply at will and with which they feel very comfortable. It is an instrument of understanding that plays on the subtleties of life and reveals meanings that are particularly close to the unique experiences of gay men.

The semiotics of masculinity and femininity reveal an intricate spectrum of behaviours for the communication of power in the service of patriarchal heterosexual relations. Although gay men do not benefit significantly in their personal lives from the hegemony that masculinity is meant to afford men, gay men do employ masculine behaviour. The meaning that gay men find in masculinity is distinctive in its sexual and ironic signification.

The gay experience of athletics is a matter of context. Entering into an athletic situation, a gay man can be an athlete whose world is dominated by purely athletic experience: pain, sweat, exertion, the joy of movement. He can be an earnest gay person running a race as a representative of gay pride. He can be a national swim team member covertly communicating with his gay teammates through ironic innuendo. He can be a solitary gay person working out in a crowded university weight room, privately savoring the ironic fact that he is in the midst of a macho temple that for him is almost exploding with sexuality.

At the beginning of this chapter, you were invited to imagine yourself as a swimmer at an international competition. You may remember that after the meet, in the showers, you exchanged an ironic glance and a knowing smile with a friend from Thunder Bay. As gay athletes, your worlds met. In those glances and smiles were distilled personal and cultural histories of homosexuality, masculinity, femininity, sex, and irony.

NOTES

1. An earlier version of this paper was presented to the Canadian Sociology and Anthropology Association on June 3, 1987, at the Learned Societies Conference at MacMaster University, Hamilton, ON.

2. Gay men are involved in both mainstream and gay community athletic milieux. Gay athletic clubs, which can be found in major cities across North America (see C. Rowland, "Games People Play: The Burgeoning World of Gay Athletics," *The Advocate*, 462, December 23, 1986, pp. 42–47, 108–109), constitute a major aspect of gay community life. These clubs offer gay men and lesbians a unique experience of athletics. Because space here is limited, I will devote this chapter to the experience of gay men in mainstream athletics. The phenomenology of gay men in athletics is an entirely new field of inquiry, both in regard to its approach and its subject. This paper is a simplified and brief outline of a complex and extensive phenomenon.

3. See M. Foucault, *The History of Sexuality: Vol. I. An Introduction*, translated by R. Hurley (New York: Vintage Books, 1978); J. Katz, *Gay/Lesbian Almanac:*

A New Documentary (New York: Harper and Row, 1983); J. Marshall, "Pansies, Perverts and Macho Men: Changing Conceptions of Male Homosexuality," in K. Plummer, editor, *The Making of the Modern Homosexual* (London: Hutchinson, 1981), pp. 133–54; K. Plummer, "Building a Sociology of Homosexuality" and "Homosexual Categories: Some Research Problems in the Labeling Perspective of Homosexuality," in K. Plummer, editor, Ibid., pp. 17–29 and 53–75; J. Weeks, *Sexuality* (Chichester, England: Ellis Horwood, 1986).

4. J. Weeks, "Discourse, Desire, and Sexual Deviance: Some Problems in a History of Sexuality," in K. Plummer, editor, ibid.

5. Ibid.

6. K. Plummer, op. cit.

7. My approach to phenomenology is drawn from Martin Heidegger (see his *Being and Time*, J. Marquarrie and E. Robinson, translators (New York: Harper and Row, 1926), pp. 49–62. He says that the term *phenomenology* refers to a method of inquiry, whereas *sociology*, *anthropology* and *psychology* refer to what is to be studied. Phenomenology, he says, directs us to the "how" of an investigation; it is the study of the way in which things appear to us.

8. C. Geertz, *The Interpretation of Cultures* (New York: Basic Books, 1973).

9. T. Carrigan, R. Connell, and J. Lee, "Toward a New Sociology of Masculinity," *Theory and Society*, vol. 4/5 (1985), p. 590.

10. M. Foucault, op. cit.

11. M. Foucault, ibid., pp. 92–93.

12. I am not suggesting that all gay men behave effeminately. In fact, nowhere in this paper do I suggest that gay men behave in a uniform fashion. As the reader will see, the fluidity of being gay precludes such a notion.

13. J. Marshall, op. cit.

14. M. Levine, "Gay Ghetto," in M. Levine, editor, *Gay Men: The Sociology of Male Homosexuality* (New York: Harper and Row, 1979), pp. 183–203.

15. Quentin Crisp, *The Naked Civil Servant* (London: Jonathon Cape, 1968), p. 114.

16. B. Kidd, "Sports and Masculinity," in M. Kaufman, editor, *Beyond Patriarchy: Essays by Men on Pleasure, Power, and Change* (Toronto: Oxford University Press, 1987), pp. 250–65; and D. Kopay and P. Young, *The David Kopay Story: An Extraordinary Self-Revelation* (New York: Arbor House, 1977).

17. R. M. Zaner and H. T. Englehardt, Jr., *Structures of the Lifeworld* (Evanston, IL: Northwestern University Press, 1974).

18. D. Muecke, *Irony and the Ironic* (London: Methuen, 1982).

19. Wayne Booth, *A Rhetoric of Irony* (Chicago: University of Chicago Press, 1974).

20. See K. Marshall, op. cit., and J. Weeks, op. cit.

21. The fluidity of being gay should be kept in mind here; that is, there are men who may practice homosexuality who view their masculine behaviors not in this gay context but in a traditional patriarchal one. Moreover, they may switch from a traditional context to a gay one from time to time, depending on the situation.

22. Wallace Stevens, *Opus Posthumous* (New York: Knopf, 1977), p. 163.

23. Thomas Hobbes, *Leviathan*, C. B. Macpherson, editor (Harmondsworth, England: Penguin Books, 1968 (1651)), p. 151.

24. John Hoberman, *Sport and Political Ideology* (Austin, TX: University of Texas Press, 1984).

MASCULINITY, VIOLENCE, AND WAR

BOB CONNELL

ONE

In 1976 there were 22 million people under arms in the world's 130-odd standing armies. The figure today may be a little higher. Probably 20 million of them are men. I have not seen any global totals by sex, but there are figures for particular countries which serve as pointers. In the major NATO forces in 1979–80, for instance, 92% of the US military forces were men; 95% of the French and British; 99.93% of the German. From what is commonly known about other countries, these are not likely to be exceptional figures. The vast majority of the world's soldiers are men. So are most of the police, most of the prison warders, and almost all the generals, admirals, bureaucrats and politicians who control the apparatus of coercion and collective violence. Most murderers are men. Almost all bandits, armed robbers, and muggers are men; all rapists, most domestic bashers; and most people involved in street brawls, riots and the like.

The same story, then, appears for both organised and unorganised violence. It seems there is some connection between being violent and being male. What is it? And what light can an analysis of masculinity, apparently a question of individual psychology, throw on the question of violence on a world scale?

There is surprisingly widespread belief that this is all "natural." Human males are genetically programmed to be hunters and killers, the argument runs. The reason is that ape-man aggression was a survival need in the prehistoric dawn,

while the ape-women clustered passively round their campfires suckling and breeding.

Right-wing inflections of this argument thus explain and justify aggression, competition, hierarchy, territoriality, patriarchy, and by inference private property, national rivalry, armies and war. Crude versions of this doctrine are part of the stock rhetoric of modern fascism. More sophisticated versions are developed by "sociobiologists" in the universities.

Remarkably, there is now a feminist version of this argument too. The line of thought is that human males are naturally predatory and violent; patriarchal power is thus an expression of men's inner nature. Rape and war become synonymous. A poster slogan reads: RAPE IS WAR, WAR IS RAPE. Even serious and thoughtful attempts to reckon with the connection between sexual dominance and war, like Penny Strange's pamphlet *It'll Make a Man of You*, talk freely of "male cosmology," "male violence," "male values" and so on.

Two things have gone wrong here. One is that biological speculation has substituted for hard analysis. A critical examination shows practically no grounding in evidence. The sociobiologists' pre-history is speculative, their anthropology highly selective, and their mechanisms of selection and inheritance simply imaginary. By equally convincing evolutionary speculation one can "prove" that men are naturally co-operative and peaceful. In fact it has been done, by Kropotkin in *Mutual Aid*.

Reprinted from *War/Masculinity*, P. Patton and R. Poole, eds. Melbourne, Australia: Intervention Publishers.

More important, perhaps, is the confusion of concepts in phrases like "male power," "male violence," "male culture," "malestream thought," "male authority." In each of these phrases a social fact or process is coupled with, and implicitly attributed to, a biological fact. The result is not only to collapse together a rather heterogeneous group (do gays suffer from "male cosmology," for instance; or boys?). It also, curiously, takes the heat off the open opponents of feminism. The hardline male chauvinist is now less liable to be thought personally responsible for what he says or does in particular circumstances, since what he says or does is attributable to the general fatality of being male.

That this is a point where argument and emotion have got tangled is not accidental. There is a basic theoretical problem here. The social categories of gender are quite unlike other categories of social analysis, such as class, in being firmly and visibly connected to biological difference. It is therefore both tempting and easy to fall back on biological explanation of any gender pattern. This naturalisation of social processes is without question the commonest mechanism of sexual ideologies. That biological difference underpins and explains the social supremacy of men over women is the prized belief of enormous numbers of men, and a useful excuse for resisting equality. Academic or pseudo-academic versions of this argument, male-supremacist "sociobiology" from Tiger's *Men in Groups* through Goldberg's *The Inevitability of Patriarchy* to the present, find a never-failing audience.

If we cannot do better than this in getting to grips with the connection between masculinity and violence, then the left might as well pack its bags and go home, turn on the VCR and play *Threads* until the missiles arrive. For if it all stems from the biological fact of maleness, there is nothing that can be done.

We can do better, and the basis for doing so is well known. It is to recognise that war, murder, rape and masculinity are social and cultural facts, not settled by biology. The patterns we have to deal with as issues of current politics

have been produced within human society by the processes of history. It is the shape of social relations, not the shape of genes, that is the effective cause. "Male" and "masculine" are very different things. Masculinity is implanted in the male body, it does not grow out of it.

This argument implies a very different approach to the nature of gender from the natural categories appealed to by both sociobiology and cultural (or eco-) feminism. Such an understanding has been emerging from the work of other groups of feminists (in Australia, research such as Game and Pringle's *Gender at Work* and Burton's *Subordination*), theorists of gay liberation (such as Fernbach's *The Spiral Path*), and others. Broadly, gender is seen as a structure of social practice, related in complex ways to biological sex but with a powerful historical dynamic of its own.

That general framework suggests two lines of approach to the question of masculinity and war. One is to investigate the social construction of masculinity. The other is to undertake a social analysis of war. In what follows I'll suggest some points about both.

TWO

Given a framework of social analysis, we can look at the familiar images and archetypes of manliness in a clearer light. They are parts of the cultural process of producing particular types of masculinity. What messages they convey are important because they help to shape new generations.

One of the central images of masculinity in the Western cultural tradition is the murderous hero, the supreme specialist in violence. A string of warrior-heroes—Achilles, Siegfried, Lancelot and so on—populate European literature from its origins. The twentieth century has steadfastly produced new fictional heroes of this type: Tarzan, Conan, James Bond, the Jackal, the Bruce Lee characters. If you walk into a shop selling comics you will find a stunning array of violent heroes: cops, cowboys, supermen, infantry sergeants, fighter pilots, boxers and so on. The best of the Good Guys, it seems, are those who pay evil-doers back in their own coin.

This connection between admired masculinity and violent response to threat is a resource that governments can use to mobilise support for war. The most systematic case in modern history was the Nazis' cult of Nordic manhood, reaching its peak in the propaganda image of the SS-man during World War II. In a different context, a cult of masculinity and toughness flourished in the Kennedy and Johnson administrations in the USA, and helped commit that country to war in Vietnam. Fasteau documents this in one of the early books to come out of the American "men's movement," *The Male Machine*. I can remember the process operating on young men of my generation in Australia, whose conservative government sent troops to support the Americans in Vietnam. Involvement in the war was presented as standing up to threat, and opponents were smeared as lily-livered effeminates. In the fullness of time support for napalm raids and carpet bombing by B-52s became the test of manliness. In the aftermath of the TWA jet hijacking, Reagan has been playing this tune again, trying to rouse American feeling against the threat of terrorism to provide a cover for his own military operations in central America.

Yet there is a good deal of scepticism in response to Reagan. And in the previous case, Western opposition to the Vietnam war did grow. Together with the Vietnamese resistance it eventually forced the American military to withdraw. The cult of masculine toughness is not all-powerful. This should alert us to some complexities in masculinity and its cultural images.

It is striking that the *Iliad* centres not on Achilles' supremacy in violence, but on his refusal to use it. And what changes his mind is not his reaction to threat, but his tenderness—his love for his friend Patroclus. Siegfried and Lancelot, not exactly gentle characters, are likewise full of hesitations, affection, and divided loyalties.

The image of heroism in modern figures like Tarzan and James Bond is a degraded one. The capacity for tenderness, emotional complexity, aesthetic feeling and so on has been deleted. More exactly, they are split off and assigned only to women, or to other, inferior types of men—such as the wimps, poofters and effeminates who evaded the Vietnamese war. (Part of the legend of Achilles was that he put on a dress and lived among women in order to evade the Trojan war.)

We know very little of the history of masculinity as distinct from the history of men; the detailed research has not been done. We know enough to understand that such changes in images of heroism are part of the historical process by which different kinds of masculinity are separated from each other, some exalted and some spurned. A crucial fact about men is that masculinity is not all of a piece. There have always been different kinds, some more closely associated with violence than others. This is why one should not talk of "male violence" or of "males" doing this and that—phrasing which smuggles back in the idea of a biological uniformity of social behaviour.

At any given moment some forms of masculinity will be hegemonic—that is, most honoured and most influential—and other forms will be marginalized or subordinated. The evidence about these forms is very scattered, as the question is only just coming into focus as a research issue. Some points are clear. Modern hegemonic masculinity is defined as heterosexual (not true of all societies or all periods of history), and sharply contrasted with homosexual masculinity (in our society the type case of subordinated masculinity). Some other forms of subordinated masculinity are temporary—like that of apprentices in a strongly-masculinized trade. There are kinds of masculinity that are not directly subordinated but rather marginalized by a process of social change that undermines their cultural presuppositions—the patriarchal masculinity of many immigrant men from Mediterranean countries is an important case in Australia at present. And there are struggles about what form of masculinity should be hegemonic—for instance the contest going on in the ruling classes of the capitalist world between professional/managerial and enterpreneurial/authoritarian masculinities. (The victory of Reaganism in the US is an important shift in the style of American patriarchy as well as in the precise locus of class power.)

THREE

In some civilisations the hegemonic forms of masculinity stress restraint and responsibility rather than violence. I believe that was true, for instance, of Confucian China. In contemporary Western society, hegemonic masculinity is strongly associated with aggressiveness and the capacity for violence. Modern feminism has shown us one of the bases for this: the assertion of men's power over women. This relationship itself has a strong component of violence. Wife-bashing, intimidation of women in the street, rape, jealousy-murder, and other patterns of violence against women are not accidental or incidental. They are widespread and systematic, arising from the tensions of a power struggle. This struggle has many turns and twists. Even in a society that defines a husband as the "head of the household," there are many families where wives actually run the show. Bashings may then result from an attempt to re-assert a damaged masculine ego. In other cases domestic violence is a direct expression of the husband's power, his belief that he can get away with anything, and his contempt for women in general or his wife in particular.

So there are many complexities and contradictions. The main axis, however, remains the social subordination of women, and men's general interest in maintaining it. The masculinity built on that bedrock is not necessarily violent—most men in fact do not bash women—but it is constructed, so to speak, with a door open towards violence.

Gay liberation has shown us another dimension: hegemonic masculinity is aggressively heterosexual. It defines itself in part by a vehement rejection of homosexuality. This rejection very often takes violent forms: arrests, frequent bash-

ings, and occasional murders. Homosexual men seem to arouse particular fear and loathing among tough "macho" men. This fact has led many to think the violence is an attempt to purge the world of what one suspects in oneself. In psychoanalytic terms, there is a current of repressed homosexual feeling buried somewhere in hegemonic masculinity. This, again, suggests the importance of the tensions and contradictions within masculinity. It is by no means a neat package.

In much of the writing about men produced by the "men's liberation movement" of the 1970s it was assumed that violence was simply an expression of conventional masculinity. Change the macho image, stop giving little boys toy guns, and violence would be reduced. We can now see that the connection of masculinity and violence is both deeper and more complex than that. Violence is not just an expression; it is a part of the process that divides different masculinities from each other. There is violence within masculinity; it is constitutive. Once again, this is not to imply that it is universal. Real men don't necessarily bash three poofters before breakfast every day. For one thing, TV does it for them. Part of the pattern of contemporary masculinity is the commercial production of symbolic violence on an unprecedented scale, from Tarzan movies to *Star Wars*, Space Invaders, World Series Cricket, and now *Rambo*.

FOUR

It is very important that much of the actual violence is not isolated and individual action, but is institutional. Much of the poofter-bashing is done by the police; much of the world's rape is done by soldiers. These actions grow readily out of the "legitimate" violence for which police forces and armies are set up. The state is an instrument of coercion: this remains true whatever else about it varies. It uses one of the great discoveries of modern history, rational bureaucratic organisation, to have policy-making centralized and execution down the line fairly uniform.

Given this, the state can become the vehicle of calculated violence based on and using hegemonic masculinity. Armies are a kind of hybrid between bureaucracy and masculinity.

But to make this connection with an undifferentiated "masculine violence"—as, say, Fernbach does in *The Spiral Path*—is to misunderstand the way armies work. Generals, notoriously, die in bed. They are not themselves "violent men," and would be bad generals if they were. Of course they need violent men under their command as front-line troops, or at least as organisers of front-line troops—men like the grim Sergeant Croft of *The Naked and the Dead* (a novel that strikingly makes the point about different masculinities).

It is the *relationship* between forms of masculinity—physically violent but subordinate to orders on the one hand, dominating and organisationally competent on the other—that is the basis of military organisation. The two need not overlap at all. Heinrich Himmler, the commander of one of the most brutal military organisations in recent history, never killed anyone personally. When present at any execution where some brains splattered on his neat SS uniform, he threw a screaming fit.

Even this is to understate the matter. In modern armies the majority of soldiers are not combatants at all. Most are in support services, as transport workers, administrators, technicians, maintenance workers, cooks, etc., and have no competence as fighters at all. The proportion of this kind of worker in armies has grown markedly over the last century and a half with the increasing technologisation of warfare, as several major developments have reduced the need for cannon-fodder and increased the need for supply workers. The US made two great contributions to the art of war in the 1940s—nuclear weapons and logistics. Logistics was certainly more militarily effective at the time. And you don't want Rambo types driving your jeeps and supply trucks.

Automatic weapons (machine-guns and quick-firing artillery), self-propelled military vehicles (tanks and aircraft), and ultimately long-distance weapons that eliminate the 'front' (strategic bombers, nuclear missiles) have successively intensified the trend. They have made more and more important in military organisations a third kind of masculinity, the professionalised, calculative rationality of the technical specialist.

The first stage of this was the rise of the "General Staff" to a central position in European military organisation by the early twentieth century. The idea of a General Staff was a group of planners, separate from the command of combat units, who worked out overall strategies as well as technical issues of supply. The "Schlieffen Plan" for the German attack on France in 1914 marked the ascendancy of staff over line commanders, In no sense did this mean a shift away from violence—the violence of war was growing on an unprecedented scale. The man who was the 20th century's most successful general, the Soviet Chief of Staff Georgi Zhukov, was notorious for his disregard for human life. He accepted huge casualties in order to gain advantage in battles of attrition at Moscow, Stalingrad and Kursk (the battles responsible for the ultimate defeat of Hitler).

The second stage was the mobilisation of physical scientists on a large scale into weapons research, culminating in the Manhattan Project. The friction within the Manhattan Project, and the crisis of conscience suffered by the nuclear physicists immediately after the explosion of the Hiroshima and Nagasaki bombs, are measures of the difficulty of the integrating this kind of worker into the military. But the huge growth of nuclear weapons research establishments in the USA and USSR since then shows that the initial difficulties have been overcome. The end of the world has been made technically possible by this achievement in human relations.

FIVE

In the past, as well as being the main actors of war, men have also been the main victims. Napoleon's wars killed mainly soldiers. The harnessing of high technology to the bureaucratic state has steadily changed this. Hitler's mass extermination campaigns, and the Anglo-American firebombing of Hamburg, Dresden and Tokyo, were an organised turning of conventional weapons to the killing of whole populations. The nuclear arsenal has been directed against whole populations from the start.

It has thus become a matter of urgency for humans as a group to undo the tangle of relationships that sustains the nuclear arms race. Masculinity is part of this tangle. It will not be easy to alter. The pattern of an arms race, i.e., mutual threat, itself helps sustain an aggressive masculinity.

Nor can the hegemonic pattern of masculinity be rejected totally. To achieve disarmament in reality means conducting a long and difficult struggle against an entrenched power structure. This calls for some of the qualities hegemonic masculinity exalts—toughness, endurance, determination and the like. It is no accident that hegemonic masculinity has been important in radical movements in the past: in unionism, in national liberation movements, and in socialist parties.

Yet we know masculinity is not fixed. It is at least conceivable that we can re-work masculinity in a way that sustains a struggle without reproducing the enemy. In much this sense feminism has been re-working femininity. In doing this it will be useful to remember the hidden riches of masculinity, as well as its horrors. There are cultural resources in subordinated masculinities, and in patterns lost or bypassed in recent history.

REFERENCES

Burton, C., *Subordination: Feminism and Social Theory*, Sydney, Allen and Unwin, 1985.

Carrigan, T., Connell, R. W. & Lee, J. "Hard and Heavy Phenomena: the Sociology of Masculinity," *Theory & Society*, 1985.

Chapkis, W., Ed., *Loaded Questions: Women in the Military*, Amsterdam, Transnational Institute, 1981.

Clark, A., *Barbarossa: The Russian-German Conflict 1941–1915*, Harmondsworth, Penguin, 1966.

Connell, R. W., "Men's bodies" in *Which Way Is Up?*, Sydney, Allen and Unwin, 1983.

Fernbach, D., *The Spiral Path: A Gay Contribution to Human Survival*, London, Gay Men's Press, 1981.

Fasteau, M. F., *The Male Machine*, New York, McGraw-Hill, 1974.

Game, A. & Pringle, R., *Gender at Work*, Sydney, Allen and Unwin, 1983.

Goldberg, S., *The Inevitability of Patriarchy*, New York, William Morrow, 1973.

Irving, D. J. C., *The Destruction of Dresden*, London, Kimber, 1963.

Kropotkin, P., *Mutual Aid* (1902), Boston, Extending Horizons, n.d.

Mailer, N., *The Naked and the Dead* (1949), London, Deutsch, 1964.

Strange, P., *It'll Make a Man of You: A Feminist View of the Arms Race*, Nottingham, Peace News/Mushroom, 1983.

Tiger, L., *Men in Groups*, New York, Random House, 1969.

Zhukov, G. K., *Marshal Zhukov's Greatest Battles*, London, Sphere, 1971.

WARS, WIMPS, AND WOMEN
TALKING GENDER AND THINKING WAR

CAROL COHN

l start with a true story, told to me by a white male physicist:

> *Several colleagues and I were working on modeling counterforce attacks, trying to get realistic estimates of the number of immediate fatalities that would result from different deployments.*[1] *At one point, we remodeled a particular attack, using slightly different assumptions, and found that instead of there being thirty-six million immediate fatalities, there would only be thirty million. And everybody was sitting around nodding, saying, "Oh yeah, that's great, only thirty million," when all of a sudden, I heard what we were saying. And I blurted out, "Wait, I've just heard how we're talking—Only thirty million! Only thirty million human beings killed instantly?" Silence fell upon the room. Nobody said a word. They didn't even look at me. It was awful. I felt like a woman.*

The physicist added that henceforth he was careful to never blurt out anything like that again.

. . .

During the early years of the Reagan presidency, in the era of the Evil Empire, the cold war, and loose talk in Washington about the possibility of fighting and "prevailing" in a nuclear war, I went off to do participant observation in a community of North American nuclear defense intellectuals and security affairs analysts—a community virtually entirely composed of white men. They work in universities, think tanks, and as advisers to government. They theorize about nuclear de-

terrence and arms control, and nuclear and conventional war fighting, about how to best translate military might into political power; in short, they create the discourse that underwrites American national security policy. The exact relation of their theories to American political and military practice is a complex and thorny one; the argument can be made, for example, that their ideas do not so much shape policy decisions as legitimate them after the fact. But one thing that is clear is that the body of language and thinking they have generated filters out to the military, politicians, and the public, and increasingly shapes how we talk and think about war. This was amply evident during the Gulf War: Gulf War "news," as generated by the military briefers, reported by newscasters, and analyzed by the television networks' resident security experts, was marked by its use of the professional language of defense analysis, nearly to the exclusion of other ways of speaking.

My goal has been to understand something about how defense intellectuals think, and why they think that way. Despite the parsimonious appeal of ascribing the nuclear arms race to "missile envy,"[2] I felt certain that masculinity was not a sufficient explanation of why men think about war in the ways that they do. Indeed, I found many ways to understand what these men were doing that had little or nothing to do with gender.[3] But ultimately, the physicist's story and others like it made confronting the role of

Reprinted from *Gendering War Talk,* Miriam Cooke and Angela Woollacott, eds. Princeton, N.J.: Princeton University Press, 1993: 227–246.

gender unavoidable. Thus, in this paper I will explore gender discourse, and its role in shaping nuclear and national security discourse.

I want to stress, this is not a paper about men and women, and what they are or are not like. I will not be claiming that men are aggressive and women peace loving. I will not even address the question of how men's and women's relations to war may differ, nor of the different propensities they may have to committing acts of violence. Neither will I pay more than passing attention to the question which so often crops up in discussions of war and gender, that is, would it be a more peaceful world if our national leaders were women? These questions are valid and important, and recent feminist discussion of them has been complex, interesting, and contentious. But my focus is elsewhere. I wish to direct attention away from gendered individuals and toward gendered discourses. My question is about the way that civilian defense analysts think about war, and the ways in which that thinking is shaped not by their maleness (or, in extremely rare instances, femaleness), but by the ways in which gender discourse intertwines with and permeates that thinking.[4]

Let me be more specific about my terms. I use the term *gender* to refer to the constellation of meanings that a given culture assigns to biological sex differences. But more than that, I use gender to refer to a symbolic system, a central organizing discourse of culture, one that not only shapes how we experience and understand ourselves as men and women, but that also interweaves with other discourses and shapes *them*—and therefore shapes other aspects of our world—such as how nuclear weapons are thought about and deployed.[5]

So when I talk about "gender discourse," I am talking not only about words or language but about a system of meanings, of ways of thinking, images and words that first shape how we experience, understand, and represent ourselves as men and women, but that also do more than that; they shape many other aspects of our lives and culture. In this symbolic system, human

characteristics are dichotomized, divided into pairs of polar opposites that are supposedly mutually exclusive: mind is opposed to body; culture to nature; thought to feeling; logic to intuition; objectivity to subjectivity; aggression to passivity; confrontation to accommodation; abstraction to particularity; public to private; political to personal, ad nauseam. In each case, the first term of the "opposites" is associated with male, the second with female. And in each case, our society values the first over the second.

I break it into steps like this—analytically separating the *existence* of these groupings of binary oppositions, from the association of each group with a gender, from the valuing of one over the other, the so-called male over the so-called female, for two reasons: first, to try to make visible the fact that this system of dichotomies is encoding many meanings that may be quite unrelated to male and female bodies. Yet once that first step is made—the association of each side of those lists with a gender—gender now becomes tied to many other kinds of cultural representations. If a human activity, such as engineering, fits some of the characteristics, it becomes gendered.

My second reason for breaking it into those steps is to try to help make it clear that the meanings can flow in different directions; that is, in gender discourse, men and women are supposed to exemplify the characteristics on the lists. It also works in reverse, however; to evidence any of these characteristics—to be abstract, logical or dispassionate, for example—is not simply to be those things, but also to be manly. And to be manly is not simply to be manly, but also to be in the more highly valued position in the discourse. In other words, to exhibit a trait on that list is not neutral—it is not simply displaying some basic human characteristic. It also positions you in a discourse of gender. It associates you with a particular gender, and also with a higher or lower valuation.

In stressing that this is a *symbolic* system, I want first to emphasize that while real women and men do not really fit these gender "ideals," the existence of this system of meaning affects all of us, nonetheless. Whether we want to or not, we see ourselves and others against its templates, we interpret our own and others' actions against it. A man who cries easily cannot avoid in some way confronting that he is likely to be seen as less than fully manly. A woman who is very aggressive and incisive may enjoy that quality in herself, but the fact of her aggressiveness does not exist by itself; she cannot avoid having her own and others' perceptions of that quality of hers, the meaning it has for people, being in some way mediated by the discourse of gender. Or, a different kind of example: Why does it mean one thing when George Bush gets teary-eyed in public, and something entirely different when Patricia Shroeder does? The same act is viewed through the lens of gender and is seen to mean two very different things.

Second, as gender discourse assigns gender to human characteristics, we can think of the discourse as something we are positioned *by*. If I say, for example, that a corporation should stop dumping toxic waste because it is damaging the creations of mother earth, (i.e., articulating a valuing and sentimental vision of nature), I am speaking in a manner associated with women, and our cultural discourse of gender positions me as female. As such I am then associated with the whole constellation of traits—irrational, emotional, subjective, and so forth—and I am in the devalued position. If, on the other hand, I say the corporation should stop dumping toxic wastes because I have calculated that it is causing \$8.215 billion of damage to eight non-renewable resources, which should be seen as equivalent to lowering the GDP by 0.15 percent per annum, (i.e., using a rational, calculative mode of thought), the discourse positions me as masculine—rational, objective, logical, and so forth—the dominant, valued position.

But if we are positioned *by* discourses, we can also take different positions *within* them. Although I am female, and this would "naturally" fall into the devalued term, I can choose to "speak like a man"—to be hard-nosed, realistic,

unsentimental, dispassionate. Jeanne Kirkpatrick is a formidable example. While we can choose a position in a discourse, however, it means something different for a woman to "speak like a man" than for a man to do so. It is heard differently.

One other note about my use of the term *gender discourse*: I am using it in the general sense to refer to the phenomenon of symbolically organizing the world in these gender-associated opposites. I do not mean to suggest that there is a single discourse defining a single set of gender ideals. In fact, there are many specific discourses of gender, which vary by race, class, ethnicity, locale, sexuality, nationality, and other factors. The masculinity idealized in the gender discourse of new Haitian immigrants is in some ways different from that of sixth-generation white Anglo-Saxon Protestant business executives, and both differ somewhat from that of white-male defense intellectuals and security analysts. One version of masculinity is mobilized and enforced in the armed forces in order to enable men to fight wars, while a somewhat different version of masculinity is drawn upon and expressed by abstract theoreticians of war.[6]

Let us now return to the physicist who felt like a woman: what happened when he "blurted out" his sudden awareness of the "only thirty million" dead people? First, he was transgressing a code of professional conduct. In the civilian defense intellectuals' world, when you are in professional settings you do not discuss the bloody reality behind the calculations. It is not required that you be completely unaware of them in your outside life, or that you have no feelings about them, but it is required that you do not bring them to the foreground in the context of professional activities. There is a general awareness that you *could not* do your work if you did; in addition, most defense intellectuals believe that emotion and description of human reality distort the process required to think well about nuclear weapons and warfare.

So the physicist violated a behavioral norm, in and of itself a difficult thing to do because it threatens your relationships to and your standing with your colleagues.

But even worse than that, he demonstrated some of the characteristics on the "female" side of the dichotomies—in his "blurting" he was impulsive, uncontrolled, emotional, concrete, and attentive to human bodies, at the very least. Thus, he marked himself not only as unprofessional but as feminine, and this, in turn, was doubly threatening. It was not only a threat to his own sense of self as masculine, his gender identity, it also identified him with a devalued status—of a woman—or put him in the devalued or subordinate position in the discourse.

Thus, both his statement, "I felt like a woman," and his subsequent silence in that and other settings are completely understandable. To have the strength of character and courage to transgress the strictures of both professional and gender codes *and* to associate yourself with a lower status is very difficult.

This story is not simply about one individual, his feelings and actions; it is about the role of gender discourse. The impact of gender discourse in that room (and countless others like it) is that some things get left out. Certain ideas, concerns, interests, information, feelings, and meanings are marked in national security discourse as feminine, and are devalued. They are therefore, first, very difficult to *speak*, as exemplified by the physicist who felt like a woman. And second, they are very difficult to *hear*, to take in and work with seriously, even if they *are* said. For the others in the room, the way in which the physicist's comments were marked as female and devalued served to delegitimate them. It is almost as though they had become an accidental excrescence in the middle of the room. Embarrassed politeness demanded that they be ignored.

I must stress that this is not simply the product of the idiosyncratic personal composition of that particular room. In other professional settings, I have experienced the feeling that something terribly important is being left out and must be spoken; and yet, it has felt almost physically impossible to utter the words, almost as

though they could not be pushed out into the smooth, cool, opaque air of the room.

What is it that cannot be spoken? First, any words that express an emotional awareness of the desperate human reality behind the sanitized abstractions of death and destruction—as in the physicist's sudden vision of thirty million rotting corpses. Similarly, weapons' effects may be spoken of only in the most clinical and abstract terms, leaving no room to imagine a seven-year-old boy with his flesh melting away from his bones or a toddler with her skin hanging down in strips. Voicing concern about the number of casualties in the enemy's armed forces, imagining the suffering of the killed and wounded young men, is out of bounds. (Within the military itself, it is permissible, even desirable, to attempt to minimize immediate civilian casualties if it is possible to do so without compromising military objectives, but as we learned in the Persian Gulf War, this is only an extremely limited enterprise; the planning and precision of military targeting does not admit of consideration of the cost in human lives of such actions as destroying power systems, or water and sewer systems, or highways and food distribution systems.)[7] Psychological effects—on the soldiers fighting the war or on the citizens injured, or fearing for their own safety, or living through tremendous deprivation, or helplessly watching their babies die from diarrhea due to the lack of clean water—all of these are not to be talked about.

But it is not only particular subjects that are out of bounds. It is also tone of voice that counts. A speaking style that is identified as cool, dispassionate, and distanced is required. One that vibrates with the intensity of emotion almost always disqualifies the speaker, who is heard to sound like "a hysterical housewife."

What gets left out, then, is the emotional, the concrete, the particular, the human bodies and their vulnerability, human lives and their subjectivity—all of which are marked as feminine in the binary dichotomies of gender discourse. In other words, gender discourse informs and shapes nuclear and national security discourse, and in so doing creates silences and absences. It keeps things out of the room, unsaid, and keeps them ignored if they manage to get in. As such, it degrades our ability to think *well* and *fully* about nuclear weapons and national security, and shapes and limits the possible outcomes of our deliberations.

What becomes clear, then, is that defense intellectuals' standards of what constitutes "good thinking" about weapons and security have not simply evolved out of trial and error; it is not that the history of nuclear discourse has been filled with exploration of other ideas, concerns, interests, information, questions, feelings, meanings and stances which were then found to create distorted or poor thought. It is that these options have been *preempted* by gender discourse, and by the feelings evoked by living up to or transgressing gender codes.

To borrow a term from defense intellectuals, you might say that gender discourse becomes a "preemptive deterrent" to certain kinds of thought.

Let me give you another example of what I mean—another story, this one my own experience:

One Saturday morning I, two other women, and about fifty-five men gathered to play a war game designed by the RAND Corporation.[8] Our "controllers" (the people running the game) first divided us up into three sets of teams; there would be three simultaneous games being played, each pitting a Red Team against a Blue Team (I leave the reader to figure out which color represents which country). All three women were put onto the same team, a Red Team.

The teams were then placed in different rooms so that we had no way of communicating with each other, except through our military actions (or lack of them) or by sending demands and responses to those demands via the controllers. There was no way to negotiate or to take actions other than military ones. (This was supposed to simulate reality.) The controllers then presented us with maps and pages covered with numbers representing each side's forces. We were also given a "scenario," a situation of escalating tensions and military conflicts, starting in the Middle East and spreading to Central Europe. We were to decide what to do, the controllers would go back and forth between the two teams to relate the other team's actions, and periodically the controllers themselves would add something that would ratchet up the conflict—an announcement of an "intercepted intelligence report" from the other side, the authenticity of which we had no way of judging.

Our Red Team was heavily into strategizing, attacking ground forces, and generally playing war. We also, at one point, decided that we were going to pull our troops out of Afghanistan, reasoning it was bad for us to have them there and that the Afghanis had the right to self-determination. At another point we removed some troops from Eastern Europe. I must add that later on my team was accused of being wildly "unrealistic," that this group of experts found the idea that the Soviet Union might voluntarily choose to pull troops out of Afghanistan and Eastern Europe so utterly absurd. (It was about six months before Gorbachev actually did the same thing.)

Gradually our game escalated to nuclear war. The Blue Team used tactical nuclear weapons against our troops, but our Red Team decided, initially at least, against nuclear retaliation. When the game ended (at the end of the allotted time) our Red Team had "lost the war" (meaning that we had political control over less territory than we had started with, although our homeland had remained completely unviolated and our civilian population safe).

In the debriefing afterwards, all six teams returned to one room and reported on their games. Since we had had absolutely no way to know why the other team had taken any of its actions, we now had the opportunity to find out what they had been thinking. A member of the team that had played against us said, "Well, when he took his troops out of Afghanistan, I knew he was weak and I could push him around. And then, when we nuked him and he didn't nuke us back, I knew he was just such a wimp, I could take him for everything he's got and I nuked him again. He just wimped out."

There are many different possible comments to make at this point. I will restrict myself to a couple. First, when the man from the Blue Team called me a wimp (which is what it felt like for each of us on the Red Team—a personal accusation), I felt silenced. My reality, the careful reasoning that had gone into my strategic and tactical choices, the intelligence, the politics, the morality—all of it just disappeared, completely invalidated. I could not explain the reasons for my actions, could not protest, "Wait, you idiot, I didn't do it because I was weak, I did it because it made *sense* to do it that way, given my understandings of strategy and tactics, history and politics, my goals and my values." The protestation would be met with knowing sneers. In this discourse, the coding of an act as wimpish is hegemonic. Its emotional heat and resonance is like a bath of sulfuric acid: it erases everything else.

"Acting like a wimp" is an *interpretation* of a person's acts (or, in national security discourse, a country's acts, an important distinction I will return to later). As with any other interpretation, it is a selection of one among many possible different ways to understand something—once the selection is made, the other possibilities recede into invisibility. In national security discourse, "acting like a wimp," being insufficiently masculine, is one of the most readily available interpretive codes. (You do not need to do participant observation in a community of defense intellectuals to know this—just look at the "geopolitical analyses" in the media and on Capitol Hill of the way in which George Bush's military intervention in Panama and the Persian Gulf War finally allowed him to beat the "wimp factor.") You learn that someone is being a wimp if he perceives an international crisis as very dangerous and urges caution; if he thinks it might not be important to have just as many weapons that are just as big as the other guy's; if he suggests that an attack should not necessarily be answered by an even more destructive counterattack; or, until

recently, if he suggested that making unilateral arms reductions might be useful for our own security.[9] All of these are "wimping out."

The prevalence of this particular interpretive code is another example of how gender discourse affects the quality of thinking within the national security community, first, because, as in the case of the physicist who "felt like a woman," it is internalized to become a self-censor; there are things professionals simply will not *say* in groups, options they simply will not argue nor write about, because they know that to do so is to brand themselves as wimps. Thus, a whole range of inputs is left out, a whole series of options is foreclosed from their deliberations.

Equally, if not more damagingly, is the way in which this interpretive coding not only limits what is *said*, but even limits what is *thought*. "He's a wimp" is a phrase that *stops* thought.[10] When we were playing the game, once my opponent on the Blue Team "recognized the fact that I was a wimp," that is, once he interpreted my team's actions through the lens of this common interpretive code in national security discourse, he *stopped thinking*; he stopped looking for ways to understand what we were doing. He did not ask, "Why on earth would the Red Team do that? What does it tell me about them, about their motives and purposes and goals and capabilities? What does it tell me about their possible understandings of *my* actions, or of the situation they're in?" or any other of the many questions that might have enabled him to revise his own conception of the situation or perhaps achieve his goals at a far lower level of violence and destruction. Here, again, gender discourse acts as a preemptive deterrent to thought.

"Wimp" is, of course, not the only gendered pejorative used in the national security community; "pussy" is another popular epithet, conjoining the imagery of harmless domesticated (read demasculinized) pets with contemptuous reference to women's genitals. In an informal setting, an analyst worrying about the other side's casualties, for example, might be asked, "What kind of pussy are you, anyway?" It need not happen more than once or twice before everyone gets the message; they quickly learn not to raise the issue in their discussions. Attention to and care for the living, suffering, and dying of human beings (in this case, soldiers and their families and friends) is again banished from the discourse through the expedient means of gender-bashing.

Other words are also used to impugn someone's masculinity and, in the process, to delegitimate his position and avoid thinking seriously about it. "Those Krauts are a bunch of limp-dicked wimps" was the way one U.S. defense intellectual dismissed the West German politicians who were concerned about popular opposition to Euromissile deployments.[12] I have heard our NATO allies referred to as "the Euro-fags" when they disagreed with American policy on such issues as the Contra War or the bombing of Libya. Labeling them "fags" is an effective strategy; it immediately dismisses and trivializes their opposition to U.S. policy by coding it as due to inadequate masculinity. In other words, the American analyst need not seriously confront the Europeans' arguments, since the Europeans' doubts about U.S. policy obviously stem not from their reasoning but from the "fact" that they "just don't have the stones for war." Here, again, gender discourse deters thought.

"Fag" imagery is not, of course, confined to the professional community of security analysts; it also appears in popular "political" discourse. The Gulf War was replete with examples. American derision of Saddam Hussein included bumper stickers that read "Saddam, Bend Over." American soldiers reported that the "U.S.A." stenciled on their uniforms stood for "Up Saddam's Ass." A widely reprinted cartoon, surely one of the most multiply offensive that came out of the war, depicted Saddam bowing down in the Islamic posture of prayer, with a huge U.S. missile, approximately five times the size of the prostrate figure, about to penetrate his upraised bottom. Over and over, defeat for the Iraqis was portrayed as humiliating anal penetration by the more powerful and manly United States.

Within the defense community discourse, manliness is equated not only with the ability to win a war (or to "prevail," as some like to say when talking about nuclear war); it is also equated with the willingness (which they would call courage) to threaten and use force. During the Carter administration, for example, a well-known academic security affairs specialist was quoted as saying that "under Jimmy Carter the United States is spreading its legs for the Soviet Union."[13] Once this image is evoked, how does rational discourse about the value of U.S. policy proceed?

In 1989 and 1990, as Gorbachev presided over the withdrawal of Soviet forces from Eastern Europe, I heard some defense analysts sneeringly say things like, "They're a bunch of pussies for pulling out of Eastern Europe." This is extraordinary. Here they were, men who for years railed against Soviet domination of Eastern Europe. You would assume that if they were politically and ideologically consistent, if they were rational, they would be applauding the Soviet actions. Yet in their informal conversations, it was not their rational analyses that dominated their response, but the fact that for them, the decision for war, the willingness to use force, is cast as a question of masculinity—not prudence, thoughtfulness, efficacy, "rational" cost-benefit calculation, or morality, but masculinity.

In the fact of this equation, genuine political discourse disappears. One more example: After Iraq invaded Kuwait and President Bush hastily sent U.S. forces to Saudi Arabia, there was a period in which the Bush administration struggled to find a convincing political justification for U.S. military involvement and the security affairs community debated the political merit of U.S. intervention.[14] Then Bush set the deadline, January 16, high noon at the OK Corral, and as the day approached conversations changed. More of these centered on the question compellingly articulated by one defense intellectual as "Does George Bush have the stones for war?"[15] This, too, is utterly extraordinary. This was a time when crucial political questions abounded: Can the sanctions work if given more time? Just what vital interests does the United States actually have at stake? What would be the goals of military intervention? Could they be accomplished by other means? Is the difference between what sanctions might accomplish and what military violence might accomplish worth the greater cost in human suffering, human lives, even dollars? What will the long-term effects on the people of the region be? On the ecology? Given the apparent successes of Gorbachev's last-minute diplomacy and Hussein's series of nearly daily small concessions, can and should Bush put off the deadline? Does he have the strength to let another leader play a major role in solving the problem? Does he have the political flexibility to not fight, or is he hell-bent on war at all costs? And so on, ad infinitum. All of these disappear in the sulfuric acid test of the size of Mr. Bush's private parts.[16]

I want to return to the RAND war simulation story to make one other observation. First, it requires a true confession: *I was stung by being called a wimp*. Yes, I thought the remark was deeply inane, and it infuriated me. But even so, I was also stung. Let me hasten to add, this was not because my identity is very wrapped up with not being wimpish—it actually is not a term that normally figures very heavily in my self-image one way or the other. But it was impossible to be in that room, hear his comment and the snickering laughter with which it was met, and not to feel stung, and humiliated.

Why? There I was, a woman and a feminist, not only contemptuous of the mentality that measures human beings by their degree of so-called wimpishness, but also someone for whom the term *wimp* does not have a deeply resonant personal meaning. How could it have affected me so much?

The answer lies in the role of the context within which I was experiencing myself—the discursive framework. For in that room I was not "simply me," but I was a participant in a discourse, a shared set of words, concepts, symbols that constituted not only the linguistic possibilities available to us but also constituted *me* in that situation. This is not entirely true, of course.

How I experienced myself was at least partly shaped by other experiences and other discursive frameworks—certainly those of feminist politics and antimilitarist politics; in fact, I would say my reactions were predominantly shaped by those frameworks. But that is quite different from saying "I am a feminist, and that individual, psychological self simply moves encapsulated through the world being itself"—and therefore assuming that I am unaffected. No matter who else I was at that moment, I was unavoidably a participant in a discourse in which being a wimp has a meaning, and a deeply pejorative one at that. By calling me a wimp, my accuser on the Blue Team *positioned* me in that discourse, and I could not but feel the sting.

In other words, I am suggesting that national security discourse can be seen as having different positions within it—ones that are starkly gender coded; indeed, the enormous strength of their evocative power comes from gender.[17] Thus, when you participate in conversation in that community, you do not simply choose what to say and how to say it; you advertently or inadvertently choose a position in the discourse. As a woman, I can choose the "masculine" (though, rational, logical) position. If I do, I am seen as legitimate, but I limit what I can say. Or, I can say things that place me in the "feminine" position—in which case no one will listen to me.

Finally, I would like to briefly explore a phenomenon I call the "unitary masculine actor problem" in national security discourse. During the Persian Gulf War, many feminists probably noticed that both the military briefers and George Bush himself frequently used the singular masculine pronoun "he" when referring to Iraq and Iraq's army. Someone not listening carefully could simply assume that "he" referred to Saddam Hussein. Sometimes it did; much of the time it simply reflected the defense community's characteristic habit of calling opponents "he" or "the other guy."[18] A battalion commander, for example, was quoted as saying "Saddam knows where we are and we know where he is. We will move a lot now to keep him off guard."[19] In these sentences, "he" and "him" appear to refer to Saddam Hussein. But, of course, the American forces had *no idea* where Saddam Hussein himself was; the singular masculine pronouns are actually being used to refer to the Iraqi military.

This linguistic move, frequently heard in discussions within the security affairs and defense communities, turns a complex state and set of forces into a singular male opponents. In fact, discussions that purport to be serious explorations of the strategy and tactics of war can have a tone which sounds more like the story of a sporting match, a fistfight, or a personal vendetta.

> *I would want to suck him out into the desert as far as I could, and then pound him to death.*[20]

> *Once we had taken out his eyes, we did what could be best described as the "Hail Mary play" in football.*[21]

> *[I]f the adversary decides to embark on a very high roll, because he's frightened that something even worse is in the works, does grabbing him by the scruff of the neck and slapping him up the side of the head, does that make him behave better or is it plausible that it makes him behave even worse?*[22]

Most defense intellectuals would claim that using "he" is just a convenient shorthand, without significant import or effects. I believe, however, that the effects of this usage are many and the implications far-reaching. Here I will sketch just a few, starting first with the usage throughout defense discourse generally, and then coming back to the Gulf War in particular.

The use of "he" distorts the analyst's understanding of the opposing state and the conflict in which they are engaged. When the analyst refers to the opposing state as "he" or "the other guy," the image evoked is that of a person, a unitary actor; yet states are not people. Nor are they unitary and unified. They comprise complex, multifaceted governmental and military apparatuses, each with opposing forces within it, each, in turn, with its own internal institutional dynamics, its own varied needs in relation to domestic politics, and so on. In other words, if the state is referred to and pictured as a unitary actor, what becomes

unavailable to the analyst and policy-maker is a series of much more complex truths that might enable him to imagine many more policy options, many more ways to interact with that state.

If one kind of distortion of the state results from the image of the state as a person, a unitary actor, another can be seen to stem from the image of the state as a specifically *male* actor.[23] Although states are almost uniformly run by men, states are not men; they are complex social institutions, and they act and react as such. Yet, when "he" and "the other guy" are used to refer to states, the words do not simply function as shorthand codes; instead, they have their own entailments, including assumptions about how men act, which just might be different from how states act, but which invisibly become assumed to be isomorphic with how states act.[24]

It also entails emotional responses on the part of the speaker. The reference to the opposing state as "he" evokes male competitive identity issues, as in, "I'm not going to let him push me around," or, "I'm not going to let him get the best of me." While these responses may or may not be adaptive for a barroom brawl, it is probably safe to say that they are less functional when trying to determine the best way for one state to respond to another state. Defense analysts and foreign policy experts can usually agree upon the supreme desirability of dispassionate, logical analysis and its ensuing rationally calculated action. Yet the emotions evoked by the portrayal of global conflict in the personalized terms of male competition must, at the very least, exert a strong pull in exactly the opposite direction.

A third problem is that even while the use of "he" acts to personalize the conflict, it simultaneously abstracts both the opponent and the war itself. That is, the use of "he" functions in very much the same way that discussions about "Red" and "Blue" do. It facilitates treating war within a kind of game-playing model, A against B, Red against Blue, he against me. For even while "he" is evocative of male identity issues, it is also just an abstract piece to moved around on a game board, or, more appropriately, a computer screen.

That tension between personalization and abstraction was striking in Gulf War discourse. In the Gulf War, not only was "he" frequently used to refer to the Iraqi military, but so was "Saddam," as in "Saddam really took a pounding today," or "Our goal remains the same: to liberate Kuwait by forcing Saddam Hussein out."[25] The personalization is obvious: in this locution, the U.S. armed forces are not destroying a nation, killing people; instead, they (or George) are giving Saddam a good pounding, or bodily removing him from where he does not belong. Our emotional response is to get fired up about a bully getting his comeuppance.

Yet this personalization, this conflation of Iraq and Iraqi forces with Saddam himself, also abstracts: it functions to substitute in the mind's eye the abstraction of an implacably, impeccably evil enemy for the particular human beings, the men, women, and children being pounded, burned, torn, and eviscerated. A cartoon image of Saddam being ejected from Kuwait preempts the image of the blackened, charred, decomposing bodies of nineteen-year-old boys tossed in ditches by the side of the road, and the other concrete images of the acts of violence that constitute "forcing Hussein [*sic*] out of Kuwait."[26] Paradoxical as it may seem, in personalizing the Iraqi army as Saddam, the individual human beings in Iraq were abstracted out of existence.[27]

In summary, I have been exploring the way in which defense intellectuals talk to each other—the comments they make to each other, the particular usages that appear in their informal conversations or their lectures. In addition, I have occasionally left the professional community to draw upon public talk about the Gulf War. My analysis does *not* lead me to conclude that "national security thinking is masculine"—that is, a separate, and different, discussion. Instead, I have tried to show that national security discourse is gendered, and that it matters. Gender discourse is interwoven through national security discourse. It sets fixed boundaries, and in so doing, it skews what is discussed and how it is thought about. It shapes expectations of other nations' actions, and in so doing it affects both our interpretations of international events and conceptions of how the United States should respond.

In a world where professionals pride themselves on their ability to engage in cool, rational, objective calculation while others around them are letting their thinking be sullied by emotion, the unacknowledged interweaving of gender discourse in security discourse allows men to not acknowledge that their pristine rational thought is in fact riddled with emotional response. In an "objective" "universal" discourse that valorizes the "masculine" and deauthorizes the "feminine," it is only the "feminine" emotions that are noticed and labeled as emotions, and thus in need of banning from the analytic process. "Masculine" emotions—such as feelings of aggression, competition, macho pride and swagger, or the sense of identity resting on carefully defended borders—are not so easily noticed and identified as emotions, and are instead invisibly folded into "self-evident," so-called realist paradigms and analyses. It is both the interweaving of gender discourse in national security thinking *and* the blindness to its presence and impact that have deleterious effects. Finally, the impact is to distort, degrade, and deter roundly rational, fully complex thought within the community of defense intellectuals and national security elites and, by extension, to cripple democratic deliberation about crucial matters of war and peace.

NOTES

I am grateful to the John D. and Catherine T. MacArthur Foundation and the Ploughshares Fund for their generous support of my research, and for making the writing of this chapter possible. I wish to thank Sara Ruddick, Elaine Scarry, Sandra Harding, and Barry O'Neill for their careful readings; I regret only that I was not able to more fully incorporate their criticisms and suggestions. Grateful appreciation is due to several thoughtful informants within the defense intellectual community. This chapter was written while I was a fellow at the Bunting Institute, and I wish to thank my sister-fellows for their feedback and support.

1. A "counterforce attack" refers to an attack in which the targets are the opponent's weapons systems, command and control centers, and military leadership. It is in contrast to what is known as a "countervalue attack," which is the abstractly benign term for *targeting* and incinerating cities—what the United States did to Hiroshima, except that the bombs used today would be several hundred times more powerful. It is also known in the business, a bit more colorfully, as an "all-out city-busting exchange." Despite this careful targeting distinction, one need not be too astute to notice that many of the ports, airports, and command posts destroyed in a counter*force* attack are, in fact, in cities or metropolitan areas, which would be destroyed along with the "real targets," the weapons systems. But this does not appear to make the distinction any less meaningful to war planners, although it is, in all likelihood, less than meaningful to the victims.

2. The term is Helen Caldicott's, from her book *Missile Envy: The Arms Race and Nuclear War* (New York: William Morrow, 1984).

3. I have addressed some of these other factors in: "Sex and Death in the Rational World of Defense Intellectuals," *Signs: Journal of Women in Culture and Society* 12, no. 4 (Summer 1987): 687–718; "Emasculating America's Linguistic Deterrent," in *Rocking the Ship of State: Towards a Feminist Peace Politics*, ed. Adrienne Harris and Ynestra King (Boulder, Colo.: Westview Press, 1989); and *Deconstructing National Security Discourse and Reconstructing Security* (working title, book manuscript).

4. Some of the material I analyze in this paper comes from the public utterances of civilian defense intellectuals and military leaders. But overtly gendered war discourse appears even more frequently in informal settings, such as conversations defense intellectuals have among themselves, rather than in their formal written papers. Hence, much of my data comes from participant observation, and from interviews in which men have been willing to share with me interactions and responses that are usually not part of the public record. Most often, they shared this information on the condition that it not be attributed, and I have respected their requests. I also feel strongly that "naming names" would be misleading to the extent that it would tend to encourage the reader to locate the problem within individual men and their particular psyches; in this paper I am arguing that it is crucial to see this as a cultural phenomenon, rather than a psychological one.

5. For a revealing exploration of the ways in which gender shapes international politics more generally, see Cynthia Enloe, *Bananas, Beaches and Bases: Making Feminist Sense of International Politics* (Berkeley: University of California Press, 1989).

6. See Cynthia Enloe, *Does Khaki Become You? The Militarization of Women's Lives* (London and Winchester, Mass.: Pandora Press, 1988); and Jean Elshtain, "Reflections on War and Political Discourse: Realism, Just War and Feminism in a Nuclear Age," *Political Theory* 3, no. 1 (February 1985): 39–57.

7. While both the military and the news media presented the picture of a "surgically clean" war in which only military targets were destroyed, the reality was significantly bloodier; it involved the mass slaughter of Iraqi soldiers, as well as the death and suffering of large numbers of noncombatant men, women, and children. Although it is not possible to know the numbers of casualties with certainty, one analyst in the Census Bureau, Beth Osborne Daponte, has estimated that 40,000 Iraqi soldiers and 13,000 civilians were killed in direct military conflict, that 30,000 civilians died during Shiite and Kurdish rebellions, and that 70,000 civilians have died from health problems caused by the destruction of water and power plants (Edmund L. Andrews, "Census Bureau to Dismiss Analyst Who Estimated Iraqi Casualties," *New York Times*, March 7, 1992, A7). Other estimates are significantly higher. Greenpeace estimates that as many as 243,000 Iraqi civilians died due to war-related causes (Ray Wilkinson, "Back from the Living Dead," *Newsweek*, January 20, 1992, 28). Another estimate places Iraqi troop casualties at 70,000 and estimates that over 100,000 children have died from the delayed effects of the war (Peter Rothenberg, "The Invisible Dead," *Lies of Our Times* [March 1992]: 7). For recent, detailed reports on civilian casualties, see *Health and Welfare in Iraq after the Gulf Crisis* (International Study Team/Commission on Civilian Casualties, Human Rights Program, Harvard Law School, October 1991), and *Needless Deaths in the Gulf War* (Middle East Watch, 1992). For a useful corrective to the myth of the Gulf War as a war of surgical strikes and precision-guided weaponry, see Paul F. Walker and

Eric Stambler, "The Surgical Myth of the Gulf War," *Boston Globe*, April 16, 1991; and ". . . And the Dirty Little Weapons," *Bulletin of the Atomic Scientists* (May 1991): 21–24.

8. The RAND Corporation is a think tank that is a U.S. Air Force subcontractor. In the 1950s many of the most important nuclear strategists did their work under RAND auspices, including Bernard Brodie, Albert Wohlstetter, Herman Kahn, and Thomas Schelling.

9. In the context of the nuclear arms race and the cold war, even though a defense analyst might acknowledge that some American weapon systems served no useful strategic function (such as the Titan missiles during the 1980s), there was still consensus that they should not be unilaterally cut. Such a cut was seen to be bad because it was throwing away a potential bargaining chip in future arms control negotiations, or because making unilateral cuts was viewed as a sign of weakness and lack of resolve. It is only outside that context of hostile superpower competition, and, in fact, after the dissolution of the Soviet threat, that President Bush has responded to Gorbachev's unilateral cuts with some (minor) American unilateral cuts. For a description and critical assessment of the arguments against unilateral cuts, see William Rose, *US Unilateral Arms Control Initiatives: When Do They Work?* (New York: Greenwood Press, 1988). For an analysis of the logic and utility of bargaining chips, see Robert J. Bresler and Robert C. Gray, "The Bargaining Chip and SALT," *Political Science Quarterly* 92, no. 1 (Spring 1977): 65–88.

10. For a discussion of how words and phrases can stop the thought process, see George Orwell, "Politics and the English Language," in *A Collection of Essays* (Garden City, N.Y.: Doubleday, 1954): 162–76.

11. Cohn, unattributed interview, Cambridge, Mass., July 15, 1991.

12. Ibid.

13. Ibid., July 20, 1991.

14. The Bush White House tried out a succession of revolving justifications in an attempt to find one that would garner popular support for U.S. military action, including: we must respond to the rape of Kuwait; we must not let Iraqi aggression be rewarded; we must defend Saudi Arabia; we cannot stand by while "vital U.S. interests" are threatened; we must establish a "new world order"; we must keep down the price of oil at U.S. gas pumps; we must protect American jobs; and finally, the winner, the only one that elicited any

real support from the American public, we must destroy Iraq's incipient nuclear weapons capability. What was perhaps most surprising about this was the extent to which it was publicly discussed and accepted as George Bush's need to find a message that "worked" rather than to actually have a genuine, meaningful explanation. For an account of Bush's decision making about the Gulf War, see Bob Woodward, *The Commanders* (New York: Simon and Schuster, 1991).

15. Cohn, unattributed interview, Cambridge, Mass., July 20, 1991.

16. Within the context of our society's dominant gender discourse, this equation of masculinity and strength with the willingness to use armed force seems quite "natural" and not particularly noteworthy. Hannah Arendt is one political thinker who makes the arbitrariness of that connection visible: she reframes our thinking about "strength," and finds strength in *refraining* from using one's armed forces (Hannah Arendt, *On Violence* [New York: Harcourt, Brace, Jovanovich, 1969]).

17. My thinking about the importance of positions in discourses is indebted to Wendy Hollway, "Gender Difference and the Production of Subjectivity," in *Changing the Subject*, ed. J. Henriques, W. Holloway, C. Urwin, C. Venn, and V. Walkerdine (London and New York: Methuen, 1984): 227–63.

18. For a revealing exploration of the convention in strategic, military, and political writings of redescribing armies as a single "embodied combatant," see Elaine Scarry, *The Body in Pain: The Making and Unmaking of the World* (New York: Oxford University Press, 1984): 70–72.

19. Chris Hedges, "War Is Vivid in the Gun Sights of the Sniper," *New York Times*, February 3, 1991, A1.

20. General Norman Schwarzkopf, National Public Radio broadcast, February 8, 1991.

21. General Norman Schwarzkopf, CENTCOM News Briefing, Riyadh, Saudi Arabia, February 27, 1991, p. 2.

22. Transcript of a strategic studies specialist's lecture on NATO and the Warsaw Pact (summer institute on Regional Conflict and Global Security: The Nuclear Dimension, Madison, Wisconsin, June 29, 1987).

23. Several analysts of international relations have commented upon the way in which "the state is a person" in international relations theory and in war discourse. For example, Paul Chilton and George Lakoff, distinguished linguists who study war, offer very use-

ful explorations of the impact of the state-as-a-person metaphor on the way in which we understand the Persian Gulf War. Yet neither of them find it noteworthy that the state is not simply any person, but a *male* person. See Paul Chilton, "Getting the Message Through: Metaphor and Legitimation of the Gulf War" (unpublished paper, 1991); George Lakoff, "The Metaphor System Used to Justify War in the Gulf" (unpublished paper, 1991).

24. For a lucid and compelling discussion of why it is an error to assume an isomorphism between the behavior and motivations of individuals and the behavior and motivations of states, see Marshall Sahlins, *The Use and Abuse of Biology* (Ann Arbor: University of Michigan Press, 1977), pp. ix–xv and 3–16.

25. Defense Secretary Dick Cheney, "Excerpts from Briefing at Pentagon by Cheney and Powell," *New York Times*, January 24, 1991, A 11.

26. Scarry explains that when an army is described as a single "embodied combatant," injury, (as in Saddam's "pounding"), may be referred to but is "no longer recognizable or interpretable." It is not only that Americans might be happy to imagine Saddam being pounded; we also on some level know that it is not really happening, and thus need not feel the pain of the wounded. We "respond to the injury . . . as an imaginary wound to an imaginary body, despite the fact that that imaginary body is itself made up of thousands of real human bodies" (Scarry, *Body in Pain*, p. 72).

27. For a further exploration of the disappearance of human bodies from Gulf War discourse, see Hugh Gusterson, "Nuclear War, the Gulf War, and the Disappearing Body" (unpublished paper, 1991). I have addressed other aspects of Gulf War discourse in "The Language of the Gulf War," *Center Review* 5, no. 2 (Fall 1991); "Decoding Military Newspeak," *Ms.*, March/April 1991, p. 81; and "Language, Gender, and the Gulf War" (unpublished paper prepared for Harvard University Center for Literary and Cultural Studies, April 10, 1991).

"SISSY" WARRIORS VS. "REAL" MEN
A PERSPECTIVE ON GAYS IN THE MILITARY

RICHARD RODRIGUEZ

It was easy for Americans to tolerate homosexuals as long as homosexuals were sissies. It is another matter altogether for many American heterosexuals to accept the very idea of sissy warriors.

All week, the bald and the bellied politicians, paragons of heterosexual propriety, worried the issue. The President was moving too fast, they said. What would happen on an aircraft carrier six months at sea? What would happen in the shower room? Would homosexual soldiers in combat be able to concentrate on killing if they were, otherwise, in love?

For most of the week, it was mainly male voices one heard. The issue of "allowing" homosexuals into the military involves both gays and lesbians.

But it was no coincidence that most of the talk centered on the homosexual male. The gay male is more upsetting to heterosexual America, always has been. He violates the cult of the male in a country that has always been more male than female in its ethos.

A woman doesn't get upset at being taken for a lesbian; it's more threatening for a woman to be told she is frigid. Ask a heterosexual male, by contrast, if he's gay, and he's likely to get very angry.

It is easier to be a tomboy in America than a sissy. Papa loves his tomboy daughter, with her soiled jeans and messed-up hair. She flatters him. Papa loathes his sissy son who goes to musical comedies with Mama.

The U.S. military could accept the notion of women in the ranks long before it ever dared imagine gays in the barracks. And though Americans are hesitant today about allowing women into combat, the notion of the sissy warrior is more profoundly disturbing.

So there they were, the thin and worried voices on the radio call-in shows. Many of these were the same people who, during the Vietnam years, blithely mocked anti-war protestors as "draft dodgers." All this week they were in the embarrassing position of having to criticize homosexuals for wanting to fight and die for their country.

Here is exactly the problem: If the sissy is, after all, a warrior, then he is as brave and as "male" as we always thought the heterosexual was.

And what does the sissy in arms tell us about the super-patriotic right-wing pinups like Rush Limbaugh or Patrick Buchanan who, for one reason or another, never enlisted?

Pity the insecure heterosexual male this week. Pity the heterosexual who grew up with the notion that he was the predator. In his mythic scheme of things, wasn't this always the truth? He was the one who went out and stalked the beasts in the forest. He was the one who protected the hearth and protected his family. In return, it was his prerogative to play the predator in matters of sex.

144

Poor Papa! Poor twice-divorced Rush Limbaugh! The last few years have not been easy ones.

Mama doesn't want to play Mommy anymore. She has a better job than Papa—she makes more money. The kids are, meanwhile, crossing sexual borders. The daughter is a better mechanic than Papa. The son shaves his legs.

These years of feminism have not been easy ones for the insecure heterosexual male. Which is why he needed the idea of the sissy, the reminder of the sissy—all pink and flowery—to laugh at. He needed the sissy to stay in the pretty closet.

Everyone knows that there are gays in the military. The question this week has been one of simply whether we want to acknowledge reality. Please stay in the closet, the insecure heterosexuals are pleading; we don't want to deal with the fact of your existence.

The notion of the sissy warrior challenges the illusion that Papa has always had about himself. For here was a sissy as predator, stalking the forest, defending the American household. Which is why, too, the discussion among men in Congress turned finally to shower stalls.

The insecure heterosexual shuddered at the prospect that he would no longer be the active sexual agent. (What had always bothered heterosexuals about homosexuals, of course, had been their promiscuity and sexual aggressiveness—the very things Papa assumed for himself.)

The Joint Chiefs of Staff put on their pretty ribbons and medals and posed glumly for photos this week, looking like Victorian fathers. Senators echoed in the marble halls: The President must slow down. We need to have congressional hearings. This difficult issue needs to be studied at length.

President Clinton decided to play along, play the moderate. But it was too late. By week's end, the idea of the sissy warrior had invaded the American imagination. The insecure heterosexual male was left frightened by the notion. Frightened, but unable to say exactly why.

PART FOUR

MEN AND WORK

In what ways is work tied to male identity? Do men gain a sense of fulfillment from their work, or do they view it as necessary drudgery? How might the organization of workplaces play on, reinforce, or sometimes threaten the types of masculinity that males have already learned as youngsters? How does the experience of work (or of not having work) differ for men of different social classes, ethnic, and sexual preference groups? And how do recent structural changes in society impact upon the masculinity–work relationship? The articles in this section address these issues and more.

As Jessie Bernard points out, the rise of urban industrial capitalism saw the creation of separate "public" and "domestic" spheres of social life. As women were increasingly relegated to working in the home, men were increasingly absent from the home, and the male "breadwinner role" was born.

The sexual division of labor, this gendered split between home and workplace, has led to a variety of problems and conflicts for women and for men. Women's continued movement into the paid labor force, higher levels of unemployment, and the rise of a more service-oriented economy have led to dramatic shifts in the quality and the quantity of men's experiences in their work. Articles by Peter R. Breggin and Christine Williams examine these shifts and their impact on men and women in the workplace—the former by looking at men who do "women's work," and the latter by using the Clarence Thomas confirmation hearings as a window into sexual harassment issues.

These economic changes have also had different impacts on different groups of men. Timothy Nonn examines the ways in which homeless men reproduce and challenge definitions of masculinity. Martin Levine and Ben Fong-Torres describe the insidious ways in which discrimination works against different groups of men, while Manuel Peña and David Collinson describe the responses to that discrimination based on race, class, sexuality, or ethnicity.

Music, 1985. Copyright © 1985 by Greg Drasler.

ARTICLE 17

THE GOOD-PROVIDER ROLE
ITS RISE AND FALL

JESSIE BERNARD

The Lord is my shepherd, I shall not want. He sets a table for me in the very sight of my enemies; my cup runs over (23rd Psalm). And when the Israelites were complaining about how hungry they were on their way from Egypt to Canaan, God told Moses to rest assured: There would be meat for dinner and bread for breakfast the next morning. And, indeed, there were quails that very night, enough to cover the camp, and in the morning the ground was covered with dew that proved to be bread (Exodus 16:12–13). In fact, in this role of good provider, God is sometimes almost synonymous with Providence. Many people, like Micawber, still wait for him, or Providence, to provide.

Granted, then, that the first great provider for the human species was God the Father, surely the second great provider for the human species was Mother, the gatherer, planter, and general factotum. Boulding (1976), citing Lee and deVore, tells us that in hunting and gathering societies, males contribute about one fifth of the food of the clan, females the other four fifths (p. 96). She also concludes that by 12,000 B.C. in the early agricultural villages, females provided four fifths of the human subsistence (p. 97). Not until large trading towns arose did the female contribution to human subsistence decline to equality with that of the male. And with the beginning of true cities, the provisioning work of women tended to become invisible. Still, in today's world it remains substantial.

Whatever the date of the virtuous woman described in the Old Testament (Proverbs 31:10–27), she was the very model of a good provider. She was, in fact, a highly productive conglomerate. She woke up in the middle of the night to tend to her business; she oversaw a multiple-industry household; *her* candles did not go out at night; there was no ready market for the high-quality linen girdles she made and sold to the merchants in town; and she kept track of the real estate market and bought good land when it became available, cultivating vineyards quite profitably. All this time her husband sat at the gates talking with his cronies.

A recent counterpart to the virtuous woman was the busy and industrious shtetl woman:

> *The earning of a livelihood is sexless, and the large majority of women . . . participate in some gainful occupation if they do not carry the chief burden of support. The wife of a "perennial student" is very apt to be the sole support of the family. The problem of managing both a business and a home is so common that no one recognizes it as special. . . . To bustle about in search of a livelihood is merely another form of bustling about managing a home; both are aspects of . . . health and livelihood. (Zborowski & Herzog, 1952, p. 131)*

In a subsistence economy in which husbands and wives ran farms, shops, or businesses together, a man might be a good, steady worker, but the idea that he was *the* provider would hardly ring true. Even the youth in the folk song

From *American Psychologist*, Vol. 36, No. 1 (January 1981), pp. 1–12. Copyright 1981 by the American Psychological Association. Reprinted by permission of the publisher and author.

who listed all the gifts he would bestow on his love if she would marry him—a golden comb, a paper of pins, and all the rest—was not necessarily promising to be a good provider.

I have not searched the literature to determine when the concept of the good provider entered our thinking. The term *provider* entered the English language in 1532, but was not yet male sex typed, as the older term *purveyor* already was in 1442. Webster's second edition defines the good provider as "one who provides, especially, colloq., one who provides food, clothing, etc. for his family; as, he is a good or an adequate provider." More simply, he could be defined as a man whose wife did not have to enter the labor force. The counterpart to the good provider was the housewife. However the term is defined, the role itself delineated relationships within a marriage and family in a way that added to the legal, religious, and other advantages men had over women.

Thus, under the common law, although the husband was legally head of the household and as such had the responsibility of providing for his wife and children, this provision was often made with help from the wife's personal property and earnings, to which he was entitled:

> He owned his wife's and children's services, and had the sole right to collect wages for their work outside the home. He owned his wife's personal property outright, and had the right to manage and control all of his wife's real property during marriage, which included the right to use or lease property, and to keep any rents and profits from it. (Babcock, Freedman, Norton, & Ross, 1975, p. 561)

So even when she was the actual provider, the legal recognition was granted the husband. Therefore, whatever the husband's legal responsibilities for support may have been, he was not necessarily a good provider in the way the term came to be understood. The wife may have been performing that role.

In our country in Colonial times women were still viewed as performing a providing role, and

they pursued a variety of occupations. Abigail Adams managed the family estate, which provided the wherewithal for John to spend so much time in Philadelphia. In the 18th century "many women were active in business and professional pursuits. They ran inns arid taverns; they managed a wide variety of stores and shops; and, at least occasionally, they worked in careers like publishing, journalism and medicine" (Demos, 1974, p. 430). Women sometimes even "joined the menfolk for work in the fields" (p. 430). Like the household of the proverbial virtuous woman, the Colonial household was a little factory that produced clothing, furniture, bedding, candles, and other accessories, and again, as in the case of the virtuous woman, the female role was central. It was taken for granted that women provided for the family along with men.

The good provider as a specialized male role seems to have arisen in the transition from subsistence to market—especially money—economies that accelerated with the industrial revolution. The good-provider role for males emerged in this country roughly, say, from the 1830s, when de Tocqueville was observing it, to the late 1970s, when the 1980 census declared that a male was not automatically to be assumed to be the head of the household. This gives the role a life span of about a century and a half. Although relatively short-lived, while it lasted the role was a seemingly rock-like feature of the national landscape.

As a psychological and sociological phenomenon, the good-provider role had wide ramifications for all our thinking about families. It marked a new kind of marriage. It did not have good effects on women: The role deprived them of many chips by placing them in a peculiarly vulnerable position. Because she was not reimbursed for her contribution to the family in either products or services, a wife was stripped to a considerable extent of her access to cash-mediated markets. By discouraging labor force participation, it deprived many women, especially affluent ones, of opportunities to achieve strength and competence. It deterred young women from acquiring productive skills. They dedicated themselves instead to winning a good provider who would "take care of" them. The wife of a more successful provider became for all intents and purposes a parasite, with little to do except indulge or pamper herself. The psychology of such dependence could become all but crippling. There were other concomitants of the good-provider role.

EXPRESSIVITY AND THE GOOD-PROVIDER ROLE

The new industrial order that produced the good provider changed not so much the division of labor between the sexes as it did the site of the work they engaged in. Only two of the concomitants of this change in work site are selected for comment here, namely, (a) the identification of gender with work site as well as with work itself and (b) the reduction of time for personal interaction and intimacy within the family.

It is not so much the specific kinds of work men and women do—they have always varied from time to time and place to place—but the simple fact that the sexes do different kinds of work, whatever it is, which is in and of itself important. The division of labor by sex means that the work group becomes also a sex group. The very nature of maleness and femaleness becomes embedded in the sexual division of labor. One's sex and one's work are part of one another. One's work defines one's gender.

Any division of labor implies that people doing different kinds of work will occupy different work sites. When the division is based on sex, men and women will necessarily have different work sites. Even within the home itself, men and women had different work spaces. The woman's spinning wheel occupied a different area from the man's anvil. When the factory took over much of the work formerly done in the house, the separation of work space became especially marked. Not only did the separation of the sexes become spatially extended, but it came to relate work and gender in a special way. The

work site as well as the work itself became associated with gender; each sex had its own turf. This sexual "territoriality" has had complicating effects on efforts to change any sexual division of labor. The good provider worked primarily in the outside male world of business and industry. The homemaker worked primarily in the home.

Spatial separation of the sexes not only identifies gender with work site and work but also reduces the amount of time available for spontaneous emotional give-and-take between husbands and wives. When men and women work in an economy based in the home, there are frequent occasions for interaction. (Consider, for example, the suggestive allusions made today to the rise in the birth rate nine months after a blackout.) When men and women are in close proximity, there is always the possibility of reassuring glances, the comfort of simple physical presence. But when the division of labor removes the man from the family dwelling for most of the day, intimate relationships become less feasible. De Tocqueville was one of the first to call our attention to this. In 1840 he noted that

> *almost all men in democracies are engaged in public or professional life; and . . . the limited extent of common income obliges a wife to confine herself to the house, in order to watch in person and very closely over the details of domestic economy. All these distinct and compulsory occupations are so many natural barriers, which, by keeping the two sexes asunder, render the solicitations of the one less frequent and less ardent— the resistance of the other more easy. (de Tocqueville, 1840, p. 212)*

Not directly related to the spatial constraints on emotional expression by men, but nevertheless a concomitant of the new industrial order with the same effect, was the enormous drive for achievement, for success, for "making it" that escalated the provider role into the good-provider role. De Tocqueville (1840) is again our source:

> *The tumultuous and constantly harassed life which equality makes men lead [becoming good providers] not only distracts them from the pas-*

sions of love, by denying them time to indulge in it, but it diverts them from it by another more secret but more certain road. All men who live in democratic ages more or less contract ways of thinking of the manufacturing and trading classes. (p. 221)

As a result of this male concentration on jobs and careers, much abnegation and "a constant sacrifice of her pleasures to her duties" (de Tocqueville, 1840, p. 212) were demanded of the American woman. The good-provider role, as it came to be shaped by this ambience, was thus restricted in what it was called upon to provide. Emotional expressivity was not included in the role. One of the things a parent might say about a man to persuade a daughter to marry him, or a daughter might say to explain to her parents why she wanted to, was not that he was a gentle, loving, or tender man but that he was a good provider. He might have many other qualities, good or bad, but if a man was a good provider, everything else was either gravy or the price one had to pay for a good provider.

Lack of expressivity did not imply neglect of the family. The good provider was a "family man." He set a good table, provided a decent home, paid the mortgage, bought the shoes, and kept his children warmly clothed. He might, with the help of the children's part-time jobs, have been able to finance their educations through high-school and, sometimes, even college. There might even have been a little left over for an occasional celebration in most families. The good provider made a decent contribution to the church. His work might have been demanding, but he expected it to be. If in addition to being a good provider, a man was kind, gentle, generous, and not a heavy drinker or gambler, that was all frosting on the cake. Loving attention and emotional involvement in the family were not part of a woman's implicit bargain with the good provider.

By the time de Tocqueville published his observations in 1840, the general outlines of the good-provider role had taken shape. It called for a hard-working man who spent most of his time at his work. In the traditional conception of the role, a man's chief responsibility is his job, so that "by definition any family behaviors must be subordinate to it in terms of significance and [the job] has priority in the event of a clash" (Scanzoni, 1975, p. 38). This was the classic form of the good-provider role, which remained a powerful component of our social structure until well into the present century.

COSTS AND REWARDS OF THE GOOD-PROVIDER ROLE FOR MEN

There were both costs and rewards for those men attached to the good-provider role. The most serious cost was perhaps the identification of maleness not only with the work site but especially with success in the role. "The American male looks to his breadwinning role to confirm his manliness" (Brenton, 1966, p. 194).[1] To be a man one had to be not only a provider but a *good* provider. Success in the good-provider role came in time to define masculinity itself. The good provider had to achieve, to win, to succeed, to dominate. He was a bread*winner*. He had to show "strength, cunning, inventiveness, endurance—a whole range of traits henceforth defined as exclusively 'masculine'" (Demos, 1974 p. 436). Men were judged as men by the level of living they provided. They were judged by the myth "that endows a money-making man with sexiness and virility, and is based on man's dominance, strength, and ability to provide for and care for 'his' woman" (Gould, 1974, p. 97). The good provider became a player in the male competitive macho game. What one man provided for his family in the way of luxury and display had to be equaled or topped by what another could provide. Families became display cases for the success of the good provider.

---

[1] Rainwater and Yancey (1967), critiquing current welfare policies, note that they "have robbed men of their manhood, women of their husbands, and children of their fathers. To create a stable monogamous family we need to provide men with the opportunity to be men, and that involves enabling them to perform occupationally" (p. 235).

The psychic costs could be high:

By depending so heavily on his breadwinning role to validate his sense of himself as a man, instead of also letting his roles as husband, father, and citizen of the community count as validating sources, the American male treads on psychically dangerous ground. It's always dangerous to put all of one's psychic eggs into one basket. (Brenton, 1966, p. 194)

The good-provider role not only put all of a man's gender-identifying eggs into one psychic basket, but it also put all the family-providing eggs into one basket. One individual became responsible for the support of the whole family. Countless stories portrayed the humiliation families underwent to keep wives and especially mothers out of the labor force, a circumstance that would admit to the world the male head's failure in the good-provider role. If a married woman had to enter the labor force at all, that was bad enough. If she made a good salary, however, she was "co-opting the man's passport to masculinity" (Gould, 1974, p. 98) and he was effectively castrated. A wife's earning capacity diminished a man's position as head of the household (Gould, 1974, p. 99).

Failure in the role of a good provider, which employment of wives evidenced, could produce deep frustration. As Komarovsky (1940, p. 20) explains, this is "because in his own estimation he is failing to fulfill what is the central duty of his life, the very touchstone of his manhood—the role of family provider."

But just as there was punishment for failure in the good-provider role, so also were there rewards for successful performance. A man "derived strength from his role as provider" (Komarovsky, 1940, p. 205). He achieved a good deal of satisfaction from his ability to support his family. It won kudos. Being a good provider led to status in both the family and the community. Within the family it gave him the power of the purse and the right to decide about expenditures, standards of living, and what constituted good providing. "Every purchase of the family—the radio, his

wife's new hat, the children's skates, the meals set before him—all were symbols of their dependence upon him" (Komarovsky, 1940, pp. 74–75). Such dependence gave him a "profound sense of stability" (p. 74). It was a strong counterpoise vis-à-vis a wife with a stronger personality. "Whether he had considerable authority within the family and was recognized as its head, or whether the wife's stronger personality . . . dominated the family, he nevertheless derived strength from his role as provider" (Komarovsky, 1940, p. 75). As recently as 1975, in a sample of 3,100 husbands and wives in 10 cities, Scanzoni found that despite increasing egalitarian norms, the good provider still had "considerable power in ultimate decision-making" and as "unique provider" had the right "to organize his life and the lives of other family members around his occupation" (p. 38).

A man who was successful in the good-provider role might be freed from other obligations to the family. But the flip side of this dispensation was that he could not make up for poor performance by excellence in other family roles. Since everything depended on his success as provider, everything was at stake. The good provider played an all-or-nothing game.

DIFFERENT WAYS OF PERFORMING THE GOOD-PROVIDER ROLE

Although the legal specifications for the role were laid out in the common law, in legislation, in legal precedents, in court decisions, and, most importantly, in custom and convention, in real-life situations the social and social-psychological specifications were set by the husband or, perhaps more accurately, by the community, alias the Joneses, and there were many ways to perform it.

Some men resented the burdens the role forced them to bear. A man could easily vent such resentment toward his family by keeping complete control over all expenditures, dispensing the money for household maintenance, and complaining about bills as though it were his wife's fault that shoes cost so much. He could, in effect, punish his family for his having to per-

form the role. Since the money he earned belonged to him—was "his"—he could do with it
what he pleased. Through extreme parsimony he
could dole out his money in a mean, humiliating
way, forcing his wife to come begging for pen-
nies. By his reluctance and resentment he could
make his family pay emotionally for the provisioning he supplied.

At the other extreme were the highly competitive men who were so involved in outdoing
the Joneses that the fur coat became more important than the affectionate hug. They "bought
off" their families. They sometimes succeeded
so well in their extravagance that they sacrificed
the family they were presumably providing for
to the achievements that made it possible (Keniston, 1965).[2]

The Depression of the 1930s revealed in
harsh detail what the loss of the role could mean
both to the good provider and to his family, not
only in the loss of income itself—which could
be supplied by welfare agencies or even by other
family members, including wives—but also and
especially in the loss of face.

The Great Depression did not mark the
demise of the good-provider role. But it did
teach us what a slender thread the family hung
on. It stimulated a whole array of programs designed to strengthen that thread, to ensure that
it would never again be similarly threatened.
Unemployment insurance was incorporated into
the Social Security Act of 1935, for example,
and a Full Employment Act was passed in 1946.
But there proved to be many other ways in
which the good-provider role could be subverted.

[2] Several years ago I presented a critque of what I called "extreme sex role specialization," including "work-intoxicated
fathers." I noted that making success in the provider role the
only test for real manliness was putting a lot of eggs into one
basket. At both the blue-collar and the managerial levels, it
was dysfunctional for families. I referred to the several attempts being made even then to correct the excesses of extreme sex role specialization: rural and urban communes,
leaving jobs to take up small-scale enterprises that allowed
more contact with families, and a rebellion again overtime
in industry (Bernard, 1975, pp. 217–239).

ROLE REJECTORS AND
ROLE OVERPERFORMERS

Recent research in psychology, anthropology,
and sociology has familiarized us with the
tremendous power of roles. But we also know
that one of the fundamental principles of role behavior is that conformity to role norms is not
universal. Not everyone lives up to the specifications of roles, either in the psychological or in
the sociological definition of the concept. Two
extremes have attracted research attention: (a)
the men who could not live up to the norms of
the good-provider role or did not want to, at one
extreme, and (b) the men who overperformed the
role, at the other. For the wide range in between,
from blue-collar workers to professionals, there
was fairly consistent acceptance of the role, however well or poorly, however grumblingly or willingly, performed.

First the nonconformists. Even in Colonial
times, desertion and divorce occurred:

*Women may have deserted because, say, their hus-
bands beat them; husbands, on the other hand,
may have deserted because they were unable or
unwilling to provide for their usually large families in the face of the wives' demands to do so.
These demands were, of course, backed by community norms making the husband's financial support a sacred duty. (Scanzoni, 1979, pp. 24–25)*

Fiedler (1962) has traced the theme of male escape from domestic responsibilities in the American novel from the time of Rip Van Winkle to
the present:

*The figure of Rip Van Winkle presides over the
birth of the American imagination; and it is fitting
that our first successful home-grown legend
should memorialize, however playfully, the flight
of the dreamer from the shrew—into the mountains
and out of time, away from the drab duties of home
. . . anywhere to avoid . . . marriage and responsibility. One of the factors that determine theme and
form in our great books is this strategy of evasion,
this retreat to nature and childhood which makes
our literature (and life) so charmingly and infuri-
atingly "boyish." (pp. xx–xxi)*

Among the men who pulled up stakes and departed for the West or went down to the sea in ships, there must have been a certain proportion who, like their mythic prototype, were simply fleeing the good-provider role.

The work of Demos (1974), a historian, offers considerable support for Fiedler's thesis. He tells us that the burdens thrust on men in the 19th century by the new patterns of work began to show their effects in the family. When "the [spatial] separation of the work lives of the husbands and wives made communication so problematic," he asks, "what was the likelihood of meaningful communication?" (Demos, 1974, p. 438). The answer is, relatively little. Divorce and separation increased, either formally or by tacit consent—or simply by default, as in the case of a variety of defaulters—tramps, bums, hoboes— among them.

In this connection, "the development of the notorious 'tramp' phenomenon is worth noticing," Demos (1974, p. 438) tells us. The tramp was a man who just gave up, who dropped out of the role entirely. He preferred not to work, but he would do small chores or other small-scale work for a handout if he had to. He was not above begging the housewife for a meal, hoping she would not find work for him to do in repayment. Demos (1974) describes the type:

> *Demoralized and destitute wanderers, their numbers mounting into the hundreds of thousands, tramps can be fairly characterized as men who had run away from their wives. . . . Their presence was mute testimony to the strains that tugged at the very core of American family life. . . . Many observers noted that the tramps had created a virtual society of their own [a kind of counterculture] based on a principle of single-sex companionship. (p. 438)*

A considerable number of them came to be described as "homeless men" and, as the country became more urbanized, landed ultimately on skid row. A large part of the task of social workers for almost a century was the care of the "evaded" women they left behind.[3] When the tramp became wholly demoralized, a chronic alcoholic, almost unreachable, he fell into a category of his own—he was a bum.

Quite a different kettle of fish was the hobo, the migratory worker who spent several months harvesting wheat and other large crops and the rest of the year in cities. Many were the so-called Wobblies, or Industrial Workers of the World, who repudiated the good-provider role on principle. They had contempt for the man who accepted it and could be called conscientious objectors to the role. "In some IWW circles, wives were regarded as the 'ball and chain.' In the West, IWW literature proclaimed that the migratory worker, usually a young, unmarried male, was 'the finest specimen of American manhood . . . the leaven of the revolutionary labor movement'" (Foner, 1979, p. 400). Exemplars of the Wobblies were the nomadic workers of the West. They were free men. The migratory worker, "unlike the factory slave of the Atlantic seaboard and the central states, . . . was most emphatically 'not afraid of losing his job.' No wife and family cumbered him. The worker of the East, oppressed by the fear of want for wife and babies, dared not venture much" (Foner, 1979, p. 400). The refer-

[3] In one department of a South Carolina cotton mill early in the center, "every worker was a grass widow" (Smuts, 1959, p. 54). Many women worked "because their husbands refused to provide for their families. There is no reason to think that husbands abandoned their duties more often than today, but the woman who was burdened by an irresponsible husband in 1890 usually had no recourse save taking on his responsibilities herself. If he deserted, the law-enforcement agencies of the time afforded little chance of finding and compelling him to provide support" (Smuts, 1959, p. 54). The situation is not greatly improved today. In divorce child support is allotted in only a small number of cases and enforced in even fewer. "Roughly half of all families with an absent parent don't have awards at all. . . . Where awards do exist they are usually for small amounts, typically ranging from $7 to $18 per week per child" (Jones, 1976, abstract). A summary of all the studies available concludes that "approximately 20 percent of all divorced and separated mothers receive child support regularly, with an additional 7 percent receiving it 'sometimes'; 8 percent of all divorced and separated women receive alimony regularly or sometimes" (Jones, 1976, p. 23).

ence to fear of loss of job was well taken; employers preferred married men, disciplined into the good-provider role, who had given hostages to fortune and were therefore more tractable.

Just on the verge between the area of conformity to the good-provider role—at whatever level—and the area of complete nonconformity to it was the nongood provider, the marginal group of workers usually made up of "the under-educated, the under-trained, the under-employed, or part-time employed, as well as the under-paid, and of course the unemployed" (Snyder, 1979, p. 597). These included men who wanted—sometimes desperately—to perform the good-provider role but who for one reason or another were unable to do so. Liebow (1966) has discussed the ramifications of failure among the black men of Tally's corner: The black man is

> under legal and social constraints to provide for them [their families], to be a husband to his wife and a father to his children. The chances are, however, that he is failing to provide for them, and failure in this primary function contaminates his performance as father in other respects as well. (p. 86)

In some cases, leaving the family entirely was the best substitute a man could supply. The community was left to take over.[4]

At the other extreme was the overperformer. De Tocqueville, quoted earlier, was already describing him as he manifested in the 1830s. And as late as 1955 Warner and Ablegglen were adding to the considerable literature on industrial leaders and tycoons, referring to their "driving concentration" on their careers and their "intense focusing" of interests, energies, and skills on these careers, "even limiting their sexual activity" (pp. 48–49). They came to be known as workaholics or work-intoxicated men. Their preoccupation with their work even at the expense

of their families was, as I have already noted, quite acceptable in our society.

Poorly or well performed, the good-provider role lingered on. World War II initiated a challenge, this time in the form of attracting more and more married women into the labor force, but the challenge was papered over in the 1950s with an "age of togetherness" that all but apotheosized the good provider, his house in the suburbs, his homebody wife, and his third, fourth, even fifth, child. As late as the 1960s most housewives (87%) still saw breadwinning as their husband's primary role (Lopata, 1971, p. 91).[5]

INTRINSIC CONFLICT IN THE GOOD-PROVIDER ROLE

Since the good-provider role involved both family and work roles, most people believed that there was no incompatibility between them or at least that there should not be. But in the 1960s and 1970s evidence began to mount that maybe something was amiss.

De Tocqueville had documented the implicit conflict in the American businessman's devotion to his work at the expense of his family in the early years of the 19th century; the Industrial Workers of the World had proclaimed that the good-provider role which tied a man to his family was an impediment to the great revolution at the beginning of the 20th century; Fiedler (1962) had noted that throughout our history, in the male fantasy world, there was freedom from the responsibilities of this role; about 50 years ago Freud (1930/1958) had analyzed the intrinsic conflict between the demands of women and the family on one side and the demands of men's work on the other:

> Women represent the interests of the family and sexual life, the work of civilization has become more and more men's business; it confronts them

---

[4]Even though the annals of social work agencies are filled with cases of runaway husbands, in 1976 only 12.6% of all women were in the status of divorce and separation, and at least some of them were still being "provided for." Most men were at least trying to fulfill the good-provider role.

[5]Although all the women in Lopata's (1971) sample saw breadwinning as important, fewer employed women (54%) than either nonemployed urban (63%) or suburban (64%) women assigned it first place (p. 91).

*with ever harder tasks, compels them to sublimi-
nations of instinct which women are not easily able
to achieve. Since man has not an unlimited amount
of mental energy at his disposal, he must accomplish his tasks by distributing his libido to the best
advantage. What he employs for cultural [occu-
pational] purposes he withdraws to a great extent
from women, and his sexual life; his constant association with men and his dependence on his relations with them even estrange him from his
duties as husband and father. Woman finds herself
thus forced into the background by the claims of
culture [work] and she adapts an inimical attitude
towards it. (pp. 50–51)*

In the last two decades, researchers have been
raising questions relevant to Freud's statement
of the problem. They have been asking people
about the relative satisfactions they derive from
these conflicting values—family and work.
Among the earliest studies comparing family–
work values was a Gallup poll in 1940 in which
both men and women chose a happy home over
an interesting job or wealth as a major life value.
Since then there have been a number of such
polls, and a considerable body of results has now
accumulated. Pleck and Lang (1979) and Hesselbart (Note l) have summarized the findings of
these surveys. All agree that there is a clear bias
in the direction of the family. Pleck and Lang
conclude that "men's family role is far more psychologically significant to them than is their
work role" (p. 29), and Hesselbart—however
critical she is of the studies she summarizes—
believes they should not be dismissed lightly and
concludes that they certainly "challenge the idea
that family is a 'secondary' valued role" (p. 14).[6]
Douvan (Note 2) also found in a 1976 replication of a 1957 survey that family values retained
priority over work: "Family roles almost uni-

formly rate higher in value production than the
job role does" (p. 16).[7]

The very fact that researchers have asked such
questions is itself interesting. Somehow or other
both the researchers and the informants seem to
be saying that all this complaining about the male
neglect of the family, about the lack of family involvement by men, just is not warranted. Neither
de Tocqueville nor Freud was right. Men do value
family life more than they value their work. They
do derive their major life satisfactions from their
families rather than from their work.

It may well be true that men derive the greatest satisfaction from their family roles, but this
does not necessarily mean they are willing to pay
for this benefit. In any event, great attitudinal
changes took place in the 1960s and 1970s.

Douvan (Note 2), on the basis of surveys in
1957 and 1976, found, for example, a considerable increase in the proportion of both men and
women who found marriage and parenthood burdensome and restrictive. Almost three fifths
(57%) of both married men and married women
in 1976 saw marriage as "all burdens and restrictions," as compared with only 42% and 47%,
respectively, in 1957. And almost half (45%) also
viewed children as "all burdens and restrictions"
in 1976, as compared with only 28% and 33% for
married men and married women, respectively,
in 1957. The proportion of working men with a

[6] Pleck and Lang (1979) found only one serious study con-
tradicting their own conclusions: "Using data from the 1973
NORC [National Opinion Research Center] General Social
Survey, Harry analyzed the bivariate relationship of job and
family satisfaction to life happiness in men classified by
family life cycle stage. In three of the five groups of husbands . . . job satisfaction had a stronger association than
family satisfaction to life happiness" (pp. 5–6).

[7] In 1978, a Yankelovich survey on "The New Work Psychology" suggested that leisure is now becoming a strict
competitor for both family and work as a source of life satisfactions: "Family and work have grown less important than
leisure; a majority of 60 percent say that although they enjoy
their work, it is not their major source of satisfaction" (p.
46). A 1977 survey of Swedish men aged 18 to 35 found that
the proportion saying the family was the main source of
meaning in their lives declined from 45% in 1955 to 41% in
1977; the proportion indicating work as the main source of
satisfaction dropped from 33% to 17%. The earlier tendency
for men to identify themselves through their work is less
marked these days. In the new value system, the individual
says, in effect, "I am more than my role. I am myself"
(Yankelovich, 1978). Is the increasing concern with leisure
a way to escape the dissatisfaction with both the alienating
relations found on the work site and the demands for increased involvement with the family?

positive attitude toward marriage dropped drastically over this period, from 68% to 39%. Working women, who made up a fairly small number of all married women in 1957, hardly changed attitudes at all, dropping only from 43% to 42%. The proportion of working men who found marriage and children burdensome and restrictive more than doubled, from 25% to 56% and from 25% to 58%, respectively. Although some of these changes reflected greater willingness in 1976 than in 1957 to admit negative attitudes toward marriage and parenthood—itself significant—profound changes were clearly in process. More and more men and women were experiencing disaffection with family life.[8]

"ALL BURDENS AND RESTRICTIONS"

Apparently, the benefits of the good-provider role were greater than the costs for most men. Despite the legend of the flight of the American male (Fiedler, 1962), despite the defectors and dropouts, despite the tavern habitué's "ball and chain" cliché, men seemed to know that the good-provider role, if they could succeed in it, was good for them. But Douvan's (Note 2) findings suggest that recently their complaints have become serious, bone-deep. The family they have been providing for is not the same family it was in the past.

Smith (1979) calls the great trek of married women into the labor force a subtle revolution—revolutionary not in the sense of one class overthrowing a status quo and substituting its own regime, but revolutionary in its impact on both the family and the work roles of men and women. It diluted the prerogatives of the good-provider role. It increased the demands made on the good provider, especially in the form of more

emotional investment in the family, more sharing of household responsibilities. The role became even more burdensome.

However men may now feel about the burdens and restrictions imposed on them by the good-provider role, most have, at least ostensibly, accepted them. The tramp and the bum had "voted with their feet" against the role; the hobo or Wobbly had rejected it on the basis of a revolutionary ideology that saw it as enslaving men to the corporation; tavern humor had glossed the resentment habitués felt against its demands. Now the "burdens-and-restrictions" motif has surfaced both in research reports and, more blatantly, in the male liberation movement. From time to time it has also appeared in the clinician's notes.

Sometimes the resentment of the good provider takes the form of simply wanting more appreciation for the life-style he provides. All he does for his family seems to be taken for granted. Thus, for example, Goldberg (1976), a psychiatrist, recounts the case of a successful businessman:

> *He's feeling a deepening sense of bitterness and frustration about his wife and family. He doesn't feel appreciated. It angers him the way they seem to take the things his earnings purchase for granted. They've come to expect it as their due. It particularly enrages him when his children put him down for his "materialistic middle-class trip." He'd like to tell them to get someone else to support them but he holds himself back. (p. 124)*

Brenton (1966) quotes a social worker who describes an upper-middle-class woman: She has "gotten hold of a man who'll drive himself like mad to get money, and [is] denigrating him for being too interested in money, and not interested in music, or the arts, or in spending time with the children. But at the same time she's subtly driving him—and doesn't know it" (p. 226). What seems significant about such cases is not that men feel resentful about the lack of appreciation but that they are willing to justify their resentment. They are no longer willing to grin and bear it.

Sometimes there is even more than expressed resentment; there is an actual repudiation of the

---

[8] Men seem to be having problems with both work and family roles. Veroff (Note 3), for example, reports an increased "sense of dissatisfaction with the social relations in the work setting" and a "dissatisfaction with the affiliative nature of work" (p. 47). This dissatisfaction may be one of the factors that leads men to seek affiliative-need satisfaction in marriage, just as in the 19th century they looked to the home as shelter from the jungle of the outside world.

role. In the past, only a few men like the hobo or Wobbly were likely to give up. Today, Goldberg (1976) believes, more are ready to renounce the role, not on theoretical revolutionary grounds, however, but on purely selfish ones:

> Male growth will stem from openly avowed, unashamed, self-oriented motivations. . . . Guilt-oriented "should" behavior will be rejected because it is always at the price of a hidden build-up of resentment and frustration and alienation from others and is, therefore, counterproductive. (p. 184)

The disaffection of the good provider is directed to both sides of his role. With respect to work, Lefkowitz (1979) has described men among whom the good-provider role is neither being completely rejected nor repudiated, but diluted. These men began their working lives in the conventional style, hopeful and ambitious. They found a job, married, raised a family, and "achieved a measure of economic security and earned the respect of . . . colleagues and neighbors" (Lefkowitz, 1979, p. 31). In brief, they successfully performed the good-provider role. But unlike their historical predecessors, they in time became disillusioned with their jobs—not jobs on assembly lines, not jobs usually characterized as alienating, but fairly prestigious jobs such as aeronautics engineer and government economist. They daydreamed about other interests. "The common theme which surfaced again and again in their histories, was the need to find a new social connection—to reassert control over their lives, to gain some sense of freedom" (Lefkowitz, 1979, p. 31). These men felt "entitled to freedom and independence." Middle-class, educated, self-assured, articulate, and for the most part white, they knew they could talk themselves into a job if they had to. Most of them did not want to desert their families. Indeed, most of them "wanted to rejoin the intimate circle they felt they had neglected in their years of work" (p. 31).

Though some of the men Lefkowitz studied sought closer ties with their families, in the case of those studied by Sarason (1977), a psychologist, career changes involved lower income and

had a negative impact on families. Sarason's subjects were also men in high-level professions, the very men least likely to find marriage and parenthood burdensome and restrictive. Still, since career change often involved a reduction in pay, some wives were unwilling to accept it, with the result that the marriage deteriorated (p. 178). Sometimes it looked like a no-win game. The husband's earlier career brought him feelings of emptiness and alienation, but it also brought financial rewards for the family. Greater work satisfaction for him in lower paying work meant reduced satisfaction with life-style. These findings lead Sarason to raise a number of points with respect to the good-provider role. "How much," he asks, "does an individual or a family need in order to maintain a satisfactory existence? Is an individual being responsible to himself or his family if he provides them with little more than the bare essentials of living?" (p. 178). These are questions about the good-provider role that few men raised in the past.

Lefkowitz (1979) wonders how his downwardly mobile men lived when they left their jobs. "They put together a basic economic package which consisted of government assistance, contributions from family members who had not worked before and some bartering of goods and services" (p. 31). Especially interesting in this list of income sources are the "contributions from family members who had not worked before" (p. 31). Surely not mothers and sisters. Who, of course, but wives?

WOMEN AND THE PROVIDER ROLE

The present discussion began with the woman's part in the provider role. We saw how as more and more of the provisioning of the family came to be by way of monetary exchange, the woman's part shrank. A woman could still provide services, but could furnish little in the way of food, clothing, and shelter. But now that she is entering the labor force in large numbers, she can once more resume her ancient role, this time, like her male counterpart the provider, by way of a monetary contribution. More and more women are doing just this.

The assault on the good-provider role in the Depression was traumatic. But a modified version began to appear in the 1970s as a single income became inadequate for more and more families. Husbands have remained the major providers, but in an increasing number of cases the wife has begun to share this role. Thus, the proportion of married women aged 15 to 54 (living with their husbands) in the labor force more than doubled between 1950 and 1978, from 25.2% to 55.4%. The proportion for 1990 is estimated to reach 66.7% (Smith, 1979, p. l4). Fewer women are now full-time housewives.

For some men the relief from the strain of sole responsibility for the provider role has been welcome. But for others the feeling of degradation resembles the feelings reported 40 years earlier in the Great Depression. It is not that they are no longer providing for the family but that the role-sharing wife now feels justified in making demands on them. The good-provider role with all its prerogatives and perquisites has undergone profound changes. It will never be the same again.[9] Its death knell was sounded when, as noted above, the 1980 census no longer automatically assumed that the male member of the household was its head.

THE CURRENT SCENE

Among the new demands being made on the good-provider role, two deserve special consideration, namely, (a) more intimacy, expressivity, and nurturance—specifications never included in it as it originally took shape—and (b) more sharing of household responsibility and child care.

As the pampered wife in an affluent household came often to be an economic parasite, so

[9]Among the indices of the waning of the good-provider role are the increasing number of married women in the labor force; the growth in the number of female-headed families; the growing trend toward egalitarian norms in marriage; the need for two earners in so many middle-class families; and the recognition of these trends in the abandonment of identification of head of household as a male.

also the good provider was often, in a way, a kind of emotional parasite. Implicit in the definition of the role was that he provided goods and material things. Tender loving care was not one of the requirements. Emotional ministrations from the family were his right; providing them was not a corresponding obligation. Therefore, as de Tocqueville had already noted by 1840, women suffered a kind of emotional deprivation labeled by Robert Weiss as "relational deficit" (cited in Bernard, 1976). Only recently has this male rejection of emotional expression come to be challenged. Today, even blue-collar women are imposing "a host of new role expectations upon their husbands or lovers. . . . A new role set asks the blue-collar male to strive for . . . deep-coursing intimacy" (Shostak, Note 4, p. 75). It was not only vis-à-vis his family that the good provider was lacking in expressivity. This lack was built into the whole male role script. Today not only women but also men are beginning to protest the repudiation of expressivity prescribed in male roles (David & Brannon, 1976; Farrell, 1974; Fasteau, 1974; Pleck & Sawyer, 1974).

Is there any relationship between the "imposing" on men of "deep-coursing intimacy" by women on one side and the increasing proportion of men who find marriage burdensome and restrictive on the other? Are men seeing the new emotional involvements being asked of them as "all burdens and restrictions"? Are they responding to the new involvements under duress? Are they feeling oppressed by them? Fearful of them?

From the standpoint of high-level pure-science research there may be something bizarre, if not even slightly absurd, in the growing corpus of serious research on how much or how little husbands of employed wives contribute to household chores and child care. Yet it is serious enough that all over the industrialized world such research is going on. Time studies in a dozen countries—communist as well as capitalist—trace the slow and bungling process by which marriage accommodates to changing conditions and by which women struggle to mold the changing conditions in their behalf. For everywhere the same picture shows up in the research: an image of women sharing the provider role and at the same time retaining responsibility for the household. Until recently such a topic would have been judged unworthy of serious attention. It was a subject that might be worth a good laugh, for instance, as when an all-thumbs man in a cartoon burns the potatoes or finds himself bumbling awkwardly over a diaper, demonstrating his—proud—male ineptness at such female work. But it is no longer funny.

The "politics of housework" (Mainardi, 1970) proves to be more profound than originally believed. It has to do not only with tasks but also with gender—and perhaps more with the site of the tasks than with their intrinsic nature. A man can cook magnificently if he does it on a hunting or fishing trip; he can wield a skillful needle if he does it mending a tent or a fishing net; he can even feed and clean a toddler on a camping trip. Few of the skills of the homemaker are beyond his reach so long as they are practiced in a suitably male environment. It is not only women's work in and of itself that is degrading but any work on female turf. It may be true, as Brenton (1966) says, that "the secure man can wash a dish, diaper a baby, and throw the dirty clothes into the washing machine—or do anything else women used to do exclusively—without thinking twice about it" (p. 211), but not all men are that secure. To a great many men such chores are demasculinizing. The apron is shameful on a man in the kitchen; it is all right at the carpenter's bench.

The male world may look upon the man who shares household responsibilities as, in effect, a scab. One informant tells the interviewer about a conversation on the job: "What, are you crazy?" his hard-hat fellow workers ask him when he speaks of helping his wife. ''The guys want to kill me. 'You son of a bitch! You are getting us in trouble.'. . . The men get really mad" (Lein, 1979, p. 492). Something more than persiflage is involved here. We are fairly familiar with the trauma associated with the invasion by women of the male work turf, the hazing women can be subjected to, and the male resentment of admitting them except

into their own segregated areas. The corresponding entrance of men into the traditional turf of women—the kitchen or the nursery—has analogous but not identical concomitants.

Pleck and Lang (1979) tell us that men are now beginning to change in the direction of greater involvement in family life. "Men's family behavior is beginning to change, becoming increasingly congruent with the long-standing psychological significance of the family in their lives" (p. 1). They measure this greater involvement by way of the help they offer with homemaking chores. Scanzoni (1975), on the basis of a survey of over 3,000 husbands and wives, concludes that at least in households in which wives are in the labor force, there is the "possibility of a different pattern in which responsibility for households would unequivocally fall equally on husbands as well as wives" (p. 38). A brave new world indeed. Still, when we look at the reality around us, the pace seems intolerably slow. The responsibilities of the old good-provider role have attenuated far faster than have its prerogatives and privileges.

A considerable amount of thought has been devoted to studying the effects of the large influx of women into the work force. An equally interesting question is what the effect will be if a large number of men actually do increase their participation in the family and the household. Will men find the apron shameful? What if we were to ask fathers to alternate with mothers in being in the home when youngsters come home from school? Would fighting adolescent drug abuse be more successful if fathers and mothers were equally engaged in it? If the school could confer with fathers as often as with mothers? If the father accompanied children when they went shopping for clothes? If fathers spent as much time with children as do mothers?

Even as husbands, let alone as fathers, the new pattern is not without trauma. Hall and Hall (1979), in their study of two-career couples, report that the most serious fights among such couples occur not in the bedroom, but in the kitchen, between couples who profess a commitment to equality but who find actually implementing it difficult. A young professional reports that he is philosophically committed to egalitarianism in marriage and tries hard to practice it, but it does not work. He even feels guilty about this. The stresses involved in reworking roles may have an impact on health. A study of engineers and accountants finds poorer health among those with employed wives than among those with nonemployed wives (Burke & Wier, 1976). The processes involved in role change have been compared with those involved in deprogramming a cult member. Are they part of the increasing sense of marriage and parenthood as "all burdens and restrictions"?

The demise of the good-provider role also calls for consideration of other questions: What does the demotion of the good provider to the status of senior provider or even mere coprovider do to him? To marriage? To gender identity? What does expanding the role of housewife to that of junior provider or even coprovider do to her? To marriage? To gender identity? Much will of course depend on the social and psychological ambience in which changes take place.

A PARABLE

I began this essay with a proverbial woman. I close it with a modern parable by William H. Chafe (Note 5), a historian who also keeps his eye on the current scene. Jack and Jill, both planning professional careers, he as doctor, she as lawyer, marry at age 24. She works to put him through medical school in the expectation that he will then finance her through law school. A child is born during the husband's internship, as planned. But in order for him to support her through professional training as planned, he will have to take time out from his career. After two years, they decide that both will continue their training on a part-time basis, sharing household responsibilities and using daycare services. Both find part-time positions and work out flexible work schedules that leave both of them time for child care and companionship with one another. They live happily ever after.

That's the end? you ask incredulously. Well, not exactly. For, as Chafe (Note 5) points out, as usual the personal is also political:

> Obviously such a scenario presumes a radical transformation of the personal values that today's young people bring to their relationships as well as a readiness on the part of social and economic institutions to encourage, or at least make possible, the development of equality between men and women. (p. 28)

The good-provider role may be on its way out, but its legitimate successor has not yet appeared on the scene.

NOTES

1. Hesselbart, S. Some underemphasized issues about men, women, and work. Unpublished manuscript, 1978.
2. Douvan, E. *Family roles in a twenty-year perspective.* Paper presented at the Radcliffe Pre-Centennial Conference, Cambridge, Massachusetts, April 2–4, 1978.
3. Veroff, J. *Psychological orientations to the work role: 1957–1976.* Unpublished manuscript, 1978.
4. Shostak, A. *Working class Americans at home: Changing expectations of manhood.* Unpublished manuscript, 1973.
5. Chafe, W. *The challenge of sex equality: A new culture or old values revisited?* Paper presented at the Radcliffe Pre-Centennial Conference, Cambridge, Massachusetts, April 2–4, 1978.

REFERENCES

Babcock, B., Freedman, A. E., Norton, E. H., & Ross, S. C. *Sex discrimination and the law: Causes and remedies*. Boston: Little, Brown, 1975.

Bernard, J. *Women, wives, mothers*. Chicago: Aldine, 1975.

Bernard, J. Homosociality and female depression. *Journal of Social Issues*, 1976, *32*, 207–224.

Boulding, E. Familial constraints on women's work roles. *SIGNS: Journal of Women in Culture and Society*, 1976, *1*, 95–118.

Brenton, M. *The American male*. New York: Coward-McCann, 1966.

Burke, R. & Wier, T. Relationship of wives' employment status to husband, wife and pair satisfaction and performance. *Journal of Marriage and the Family*, 1976, *38*, 279–287.

David, D. S. & Brannon, R. (Eds.). *The forty-nine percent majority: The male sex role*. Reading, Mass.: Addison-Wesley, 1976.

Demos, J. The American family in past time. *American Scholar*, 1974, *43*, 422–446.

Farrell, W. *The liberated man*. New York: Random House, 1974.

Fasteau, M. F. *The male machine*. New York: McGraw-Hill, 1974.

Fiedler, L. *Love and death in the American novel*. New York: Meredith, 1962.

Foner, P. S. *Women and the American labor movement*. New York: Free Press, 1979.

Freud, S. *Civilization and its discontents*. New York: Doubleday-Anchor, 1958. (Originally published, 1930.)

Goldberg, H. *The hazards of being male*. New York: New American Library, 1976.

Gould, R. E. Measuring masculinity by the size of a paycheck. In J. H. Pleck & J. Sawyer (Eds.). *Men and masculinity*. Englewood Cliffs, N.J.: Prentice-Hall, 1974. (Also published in *Ms.*, June 1973, pp. 18ff.)

Hall, D. & Hall, F. *The two-career couple*. Reading, Mass.: Addison-Wesley, 1979.

Jones, C. A. *A review of child support payment performance*. Washington, D.C.: Urban Institute, 1976.

Keniston, K. *The uncommitted: Alienated youth in American society*. New York: Harcourt, Brace & World, 1965.

Komarovsky, M. *The unemployed man and his family*. New York: Dryden Press, 1940.

Lefkowitz, B. Life without work. *Newsweek*, May 14, 1979, p. 31.

Lein, L. Responsibility in the allocation of tasks. *Family Coordinator*, 1979, *28*, 489–496.

Liebow, E. *Tally's corner*. Boston: Little, Brown, 1966.

Lopata, H. *Occupation housewife*. New York: Oxford University Press, 1971.

Mainardi, P. The politics of housework. In R. Morgan (Ed.), *Sisterhood is powerful*. New York: Vintage Books, 1970.

Pleck, J. H. & Lang, L. Men's family work: Three perspectives and some new data. *Family Coordinator*, 1979, *28*, 481–488.

Pleck, J. H. & Sawyer, J. (Eds.), *Men and masculinity*. Englewood Cliffs, N.J.: Prentice-Hall, 1974.

Rainwater, L. & Yancy, W. L. *The Moynihan report and the politics of controversy*. Cambridge, Mass.: M.I.T. Press, 1967.

Sarason, S. B. *Work, aging, and social change*. New York: Free Press, 1977.

Scanzoni, J. H. *Sex roles, life styles, and childbearing: Changing patterns in marriage and the family*. New York: Free Press, 1975.

Scanzoni, J. H. An historical perspective on husband-wife bargaining power and marital dissolution. In G. Levinger & O. Moles (Eds.), *Divorce and separation in America*. New York: Basic Books, 1979.

Smith, R. E. (Ed.), *The subtle revolution*. Washington, D.C.: Urban Institute, 1979.

Smuts, R. W. *Women and work in America*. New York: Columbia University Press, 1959.

Snyder, L. The deserting, non-supporting father: Scapegoat of family non-policy. *Family Coordinator*, 1979, *38*, 594–598.

Tocqueville, A. de. *Democracy in America*. New York: J. & H. G. Langley, 1840.

Warner, W. L. & Ablegglen, J. O. *Big business leaders in America*. New York: Harper, 1955.

Yankelovich, D. The new psychological contracts at work. *Psychology Today*, May 1978, pp. 46–47; 49–50.

Zborowski, M. & Herzog, E. *Life is with people*. New York: Schocken Books, 1952.

"ENGINEERING HUMOUR":
MASCULINITY, JOKING AND CONFLICT IN SHOP-FLOOR RELATIONS

DAVID L. COLLINSON

This article examines the interrelationship between humour and masculinity in the social relations of an all-male, shop-floor workforce. The analysis seeks not only to highlight the collective elements of this joking culture, but also to explore the contradictions and divisions which also characterized shop-floor relations.

It could be argued that the recurrent research finding of employee 'light-heartedness' demonstrates either that workers are generally satisfied with their fragmented tasks in the labour process or that they are able to 'let off steam' and so dissipate their frustration with deskilled and routinized jobs. For example, Roy (1958) describes how four machinists avoided 'going nuts' in the face of the 'beast of monotony' by constructing an informal group culture characterized by mock aggression and incessant teasing. Humour may also be the means by which *social* frustration and conflict can be expressed in ways that reduce hostility and maintain social order. Burawoy (1979) discovered that racial prejudice between blacks and whites was articulated in jokes on the shop-floor. Since the production process demanded a degree of worker co-operation, overt racial hostility had to be minimized and was therefore diluted in humour. Yet there is also a substantial amount of evidence suggesting that joking does not always constitute a shortcut to consensus and social harmony.

Willis' (1977) analysis of school counter-culture is particularly revealing in exposing the oppositional and collective properties of joking. He highlights how 'piss-taking' and intimidatory joking at school are creative elements in the oppositional group logic of the 'lads'. Their informal resistance provides an alternative definition of what it means to be successful to that offered by the dominant values of the education system. Willis (1977) shows how the 'false promise' of upward mobility through educational success is scorned by the lads, who pursue more immediate forms of gratification, excitement, and the establishment of male identity. The ability to produce a laugh is a defining characteristic of group membership. This working class joking culture establishes a non-conformist, highly masculine, sense of identity for its members, which celebrates practical manual work, and ridicules passive, unmanly mental work, both in school and employment.

Willis' (1979) analysis is particularly illuminating in its linkage of working class group culture, masculinity, joking and resistance. Nevertheless, it contains a tendency to *romanticize* the lads' joking culture. This is revealed in a failure to explore fully, the contradictions of both the joking culture itself and the search to secure a masculine identity that is mediated through shop-floor humour. Admittedly, he highlights the paradoxical consequence of the

Reprinted from *Organization Studies*, September 1988: 181–199 © 1988 EGOS.

lads' resistance, which, in celebrating working class life as a form of freedom, encourages them to seek out precisely those manual jobs, through which their subordination is guaranteed. Yet the internal divisions of the group culture and the destructive and self-defeating consequences of the search to realise this masculine identity are left under-explored.

In failing to question the lads' proud boastings and often apocryphal accounts of their culture, Willis (1977) neglects to examine the deep-seated social and psychological insecurities which reflect and reinforce their concern to establish and embellish gender and group identity. In one-sidedly treating identify constructions as expressions of resistance, 'the darker side' of shop-floor humour tends to be neglected in Willis' (1977) analysis. As the following case study will demonstrate, the preoccupation with defending and protecting self through humour is a powerful logic, that not only defines the boundaries of, but can also generate divisions within, the group.

The data emerged out of research conducted between 1979 and 1983 in a lorry-making factory in the North West of England (Collinson, 1981). The research, which was approved by the management, concentrated in the components division of the plant. This consisted of the departments of fabrication; axle assembly; toolroom; loading bay; paint spray; stores and two machine shops. The division employed an exclusively male workforce of 250, the vast majority of whom were classified as skilled engineers. Interviews with over sixty of these workers were conducted by the writer on a regular basis and were supplemented by non-participant observation. The primary focus of the research was management/shop-floor industrial relations. Yet, as the research progressed, a recognition of the significance of humour, in this all-male, shop-floor context, simultaneously emerged. The humour of the components division was a crucial mechanism through which shop-floor relations and practices were mediated. It reflected and reinforced the central values and practices of these male manual workers and contained elements of resistance and control, creativity and destructiveness. These contrasting elements of the joking culture will now be elaborated in turn.

HUMOUR AS RESISTANCE

Shop-floor humour was in part a form of resistance both to the tightly controlled repetitious work tasks and to the social organization of production within the company. The spontaneous and cutting creativity of shop-floor banter was indeed conditioned by a desire to make the best of the situation and to enjoy the company of others. Many of the workers themselves saw the humorous repartee as a way of dealing with the monotonous work itself, as one told me,

> *'Some days it feels like a fortnight. A few years ago I got into a rut. I had to stop myself getting bored so I increased the number of pranks at work.'*

'Having a laff' allowed these men to resist their mundane circumstances, providing the illusion of separation from an otherwise alienating situation. In addition, this frivolity and absurdity reflected and reinforced a shared sense of self and group identity and differentiation. This was illustrated by the following comment,

> *'He's writing a book about this place, it'll be a best seller, bigger than Peyton Place with all the characters in here!'*

The men were concerned to show that they were 'big enough' to laugh at themselves. Joking reflected the nature of the person. This collective self identity as a community of comedians was strengthened by the reputations of its members. These were often preserved in nicknames that were based on exaggerated and stereotypes personal characteristics. Their daily use in shop-floor discourse helped to create a mythical and imaginary world that sustained a distance from boredom and routine.

'Fat Rat', 'Bastard Jack', 'Big Lemon' and 'The Snake' were names conjured up daily in the components division. 'Electric Lips' was unable to keep secrets. 'Pot Harry' was so nicknamed because, as a teaboy, thirty years before, he had dropped and broken all the drinking 'pots'. 'Tom Pepper' was reputed to have never spoken the truth in his life. Another man was known as 'Yoyo' because of his habit of walking away and then returning during a conversation and even in mid-sentence. His 'Yoyo' record had been calculated as fifteen returns in one conversation. Although exaggerated, these culture identities contributed to shop-floor cohesion by developing a shared sense of masculinity. For only 'real men' would be able to laugh at themselves by accepting highly insulting nicknames.

The joking culture also facilitated manual workers' self-differentiation from, and antagonism to, white collar staff and managers. This defensive stance was partly the result of the conditions of shop-floor experience, which threatened the workers' sense of dignity. Of all company employees, those on the shop-floor worked the longest hours in the most insecure and tightly controlled jobs, enjoyed the worst canteen and car park facilities and the poorest holiday, pension and sickness provision. These conditions confirmed to shop-floor workers that they were the least valued and most easily disposable of employees.

'Dirty Bar' displayed how manual workers typically dealt with this degrading experience. He emphasized how manual work was the very essence of masculinity,

'Fellas on the shop-floor are genuine. They're the salt of the earth, but they're all twats and nancy boys in th'offices.'

Like 'the lads', the fellas on the shop-floor perceived their own joking culture to be a symbol of freedom and autonomy, which contrasted with the more reserved work conditions and character of the office staff. The uncompromising banter of the shop-floor, which was permeated by uninhibited swearing, mutual ridicule, displays of sexuality and 'pranks', was contrasted, exaggerated and elevated above the middle-class politeness,

cleanliness and more restrained demeanor of the offices. Ironically, when compared with others, the subordinated world of the shop-floor came to be seen as a free space in which the 'true self' could be expressed, as another worker put it,

'You can have a load of fun on the shop-floor, but in the offices, they're not the type to have a laff and a joke. You can't say 'you fucking twat!'' in the offices.'

In a similar way, the joking culture reflected and reinforced the sense of 'us and them' in relations with the management. The perceived conformism of managers and their reputed inability to make decisions led to them being nicknamed 'the yes men', and to being ridiculed as effeminate. On one occasion, as a result of a workforce 'go-slow', a significant shortfall occurred on management's projected production levels. This stimulated the axle shop steward to joke,

'(The production manager) will have a baby when he sees these figures.'

Shop-floor humour directed at managers was usually concerned to negate and distance them, as evident in the following joke found on a trade union noticeboard:

When the body was first made all parts wanted to be SUPERVISORS.

The Brain insisted. 'Since I control everything and do all the thinking, I should be Supervisor.' The Feet said, 'Since we carry man where he wants to go, we should be Supervisors.' The Hands said, 'Since we do all the work and earn all the money to keep the rest of you going, we should be Supervisors.' The Eyes too staked their claim, 'Since we must watch out for all of you, we should be Supervisors.'

An so it went on: the Heart; the Ears and finally . . . the BUM! How all the other parts laughed to think the Bum should be Supervisor!!!

Thus the Bum became mad and refused to function. The Brain became feverish: the Eyes crossed and ached: the Legs got wobbly and the Stomach went sick.

ALL pleaded with the Brain to relent and let the Bum be Supervisor. And so it came to be. That all

the other parts did their work and the Bum simply Supervised and passed a load of CRAP.

* * *

MORAL: *You don't have to be a Brain to be a Supervisor—only a Bum.*

The irony that three foremen had not been informed of a course in communication skills, to which they had been assigned, was not lost on many shop-floor workers. In general, however, shop-floor humour tended to remain within the confines of the group culture.

By contrast, management repeatedly sought to engage shop stewards in humorous interaction. Yet, the stewards were aware that managerial humour was intended to obscure conflict behind personalized relations, which tried to deny the hierarchical structure of status and power. Hence they avoided participating, for as the AUEW convenor explained,

> 'You've always got to retain a difference from management because they try to draw you in.'

Six years earlier the company had been taken over by an American multinational. The personal approach of the new regime had been rejected by the stewards,

> 'At first they tried to come on a bit, but we didn't think much of their jokes.'

As part of the American's campaign to win the trust of the workforce, a company in-house magazine was introduced. The paper was dismissed widely as a 'Let's be pals act' and nicknamed by the convenor as 'Goebbel's Gazette.' This criticism stimulated a 'jokey' response in the paper by the editors,

> 'Did you know that 'X' is being called Goebbel's Gazette in some quarters?'
> 'No I didn't, but thank you for bringing it to my Achtung'
> 'Don't get me wrong, but it is propaganda isn't it?'
> 'If propaganda is informing everyone on topics which previously were known to only a handful of people, the answer is "Yes". We do concentrate on

the plus points of the company, but so what? Our performance compares favourably with the company's plants anywhere in the world, so why present any other picture?'

The intention of managerial humour, to reduce conflict and emphasize organizational harmony, had the opposite effect of merely reinforcing the polarization between management and shop-floor.

HUMOUR AS CONFORMITY

The joking culture was based as much on the internal demands of group conformity as on collective resistance. These demands were embedded in specific rules that simulated the 'laws' of natural selection. Social 'survival of the fittest' was the underlying principle behind the pressure to be able to give and take a joke, to laugh at oneself and expect others to respond likewise to cutting remarks. The men in the components division were concerned to be how others expected them to be. Defensively engaged in the mock battles of male sparring, bluff and bravado, it was expected that these workers would be aggressive, critical and disrespectful, so as to create embarrassment in others. For this was the symbolic scalp of the successful 'piss-take', as one engineer explained,

> 'You've got to give it or go under. It's a form of survival, you insult first before they get one back. The more you get embarrassed, the more they do it, so you have to fight back. It can hurt deep down, although you don't show it.'

and his workmate interjected 'you'll learn fuck all there!' to which he responded 'You see what I mean, you've got to get the knife in the back first.' Behind this image of toughness, masculinity and an apparent ability to withstand ridicule from others was an acknowledgement that the jibes could, and did sometimes, hurt, as one man privately conceded,

> 'I detest being embarrassed, so I take the piss out of the others.'

Nevertheless, in adhering to the rules of social survival, workers prided themselves on their predatory ability to 'pounce' on the weaknesses of their colleagues, so as to 'wind them up', as Jack exemplified,

> 'I can get Fred going easy. Friday, I pointed to the foreman's cabin and said, "I can remember when you said, That was going to be mine!" Then he was at it all afternoon.'

Some were 'bullet makers' and some were 'firers' of the joking attacks, which were considered to be skilled penetrations of other's weaknesses. Practical jokes in particular 'sounded out' their victims, who had to show that they could 'stand' being the object of humour. For example, an amateur weightlifter was assured that he would not be able to lift Allan, because the latter could increase his weight at will. The weightlifter failed. This was because Allan had nailed his shoes to the duckboard and therefore the man was trying to lift Allan, the board, and himself. The element of surprise was also exploited to maximum effect in practical jokes, like the 'plastic spider trick', as Allan again outlined,

> 'It was fucking essence with Brown and the spider. It was his first day back from illness and he was reading so we lowered it over his shoulder. He finished up fighting with it.'

Newcomers to the shop-floor, in particular, were quickly informed of the requirements for group acceptance. Apprentices, for example, had to negotiate a series of degrading and humiliating initiation ceremonies. Such ceremonies were viewed by their perpetrators as worthwhile experience, and as real learning about taking a joke and being a man. Being able to take a joke was a sign that the lessons of the shop-floor had been learnt.

Exposure to the joking culture, not only instructed new members on how to act and react, but also constituted a test of the willingness of initiates to be part of the male group and to accept its rules. For example, one apprentice had to sing Christmas carols to the rest of the work-force as part of his initiation in 'bringing me out of meself',

> 'There were three of us. It was embarrassing but everybody does it, so you accept it, you've got to "laff back", it's the only way. I used to get embarrassed easy, but not now here.'

Similarly, pancake Tuesday was celebrated by 'greasing the bollocks' of the apprentices with emulsion and then 'locking them in the shithouse, bollock naked.' The lads had to 'take it', in order to survive on the shop-floor. Having graduated through these degradation ceremonies, they would be recognized as mature men worthy of participating fully in the shop-floor culture and banter. That is, if they could also 'take' the daily practical jokes, for which their lack of knowledge made them ideal victims, as one engineer exemplified,

> 'I like shocking the apprentices. A classic is sending one of the lads for a "a long stand". They go over and say, "Bob sent me for a long stand". The other bloke'll say "O.K.' and then after a while he'll say, "Is that long enough?" "Fucking hell" the apprentice will think.'

But some failed the test as the same engineer complained,

> 'The new apprentice is religious and looks away from women. I'm really pissed-off with him because you can't have a caper with him.'

Those who were perceived to be 'different' were either kept at a distance, or had to accept incorporation into the joking culture on its own terms. For example, the story of one lad, who entered the company with 'diplomas galore', was often recited,

> 'They had a French letter on his back by ten o'clock. They had him singing and dancing in the loo with the pretext of practicing for a pantomime . . . we soon brought him round to our way of thinking.'

These practical jokes enabled manual workers to alleviate any feelings of inferiority by undermining the sense of superiority assumed to be harboured by this lad.

I too had to be trained to 'think correctly', and was rechristened by members of the culture, who were attempting to transcend the uncertainty and 'strangeness' of my presence and observation of their world. Surprised that anyone could be paid 'just for going around talking to people', I was seen as 'something to do with psychiatry', which my new shop-floor nicknames reflected. Different areas of the factory created different names for me, such as 'Dr. Bob', 'the Headshrinker', 'Rand and Rave', (rhymes with Dave) 'The Absent-minded Professor' and 'The Lardee-da University Lad'. When these comments became open criticisms, it seemed to represent a humorous sign of partial acceptance, at least on their terms, into the cultural fabric. Yet, the motive was not merely the production of humour. Behind such comments as 'Keep your business out of our fucking nose' and 'He'll have you talking all day will this sod!' was a real warning that I was 'sniffing' in places that ought to remain private. It also reflected the suspicion about my motives for research. For example, my visits were half jokingly interpreted as 'fact-finding missions' to 'get the mood of the shop-floor' for management, 'Why else would they let you in?' I was asked. The comments that followed my initiation tended to be directed at the issues which seemed to differentiate them from me, often concentrating on undermining what was assumed to be important to me,

'This cunt thinks that a manual labourer is a Spanish bullfighter! Your tutor must have some trouble with you! . . . He went to Dublin University this lazy cunt! . . . This twat's a spy for E.R.F. . . . Fancy talking to this fucker outside, it's alright when you're paid to do it, but there'd be no way outside! . . . Are you going to call this book, "How I Wasted Twelve Months"?'

The jokes maintained a very conscious sense of difference and ideological support for their own world. Hence when washing my hands in the toilet I was asked, with great concern, 'Have you fallen over?' The implication being that, as a 'mental worker', this could be the only possible

way of getting my hands dirty. It is important to recognize that despite the overtly humorous exterior of these comments, another more serious meaning lurked beneath the surface. Workers retained a masculine pride in their manual, productive skills and practical experience, remaining suspicious of purely theoretical ideas that were seen as inferior to 'commonsense.' Like the apprentices, initiation was also facilitated, by practical jokes. On more than one occasion, I spent much of the day unknown to myself carrying flowers made from paper cups on my back. The news that I had been enrolled into the distinguished order, below, seemed to be final confirmation that I was not as clever as they thought, I thought, I was. One worker asked me for tenpence on the pretext of buying a cup of coffee. In receipt, I was given the following card,

You were just conned out of 10p and you are now a member of the

DUMB FUCKERS CLUB

In order to resign from this honourable and distinguished organisation, you must pass the Membership Card on to another Cunt like yourself and your fee will be refunded.

Should you fail to get a refund, you will automatically become president and bestowed the honour of being the

DUMBEST FUCKER IN TOWN

Such ridicule facilitated the display of tough masculinity and the testing of these same qualities in others. The rules of the joking culture reflected the content of much shop-floor discourse, which centred on a preoccupation with male sexuality and the differentiation of working class men from women.

Within the all-male environment of the components division, masculine sexual prowess was a pervasive topic. Mediated through bravado and joking relations, a stereotypical image of self, which was assertive, independent, powerful and sexually insatiable was constructed and protected. By contrast, women were dismissed as passive, dependent and only interested in catching a man. These images contributed to male unity on the shop-floor and constituted a powerful pressure, to which shop-floor workers were required to conform.

Photos of female nudes could be found on most shop-floor walls in the division. Many of these had been supplied by the 'Porn King' who maintained a 'sex library' of magazines for shop-floor edification. In addition, proud boasts and comments such as the following were part of the daily fabric of shop-floor interaction:

'I've had many a jump at the local train station.'
'Men come from the womb and spend the rest of their lives trying to get back in'.
'You'll never win with women because they're sitting on a goldmine. They'll always have the power.'
'At school I was very shy. I went red if the girls talked to me. If they talk to me now, I'll shag them!'

Such statements confirmed to manual workers and their colleagues who, and what, they were, i.e. tough, autonomous and invulnerable men who simply expressed their predatory nature in joking about sexual matters.

Two primary and typical forms of male sexuality, related to the conventional male life-cycle, permeated shop-floor discourse. Younger men tended to display a fetishization of sexuality and a reduction of women to sexual objects. This was exemplified by the 'sexploitative' mentality of twenty-three-year-old 'Boris'. Much of his shop-floor contact was spent embellishing his infamous reputation as a self-defined 'super-stud'. He maintained a 'sex diary' which listed all his past 'conquests'. Concerned to 'trap' females, Boris graded out of ten the 'performance' of his twenty 'victims'. A 'scientific analysis' revealed that the older the woman (especially if she was married), the higher she was graded. Boris proudly boasted of his escapades and the 'carpet burns on my knees.' But his exaggerated accounts of sexual exploits were received with disbelief and ridicule. A recurrent comment by Ernie was,

'He's a Don Juan is Boris . . . When he's had Juan he's Don!'

Alternatively, older manual workers often prioritized their domestic power as the family bread-winner. Accordingly, they treated work primarily as a means of securing an income. This role of the provider invariably constituted a crucial element of masculine self-respect, as 'Dirty Bar' indicated,

'I think you should be useful with your life. I love family responsibility. I would have ten kids, if I could afford them. It's easy to have kids, but it takes a man to bring them up.'

The older men's joking reflected their concern with the preservation of male authority in the home and with economic instrumentalism at work. For example, a majority of those interviewed claimed that they did not reveal the size of their wage packet to their wives. The few who admitted that they did, were attacked unmercifully. Fred, a general labourer, was ridiculed by Jack, the axle shop steward, for 'tipping' his wage packet. The former's henpecked home-life was always an amusing theme on which to draw, as Jack outlined,

'She has Fred chasing his own tail at home. See what an effect it has on him, he's in a daze, he's had a sheltered life. He'd prefer to read a book than have sex!

This contrasts with Jack, who had kept his wages secret from his wife throughout their eleven married years,

'I don't think a woman should see your wage packet. It's a matter of understanding in our house. She understands I am in command.'

The emphasis of the joking culture therefore shifted from 'trapping' to 'tipping', from sexuality to domestic power. As one older worker explained,

'At eighteen I thought they were good for screwing. Now I realise they've other uses.'

One male self-identity, as sexually rampant, was superceded by another, that of the responsible family breadwinner. In both cases, however, shop-floor workers were expected to subscribe to the masculine assumptions of the joking culture. Yet these demands to conform inevitably generated a form of reluctant compliance from some workers which rendered shop-floor unity at best precarious and fragile. The oppositional values of personal freedom, masculine independence and autonomy, enshrined in the breadwinner role, contributed to these divisions, in particular, by compounding the separation between the 'public' sphere of work and the 'private' world of home. The collective experience of shared masculinity at work often contradicted the individualistic orientation to life outside.

For example, the profuse swearing of the men on the shop-floor contrasted sharply with their behaviour outside, as other research has discovered (e.g. Pitt 1979; Cockburn 1983). In the presence of women, it was often considered a 'mark of respect' to refrain from swearing. One axle assembler, infamous for his 'foul-mouthed grumpiness', exemplified this contrast between the collectivity of work and the private individualism of home,

> *'I'm noted for swearing in here, but I'd never swear in the house. At work we're all lads together. It's natural isn't it? But I can easily stop it. You can't swear at home, so you let it out at work.'*

Similar assumptions were revealed in the following shop-floor banter,

> *'There's two parts to me. I'm free and easy here. At work I swear and sing my head off, and in the games room, but if women are present I won't, it's respect. I don't like to hear a woman swear.'*

Bert, who was divorced, interjected, 'I used to tell mine to fuck off.' Steve, who was married, replied 'Aye, that's why he's separated.' Bert, 'Yea, but he has to put his hand up to speak to his missus'. Although he was a major participant in the piss-taking, Bert also revealed privately, the extent to which relations between the men remained superficial and distant, despite their collective appearance,

> *'Yea, they take the piss out of you here, but it would not bother me if they were a load of strangers.'*

Moreover some respondents conceded that their involvement in macho joking was merely a performance designed to comply with the demands of the culture,

> *'It's accepted to swear here. You want to feel accepted but it's a false picture. They think it's soft to stir tea with a spoon. You've got to use your ruler, so you don't look effeminate . . . But the real me is the one at home where I don't swear.'*

Similarly, workers sometimes objected to the use of shop-floor nicknames in their 'private' leisure time, as 'Dirty Bar' complained,

> *'In a pub recently the landlord said, 'Ah Dirty Bar, and this must be Mrs. Dirty Bar!' Now that is too personal. I don't mind being called "Dirty Bar" in work . . . well there's nothing I can do about it. If I don't like it, they'll call it me behind my back. But I won't accept it outside.'*

The whole masculine style of shop-floor joking was aimed at testing and displaying the individual's inner strength to withstand teasing and ridicule. Yet, paradoxically, many of the men who subscribed to the culture and articulated its demands could not, in fact, handle them. The pressing and pervasive desire to secure male dignity in the eyes of others was repeatedly found to be incompatible with a concern to display impregnability and a disregard for the crit/witicisms of others. The sensitivity of working-class male identity meant that joking was often misinterpreted, when used as a pretence of hostility, and construed correctly when employed to 'make a point'. Invariably, the result was that its victim would snap'. Snapping was the cultural term of a successful breaking down of another's defences. 'Billy Snap' was so named because he very quickly failed to see the joke. Colleagues sometimes had to be 'wiped up off the floor' after making Billy the butt of their jokes. 'Losing your rag' was almost as commonplace as 'having a joke' in these shop-floor relations.

Workers themselves differentiated between 'taking the piss' on the one hand, and 'one-up-manship' and 'malicious piss-taking', on the other. The result of the latter was division, as one scapegoated worker in the paint-spray shop illustrated,

'I've never known a more awkward lot than in the other room. Fellas there like to laff at your own failure. They enjoy taking the piss in a different way. It's serious not funny. We've not spoken to them for weeks and weeks.'

In the case of 'Deaf Dave', the joking resulted in his total emotional breakdown. In conforming to the 'macho' verbal violence that denied any concern for its victim, Dave had his 'leg pulled' and took 'the pain' 'like a man'. But his disability made him an easy target for the practical joke and one day the men went too far. His locker was removed and hidden on three separate occasions, but then replaced each time before Dave returned with the foreman. On the third occasion, Dave broke down. After the incident, although he continued to claim 'it's a good job I can take it', receiving only unsympathetic replies such as 'you fucking have to mate!' the men tended to turn their attention elsewhere for a scapegoat.

The concern to differentiate self on the criteria of being able to laff and take a joke was not confined to those employees outside the shop-floor, as one axle fitter illustrated,

'Them in the bottom shop, they're only after the money. They're a bunch of miserable fuckers, but we're a breed on our own in here "Lostock" (another section of the plant) are even worse. They're very vindictive.'

This statement reveals a tension between the informal culture of 'having a laff' and the formal collective bonus system which encouraged workers to pursue high wages. It is a tension that reflects a conflict between two different forms of resistance and two separate manifestations of masculinity. First, there was the *collective* group culture of piss-taking, which was united in a shared masculinity and in the avoidance, or at

least restriction, of work output. Second, there was the individual economic instrumentalism which distanced self, while maximizing wages, in order to provide for dependents in the home. It is along these conflicting axes that the most serious shop-floor conflicts occurred. The pressure of the bonus scheme and the preoccupation with male identity combined to generate disputes between specific workers in all seven departments where research took place.

HUMOUR AS CONTROL

Conflict in the Components Division was often the result of veiled insults, mediated through ambiguous piss-takes, which implied that other men were either miserable or lazy. In such cases, the pressure to conform to routine shop-floor values and practices was thereby transformed into worker strategies of mutual control and discipline. In the bottom machine shop, for example, several men had not spoken to each other for a number of years. One man had threatened to go to the foreman because another continually criticized him for being a 'lazy bastard'. In the axle department an apprentice was constantly attacked because he was a 'lazy cunt'. One older worker was particularly sarcastic, as he asked me,

'Has he told you about his dreams, 'cos that's all he does here!'

This was just one example of a steady stream of cutting remarks designed to act as a social control over 'deviants'. The precariousness and fragility of shop-floor identity repeatedly led to the collapse of work relationships, as the 'bullets' hit their target and workers began to 'snap'. For example, Jimmy 'Silver Sleeve' (he did not use a handkerchief) and Tony were school chums, drinking partners and workmates. Yet conflict broke out between them,

'Tony likes to give it, but snaps sometimes when I do it back. Once he really snapped. "That's enough" he said "or I'll drop you!", I said,

"Right, let's get out on the croft". He didn't speak to me for three days, then he was alright again.'

The dispute centred on Jimmy's accusation about Tony's laziness, as the former continued,

'They're a motley crew in the stores. Some there I wouldn't pay in marbles! They just go to work to clown about half the time!'

In the top machine shop two distinct groups of antagonistic workers emerged. A younger section comprised 'Dirty Bar', Boris, Allan, 'Silent Night' and Brian, while an older group, close to retirement, included 'Eyebrow' and 'Ronnie Barker'. The former faction were heavily embroiled in piss-taking, but the latter were more serious and reserved. The relationship between 'Ronnie Barker' and 'Silent Night' had deteriorated after the latter had sent the rate-fixer to re-time 'Ronnie's job' with the implication that he was lazy. Ronnie complained,

'It's childish, they're like little kids. I don't speak to Brian. He started it, but then he couldn't take it. People in glass houses shouldn't throw stones. When I started back, he said, "You're a cunt, getting personal". But you've got to go one better.'

Concerned to protect himself from such piss-taking, Ronnie was unable to acknowledge the extent to which he also lived in a 'glass house.'

Similarly, a dispute between 'Dirty Bar' and 'Eyebrow' degenerated into a 'slanging match' in the foreman's office. They had been 'good mates' and 'Eyebrow' had originally helped 'Dirty Bar' with his work. Then 'Dirty Bar' started to call 'Eyebrow' a 'miserable cunt', who 'thinks he does all the work', while the latter responded,

'You always get this aggro creeping in. Dirty Bar was a piss-taker, that's alright, but if he gets a bollocking back, he didn't like it.'

The following practical joke by 'Dirty Bar' had exacerbated this rift,

'Eyebrow was off for a week. So we stuffed his overalls, put a face on it, pen and paper open on the crossword page, fag in his mouth and glasses.

When he came back, he didn't speak to a few for a week or so.'

With both accusing each other of laziness, the relationship collapsed completely as 'Eyebrow' shut a door in the face of 'Dirty Bar', who was carrying steel sheets and the latter responded by supplying the former with 'bent, dirty, wrong length bars and the worst quality I can find' (hence his nickname).

Another breakdown in work relationships was also mediated through a clash of the two shop-floor practices of 'having a laff' and of 'maximizing wages'. Len in the top machine shop was particularly proud of his reputation as a 'character'. He sought to reconfirm his self image as 'the works idiot' within the everyday joking banter of the shop-floor. Being the butt of the majority of jokes confirmed to Len his popularity and prestige, as he explained,

'I'm one of the characters in here. A lot are just another brick in the wall, but I stand out . . . There's been at least three punch-ups in here. I've been involved in action . . . mainly running away!'

He recounted the following story with pride,

'Tony followed me into the loo and shouted my name. When he heard me voice, over came a bucket of water!'

Did that upset you?

'No, that was a bit of fun. He was me mate. And I'd asked for it. I'd said his wife was like a pig . . . but she is a bit!'

During interviews with Len, numerous people would come up to 'rib' him, and criticize him for skiving,

'Your [sic] just like your Dad. I used to pull him off the ceiling twice a day! You won't get any sense out of him! It's a wonder they make a profit with him working here! Get some work done!'

Len's usual defence was to attack others for their laziness. He had nicknamed one worker on an adjacent lathe as 'No Bonus Stanley'.

'You're not as clever as you think you are. Stan is much more intelligent because he earns a hundred quid a week for doing nothing, but you get nowt!'

Once again, what began as the pretence of hostility collapsed as the serious messages underlying this piss-taking surfaced. Tom was Len's main assailant. In response, Len had nicknamed him 'Council Flat Tommy', whom he described, in the following pejorative statement,

'He's very simple. He lives in a council house and dips his bread in his fucking beer. "Tom Hops" they call him. I never let anyone call me simple because I'm a property owner. They say they wouldn't like the responsibility, but it would worry me having a council house. That (pointing to Tom) is an example of what this place does to you after twelve years.'

Involving myself in what I understood to be a strongly developed form of joking disrespect, I asked Tom, 'What do you think of Len?' He replied, 'I don't.'

Soon after this altercation neither person was prepared to talk to the other. Len's defence had been to criticize Tommy for failing in his role of male provider. For several respondents, house ownership was an important source of independence and male dignity as the family breadwinner. When Tom reported Len for skiving, the latter responded,

'This fella is a malicious liar. He's just thick. I'm not dealing with such rubbish. My critics are all council house halfwits!'

As a result of these shop-floor battles for dignity, which emerge in jokes but collapse into mutual disdain, hierarchical control becomes unnecessary, as Len pointed out,

'The men are the gaffers now. They watch each other like hawks. The nature of the blokes is such that they turn on each other. Human nature plays against itself. You're more worried about what the men think than the gaffers . . . I'm just as bad if there's someone not working.'

For a while, the group sanctioning led by Tommy coerced Len to work harder and to resign from the joking game. Old habits die hard, however, and the inevitable sarcasm returned. One morning, two months later I was confronted by a raging Len, who shouted at me, 'I may be a silly cunt but at least I own my own house.' It was explained to me later that Tommy had set Len up' by informing him that I had said, 'I see that silly cunt is still here!' The banter had stopped only temporarily.

CONCLUSION

This article has highlighted three specific aspects of the joking culture. First, humour was shown to operate as one medium through which collective solidarity to *resist* boredom, the organizational status system and managerial control emerged. Second, shop-floor joking was found to embody considerable social pressure to *conform* to its central preoccupation with working-class masculinity. Manual workers were required to display a willingness, for example, to give and take a joke, to swear, to be dismissive of women, and to retain their domestic authority. Third, the research discovered that shop-floor humour became a means by which workers sought to *control* those perceived to be not 'pulling their weight'. Accordingly, a romanticized account of the culture had to be avoided since deepseated and longstanding shop-floor conflicts emerged out of joking relationships that went 'too far'. Clearly the bonus scheme, which was calculated on a collective basis (see Collinson 1981), reinforced some workers' concern to control and discipline colleagues. However, the preoccupation with masculine working-class identity, expressed in 'having a laff' at work, or in maximizing wages to provide for domestic dependents, was an equally crucial factor which compounded shop-floor divisions. The collective bonus scheme merely exposed the precariousness of masculine identity on the shop-floor and revealed the fragility of shop-floor collectivity.

The privatized male identity as family breadwinner also contributed to a weakening of shop-floor solidarity. Indeed these additional domestic responsibilities constituted an important difference between the working class 'lads' of the school counter-culture highlighted by Willis (1977) and the 'fellas' on the shop-floor. For the latter, the pressures to conform were greater because of the threat of job loss and the probable need to 'provide for a family'. Hence it was more difficult for the fellas to engage in similar oppositional practices to those of the 'lads', who could see no material vested interests in remaining at school. The danger of romanticizing working-class shop-floor culture is therefore all the more important to avoid. The material realities of shop-floor life, combined with the symbolic preoccupation with working-class masculinity resulted in relationships between the men that were largely defensive and superficial. This was no basis to establish the mutual closeness, commitment and respect from which effective, collective shop-floor resistance could emerge. The evidence presented highlights the importance of theorizing the social construction of gender identity as a means of analyzing much of both the creativity and the 'dark side' of organizational humour.

Ultimately, in this company, the pervasive concern to differentiate a highly masculine sense of self from the organization through joking and other working-class cultural relations contradicted the reality or organizational power and managerial control. This was illustrated most sharply in 1983 when closure of the components plant was announced with the loss of 153 jobs. Rather than reinforcing the male solidarity of the shop-floor, to fight at the minimum for improved redundancy payments, this decision merely exacerbated the fragmentation of the workforce. Despite, or perhaps indeed because of, the central values of the joking culture, which emphasized personal virility, privatized freedom and masculine independence, workers voted to accept the lump-sum package without a fight. Ironically, their resistance had finally been exposed as little more than a joke.

NOTE

The author would like to thank Jeff Hearn and David Morgan for their comments on a earlier draft of this paper.

REFERENCES

Burawoy, Michael
1979 *Manufacturing consent*. Chicago: University of Chicago Press.
Cockburn, Cynthia
1983 *Brothers: Male dominance and technological change*. London: Pluto Press.
Collinson, David L.
1981 'Managing the shop-floor'. Unpublished Msc, Department of Management Sciences, UMIST, Manchester.
Linstead, Steve
1985 'Jokers wild: the importance of humour in the maintenance of organizational culture'. *The Sociological Review* 33/4 (November): 741–767.

Pitt, Malcolm
1979 *The world on our backs*. London: Lawrence and Wishart.
Roy, Donald F.
1958 'Banana time: job satisfaction and informal interaction'. *Human Organisation* 18: 158–168.
Willis, Paul
1977 *Learning to labour*. London: Saxon House.
Willis, Paul
1979 'Shop-floor culture, masculinity and the wage form' in *Working class culture*. J. Clarke, C. Critcher, and R. Johnson (eds.), 185–198. London: Hutchinson.

CLASS, GENDER, AND MACHISMO:
THE "TREACHEROUS-WOMAN" FOLKLORE
OF MEXICAN MALE WORKERS

MANUEL PEÑA

Mexican machismo and its vulgar folklore have long been of interest to students of Mexican culture. This article, based on research among a group of undocumented male workers, reexamines one aspect of this folklore—its degradation of women—and proposes that, besides legitimizing the oppression of women, it plays an ideological role in class conflict. The article argues that, as a signifying system unique to working-class male culture, the folklore of machismo symbolically conflates class and gender by shifting the point of conflict from the public domain of the former to the domestic domain of the latter.

Interpretation proper . . . always presupposes, if not a conception of the unconscious itself, then at least some mechanism of mystification or repression in terms of which it would make sense to seek a latent meaning behind a manifest one, or to rewrite the surface categories of a text in the stronger language of a more fundamental interpretive code. (Jameson 1981, 60)

The twentieth-century Mexican *canción-ranchera*[1] is noted for the prevalence of one theme—*la mujer traicionera* (the treacherous woman)[2] and other complementary stereotypes. Stereotypical, also, is the eternal lament of these songs, which is accompanied by the ever-present *copa de vino*—the wine glass—to help the forlorn lover drown his despair. If we were to interpret the ranchera at face value, we might conclude that Mexican women are a treacherous and de-

based lot and that Mexican men are emotional weaklings who readily succumb to alcoholism to obliterate their sorrows. Neither of these conclusions would be correct. If anything, the traditional Mexican woman is faithful to a fault, although the second assumption, the Mexican's strong attraction to alcohol, may stand closer scrutiny.

What, then, are we to make of the theme of the treacherous woman and similar debased-female stereotypes, such as that of the perverted wench? These are prevalent not only in the canción ranchera but also in a kind of folklore that forms the subject of this article—the folklore of machismo (Paredes 1966). The article explores the theme of the treacherous woman in the folklore of machismo and its relationship to Mexican working-class male ideology. It proposes that, in addition to legitimizing the oppression

Reprinted from *Gender & Society*, Vol. 5 No. 1, March 1991: 30–46 © 1991 Sociologists for Women in Society.

of women, the folklore symbolically conflates class and gender, shifting the point of conflict from the former, which is shrouded in mystification, to the latter, which is more susceptible to conscious ideological manipulation.

The interpretation offered here differs from previous analyses of Mexican machismo, Paredes (1966), for example, attributed much of the symbolism of the folklore of machismo to Mexican middle-class men and their reaction to the overbearing presence of the Americans and their sense of cultural superiority. Paz (1961), Ramos (1962), and other scholars have analyzed Mexican machismo generally as the psychohistorical product of a traumatic Spanish conquest. I agree with Paredes that machismo is a universal phenomenon and not the result of conquest trauma; however, I do not think it is primarily an expression of Mexican middle-class men's resentment toward Americans. In fact, as Ramos (1962) and others have observed, the style of discourse in which macho folklore best flourishes—vulgar language, sadistic insults, the utter degradation of women—is more characteristic of working-class men than their middle-class counterparts.

This article argues that the folkloric theme of the treacherous woman is a key element in the ideology of machismo and that both are intimately tied to Mexican working-class, male culture. This ideology derives its power not from the psychohistorical effects of a conquest trauma, as Ramos and others have proposed, but from the specific conditions that have historically shaped Mexican culture—extreme economic exploitation and its attendant deprivation and alienation. The article uses a historical-materialist theory to link class, gender, and culture and thereby reveals the connection among folklore, the ideology of machismo, and the oppressed economic condition of the Mexican male worker.

ON METHOD

The data for the article were collected during fieldwork I conducted between 1986 and 1988 among Mexican immigrant men who worked for a large agribusiness firm near Fresno, California. The firm, which I shall call S&J Growers, employed about 450 men and women during the peak summer season—harvesting, packing, and shipping a variety of fruits and nuts. All the women (a total of about 50), as well as a handful of men, were employed in the packing shed. The remainder of the men worked in the fields and orchards. The vast majority of the workers were undocumented at the time I began the fieldwork. However, most of them became eligible for amnesty under the provisions of the U.S. Immigration Reform and Control Act of 1986, and by 1988 many of the men and women at S&J Growers had been granted amnesty.

I conducted the research exclusively among the men who worked in the orchards. Most of that research was carried out during the summers of 1986 and 1987, when I logged more than 400 hours picking fruit alongside the men who collaborated with me in this study. They knew the *patrón* had given me permission to collect "stories and jokes" from them, which made it easier for me to intervene in their work routine. During my first days in the field, I would walk up to a group of workers, introduce myself, and begin picking fruit next to them. I would then engage them in casual conversation to get acquainted. Later, as I became more familiar to the men and they more open with me, I started bringing a portable cassette recorder to the field. With microphones discreetly concealed in my shirt pocket, I taped a number of conversations, as well as over 100 assorted jokes, riddles, and rhymes, known collectively as *charritas* to the workers.

Among the charritas collected is the subcategory with which this article is concerned—*charritas coloradas* (red jokes)—which form the core of the folklore of machismo and whose unvarying message is "sadism toward women and symbolic threats of sodomy toward other males" (Paredes 1966, 121). I should point out that the workers were at first reluctant to share these often-risqué charritas with me. In due time, however, this type of humor surged to the forefront, and once the workers convinced themselves that I was especially interested in charritas coloradas, these became the dominant genre performed.

The methods I employed in my research—participation and observation—were keyed to the performance context of the charritas as a generator of meaning and interpretation. The charritas cannot be properly analyzed outside that context. Any given context, however, is inevitably altered by the ethnographer's biases. As advocates of reflexive anthropology have often reminded us, ethnography is not the science of cultural analysis but the art of writing "partial truths" (Clifford 1986, 7). Thus, although the limitations inherent in the fieldwork enterprise do not, by any means, invalidate our interpretations, they do commit us to one-sided accounts, since it is impossible for the ethnographer to know and portray a whole way of life (Clifford 1986, 7–8). This interpretive ethnography is no exception.

CHARRITAS AND TREACHEROUS WOMEN

As Paredes correctly noted (1966), the woman is singled out for a special, if ignominious, role in the folklore of machismo. Typically, in the charrita colorada she may be reduced to a state of absolute sexual passivity, an unwitting object for the sadistic amusement of the macho.[3] Or, as is more common in the canción ranchera, she may be portrayed as a heartless wench who betrays her lover without the slightest sense of remorse.[4] In either case, the folkloric portrayal stands in stark contrast to the normative expectations of the idealized Mexican woman—the mother described by Díaz-Guerrero (1975, 3) as the source of boundless love and "absolute self-sacrifice."

The charritas analyzed in the following pages illustrate both portrayals. The immediate context in which they were performed is important, because all of them were embedded in discourse with clear implications for gender relations as conceived by these male workers. For example, during a conversation with four men, aged 18 to 25, regarding the differences between Mexican

and Mexican-American women, a number of points were raised with respect to gender roles and the relationship that should obtain between men and women. In the context of this relationship, the man proclaimed the superiority of the Mexican woman over her Mexican-American counterpart, whom they considered lazy, footloose, unfaithful, and generally insubordinate to men's authority. One of the workers complained that Mexican-American women, or Chicanas, were *muy libertinas*—"too unrestrained or licentious":[5]

I don't want the same thing to happen to me as it did to a neighbor, who married a woman from here, and not even with blows could he control her, to keep her from running around like a harlot.

Another worker summed up the tenor of the discussion with the following assessment:

Over there [in Mexico] one has command over them, and scolds them and all that. But not here; if she feels that things don't suit her, she gets out and leaves.

At length, the conversation took on a lighter vein, and it was then that one of the men made the offensive but tongue-in-cheek observation that, "las chicanas son más putas que las gallinas [Chicanas are worse whores than hens]." Taking my cue from this folkloric statement, I asked for some charritas about women. The two that follow were particularly keyed to the conversation of the moment. The first one articulates the theme of the treacherous woman, who, out of sheer perversity, picks up and walks out on her man to go and enjoy the "fast life":

A man was left by his wife—she liked the fast life [le gustaba el pedo]. And the man lost himself in drinking. He would get drunk, and he would get like this, sitting down, with his slobber [baba] coming out of his mouth. And he was sitting on a chair like this [the performer mimics a drunk man], with slobber all the way down. And somebody said to him, "Señor, ¡la baba, la baba!" "Sí," he answered, "sí lavaba—y planchaba y todo, pero se me fué, ¡la hija de la chingada!"

The humor in this charrita lies in its word play, of course. When the man is alerted to the slobber drooling from his mouth (¡la baba, la baba!), he interprets what he hears as a question related to his wife's competence as a home-maker: *¿lavaba, lavaba?*—"Did she wash [clothes]?" To which he replies, "Yes, she washed—and she ironed and everything, but she left me, the bitch."

As soon as the laughter and other gratuitous remarks elicited by this charrita died down, an-other worker volunteered the following one, in which the woman is depicted as a debased, sex-driven pervert who in the end gets more than she has bargained for. The repeated references to her as a *vieja* (here, a whorelike figure) underscore her depraved, perverse character:

There was this woman who liked the thing, you know, who liked for men to stick the thing in her. And then she came to a field like this [gesturing to-ward the field around us], where there was a lot of raza [Mexican men]. She says, "I've come for one who is really big, who can fill me up," she says. No, well, they all started to show up. "Let's see here, Carlos [the author of the first charrita], you who have such a big one." No, they all showed up, and she sized them all, and the vieja would say, "No, I want a bigger one." And they all came, one after another. And she says, "No, bigger." "No," they say, "bring Gollo." So Gollo arrives and he was really big. So he starts to get down on her, until he left her so worn out she couldn't even get up, the vieja. He was so big, he left her all hurt—but he won the bet. So she starts walking, all hurt, she couldn't even walk, when a robber comes out with a knife and says, "El dinero, o la degollo." "¡No, no," she cries, "la de Gollo ya no, la de Gollo ya no!"

In this charrita, again, the humor revolves around a linguistic misinterpretation: *El dinero o la degollo* translates into "the money or I'll de-capitate you [*la degollo*]." However, the woman, still reeling from Gollo's sexual assault, confuses la degollo for the identically sounding but even more terrifying *la de Gollo*—Gollo's "it," that is, his penis. The robber's threat is thus heard as, "The money, or you get Gollo's penis [again]."

In the end, besides debasing the woman, the charrita redeems macho pride, which is embod-ied in the symbol of male prowess, Gollo's enor-mous penis (cf. Paredes 1966, 121; Paz 1961, 82; Ramos 1962, 59–60). The men were obviously aware of all these implications, and their cheers and raucous laughter left no doubt that they en-joyed seeing their side triumph in this small skirmish between men and women.

Charritas often bolster common beliefs about gender relations. For example, I was engaged in conversation with three workers, one in his late teens, the other two in their 30s. Again, at my ini-tiative the conversation turned to relations be-tween men and women, especially in Chicano versus Mexican marriages:

MP: Are you telling me that the woman from here is more difficult to get along with than the woman from over there?

J: I believe so. The woman from over there will follow you wherever you want. The one from here, if she doesn't want to, she won't go. She stays here. You marry a young one from here and two, three years later you're single. You come here, they go out dancing. "Your wife, where is she?" She goes here, she goes there.

B: You know what advantage the women have here? The women from here, the ones who are alone who have been left [by their hus-bands] are supported by welfare. And over there they are not. That's why they [women in Mexico] don't leave you.

At this point, the conversation switched to the men's explanations as to why Chicanos do not come out to the fields to work, but moments later one of the men engaged in the conversation re-membered that a fellow working nearby had made up a charrita especially for me. He called him over and had him recite it for all present. It was a rhyme:

At the top of that mountain
I have a carton of beer;
open your legs Teresa,
'cause I'm coming at you headlong.

While this charrita does not depict the woman as treacherous or debased, it does reduce her to a pliant, submissive creature whose function, at least implicitly, is to satisfy the sexual whims of her man. Coming as it did moments after a serious discussion about women, it reinforced the general tone of the conversation from the men's point of view: It is a man's inalienable right to exercise control over a woman, to possess her sexually when he wishes—in effect, to render her defenseless and penetrate her at will. The men appreciated the performer's inventiveness and his artistic handling of the topic and rewarded him with claps and cheers of approval.

Several more charritas followed on the heels of this one, as the men around us began to warm up to the session. One, offered by el Jarocho, a man well known even among these hardened workers as a real "macho," was particularly clever and subtle:

Pussy [culito], when you were mine
you sounded like a [tight] wooden rattle.
Now that you're no longer mine
you sound like a cow's ass [culote]

Lusty cheers of approbation followed el Jarocho's performance, as the men evidently identified with the rhyme's message, which in the original Spanish accentuates the woman's transformation from virgin to wornout hag by a subtle linguistic shift—the diminutive culito replaced by the augmentative culote. The cause of the change is ambiguous: It is either the result of the man's formidable penis or her fickle and dissolute life. Given the scornful tone of the rhyme, the latter seems the more correct interpretation. Heightening the effect is the extreme vulgarity of the rhyme, which dehumanizes the woman by reducing her to the level of an animal.

Their treatment of women aside, and the enjoyment the men derived from them, charrita colorada performances often led to exchanges of sadistic insults that at times resulted in half-serious, half-playful duels—particularly among the younger men. On the surface, these insults,

mock fights, and macho humor could be interpreted as expressions of sexual deviance, interpersonal hostility, or even the psychocultural inferiority that Ramos (1962) and others have attributed to Mexican men. More fundamentally, however, they signify an unconscious betrayal of the profound social conflict and resentment that existed in the lives of the joke tellers. In short, they were symbolic manifestations of a complex social reality enmeshed in the interplay of class, gender, and culture.

PELADOS, MACHISMO AND PSYCHOHISTORY: A CRITICAL REASSESSMENT

Working-class men like those I have been describing here, as well as the culture of machismo associated with them, have hardly gone unnoticed in previous Mexican (and American) scholarship. Samuel Ramos, the respected Mexican philosopher, was an early and influential critic, being principally responsible for developing a portrait of Mexican man and culture that has long resisted challenge. That portrait needs to be reassessed, in light of this and other recent research (Colombres 1982).

In a highly influential book, *El perfil del hombre y la cultura en Mexico* (1934; English version, *Profile of Man and Culture in Mexico*, published in 1962), Ramos dealt at length with the culture of machismo and the "best model for its study"—the *pelado* of proletarian origins (Ramos 1962, 58). *El perfil* drew a stark portrait of the pelado—the penniless, dissolute, glib-tongued character immortalized by the comic Cantinflas. More than that, for Ramos the pelado was the purest incarnation of the Mexican "national character"—a resentful, distrusting misanthrope with a constant need to vent his deep-seated feelings of hostility and inferiority on enemies seen and unseen. Ramos excoriated this perennial child of Mexico's extreme social-class disparity, castigating him for his warped machismo and crude life-style. In short, for Ramos the pelado is nothing more than "a form of human rubbish from the great city . . . a being without substance" (1962, 61–62).

From a sociological perspective, male proletarian workers like those at S&J Growers are no different from Ramos's pelado. Indeed, the popular perception of the modern proletarian man, which derives in great part from Ramos's analysis, does not differ significantly from the latter's original characterization of the pelado. The mass media portrays the modern male proletarian as Ramos did his predecessor—a culturally crude and violent macho. Yet the present research suggests a more complex picture of this quintessential Mexican than Ramos or the media have perceived. For instance, in everyday life most of the men at S&J Growers, at least, were not nearly as violent as Ramos's pelados—those "explosive beings with whom relationship is dangerous" (1962, 59). Nor, for that matter, were they as callous toward women as the folklore of machismo would suggest, if taken at face value.

In fact, the men who delighted in the performance of charritas and other types of macho humor also evinced the other side of machismo—the typically Mexican sense of *respeto* that idealizes women. Like Mexican men everywhere, these workers bestowed an inordinate share of courtesy, protectiveness, and even reverence upon their mothers, sisters, wives, and "significant others," as long as their male supremacy was not challenged (cf. Díaz-Guerrero 1975, 1–15, 89–111; Mirandé 1988). In particular, the older married men who had families in Mexico expressed their concerns about making enough money to send back home, being away from their growing children for long periods, and burdening their wives with added domestic responsibilities while they were absent.

Yet their code of machismo impelled the men toward cultural behavior that can only be termed destructive. They drank and celebrated with abandon, often with disastrous results, such as bloody fights and vehicular accidents. Almost invariably, alcohol intensified their feelings of machismo and the crudities associated with it—vulgarity, sadistic behavior, blind anger—all

those cultural negatives that Ramos originally attributed to the pelado. And, like the pelado, these agricultural workers arrogated to themselves a special kind of virility, "creating thereby the illusion that personal valor is the Mexican's particular characteristic" (Ramos 1962, 63).

According to Ramos, the liabilities associated with the culture of machismo are deeply rooted in Mexican psychohistory, which spawned a collective inferiority complex that coalesced early on in the personality of the proletarian pelado. For this critic of Mexican culture, all the manifestations of the Mexican man's inferiority—his distrust, aggressiveness, resentment, timidity, deception, crude language, and all the rest of the Mexican's imputed cultural ills—can be traced to the original rape of the Indian mother by the Spanish conquistador.

Ramos's psychohistorical theory continues to inform more recent but no less pessimistic analyses of the Mexican man (Echanove Trujillo 1973; Goldwert 1983; Paz 1961). In focusing on conquest and colonization as the ultimate causes of cultural disharmony, these analyses ignore the intricate relationship among class, gender, and culture and the possible role these may play in the development of Mexican machismo. Instead, to psychohistorically minded analysts, the Mexican man's pent-up anger, gross language, and distrust must be "psychic transformations . . . instinctive tricks devised to protect the ego from itself" (Ramos 1962, 66), that is, from facing up to the fact that the Mexican has a deeply rooted inferiority complex.

The men I worked with did at times display the pent-up anger, the distrust, and all the behavior of the pelado that so vexed Ramos. Like the pelado, they displayed their "black resentment" toward "every quarter that has been hostile to them" (Ramos 1962, 59). Sometimes free-floating, this resentment surfaced in acts of aggression such as drunken fights; sometimes it was directed at convenient targets such as the Mexican American, whom they criticized incessantly. Occasionally, I saw this anger aimed directly at those whom the workers felt were exploiting them, from abusive foremen to the *patrones* who exercised arbitrary power over them. Resentment toward the latter was the most seething, yet suppressed. I saw it flash momentarily in the defiant faces of young men summarily dismissed for not conforming to the management's strict grooming requirements— no beards, long sideburns, or hair below the shirt collar. The men also spoke angrily of comrades being paid less than the newly legislated minimum wage. Yet, as one man bitterly complained, "We are a bunch of chickens; we don't know how to unite and protest against injustice."

Resentment thus flowed like a powerful undercurrent in the stream of these undocumented workers' culture. It was expressed as well in sublimated ways—the real "psychic transformations" out of which the folklore of machismo is spun. An interpretive question arises: To what extent are cultural expressions like the folklore of machismo symbolic alibis for sources of frustration rooted in other spheres of these workers' lives? I am not pointing here to inferiority complexes born of the rape of ancestral mothers by Spanish conquistadors (to borrow Paredes's colorful phrase), but to the daily adversities thrown up against the workers by an economic system that condemns them to perpetual struggle, impoverishment, and alienation.

If the folklore of machismo is not the product of psychohistory but a reflection of fundamental economic structures, why the psychic transformation? Why, in other words, should the folklore be so obsessed with the degradation of women, when the source of resentment is class exploitation? This leads us to the heart of the interpretive challenge. Are we, after all, dealing here with a latter-day version of Ramos's pelado, who is not only the essence of the Mexican national character, but "a most vile category of social fauna" (Ramos 1962, 58)? I would assert otherwise. In their daily struggle these men are, as a group, not lacking in responsibility, initiative, compassion—in short, the full range of human qualities that Ramos found so wanting in the pelado.

TREACHEROUS WOMEN AND THE DISPLACEMENT OF CLASS CONFLICT

In alluding to the charritas as a form of symbolic alibi, I had in mind a form of communication that ideologically displaces a given type of social relationship (in this case, a class relationship) while transposing it from its concrete actualization in a "realized signifying system" (Williams 1981, 207). Such a signifying system is intrinsic to the economic system that produces it, in that it serves at the level of discourse to "realize," mediate, or be an alibi for the set of social relations circumscribed by that order.

Examples of signifying systems include currency, literature, art, and even shelter, which assumes a powerful signifying function the more it reflects the social status of its owner (Williams 1981). In fact, any object, when "disengaged from its mere actuality and used to impose meaning upon experience" (Geertz 1973, 45) can serve this signifying function. However, the process of signification is not uncomplicated: Between the world of social relations and its cultural articulation lies a jungle of ambiguities, metaphysical subtleties, and even subterfuge, which can exert a powerful, distorting effect on communication and set the stage for the development of ideology, as Marx defined the term.

As an expression of working-class culture, the folklore of machismo can be considered a realized signifying system (while keeping in mind its potential for ideological displacement). As a signifier, or, what Jameson (1981) might term an *ideologeme*, it points to, but simultaneously displaces, a class relationship and its attendant conflict. At the same time, it introduces a third element, the gender relationship, which acts as a mediator between signifier (the folklore) and signified (the class relationship). Additionally, as a signifier for class conflict, the folklore of machismo should be considered one component in a broader, though inchoate, communicative strategy, whose function is the "defense of patterns of belief and value" (Geertz 1973, 231)— that is, the defense of men's basic sense of social solidarity in the face of life's adversities. In sum, like other everyday expressions—their opinions about Mexican Americans, for example—the male workers' folklore is part of a larger ideology that ultimately coincides with their subordinate class position and its orientation toward life.

Gender enters the analysis through the beliefs that these men hold about the family and the subordinate status that women should occupy. These beliefs verify what Kelly wrote about the working-class family:

The family in modern society has served as the domain for the production and training of the working class. . . . And it has served to compensate the worker whose means of subsistence were alienated from him but who could have private property in his wife. *(1984, 15; emphasis added)*

To men oppressed by the organization of labor and maldistribution of social wealth and power in society after society, the dual order of patriarchal society provides in many . . . instances the satisfaction of dominion over women. (1984, 61; emphasis added)

In the modern world of capitalist, male-dominant economic systems and the ideologies that sustain them, the subordinate sectors of society have at least three options in responding to their subordination, depending on the sociohistorical moment. They may, as one alternative, propagate ideas that openly challenge, at least in part, the ideology of the dominant groups (Deckard 1979; Gramsci 1971; Swingewood 1977). They may, as a second alternative, adopt beliefs and values that are in large part a surrender to the hegemony of the ruling classes—a phenomenon particularly evident in advanced capitalist nations (Habermas 1970; Marcuse 1964). Or, as is the case with the workers being discussed here, the men of a subordinate class may invent cultural strategies that, through a crucial process of ideological displacement, *shift the point of conflict* from the public domain of class relations between men to the private domain of domestic relations between men and women. This shift is critical to an interpretation of the folklore of machismo.

First, we may suggest that the obedience and servitude Mexican working-class men expect of their women is an integral part of the principle of compensation, understood in both its economic and psychocultural sense. However, in neither sense is this compensation adequate, as it does not resolve the problem of economic deprivation based on class inequality. Worse, the male workers cannot consciously challenge this state of affairs, for they are not equipped, culturally or politically, to recognize the structural basis of that inequality. They cannot even identify the conflict zone that marks the boundary between the two competing, inherently antagonistic classes in capitalist society, for it is no longer the locus of conflict (Habermas 1970, 109).

Indeed, the ideological system that governs life in postcapitalist society has successfully banished from all consciousness the notion of "domination . . . exercised in such a manner that one class subject confronts another as an identifiable group . . . [However] this does not mean that class antagonisms have been abolished but that they have become *latent*" (Habermas 1970, 109, emphasis in original). The conflict zone has thus been displaced; the regnant bourgeois ideology of "classless inequality" has shifted the point of contestation from the class boundary, where it belongs, to the "underprivileged regions of life"— to the oppressed class itself. The members of the oppressed class reformulate class distinctions and antagonisms, giving them new shape in subtraditions that may not directly address class inequality, but are nonetheless consonant with their experiences and orientations. It is in this realm of social life that ideologically mediated signifying systems work themselves out.

In the case under discussion, the persistent class inequality that Mexican working-class men face, immune as it is from cultural penetration, deflects the political unconscious (Jameson 1981) toward a more overt, less mystified (though no less ideological) source of conflict and inequality—the relationship between men and women. Fully cognizant of his supremacy in the latter relationship, the working-class man wrings every bit of compensation out of his advantage, which he enhances by symbolically conflating two distinct relationships—class and gender. The folklore of machismo plays a critical role in this conflation. Through the process of ideological displacement, the folklore shifts attention from its latent text, a class relationship that it signifies but cannot articulate, and focuses that attention on its manifest text, a gender relationship that it articulates but does not signify.

It is thus in the realm of gender relations that class conflict is reformulated and given new cultural purpose—the total subjugation of women. In consequence, oppressive yet tolerated cultural practices thrive: physical and psychological violence against women—in the form of beatings and the denial of personal autonomy—as well as symbolic violence, in the form of degrading but richly elaborated cultural expression like the folklore of machismo and its treacherous-woman stereotype.

CONCLUSION: THE LIMITS OF AN IDEOLOGY

It may be a bleak commentary on gender relations, but the folklore and other expressed attitudes of the workers at S&J Growers would seem to indicate that Mexican working-class men are a perfect empirical case of Kelly's compensation principle. As noted, they have a most sexist orientation toward gender relations and view the woman as simply part of man's dominion, to be completely subjected to his will. To the workers this relationship is a perfectly natural development and a just form of "compensation" for their sacrifice. Countless times the men reiterated their belief in the justification for such an arrangement. As one man put it, "The woman should be subject to the man—the man to work and the woman to the house chores." Another worker summed up the general attitude with this statement: "The man has a right to his 'slips' [*resvaladitas*], the woman is supposed to bear it."

On the face of it, these statements would seem to be nothing more than crude rational-

izations for a system of inequality based not on class, but on gender, since the advantages that men gain from sexism—as a sui generis phenomenon—cut across class lines. More important, the recognition that male sexism is an integral component in gender relations enables us to address a charge made by critics of the approach advocated here—that the folklore of machismo cannot be a signifier for class conflict, since it is not unique to working-class men. That its performance is not uncommon among the men of the dominant classes is true enough, but have these men nothing to gain from perpetuating the myth of the treacherous woman? By contrast, as I have tried to show, for working-class men the obsession with machismo goes beyond gender domination and, in fact, links up ideologically with the problem of class inequality.

The men themselves were at least dimly aware of the complexities and contradictions inherent in their culture of machismo. For instance, when asked why the charrita colorada was so popular among his peers, an older informant replied, "We carry on like this to make light of things for a moment, to forget the problems of life for a moment—the toil, the struggle." Another worker, politically more sophisticated than his peers, observed, "This is pure bullshit; the problems of life are not solved by this [charritas and macho humor generally]." Addressing his companions' sense of male supremacy and its sexist humor, a man (one of the few married to a Chicana) stated his opinion succinctly: "I believe one does it all for the sake of machismo—as if we have to prove that we are men."

Other similar statements, generally voicing the workers' acute awareness of their economic insecurity *and* their need to "prove that we are men," indicate that they are not oblivious to the forces that keep them in a sate of poverty. Such statements also point toward an awareness, however diffuse, that the precariousness of their economic status, along with the frustration this status generates, is a major factor contributing to the men's vociferous defense of their privileged male roles on the one hand, and their gross insensitivity to the needs and rights of women on the other. Their embattled position—their desire to control women and their fear of losing that control—is plainly evident in their disapproval of changes they perceive among Mexican-American women, whom they consider muy *libertinas.*

The workers' negative attitude toward the Chicana is interwoven into the theme of the treacherous woman. While the latter exists for the most part as a fictitious element in the folklore of machismo (after all, *real* Mexican women are *not* that way), for these men it acquires a measure of verisimilitude when projected onto the Mexican-American woman. In short, the Chicana not only serves as a handy scapegoat for the workers' worst fears, but her perceived insubordination provides a convenient prop on which to hang the ideology of machismo. Given their sexist attitude, it is not surprising that the men at S&J Growers were especially critical of Mexican-American men for letting their "natural" authority over women erode by giving in to their demand for equality. Most important, they feared that these changes were being exported to Mexico and that soon women there would also "want to be like men."

Caught in a bind between the sexist, patriarchal culture they espouse, the discontent and powerlessness they feel as a result of their subordinate economic status (with its constant threat to their masculine pride), and the inexorable shift in gender relations that a changing capitalist society promotes, the workers at S&J Growers have responded with a familiar defense. They have succumbed to the displaced compensation that the ideology of machismo provides, no matter how self-defeating. In serious, reflective conversation the workers attempted, at least, to rationalize this machismo and its open acceptance of the subordination of women. They argued that the man works long hours, he protects his family from hardship, he therefore deserves the woman's unswerving devotion and maybe a *parranda* (binge) with his fellows once a week. In the folk-

lore of machismo's distorted message, however, rational explanations vanished. Instead, the rhetorical power of the folkloric performance morally and sexually degraded women, thereby validating what these workers felt was their last birthright as sovereign *mejicanos*—their supreme machismo.

An exaggerated sense of machismo links undocumented male workers to the pelado and other notorious figures in Mexican history (e.g., the nineteenth-century *léparo*). But still another, grimmer experience cements the link among these proletarian outcasts—extreme exploitation, at both the economic and the cultural level. Serrón expressed this truth bluntly: "[Economic] exploitation is a fact of Mexican life—a sad, disfiguring, warped, and tragic fact of life in everyday Mexico" (1980, 197). And, as in other capitalist countries, in Mexico economic exploitation works hand in hand with cultural exploitation. Through the latter, the classes that control economic life also control the tenor of public discourse, creating a formidable brake against any counterdiscourse that might raise the consciousness of the dispossessed masses vis-à-vis the class dynamics that maintain them in subordination (Vellinga 1979).

Possessing neither the class consciousness nor the political means to end their exploitation, the Mexican male workers of the late twentieth century do not seem to have developed much in the way of cultures that contest the established order. They have yielded instead to the sexist ideology of machismo, which also serves the interests of the ruling classes by imposing cultural limits on a working-class consciousness that might develop solidarity between women and men. The range of this working-class consciousness reduced, these male proletarians translate their economic subordination into symbolic expression that voices their class resentment in terms that are culturally rewarding, if politically displaced. It is in this context that folkloric images of heartless, deceitful women who drive men to the depths of alcoholic despair play out their grim, mythic role.

NOTES

1. The canción ranchera derives from a type of folk-song known until the 1930s as a *canción típica mexicana*. Since the 1930s, it has been commercially manufactured primarily for the consumption of the working class. The theme of the treacherous woman appears in countless canciones dating as far back as the nineteenth century. However, it did not become dominant until the advent of the canción ranchera proper.

2. The Spanish word *traicionera* has multiple connotations, which are difficult to translate precisely. In popular usage, as a referent for a woman who has been unfaithful to her lover, traicionera may be closer to the English words *perfidious, unfaithful*, or *betraying*. Nonetheless, despite the imprecision, *treacherous* glosses a wider range of meanings than the other words, and so that is the term used in this article.

3. Compare Paz (1961) on the *chingón*: "The *chingón* is the macho, the male; he rips open the *chingada*, the female, who is pure passivity, defenseless against the exterior world" (p. 77).

4. The following stanzas are from *La mancornadora*, an old canción of unknown origin, and *La traicionera*, composed by the apotheosis of the ranchera genre, the late, idolized composer, José Alfredo Jiménez.

La mancornadora

Ando ausente del bién que adoré,
apasionado por una mujer;
solo tomando disipi mis penas
con las copas llenas para divagar.

. . . .

Y si tú fueras legal con mi amor,
tú gozarías de mi protección;
pero en el mundo tú fuiste traidora,
la mancornadora de mi corazón.

La traicionera

Nunca creí que esa ingrata
me fuera tan traicionera;
'qué la traición que me hiciste
no se queda como quiera;
recuerda que me juraste
una pasión verdadera.

The Ensnaring Woman

I'm away from the love I adore,
impassioned over a woman;
only drinking can I dispel my sorrows
with filled glasses to distract me.

. . . .

And if you were sincere with my love,
you would enjoy my protection;
but in the world you were a betrayer,
the one who ensnared my heart.

The Betraying Woman

I never believed that cruel woman
would turn out so treacherous;
for the treachery you did to me
will not remain just like that;
remember you solemnly promised me
a sincere passion.

5. All quotations are my translations from the Spanish.

REFERENCES

Clifford, James. 1986. Introduction: Partial truths. In *Writing culture: The poetics and politics of ethnography*, edited by James Clifford and George E. Marcus. Berkeley: University of California Press.

Colombres, Adolfo, ed. 1982. *La cultura popular*. Mexico, D. F.: Premia Editora.

Deckard, Barbara Sinclair. 1979. *The women's movement: Political, socioeconomic, and psychological issues*. New York: Harper & Row.

Díaz-Guerrero, Rogelio R. 1975. *The psychology of the Mexican: Culture and personality*. Austin: University of Texas Press.

Echanove Trujillo, Carlos. 1973. *Sociología mexicana*. Mexica, DF: Editorial Porrua.

Geertz, Clifford. 1973. *The interpretation of cultures*. New York: Basic Books.

Goldwert, Marvin. 1983. *Machismo and conquest: The case of Mexico*. Lanham, MD: University Press of America.

Gramsci, Antonio. 1971. *Selections from the prison notebooks*, translated by Q. Hoare and G. N. Smith. New York: International Publishers.

Habermas, Jürgen. 1970. *Toward a rational society: Student protest, science, and politics*. Boston: Beacon.

Jameson, Fredric. 1981. *The political unconscious: Narrative as a socially symbolic act*. Ithaca, NY: Cornell University Press.

Kelly, Joan. 1984. *Women, history, and theory*. Chicago: University of Chicago Press.

Marcuse, Herbert. 1964. *One-dimensional man*. Boston: Beacon.

Mirandé, Alfredo. 1986. Qué gacho es ser macho: It's a drag to be a macho man. *Aztlan: A Journal of Chicano Studies* 17:63–89.

Paredes, Américo. 1966. The Anglo-American in Mexican folklore. In *New voices in American studies*, edited by Ray B. Browne and Donald H. Wenkelman. Lafayette, IN: Purdue University Press.

Paz, Octavio. 1961. *The labyrinth of solitude*. New York: Grove.

Ramos, Samuel. 1934. *El perfil del hombre y la cultura en México* (Profile of man and culture in Mexico). Mexico, D. F.: Imprenta Mundial.

———. 1962. *Profile of man and culture in Mexico*. Austin: University of Texas Press.

Serrón, Luis A. 1980. *Scarcity, exploitation, and poverty: Malthus and Marx in Mexico*. Norman: University of Oklahoma Press.

Swingewood, Alan. 1977. *The myth of mass culture*. London: Macmillan.

Vellinga, Menno. 1979. *Economic development and the dynamics of class: Industrialization, power and control in Monterrey, Mexico*. Assen, The Netherlands: Van Gorcum.

Williams, Raymond, 1981. *The sociology of culture*. New York: Schocken Books.

ABUSE OF PRIVILEGE:
SEXUALITY AFTER THOMAS/HILL

PETER R. BREGGIN

He is the hard-driving, professional, compulsively responsible man who holds others to a high standard. Few know him intimately, but all recognize his accomplishments. He has a kind of aloofness or superiority that may put some people off, but it impresses most. If anything, people are flattered when he *doesn't* look down on them. Then people are shocked when he is accused of taking sexual advantage.

Here in Washington, he is the stuff of daily headlines: John Tower, Edward Kennedy, Gary Hart. Or we may recall him less notoriously, as John Fedders, the high-ranking government bureaucrat exposed for beating his wife. He had the gall to go to court for a percentage of her royalties when she wrote a book about his abuses.

She is almost always younger than the man, less secure, perhaps equally ambitious, but with a long way to go before people stop saying, "She has a lot of *potential*." Her dignity makes her a sexual challenge to him. And in addition to her other attractions, there is a youthful vulnerability about her that is attractive to some men, a kind of obvious neediness, even a desire to look up to a man. Especially important, she is not intimate with anyone else at work; he can risk exposing his other side to her. She is a secretary, a student, a rising young professional. In the Senate, *he* may be a young page.

As a psychiatrist and as a professor teaching graduate seminars at George Mason University on the male abuse of women and children, I watched with special interest as the explosive question of sexual harassment took center stage at Supreme Court Justice Clarence Thomas's recent confirmation hearings. There was so much psychological talk that was so far off the mark. Much of it came down to this: It's inconceivable that a seemingly honorable man could do something so outrageous and self-destructive as talk obscenely to one of his employees; and when he is addressed "Your Honor," the contradiction seems unbearable. It was also inconceivable that a seemingly rational woman could accept such abuse, follow the man to another job, and then maintain any kind of relationship with him over the years.

Notice that both players are uncommon enough to be considered worthy of note: the honorable man and the rational woman. But which identity is more suspect? To judge from the Senate vote and public opinion polls, honorable man outlasts rational woman. Anita Hill, we are reassured to learn, is not so sane after all. She is so self-deluded that she can even fool herself into passing a lie detector test with flying colors.

Consider a similar scenario in a society where honorable men were thought to be the norm: Vienna at the turn of the twentieth century. As former psychoanalyst Jeffrey Moussaieff Masson disclosed in *Freud: The Assault on Truth*, Freud quickly discovered that his female patients, who came from some of Europe's finest families, had

Reprinted from TIKKUN MAGAZINE, A BI-MONTHLY JEWISH CRITIQUE OF POLITICS, CULTURE, AND SOCIETY. Subscriptions are $31.00 per year from TIKKUN, 251 West 100th Street, 5th floor, New York, NY 10025.

been sexually abused as children, usually by their fathers or other trusted older men. Freud enthusiastically reported this to his colleagues at the Society for Psychiatry and Neurology in Vienna in 1891, but his fellow physicians shunned him, and warned that such ideas would ruin him professionally. Those men of medical authority came to the defense of the generic honorable man, the Victorian father, and were unwilling to admit his abuses. We can only surmise how many of them were indulging in the same practices.

Under this concerted professional pressure, Freud altered his theory. Young girls weren't being sexually abused by their fathers, he concluded. They suffered from unrequited love for their fathers and fantasized the sexual relationships with them. And so the Oedipus complex was born, and generations of young girls bore the onus of allegedly harboring illicit desires for their fathers when they themselves were victims of sexual abuse. And so the method was established for dismissing the charges of Anita Hill against the Honorable Clarence Thomas.

Of course, many intermediate refinements of psychoanalytic and psychiatric practice have also set the stage for Anita Hill's degradation. In modern textbooks, women who suffer the daily outrages of male domination are pathologized as "self-defeating personalities." As I describe in my book *Toxic Psychiatry*, modern and seemingly gender-neutral explanations of women's psychological maladies offered by biochemical psychiatry are more insidious. The high rate of depression among women has nothing to do with their experiences in a male-dominated social order; it's a physiological condition, to be treated with drugs and electroshock therapy.

Modern biopsychiatry remains the prototype of hierarchical power. The psychiatrist is whole and above it all, the patient defective; the psychiatrist diagnoses and treats, and the patient accepts and submits to control. And, of course, the psychiatrist "means well," even as he degrades and coerces. The righteous-male-turned-diagnostician came out in full force at the hearings, as even "lay" observers took it upon themselves to pin psychiatric labels on Anita Hill. Sometimes they did not veil their rage; but at other times, they forgave her in the tradition of psychiatry for not knowing what she was doing. And in the tradition of the insanity defense, they helpfully suggested that Hill didn't know that she was making it all up.

Anita Hill fared no better than Freud's first female patients. Unlike Freud, she found the courage to step forth as both messenger and victim to tell the august body of men that one of their peers was an abuser of women. Once again in the U.S. Senate, the generic honorable man, now in the person of Clarence Thomas, was exonerated by his peers, while the victim was accused of lustful fantasy. The woman's accusation was reinterpreted to make it appear her own lustful wish, and the older, dominant male was found pure. That no one suggested a biochemical imbalance in Anita Hill's brain merely means that the Senate was not up on the latest diagnostic fad.

It makes no difference that the woman in this case is in her own right an enormously respectable person, a lawyer and professor. That, perhaps, is the most vicious lesson these singularly vicious hearings sought to drive home: No matter how much a woman accomplishes in the man's world, she remains only *seemingly* rational. When she identifies sexual abuse from an honorable man, she is still doomed to be declared mentally ill.

I am in no position to say with certainty who has lied, Judge Thomas or Professor Hill. But drawing on the research and insights provided by the field of victimology, I can observe that the pattern of behavior we have witnessed fits the standard pattern of sexual abuse in nearly every way. As we shall see, Judge Thomas and his supporters acted like typical perpetrators and Professor Hill like a typical victim—at least until she finally grew mature and powerful enough in her own right to rise above the role. And most of the Senate and the American people responded as the majority has always done, by identifying with the angry, outraged, honorable man.

But weren't the Judge's supporters right? As Senator Orrin Hatch (R–Utah) suggested, wouldn't a man like him have to be a "psychopathic fiend or pervert" before he'd risk his reputation by so outrageously abusing an employee? According to Hatch, men like that could only be found in the loony bin. How easily Washington has forgotten its own history of abuse, peopled with embarrassing figures such as Richard Berendzen, the president of American University, who made shocking, sexually sadistic phone calls to women, describing the torture of small children in a basement. Berendzen wasn't in a loony bin; he was in the seat of power. In a society in which more than a third of women have been sexually exploited as children and one in four women will be raped, sexual abuse is the province not of madmen but of Everyman. Woman after woman at the hearings admitted to having been sexually humiliated by men in authority.

How does "the man" feel and act when he is finally exposed? Or when he sees that another man he values is exposed? The hearings disclosed the narrow spectrum of responses, from professed sensitivity to unbridled resentment and accusation aimed at Hill. Unhappily, patriarchal man—and perhaps the perpetrator himself—triumphed. The Judge was outraged, accused the world of conspiring against him, denied even lusting in his heart, redefined the issue as racial prejudice against him, rather than gender persecution of a woman, and refused to listen to the accusations.

None of this is new to men, especially the refusal to listen. We now have a Supreme Court justice who wouldn't even deign to *hear* his accuser. As attorney John Doggett III, one of the Judge's most vociferous male supporters, declared under oath, "She isn't worth it."

Indeed, Doggett went on to offer his own psychoanalytic diagnosis: Hill was obsessed with men, and deluded about their interest in her. On the flimsiest of evidence, a brief encounter at a party, Doggett fancied that Hill lusted after him despite his rejection of her. The exemplary patriarch, the white-haired, retired law-school dean

Charles Kothe (who was also a close friend to the Judge), said it was inconceivable that she wouldn't have confided in him about it if it were true. Several men patronized her by conceding that she might *think* she'd been abused. Thus they congratulated themselves on their sensitivity while remaining obtuse to the realities of male abuse.

If many of the men behaved as perpetrators typically do, most of the victims also conformed to their psychological profiles, including Professor Hill. As a young woman in her twenties, she had been too frightened, ashamed, and proud to reveal the details, even to her friends. She took no notes, because victims want to forget rather than to remember, and almost never have the foresight or determination to make a record for the future. I have said it to innumerable patients and friends: "Write it down, write it down." But the act of writing it down lends the trauma too much reality and approaches too closely that next dangerous step of public disclosure. She only wants to go on as best she can, to be as self-reliant and as self-possessed as she was taught to be, and to avoid flaunting her grievances.

Then, years later, the victim tries to come to grips with the experience. At first the details come slowly. She tells the story once, twice, three times, each time recalling more detail. She is not making it up. On the contrary, it takes courage to continue dredging it all up. Besides, she knows no one will believe the more outrageous details, not when they involve her father, her minister, her doctor, her esteemed boss.

Nor does she rebel against her abuser. In nearly every case of sexual abuse in families, schools, and the workplace, the victim is, in reality, dependent upon her abuser. Her relative powerlessness indeed forms much of her appeal to him. She wants his approval; she needs his help. Of necessity and through her upbringing, she learns to live in dread of his anger and rejection. And why should she have to quit? She wants this job. Women like her have won the legal right to keep their jobs without having to submit to harassment.

As a rational person, she doesn't want to threaten her career by alienating a powerful boss, or to settle for an inferior position elsewhere simply to escape from something that could reemerge in her workplace at any time. Rationally, it makes sense for her to bite the bullet. Historically, men have used their connections to get ahead. Should she do anything less? And having endured that abuse, why shouldn't she stay casually in touch in order to forward her career?

Thinking in a way men find difficult to understand, she values her relationship with him. As disgusting as it might seem at times, she keeps hoping he will stop. Then she can continue her professional relationship with him and continue advancing her career, which is so dependent upon his good will. Like many women, she knows she gets men to do things for her not just because of her intelligence, accomplishments, or credentials, but because of how well she pleases them.

An unusually confident man might stand up to a boss who is mistreating him and say "cut it out" and even get away with it. But a woman knows that a man confronted by a woman feels humiliated by her. He acts like *he's* the aggrieved party and may become dangerously angry. In the words of legal scholar Catharine MacKinnon, "Hell hath no fury like a man exposed."

The woman who makes a complaint about sexual abuse from her father, brother, or boss knows that she cannot even count on her mother, sisters, or coworkers to support her. Many are simply too intimidated; some are in denial about what has been done to them; some have succumbed to the "men-will-be-men" strain of fatalism that permeates our culture; and still others persist in holding the victim responsible. And fear of the angry male authority ensures that few subordinates of either sex will side with the victim.

Without an old-boy network to support them, women have good reason to be more afraid than men to stick out their necks. In countless ways, patriarchal society has declared them by their very nature inferior. And many female co-workers, struggling to get ahead, may envy the woman who does succeed, and falsely accuse her of doing so on the basis of sexual favors. As we saw at the Thomas hearings, women may try to compete over who is truly "close" to the male authority. And while the Thomas hearings focused on the plight of the professional woman, consider the still-greater vulnerability of the vast majority of women who struggle to earn a meager wage while supporting their children.

That, indeed, is the lesson of the hearings: Men abuse women. They do it in the home, the school, the workplace and, yes, the U.S. Senate, even as they are being televised. Then they act disbelieving and even outraged when they are accused of it. Eventually they chalk it up to the insanity of even the most clearly rational woman. Afterward, they self-righteously commiserate with each other over how much pain the whole thing has caused them.

But there's another dismal lesson: There were no heroic men at the Thomas hearings. Men may clamor in the defense of each other, and sometimes to the defense of a clearly defeated and harmless woman. When a woman stands up to men in the male domain, however, she must do so alone.

Many of us awaited the hearings with hope. There would be a renewed dedication to the equal rights and dignity of women, and specifically to acknowledging and redressing male abuse of women. *One brave woman, Anita Hill, would lead us all toward redemption.* Instead, we saw Hill cast once more in the role of victim rather than redeemer; a person as vulnerable as she was courageous, trying her best to cope with accusation, disbelief, indifference, diagnosis, hostility, and an occasional patronizing gesture of support. No one, absolutely no one, stood up in outrage on her behalf. Led by the raging Thomas, the Republicans seized the day.

Like children unable to side with their siblings in the face of oppressive parents, men and women throughout America became unable to side with Anita Hill. In the opinion polls, they sided against her out of a fear of authority and a lack of leadership. Had one senator been truly honorable, had he been heroic in defense of Anita Hill, Americans might have been moved to take his example to heart.

Some good will come out of the hearings. There will be an increased caution on the part of a few men in the workplace. An occasional man and many women will find themselves appalled by the senators and inspired by Anita Hill. But the benefits will be limited because men, thus far, seem little affected.

As Senator Barbara Mikulski (D–Md.) declared during the confirmation debate, it's time for men to do more. We can start by getting angry at ourselves for the way we've been controlling and abusing women for ten thousand years or more. Then we can get angry about our failure to stand up to other men in defense of women and their rights.

If candidacy for high office was truly open only to men who had never abused a woman, most men would be disqualified. What we need are repentant men, men willing to examine themselves and to reject a system that's organized to their benefit at the expense of all women. Only then will women begin to get a fair hearing anywhere in society.

But what is a "repentant" man? He is not a man who caves in with guilt and shame, and supplicates himself before women. He is not a politician who apologizes under the heat of an upcoming election. In regard to personal relationships with women, he knows he can transform himself just to reject the role of superior. He knows that he, like all men, has taken advantage of the power imbalance between men and women. He recognizes that he has not done enough to rest the sexual abuse of women.

Having repented, he takes action. He refuses to take advantage of the imbalance of power inherent in mixed-gender relationships. He is willing and able to discuss honestly issues of patriarchy and male domination—to confront and reject the male abuse of women and children in the public as well as the private sphere.

The repentant man is, of course, open and vulnerable. But now, after the debacle of the Thomas hearings, vulnerability seems the easy part. Men need to begin confronting other men in order to stop them from abusing women. Had more men done so during the Thomas hearings—and had *any* of the senators on the Judiciary Committee done so—the U.S. Senate could have presided over a new dawn in gender relations. Instead, it rallied to protect and reassert business as usual in the male-dominated halls of power.

THE GLASS ESCALATOR
HIDDEN ADVANTAGES FOR MEN IN THE "FEMALE" PROFESSIONS

CHRISTINE L. WILLIAMS

This paper addresses men's underrepresentation in four predominantly female professions: nursing, elementary school teaching, librarianship, and social work. Specifically, it examines the degree to which discrimination disadvantages men in hiring and promotion decisions, the work place culture, and in interactions with clients. In-depth interviews were conducted with 99 men and women in these professions in four major U.S. cities. The interview data suggest that men do not face discrimination in these occupations; however, they do encounter prejudice from individuals outside their professions. In contrast to the experience of women who enter male-dominated professions, men generally encounter structural advantages in these occupations which tend to enhance their careers. Because men face different barriers to integrating nontraditional occupations than women face, the need for different remedies to dismantle segregation in predominantly female jobs is emphasized.

The sex segregation of the U.S. labor force is one of the most perplexing and tenacious problems in our society. Even though the proportion of men and women in the labor force is approaching parity (particularly for younger cohorts of workers) (U.S. Department of Labor 1991:18), men and women are still generally confined to predominantly single-sex occupations. Forty percent of men or women would have to change major occupational categories to achieve equal representation of men and women in all jobs (Reskin and Roos 1990:6), but even this figure underestimates the true degree of sex segregation. It is extremely rare to find specific jobs where equal numbers of men and women are engaged in the same activities in the same industries (Bielby and Baron 1984).

This research was funded in part by a faculty grant from the University of Texas at Austin. I also acknowledge the support of the sociology departments of the University of California, Berkeley; Harvard University; and Arizona State University. I would like to thank Judy Auerbach, Martin Button, Robert Nye, Teresa Sullivan, Debra Umberson, Mary Waters, and the reviewers at *Social Problems* for their comments on earlier versions of this paper.
 Reprinted from *Social Problems*, Vol. 39, No. 3, August 1992, pp. 253–267 by permission.

Most studies of sex segregation in the work force have focused on women's experiences in male-dominated occupations. Both researchers and advocates for social change have focused on the barriers faced by women who try to integrate predominantly male fields. Few have looked at the "flip-side" of occupational sex segregation: the exclusion of men from predominantly female occupations (exceptions include Schreiber 1979; Williams 1989; Zimmer 1988). But the fact is that men are less likely to enter female sex-typed occupations than women are to enter male-dominated jobs (Jacobs 1989). Reskin and Roos, for example, were able to identify 33 occupations in which female representation increased by more than nine percentage points between 1970 and 1980, but only three occupations in which the proportion of men increased as radically (1990:20–21).

In this paper, I examine men's underrepresentation in four predominantly female occupations—nursing, librarianship, elementary school teaching, and social work. Throughout the twentieth century, these occupations have been identified with "women's work"—even though prior to the Civil War, men were more likely to be employed in these areas. These four occupations, often called the female "semi-professions" (Hodson and Sullivan 1990), today range from 5.5 percent male (in nursing) to 32 percent male (in social work). (See Table 1.) These percentages have not changed substantially in decades. In fact, as Table 1 indicates, two of these professions—librarianship and social work—have experienced declines in the proportions of men since 1975. Nursing is the only one of the four experiencing noticeable changes in sex composition, with the proportion of men increasing 80 percent between 1975 and 1990. Even so, men continue to be a tiny minority of all nurses.

Although there are many possible reasons for the continuing preponderance of women in these fields, the focus of this paper is discrimination. Researchers examining the integration of women into "male fields" have identified discrimination as a major barrier to women (Jacobs 1989; Reskin 1988; Reskin and Hartmann 1986). This discrimination has taken the form of laws or institutionalized rules prohibiting the hiring or promotion of women into certain job specialties. Discrimination can also be "informal," as when women encounter sexual harassment, sabotage, or other forms of hostility from their male coworkers resulting in a poisoned work environment (Reskin and Hartmann 1986). Women in nontraditional occupations also report feeling stigmatized by clients when their work puts them in contact with the public. In particular, women in engineering and blue-collar occupations encounter gender-based stereotypes about their competence which undermine their work performance (Epstein 1988; Martin 1980). Each of these forms of discrimination—legal, informal, and cultural—contributes to women's underrepresentation in predominantly male occupations.

The assumption in much of this literature is that any member of a token group in a work setting will probably experience similar discrimi-

TABLE 1 Percent Male in Selected Occupations, Selected Years

PROFESSION	1990	1980	1975
Nurses	5.5	3.5	3.0
Elementary teachers	14.8	16.3	14.6
Librarians	16.7	14.8	18.9
Social workers	31.8	35.0	39.2

Source: U.S. Department of Labor. Bureau of Labor Statistics. *Employment and Earnings* 38:1 (January 1991), Table 22 (Employed civilians by detailed occupation), 185; 28:1 (January 1981), Table 23 (Employed persons by detailed occupation), 180; 22:7 (January 1976), Table 2 (Employed persons by detailed occupation), 11.

natory treatment. Kanter (1977), who is best known for articulating this perspective in her theory of tokenism, argues that when any group represents less than 15 percent of an organization, its members will be subject to predictable forms of discrimination. Likewise, Jacobs argues that "in some ways, men in female-dominated occupations experience the same difficulties that women in male-dominated occupations face" (1989:167), and Reskin contends that any dominant group in an occupation will use their power to maintain a privileged position (1988:62).

However, the few studies that have considered men's experience in gender atypical occupations suggest that men may not face discrimination or prejudice when they integrate predominantly female occupations. Zimmer (1988) and Martin (1988) both contend that the effects of sexism can outweigh the effects of tokenism when men enter nontraditional occupations. This study is the first to systematically explore this question using data from four occupations. I examine the barriers to men's entry into these professions; the support men receive from their supervisors, colleagues and clients; and the reactions they encounter from the public (those outside their professions).

METHODS

I conducted in-depth interviews with 76 men and 23 women in four occupations from 1985–1991. Interviews were conducted in four metropolitan areas: San Francisco/Oakland, California; Austin, Texas; Boston, Massachusetts; and Phoenix, Arizona. These four areas were selected because they show considerable variation in the proportions of men in the four professions. For example, Austin has one of the highest percentages of men in nursing (7.7 percent), whereas Phoenix's percentage is one of the lowest (2.7 percent) (U.S. Bureau of the Census 1980). The sample was generated using "snowballing" techniques. Women were included in the sample to gauge their feelings and responses to men who enter "their" professions.

Like the people employed in these professions generally, those in my sample were predominantly white (90 percent).[1] Their ages ranged from 20 to 66 and the average age was 38. The interview questionnaire consisted of several open-ended questions on four broad topics: motivation to enter the profession; experiences in training; career progression; and general views about men's status and prospects within these occupations. I conducted all the interviews, which generally lasted between one and two hours. Interviews took place in restaurants, my home or office, or the respondent's home or office. Interviews were tape-recorded and transcribed for the analysis.

Data analysis followed the coding techniques described by Strauss (1987). Each transcript was read several times and analyzed into emergent conceptual categories. Likewise, Strauss' principle of theoretical sampling was used. Individual respondents were purposively selected to capture the array of men's experiences in these occupations. Thus, I interviewed practitioners in every specialty, oversampling those employed in the *most* gender atypical areas (e.g., male kindergarten teachers). I also selected respondents from throughout their occupational hierarchies—from students to administrators to retirees. Although the data do not permit within group comparisons, I am reasonably certain that the sample does capture a wide range of experiences common to men in these female-dominated professions. However, like all findings based on qualitative data, it is uncertain whether

---

1. According to the U.S. Census, black men and women comprise 7 percent of all nurses and librarians, 11 percent of all elementary school teachers, and 19 percent of all social workers (calculated from U.S. Census 1980: Table 278, 1–197). The proportion of blacks in social work may be exaggerated by these statistics. The occupational definition of "social worker" used by the Census Bureau includes welfare workers and pardon and parole officers, who are not considered "professional" social workers by the National Association of Social Workers. A study of degreed professionals found that 89 percent of practitioners were white (Hardcastle 1987).

the findings generalize to the larger population of men in nontraditional occupations.

In this paper, I review individuals' responses to questions about discrimination in hiring practices, on-the-job rapport with supervisors and co-workers, and prejudice from clients and others outside their profession.

DISCRIMINATION IN HIRING

Contrary to the experience of many women in the male-dominated professions, many of the men and women I spoke to indicated that there is a *preference* for hiring men in these four occupations. A Texas librarian at a junior high school said that his school district "would hire a male over a female."

I: Why do you think that is?

R: Because there are so few, and the . . . ones that they do have, the library directors seem to really . . . think they're doing great jobs. I don't know, maybe they just feel they're being progressive or something, [but] I have had a real sense that they really appreciate having a male, particularly at the junior high. . . . As I said, when seven of us lost our jobs from the high schools and were redistributed, there were only four positions at junior high, and I got one of them. Three of the librarians, some who had been here longer than I had with the school district, were put down in elementary school as librarians. And I definitely think that being male made a difference in my being moved to the junior high rather than an elementary school.

Many of the men perceived their token status as males in predominantly female occupations as an *advantage* in hiring and promotions. I asked an Arizona teacher whether his specialty (elementary special education) was an unusual area for men compared to other areas within education. He said,

> Much more so. I am extremely marketable in special education. That's not why I got into the field.

> But I am extremely marketable because I am a man.

In several cases, the more female-dominated the specialty, the greater the apparent preference for men. For example, when asked if he encountered any problem getting a job in pediatrics, a Massachusetts nurse said,

> No, no, none. . . . I've heard this from managers and supervisory-type people with men in pediatrics: "It's nice to have a man because it's such a female-dominated profession."

However, there were some exceptions to this preference for men in the most female-dominated specialties. In some cases, formal policies actually barred men from certain jobs. This was the case in some rural Texas school districts, which refused to hire men in the youngest grades (K–3). Some nurses also reported being excluded from positions in obstetrics and gynecology wards, a policy encountered more frequently in private Catholic hospitals.

But often the pressures keeping men out of certain specialties were more subtle than this. Some men described being "tracked" into practice areas within their professions which were considered more legitimate for men. For example, one Texas man described how he was pushed into administration and planning in social work, even though "I'm not interested in writing policy; I'm much more interested in research and clinical stuff." A nurse who is interested in pursuing graduate study in family and child health in Boston said he was dissuaded from entering the program specialty in favor of a concentration in "adult nursing." A kindergarten teacher described the difficulty of finding a job in his specialty after graduation: "I was recruited immediately to start getting into a track to become an administrator. And it was men who recruited me. It was men that ran the system at that time, especially in Los Angeles."

This tracking may bar men from the most female-identified specialties within these professions. But men are effectively being "kicked upstairs" in the process. Those specialties considered more legitimate practice areas for men also tend to be the most prestigious, better paying ones. A distinguished kindergarten teacher, who had been voted city-wide "Teacher of the Year," told me that even though people were pleased to see him in the classroom, "there's been some encouragement to think about administration, and there's been some encouragement to think about teaching at the university level or something like that, or supervisory-type position." That is, despite his aptitude and interest in staying in the classroom, he felt pushed in the direction of administration.

The effect of this "tracking" is the opposite of that experienced by women in male-dominated occupations. Researchers have reported that many women encounter a "glass ceiling" in their efforts to scale organizational and professional hierarchies. That is, they are constrained by invisible barriers to promotion in their careers, caused mainly by sexist attitudes of men in the highest positions (Freeman 1990).[2] In contrast to the "glass ceiling," many of the men I interviewed seem to encounter a "glass escalator." Often, despite their intentions, they face invisible pressures to move up in their professions. As if on a moving escalator, they must work to stay in place.

A public librarian specializing in children's collections (a heavily female-dominated concentration) described an encounter with this "escalator" in his very first job out of library school. In his first six-months' evaluation, his supervisors commended him for his good work in storytelling and related activities, but they criticized him for "not shooting high enough."

Seriously. That's literally what they were telling me. They assumed that because I was a male—and they told me this—and that I was being hired right out of graduate school, that somehow I wasn't doing

2. In April 1991, the Labor Department created a "Glass Ceiling Commission" to "conduct a through study of the underrepresentation of women and minorities in executive, management, and senior decision-making positions in business" (U.S. House of Representatives 1991:20).

the kind of management-oriented work that they thought I should be doing. And as a result, really they had a lot of bad marks, as it were, against me on my evaluation. And I said I couldn't believe this!

Throughout his ten-year career, he has had to struggle to remain in children's collections.

The glass escalator does not operate at all levels. In particular, men in academia reported some gender-based discrimination in the highest positions due to their universities' commitment to affirmative action. Two nursing professors reported that they felt their own chances of promotion to deanships were nil because their universities viewed the position of nursing dean as a guaranteed female appointment in an otherwise heavily male-dominated administration. One California social work professor reported his university canceled its search for a dean because no minority male or female candidates had been placed on their short list. It was rumored that other schools on campus were permitted to go forward with their searches—even though they also failed to put forward names of minority candidates—because the higher administration perceived it to be "easier" to fulfill affirmative action goals in the social work school. The interviews provide greater evidence of the "glass escalator" at work in the lower levels of these professions.

Of course, men's motivations also play a role in their advancement to higher professional positions. I do not mean to suggest that the men I talked to all resented the informal tracking they experienced. For many men, leaving the most female-identified areas of their professions helped them resolve internal conflicts involving their masculinity. One man left his job as a school social worker to work in a methadone drug treatment program not because he was encouraged to leave by his colleagues, but because "I think there was some macho shit there, to tell you the truth, because I remember feeling a little uncomfortable there . . . ; it didn't feel right to me." Another social worker, employed in the mental health services department of a large urban area in California, reflected on his move into administration:

> *The more I think about it, through our discussion, I'm sure that's a large part of why I wound up in administration. It's okay for a man to do the administration. In fact, I don't know if I fully answered a question that you asked a little while ago about how did being male contribute to my advancing in the field. I was saying it wasn't because I got any special favoritism as a man, but . . . I think . . . because I'm a man, I felt a need to get into this kind of position. I may have worked harder toward it, may have competed harder for it, than most women would do, even women who think about doing administrative work.*

Elsewhere I have speculated on the origins of men's tendency to define masculinity through single-sex work environments (Williams 1989). Clearly, personal ambition does play a role in accounting for men's movement into more "male-defined" arenas within these professions. But these occupations also structure opportunities for males independent of their individual desires or motives.

The interviews suggest that men's underrepresentation in these professions cannot be attributed to discrimination in hiring or promotions. Many of the men indicated that they received preferential treatment because they were men. Although men mentioned gender discrimination in the hiring process, for the most part they were channelled into the more "masculine" specialties within these professions, which ironically meant being "tracked" into better paying and more prestigious specialties.

SUPERVISORS AND COLLEAGUES: THE WORKING ENVIRONMENT

Researchers claim that subtle forms of work place discrimination push women out of male-dominated occupations (Jacobs 1989; Reskin and Hartmann 1986). In particular, women report feeling excluded from informal leadership and decision-making networks, and they sense hostility from their male co-workers, which

makes them feel uncomfortable and unwanted (Carothers and Crull 1984). Respondents in this study were asked about their relationships with supervisors and female colleagues to ascertain whether men also experienced "poisoned" work environments when entering gender atypical occupations.

A major difference in the experience of men and women in nontraditional occupations is that men in these situations are far more likely to be supervised by a member of their own sex. In each of the four professions I studied, men are overrepresented in administrative and managerial capacities, or, as is the case of nursing, their positions in the organizational hierarchy are governed by men (Grimm and Sterm 1974; Phenix 1987; Schmuck 1987; Williams 1989; York, Henley and Gamble 1987). Thus, unlike women who enter "male fields," the men in these professions often work under the direct supervision of other men.

Many of the men interviewed reported that they had good rapport with their male supervisors. Even in professional school, some men reported extremely close relationships with their male professors. For example, a Texas librarian described an unusually intimate association with two male professors in graduate school:

> *I can remember a lot of times in the classroom there would be discussions about a particular topic or issue, and the conversation would spill over into their office hours, after the class was over. And even though there were . . . a couple of the other women that had been in on the discussion, they weren't there. And I don't know if that was preferential or not . . . it certainly carried over into personal life as well. Not just at the school and that sort of thing. I mean, we would get together for dinner . . .*

These professors explicitly encouraged him because he was male:

I: Did they ever offer you explicit words of encouragement about being in the profession by virtue of the fact that you were male? . . .

R: Definitely. On several occasions. Yeah. Both of these guys, for sure, including the Dean who was male also. And it's an interesting point that you bring up because it was, oftentimes, kind of in a sign, you know. It wasn't in the classroom, and it wasn't in front of the group, or if we were in the student lounge or something like that. It was . . . if it was just myself or maybe another one of the guys, you know, and just talking in the office. It's like . . . you know, kind of an opening-up and saying, "You know, you are really lucky that you're in the profession because you'll really go to the top real quick, and you'll be able to make real definite improvements and changes. And you'll have a real influence," and all this sort of thing. I mean, really, I can remember several times.

Other men reported similar closeness with their professors. A Texas psychotherapist recalled his relationships with his male professors in social work school:

> I made it a point to make a golfing buddy with one of the guys that was in administration. He and I played golf a lot. He was the guy who kind of ran the research training, the research part of the master's program. Then there was a sociologist who ran the other part of the research program. He and I developed a good friendship.

This close mentoring by male professors contrasts with the reported experience of women in nontraditional occupations. Others have noted a lack of solidarity among women in nontraditional occupations. Writing about military academies, for example, Yoder describes the failure of token women to mentor succeeding generations of female cadets. She argues that women attempt to play down their gender difference from men because it is the source of scorn and derision.

> Because women felt unaccepted by their male colleagues, one of the last things they wanted to do was to emphasize their gender. Some women thought that, if they kept company with other women, this would highlight their gender and would further isolate them from male cadets. These women desperately wanted to be accepted

> as cadets, not as women cadets. Therefore, they did everything from not wearing skirts as an option with their uniforms to avoiding being a part of a group of women. (Yoder 1989:532)

Men in nontraditional occupations face a different scenario—their gender is construed as a *positive* difference. Therefore, they have an incentive to bond together and emphasize their distinctiveness from the female majority.

Close, personal ties with male supervisors were also described by men once they were established in their professional careers. It was not uncommon in education, for example, for the male principal to informally socialize with the male staff, as a Texas special education teacher describes:

> Occasionally I've had a principal who would regard me as "the other man on the campus" and "it's us against them," you know? I mean, nothing really that extreme, except that some male principals feel like there's nobody there to talk to except the other man. So I've been in that position.

These personal ties can have important consequences for men's careers. For example, one California nurse, whose performance was judged marginal by his nursing supervisors, was transferred to the emergency room staff (a prestigious promotion) due to his personal friendship with the physician in charge. A Massachusetts teacher acknowledged that his principal's personal interest in him landed him his current job.

I: You had mentioned that your principal had sort of spotted you at your previous job and had wanted to bring you here [to this school]. Do you think that has anything to do with the fact that you're a man, aside from your skills as a teacher?

R: Yes, I would say in that particular case, that was part of it. . . . We have certain things in common, certain interests that really lined up.

I: Vis-à-vis teaching?

R: Well, more extraneous things—running specifically, and music. And we just seemed to get along real well right off the bat. It is just kind of a guy thing; we just liked each other . . .

Interviewees did not report many instances of male supervisors discriminating against them, or refusing to accept them because they were male. Indeed, these men were much more likely to report that their male bosses discriminated against the *females* in their professions. When asked if he thought physicians treated male and female nurses differently, a Texas nurse said:

> I think yeah, some of them do. I think the women seem like they have a lot more trouble with the physicians treating them in a derogatory manner. Or, if not derogatory, then in a very paternalistic way than the men [are treated]. Usually if a physician is mad at a male nurse, he just kind of yells at him. Kind of like an employee. And if they're mad at a female nurse, rather than treat them on an equal basis, in terms of just letting their anger out at them as an employee, they're more paternalistic or there's some sexual harassment component to it.

A Texas teacher perceived a similar situation where he worked:

> I've never felt unjustly treated by a principal because I'm a male. The principals that I've seen that I felt are doing things that are kind of arbitrary or not well thought out are doing it to everybody. In fact, they're probably doing it to the females worse than they are to me.

Openly gay men may encounter less favorable treatment at the hands of their supervisors. For example, a nurse in Texas stated that one of the physicians he worked with preferred to staff the operating room with male nurses exclusively—as long as they weren't gay. Stigma associated with homosexuality leads some men to enhance, or even exaggerate their "masculine" qualities, and may be another factor pushing men into more "acceptable" specialties for men.

Not all men who work in these occupations are supervised by men. Many of the men interviewed who had female bosses also reported high levels of acceptance—although levels of intimacy with women seemed lower than with

other men. In some cases, however, men reported feeling shut-out from decision making when the higher administration was constituted entirely by women. I asked an Arizona librarian whether men in the library profession were discriminated against in hiring because of their sex:

> Professionally speaking, people go to considerable lengths to keep that kind of thing out of their [hiring] deliberations. Personally, is another matter. It's pretty common around here to talk about the "old girl network." This is one of the few libraries that I've had any intimate knowledge of which is actually controlled by women. . . . Most of the department heads and upper level administrators are women. And there's an "old girl network" that works just like the "old boy network," except that the important conferences take place in the women's room rather than on the golf course. But the political mechanism is the same, the exclusion of the other sex from decision making is the same. The reasons are the same. It's somewhat discouraging . . .

Although I did not interview many supervisors, I did include 23 women in my sample to ascertain their perspectives about the presence of men in their professions. All of the women I interviewed claimed to be supportive of their male colleagues, but some conveyed ambivalence. For example, a social work professor said she would like to see more men enter the social work profession, particularly in the clinical specialty (where they are underrepresented). Indeed, she favored affirmative action hiring guidelines for men in the profession. Yet, she resented the fact that her department hired "another white male" during a recent search. I questioned her about this ambivalence:

I: I find it very interesting that, on the one hand, you sort of perceive this preference and perhaps even sexism with regard to how men are evaluated and how they achieve higher positions within the profession, yet, on the other hand, you would be encouraging of more men to enter the field. Is that contradictory to you, or . . . ?

R: Yeah, it's contradictory.

It appears that women are generally eager to see men enter "their" occupations. Indeed, several men noted that their female colleagues had facilitated their careers in various ways (including mentorship in college). However, at the same time, women often resent the apparent ease with which men advance within these professions, sensing that men at the higher levels receive preferential treatment which closes off advancement opportunities for women.

But this ambivalence does not seem to translate into the "poisoned" work environment described by many women who work in male-dominated occupations. Among the male interviewees, there were no accounts of sexual harassment. However, women do treat their male colleagues differently on occasion. It is not uncommon in nursing, for example, for men to be called upon to help catheterize male patients, or to lift especially heavy patients. Some librarians also said that women asked them to lift and move heavy boxes of books because they were men. Teachers sometimes confront differential treatment as well, as described by this Texas teacher:

> As a man, you're teaching with all women, and that can be hard sometimes. Just because of the stereotypes, you know. I'm real into computers . . . and all the time people are calling me to fix their computer. Or if somebody gets a flat tire, they come and get me. I mean, there are just a lot of stereotypes. Not that I mind doing any of those things, but it's . . . you know, it just kind of bugs me that it is a stereotype, "A man should do that." Or if their kids have a lot of discipline problems, that kiddo's in your room. Or if there are kids that don't have a father in their home, that kid's in your room. Hell, nowadays that'd be half the school in my room (laughs). But you know, all the time I hear from the principal or from other teachers, "Well, this child really needs a man . . . a male role model" (laughs). So there are a lot of stereotypes that . . . men kind of get stuck with.

This special treatment bothered some respondents. Getting assigned all the "discipline problems" can make for difficult working conditions, for example. But many men claimed this differential treatment did not cause distress. In fact, several said they liked being appreciated for the special traits and abilities (such as strength) they could contribute to their professions.

Furthermore, women's special treatment sometimes enhanced—rather than poisoned—the men's work environments. One Texas librarian said he felt "more comfortable working with women than men" because "I think it has something to do with control. Maybe it's that women will let me take control more than men will." Several men reported that their female colleagues often cast them into leadership roles. Although not all savored this distinction, it did enhance their authority and control in the work place. In subtle (and not-too-subtle) ways, then, differential treatment contributes to the "glass escalator" men experience in nontraditional professions.

Even outside work, most of the men interviewed said they felt fully accepted by their female colleagues. They were usually included in informal socializing occasions with the women—even though this frequently meant attending baby showers or Tupperware parties. Many said that they declined offers to attend these events because they were not interested in "women's things," although several others claimed to attend everything: The minority men I interviewed seemed to feel the least comfortable in these informal contexts. One social worker in Arizona was asked about socializing with his female colleagues:

I: So in general, for example, if all the employees were going to get together to have a party, or celebrate a bridal shower or whatever, would you be invited along with the rest of the group?

R: They would invite me, I would say, somewhat reluctantly. Being a black male, working with all white females, it did cause some outside problems. So I didn't go to a lot of functions with them . . .

I: You felt that there was some tension there on the level of your acceptance . . . ?

R: Yeah. It was OK working, but on the outside, personally, there was some tension there. It never came out, that they said, "Because of who you are we can't invite you" (laughs), and I wouldn't have done anything anyway. I would have probably respected them more for saying what was on their minds. But I never felt completely in with the group.

Some single men also said they felt uncomfortable socializing with married female colleagues because it gave the "wrong impression." But in general, the men said that they felt very comfortable around their colleagues and described their work places as very congenial for men. It appears unlikely, therefore, that men's underrepresentation in these professions is due to hostility towards men on the part of supervisors or women workers.

DISCRIMINATION FROM "OUTSIDERS"

The most compelling evidence of discrimination against men in these professions is related to their dealings with the public. Men often encounter negative stereotypes when they come into contact with clients or "outsiders"—people they meet outside of work. For instance, it is popularly assumed that male nurses are gay. Librarians encounter images of themselves as "wimpy" and asexual. Male social workers describe being typecast as "feminine" and "passive." Elementary school teachers are often confronted by suspicions that they are pedophiles. One kindergarten teacher described an experience that occurred early in his career which was related to him years afterwards by his principal:

He indicated to me that parents had come to him and indicated to him that they had a problem with the fact that I was a male. . . . I recall almost exactly what he said. There were three specific concerns that the parents had: One parent said, "How can he love my child; he's a man." The second thing that I recall, he said the parent said, "He has a beard." And the third thing was, "Aren't you concerned about homosexuality?"

Such suspicions often cause men in all four professions to alter their work behavior to guard against sexual abuse charges, particularly in those specialties requiring intimate contact with women and children.

Men are very distressed by these negative stereotypes, which tend to undermine their self-esteem and to cause them to second-guess their motivations for entering these fields. A California teacher said,

If I tell men that I don't know, that I'm meeting for the first time, that that's what I do, . . . sometimes there's a look on their faces that, you know, "Oh, couldn't get a real job?"

When asked if his wife, who is also an elementary school teacher, encounters the same kind of prejudice, he said,

No, it's accepted because she's a woman. . . . I think people would see that as a . . . step up, you know. "Oh, you're not a housewife, you've got a career. That's great . . . that you're out there working. And you have a daughter, but you're still out there working. You decided not to stay home, and you went out there and got a job." Whereas for me, it's more like I'm supposed to be out working anyway, even though I'd rather be home with [my daughter].

Unlike women who enter traditionally male professions, men's movement into these jobs is perceived by the "outside world" as a step down in status. This particular form of discrimination may be most significant in explaining why men are underrepresented in these professions. Men who otherwise might show interest in and aptitudes for such careers are probably discouraged from pursing them because of the negative popular stereotypes associated with the men who work in them. This is a crucial difference from the experience of women in nontraditional professions: "My daughter, the physician," resonates far more favorably in most people's ears than "My son, the nurse."

Many of the men in my sample identified the stigma of working in a female-identified occupation as the major barrier to more men entering their professions. However, for the most part, they claimed that these negative stereotypes were not a factor in their own decisions to join these occupations. Most respondents didn't consider entering these fields until well into adulthood, after working in some related occupation. Several social workers and librarians even claimed they were not aware that men were a minority in their chosen professions. Either they had no well-defined image or stereotype, or their contacts and mentors were predominantly men. For example, prior to entering library school, many librarians held part-time jobs in university libraries, where there are proportionally more men than in the profession generally. Nurses and elementary school teachers were more aware that mostly women worked in these jobs, and this was often a matter of some concern to them. However, their choices were ultimately legitimized by mentors, or by encouraging friends or family members who implicitly reassured them that entering these occupations would not typecast them as feminine. In some cases, men were told by recruiters there were special advancement opportunities for men in these fields, and they entered them expecting rapid promotion to administrative positions.

I: Did it ever concern you when you were making the decision to enter nursing school, the fact that it is a female-dominated profession?

R: Not really. I never saw myself working on the floor. I saw myself pretty much going into administration, just getting the background and then getting a job someplace as a supervisor and then working, getting up into administration.

Because of the unique circumstances of their recruitment, many of the respondents did not view their occupational choices as inconsistent with a male gender role, and they generally avoided the negative stereotypes directed against men in these fields.

Indeed, many of the men I interviewed claimed that they did not encounter negative professional stereotypes until they had worked in these fields for several years. Popular prejudices can be damaging to self-esteem and probably push some men out of these professions altogether. Yet, ironically, they sometimes contribute to the "glass escalator" effect I have been describing. Men seem to encounter the most vituperative criticism from the public when they are in the most female-identified specialties. Public concerns sometimes result in their being shunted into more "legitimate" positions for men. A librarian formerly in charge of a branch library's children's collection, who now works in the reference department of the city's main library, describes his experience:

R: Some of the people [who frequented the branch library] complained that they didn't want to have a man doing the storytelling scenario. And I got transferred here to the central library in an equivalent job . . . I thought that I did a good job. And I had been told by my supervisor that I was doing a good job.

I: Have you ever considered filing some sort of lawsuit to get that other job back?

R: Well, actually, the job I've gotten now . . . well, it's a reference librarian; it's what I wanted in the first place. I've got a whole lot more authority here. I'm also in charge of the circulation desk. And I've recently been promoted because of my new stature, so . . . no, I'm not considering trying to get that other job back.

The negative stereotypes about men who do "women's work" can push men out of specific jobs. However, to the extent that they channel men into more "legitimate" practice areas, their effects can actually be positive. Instead of being a source of discrimination, these prejudices can add to the "glass escalator effect" by pressuring men to move *out* of the most female-identified areas, and *up* to those regarded more legitimate and prestigious for men.

CONCLUSION: DISCRIMINATION AGAINST MEN

Both men and women who work in nontraditional occupations encounter discrimination, but the forms and consequences of this discrimination are very different. The interviews suggest that unlike "nontraditional" women workers, most of the discrimination and prejudice facing men in the "female professions" emanates from outside those professions. The men and women interviewed for the most part believed that men are given fair—if not preferential—treatment in hiring and promotion decisions, are accepted by supervisors and colleagues, and are well-integrated into the work place subculture. Indeed, subtle mechanisms seem to enhance men's position in these professions—a phenomenon I refer to as the "glass escalator effect."

The data lend strong support for Zimmer's (1988) critique of "gender neutral theory" (such as Kanter's [1977] theory of tokenism) in the study of occupational segregation. Zimmer argues that women's occupational inequality is more a consequence of sexist beliefs and practices embedded in the labor force than the effect of numerical underrepresentation per se. This study suggests that token status itself does not diminish men's occupational success. Men take their gender privilege with them when they enter predominantly female occupations: this translates into an advantage in spite of their numerical rarity.

This study indicates that the experience of tokenism is very different for men and women. Future research should examine how the experience of tokenism varies for members of different races and classes as well. For example, it is likely that informal work place mechanisms similar to the ones identified here promote the careers of token whites in predominantly black occupations. The crucial factor is the social status of the token's group–not their numerical rarity—that determines whether the token encounters a "glass ceiling" or a "glass escalator."

However, this study also found that many men encounter negative stereotypes from persons not directly involved in their professions. Men who enter these professions are often considered "failures," or sexual deviants. These stereotypes may be a major impediment to men who otherwise might consider careers in these

occupations. Indeed, they are likely to be important factors whenever a member of a relatively high status group crosses over into a lower status occupation. However, to the extent that these stereotypes contribute to the "glass escalator effect" by channeling men into more "legitimate" (and higher paying) occupations, they are not discriminatory.

Women entering traditionally "male" professions also face negative stereotypes suggesting they are not "real women" (Epstein 1981; Lorber 1984; Spencer and Podmore 1987). However, these stereotypes do not seem to deter women to the same degree that they deter men from pursuing nontraditional professions. There is ample historical evidence that women flock to male-identified occupations once opportunities are available (Cohn 1985; Epstein 1988). Not so with men. Examples of occupations changing from predominantly female to predominantly male are very rare in our history. The few existing cases—such as medicine—suggest that redefinition of the occupations as appropriately "masculine" is necessary before men will consider joining them (Ehrenreich and English 1978).

Because different mechanisms maintain segregation in male- and female-dominated occupations, different approaches are needed to promote their integration. Policies intended to alter the sex composition of male-dominated occupations—such as affirmative action—make little sense when applied to the "female professions." For men, the major barriers to integration have little to do with their treatment once they decide to enter these fields. Rather, we need to address the social and cultural sanctions applied to men who do "women's work" which keep men from even considering these occupations.

One area where these cultural barriers are clearly evident is in the media's representation of men's occupations. Women working in traditionally male professions have achieved an unprecedented acceptance on popular television shows. Women are portrayed as doctors ("St. Elsewhere"), lawyers ("The Cosby Show," "L.A.

Law"), architects ("Family Ties"), and police officers ("Cagney and Lacey"). But where are the male nurses, teachers and secretaries? Television rarely portrays men in nontraditional work roles, and when it does, that anomaly is made the central focus—and joke—of the program. A comedy series (1991–92) about a male elementary school teacher ("Drexell's Class") stars a lead character who *hates children!* Yet even this negative portrayal is exceptional. When a prime time hospital drama series ("St. Elsewhere") depicted a male orderly striving for upward mobility, the show's writers made him a "physician's assistant," not a nurse or nurse practitioner—the much more likely "real life" possibilities.

Presenting positive images of men in nontraditional careers can produce limited effects. A few social workers, for example, were first inspired to pursue their careers by George C. Scott, who played a social worker in the television drama series, "Eastside/Westside." But as a policy strategy to break down occupational segregation, changing media images of men is no panacea. The stereotypes that differentiate masculinity and femininity, and degrade that which is defined as feminine, are deeply entrenched in culture, social structure, and personality (Williams 1989). Nothing short of a revolution in cultural definitions of masculinity will effect the broad scale social transformation needed to achieve the complete occupational integration of men and women.

Of course, there are additional factors besides societal prejudice contributing to men's underrepresentation in female-dominated professions. Most notably, those men I interviewed mentioned as a deterrent the fact that these professions are all underpaid relative to comparable "male" occupations, and several suggested that instituting a "comparable worth" policy might attract more men. However, I am not convinced that improved salaries will substantially alter the sex composition of these professions unless the cultural stigma faced by men in these occupations diminishes. Occupational sex segregation is remarkably resilient, even in the face of devastating economic hardship. During the Great

Depression of the 1930s, for example, "women's jobs" failed to attract sizable numbers of men (Blum 1991:154). In her study of American Telephone and Telegraph (AT&T) workers, Epstein (1989) found that some men would rather suffer unemployment than accept relatively high paying "women's jobs" because of the damage to their identifies this would cause. She quotes one unemployed man who refused to apply for a female-identified telephone operator job:

> *I think if they offered me $1000 a week tax free, I wouldn't take that job. When I . . . see those guys sitting in there [in the telephone operating room], I wonder what's wrong with them. Are they pansies or what? (Epstein 1989: 577)*

This is not to say that raising salaries would not affect the sex composition of these jobs. Rather, I am suggesting that wages are not the only—or perhaps even the major—impediment to men's entry into these jobs. Further research is needed to explore the ideological significance of the "woman's wage" for maintaining occupational stratification.[3]

At any rate, integrating men and women in the labor force requires more than dismantling barriers to women in male-dominated fields. Sex segregation is a two-way street. We must also confront and dismantle the barriers men face in predominantly female occupations. Men's experiences in these nontraditional occupations reveal just how culturally embedded the barriers are, and how far we have to travel before men and women attain true occupational and economic equality.

3. Alice Kessler-Harris argues that the lower pay of traditionally female occupations is symbolic of a patriarchal order that assumes female dependence on a male breadwinner. She writes that pay equity is fundamentally threatening to the "male worker's sense of self, pride, and masculinity" because it upsets his individual standing in the hierarchical ordering of the sexes (1990:125). Thus, men's reluctance to enter these occupations may have less to do with the actual dollar amount recorded in their paychecks, and more to do with the damage that earning "a woman's wage" would wreak on their self-esteem in a society that privileges men. This conclusion is supported by the interview data.

REFERENCES

Bielby, William T., and James N. Baron
1984 "A woman's place is with other women: Sex segregation within organizations." In *Sex Segregation in the Workplace: Trends, explanations, remedies*, ed. Barbara Reskin, 27–55. Washington, D.C.: National Academy Press.

Blum, Linda M.
1991 *Between Feminism and Labor: The Significance of the Comparable Worth Movement*. Berkeley and Los Angeles: University of California Press.

Carothers, Suzanne C., and Peggy Crull
1984 "Contrasting sexual harassment in female-dominated and male-dominated occupations." In *My Troubles are Going to have Trouble with Me: Everyday Trials and Triumphs of Women Workers*, ed. Karen B. Sacks and Dorothy Remy, 220–227. New Brunswick, N.J.: Rutgers University Press.

Cohn, Samuel
1985 *The Process of Occupational Sex-Typing*. Philadelphia: Temple University Press.

Ehrenreich, Barbara, and Deirdre English
1978 *For Her Own Good: 100 Years of Expert Advice to Women*. Garden City, N.Y.: Anchor Press.

Epstein, Cynthia Fuchs
1981 *Women in Law*. New York: Basic Books.
1988 *Deceptive Distinctions: Sex, Gender and the Social Order*. New Haven, Conn.: Yale University Press.
1989 "Workplace boundaries: Conceptions and creations." *Social Research* 56: 571–590.

Freeman, Sue J. M.
1990 *Managing Lives: Corporate Women and Social Change*. Amherst, Mass.: University of Massachusetts Press.

Grimm, James W., and Robert N. Stern
1974 "Sex roles and internal labor market structures: The female semi-professions." *Social Problems* 21: 690–705.

Hardcastle, D. A.
1987 "The social work labor force." Austin, Tex.: School of Social Work, University of Texas.

Hodson, Randy, and Teresa Sullivan
1990 *The Social Organization of Work*. Belmont, Calif.: Wadsworth Publishing Co.

Jacobs, Jerry
1989 *Revolving Doors: Sex Segregation and Women's Careers*. Stanford, Calif.: Stanford University Press.

Kanter, Rosabeth Moss
1977 *Men and Women of the Corporation*. New York: Basic Books.

Kessler-Harris, Alice
1990 *A Woman's Wage: Historical Meanings and Social Consequences*. Lexington, Ky.: Kentucky University Press.

Lorber, Judith
1984 *Women Physicians: Careers, Status, and Power*. New York: Tavistock.

Martin, Susan E.
1980 *Breaking and Entering: Police Women on Patrol*. Berkeley, Calif.: University of California Press.
1988 "Think like a man, work like a dog, and act like a lady: Occupational dilemmas of policewomen." In *The Worth of Women's Work: A Qualitative Synthesis*, ed. Anne Statham, Eleanor M. Miller, and Hans O. Mauksch, 205–223. Albany, N.Y.: State University of New York Press.

Phenix, Katharine
1987 "The status of women librarians." *Frontiers* 9: 36–40.

Reskin, Barbara
1988 "Bringing the men back in: Sex differentiation and the devaluation of women's work." *Gender & Society* 2: 58–81.

Reskin, Barbara, and Heidi Hartmann
1986 *Women's Work, Men's Work: Sex Segregation on the Job*. Washington, D.C.: National Academy Press.

Reskin, Barbara, and Patricia Roos
1990 *Job Queues, Gender Queues: Explaining Women's Inroads into Male Occupations*. Philadelphia: Temple University Press.

Schmuck, Patricia A.
1987 "Women school employees in the United States." In *Women Educators: Employees of Schools in Western Countries*, ed. Patricia A. Schmuck, 75–97. Albany, N.Y.: State University of New York Press.

Schreiber, Carol
1979 *Men and Women in Transitional Occupations*. Cambridge, Mass.: MIT Press.

Spencer, Anne, and David Podmore
1987 *In A Man's World: Essays on Women in Male-dominated Professions*. London: Tavistock.

Strauss, Anselm L.
1987 *Qualitative Analysis for Social Scientists*. Cambridge, England: Cambridge University Press.
U.S. Bureau of the Census
1980 *Detailed Population Characteristics*, Vol. 1, Ch. D. Washington, D.C.: Government Printing Office.
U.S. Department of Labor. Bureau of Labor Statistics
1991 *Employment and Earnings*. January. Washington, D.C.: Government Printing Office.
U.S. Congress. House
1991 *Civil Rights and Women's Equity in Employment Act of 1991*. Report. (Report 102-40, Part I.) Washington, D.C.: Government Printing Office.
Williams, Christine L.
1989 *Gender Differences at Work: Women and Men in Nontraditional Occupations*. Berkeley, Calif.: University of California Press.
Yoder, Janice D.
1989 "Women at West Point: Lessons for token women in male-dominated occupations." In *Women: A Feminist Perspective*, ed. Jo Freeman, 523–537. Mountain View, Calif.: Mayfield Publishing Company.
York, Reginald O., H. Carl Henley, and Dorothy N. Gamble
1987 "Sexual discrimination in social work: Is it salary or advancement?" *Social Work* 32: 336–340.
Zimmer, Lynn
1988 "Tokenism and women in the workplace." *Social Problems* 35: 64–77.

WHY ARE THERE NO MALE ASIAN ANCHOR*MEN* ON TV?

BEN FONG-TORRES

Connie Chung, the best-known Asian TV newswoman in the country, is a co-anchor of *1986*, a primetime show on NBC. Ken Kashiwahara, the best-known Asian TV newsman, has been chief of ABC's San Francisco bureau for seven years; his reports pop up here and there on ABC's newscasts and other newsrelated programs.

Wendy Tokuda, the best-known Asian TV newswoman in the Bay Area, is a co-anchor of KPIX's evening news. David Louie, the most established Asian TV newsman, is a field reporter, covering the Peninsula for KGO.

And that's the way it is: among Asian American broadcasters, the glamor positions—the anchor chairs, whose occupants earn more than $500,000 a year in the major markets—go to the women; the men are left outside, in the field, getting by on reporters wages that top out at about $80,000.

The four Bay Area television stations that present regular newscasts (Channels 2, 4, 5 and 7) employ more than 40 anchors. Only two are Asian Americans: Tokuda and Emerald Yeh, a KRON co-anchor on weekends. There is no Asian male in an anchor position, and there has never been one. (Other Asian women who have anchored locally are Linda Yu [KGO] and Kaity Tong [KPIX], now prime-time anchors in Chicago and New York.)

None of the two dozen broadcasters this reporter spoke to could name a male Asian news anchor working anywhere in the United States.

Don Fitzpatrick, a TV talent headhunter whose job it has been for four years to help television stations find anchors and reporters, maintains a video library in his San Francisco office of 9000 people on the air in the top 150 markets.

There are, in fact, several reasons proposed by broadcasters, station executives, talent agents and others.

- Asian men have been connected for generations with negative stereotypes. Asian women have also been saddled with false images, but, according to Tokuda, "In this profession, they work for women and against men."
- Asian women are perceived as attractive partners for the typical news anchor: a white male. "TV stations," says Henry Der, director of Chinese for Affirmative Action, "have discovered that having an Asian female with a white male is an attractive combination." And, adds Sam Chu Lin, a former reporter for both KRON and KPIX, "they like the winning formula. If an Asian woman works in one market, then another market duplicates it. So why test for an Asian male?"
- Asian women allow television stations to fulfill two equal-opportunity slots with one hiring. As Mario Machado, a Los Angeles-based reporter and producer puts it, "They get two minorities in one play of the cards. *They* hit the jackpot."

- Asian males are typically encouraged by parents toward careers in the sciences and away from communications.
- Because there are few Asian men on the air, younger Asian males have no racial peers as role models. With few men getting into the profession, news directors have a minuscule talent pool from which to hire.

And, according to Sumi Haru, a producer at KTLA in Los Angeles, the situation is worsening as stations are being purchased and taken over by large corporations. At KTTV, the ABC affiliate, "The affirmative action department was the first to go." At her own station, the public affairs department is being trimmed. "We're concerned with what little Asian representation we have on the air," said Haru, an officer of the Association of Asian-Pacific American Artists.

HONORS THESIS

Helen Chang, a communications major at UC Berkeley now working in Washington, DC, made the missing Asian anchorman the subject of her honors thesis. Chang spoke with Asian anchorwomen in Los Angeles, Chicago and New York as well as locally. "To capsulize the thesis, "she says, "it is an executive decision based on a perception of an Asian image. On an executive decision level, the image of the Asian woman is acceptable."

"It's such a white bread medium; it's the survival of the blandest," says a male Asian reporter who asked to remain anonymous. A native San Franciscan, this reporter once had ambitions to be an anchor, but after several static years at his station, "I've decided to face reality. I have a white man's credentials but it doesn't mean a thing. I'm not white. How can it not be racism?"

"Racism is a strong word that scares people," says Tokuda.

"But whatever's going on here is some ugly animal. It's not like segregation in the south. What it is is very subtle . . . bias."

To Mario Machado, it's not that subtle. Machado, who is half Chinese and half Portuguese, is a former daytime news anchor in Los Angeles who's had the most national television exposure after Kashiwahara. Being half-Chinese, he says, has given him no advantage in getting work. "It's had no bearing at all. There's a move on against Asians, period, whether part-Asian or full Asian."

TV executives, he charges, "don't really want minority males to be totally successful. They don't want minority men perceived as strong, bright, and articulate. We can be cute second bananas, like Robert Ito on *Quincy*. But having an Asian woman—that's always been the feeling from World War II, I guess. You bring back an Asian bride, and she's cute and delicate. But a strong minority man with authority and conviction—I don't think people are ready for that."

WAR IMAGE

Bruno Cohen, news director at KPIX, agrees that "for a lot of people, the World War II image of Japanese, unfortunately, is the operative image about what Asian males are all about."

That image, says Serena Chen, producer and host of *Asians Now!* on KTVU, was one of danger. "They may be small, but they're strong. So watch out, white women!"

The Vietnam war and recent movies like *Rambo*, Machado says, add to the historic negativity. "You never went to war against Asian women," he says. "You always went to war against Asian men."

Today, says Tokuda, Asian men are saddled with a twin set of stereotypes. "They're either wimpy—they have real thick glasses and they're small and they have an accent and they're carrying a lot of cameras—or they're a murderous gangster." "Or," says Les Kumagai, a former KPIX intern now working for a Reno TV station, "they're businessmen who are going to steal your jobs."

"The Asian woman is viewed as property, and the Asian male has been denied sexuality," says Chen. "Eldridge Cleaver created a theory of the black male being superglorified in the physical and superdecreased in the mental. It's very difficult for people to see a successful black male unless he's an athlete or a performer. If he's in a corporate situation, everyone says, 'Wow, he's the product of affirmative action.' That theory holds that in this society, people who have potential to have power have to be male, and have both mental and physical [strength] to be the superior male. In this society, they took away the black male's mental and gave him his physical. The Asian male has been denied the physical and given the mental."

Veteran KRON reporter Vic Lee listens to a tally of stereotypes and images associated with Asian men. "All those reasons limit where an Asian American can work. I've always said to my wife, if I'm fired here, there're only a couple of cities I can go to and get a job based on how well I do my work, not how I look or what color my skin is. There are cities with Asian American populations, and you can count them on one hand: Seattle, Los Angeles, New York, Boston, and possibly Washington.

"The rest of the country? You might as well forget Detroit. They *killed* a [Chinese] guy just 'cause he looked Japanese." Lee is referring to Vincent Chin, who was beaten to death by two white auto workers who mistook him for a Japanese and blamed him for their unemployment.

"EXOTIC" FEMALES

In contrast to the threatening Asian male, says Les Kumagai, "Females are 'exotic.' They're not threatening to non-Asian females and they're attractive to non-Asian males. You're looking to draw the 18-to-45-year-old female demographic for advertising. You just won't get the draw from an Asian male."

To Tokuda, the Asian woman's persisting stereotype is more insidious than exotic. "It's the Singapore girl: not only deferential but submissive. It's right next to the geisha girl."

At KGO, says one newsroom employee, "somebody in management was talking about

[recently hired reporter] Janet Yee and blurted out, 'Oh, she's so cute.' They don't care about her journalistic credentials. . . . That type of thinking still persists."

AGGRESSIVE

Janet Yee says she can take the comment as a compliment, but agrees that it is "a little dehumanizing." Yee, who is half Chinese and half Irish-Swedish, says she doesn't get the feeling, at KGO, that she was hired for her looks. Stereotypes "are the things I've fought all my life," she says, adding that she isn't at all submissive and deferential. "I'm assertive and outgoing, and I think that's what got me the job."

Emerald Yeh, who worked in Portland and at CNN (Cable News Network) in Atlanta before joining KRON, says she's asked constantly about the part being an Asian woman played in her landing a job. "The truth is that it's a factor, but at the same time, there is absolutely no way I can keep my job virtually by being Asian."

Despite the tough competition for jobs in television, Yeh, like Tokuda and several peers in Los Angeles, is vocal about the need to open doors to Asian men. "People think Asians have done so well," she says, "but how can you say that if one entire gender group is hardly visible?"

George Lum, a director at KTVU who got into television work some 30 years ago at Channel 5, has a theory of his own. "The Asian male is not as aggressive as the Asian female. In this business you have to be more of an extrovert. Men are a little more passive."

Headhunter Don Fitzpatrick agrees. "Watching my tapes, women in general are much more aggressive than men. . . . My theory on that is that—say a boy and girl both want to get into television, and they have identical SATs and grade point average. Speakers tell them, you'll go to Chico or Medford and start out making $17,000 to $18,000 a year. A guy will say, 'This is bull. If I stay in school and get into accounting or law . . .' And they have a career change. A woman will go to Chico or Medford and will get into LA or New York."

"In Helen Chang's paper," recalls Tokuda, "she mentions the way Asian parents have channeled boys with a narrow kind of guidance."

"With Japanese kids," says Tokuda, "right after the war, there was a lot of pressure on kids to get into society, on being quiet and working our way back in." In Seattle, she says, "I grew up with a whole group of Asian American men who from the time they were in junior high knew they were going to be doctors—or at least that they were gonna be successful. There was research that showed that they were very good in math and sciences and not good in verbal skills. With girls there's much less pressure to go into the hard sciences."

Most of the men who do make it in broadcasting describe serendipitous routes into the field, and all of them express contentment with being reporters. "Maybe I'm covering my butt by denying that I want to anchor," says Kumagai, "but I do get a bigger charge being out in the field."

Still, most Asian male reporters do think about the fame and fortune of an anchor slot. Those thoughts quickly meet up against reality.

David Louie realizes he has little chance of becoming the 6 o'clock anchor. "I don't have the matinee idol look that would be the most ideal image on TV. Being on the portly side and not having a full head of hair, I would be the antithesis of what an anchorman is supposed to look like."

Kind of like KPIX's Dave McElhatton? Louie laughs. "But he's white," he says, quickly adding

that McElhatton also has 25 years of experience broadcasting in the Bay Area.

At least Louie is on the air. In Sacramento, Lonnie Wong was a reporter at KTXL (Channel 40), and Jan Minagawa reported and did part-time anchoring at KXTV (Channel 10). Both have been promoted into newsroom editing and production jobs. And neither is thrilled to be off the air.

Wong, who says he was made an assignment editor because, among reporters, he had "the most contacts in the community," says his new job is "good management experience. But I did have a reservation. I was the only minority on the air at the station; and I know that's valuable for a station."

Minagawa's station, KXTV, does have an Asian on the air: a Vietnamese woman reporter named Mai Pham. "That made the decision easier," says Minagawa, who had been a reporter and fill-in anchor for seven years. A new news director, he says, "had a different idea of what should be on the air" and asked him to become a producer. "I didn't like it, but there was nothing I could do."

Mitch Farris rejects any notion of a conspiracy by news directors against Asian American men. In fact, he says, they are "desperate" for Asian male applicants. "Just about any news director would strive to get an Asian on the air and wouldn't mind a man."

To which Machado shouts, "We're here! We're here! We're looking for work."

THE STATUS OF GAY MEN IN THE WORKPLACE

MARTIN P. LEVINE

Work poses manifold meanings in modern American life (Julian and Kornblum, 1983:489–492). On one hand, it denotes the quality of our economic well being. For most of us, our job determines how much money we make, and this in turn affects how well we live. Work also signifies our social status. What we do for a living strongly influences how other people evaluate and rank us. And finally, work affects how we think about ourselves. What we do often determines how we feel about who we are.

Jobs hold additional meanings for men. For them, work demonstrates manliness (Pleck, 1982; Doyle, 1983). To prove their masculinity, men attempt to be breadwinners. This test applies most strongly for men, typically blue collar workers, who adhere to the traditional male role (Le Masters, 1975). These men demonstrate their manliness by earning enough to support a wife and family. Men who follow the modern male role, usually white collar workers or "yuppies," emphasize professional success (Ehrenreich, 1983; Gould, 1974). These men prove their masculinity by achieving corporate power, professional recognition, and high earnings.

Gay men experience great difficulty in meeting this manly test. The deep-seated cultural antipathy towards men who love men, called homophobia, prevents homosexuals from obtaining good jobs. Homophobia drives gay men into nonprestigious, low paying, white collar or service jobs, which are commonly regarded as unsuitable for men (Harry, 1982:181–183; Harry and DeVall, 1978:159–160). This, in turn, reinforces the popular impression of homosexuals as effeminate.

This article explores the status of homosexuals in the work force. After examining the prevailing stereotypes of gay men, I will consider the effect of these stereotypes on attitudes towards the hiring of homosexuals, and then examine how these attitudes provoke employment discrimination against gay men.

STEREOTYPES OF HOMOSEXUALS

Americans view homosexuals as "failed men."[1] Most of us equate masculinity with heterosexuality and believe that "real men" love women. We accordingly associate homosexuality with a spoiled masculinity—with a lack of the physical, emotional, or social characteristics of real men.[2]

The stereotypes of homosexuals incorporate these assumptions and include several interrelated images of gay men: (1) the swishy pansy, (2) the cultivated fop, (3) the diseased pervert, and (4) the immoral degenerate. The first two stereotypes link homosexuality with unmasculine behaviors and interests. As swishy pansies, gay men prance with mincing gaits, shriek in lisping voices, and dress in womanly garb. Their physiques, moreover, are puny and thin.[3] As cultivated fops, gays revel in haute cuisine, couture, and culture. They adore trendy food and nightspots, decorate and dress in the latest styles, and flock to the ballet, opera, and theater.[4] The last two stereotypes link homosexuality with unmanly illnesses and vices. As diseased perverts, gay men suffer from twisted erotic desires and illnesses. Their deranged upbringing fosters unnatural sexual interests, compulsive promiscuity, and susceptibility to AIDS.[5] As immoral degenerates, gay men are sex crazed, substance abusing, molesters of children. Their twisted emotions provoke uncontrollable urges for sex, liquor, and drugs, which prompts them to drink, snort cocaine, and molest young boys.[6]

ATTITUDES TOWARDS THE EMPLOYMENT OF HOMOSEXUALS

These stereotypes account for our conflicting attitudes towards the employment of gay men. On one hand, we endorse the principle of equal job opportunities for homosexuals (Schneider and Lewis, 1984:18). Americans have recently accepted the doctrine of equal opportunity in the work place, which by extension fosters support for equal job opportunities for racial, religious, and sexual minorities (Schneider and Lewis, 1984:18). A recent poll, for instance, found that nearly two-thirds of the public favored equal rights in the labor force for homosexuals (Gallup, 1982). On the other hand, we also favor banning gay men from particular lines of work. Americans oppose employing homosexuals for either jobs typically done by men, or jobs involving maternal duties (Schneider and Lewis, 1984:18).

Homophobic stereotypes account for these attitudes. Americans perceive homosexuals as swishy pansies and cultivated fops, and therefore consider gay men as unfit for the jobs traditionally assigned to men (Harry, 1982:181–183). "Men's work" expresses, stereotypically masculine traits like rationality, toughness, and aggressiveness, which tend to be concentrated in high status, better paying, blue or white collar fields (Davidson and Gordon, 1979:72–75). Public opinion polls record extensive opposition to homosexuals doing men's work. By large pluralities, we disapprove of gay men working as judges, doctors, policemen, and government officials (Levitt and Klassen, 1974; Schneider and Lewis, 1984:18).

The stereotypes foster the belief that homosexuals *are* suitable for traditionally feminine jobs, "women's work" (Davidson and Gordon, 1979:72–75). These jobs embody traditionally feminine attributes like domesticity, compassion, and dependency. All of these jobs tend to be in low status, poorly paying, white collar or service fields (Benokratis and Feagin, 1985:52–53). Polls indicate widespread support for gay men doing nutrient, decorative, or expressive forms of women's work. By overwhelming majorities, we approve of homosexuals working as artists, beauticians, musicians, florists, and retail clerks (Schneider and Lewis, 1984:18; Levitt and Klassen, 1974). These jobs can be classified as "sissy work."

We do not, however, regard gay men as fit for all kinds of women's work. Americans also believe that homosexuals are diseased perverts and immoral degenerates, which evokes strong opposition to gay men doing jobs involving such maternal responsibilities as intimate contact, moral training, and the care of children. We believe that homosexuals are too "sick" for these jobs—their perverted nature will lead them to corrupt or molest young people. By huge pluralities, we disapprove of homosexuals working as clergy, teachers, principals, and camp counselors (Schneider and Lewis, 1984:18; Gallup, 1987).

EMPLOYMENT DISCRIMINATION AGAINST GAY MEN

Homophobic stereotypes provoke discriminatory practices against gay men in the work place (National Gay Task Force, 1981). Work associates share the cultural stereotypes of gay men, which cause them to hold extremely negative perceptions of homosexual workers. For example, employers and co-workers view gay men as swishy pansies and debauched lechers and they therefore believe that homosexual workers would dress like women and sexually harass people on the job (Maddocks, 1969:101–102). Employers also regard gay men as diseased perverts and they consequently believe that homosexual workers would be emotionally unstable, which would result in high rates of absenteeism and low rates of productivity (Weinberg and Williams, 1974:223–228; Bellard Weinberg, 1978:141–142).

These images affect the attitudes of workplace associates towards the employment of gay men in particular jobs. Employers and co-workers hold similar attitudes towards this issue as the general public, believing gay men to be unsuitable for traditionally masculine or maternal lines of work but fit for "sissy" jobs.

AIDS fosters additional negative perceptions of gay employees. Misconceptions about the nature of this disease appear to be fairly widespread. Despite all the evidence that AIDS cannot be spread by casual contact, many Americans believe that AIDS can be spread through such casual means as handshakes, bathroom facilities or shared work spaces (Institute of Medicine, 1988:67; Jennings, 1988:66).

This misconception influences the attitudes of workplace associates toward homosexual workers. Employers and coworkers view gay men as diseased perverts who are infected with the AIDS virus and consequently fear that homosexual employees will give them AIDS. In addition, employers worry about the high medical costs and lost productivity incurred by people afflicted with this disease Leonard 1975; Smothers, 1988; Hamilton et al., 1987).

These attitudes prompt job discrimination against gay men. This victimization can be either direct or indirect (Harry and De Vall, 1978:159). In direct job discrimination, workplace associates either harass gay men or discriminate against them in hiring, retention, and advancement. In indirect job discrimination, fear of victimization drives homosexuals into stereotypically "sissy" lines of work.

Direct Job Discrimination

This form of employment discrimination occurs primarily in jobs considered unsuitable for gay men. Many employers, in typically male or ma-

ternal fields, consider homosexuality grounds for not hiring, promoting, or retaining otherwise qualified individuals (Maddock 1969). They consequently refuse to employ, advance, or retain gay men.

The practice of direct job discrimination varies according to openness about sexual orientation. Homosexuals differ in their ability to hide their sexual preference from work associates (Bell and Weinberg, 1978). Sociologists use the terms "discredited" and "discreditable" to describe these differences (Goffman, 1963:4). Discredited gay men are unable to hide their sexual orientation from work associates. The reasons for this are twofold: First, discredited men may be labeled homosexual in the official records of the courts, armed forces, and medical facilities. Employers regularly check these records, and consequently discover the homosexuality of discredited men (Levine, 1979). These men are involuntarily discredited.[7] Second, feelings of pride, self-affirmation or intimacy may compel discredited men to reveal their sexual preference to work associates (Troiden, 1988). These men are voluntarily discredited. Discreditable gay men are able to hide their sexual orientation from work associates. Employers and coworkers consequently are unaware of their sexual preference. Discredited and discreditable gay men are victimized differently during hiring procedures and after employment.

Hiring Procedures

Employers do not want to hire homosexuals. They therefore routinely ask questions during the hiring process that expose the homosexuality of discredited and discreditable men. These questions appear on standard application and interview forms. Nearly all forms ask prospective employees about their personal interests and background. More specifically, they inquire about prior criminal, military, medical, marital, and residential experiences. They also ask about hobbies and community service.

These questions place involuntarily discredited men in a classic double bind. If they answer the questions truthfully, they will disclose their sexual orientation and lose the job:

> *I applied for a job at G.E. and told them about my discharge. He said he could have hired me if I had served my time in prison for murder but not with that discharge. The department stores told me, we're sorry but we don't employ homosexuals (Williams and Weinberg, 1971:116).*

If they lie and hide their homosexuality, they will be terminated once the records are checked.

The questions concerning personal interests threaten the hiring of voluntarily discredited men. These men typically reveal their sexual preference while discussing pastimes or community service. To illustrate, they may state that they volunteer for a local gay charity. The effects of voluntary disclosure are documented in two recent studies. Adam (1982) investigated the hiring practices of law firms in Ontario, Canada. He sent each firm an application form and resume for an entry level position known as articling, which is open to recent law school graduates. The applications and resumes were identical except for the sex and sexual preference of the applicant. Sexual orientation was indicated by listing "active in local Gay People's Alliance" under the Personal Background section of the resume. The findings reveal that homosexual applicants were the least likely to obtain interviews; heterosexual men received 1.6 times more interview offers than gay men. The American Sociological Association's Task Group on Homosexuality investigated the employment practices of American sociology departments (Huber, 1982). The Task Group asked the heads of these departments about their ability to hire sociologists who were self-proclaimed gay or lesbian rights activists. More than half of the chairs reported that employing such activists would cause serious problems or that it just could not be done.

The questions about marital status, living arrangements, medical histories, and personal interests jeopardize the employment of discreditable gay men. Employers regard particular answers to these questions as evidence of homo-

sexuality. They assume that men who state that they have never married, live with a male roommate, or dwell in a gay neighborhood are homosexual, as are men who report frequent exposures to sexually transmitted diseases or interest in the arts. These statements typically cost men the position.

Job interviews also endanger the hiring of discreditable gay men. Employers commonly check the applicant's demeanor and appearance for signs of homosexuality during the interview. They presume that men who are effeminate, well-dressed, or slightly built are gay, and consequently refuse to employ them.

Placement agencies further threaten employment (Brown, 1976:163; Zoglin, 1974). These agencies regularly scrutinize prospective employees' application forms and interviews for evidence of homosexuality. Men evincing these signs are thought to be gay, and their forms are coded with a letter or number signifying homosexuality. Most agencies will not refer suspected homosexuals to potential employers because they believe that such referrals would damage business with these employers.

After Employment

Workplace associates, moreover, do not want to retain or promote gay men. They consequently ask questions after hiring that reveal the homosexuality of discredited and discreditable gay men. These questions appear in either standard personnel investigations or on-the-job conversations. Almost all employers conduct periodic investigations into the background of their staff, usually for purposes of promotion or retention. These investigations commonly inquire about arrest records, sexual orientation, and personal life.

The arrest questions expose the homosexuality of involuntarily discredited men. Many of these men have been arrested after hiring for such homosexual offenses as sodomy, solicitation for illegal sexual conduct, or loitering for purposes of engaging in deviant sexual intercourse (Boggan, et al., 1983).[8] Employers discover these arrests while checking police records, and therefore detect the men's homosexuality, which may cost them the job or promotion.

The questions about sexual preference jeopardizes the employment of discreditable men. Many employers require these men to answer direct questions about their sexual orientation during polygraph (lie-detector) tests that disclose false replies to the questions. Employers frequently fire or deny promotions to men whose test results indicate that they lied about being gay.

Polygraph tests put discreditable gay men in a "no-win" situation. If they take the test, they will disclose their homosexuality and lose their job or promotion. If they refuse to be tested, they will also be fired or denied promotion:

> *I had to turn down a job offer which was conditional on my agreement to take a lie-detector test, because I was afraid they would ask The Question (Jay and Young, 1979:706).*

The questions about personal lives further threaten the jobs of discreditable men. Employers typically question these men about their living arrangements, recreational interests, and friendship circles. They perceive certain kinds of answers to these questions as evidence of homosexuality. They presume that men who report living with other men, attending cultural events, or associating with gay people, organizations or gathering places are homosexual. These answers cost men the job or promotion.

Industrial intelligence agencies are often used to verify the answers concerning personal lives (Levine, 1979). These agencies frequently utilize investigative procedures that encroach upon constitutional rights to privacy. Some of these procedures include secretly monitoring daily activities and interrogating family, friends, and neighbors:

> *Lloyd, at age fifty-three, had worked his way up from a door-to-door salesman for a large insurance company to the point where in 1973, he was about to be promoted to a vice-presidency. . . . Lloyd was a homosexual who had been living for twelve years with a man he told neighbors and vis-*

> *itors was his cousin. In 1968 Lloyd's lover was crippled in an automobile accident and confined for the rest of his life to a wheelchair. Lloyd made him the beneficiary of his own life insurance policy, explaining to the company that he had an obligation to provide for a relative who was no longer able to work.*
>
> *As part of a final check on the man they were about to promote, the senior officers sent an investigator to speak with Lloyd's neighbors and to interview people in his "cousin's" hometown. The investigator used the standard ploy—the young man was about to become the beneficiary of an $80,000 insurance policy. His former neighbors talked freely, and the investigator soon learned that the man was in fact not related to Lloyd. Back in Lloyd's town, he learned that the two men had been living together for years. With the investigator's report in hand, the company officials called Lloyd in and demanded his immediate resignation. The word homosexual was not mentioned; they were too polite for that (Brown, 1976:151–152).*

The media also informs employers about discreditable men's homosexuality. In many localities, news editors regard arrests for homosexual offenses and gay rights demonstrations as major news features. They consequently spotlight these arrests and demonstrations as front page or lead stories. These stories, moreover, usually include the names, addresses, occupations, and occasionally pictures of the offenders and demonstrators. Employers see these stories, discover an employee's homosexuality, and fire or deny this man a promotion:

> *I was fired from my job I held for thirteen years (engineering management) because I am homosexual. They discovered this when a letter I wrote decrying oppression was published in the local newspaper (Jay and Young, 1979:705).*

Co-workers also endanger the employment of discreditable men. Work associates are often the first to recognize that a colleague is gay (Harry and De Vall, 1978:161–162). Their suspicions arise from the disclosures men make about their private lives during on-the-job conversations.[9] For example, the men may show little interest in sports, dating or sex talk, or they may receive frequent telephone calls from male friends or roommates. Co-workers discriminate against men they presume to be gay. They either harass them into quitting or pressure employers into firing them:

> *On the job I was ridiculed and made the butt of jokes until I retaliated by losing my head and temper over something minor, resulting in my dismissal (Jay and Young, 1979:705).*

> *The other people used to abuse me because of it. Finally I got tired of pussyfooting around and complained about it and they told me I was through (Bell and Weinberg, 1978:144).*

In addition, they may use this knowledge to advance their career at the expense of the man thought to be gay:

> *The guy was after my job. He suspected I was gay and started to spread it through the office, making all sorts of wisecracks, trying to damage my reputation. Eventually, the atmosphere in the office grew very hostile (Interview with author).*

Homosexuals are further victimized in terms of job responsibilities. Many gay men find their work assignments curtailed after employers discover their homosexuality. They may be demoted to a less responsible position or transferred to a job beneath their qualifications (Zoglin, 1974):

> *The owner of a Portland-based international firm recruited a 44-year-old man for a position as director of marketing. The owner found out that this man was homosexual and wanted to fire him immediately, but because the company was in financial difficulty he was kept on. After a year his responsibilities were gradually taken from him until he resigned (Task Force on Sexual Preference, 1978:47).*

Special Cases of Direct Job Discrimination: Occupational Licenses and Security Clearances

A wide range of jobs, in both private industry and the civil service, demand occupational licenses or security clearances. According to one count

(Boggan, et al., 1983:25), over 350 different fields require occupational licenses, including such diverse trades as doctor, teacher, and barber—and about 7 million people work in licensed jobs. In addition, many positions within the Defense and State Department demand security clearances, as do thousands of jobs in security-related research and manufacturing industries. Approximately 2.2 million people work in these industries (Boggan, et al., 1983:53).

The agencies authorized to grant occupational licenses routinely discriminate against gay men. Virtually every jurisdiction has created special boards for administering occupational licensing. These boards issue licenses, which are certificates stating that an individual is authorized to engage in a particular occupation, on the basis of legally proscribed professional and moral standards. The professional standards specify certain skill levels, age requirements, work experiences, and educational backgrounds. The moral standards prohibit licensing people who either lack "good moral character" or have committed criminal offenses or unprofessional conduct. The boards construe homosexuality as evidence of "moral failure" and consequently revoke or refuse to grant licenses to gay men, which prevents them from working in their field:

> *My chief of service, a well-meaning but misguided man who had used me as a resident for four years, had a delayed guilt reaction for having "harbored" a homosexual. He decided that he must tell the truth for the good of all concerned. So he informed the ACS (American College of Surgeons) and my specialty board that I was a homosexual. To their credit, the ACS approved my membership, making me an FACS (Fellow of the American College of Surgeons). The specialty board, however, turned down my request to take the exam on the grounds of "poor moral character . . . This lack of formal certification meant I might not be reappointed to my hospital and raised questions about my competency. It delayed my career as a neurosurgeon (Brown, 1976:154).*

> *My arrest record [for a homosexual offense] caused my California teachers' license to be re-*

scinded. *I'm not allowed to teach in the public schools because of it (Bell and Weinberg, 1978:144).*

Homosexuals are also regularly victimized in the awarding of security clearances. A handful of government agencies (such as the federal Defense Industrial Security Office and the Civil Service Commission) grant such clearances, which are documents permitting the holder access to classified information about matters pertaining to the national security. These agencies perceive homosexuality as a threat to the national security. First, they believe that gay men are too emotionally unstable to keep classified information secret. Second, they believe that gay men can be easily blackmailed into divulging official secrets through threats of exposing their homosexuality (Walters, 1986). The agencies thus revoke or refuse to issue security clearances to gay men, which prevents them from working in their field:

> *I lost my security clearance and am unable to get one. My field was industrial health, radioactive stuff. It requires a security clearance. Anyone that could use me has defense contracts and because they have defense contracts they can't use me. I applied for three or four jobs and they asked for my discharge [Undesirable discharge for homosexuality] and said, "Sorry, we can't use you" (Williams and Weinberg, 1971:118).*

The rationale for such discriminatory actions is seriously flawed. There is no evidence that gay men are more emotionally disturbed than straight males. Studies of matched samples of homosexual and heterosexual men show equal rates of psychopathology in both groups (Bell and Weinberg, 1978). Furthermore, gay men are not uniformly vulnerable to blackmail. Voluntarily discredited men cannot be blackmailed about something that is evident. In addition, discreditable men are susceptible only because disclosure of their homosexuality would cost their job. Employment discrimination not homosexuality makes them vulnerable to blackmail.

Coping Strategies

Sociologists classify the tactics homosexuals use to cope with direct job discrimination as techniques for avoiding stigmatization (Goffman, 1963; Humphrey, 1972; ch 8). These strategies enable gay men to evade or lessen victimization. The most widely used tactics include passing, covering, and minstrelization.

Passing as heterosexual is probably the most commonly utilized technique, and is favored mainly by discreditable men (Troiden, 1988:52; Humphreys, 1972:28). In passing, homosexuals conceal their sexual orientation from work associates, which leads employers and coworkers to think that they are heterosexual. Gay men hide their sexual preference through subterfuge, suppression, and nondisclosure. Subterfuge involves overt pretenses of heterosexuality. To convince work associates that they are straight, homosexuals actively pretend to be heterosexual. For example, they may comment about the physical attractiveness of female associates, participate in the traditional lunch-time pastime of "girl-watching," or bring female dates to job-related social events:

> *I will often be eating lunch with one of the vice presidents or the controller or somebody, and the talk will get to sex—as it always does. I will play along. For example, when we comment on girls, they all know what my type is (Zoglin, 1974:27).*

Dates, moreover, usually pose as girl-friends, fiancees, and even wives:

> *I work in an extremely homophobic organization. To protect myself, I married a woman. She was an illegal alien and married me to stay in the country. I married her for a cover. Everyone at work thinks I am straight because I am married (Interview with author).*

Suppression entails concealment of evidence of homosexuality. To keep their sexual orientation secret, gay men consciously hide features of their private lives that are considered signs of homosexuality. For example, they purposefully avoid telling work associates that they have male roommates, vacation in gay resorts, or attend the opera. Finally, nondisclosure involves covertness about erotic preference. In this strategy, gay men stop either pretending to be straight or concealing signs of their homosexuality. They instead behave as naturally as they can without revealing their sexual orientation.

Covering constitutes the second most widely used tactic for evading discrimination. In covering, homosexuals convince work associates that they are "normal" by dressing and acting like conventionally masculine men. This strategy enables discredited men to show employers and coworkers that they are not like stereotypical homosexuals, which hopefully thwarts victimization. It also allows discreditable men to deflect any suspicions about their sexual orientation:

> My image at work is decidedly conservative. I always wear dark Brooks Brothers suits, with cuffed pants, button-down shirts, and tortoise shell glasses. I always talk about sports. My act is so straight that no one would think that I am gay (Interview with author).

Passing and covering entail significant psychological and occupational costs. Both techniques involve careful, even torturous, monitoring of behavior and talk, which generates tremendous feelings of strain and inauthenticity. Anxiety over the possibility of exposing one's homosexuality and then being discriminated against further heightens the anguish (Weinberg and Williams, 1974:226–228). In addition, these techniques require social distance from employers and coworkers, which impedes advancement because promotion often depends on socializing or being friendly with work associates.

Discredited men also avoid victimization through minstrelization. In this strategy, gay men either seek jobs or form businesses (typically small retail establishments) in culturally approved fields dubbed sissy work (Whitam and Marthy, 1986:84–86). These occupations embody traditionally feminine behaviors and are considered suitable for homosexuals (Table 1):

> Women usually expect a hairdresser to be homosexual. They aren't threatened by it (Bell and Weinberg, 1978:145).

> There are a number of gays in interior decorating, and it makes things easier in terms of the rest of society. They kind of expect it (Bell and Weinberg, 1978:145).

Furthermore, being gay is generally an asset in these fields because homosexuals actively hire and advance one another (Harry and De Vall, 1978:156):

TABLE 1   Sissy Work

FEMININE FIELD	OCCUPATIONS
Nurturient Jobs	
Helping professions	Nurse, librarian, secretary
Domestic work	Cook, counterman, airline steward, bellhop, bartender, waiter, orderly
Decorative Jobs	
Home-related	Interior decorator, florist
Grooming	Fashion designer, hairdresser, model
Commercial arts	Graphic designer, window display
Expressive Jobs	
Arts	Dancer, musician, artist
Entertainment	Actor, singer

Note. The listed occupations are illustrative, not exhaustive.

Most people in display are queer. It's been easier at times to get ahead because I am homosexual (Bell and Weinberg, 1978:145).

Indirect Job Discrimination

Minstrelization constitutes a form of indirect job discrimination and negatively affects the occupational position of gay men. To shield themselves from possible discrimination, some homosexuals avoid jobs in which they anticipate victimization, and instead choose fields in which they are tolerated:

My whole goals are affected. I have to choose a job where I won't be discriminated against (Bell and Weinberg, 1978:144).

They accordingly shun higher-status, better-paying lines of men's work for lower-status, poorly-paying forms of sissy work:

Homosexuality forced me out of the service and caused me to become a hairdresser because here only I could be myself (Saghir and Robins, 1973:174).

Moreover, these jobs tend to be below their educational qualifications (Harry and De Vall, 1978:157–160):

There are plenty of gay Ph.D's waiting tables in San Francisco (Interview with author).

The unusual occupational distribution of gay men flows from indirect discrimination (Levine, 1979). Researchers consistently report high levels of educational attainment among gay men (Harry and De Vall, 1978:155). For example, more than two thirds of Harry and De Vall's (1978:155) homosexual respondents—and about three quarters of Bell and Weinberg's (1978:277) had at least some college education. Yet gay men are often unable to convert their educational qualifications into high income and status jobs. Indirect discrimination forces them to cluster in marginal white collar or service jobs (Harry and De Vall, 1978:156–157).

Extent of Discrimination

No one knows exactly how often gay men are victimized in the workplace. Our inability to do representative sampling in the homosexual community prevents us from obtaining precise measures of this problem (Levine, 1979). Representative sampling requires knowing the size and location of the population under investigation. These parameters are unknown for the gay community. (No exhaustive listings of the homosexual population are presently available.)

There are, however, some empirical studies of homosexual behavior that provide limited data on the magnitude of this problem. (These studies are listed in Table 2.) All of these studies used questionnaires to investigate the social and psychological adjustment of gay men. The questionnaires, moreover, included a few items about employment discrimination. For example, four of the 145 questionnaire items in Weinberg and William's (1974) research—and three out of the 528 items in Bell and Weinberg's (1978) study pertain to job discrimination.

The picture that emerges from these data shows that gay men anticipate and encounter significant victimization in the workplace. More

TABLE 2   Extent of Perceived Adverse Career Consequences of Homosexuality among Gay Men

STUDIES	GAY MEN PERCEIVING ADVERSE CAREER CONSEQUENCES (%)
Williams and Weinberg (N = 63)	29
Saghir and Robins (N = 89)	32
Weinberg and Williams (N = 1057)	30
Bell and Weinberg (N = 665)	25
All four studies (N = 1874)	30

than three quarters of the homosexuals interviewed in Weinberg and William's (1974:106) research feared that there would be problems at work if it became known that they were gay. The men worried primarily about punitive reactions from work associates. Almost half felt that their employers would be intolerant or rejecting; about two fifths expected co-workers to behave similarly.

The studies that uncovered actual instances of discrimination demonstrated that such fears are not groundless. In Williams and Weinberg's (1971:98) work, 16 percent of the respondents lost or were refused jobs because of their homosexuality. Similar figures appear in other studies. Saghir and Saghir (1973:174) discovered that 16 percent of their sample was fired or asked to resign after detection of their sexual orientation. In a later study, Weinberg and Williams (1974:109) found that 16 percent of their respondents lost a job after their homosexuality became known. Finally, Bell and Weinberg (1978:362) reported somewhat lower figures—7 percent of their sample lost or almost lost a job due to erotic preference, and 6 percent were denied better work assignments.

The studies also showed that a considerable percentage of homosexuals believed that their sexual orientation has adversely affected their careers by making them vulnerable to discrimination. Nearly one third of Weinberg and Williams' (1974:108) sample felt that their homosexuality caused them problems on the job. This proportion holds in two other studies. Approximately one third of Saghir and Robin's (1973:172) sample believed that their sexual preference limited their choice of work or their career advancement. In addition, almost a third of William's and Weinbergs' (1971:98) respondents felt that their sexual orientation negatively influenced their economic lives. Likewise, one quarter of Bell and Weinberg's (1978:361) sample believed that their homosexuality adversely affected their careers.

Two of the studies collected data on coping strategies among homosexual workers. Most gay men passed for heterosexual on the job. Nearly three quarters of Weinberg and Williams' (1974:106) respondents—and more than half of Bell and Weinberg's (1978:96) concealed their sexual orientation from employers. Passing appears to be less common with co-workers. Only two fifths of Weinberg and Williams' (1974:106) sample—and one third of Bell and Weinberg's (1978:296) hid their homosexuality from all of their coworkers.

When taken together, these studies afforded a somewhat muddled picture of the scope of employment discrimination. We can, however, obtain a clearer image through a secondary analysis of the data presented in all four studies. We can reanalyze this data to compute approximate measures of victimization because all of the studies posed similar questions about job discrimination and looked at similar samples. (All of the researchers used large but nonrepresentative samples recruited from gay organizations and gathering places, and all of the samples came from urban areas.)

In determining the overall extent of the victimization, we defined perceived adverse consequences on the belief that homosexuality negatively affected careers, and actual discrimination, as firing, nonhiring, or nonpromotion. We calculated the percentages of gay men who perceived adverse consequences or experienced discrimination by dividing the number of respondents in all of the studies which asked questions about these factors by the number who answered these questions affirmatively (Tables 2 and 3).

Nearly one third of the homosexuals surveyed felt that their sexual preference had negatively affected their careers, and almost one sixth of the men had actually experienced job discrimination. The only comparable estimates for lesbians are quite similar, with 31 percent of the lesbians surveyed anticipating victimization in the workplace and 13 percent actually encountering discrimination (Levine and Leonard, 1984).

Although certainly imposing, these figures offer only an imprecise measure of the extent to which gay men are victimized in employment,

TABLE 3   Extent of Actual Employment
Discrimination among Gay Men

STUDIES	GAY MEN EXPERIENCING DISCRIMINATION (%)
Williams and Weinberg (N = 63)	16
Saghir and Robins (N = 89)	16
Weinberg and Williams (N = 1057)	16
Bell and Weinberg (N = 665)	7
All four studies (N = 1874)	13

and most likely represent a low estimate. There are three reasons for making this claim. First, all the data come from self-report studies in which gay men are queried about their experiences with job discrimination. Yet homosexuals are often unaware of being discriminated against on the job (Harry and De Vall, 1978:161). Employers may be too frightened of adverse public reaction or may be too embarrassed to acknowledge that sexual orientation is the reason for not hiring, promoting, or retaining a gay man. They therefore conceal the real motive for taking discriminatory actions by stating that, for example, the position has already been filled or that the homosexual employee was incompetent or unqualified. Second, the gay men participating in these studies lived in cities where, according to various polls, residents are far more accepting of homosexuality than nonurban dwellers (Schneider and Lewis, 1984; Gallup, 1987). In fact, all of these studies included men who lived in San Francisco or New York, cities well known for their acceptance of homosexuality.

CONCLUSION

Whatever the precise statistic may be, homosexuals are clearly victimized in the workplace. Homophobic stereotypes cause employers and co-workers to routinely discriminate against gay men in traditionally masculine lines of work. To cope with this victimization, homosexuals use psychologically taxing or professionally damaging tactics. Moreover, fear of discrimination drives many gay men away from men's work and into sissy jobs, which functions to reinforce prevailing images of gay men as effeminate.

Not only does this discrimination waste promising talents, it also seriously reduces life chances of homosexuals. Many talented and qualified gay men are working at positions far beneath their capabilities because of job discrimination, which robs our society of their potential contributions. In addition, discrimination erodes the ability of homosexuals to earn a living which adversely affects their life-style and self-esteem.

Anti-discrimination laws and policies are needed to curtail the victimization of gay men. A handful of localities have passed laws—and a number of companies have formulated personal policies barring employment discrimination on the basis of sexual orientation. It is time that these laws and policies become commonplace.

NOTES

1. I am indebted to Michael S. Kimmel for the concept of homosexuals as failed men.
2. Many Americans believe that homosexuals lack the genetic, hormonal, or familial makeup of real men, which is why they become gay. Familial explanations are perhaps the most popular of these perceptions. It is commonly believed that gay men grow up in households in which parents fail to follow traditional roles. Their mothers are overbearing and dominating; and their fathers, weak and passive, which causes homosexuals to hate women, love men and turn gay. Bell, et al. (1981) found no relationship between this kind of upbringing and adult homosexuality. Approximately equal number of homosexuals and heterosexuals grew up in such family settings.

3. Research indicates that most gay men are appropriately masculine in demeanor and appearance. Saghir and Robins (1973:106–8) evaluated the effeminacy of their homosexuals respondents, and found that only one sixth of their sample manifested womanly attributes.

4. The extent to which gay men display these interests is presently unknown. As best we can tell, such interests are not typical of all gay men. Saghir and Robins (1973:175) found that about two thirds of their respondents were interested in individual sports (e.g., swimming, tennis). About half were interested in the arts; a quarter in constructional hobbies like carpentry, and one tenth, in domestic pursuits (e.g., cooking, sewing).

5. Mental health professionals no longer classify homosexuality as an emotional disorder. In 1973, the American Psychiatric Association removed homosexuality from its official listing of mental illnesses. Heterosexuals are also vulnerable to AIDS; men and women can get AIDS from unprotected (without a condom) vaginal or anal intercourse.

6. Research demonstrates that homosexuals are not hypersexual pedophiles. Bell and Weinberg (1978) found that their homosexual sample was not overly interested in sex. DeFrancis (1976) reports that most instances of child molestation involve heterosexual men and young girls.

7. The evidence suggests that considerable numbers of gay men are involuntarily discredited. Forty one percent of the homosexuals questioned by Weinberg and Williams (1974:108) stated that they had been officially labeled as gay. The police and the military appear to be the most frequent labelers. Twenty-five percent of the men reported being arrested for reasons related to their homosexuality. Saghir and Robins (1973:161) found, in a different study, that 20 percent of their sample bad received a draft deferment or less than honorable discharge from the military for being gay.

8. The legal problems of homosexuals flow from the criminalization of the same-sex contact. Sexual relations between two men is considered a crime in nearly half the states. Moreover, many states criminalize solicitation or loitering for purposes of same-sex contact. These laws make gay men vulnerable to arrest (Boggan, et al., 1983).

9. Co-workers routinely share or overhear information about each other's lives. For example, they may regularly discuss their families, relationships, and pastimes with one another during coffee breaks or lunch hours. Such disclosures may cause them to suspect that an associate is homosexual.

REFERENCES

Adam, Barry D. 1981. "Stigma and Employability: Discrimination by Sex and Sexual Orientation in the Ontario Legal Profession." *Canadian Review of Sociology and Anthropology* 18(2): 216–221.

Bell, Alan P., and Martin S. Weinberg. 1978. *Homosexualities: A Study of Diversity Among Men and Women*. New York: Simon & Schuster.

———, Martin S. Weinberg, and Sue Kiefer Hammersmith. 1981. *Sexual Preference: Its Development in Men and Women*. Bloomington, IN: Indiana University Press.

Benodraitis, Nijole V., and Joe R. Feagin. 1986. *Modern Sexism: Blatant, Subtle, and Covert Discrimination*. Englewood Cliffs, N.J.: Prentice-Hall.

Boggun, E. Carrington, Marilyn G. Haft, Charles Lister, John P. Rupp, and Thomas Stoddard. 1983. *The Rights of Gay People: Revised Edition*. New York: Bantam Books.

Brown, Howard. 1976. *Familiar Faces, Hidden Lives*. New York: Harvest/HBJ.

Chafetz, Janet Saltzman. 1974. *Masculine/Feminine or Human? An Overview of the Sociology of Sex Roles*. Itasca, IL: F. E. Peacock.

Davidson, Laurie, and Laura Kramer Gordon. 1979. *The Sociology of Gender*. Chicago: Rand McNally

DeFrancis, Vincent. 1976. *Protecting the Child Victim of Sex Offenders*. Denver: The American Humane Association Children's Division.

Doyle, James A. 1983. *The Male Experience*. Dubuque, Iowa: Wm. C. Brown.

Ehrenreich, Barbara. 1983. *The Hearts of Men: American Dreams and the Flight From Commitment*. Garden City, N.Y.: Anchor.

Gallup, 1982. "Homosexuality." *The Gallup Report* 205 (October): 3–19.

———. 1987. "Homosexuality." *The Gallup Report* 258 (March): 12–18.

Goffman, Erving. 1963. *Stigma: Notes on the Management of Spoiled Identity*.

Gould, Robert. 1976. "Measuring Masculinity by the Size of a Paycheck." In *The Forty-Nine Percent Majority: The Male Sex Role*, edited by Deborah S. David and Robert Branan, 113–117. Reading, MA: Addison-Wesley.

Hamilton, Joan O. C., Julie Flynn, Patrick Houston, and Reginald Rhein, Jr. "The AIDS Epidemic and Business." *Business Week* March 23, 1987: 122–126.

Harry, Joseph. 1982. *Gay Children Grown Up: Gender Culture and Gender Deviance*. New York: Praeger.

——— and William B. De Vall. 1978. *The Social Organization of Gay Males*. New York: Praeger.

Huber, Joan, Chair. 1982. "Report of the American Sociological Association's Task Group on Homosexuality." *American Sociologist* 17(3): 164–88.

Humphreys, Laud. 1972. *Out of the Closets: The Sociology of Homosexual Liberation*. Englewood Cliffs, N.J.: Prentice-Hall.

Institute of Medicine. 1988. *Confronting AIDS: Update 1988*. Washington, D.C.: National Academy Press.

Jay, Karla, and Allen Young. 1979. *The Gay Report*. New York: Summit Books.

Jennings, Chris. 1988. *Understanding and Preventing AIDS: A Book for Everyone, Second Edition*. Cambridge, MA: Health Alert Press.

Julian, Joseph, and William Kornblum. 1983. *Social Problems: Fourth Edition*. Englewood Cliffs, N.J.: Prentice-Hall.

Le Masters, E. E. 1975. *Blue-Collar Aristocrats: Life Styles of a Working-Class Tavern*. Madison, WI: University of Wisconsin Press.

Leonard, Arthur S. 1985. "Employment Discrimination Against Persons with AIDS." *University of Dayton Law Review* 10(681): 689–96.

Levine, Martin P. 1979. "Employment Discrimination Against Gay Men." *International Review of Modern Sociology* 9(5–7): 151–63.

——— and Robin Leonard. 1984. "Discrimination Against Lesbians in the Work Force." *Signs* 9(4): 700–710.

Levitt, Eugene E., and Albert D. Klasser, Jr. 1974. "Public Attitudes Toward Homosexuality: Part of the 1970 National Survey of the Institute for Sex Research." *Journal of Homosexuality* 1(1): 131–134.

Maddocks, Lewis I 1969. "The Law and the Church vs. the Homosexual." In *The Same Sex: An Appraisal of Homosexuality*, edited by Ralph W. Weltge, 95–112. Philadelphia: United Church Press.

National Gay Task Force. 1981. "You and Your Job— A Gay Employee's Guide to Discrimination." New York: National Gay Task Force.

Pleck, Joseph R. 1981. *The Myth of Masculinity*. Cambridge, MA: MIT Press.

Saghir, Marcel T., and Eli Robins. 1973. *Male and Female Homosexuality*. Baltimore: Williams & Wilkins.

ARTICLE 24

HITTING BOTTOM
HOMELESSNESS, POVERTY,
AND MASCULINITY

TIMOTHY NONN

In the dangerous and impoverished Tenderloin district of San Francisco live the men we consider failures. Urban deterioration and public neglect has created a "dumping-ground for unwanted individuals" (North of Market Planning Coalition 1992: 4). Low rents attract immigrants, welfare recipients, and low-income workers. The population is about 40 percent white, one-third Asian American, and one-tenth black and Latino, respectively. There are severe problems with homelessness, AIDS, violence, substance abuse, and unemployment.

In studies of men, poor men are rarely the object of research.[1] This article examines the coping mechanisms poor men develop to resolve their status as "failed men": First, to overcome stigmatization and regain self-worth, Tenderloin men develop "counter-masculinities" within distinct groups; second, some men develop new values in response to a multiplicity of masculinities that allow them to transcend separate groups and identify with the Tenderloin community.

Using a snowball sample, twenty men were interviewed during a six-month period, including twelve whites, six blacks, and two Latinos; twelve were heterosexual, and eight were homosexual. Their ages ranged from twenty-nine to fifty-four; the majority had a high-school education. Many had been homeless, but most were now living in single-room occupancy hotels. Twelve were single, seven were divorced or separated, and one was married. Several have left children behind. Their interactions with women at the time of the interview were very limited. Few had contact with families or had long-term relationships with women.

Each interview lasted about two hours and included a questionnaire that examined attitudes about gender, race, and sexuality. In the study, I examined how Tenderloin men, as groups, interacted with other men.

FAILED MEN

A discussion of failure among men must begin with hegemonic masculinity. R. W. Connell writes:

> *Hegemonic masculinity is constructed in relation to women and to subordinated masculinities. These other masculinities need not be as clearly defined—indeed, achieving hegemony may consist precisely in preventing alternatives gaining cultural definition and recognition as alternatives, confining them to ghettos, to privacy, to unconsciousness. (Connell 1987: 186)*

Connell defines hegemonic masculinity as men's dominance over women. While individuals may change, men's collective power remains embedded in social and cultural institutions. Michael Messner interprets change among white, middle-class men as a matter of personal lifestyle rather than a restructuring of power and politics (Messner 1993).

Hegemonic masculinity is the standard by which Tenderloin men are judged. The media refers to them as "thugs and bums."[2] Forced to live amidst poverty, drugs, and violence, they are stripped of or denied access to a masculine identity constructed around the role of "the good provider" (see Bernard in this book). As white heterosexuals, they are stripped of an identity associated with privilege and power. As gays or men of color, they are denied access to a masculine ideal associated with heterosexual whites. George, a divorced black Vietnam veteran, says:

Now, we're talking about that segment of the male population that have been taught some of the same things that all men are taught. So they were straight-up abject failures.[3]

Tenderloin men sometimes refer to each other as "invisible." George describes a homeless man's life:

I call it the "invisible-man syndrome." That's what you become. Most homeless, but not all, self-medicate. It's that thing that you can turn to when you're suffering. You feel disenfranchised from society. You feel less than human. It tells him—in between those periods where he has some lucidity, in between drug or alcohol bouts—that he is a total failure.

Allan, a forty-six-year-old heterosexual white man, recounts the experience of trying to cash a small check:

[I went] into the bank to cash a two-dollar check and had to deal with people's feedback. I just want to be invisible. I'm real embarrassed about that. About my economic status. . . . When I was stripped of all those material things that I was taught were the measure of success, and everybody rejected me—even though as a person I hadn't changed—I saw the sort of shallowness. It was very painful and very hard.[4]

Tenderloin men face a lonely end. Before death—having been stripped of everything that qualifies a man for full participation in society—there is the shame of surviving as less than a man. Tenderloin men belong to a "shamed group" (Goffman 1963: 23). David, a heterosexual black homeless man, describes their daily struggle:

The thing that really hurts and holds people down is when they give completely up. When you give completely up that means you take your energy and give it to drugs or alcohol. . . . Some homeless men have lost their self-esteem. They have been down for so long. And the system has played this game of chess with them for so long. They've just said, "Oh, forget it." They say, "We'll sell drugs. So if I go to jail, I still have a home." So it don't make any difference. They feel rejected.[5]

Tenderloin men feel trapped in the role of failure.[6] Many hang out day and night on streets "drinking and drugging," talking and begging. The ubiquitous drug trade, routine violence, and crushing poverty combine to form an atmosphere of continual dread and hopelessness within the neighborhood. The men wait in line for hours at churches to receive food, clothing, and lodging. Because it is equally painful to be seen as to be invisible, they are silent and avoid eye contact. They spend a lot of time waiting. The wait transforms them. They dress in a similar ragged way. They walk and talk in a dispirited way. Their faces have the same blank stare or menacing hardness. Some turn into predators in search of victims.[7] Others turn into victims in search of sympathy. George says:

Your antenna is up for people feeling sorry for you. Part of you becomes a predator. The predator part wants to take advantage. So you can get resources to continue your downward spiral to total destruction. The other part of you feels ashamed because you have violated every man-code that you were ever taught. So you're stuck on stupid. You get to a point where you don't know what to do. You don't give a shit no more about how you're perceived. You can walk down the street smelling like a billy goat. Stuff hanging all over you. You haven't had access to basic hygiene in days and sometimes weeks. You don't care. And the looks don't bother you anymore because you ain't nobody. The productive citizens have that way of not looking at you anyway because you're the invisible man.

The invisibility of Tenderloin men is part of "a pervasive two-role social process" in which failure and success are interrelated (Goffman

1963: 138). They are stigmatized merely by living in an area decimated by poverty, sex and drug markets, and high levels of crime and violence. William Julius Wilson calls them "the permanent underclass" (Wilson 1987: 7). Samuel, a forty-year-old homosexual black man, describes their plight more poignantly: "You're always going to need a place where the lonely souls can go."[8]

Trapped at the bottom of society and stigmatized as failures, Tenderloin men have limited opportunities to claim an identity that fosters self-worth. Charles, a fifty-year-old white gay man, says: "Once you go in there, it's like being an untouchable. You're stigmatized as being this type of sleazy person that does dope and needles, and the whole thing."[9] After a man is stripped of or denied access to symbols of masculinity that confer power and privilege—job, car, home, and family—life becomes a series of challenges to his existence. Some escape the Tenderloin by getting clean, finding work, and moving out. Others descend further into self-destructive behavior and die. Those who remain must adapt to the Tenderloin.

COUNTER-MASCULINITIES

Counter-masculinities—developed in response to hegemonic masculinity—are coping mechanisms that provide Tenderloin men with a sense of self-worth.[10] A typology of counter-masculinities was found among three groups of Tenderloin men: heterosexual whites, heterosexual blacks and Latinos, and homosexual blacks and whites.

Heterosexual White Men: Urban Hermits

Heterosexual whites are the only men that do not identify with their own group. In the introduction to this book, Michael Kimmel writes that white men see themselves as "the generic person" because "the mechanisms that afford us privilege are very often invisible to us." To escape from the stigma of failure, the "urban hermit" structures identity around the value of self-sufficiency. Power is interpreted as individual achievement. Oscar, a fifty-year-old divorced heterosexual white man, describes a sense of failure:

It's a difficult struggle. But you can't blame anybody but yourself. Because it is you yourself. Like with me. It's me myself that has the illness. Not the people of the government. Not the people of the different businesses. And things like that. It's me.[11]

Although receiving disability benefits, Oscar views himself as self-sufficient and criticizes blacks on welfare for lacking motivation. Men of color similarly criticize whites. Ned, a forty-year-old single heterosexual black man, says:

I feel that most of them have given up. They don't really care or try. I try to respect all men. But it's difficult to understand why a white man would give up on himself given a society that is made for them.[12]

Virtually all heterosexual white men interpret their present hardship as the result of personal failure. Richard Sennett and Jonathan Cobb argue that the "code of respect" in American society demands that "a man should feel responsibility for his own social position—even if, in a class society, he believes men in general are deprived of the freedom to control their lives." Failure is defined according to cultural values in which a man is expected to have the desire and opportunity to work (Sennett and Cobb 1972: 36).

Urban hermits spend most of their time alone in hotel rooms. Many frequent bars and restaurants where they complain that criminals have "taken over" the area and demand that police "clean up the streets."[13] Unable to reconcile belief in white male superiority and life among the disenfranchised, most believe society is falling apart. Frank, a single heterosexual white man, describes whites:

Their spirits are broken. They're outcasts of their families from all over the country. They're in disarray. They're drifting. Some of them never came back from Vietnam. Some of them are screwed up on drugs. It seems to me that America isn't like it used to be. When I grew up it was changing . . . it was breaking apart. My family broke apart, anyway. It was hard on me. They're outcasts from all over the country, and they gravitate here.[14]

Heterosexual white men experience a high level of cultural shock in moving to the Tenderloin.[15] A walk to the store is a challenge to their self-esteem. They confront black and Latino men who threaten their sense of racial superiority and gays who threaten their sexual identity. Oscar believes gays challenge divine law. He says:

God decided he wanted a man to look like a man and a woman to look like a woman. It's not his fault if some men act like women and women act like men. It's the fault of the people themselves. The people can go without acting that way if they don't want to and they can act that way if they want to. It's up to them.[16]

Heterosexual whites are confused and angry because others appear to violate social norms. Most retreat into isolation. A few imitate other men's behavior. Brad, a twenty-nine-year-old single, heterosexual white man, admires the "sense of family" among Latinos.[17] Many appreciate the nurturing qualities of gays. But other men criticize whites for not knowing themselves. Miguel, a divorced fifty-year-old heterosexual Latino man, says:

The white man tries too hard to make friends. . . . If you're going to come in here and start trying to be black, they see that already. You're not! But here's a guy and he's trying to talk like us and be cool. It's a front. We know that. Hey, come on. I mean I've studied white folks before, and I know that's not the way white people are supposed to be.[18]

Wanting to belong, and forced to confront their prejudices, heterosexual whites discover that genuineness is vital. But it is difficult for them to adapt. Quinn, a fifty-four-year-old gay white man, says whites are aloof because: "White is right. White isn't going to be criticized. White isn't going to be stopped by police.[19]

The counter-masculinity of the urban hermit discloses an inability to cope with diversity of race, culture, and sexual orientation. As a coping mechanism, it resists the stigma of failure but undermines identity by organizing social relations around poles of independence and dependence. In the Tenderloin, interdependence is both a reality and a necessity. What heterosexual whites view as self-sufficiency, others view as arrogance. Because the urban hermit is seen as an outcast among outcasts, failure and alienation are not overcome through self-sufficiency.

Heterosexual Black and Latino Men: Cool Pose

Heterosexual blacks and Latinos dominate street life and display what Majors and Billson (1992) call "cool pose." Cool pose is a counter-masculinity that structures identity around the value of respect. Power is interpreted as group solidarity in a racist society. Blacks and Latinos establish social position by displaying aggressiveness or showing deference (Almaguer 1991: 80). Miguel claims the system of respect maintains harmony: "You don't have to trust someone. You just respect them." George uses a hypermasculine facade to obtain respect and to fend off predators. He says:

One of the techniques you use—and this is a prison technique—is getting big. You work out hard. You carry yourself in an intimidating manner. Your body language says, "I'll kill you if you even think about approaching my space."

The mask of hypermasculinity establishes a man's position in his group.[20] Miguel describes putting on his mask:

Whenever I walk, I look mean. I make my face look like I got an attitude. Like I just got ripped off. I don't look at the person. I look through them. I'm cutting him. And this guy's thinking, "Hmmm. Let me move out of the way." You could get busted. "Oh, you ain't that tough." But out there you gotta act that way.

"Getting busted" means that someone is able to see through a man's mask. Whites have difficulty distinguishing between actual threats and posturing by blacks and Latinos, and often feel threatened. But Jack, a heterosexual black man, explains that cool pose conceals a sense of failure among men of color living in a white-dominated society:

> The one thing I hear from white guys is, "You guys act like you're so proud." They don't realize why we're doing it. It's to survive amongst our own peers. We feel just as bad as he does. The white guy resents that; "How in the hell can he act like that and I'm white? I come from the superior race and I can't act like that. I feel dead." They come from two different worlds.[21]

Ned interprets cool pose in relation to a definition of masculinity that excludes black men in American society:

> A black man has to be tough out there on the street. The reason they have to be that way is that they don't have any other outlet for their manhood. They can't show their manhood by being a success economically because society simply will not give them a chance. I mean a black man is even lucky to have a full-time—or even a part-time—job. So he has to show his manhood by acting physically tough. Because mentally tough won't get him anywhere. But there has been no reason that white men have had to be physically tough because they've been able to show their manhood through their nine-to-five. Going to work every day. And making a living.

Cool pose is depicted as "a creative strategy devised by African-American males to counter the negative forces in their lives" (Majors and Billson 1992: 105). Yet, the counter-masculinity of cool pose does not allow heterosexual black and Latino men to escape from failure by structuring identity around the value of respect. While the coping mechanism of cool pose weakens the stigma of failure, it undermines identity by organizing social relations around poles of dominance and submission. What heterosexual men of color view as respect, others view as hostility. By adopting an identity based upon fear and violence, men

of color in the Tenderloin in part contribute to their own alienation from other groups and society at large. They are further marginalized in an environment where different social groups demand to live in equality with one another.

Homosexual Black and White Men: Perfect Copy

Gays in the Tenderloin blur gender and sexual boundaries by constructing identity around performance of a series of roles. "Perfect copy" of hypermasculinity redefines and subverts masculinity (Butler 1990: 31). Klaus, a thirty-four-year-old gay white man, interprets his experience with heterosexual men in the Tenderloin:

> They feel like their manhood or sexuality has been threatened because I'm more butch than they are. I am more of a man than a straight man can be around here. They're threatened. Not only to me but to themselves.[22]

Gays structure identity around the value of acceptance. Power is interpreted as inclusion of persons who challenge gender and sexual categories. Because identity is in flux, and gender and sexual identity are rendered uncertain, "homosexuality undermines masculinity" (Edwards 1990: 114). Larry, a thirty-three-year-old gay white man, says heterosexuals are simultaneously confused and intrigued by gays:

> I think [they] are very jealous of gay men because we're so open and free with our feelings. We speak what we have to say. We don't hide our feelings. We cry at sad movies. Heterosexual men think that men don't cry. But if you go drinking with them, get them drunk or high, they're the first ones that throw their legs in the air or whip out their cocks in front of you and say, "Here. Suck this."[23]

Another gay man believes single heterosexuals are in a predicament because they normally rely on women to provide them with gender identity. Charles says:

> Most men depend on women to define that role for them. So a man is what a woman defines him to

be. So if you don't have a woman in your life to define you as a man, then you have to depend on all these macho apparatuses. Then you have to prove to other men that you are a man.

Transgenders pose a new challenge by further blurring gender and sexual boundaries. Thomas, a twenty-nine-year-old gay black man, says some men respond favorably:

It seems to be a turn-on. Especially if everything is in order—the appearance is almost perfect. Woman have a lot to do just getting dressed in the morning. Hair, makeup, clothing, shoes. Everything has to be just right. It's not like men. We can just put on a pair of jeans and a T-shirt. And out the door. I've noticed this especially with straight men. They seem to be really impressed.[24]

Identity is a series of roles that gays perfect in daily encounters. Transgenders further complicate identity when "some transgendered persons consider themselves heterosexual, while others consider themselves homosexual" (Koenig 1993: 10). The counter-masculinity of perfect copy challenges hegemonic masculinity through a multitude of replicated masculinities that blur sexual and gender boundaries. Performance of a series of roles creates security in a homophobic society by destabilizing and redefining social relations. But perfect copy of hypermasculine (or hyperfeminine) roles implies a reliance upon hegemonic masculine ideals. While the coping mechanism of perfect copy resists the stigma of failure, it undermines identity by organizing social relations around poles of performance and observation. Perfect copy contributes to further alienation of gays, because what they view as acceptance, others view as licentiousness.

Counter-masculinities are coping mechanisms that aid Tenderloin men in regaining a sense of self-worth while preventing them from overcoming alienation from other groups of men. For Tenderloin men, masculine identity develops around specific value systems in response to the social system of hegemonic masculinity and an immediately hostile environment (Tong 1971: 8). Paradoxically, counter-masculinities offer resistance to hegemonic masculinity while deepening social divisions. Since the contradictions of counter-masculinities stem from inequitable relations of power, what unites men as a group separates them as a community. The urban hermit devalues interdependence in favor of self-sufficiency; cool pose devalues equality in favor of dominance; and perfect copy devalues mutuality in favor of performance. A new value system constructed around shared power is required to unite Tenderloin men into a community.

VERSATILE MASCULINITY

Versatile masculinity is a unique masculine identity that emerges from everyday encounters of Tenderloin men as they collectively resolve the contradictions of counter-masculinities. Versatile masculinity allows men to identify with a transcendent set of values without destroying their group identity or value systems. This new set of values—while not distinctively masculine—is the basis of a masculine identity that binds Tenderloin men together in genuine community.

Versatile masculinity is not a fixed identity but a growing capacity for relating to difference.[25] As a fluid construction that sorts and combines practices, values, and attitudes in a strategic movement, it enables men to flourish in a diverse and dynamic environment. *Most important, it is not a way of being but a way of becoming in relationships.* David calls it being "flexible":

So many people [were] raised a certain way, and it stays with them. That's the only way they know. Instead of looking over the whole situation and see this and that. That's the way you have to live. Especially if you're living homeless on the streets. You have to be able to be flexible. Maybe this guy does things a different way. Maybe I can help him do this and he can help me do that. That's where you have to come in and learn it. That's what certain people call "streetwise." Streetwise people are just movable. They're just flexible.

Versatile masculinity does not undermine the different values of Tenderloin men but relates them to a transcendent set of values: honesty, caring, interdependence, and respect. H. Richard Niebuhr writes that ultimate value is not identifiable with a particular mode of being but "is present whenever being confronts being, wherever there is becoming in the midst of plural, interdependent, and interacting existences. It is not a function of being as such but of being in relation to being" (Niebuhr 1970: 106–7).

Similarly, versatile masculinity creates unity from diversity. Jack believes that acceptance of difference is essential to survival:

All people are equal. All things are relative. If you exterminate Jews, you exterminate me and you. . . . They're all of our cultures, are relative to keep us together. If I'm not afraid to learn about your culture then I got something to learn. Something that is relative. If everybody was alike, we'd be in trouble. We'd be in real trouble.

As marginalized persons, Tenderloin men are innovative survivors who manifest "creative strategies for survival that then open up new possibilities for everyone" (Duberman 1993: 24). But their experience reveals that only after a man has reached bottom—after he is stripped of or denied access to a masculine identity that provides him with a sense of innate superiority—will he change. Quinn says:

You bottom out. And you go through the bottom of the barrel and you come up again. You learn a different type of survival skills. . . . But going from the bottom and coming through you run into criminals, junkies, crazies, and everything else. . . . It doesn't make you less of a person. Actually, it can make you a stronger person. And more sensitive.

Versatile masculinity includes three conditions: (1) A man must be stripped of or denied access to a hegemonic masculine identity; (2) a man must adopt a counter-masculinity to reconstruct his identity and resist hegemonic masculine values that stigmatize him as a failure; and (3) a man must experience a multiplicity of masculinities that compel him to develop an identity based on acceptance of difference. When these conditions exist, versatile masculinity drives men to overcome their differences and create a community based on the following values.

Honesty

For Tenderloin men, honesty means genuineness. It is a process of "coming to critical consciousness" (Hooks 1990: 191). Tenderloin men sometimes discard illusions that contribute to lack of self-esteem. Hank, a thirty-six-year-old divorced, heterosexual white man, says:

I realized that the only way I was going to get clean and sober, and really become a disciple of Christ, was to clean up my act. To become truly honest. Beginning with admitting to myself that I was full of shit. That I was living a lie. Just a lie.[26]

Brad says:

I feel like if you're genuine with people there's some recognition within them. Or they see something. I know it's happened to me when I just met somebody who is for real and I've been acting like a fool or not being true to myself. It kind of makes me go, "Oh!" and "Yeah!"

In the Tenderloin, because men use every imaginable act to hide from themselves and society, they can easily recognize genuineness. Quinn says: "An honest person is going to recognize another honest person and see a phony."

Caring

Many Tenderloin men have HIV/AIDS. Samuel, who is beginning to display symptoms, has given himself a final task before he dies. He says:

I'm having a big struggle with a transvestite named Carol who rips me off every second she has a chance to. I keep going back to her. And I tell her, "You got me, girl. But you didn't really have to do that. If you wanted it, just ask me for it. I'll give it to you. And if not, then you can rip me off." She's turned out to be one of my best friends. It's all she's ever known in her life. She's always lived in the ghetto. This is my personal struggle. My personal fight is to just take that one person and make her realize that she doesn't have to keep two steps ahead of me in order to get what's mine. Because it's all materialistic. If what I have you need, you can have. All you have to do is just ask for it.

Poverty, ostracism, and illness have brought men together to provide and receive care from one another. Allan describes his life at one of the worst slum hotels in the Tenderloin:

At the Victoria, people will come in who are very different from one another, and sit down and talk and joke with one another. I don't think you could say that those interactions are insincere, or [occur] simply because they're close together. They like each other. They've discovered that we're all human beings with the same needs and very interesting differences. It's an acknowledgment that they're worthwhile. The kinds of sharing of people who don't have a lot to give is striking.

The work of caring is rare among men in our society, because compassion is a value identified with women. For Tenderloin men, caring for one another is tremendously empowering.

Interdependence

Men forced to live at the bottom of society feel insignificant and powerless. A common phrase heard on the streets is "the small people." Masculinity is redefined as an identity based on interdependence. Thomas says:

Here you kind of like take care of your own. You kind of have to take care of each other here just so everybody survives. If one person doesn't survive, there's a big effect on everybody.

Respect

The most important lesson that Tenderloin men learn is respect for the intrinsic worth of each person. Masculinity includes an identification with humanity rather than only with one's group. This process (especially for heterosexual whiter) begins with a period of cultural shock. Eduardo, a thirty-three-year-old single, heterosexual Latino man, says new residents overcome fear when they "start standing in the soup lines and staying in hotels. You realize that the homeless

are not unlike you or I. They're human. You become part of the community."[27] Larry—who once worked as a male prostitute in the Tenderloin—believes faith overcomes barriers between people. He says:

Mary Magdalene was a prostitute. There are many women and men in this city that are prostitutes. There's nothing wrong with that. They're human beings first. Their titles come afterward. We weren't born what we are today. We were born human beings first. Then we were educated and trained to become who we are. But before we are what we are, we're humans first. A lot of people have lost that track. Lost that faith. To see what the hell we were or where we came from.

George says we all are faced with a choice:

Basically, they are human beings. The one thing that we have been given is the ability to make choices. That's what separates us from other animals. Outside forces may have an effect, and usually do have an effect, on the choices we have to make. But the fact is, we get to make those choices. So make those choices as a winner—not so much as a winner—but as a human being.

SUMMARY

Tenderloin men construct new masculine identities to resist a sense of failure and to create a sense of belonging. Versatile masculinity develops from their need to safely coexist in a hostile environment, but it also provides a basis for shared power and love in relationships. The Tenderloin men who transform themselves from "failed men" into human beings display a capacity not merely to survive, but also to flourish in a context of adversity and diversity. This is aptly demonstrated by the tenants of a Tenderloin residential hotel—many of whom were once homeless and substance abusers—who have built a beautiful rooftop garden. A resident says it's "a little bit of magic in the Tenderloin." Another is happy to see "a new spirit in this neighborhood" (Maitland 1993). In the Tenderloin, a small space has gradually emerged where men are free to change.

NOTES

1. There are several noteworthy works that examine the lives of poor and working-class men. See Eugene V. Debs, *Walls and Bars* (Chicago: Charles H. Kerr and Company, 1973); George Orwell, *Down and Out in Paris and London* (New York: Berkeley Medallion, 1959); James Agee and Walker Evans, *Let Us Now Praise Famous Men* (Boston: Houghton Mifflin Company, 1939); Studs Terkel, *Hard Times: An Oral History of the Great Depression* (New York: Washington Square Press, 1970); Elliot Liebow, *Tally's Corner* (Boston: Little, Brown and Company, 1967); William Julius Wilson, *The Truly Disadvantaged: The Inner City, the Underclass, and Public Policy* (Chicago: University of Chicago Press, 1987): Lillian Rubin, *Worlds of Pain: Life in the Working-Class Family* (New York: Basic Books, 1976); Richard Sennet and Jonathan Cobb, *The Hidden Injuries of Class* (New York: Vintage Books, 1972).

2. Local newspapers regularly describe Tenderloin residents in derogatory terms. See "Cheap wine ban sought in Tenderloin," *San Francisco Chronicle*, 5 April 1989; "Group wants Tenderloin as family neighborhood," *San Francisco Chronicle*, 21 July 1992; "Community policing," *San Francisco Chronicle*, 20 November 1992.

3. Interview with George on 30 April 1993. All names are fictitious.

4. Interview with Allan on 22 June 1993.

5. Interview with David on 1 May 1993.

6. Interview with Peter, a recently married, forty-eight-year-old heterosexual while man, on 27 July 1993.

7. The term "predator" is commonly used to refer to persons (often drug users) who prey on the more vulnerable sectors of the Tenderloin neighborhood, such as the elderly, children, and tourists.

8. Interview with Samuel on 26 August 1993.

9. Interview with Charles on 28 July 1993.

10. Thomas J. Gershick and Adam S. Miller (1993: 5) similarly interpret masculinities of disabled men as coping mechanisms that rely upon, reformulate, or reject the standard of hegemonic masculinity.

11. Interview with Oscar on 19 June 1993.

12. Interview with Ned on 26 July 1993.

13. Interviews with Oscar on 24 April and 19 June 1993.

14. Interview with Frank on 13 August 1993.

15. Bruno Bettelheim (1960: 120) reports that of Jews sent to Nazi concentration camps, middle-class German men experienced the greatest level of initial shock and were the least adaptable prisoners.

16. Interview with Oscar on 19 June 1993.

17. Interview with Brad on 28 July 1993.

18. Interview with Miguel on 23 July 1993.

19. Interview with Quinn on 29 July 1993.

20. Pleck (1987: 31) defines "hypermasculinity" as exaggerated, extreme masculine behavior.

21. Interview with Jack on 23 April 1993.

22. Interview with Klaus on 13 March 1993.

23. Interview with Larry on 16 July 1993.

24. Interview with Thomas on 28 August 1993.

25. Versatility is defined as "the faculty or character of turning or being able to turn readily to a new subject or occupation," or "many-sidedness." In *The Compact Edition of the Oxford English Dictionary* 1971, Oxford University Press.

26. Interview with Hank on 31 July 1993.

27. Interview with Eduardo on 14 May 1993.

REFERENCES

Almaguer, Tomas. 1991. "Chicano Men: A Cartography of Homosexual Identity and Behavior." *Differences* 3(2).

Bernard, Jessie. 1995. "The Good-Provider Role." In Michael S. Kimmel and Michael A. Messner, eds., *Men's Lives*. New York: Macmillan.

Bettelheim, Bruno. 1960. *The Informed Heart: Autonomy in a Mass Age*. New York: The Free Press.

Butler, Judith. 1990. *Gender Trouble: Feminism and the Subversion of Identity*. New York: Routledge & Kegan Paul.

Connell, R. W. 1987. *Gender and Power*. Stanford, CA: Stanford University Press.

Duberman, Martin. 1993. "A Matter of Difference." *Nation*, 5 July.

Edwards, Tim. 1990. "Beyond Sex and Gender: Masculinity, Homosexuality and Social Theory." In Jeff Hearn and David Morgan, eds., *Men, Masculinities, and Social Theory*. London: Unwin Hyman.

Gershick, Thomas J., and Adam S. Miller. 1994. "Coming to Terms: Masculinity and Physical Disability." In M. Kimmel and M. Messner, eds., *Men's Lives*, 3rd edition. Boston: Allyn & Bacon.

Goffman, Erving. 1963. *Stigma: Notes on the Management of Spoiled Identity*. New York: Touchstone.

hooks, bell. 1990. "Feminism: A Transformational Politic." In Deborah L. Rhode, ed., *Theoretical Perspectives on Sexual Difference*. New Haven: Yale University Press.

Koenig, Karen. 1993. "Transgenders Unite to Fight for Justice and Recognition." *Tenderloin Times*, August.

Maitland, Zane. 1993. "Tenderloin Hotel Has a Rooftop Garden." *San Francisco Chronicle*, 23 July.

Majors, Richard, and Janet Mancini Billson. 1992. *Cool Pose: The Dilemmas of Black Manhood in America*. New York: Lexington Books.

Messner, Michael A. 1993. " 'Changing Men' and Feminist Politics in the United States." *Theory and Society*, August/September.

Niebuhr, H. Richard. 1970. *Radical Monotheism and Western Culture*. New York: Harper Torchbooks.

North of Market Planning Coalition (NOPC). 1992. *Final Report: Tenderloin 2000 Survey and Plan*. San Francisco: NOPC.

Pleck, Joseph H. 1987. "The Theory of Male Sex-Role Identity: Its Rise and Fall, 1936 to the Present." In Harry Brod, ed., *The Making of Masculinities: The New Men's Studies*. New York: Routledge & Kegan Paul.

Sennett, Richard, and Jonathan Cobb. 1972. *The Hidden Injuries of Class*. New York: Vintage Books.

Tong, Ben. 1971. "The Ghetto of the Mind: Notes on the Historical Psychology of Chinese America." *Amerasia Journal*, 1(3). November.

Wilson, William Julius. 1987. *The Truly Disadvantaged: The Inner City, the Underclass, and Public Policy*. Chicago: University of Chicago Press.

PART FIVE

MEN AND HEALTH:
BODY AND MIND

Why did the gap between male and female life expectancy increase from two years in 1900 to nearly eight years today? Why do men suffer heart attacks and ulcers at such a consistently higher rate than women do? Why are auto insurance rates so much higher for young males than for females of the same age? Are mentally and emotionally "healthy" males those who conform more closely to traditional cultural prescriptions for masculinity, or is it the other way around?

The articles in this section, though focusing on different specific topics, tend to follow and develop the argument of the men's liberation movement of the mid-1970s: Men do enjoy privileges in patriarchal society, but they often pay a heavy price. Narrow, emotionally inexpressive cultural prescriptions for masculinity are not only "stressful," they are in fact "lethal" for men. Harrison, Chin, and Ficarrotto explore the specific causes of men's lower life expectancy—higher rates of heart disease, cancer, and death by accident or suicide. Three-quarters of the reasons for men's earlier deaths, they argue, have to do with "the male sex role": men rarely ask for help at early signs of physical or emotional troubles; men may deal with stresses by internalizing them and/or by turning to alcohol, tobacco, or other drugs; men take more unnecessary risks driving cars, in their work and in recreation; and men are more successful in their attempts at suicide than are women. Gloria Steinem's humorous meditation on menstruation and masculinity underscores the seriousness of the ways in which men ignore their own health and cast women's bodies as the "other." In the next article, Barry Glassner demonstrates how dominant conceptions of masculinity are encoded in and symbolized by the development of muscular male bodies.

Alongside these dominant cultural conceptions of masculinity, there have always been masculinities that have been marginalized and subordinated. Tom Gerschick and Adam Miller's insightful essay explores the meanings of manhood among those men who are physically challenged.

South Boston, 1982. Copyright © 1982 Sage Sohier.

WARNING: MASCULINITY MAY BE DANGEROUS TO YOUR HEALTH

JAMES HARRISON
JAMES CHIN
THOMAS FICARROTTO

In 1900, life expectancy in the United States was 48.3 years for women and 46.3 years for men. In 1984, it was 78.2 years for women and 71.2 years for men (U.S. Department of Health and Human Services, 1987). During this 84-year period life expectancy for both men and women increased by more than 24 years, whereas the difference increased from 2 years in 1900 to 7 years in 1984, consistently favoring women.

This difference grew consistently larger during the course of this century, reaching a peak difference between sexes of 7.8 years in 1975 and 1979. (Recent data suggest, however, that women's advantage is decreasing.)

The gains in life expectancy for both men and women can be attributed to better nutrition and improved health care. But how can the difference between men's and women's life expectancies and the consistent increase in the size of this difference during this century be explained?

Two general perspectives—a biogenetic and a psychosocial—can be distinguished. The former attributes men's greater mortality to genetic factors (Montagu, 1953). The latter attributes men's greater mortality in large part to lethal aspects of the male role (Jourard, 1971). This article will evaluate these two perspectives, and assess what can most reliably be said about the consequence of male role behavior for life expectancy.

In comparison to women, there is for men a higher perinatal and early childhood death rate, a higher rate of congenital birth defects, a greater vulnerability to recessive sex-linked disorders, a higher accident rate during childhood and all subsequent ages, a higher incidence of behavioral and learning disorders, a higher suicide rate, and a higher metabolism rate, which may result in greater energy expenditure and a consequent failure to conserve physical resources. In the biogenetic perspective, this broad range of reported physical, psychological, and social sex differences is interpreted as a direct or mediated consequence of genetic differences. These differences are understood to be causally and cumulatively related, and to result in a higher mortality rate for men. There is a quality of inevitability in this perspective—biology is seen as destiny with a vengeance—but in this case males are understood to be in the less favored position. Taken all together, and without consideration of other factors, this perspective constitutes a plausible explanatory system for an array of apparently correct data.

In contrast, the alternative psychosocial perspective hypothesizes that the greater mortality rate of men is at least partially a consequence of the demands of the male role and emphasizes the ways in which male role expectations have a deleterious effect on men's lives, and possibly contribute to men's higher mortality rate. One of the complexities of this sociocultural hypothesis is the problem of specifying what is meant by "male role expectations." This is no simple task.

DEFINING THE MALE ROLE

Brannon (1976) has provided the most detailed and systematic attempt to delineate the various components of the male role. Although noting its elusive quality and the apparent contradictions within it, he abstracts four themes or dimensions that seem to be valid across all specific manifestations of stereotyped male role behavior. He characterizes these components in four short phrases:

1. No Sissy Stuff: the need to be different from women.
2. The Big Wheel: the need to be superior to others.
3. The Sturdy Oak: the need to be independent and self-reliant.
4. Give 'Em Hell: the need to be more powerful than others, through violence if necessary.

Clearly men express more positive and socially valued characteristics than described by these four themes. The attempt to define a normative role specific for only one sex necessarily results in a distorted model of human potential. The fiction that men and women are opposites is perpetuated. The recognition that men and women are essentially similar in what constitutes their humanity although manifesting a range of individual differences both within and between each sex is ignored. It is consequently possible to understand why the attempt to conform to male role expectations has negative consequences for men.

Jourard (1971) assumed that men's basic psychological needs are essentially the same as women's: all persons need to be known and to know, to be depended upon and to depend, to be loved and to love, and to find purpose and meaning in life. The socially prescribed male role, however, requires men to be noncommunicative, competitive and nongiving, and inexpressive, and to evaluate life success in terms of external achievements rather than personal and interpersonal fulfillment. All men are caught in a double bind. If a man fulfills the prescribed role requirements, his basic human needs go unmet; if these needs are met, he may be considered, or consider himself, unmanly. Jourard contended that if these needs are not met, persons risk emotional disorder, they may ignore somatic signals with a resultant failure to seek health care, possibly develop greater vulnerability to illness, and even lose the will to live.

Going beyond Jourard's general assessment, Rosenfeld (1972) has argued that the growing-up process by which boys become men has been made into an achievement or a task rather than a natural unfolding of human potentiality. By what criteria can a boy ever know that he has fulfilled the requirements of the male role? Adults are of little help in clarifying expectations for children, because they too are confused by apparent uncertainties about and inconsistency within male role expectations. Hartley (1959) long since observed that unclear sex-role expectations for children are a major source of anxiety. If severe enough and persistent, such anxiety may lead to serious emotional difficulty that may cause, or contribute to, behavioral and learning disorders.

One way children cope with anxiety derived from sex-role expectations is the development of compensatory masculinity (Tiller, 1967). Compensatory masculine behaviors range from the innocent to the insidious. Boys naturally imitate the male models available to them and can be observed overemphasizing male gait and verbal patterns. But if the motive is a need to prove the right to male status, more destructive behavioral patterns may result, and persist into adulthood. Boys are often compelled to take risks that result in accidents; older youth often begin smoking and drinking as a symbol of adult male status (Farrell, 1974); automobiles are often utilized as an extension of male power; and some men find confirmation of themselves in violence toward those whom they do not consider in conformity to the male role (Churchill, 1967). A convincing case has been made by both Fasteau (1974) and Komisar (1976) that readiness to settle international conflict by war rather than diplomacy is a function of prevalent male role expectations.

In addition, the requirements of the male work role have also been implicated as a cause of men's greater mortality. It has been suggested that stress and the competition to get ahead may result in greater vulnerability for men (Slobogin, 1977).

DATA RELEVANT TO THE BIOGENETIC AND PSYCHOSOCIAL HYPOTHESIS[1]

Madigan's early study (1957) remains influential in defense of the biogenetic perspective because its claimed empirical basis gave it evidential status that the psychosocial hypothesis has only recently begun to amass. The current debate is rightly focused on data about rates of conception, birth, and death that can be attributed to genetic causes, on the one hand, and data about rates of death that can be correlated with sex-role-related behavior.

Rates of Conception and Prenatal Mortality

In spite of the theoretically equal opportunity for parity in male and female conceptions (the primary sex ratio), the known ratio of male to female births (the secondary sex ratio) consistently favors males. This ratio is reported variously as between 103:100 and 106:100 (Tricomi, Serr, & Solish, 1960; Parkes, 1967; Stoll, 1974). The preponderance of evidence suggests that the sex ratio at conception favors males to an even greater degree, but due to greater loss of males during pregnancy the amount of excess males at birth is reduced. Most studies show a higher ratio of males to females in induced abortions, which indicates a higher conception rate for males, and an even higher ratio of males to females in spontaneous abortions, which suggests that the male fetus is less viable. Accordingly the ratio of male to female conceptions is estimated to be between 108:100 and 120:100. It is therefore assumed that the male fetus is more vulnerable *in utero*.

Greater male mortality continues during early childhood: utilizing 1982 data, the ratio of male to female deaths due to certain causes in infancy is 140:100; and the ratio of male to female deaths at all ages, but attributable to congenital abnormalities, is 118:100. Due to an excess of male over female deaths from all causes, parity is achieved in the sexes ratio during the 25–34 year decade (Parkes, 1967). The excess of male over female deaths continues (see Table 1), resulting in an increasing ratio of females to males alive as age advances.

In sum, the genetic evidence suggests that the male fetus and the male neonate are more vulnerable prior to the time when sociocultural factors could exert an influence sufficient to account for a significant amount of the variance. These innate factors, however, are not sufficient to reduce the sex ratio to parity, since parity is not reached until early adulthood, the time of expected procreation. Subsequent to childhood the excess of the male over the female death rate cannot be attributed solely to biological differences between the sexes.

The greater *in utero* and perinatal mortality of males, along with the slightly higher mortality of males at later ages due to congenital anomalies, suggests the operation of a biological factor that may contribute to the overall higher

1. Several methodological considerations should be noted: First, the psychosocial hypothesis utilizes a conception of causality involving the complex interaction of biological, psychological, and social factors. When assessing the claims of the psychosocial hypothesis, it is difficult to determine the degree to which illness is a consequence of any one factor, or an interaction among a combination of factors. Second, age must be taken into consideration when accounting for sex differences in mortality. For example, in middle life the incidence of death attributable to heart disease is greater for men than women. In old age the cause of death is frequently heart failure for both sexes. When data for all ages are taken together, the large sex differences at different ages are obscured. Third, sex differences in morbidity may be subject to observational and reporting errors, as well as response bias. In addition, mental illness contributes to physical illness, suicide, and death by accidental cause. Although women are assumed to suffer from mental illness more than men, this notion has been seriously challenged by health professionals (see Harrison, 1975). Finally there are limitations on the use of mortality data. Methods and criteria for collection have changed over time, and adequate data are still unavailable for many nonindustrial societies. Therefore comparisons over time and across cultures are made difficult.

TABLE 1   Ratio of Male to Female Deaths
(1982 Data)[a]

AGE IN YEARS	MALE:FEMALE
Under 1	125:100
1–4	123:100
5–14	153:100
15–24	289:100
25–34	257:100
35–44	189:100
45–54	185:100
55–64	190:100
65–74	164:100
75–84	164:100
85 +	123:100

[a]Recalculated from data in *Vital Statistics of the United States*, 1982 (USDHHS, 1986).

mortality rate of men. In the absence of evidence to demonstrate the operation of social factors, a biologically reductionist explanation appears plausible. For this reason it is essential to examine the available data in which the possible effect of social factors can be discerned.

Current Adult Mortality

Mortality data, examined in terms of sex differences in specific causes of death, provide the best evidence for the psychosocial hypothesis. In his early study, Madigan (1957) attempted to determine why men had not benefited from technological advances in health care to the same extent as women. He compared the mortality rates in a sample of cloistered members of religious orders with population rates and he hypothesized that the life expectancy of the male "religious" would approach that of the female "religious" and exceed that of men in the general population, if differential mortality rates were due to male role-induced stress. He found no large departure of his subjects from population norms, and concluded that role strain makes only a small contribution to the differences and that biological factors are the chief source of variance.

Madigan recognized that the men and women subjects did not live under identical conditions—

that cloistered men were more likely to drink and to smoke than women, for example. He overlooked completely, however, the consequences of the male subject's socialization into male role patterns prior to entering the religious orders, and the further possibility that a cloistered existence may have contributed to rather than reduced the strain that they experienced.

Enterline (1961) argued that a reductionist biological view could not be sustained when variations over time in specific causes of death in different age groups were examined. He identified several trends in the differential death rate between 1929 and 1958 that could not be simply attributed to biological causes: an increase in deaths due to lung cancer and coronary heart disease among 45- to 64-year-old males. Though he was not able to provide an explanatory hypothesis for these differences, in the absence of a satisfactory biological explanation Enterline concluded that environmental determinants were a more likely explanation.

Conrad (1962) extended the analysis of the determinants of differential mortality rates by specifically considering sociological factors. He identified a variety of means by which male role behaviors may contribute to the higher mortality rates of men: the higher accidental death rate at all ages, the greater physical and emotional strain of the male economic role, and the greater exposure to industrial hazards and contaminants.

Waldron and Johnson (Waldron, 1976, 1983a, 1983b; Waldron & Johnson, 1976) have focused attention on sex differences in causes of death by ranking all causes accounting for more than 1% of all deaths in descending order according to the ratio of male to female deaths. In their presentation the first seven categories and the ratio of male to female deaths in each were as follows:

1. Malignant neoplasm of the respiratory system (5.9:1).
2. Other bronchopulmonic disease (4.9:1).
3. Motor vehicle accidents (2.8:1).
4. Suicide (2.7:1).
5. Other accidents (2.4:1).
6. Cirrhosis of the liver (2.0:1).

7. Arteriosclerotic heart disease, including coronary disease (2.0:1).

All seven categories have sex-role behavior correlates, for example, the greater incidence and frequency of smoking, drinking, and propensity toward risk taking and violence among men.

The present discussion utilizes Waldron's interpretive framework, but is based on more recent data (Tables 2 and 3). The criteria for inclusion of categories of cause of death in Tables 2 and 3 were (1) the 15 major headings defined in the *Vital Statistics* as the leading causes of death, (2) following Waldron, all subcate-

TABLE 2   Causes of Death (1972 Data)[a]

	MALE/FEMALE RATIO[b]	MALE/FEMALE RATIO	PERCENTAGE OF DEATHS
Diseases of the heart	418.5:310.3	1.35	38.5
Acute myocardial infarction	221.5:124.7	1.78	18.2
Chronic ischemic heart disease	157.9:151.4	1.04	16.3
Other	21.2:15.6	1.36	1.9
Malignant neoplasms	185.7:147.2	1.26	17.6
Bucal cavity and pharynx	5.3:2.0	2.65	0.4
Digestive organs	50.3:41.9	1.20	4.9
Respiratory system	60.3:14.8	4.07	3.9
Breasts	0.3:29.2	0.01	1.6
Genital organs	18.9:21.7	0.87	2.2
Urinary organs	10.5:4.8	2.19	0.8
Other	21.6:18.5	1.17	2.1
Lymphatic and hemato-poictic tissue	10.5:8.4	1.25	1.0
Cerebrovascular diseases	94.0:110.5	0.85	10.9
Cerebral hemorrhage	17.1:18.2	0.94	1.9
Cerebral thrombosis	24.9:30.2	0.82	2.9
Other	51.6:61.6	0.84	6.1
Accidents	78.6:33.4	2.35	5.9
Motor vehicle	39.6:15.1	2.62	2.9
Other	39.0:18.4	2.12	3.0
Influenza and pneumonia	34.2:26.1	1.31	3.2
Diabetes mellitus	15.6:21.4	0.73	2.0
Certain causes in infancy	19.5:13.2	1.48	1.7
Cirrhosis of the liver	21.1:10.4	2.03	1.7
Arteriosclerosis	13.5:17.6	0.77	1.7
Bronchitis, emphysema, asthma	23.3:6.7	3.48	1.6
Suicide	17.5:6.8	2.57	1.3
Homicide	15.4:3.7	4.16	1.0
Congenital abnormalities	7.7:6.4	1.20	0.8
Nephritis and nephrosis	4.6:3.6	1.27	0.4
Peptic ulcer	5.1:2.5	2.04	0.4
All other	61.1:45.6	1.34	11.6

[a]Calculated from data in USDHEW (1976).
[b]Rate per 100,000 population.

TABLE 3   Causes of Death (1982 Data)[a]

	MALE/FEMALE RATIO[b]	MALE/FEMALE RATIO	PERCENTAGE OF DEATHS
Diseases of the heart	353.9:299.6	1.18	38.3
Acute myocardial infarction	151.3:101.3	1.49	14.7
Old myocardial infarction and other chronic ischemic heart disease	113.2:108.7	1.04	13.0
Other forms of heart disease	72.4:69.3	1.04	8.3
Hypertensive heart disease	7.9:10.0	0.79	1.1
Malignant neoplasms[a]	207.6:167.8	1.23	22.0
Bucal cavity and pharynx[c]	5.2:2.2	2.50	0.4
Digestive organs[c]	52.3:45.0	1.15	5.7
Respiratory system[c]	73.7:28.0	2.63	5.9
Breasts[c]	0.2:31.4	0.01	1.9
Genital organs[c]	21.9:19.2	1.14	2.4
Urinary organs[c]	10.7:5.3	2.01	0.9
Other[c]	24.8:21.2	1.17	2.7
Lymphatic and hematopoietic tissue[c]	10.5:9.2	1.14	1.2
Cerebrovascular diseases[c]	56.7:78.8	0.72	8.0
Cerebral hemorrhage[c]	8.1:9.1	0.89	1.0
Cerebral thrombosis[c]	10.0:14.3	0.69	1.4
Other[c]	38.6:55.4	0.69	5.5
Accidents[c]	58.4:23.8	2.45	4.8
Motor vehicle[c]	29.5:10.6	2.78	2.3
Other[c]	28.9:13.2	2.18	2.4
Chronic obstructive pulmonary disease and allied conditions	35.2:16.9	2.08	3.0
Bronchitis, emphysema, and asthma[c]	11.1:5.8	1.91	1.0
Pneumonia and influenza[c]	22.5:19.8	1.13	2.5
Diabetes mellitus[c]	12.6:17.1	0.73	1.4
Suicide[c]	19.2:5.6	3.42	1.4
Chronic liver disease and cirrhosis[c]	15.9:8.2	1.93	1.4
Arteriosclerosis[c]	9.4:13.6	0.69	1.4
Homicide and legal intervention[c]	15.4:4.2	3.66	1.1
Certain conditions originating in perinatal period	10.5:7.5	1.40	1.1
Nephritis, nephrotic syndrome, and nephrosis	8.1:7.5	1.08	0.9
Congenital abnormalities[c]	6.4:5.4	1.18	0.7
Septicemia	4.9:5.1	0.96	0.6
All other			11.2

[a]Calculated from data in USDHS (1986).

[b]Rate per 100,000 population.

[c]Comparable to Table 2 (1972 data) categories.

gories that account for more than 1% of all deaths, and (3) subcategories that have high sex ratios.

There are several significant points of contrast with Waldron's presentation. The data in Tables 2 and 3 are ranked by percentage of deaths attributed to each cause, rather than by rank of the sex ratio, and it is not possible to know how all Waldron's categories compare with those here. In addition, Waldron omitted entirely the cerebrovascular category that accounts for 10.9% of all deaths in our 1972 data and 8.0% of all deaths in our 1982 data, and which in all subcategories account for more female than male deaths. The male to female ratio for homicides accounted for more than 1% of all deaths in 1972 and 1982 with a male to female ratio of 4.16:1 and 3.66:1, respectively, which would have qualified this cause of death for second place had the data been ranked as in Waldron's presentation.

It is also noteworthy that the *Vital Statistics* for the years 1972 through 1982 were analyzed for each of the 1972 major causes of death and it was determined that the 1982 statistics were within the limits of a linear trend model. This analysis was complicated by changes in categorization of major causes of death that began in the 1979 *Vital Statistics* with the implementation of the use of the Ninth Revision of the International Classification of Diseases, 1975. Only those causes of death indicated by footnote c in Table 3 are directly comparable to similar categories in Table 2. Given these caveats, it was concluded that the statistics for the major causes of death in 1982 that also appeared within the 15 major causes of death in 1972 were not artifactual but consistent with trends through these years.

Examination of the differential mortality rates alone reveals nothing about the antecedents of specific causes of death. The importance of Waldron's analysis is her discussion of these antecedents in relationship to sex-role-related behaviors. Fulfilling the requirements of the male role is characterized as an achievement, not simply the consequences of natural growth and development; it is often bought at the cost of risk and stress. Anxiety about failure to achieve may result in compensatory behaviors designed to show outward conformity to the role. Compensatory behaviors involve risk-taking of various kinds that may lead to accidents, exhibition of violence, excessive consumption of alcohol, and smoking. Reciprocally, anxiety about failure to achieve male role requisites may result in denial of dimensions of human experience more stereotypical[ly] associated with women's role. This denial may result in the suppression of gentleness and emotion. These specific male behaviors seem to be significant antecedents to all the major causes of death in which male death rates exceed those of women by a ratio of 2:1, a convention established by Waldron as a criterion of a large sex difference.

Diseases of the Heart

In contrast to Waldron's 1967 data, the ratio of male to female deaths does not exceed that 2:1 ratio in the 1972 or 1982 data when considering all ages combined. The higher coronary heart disease (CHD) death rates among the elderly, however, obscure large sex differences in mortality ratios for the younger age groups. For instance, for individuals between the ages of 20–44 years old in 1982, the sex-mortality ratio exceeds 4:1 for acute myocardial infarction and for old myocardial infarction; in the same year, it exceeds 2:1 for hypertensive heart disease.

A biogenetic explanation posits that the female advantage in CHD mortality can be attributed to the protective effects of endogenous sex hormones. This argument is based on several investigations that have found that postmenopausal and oophorectomized women (women who have had their ovaries removed) are at an increased risk for CHD (Waldron, 1976, 1983a). Research supporting a biogenetic explanation, however, has been criticized on the basis of methodological flaws and inconsistent findings.

Evidence that links men's greater vulnerability to CHD to sex differences in smoking patterns, as well as to sex differences in aggressive, "hard-driving," behavior, appears to be a stronger argument explaining the sex differential in CHD mortality.

Of the three major risk factors for CHD, cigarette smoking is far more prevalent in the American population than either hypertension or elevated serum cholesterol (U.S. Surgeon General, 1983). Generally, in the past a greater percentage of men have smoked cigarettes compared to women. The proportion of smokers, however, has declined steadily between 1960 and 1980 in both men and women. This decline was steeper among men than among women. In 1970, male smokers smoked 4.1 more cigarettes per day than female smokers, but in 1980 men smoked only 2.0 more cigarettes per day than did women. Although a greater percentage of men still smoked cigarettes in 1980, and continued to smoke a greater average number of cigarettes per day, the differences between the sexes in 1980 was less than that observed a decade earlier (U.S. Surgeon General, 1983). Thus, as the smoking patterns of women become more similar to that of men, we might expect differences between men's and women's death rates as a consequence of smoking-related causes to diminish.

Behavioral patterns are also related to differential risks for heart disease. The Coronary Prone Behavior Pattern, Type A behavior (Friedman & Rosenman, 1974) is characterized by competitive achievement, striving, time urgency, and a potential for hostility. Type A behavior has been associated with an increased risk of CHD mortality in both men and women (Cooper, Detre, & Weiss, 1981; Booth-Kewley & Friedman, 1987).

Considering the major components of Type A behavior, such as excessive aggressiveness and competitiveness, one might suggest that Type A behaviors are associated with traditional masculine sex-role characteristics. At least six investigations have found positive correlations between Type A behavior and self-rated masculine sex-role characteristics in both male and female students (Blascovitch, Major, & Katkin,

1981; DeGregorio & Carver, 1980; Grimm & Yarnold, 1985; Nix & Lohr, 1981; Stevens, Pfost, & Ackerman, 1984; Zeldow, Clark, & Daugherty, 1985).

Although Type A behavior has been cited as being more prevalent among men than women (see Chesney, 1983), women are by no means exempt from the development of Type A behavior. Sex differences in Type A behavior are apparently reduced once a comparison is made between men and women engaged in similar vocational activities (Ficarrotto & Weidner, 1987). In addition, employment outside the home appears to be a crucial factor in the expression of Type A behavior in women, and higher status occupations among women appear to be associated with higher Type A scores (Morell & Katkin, 1982). Thus, it appears that "sex differences" in Type A behavior might have less to do with gender and more to do with whether a person's putative societal role can be defined as traditional male.

It should be noted that several prospective studies have failed to find a link between Type A behavior and CHD mortality (see Chesney, Hecker, & Black, 1987). In fact, Ragland and Brand (1988) found that among men who had already suffered a heart attack, Type A behavior was not associated with subsequent CHD mortality. It appears that certain components of the Type A pattern, such as hostility, might be more directly related to CHD mortality than overall Type A scores (Wright, 1988). Interestingly, men display more hostility than do women (Maccoby & Jacklin, 1974; Pleck, 1981; Waldron, 1976; Weidner, Friend, Ficarrotto, & Polowczyk, 1988). This raises the question of whether sex differences in hostility may contribute to men's higher CHD risk.

Malignant Neoplasms

Taking all types of cancer together, men are slightly more vulnerable than women. Utilizing Waldron's criterion, sex differences greater than 2:1 emerge in only four subcategories of malignant neoplasms. Of these, breast cancer is the only category in which women's risk is greater than men's, which seems largely a consequence of endocrine differences. The incidence of all other loci for cancer is greater for men.

Most relevant for this discussion, however, is the male to female ratio for cancer of the mouth and pharynx, 2.65 in 1972 and 2.50 in 1982, and of the respiratory system, 4.07 in 1972 and 2.63 in 1982. Both types of cancer are related to smoking, for which a higher rate is documented for men. Studies of the prevalence of smoking just prior to the 1982 data show that the amount of daily smoking among women was approaching that of men and that the age of onset for smoking was getting earlier for both sexes (Schuman, 1977).

The ratio of cancer of the urinary organs was 2.19 in 1972 and 2.01 in 1982. There is evidence that a high level of smoking increases the risk of cancer of the ureter, and is related to cancer of the bladder at all levels of smoking (USDHEW, 1973, 1974, 1975).

It is also important to note that due to different work roles men are also exposed more often and at a higher level to industrial carcinogens.

Other Respiratory Diseases

In 1982, men still smoked more than women, according to all the parameters by which smoking could be measured. The relevance of this difference is seen again in the 3.48 ratio (1972) and 1.91 ratio (1982) of male to female deaths attributable to bronchitis, emphysema, and asthma. Research findings are consistent across national and ethnic groups. Smokers have higher death rates from chronic bronchitis and emphysema proportionately to the number of cigarettes smoked. Smokers are also more frequently subject to other respiratory infections than nonsmokers and require a longer convalescence (USDHEW, 1973, 1974, 1975). In addition, exposure to air pollution and/or industrial pollutants potentiates the effect of smoking.

Cirrhosis of the Liver

More men than women drink alcohol and more men than women drink to excess by an approximate ratio of 4:1 (Cahalan, 1970; McClelland et al., 1972). Alcohol serves both as a symbolic manifestation of compensatory masculinity and as an escape mechanism from the pressure to achieve. It is not surprising that males should die from causes of death associated with excessive drinking to a greater degree than women; the ratio of cirrhosis of the liver is 2.03(1972) and 1.93(1982).

Deaths Due to External Causes

Men die more frequently than women from four external causes of death: motor vehicle accidents, 2.62 in 1972 and 2.78 in 1982; other accidents, 2.12 in 1972 and 2.18 in 1982; suicide, 2.57 in 1972 and 3.42 in 1982; and homicide, 4.16 in 1972 and 3.66 in 1982. Abuse of alcohol is clearly implicated in many automobile fatalities, and is very likely a factor in other deaths due to external causes. The consistent excess of male to female deaths due to accidents of other kinds has led some interpreters to presume an innate accident-prone tendency among males. This interpretation, however, is inconsistent with the emphasis on greater skill development among males in this culture. Consequently the greater accident rate can be accounted for more readily by the different socialization of males to perform high-risk activities, the popular assumption that male children are tougher than females, and the subsequent development of compensatory masculine behavior among men as a means of validating their status as males (Cicone & Ruble, 1978).

The greater vulnerability of males to death by suicide and homicide can be understood as a consequence of the greater socialization of men to aggressive and violent behavior. This is especially notable in contrast to the greater rate of suicide attempts by women, which appear to be requests for help rather than a determination to end life. Women more frequently utilize less violent and less effective means of attempting suicide. In sum, differences in the sex ratio of all external causes of death, which account for more than 1% of all deaths, are plausibly related to sex-role socialization.

CONCLUSIONS

A critical reading of presently available evidence confirms that male role socialization contributes to the higher mortality rate of men. Recognizing the multiplicity of variables within the chain of causality, Waldron (1976) estimates that three-fourths of the difference in life expectancy can be accounted for by sex-role-related behaviors that contribute to the greater mortality of men. She estimates that one-third of the differences can be accounted for by smoking, another one-sixth by coronary prone behavior, and the remainder by a variety of other causes. Using more precise statistical techniques to analyze differences in male/female mortality rates in terms of antecedents to specific causes of death, Retherford (1972) attributes half of the differences to smoking alone.

Waldron's estimate that three-fourths of the current 7.0 year difference in life expectancy is attributable to socialization is plausible and concordant with the difference in life expectancy at the turn of the century of approximately 2 years. The evidence we have reviewed suggests that this portion of the variance may be attributable to biogenetic determinants (1983a). However, any biogenetic factor is exacerbated by male role socialization. Parents assume that male children are tougher, when in fact they may be to some degree more vulnerable than female children. Male children are also more likely to develop a variety of behavioral difficulties such as hyperactivity, stuttering, dyslexia, and learning disorders of various kinds. Maccoby and Jacklin's (1974) review of research on childhood sex differences lends little support to the view that these observed sex differences are genetically determined. Insofar as they may be biogeneti-

cally predisposed, certainly the development of more functional behavioral patterns should be the goal of the socialization process. Male socialization into aggressive behavioral patterns seems clearly related to the higher death rate from external causes. Male anxiety about the achievement of masculine status seems to result in a variety of behaviors that can be understood as compensatory.

During the period in which the ratio between men's and women's life expectancy has worsened, social policy in the United States, especially in preparation for war and national defense, has been overwhelmingly directed toward reinforcement and support of the stereotyped male role (Fasteau, 1974; Filene, 1974). Recognition of the lethal aspects of the male role has had to await the emergence of a critical theory of sex-role socialization free of the ideological commitment to the status quo. This has been inspired by a critique of traditional psychological research inspired by the feminist movement (Harrison, 1975) and has been focally articulated for men's roles by Pleck (1976, 1981).

In the psychosocial perspective, sex differences, apart from those specifically associated with reproductive function, are understood to be smaller, less biologically based, and less socially significant. This is demonstrated by the greater range of difference within each sex than the average differences between the sexes. Differences in learned personality traits are understood not to be a necessary function of the development of sexual identity, but rather a consequence of social expectation. Finally, learning only stereotypical sex-typed traits is understood to be a handicap rather than an asset.

Traditional sex-role ideology serves as a rationale for the inevitability of psychological sex differences and the traditional division of family, work, and social responsibilities. The newer role liberation perspective provides not only the basis of reassessment of psychological characteristics and social arrangements, but also a basis for the reinterpretation of many previously observed sex differences (Pleck, 1976, 1981;

Miller, 1976). Research suggests that it is not so much biological gender that is potentially hazardous to men's health but rather specific behaviors that are traditionally associated with the male sex role that can be taken on by either gender (Weidner et al., 1988; Wright, 1988). Recent data indicating a slight trend of convergence between sexes in mortality due to specific causes correlated with the convergence of smoking habits between the sexes are supportive of the psychosocial hypothesis. As plausible as this conclusion is, it is nevertheless tentative given the multivariate nature of public health data that need to be thoroughly researched along with prospective health and gender studies (Stillion, 1985).

Contemporary research has failed to demonstrate the existence of important intrinsic psychological differences between men and women. However, research on sex-role stereotypes demonstrates the persistence of the belief in such differences in personality traits (Rosencrantz, Vogel, Bee, Brovermann, & Brovermann, 1968).

This continuing belief brings to mind W. I. Thomas's famous dictum: "If men [people] define situations as real, they are real in their consequences" (1928, p. 572). It is time that men especially begin to comprehend that the price paid for belief in the male role is shorter life expectancy. The male sex-role will become less hazardous to our health only insofar as it ceases to be defined as opposite to the female role, and comes to be defined as one genuinely human way to live.

Ironically, Madigan, whose work (1957) continues to have an undeserved credibility in discussions of this issue, supported the best possibility of extending male life expectancy. For him, as for many in our society, a technological solution was more probable than the "profound cultural revolution" that he recognized the psychosocial thesis required. But it is precisely that profound cultural revolution that is our need. The best hope for both men and women is overcoming a view of development that turns maturation into a polarized sex-typed achievement.

REFERENCES

Blascovitch, J., Major, B., & Katkin, E. Sex role orientation and Type-A behavior. *Personality and Social Psychology Bulletin*, 1981, 7, 600–604.

Booth-Kewley, S., & Friedman, II. Psychological predictors of heart disease: A qualitative review. *Psychological Bulletin*, 1987, 10, 343–362.

Brannon, R. C. No "sissy stuff": The stigma of anything vaguely feminine. In D. David & R. Brannon (Eds.), *The Forty-Nine Percent Majority*. Reading, MA: Addison-Wesley, 1976.

Broverman, I., Broverman, D., Clarkson, F., Rosencrantz, P., & Vogel, S. 1970. "Sex Role Stereotypes and Clinical Judgments of Mental Health." *Journal of Consulting Psychology 34*: 1–7.

Cahalan, D. *Problem Drinkers*. San Francisco: Jossey-Bass, 1970.

Chesney, M. Occupational setting and coronary prone behavior in men and women. In T. Dembroski, G. Schmidt, & G. Blumchen (Eds.), *Biobehavioral Bases of Coronary Heart Disease*, pp. 79–90. New York: Karger, 1983.

Chesney, M. A., Hecker, M. H., Black, G. W. "Coronary-Prone Components of Type-A Behavior in the W.C.G.S.: A New Methodology." In B. K. Houston & C. R. Snyder (eds.) *Type-A Behavior Pattern: Current Trends and Future Directions*. New York: John Wiley, 1987, pp. 1–31.

Churchill, W. *Homosexuality in a Cross Cultural Perspective*. Englewood Cliffs, NJ: Prentice-Hall, 1967.

Cicone, M., & Ruble, D. Beliefs about males. *The Journal of Social Issues*, 1978, 34, 5–16.

Conrad, F. Sex roles as a factor in longevity. *Sociology and Social Research*, 1962, 46, 195–202.

Cooper, T., Detre, T., & Weiss, S. Coronary prone behavior and coronary heart disease: A critical review. *Circulation*, 1981, 63, 1199–1215.

DeGregorio, E., & Carver, C. Type A behavior, sex role orientation, and psychological adjustment. *Journal of Personality and Social Psychology*, 1980, 39, 286–293.

Enterline, P. Causes of death responsible for recent increases in sex mortality differentials in the United

States. *Milbank Memorial Fund Quarterly*, 1961, *39*, 312–328.

Farrell, W. *The Liberated Man*. New York: Random House, 1974.

Fasteau, M. *The Male Machine*. New York: McGraw-Hill, 1974.

Ficarrotto, T., & Weidner, G. Sex differences in coronary heart disease mortality: A psychosocial perspective. Unpublished manuscript, 1987.

Filene, P. *Him/Her/Self: Sex Roles in Modern America*. New York: Harcourt, Brace, Jovanovich, 1974.

Friedman, M., & Rosenman, R. *Type A behavior and your heart*. Greenwich, CT: Fawcett Publications, 1974.

Grimm, L., & Yarnold, P. Sex typing and the coronary prone behavior pattern. *Sex Roles*, 1985, *12*, 171–177.

Harrison, J. A critical evaluation of research on "masculinity/femininity." Doctoral dissertation, New York University, 1975. *Dissertation Abstracts International*, 1975, *36*, 1903B. (University Microfilms No. 75-22890.)

Hartley, R. Sex role pressures in the socialization of the male child. *Psychological Reports*, 1959, *5*, 457–468.

Jourard, S. *The Transparent Self*. New York: Van Nostrand, 1971.

Komisar, L. Violence and the masculine mystique. In D. David and R. Brannon (Eds.), *The Forty-Nine Percent Majority*. Reading, MA: Addison-Wesley, 1976.

Maccoby, E., & Jacklin, C. *The Psychology of Sex Differences*. Stanford, CA: Stanford University Press, 1974.

Madigan, F. Are sex mortality differentials biologically caused? *Millbank Memorial Fund Quarterly*, 1957, *35*, 202–223.

McClelland, D., et al. *The Drinking Man*. Riverside, NJ: Free Press, 1972.

Miller, J. *Towards a New Psychology of Women*. Boston, MA: Beacon Press, 1976.

Montagu, A. *The Natural Superiority of Women*. New York: Macmillan, 1953.

Morell, M., & Katkin, E. Jenkins activity survey scores among women of different occupations. *Journal of Consulting and Clinical Psychology*, 1982, *50*, 588–589.

Nathanson, C. Illness and the feminine role: A theoretical review. *Social Science and Medicine*, 1975, *9*, 57–62.

Nix, J., & Lohr, J. Relationship between sex, sex role characteristics, and coronary prone behavior in college students. *Psychological Reports*, 1981, *48*, 739–744.

Parkes, A. The sex-ratio in man. In A. Allison (Ed.), *The Biology of Sex*. Baltimore, MD: Penguin Books, 1967.

Pleck, J. The male sex role: Definitions, problems, and sources of change. *Journal of Social Issues*, 1976, *32*(3), 155–163.

Pleck, J. *The Myth of Masculinity*. Cambridge, MA: The MIT Press, 1981.

Ragland, D., & Brand, R. Type A behavior and mortality from coronary heart disease. *New England Journal of Medicine*, 1988, *318*, 65–69.

Retherford, R. Tobacco smoking and the sex mortality differential. *Demography*, 1972, *9*, 203–216.

Rosenfield, A. Why men die younger. *Readers Digest*, 1972, 121–124.

Rosenkrantz, P., Vogel, S., Bee, H., Brovermann, I., & Brovermann, D. Sex-role stereotypes and self-concepts in college students. *Journal of Consulting and Clinical Psychology*, 1968. *32*, 287–295.

Schuman, L. Patterns of smoking behavior. In Jarvik, M., Cullen, J., Gritz, E., Vogt, T., & West, L. (Eds.), *Research on Smoking Behavior*. NIDA Research Monograph 17. Washington, DC: U.S. Government Printing Office, 1977.

Slobogin, K. Stress. *The New York Times Magazine*. November 20, 1977, 48–50, 96, 98, 100, 102, 104, 106.

Stevens, M., Pfost, K., & Ackerman, M. The relationship between sex role orientation and the Type A behavior pattern: A test of the main effect hypothesis. *Journal of Clinical Psychology*, 1984, *40*, 1338–1341.

Stillion, J. *Death and the Sexes*. Washington, D.C.: Hemisphere Publishing Corp., 1985.

Stoll, C. *Female and Male*. Dubuque, IA: Wm. C. Brown, 1974.

Thomas, W. *The Child in America*. New York: Alfred A. Knopf, 1928.

Tiller, P. Parental role division and the child's personality. In E. Dahlstrom (Ed.), *The Changing Roles of Men and Women*. Boston, MA: Beacon, 1967.

Tricomi, V., Serr, O., & Solish, C. The ratio of male to female embryos as determined by the sex chromatin. *American Journal of Obstetrics and Gynecology*, 1960, *79*, 504–509.

United States Department of Health Education and Welfare. *The Health Consequences of Smoking*. Washington, DC: The U.S. Government Printing Office, 1973, 1974, 1975.

United States Department of Health Education and Welfare. *Vital Statistics of the United States*. 1972 (Vol. 2). Washington, DC: U.S. Government Printing Office, 1976.

U. S. Department of Health and Human Services. *The Health Consequences of Smoking: Chronic Obstructive Lung Disease: A Report of the U.S. Surgeon General*, 1984. Rockville, MD: Public Health Service, Office on Smoking and Health; Washington, D.C., 1984. (D.H.H.S. [PHS] 84-50205)

United States Department of Health and Human Services. *Vital Statistics of the United States*, 1982 (Vol. 2). Washington, DC: U.S. Government Printing Office, 1987.

United States Department of Health and Human Services. *Vital Statistics of the United States,* 1984 (Pre-Publication Monograph). Washington, DC: U.S. Government Printing Office, 1987.

Verbrugge, L. M. 1980. "Recent Trends in Sex Mortality Differentials in the United States." *Women and Health 5*: 17–37.

Waldron, I. Why do women live longer than men? *Journal of Human Stress*, 1976, *2*, 1–13.

Waldron, I. Sex differences in human mortality: The role of genetic factors. *Social Science and Medicine*, 1983a, *17*, 321–333.

Waldron, I. Sex differences in illness incidence, prognosis and mortality: Issues and evidence. *Social Science and Medicine*, 1983b, *17*, 1107–1123.

Waldron, I., & Johnson, S. Why do women live longer than men? *Journal of Human Stress*, 1976, *2*, 19–29.

Weidner, G., Friend, R., Ficarrotto, T., Mendell, N. R. Hostility and cardiovascular reactivity to stress in women and men. *Psychosomatic Medicine*, 1988.

Wright, L. The Type A behavior pattern and coronary artery disease: Quest for the active ingredients and the elusive mechanisms. *American Psychologist*, 1988, *43*, 2–14.

Zeldow, P., Clark, D., & Daugherty, S. Masculinity, femininity, Type A behavior and psychosocial adjustment in medical students. *Journal of Personality and Social Psychology*, 1985, *45*, 481–492.

IF MEN COULD MENSTRUATE

GLORIA STEINEM

A white minority of the word has spent centuries conning us into thinking that a white skin makes people superior—even though the only thing it really does is make them more subject to ultraviolet rays and to wrinkles. Male human beings have built whole cultures around the idea that penis-envy is "natural" to women—though having such an unprotected organ might be said to make men vulnerable, and the power to give birth makes womb-envy at least as logical.

In short, the characteristics of the powerful, whatever they may be, are thought to be better than the characteristics of the powerless—and logic has nothing to do with it.

What would happen, for instance, if suddenly, magically, men could menstruate and women could not?

The answer is clear—menstruation would become an enviable, boastworthy, masculine event:

Men would brag about how long and how much.

Boys would mark the onset of menses, that longed-for proof of manhood, with religious ritual and stag parties.

Congress would fund a National Institute of Dysmenorrhea to help stamp out monthly discomforts.

Sanitary supplies would be federally funded and free. (Of course, some men would still pay for the prestige of commercial brands such as John Wayne Tampons, Muhammad Ali's Rope-a-dope Pads, Joe Namath Jock Shields—"For Those Light Bachelor Days," and Robert "Baretta" Blake Maxi-Pads.)

Military men, right-wing politicians, and religious fundamentalists would cite menstruation ("*men*-struation") as proof that only men could serve in the Army ("you have to give blood to take blood"), occupy political office ("can women be aggressive without that steadfast cycle governed by the planet Mars?"), be priests and ministers ("how could a woman give her blood for our sins?"), or rabbis ("without the monthly loss of impurities, women remain unclean").

Male radicals, left-wing politicians, and mystics, however, would insist that women are equal, just different; and that any woman could enter their ranks if only she were willing to self-inflict a major wound every month ("you *must* give blood for the revolution"), recognize the preeminence of menstrual issues, or subordinate her selfness to all men in their Cycle of Enlightenment.

Street guys would brag ("I'm a three-pad man") or answer praise from a buddy ("Man, you lookin' *good!*") by giving fives and saying, "Yeah, man, I'm on the rag!"

TV shows would treat the subject at length. ("Happy Days": Richie and Potsie try to convince Fonzie that he is still "The Fonz," though he has missed two periods in a row.) So would newspapers. (SHARK SCARE THREATENS MENSTRUATING MEN. JUDGES CITES MONTHLY STRESS IN PARDONING

RAPIST.) And movies. (Newman and Redford in "Blood Brothers"!)

Men would convince women that intercourse was *more* pleasurable at "that time of the month." Lesbians would be said to fear blood and therefore life itself—though probably only because they needed a good menstruating man.

Of course, male intellectuals would offer the most moral and logical arguments. How could a woman master any discipline that demanded a sense of time, space, mathematics, or measurement, for instance, without that in-built gift for measuring the cycles of the moon and planets—and thus for measuring anything at all? In the rarefied fields of philosophy and religion, could women compensate for missing the rhythm of the universe? Or for their lack of symbolic death-and-resurrection every month?

Liberal males in every field would try to be kind: the fact that "these people" have no gift for measuring life or connecting to the universe, the liberals would explain, should be punishment enough.

And how would women be trained to react? One can imagine traditional women agreeing to all these arguments with a staunch and smiling masochism. ("The ERA would force housewives to wound themselves every month": Phyllis Schlafly. "Your husband's blood is as sacred as that of Jesus—and so sexy, too!": Marabel Morgan.) Reformers and Queen Bees would try to imitate men, and *pretend* to have a monthly cycle. All feminists would explain endlessly that men, too, needed to be liberated from the false idea of Martian aggressiveness, just as women needed to escape the bonds of menses-envy. Radical feminists would add that the oppression of the nonmenstrual was the pattern for all other oppressions. ("Vampires were our first freedom fighters!") Cultural feminists would develop a bloodless imagery in art and literature. Socialist feminists would insist that only under capitalism would men be able to monopolize menstrual blood. . . .

In fact, if men could menstruate, the power justifications could probably go on forever.

If we let them.

MEN AND MUSCLES

BARRY GLASSNER

America was built of male muscle, at least according to our popular lore. The standard version of our early years speaks of rugged pioneers fighting the forces of nature and mastering savages with their bare hands. American industry likewise is understood to have been the product of male brawn. The captains of industry in the late nineteenth and early twentieth centuries were portrayed as almost animalistic in their physical power and drive. Aspiring young men were urged to display their own commitment to the same values. A 1920s manual for salesmen, like some of its counterparts in the 1980s, recommended exercises each morning, because muscular strength "imparts a feeling of enthusiasm, physical vigor and power of decision that no other faculty can give."

Bernarr Macfadden, creator of the physical culture movement early in this century, exhorted men to realize that "it lies with you, whether you shall be a strong virile animal . . . or a miserable little crawling worm."

During the world wars, male strength was equated—in political speeches and posters—with patriotism. And men who grew up just after the World War II remember vividly the Charles Atlas ads in comic books of the period. "I manufacture weaklings into MEN," read the headline on the back page of a 1952 issue of *The Fighting Leathernecks* (ten cents a copy). Beside a huge picture of Atlas, "the world's most perfectly developed man," appeared the famous story of how he used to be a ninety-seven-pound weakling. The choice every man had to face is made explicit in these ads: he could either keep his "skinny, pepless, second-rate body" or turn it over to Atlas (or the high school coach or the trainer at the local gym), who would "cram it so full of handsome, healthy, bulging new muscle that your friends will grow bug eyed."

Generations of boys have received the message loud and clear. Sociologist James Coleman asked high school boys in the early sixties how they would like to be remembered. Nearly half chose "athletic star," far more than opted for "brilliant student" or even "most popular." Neither hippies nor drugs nor the women's movement has changed things very much since. When the same question was asked of high schoolers in the seventies and again in the eighties, the same results were obtained: close to half answered "athletic star." What's more, in contemporary studies of college students, muscular men have been shown to be better liked by others and happier with themselves than their less well-developed classmates.

Boys suffer if they can't or won't accept the obligation to develop manly physiques. Every one of 256 nonmuscular adolescent boys examined in one study suffered mood or behavior problems connected to feelings of physical inadequacy. *Sissy* is, after all, a much more negative term than *tomboy*. While a girl is expected to outgrow her tomboyism, a boy who doesn't act boyish may well be sent to a psychiatrist for help. So a boy must prove decisively his commitment to masculinity, and the primary way to do it is through athletics and muscularity.

Muscles are *the* sign of masculinity. Author Nancy Huston has pointed out that women are distinguished from men by their ability to give birth, but men have no parallel "mark" of their gender. To fill in for this lack of a distinctive male trait, Huston says, many cultures have granted physical strength to boys and men as a characteristic uniquely their own. Over the years, innumerable scientific and superstitious explanations have been advanced purporting to prove it was God or Nature that made males stronger than females.

Because of the great meaning attached to muscles, nonathletic boys often grow into insecure men. In an "About Men" column in *The New York Times Magazine*, Mark Goodson, the television producer, wrote humorously about the drawbacks of disliking sports. Soon after arriving in New York in the 1940s, "hungry, anxious, in need of work," he was offered a job hosting a sports quiz. "I felt the blood leave my face," he recalls, but he accepted the assignment. Every Monday night for twenty-six weeks he feigned an interest in the subject, well enough that the radio station offered him a job announcing a baseball game. Never having been to a baseball game, he rushed out to buy a book on the rules of the game. "As I got to the tenth page, I collapsed," he reports. Much as I needed the money, I knew there was no way that I could manage this bluff."

Goodson built a TV production empire despite such setbacks, and he jokes about them now. But he also recognizes that to be male and nonathletic is serious business. "I approach this subject with a light touch, but in truth," he writes, "it has been a problem that has plagued me for most of my life." From early childhood until late adulthood, he hid his disinterest and inability for fear of seeming homosexual. Yet "even after three marriages, three children, and some in between love affairs, plus the sure knowledge that I adore women, I still feel, from time to time, that, somehow, I must be lacking in the right male genes."

One irony, of course, is that for many years now it has not been much easier for a man to be nonathletic if he's gay than if he's straight. The ideal man within the gay world, as in the heterosexual, is powerfully built. "What a shock I had when I came out," said Jim, a twenty-nine-year-old real estate agent I interviewed at the San Francisco apartment he shares with his lover.

Jim had waited until his junior year in college to become involved in the gay community. One aspect of coming out that he'd eagerly anticipated was the opportunity to dress the way he wanted. As far back as he could remember he'd been careful not to wear flamboyant clothes and to camouflage his thin arms and concave chest with a sports coat or sweater.

"I was basically a sissy as a kid," he told me, "and I had a lot of defenses about it. I would get stomachaches from having to play baseball. The whole idea of having to play games at recess or gym class was too much for me. I made a big distinction between intellect and athletics. I always felt that I was a head person and not a body person. Most of the boys in the little Wisconsin town where I grew up were very jock-y. Since I wasn't that, I kept to myself and read a lot and drew pictures. Fortunately, my family never gave me problems about who I was."

Still, Jim was anxious and unhappy during childhood. He remembers crying in the school bathroom in third grade because some boys had mocked him. After that, he practiced a tougher swagger and spiced up his speech with words like "shit" and "pussy."

Things changed in junior high. For starters, there was no more "recess," so he wasn't forced to play ball games; and for another, he found a new role for himself. The boys and girls started mixing with one another, awkwardly, and Jim served as a go-between. He was handsome, but he didn't go after girls sexually, and thus the girls considered him both appealing and trustworthy. For their part, the boys appreciated having a guy around who was neither a nerd nor a competitor.

Still, the idea that he might appear effeminate was abhorrent to him. Once the other kids starting dating, he made sure he always had a girl-friend—Catholic girls who, all the boys knew, would never let anyone past first base.

So it was with great anticipation of ending his long years of inauthenticity that he went public with his homosexuality midway through college. He'd had one affair with a man prior to that time but had kept his feelings secret.

"I'd been active in the ecology movement on campus, so I decided that a good way to come out would be through politics. I joined a gay rights group, and of course those were guys who were immersed in gay culture. Most of them at that time were very hard types, and I didn't know what I was getting into. They told me that it would just be a matter of time before I would become a sophisticated S-and-M'er. In a couple of months I would understand why it was correct to be tough and wear leather all the time."

"I tried to make it happen," he laughed, "but there was no way. It took me a few years and a set of barbells to accept that that wasn't me. It's taken even longer to accept the fact that gay men expect one another to dress in tight shirts and tight pants that emphasize their asses and their chests and their dicks. I mean, I've gotten comfortable dressing like that to be camp at a party, but I wouldn't dress that way to walk around Castro Street or go to work."

Instead, Jim dresses unusually "straight," even preppy. For our meeting he wore a cotton V-neck sweater and loose-fitting slacks, neither of which threw into relief any part of his body. On the other hand, Jim hasn't exactly stayed undeveloped. Partly as a result of the AIDS epidemic, the strong-and-healthy look is very much the order of the day where Jim lives. In addition to the barbells he bought in college, he owns a small trampoline and a sit-up board, and while he doesn't relish the thirty minutes every morning he spends exercising, he admitted it's made him happier with himself and has kept his partner interested.

BICEPS MAKE THE MAN

Gay men are by no means the only ones to have experienced conflicts over a lack of muscles. A national survey of 62,000 readers of *Psychology Today* found that a man's self-esteem correlates directly with having a muscular upper body. And in experiments in which male college students are given weight training, as the men grow stronger they become more outgoing and their degree of satisfaction with themselves increases.

Yet there is great variation in how men cope with the physical ideals placed upon them. Some men devote most of their lives to building up their bodies, while others scarcely exercise at all. Generally, a man's choice of one of these options or the other, or something in between, depends on what other people made of his body earlier in his life.

Those who suffer as adults are men who somehow never got into athletics while growing up but always felt parental and community pressure to do so. "I make a great pretense of being happy with these arms," said Larry, the thirty-six-year-old owner of an advertising agency in Atlanta, as he demonstrated how thin his left arm is by cupping the thumb and middle finger of his right hand almost completely around his upper arm. "I kid my friends who work out. I tell them, 'Biceps are just ugly bulges.' But the truth is, I'm not happy with my body.

"There's an event that sticks in my mind," he continued. "Nineteen seventy-two. We'd just graduated from Oberlin, and about a dozen of us took over the summer house of somebody's parents on a private lake in upstate New York for a week. One afternoon they all decided to go skinny-dipping. I begged off at first. I don't take off my clothes even in front of people I'm totally comfortable with. I make love in the dark when I have a choice in the matter. But those were the days of free sex and do-your-own-thing, and it wasn't considered cool to be hung up about nudity. They hassled me until I finally stripped and jumped in the water.

"It was about the worst experience of my life. First off, the other guys all had better bodies than I did. My stomach stuck out, even then, and I had no shoulders or chest, and of course, no biceps." Larry laughed nervously.

"The thing that really did me in was when an ex-girlfriend of mine swam by with the man she was living with at the time and made a comment about how I won the funniest-shape-of-the-day award. It was as if someone had run me over with a Mack truck. I felt embarrassed and betrayed."

Fifteen years later, and Larry still has a puny body he's ashamed about. Now not only doesn't he go skinny-dipping, he doesn't even go swimming. But he's not unattractive. In fact, he has a pleasant face and a full head of wavy black hair. One could easily imagine that if he stood up straight and added an inch or two of muscle in strategic spots, he's look great in the stylish clothes he wears.

Why doesn't Larry simply work out a few hours a week so that he can feel decent about himself physically? He was unable to answer that question directly. The answer came out, nonetheless, at another point in our discussion, when he described his parents and the nature of his relationship with them as a child. His mother used to criticize him for not being the son she'd imagined having, but anytime he showed some independence or virility, she was unsatisfied with his performance.

As he described it: "Either you played ball with the other kids or you weren't a Real Man. My mother's brother Don was a Real Man. He's been a guard for the basketball team. He's very tall and very fast. He ran a marathon this summer to celebrate his sixtieth birthday. My mother was very pretty in high school, very 'popular,' and she wanted me to be the same. If I'd had a sister, or even if there'd been another boy for her to lay it on, maybe I wouldn't have felt so pressured. I think I wimped out of sports just to spite her constant chirping about how I ought to be more like my Uncle Don."

At the same time, Larry's father, a man who was already distant, became even more so on the few occasions when Larry shelved his stamp collection and put on a baseball mitt. And at an early age Larry noticed that his mother was affectionate with his father only when his father was sick, a handy trick Larry came to deploy himself.

It's clear that in the crevices of Larry's adult mind there lives the belief that he cannot be fit without losing the attention of those he depends on. In his experience, to be fit was to yield to the wishes of an overpowering mother, whereas to be weak was to gain attention from the most important man in his world. This is just the opposite of many boys, who seduce Mom and buddy up to Dad by playing sports.

Larry survived high school thanks to an extracurricular activity that allowed him to relate to his father and to other males. He took up photography, a longstanding hobby of his father's. Working for the school yearbook, he was assigned to photograph football and basketball games. He became friends with other staffers, and in his senior year he was appointed editor. "The yearbook room was my safe zone, the camera was my weapon," he said.

At artsy Oberlin College in the late sixties, his camera attracted the attention of desirable women. It wasn't until that episode at the lake that he started to pay a price again for his physique.

He was safe in high school and college in part because the culture had changed. Some decades are better than others for men like Larry; fashions in brawn wax and wane. During certain periods, American body trends reward less muscular men. Historians have documented several such periods, including the years just after the Civil War, and the 1960s. At other times, including the early years of this century and the seventies and eighties, American men have been required to be overtly strong in order to be received as attractive and healthy.

Physical fashions for men reflect national political trends. During the Vietnam War, men's bodies took on special significance. In fact, the war was *over* bodies. Each side claimed victory less on the basis of territory taken than on "body counts." Those who opposed the war actively deployed their bodies in the service of opposition. Some were beaten up in protests in Chicago, and many more recast their bodies into symbols of defiance—wearing long hair, beards, and odd clothes that distinguished them from Marines. Suddenly, men who'd enjoyed athletics in high-school were viewed as no sexier than their comrades who'd earlier been teased for throwing a ball like a girl. Muscles didn't necessarily contribute much to an antiwar image.

After the war, the oppositional look largely disappeared. The current ideal American male body stands as a symbol of reunification. *We have the same basic values*, the post-Vietnam body proclaims, and these are manifest in the trim, strong figure we admire in our men (and, to a limited degree, in our women). *Our goals are identical*, the post-Vietnam body reassures: liberal or conservative, black or white, we just want to be secure and prosperous and in charge of our own destiny. The American body politic, once torn asunder, is mended.

"Muscles have come to *mean* something again: an obsession with the beauty of health and a growing impatience with having sand kicked in our face have combined to give back to muscles a national symbolic credibility," Charles Gaines observed in *Esquire*.

But let's return to Larry, who hasn't fared at all well during the age of brawn. Just after college he married a graphic artist, who helped him set up his ad agency until she grew bored and status-hungry and went back to school for an MBA. A few years ago, she left Larry for someone she met at the health club where she has a corporate membership.

According to Larry, it's hard to have much success on the singles scene when you're out of shape. An analysis I conducted of "personals" ads in ten newspapers and magazines from across the U.S. and from London bears him out. Words like "athletic" and "well-built" appear in a majority of the men's descriptions of themselves and women's descriptions of their desired mates.

Women who advertise in these publications are primarily upper-middle-class, well educated, and looking for men of the same stripe. Since they've broken out of traditional roles themselves to some extent, they might be expected to be more receptive to less traditionally masculine men. In fact, they often prefer to have rather macho men around, perhaps to offset their fears

that they may not be sufficiently feminine. Christine, for instance, the corporate vice-president, made it very clear she has no interest in "pale hairless guys who make great pasta," whom she calls "newts." She dates tall, well-built, handsome fellows. "I don't need to be taken care of," she said, "and I can forge my own way and make a lot of money. I'd sort of like the feminine side of me reinforced by being with a man who is more male than I am. Dealing with a man who has a real female side is unsettling."

Politically left-leaning women can also be suspicious of men with sunken chests. One woman I interviewed, who has refused to wear makeup her entire adult life on the grounds that the cosmetics industry is a capitalist plot to enslave women, said sternly about men: "The obligation to be beautiful is oppressive, the obligation to be strong is empowering. A woman who refuses to 'fix her face' is simply rejecting patriarchal oppression, but a man who refuses to build up his body isn't making any kind of statement at all, except that he's lazy."

FEAR MAKES THE BICEPS

Given their poor reception in the outside world, men who are physically weak understandably experience low self-confidence. What's surprising is that their mirror opposites—the hunks and superjocks—often suffer from the same problem.

Perhaps the single greatest force that keeps men working out is insecurity. This is evident in those who exercise chiefly because they're afraid of heart disease. But almost all avid male exercisers are engaged in a passionate battle with their own sense of vulnerability. Herein lies an important distinction between men and women. For both, the key motivation to exercise is improved self-esteem, but the genders differ on what they believe produces these benefits. When surveyed as to why they exercise, women talk about accomplishment, beauty, affiliation with others; men say they're motivated by the chance to pit themselves against nature or other men and to confront physical danger. In other words, men seek to prove to themselves and others that they can survive, that they're winners.

The harder a man exercises, the more he may be trying to overcome his feelings of inadequacy or helplessness. Most bodybuilders in a study conducted in southern California were found to have been stutterers, dyslexics, thin, fat, short, nearsighted, or otherwise unacceptable to their parents when they were children. The author of the study, sociologist Alan Klein, proposes that body-building serves as a kind of "therapeutic narcissism." Through it, those who feel deeply insecure are offered a way to devote their full attention to making themselves big, strong, and commanding of attention.

I developed a vivid appreciation for the sweat-for-salvation aspect of male fitness when I visited a place where a high concentration of America's best-developed men live—a maximum security prison. There I met a man named Nathan, who is famous in several California prisons as an advocate for strengthening and perfecting the body while in jail.

Attractive and well-groomed, Nathan wore a short-sleeved yellow Lacoste shirt along with his starched gray prison pants and gave off a scent of expensive cologne. His closely cropped beard was cut precisely to complement his square features and his short curly black hair, which had obviously been styled by a talented barber. (He had an arrangement, he explained, with an inmate who had worked in a Hollywood hair salon prior to his conviction on drug charges.) Nathan's huge arms, covered with blue tattoos of eagles and naked women, offered a strange counterpoint to his fastidious grooming.

In a small room off the main visiting area, I asked Nathan to describe the different types of men who build up their bodies in jail.

"You got the superheavyweights, over six feet and massively built," he began, over the constant hum of prisoners yelling from the cell blocks in the adjoining buildings. "Then you got the real short guys. The tall ones are usually pretty smart—they don't have a college education, but they have common sense. They don't want to be

overly aggressive, they just want to keep people away and do their time. The short ones usually are abrasive. They're looking for trouble. They've got that Napoleon complex. Then you've got the guys that want to box. They go through a very rigorous boxing discipline. They run, they practice all the boxing techniques, jump rope, hit the heavy bag."

Nathan estimated that two-thirds of the inmates at the prisons he's been in are seriously involved in exercise of some type. "When you come to jail you have a lot of time on your hands," he said at first. But as he talked on about prison life, and his own biography, a more complex picture emerged.

"When you're in the streets," he said, "you have a lot of time, but it's not structured into roll calls and meals, so it seems to go very fast. In here you're really conscious of time, and one of the pastimes that you can see some results from is lifting weights. You see people around you and you say, 'Wow, that looks nice, that guy has a nice build.' The way he carries himself, the way he walks, the way people respect him. And when you get big it gives you an artificial sense of security."

In what way is it artificial? I asked, feeling oddly comfortable after only ten or fifteen minutes with this Herculean man whom I knew to have been convicted of murder.

"It's artificial because you have to defeat the fear within your heart," he answered. "How big or small you are doesn't have anything to do with it. I had nineteen-and-a-half-inch arms at one point, but I couldn't pacify the fear in my heart, and people could see that."

His personal fear, he went on to explain, is that he'll spend his entire life in jail. He was first locked up, in a mental hospital, when he was five and a half years old. On that occasion he'd been playing with matches; he set fire to a sheet and his family's apartment went up in flames. His father, who was confined to bed for a back injury, died in the blaze. "My mother wanted to love me," he said with practiced dispassion, having relayed the story many times, "but she couldn't because she blamed me for the death of my father."

Nathan was cast out by his mother and didn't fare much better in his neighborhood. His light-brown skin and his ethnic background marked him for trouble from the time he was a young child. His father had come from the Cape Verde Islands and his mother from Brazil. In the barrio where Nathan grew up, "people had names like Carlos and José, and here I was Nathan. Kids used to think I was white because I'm so light, and there I was being acculturated into the Chicano culture, yet I couldn't identify with them physically. Everywhere I went it was understood I wasn't one of them."

Most of his formative years were spent in juvenile detention facilities. He was angry and confused, and he struck out with acts of violence ranging from schoolyard fights to armed robbery.

During one of his longer stays on the outside, at age twelve, Nathan shot heroin. He continued off and on until he hit forty, when he took up yoga and physical fitness in prison. The inmate who taught the yoga course espoused the view that drugs are poison and drug users pathetic creatures.

After his release on parole, Nathan became a community crusader against drugs, combing the streets for strung-out kids he could Pied Piper into his martial arts classes, which he conducted free at a recreation center in Watts. The more respect Nathan got in the neighborhood from his physical abilities, the more grandiose he grew, and within a few months he was preaching about "eradicating drugs from the face of the earth."

One afternoon, when an adolescent follower arrived with the news that another was in a coma from an overdose, Nathan went looking for the drug dealer who had sold him the stuff. He beat the man up badly and left him bleeding in an alley. The man died a few hours later, and Nathan was sentenced to twenty-five years to life for murder.

"Once I was back in the joint," Nathan remembered, "I borrowed some law books. I knew

I'd spend the rest of my life in the joint unless I could find a way to get around this sentence. But it was hard to concentrate because I was on an open block. You have TVs and radios on full-blast and people yelling twenty-four hours a day, seven days a week. I had to be able to pull myself inward and digest this material, to think of an approach to use at my defense."

Nathan initiated a daily regimen of physical development and purification which he still continues. He says it gave him the willpower to study the law and to argue successfully before the parole board in 1985 that his sentence should be reduced to six to twelve years.

Today, Nathan's routine goes something like this. He rises at 5:00 A.M., when the cell block is still reasonably quiet. Without making enough noise to wake anyone, he repeats twelve times each a series of special exercises that combine calisthenics and yoga. In describing these to me, he left his chair and demonstrated. Assuming a squatting position, he took a very deep breath that expanded his chest muscles to their fullest; he held this for a few seconds, then gracefully raised himself upward to a full standing position, from which he bent forward while slowly exhaling, until his palms touched the floor.

On his way back up, Nathan caught a glimpse of the concerned expression on the face of the guard outside our cubicle and sat down again. He continued his description: "As you see, I don't look anything like yogis. If you see them in a book, they look like they're malnourished, whereas my body is well-developed everywhere. Yet I can put my elbows on the ground from a standing position with my knees locked. I'm superflexible. In America you want to have a good, healthy, rich image, not malnourished. My concept is that you can maintain that look and at the same time have flexibility."

After his predawn exercises, which take an hour, Nathan eats breakfast in his cell. He refuses to eat in the mess hall he said, because the food isn't healthy. Instead, with money or cigarettes earned from advising other inmates on legal matters, he orders health foods through the prison commissary. Friends who work in the mess hall also bring him milk, fish, and vegetables a few times a week.

After lineup, he attends a class offered in the prison by a local university. At the juvenile detention facilities where Nathan grew up, schooling was provided only a few hours a day; the rest of the time Nathan hauled coal and cut grass. His formal education was poor at best, and so it's no minor accomplishment that at the time I met him, he was about to graduate from college as valedictorian of his prison class of twenty-eight.

He credited his educational achievement to his bodily discipline. "It really opened my mind and gave me a sense of direction and a focus for my energies," he said. Classes in the prison are offered in the mornings and early evenings. In between, nonstop from 1:00 until 5:00 P.M., Nathan can be found in the jailyard working out with a group of inmates who have taken up his fitness system. They run a few laps to limber up, then move into the same sorts of exercises Nathan performs alone in his cell.

Life in a hot, violent, noisy prison is hell for anyone. Still, Nathan has a busy and secure life behind bars. "This has become like a womb for me, where I can function and be successful," he let drop at one point in the interview. Each time he's been released, he's come unhinged within a few months. As an adolescent, "just having been in prison was a status symbol. When I went home they had a party and everybody said, 'There goes a sure-enough bad dude.' I felt great. Then, two days later, I had to prove myself all over, and I'd get into trouble again." As an adult who has spent so much time behind bars, he says he can't maintain routines when he's on the outside. "I overindulge. I stay out every night dancing and having sex, trying to make up for lost time. I become totally fatigued, and then I feel bad because I'm not keeping my mind and body as sharp as I know I'm supposed to. I get paranoid and confused on the street."

It may be ironic, and it's surely unfortunate, but Nathan feels more at home in jail than he does on the outside. Behind bars he can maintain some measure of self-respect and control, thanks to his fitness regimen. His exercise program has given his life order and predictability and is a source of personal pride.

CALMING THE STORM

Among the law-abiding men I interviewed who exercise obsessively for periods of weeks or months, the same basic motivations apply. They discipline themselves through fitness in order to stave off the impending chaos they confront in their daily lives.

A case in point is Roger, a forty-two-year-old Chicago lawyer. While growing up, he played softball in the neighborhood; in college he did nothing beyond a morning wakeup routine of push-ups and sit-ups; and in law school he "hardly had time to eat." Although Roger was in the top quarter of his University of Chicago Law School class, he was terrified he'd fail the bar exam, as his older brother had. He countered his fears by bingeing on exercise. "I've played racquetball exactly twenty-two times in my life, and they were all within the space of the last three weeks before my bar exam," he reported. "Racquetball made me feel better. When I couldn't study, it loosened me up. I didn't play particularly *well*, but nobody played *harder*. I broke several racquets and messed up my arm pretty badly a couple of times."

That was the first of three times in the past fifteen years that Roger has gone on and off the exercise wagon. From the day he received notification that he'd passed the bar, about the only exercise Roger got was lifting heavy law books in the back offices of a large firm—until, that is, his second exercise blitz, which began a couple of years out of law school when he found himself unable to sleep the nights before he was to do battle with another lawyer in court. He'd awaken at four in the morning, his jaws clenched and his stomach knotted. In the middle of an argument in the courtroom the next day, his mouth would go dry and he'd lose his train of thought. Once a judge asked him to approach the bench and in a peevish voice advised Roger to request that his firm send him to a public speaking course.

Instead, Roger took up running. On his way back from court, he bought an expensive pair of Etonics, and each morning thereafter he ran three or four miles around Grant Park before going to his office in the Loop. "My father had had a heart attack at a young age," he said. "With all the reports coming out at that time about the benefits of running, I decided to join in." Before long he was doing eight miles a day, then ten and twelve. Some days he didn't feel like running but would run anyway: "A mile into the run I would get that feeling of relaxation, of going on forever, a real kind of power." And he was able to sleep at night and to present a strong case in court.

By the end of his third year out of law school Roger was, in his own words, "a damned good trial attorney. Within a year, his confidence firmly in place, the running fell off to a few miles every other day, then diminished to nothing. He blames the long hours at work required to make partner.

Except for a taste of golf, which he found boring, Roger again went without exercise until a year before our interview. The event that precipitated this, his third exercise spree, was sudden rejection by a long-term girlfriend. As an antidote to the pain and vulnerability he felt, Roger hired a private exercise trainer known in Chicago executive circles to be unsparing, even sadistic, in his drive to get his clients back in shape. For ten months prior to our meeting, the trainer had greeted Roger every Monday, Wednesday, and Thursday at 6:00 P.M. upon Roger's arrival home from work, and Saturdays at 4:00 P.M. For a grueling hour he orchestrated Roger's workout in the gym they set up in the spare bedroom of Roger's Lake Shore apartment. "I never would have thought it possible that I could be in such great physical condition," Roger claimed. "I feel great and I look great."

Nevertheless, when I met him he was already showing signs that the end of this current exercise cycle was in sight. He told me of plans to

decrease the number of training sessions each week; and although he "swore off women" after his disappointment the year before, a few weeks prior to our interview he began sleeping regularly with a thirty-two-year-old physician.

Men who exercise for purposes of deliverance (like Roger and Nathan), as well as those who abstain from exercise (like Larry), differ in an important regard from men who are at neither of those extremes. Exercise is not a highly charged activity for those who pursue it in a more moderate way. They don't attach magical significance to lifting heavy objects or hitting balls.

A hallmark of a sane exercise program is that it is integrated into a person's daily life. It's just something a man does, like eating lunch or getting a haircut. He goes to the Y or health club regularly to play basketball or handball or pump a little iron with his buddies. And although his sports activities may take up a fair amount of leisure time, he foregoes them if a family or business emergency takes precedence.

At times—when he's angry with someone at work, for instance—he may play rough and injure himself, but the displacement of frustration is not what his athleticism is about. The role of athletics in his life is much more basic than that. Typically he has been involved with sports since childhood. He loves to reminisce about a particular game from his youth, or the day his dad installed a hoop on the garage at the end of the driveway when he was five or six. He has a vivid memory of his father placing the massive basketball in his arms and lifting him up so he could sink it through the basket. In the twenty or thirty or forty years since, there's never been a period when he hasn't played some kind of sport; in high-school he may even have made it onto a team. And he devotedly follows college and pro teams on TV.

Lifelong jocks are living evidence for a current view of human development called, appropriately enough, "continuity theory." It holds that our interests during adulthood are usually extensions of what we enjoyed as children. Continuity theory disputes the myth perpetrated by sports magazines and health clubs—that a devoted couch potato can, with a bit of willpower, transform himself at age forty into a championship marathon runner or ball player. Men who try athletics for the first time during adulthood seldom succeed; like Roger, they don't stick with any activity very long.

Several studies show that men who engage in exercise on a regular basis as adults also did so during their childhood or adolescence. One of the best predictors of whether a man will be athletic in midlife (and later) is whether his father participated in sports and brought him up to do so as well.

Men who've grown up athletic are the great beneficiaries of the American male role. When social scientists track down high school athletes ten or more years after graduation, they find them holding better-paying, higher-status jobs than their classmates from similar socioeconomic backgrounds. Their body image and self-esteem are greater too.

Who can say whether these positive outcomes are the result of their athleticism or are coincidental with it? Whichever it may be, other men envy these men their comfort with their masculinity and their physiques, and women wish it were as easy for them to stay pretty as it is for these men to stay handsome. How unfair, I've heard women complain, that such men need merely continue to play the games of their youth, while to maintain their beauty women must spend hours in beauty salons having perms, facials, manicures, and pedicures; must starve themselves on diets; must wear uncomfortable shoes . . . and on top of all that, exercise whether they enjoy it or not.

Although some men do fit that picture, they're a small minority. Most men, even if they've kept themselves reasonably fit, are privately insecure about their looks and more vain than others imagine them to be.

COMING TO TERMS:
MASCULINITY AND PHYSICAL DISABILITY

THOMAS J. GERSCHICK
ADAM STEPHEN MILLER

Men with physical disabilities are marginalized and stigmatized in American society. The image and reality of men with disabilities undermines cultural beliefs about men's bodies and physicality. The body is a central foundation of how men define themselves and how they are defined by others. Bodies are vehicles for determining value, which in turn translates into status and prestige. Men's bodies allow them to demonstrate the socially valuable characteristics of toughness, competitiveness, and ability (Messner 1992). Thus, one's body and relationship to it provide a way to apprehend the world and one's place in it. The bodies of men with disabilities serve as a continual reminder that they are at odds with the expectations of the dominant culture. As anthropologist Robert Murphy (1990: 94) writes of his own experiences with disability:

> *Paralytic disability constitutes emasculation of a more direct and total nature. For the male, the weakening and atrophy of the body threaten all the cultural values of masculinity: strength, activeness, speed, virility, stamina, and fortitude.*

This article seeks to sharpen our understanding of the creation, maintenance, and recreation of gender identities by men who, by birth, accident, or illness, find themselves dealing with a physical disability. We examine two sets of social dynamics that converge and clash in the lives of men with physical disabilities. On the one side, these men must deal with the presence and pressures of hegemonic masculinity, which demands strength. on the other side, societal members perceive people with disabilities to be weak.

For the present study, we conducted in-depth interviews with ten men with physical disabilities in order to gain insights into the psychosocial aspects of men's ability to come to terms with their physical and social condition. We wanted to know how men with physical disabilities respond to the demands of hegemonic masculinity and their marginalization. For instance, if men with disabilities need others to legitimate their gender identity during encounters, what happens when others deny them the opportunity? How do they reconcile the conflicting expectations associated with masculinity and disability? How do they define masculinity for themselves, and what are the sources of these definitions? To what degree do their responses contest and/or perpetuate the current gender order? That is,

Reprinted from *Masculinities*, 2(1) 1994.

We would like to thank our informants for sharing their time, experiences, and insights. Additionally, we would like to thank the following people for their comments on earlier drafts of this work: Sandra Cole, Harlan Hahn, Michael Kimmel, Michael Messner, Don Sabo, and Margaret Weigers. We, of course, remain responsible for its content. Finally, we are indebted to Kimberly Browne and Erika Gottfried for background research and interview transcriptions. This research was supported by a grant from the Undergraduate Research Opportunity Program at the University of Michigan.

what are the political implications of different gender identities and practices? In addressing these questions, we contribute to the growing body of literature on marginalized and alternative gender identities.

We will first discuss the general relationship between physical disability and hegemonic masculinity. Second, we will summarize the methods used in this study. Next, we will present and discuss our central findings. Finally, we discuss how the gender identities and life practices of men with disabilities contribute to the politics of the gender order.

HEGEMONLC MASCULINITY AND PHYSICAL DISABILITY

Recently, the literature has shifted toward understanding gender as an interactive process. Thus, it is presumed to be not only an aspect of what one *is*, but more fundamentally it is something that one *does* in interaction with others (West and Zimmerman 1987). Whereas previously, gender was thought to be strictly an individual phenomenon, this new understanding directs our attention to the interpersonal and institutional levels as well. The lives of men with disabilities provide an instructive arena in which to study the interactional nature of gender and its effect on individual gender identities.

In *The Body Silent*, Murphy (1990) observes that men with physical disabilities experience "embattled identities" because of the conflicting expectations placed on them as men and as people with disabilities. On the one side, contemporary masculinity privileges men who are strong, courageous, aggressive, independent and self-reliant (Connell 1987). On the other side, people with disabilities are perceived to be, and treated as, weak, pitiful, passive, and dependent (Murphy 1990). Thus, for men with physical disabilities, masculine gender identity and practice are created and maintained at the crossroads of the demands of contemporary masculinity and the stigmatization associated with disability. As such, for men with physical disabilities, being

recognized as masculine by others is especially difficult, if not impossible, to accomplish. Yet not being recognized as masculine is untenable because, in our culture, everyone is expected to display an appropriate gender identity (West and Zimmerman 1987).

METHODS

This research was based on in-depth interviews with ten men. Despite the acknowledged problem of identity management in interviews, we used this method because we were most interested in the subjective perceptions and experiences of our informants. To mitigate this dynamic, we relied on probing questions and reinterviews. Informants were located through a snowball sample, utilizing friends and connections within the community of people with disabilities. All of our informants were given pseudonyms, and we further protected their identity by deleting nonessential personal detail. The age range of respondents varied from sixteen to seventy-two. Eight of our respondents were white, and two were African American. Geographically, they came from both coasts and the Midwest. All were "mobility impaired," and most were para- or quadriplegics. Given the small sample size and the modicum of diversity within it, this work must necessarily be understood as exploratory.

We interviewed men with physical disabilities for three primary reasons. First, given the diversity of disabilities and our modest resources, we had to bound the sample. Second, mobility impairments tend to be more apparent than other disabilities, such as blindness or hearing loss, and people respond to these men using visual clues. Third, although the literature in this area is scant, much of it focuses on men with physical disabilities.

Due to issues of shared identities, Adam did all the interviews. Interviews were semi-structured and tape-recorded. Initial interviews averaged approximately an hour in length. Additionally, we contacted all of our informants at least once with clarifying questions and, in some cases, to test ideas that we had. These follow-ups lasted approximately thirty minutes. Each informant received a copy of his interview transcript to ensure that we had captured his perspective accurately. We also shared draft copies of this chapter with them and incorporated their insights into the current version.

There were two primary reasons for the thorough follow-up. First, from a methodological standpoint, it was important for us to capture the experience of our informants as fully as possible. Second, we felt that we had an obligation to allow them to control, to a large extent, the representation of their experience.

Interviews were analyzed using an analytic induction approach (Denzin 1989; Emerson 1988; Katz 1988). In determining major and minor patterns of masculine practice, we used the responses to a series of questions including, What is the most important aspect of masculinity to you? What would you say makes you feel most manly or masculine? Do you think your conception of masculinity is different from that of able-bodied men as a result of your disability? If so, how and why? If not, why not? Additionally, we presented our informants with a list of characteristics associated with prevailing masculinity based on the work of R. W. Connell (1987, 1990a, 1990b, 1991) and asked them to rate their importance to their conception of self. Both positive and negative responses to this portion of our questionnaire guided our insight into how each man viewed his masculinity. To further support our discussion, we turned to the limited academic literature in this area. Much more helpful were the wide range of biographical and autobiographical accounts of men who have physical disabilities (see, for instance, Murphy 1990; Callahan 1989; Kriegel 1991; Hahn 1989; and Zola 1982).

Finally, in analyzing the data we were sensitive to making judgments about our informants when grouping them into categories. People with disabilities are shoehorned into categories too much as it is. We sought to discover what was common among their responses and to highlight what we perceived to be the essence of their views. In doing so, we endeavored to provide a conceptual framework for understanding the responses of men with physical disabilities while trying to be sensitive to their personal struggles.

DISABILITY, MASCULINITY, AND COMING TO TERMS

While no two men constructed their sense of masculinity in exactly the same way, there appeared to be three dominant frameworks our informants used to cope with their situations. These patterns can be conceived of in relation to the standards inherent in dominant masculinity. We call them the three Rs: *reformulation*, which entailed men's redefinition of hegemonic characteristics on their own terms; *reliance*, reflected by sensitive or hypersensitive adoptions of particular predominant attributes; and *rejection*, characterized by the renunciation of these standards and either the creation of one's own principles and practices or the denial of masculinity's importance in one's life. However, one should note that none of our interviewees *entirely* followed any one of these frameworks in defining his sense of self. Rather, for heuristic reasons, it is best to speak of the major and minor ways each man used these three patterns. For example, some of our informants relied on dominant standards in their view of sexuality and occupation but also reformulated the prevailing ideal of independence.

Therefore, we discuss the *primary* way in which these men with disabilities related to hegemonic masculinity's standards, while recognizing that their coping mechanisms reflected a more complex combination of strategies. In doing so, we avoid "labeling" men and assigning them to arbitrary categories.

Reformulation

Some of our informants responded to idealized masculinity by reformulating it, shaping it along the lines of their own abilities, perceptions, and strengths, and defining their manhood along these new lines. These men tended not to contest these standards overtly, but—either consciously or unconsciously—they recognized in their own condition an inability to meet these ideals as they were culturally conceived.

An example of this came from Damon, a seventy-two-year-old quadriplegic who survived a spinal-cord injury in an automobile accident ten years ago. Damon said he always desired, and had, control of his life. While Damon required round-the-clock personal care assistants (PCAs), he asserted that he was still a very independent person:

> *I direct all of my activities around my home where people have to help me to maintain my apartment, my transportation, which I own, and direction in where I go. I direct people how to get there, and I tell them what my needs will be when I am going and coming, and when to get where I am going.*

Damon said that his sense of control was more than mere illusion; it was a reality others knew of as well. This reputation seemed important to him:

> *People know from Jump Street that I have my own thing, and I direct my own thing. And if they can't comply with my desire, they won't be around. . . . I don't see any reason why people with me can't take instructions and get my life on just as I was having it before, only thing I'm not doing it myself. I direct somebody else to do it. So, therefore, I don't miss out on very much.*

Hegemonic masculinity's definition of independence privileges self-reliance and autonomy. Damon required substantial assistance: indeed, some might term him "dependent." However, Damon's reformulation of the independence ideal, accomplished in part through a cognitive shift, allowed him to think otherwise.

Harold, a forty-six-year-old polio survivor, described a belief and practice akin to Damon's. Also a quadriplegic, Harold similarly required PCAs to help him handle daily necessities: Harold termed his reliance on and control of PCAs "acting through others":

> *When I say independence can be achieved by acting through other people, I actually mean getting through life, liberty, and the pursuit of happiness while utilizing high-quality and dependable attendant-care services.*

As with Damon, Harold achieved his perceived sense of independence by controlling others. Harold stressed that he did not count on family or friends to do favors for him, but *employed* his PCAs in a "business relationship" he controlled. Alternatives to family and friends are used whenever possible because most people with disabilities do not want to burden or be dependent on their families any more than necessary (Murphy 1990).

Social class plays an important role here. Damon and Harold had the economic means to afford round-the-clock assistance. While none of our informants experienced economic hardship, many people with disabilities depend on the welfare system for their care, and the amount and quality of assistance they receive make it much more difficult to conceive of themselves as independent.

A third man who reformulated predominant demands was Brent, a forty-five-year-old administrator. He told us that his paraplegic status, one that he had lived with since he was five years old, had often cast him as an "outsider" to society. This status was particularly painful in his late adolescence, a time when the "sexual revolution" was sweeping America's youth:

> *A very important measure of somebody's personhood—manhood—was their sexual ability. . . . What bothers me more than anything else is the stereotypes, and even more so, in terms of sexual desirability. Because I had a disability, I was less desirable than able-bodied people. And that I found very frustrating.*

His experiences led him to recast the hegemonic notion that man's relations with a partner should be predominantly physical. As a result, he stressed the importance of emotional relations and trust. This appeared to be key to Brent's definition of his manhood:

For me, that is my measure of who I am as an individual and who I am as a man—my ability to be able to be honest with my wife. Be able to be close with her, to be able to ask for help, provide help. To have a commitment, to follow through, and to do all those things that I think are important.

As Connell (1990a) notes, this requires a capacity to not only be expressive, but also to have feelings worth expressing. This clearly demonstrates a different form of masculine practice.

The final case of reformulation came from Robert, a thirty-year-old survivor of a motorcycle accident. Able-bodied for much of his life, Robert's accident occurred when he was twenty-four, leaving him paraplegic. Through five years of intensive physical therapy, he regained 95 percent of his original function, though certain effects linger to this day.

Before his accident, Robert had internalized many of the standards of dominant masculinity exemplified by frequenting bars, leading an active sex life, and riding a motorcycle. But, if our research and the body of autobiographical works from men with physical disabilities has shown anything, it is that coming to terms with a disability eventually changes a man. It appeared to have transformed Robert. He remarked that, despite being generally "recovered," he had maintained his disability-influenced value system:

I judge people on more of a personal and character level than I do on any physical, or I guess I did; but, you know, important things are guys that have integrity, guys that are honest about what they are doing, that have some direction in their life and know . . . peace of mind and what they stand for.

One of the areas that Robert said took the longest to recover was his sexuality—specifically, his confidence in his sexual ability. While Robert said sexual relations were still important to him, like Brent he reformulated his previous, largely hegemonic notion of male sexuality into a more emotionally and physically egalitarian model:

I've found a whole different side to having sex with a partner and looking at satisfying the partner rather than satisfying myself; and that has taken the focus off of satisfying myself, being the big manly stud, and concentrating more on my partner. And that has become just as satisfying.

However, reformulation did not yield complete severance from prevailing masculinity's standards as they were culturally conceived. For instance, despite his reformulative inclinations, Robert's self-described "macho" attitude continued in some realms during his recovery. He, and all others we interviewed, represented the complexity of gender identities and practices; no man's masculinity fell neatly into any one of the three patterns.

For instance, although told by most doctors that his physical condition was probably permanent, Robert's resolve was unyielding. "I put my blinders on to all negative insight into it and just totally focused on getting better," he said. "And I think that was, you know, a major factor on why I'm where I'm at today." This typified the second pattern we identified—reliance on hegemonic masculinity's standards. It was ironic, then, that Robert's tenacity, his never-ending work ethic, and his focused drive to succeed were largely responsible for his almost-complete recovery. While Robert reformulated much of his earlier sense of masculinity, he still relied on this drive.

Perhaps the area in which men who reformulate most closely paralleled dominant masculinity was the emphasis they placed on their occupation. Our sample was atypical in that most of our informants were professionally employed on a full-time basis and could, therefore, draw on class-based resources, whereas unemployment among people with disabilities is very high. Just as societal members privilege men who are accomplished in their occupation, Harold said he finds both "purpose," and success, in his career:

No one is going to go through life without some kind of purpose. Everyone decides. I wanted to be a writer. So I became a writer and an observer, a trained observer.

Brent said that he drew much of his sense of self, his sense of self-esteem, and his sense of manhood from his occupational accomplishments. Initially, Brent denied the importance of the prevailing ideal that a man's occupational worth was derived from his breadwinner status:

> It is not so important to be the breadwinner as it is to be competent in the world. You know, to have a career, to have my name on the door. That is what is most important. It is that recognition that is very important to me.

However, he later admitted that being the breadwinner still was important to him, although he denied a link between his desires and the "stereotypical" conception of breadwinner status. He maintained that "it's still important to me, because I've always been able to make money." Independence, both economic and physical, were important to all of our informants.

Rejection of hegemonic ideals also occurred among men who primarily depended on a reformulative framework. Harold's view of relationships with a partner dismissed the sexually powerful ideal: "The fact of the matter is that I'm not all that upset by the fact that I'm disabled and I'm a male. I mean, I know what I can do." We will have more to say about the rejection of dominant conceptions of sexuality later.

In brief summary, the subset of our informants whose primary coping pattern involved reformulation of dominant standards recognized their inability to meet these ideals as they are culturally conceived. Confident in their own abilities and values, and drawing from previous experience, they confronted standards of masculinity on their own terms. In doing so, they distanced themselves from masculine ideals.

Reliance

However, not all of the men with physical disabilities we interviewed depended on a reformulative approach. We found that many of our informants *were* concerned with others' views of their masculinity and with meeting the demands of hegemonic masculinity. They primarily used the second pattern, reliance, which involves the internalization of many more of the ideals of predominant masculinity, including physical strength, athleticism, independence, and sexual prowess. Just as some men depended on reformulation for much of their masculine definition, others, despite their inability to meet many of these ideals, relied on them heavily. As such, these men did not seem to be as comfortable with their sense of manhood; indeed, their inability to meet society's standards bothered them very much.

This subset of our informants found themselves in a double bind that left them conflicted. They embraced dominant conceptions of masculinity as a way to gain acceptance from themselves and from others. Yet, they were continuously reminded in their interactions with others that they were "incomplete." As a result, the identity behind the facade suffered; there were, then, major costs associated with this strategy.

The tension between societal expectations and the reality of men with physical disabilities was most clearly demonstrated by Jerry, a sixteen-year-old who had juvenile rheumatoid arthritis. While Jerry was physically able to walk for limited distances, this required great effort on his part; consequently, he usually used a wheelchair. He was concerned with the appearance of his awkward walking. "I feel like I look a little, I don't know, more strange when I walk," he said.

The significance of appearance and external perception of manliness is symptomatic of the difficulty men with physical disabilities have in developing an identity and masculinity free of others' perceptions and expectations. Jerry said:

> I think [others' conception of what defines a man] is very important, because if they don't think of you as one, it is hard to think of yourself as one; or, it doesn't really matter if you think of yourself as one if no one else does.

Jerry said that, particularly among his peers, he was not perceived as attractive as the able-bodied teenagers; thus, he had difficulty in male-female relations beyond landing an occasional date. "[The girls believe] I might be a 'really nice person,' but not like a guy per se," he said. "I think to some extent that you're sort of gender-less to them." This clearly represents the emasculation and depersonalization inherent in social definitions of disability.

However, Jerry said that he faced a more persistent threat to his autonomy—his independence and his sense of control—from others being "uncomfortable" around him and persisting in offering him assistance he often did not need. This made him "angry, though he usually did not refuse the help out of politeness. Thus, with members of his social group, he participated in a "bargain": they would socialize with him as long as he remained in a dependent position where they could "help" him.

This forced, situational passivity led Jerry to emphasize his autonomy in other areas. For instance, Jerry avoided asking for help in nearly all situations. This was directly tied to reinforcing his embattled manhood by displaying outward strength and independence:

If I ever have to ask someone for help, it really makes me like feel like less of a man. I don't like asking for help at all. You know, like even if I could use some, I'll usually not ask just because I can't, I just hate asking. . . . [A man is] fairly self-sufficient in that you can sort of handle just about any situation, in that you can help other people, and that you don't need a lot of help.

Jerry internalized the prevailing masculine ideal that a man should be independent; he relied on that ideal for his definition of manhood. His inability to meet this ideal—partly through his physical condition, and partly from how others treated him—threatened his identity and his sense of manhood, which had to be reinforced even at the expense of self-alienation.

One should not label Jerry a "relier" simply because of these struggles. Being only sixteen years of age—and the youngest participant in our study—Jerry was still developing his sense of masculinity; and, as with many teenagers both able-bodied and disabled, he was trying to fit into his peer group. Furthermore, Jerry will continue to mature and develop his self-image and sense of masculinity. A follow-up interview in five years might show a degree of resolution to his struggles.

Such a resolution could be seen in Michael, a thirty-three-year-old manager we interviewed, who also internalized many of the standards of hegemonic masculinity. A paraplegic from an auto accident in 1977, Michael struggled for many years after his accident to come to terms with his condition.

His struggles had several sources, all tied into his view of masculinity's importance. The first was that, before his accident, he accepted much of the dominant conception of masculinity. A high-school student, farm hand, and football and track star at the time, Michael said that independence, relations with the women he dated, and physical strength were central to .his conception of self.

After his accident, Michael's doctors told him there was a 50-50 chance that he would regain the ability to walk, and he clung to the hope. "I guess I didn't understand it, and had hope that I would walk again," he said. However, he was "depressed" about his situation, "but not so much about my disability, I guess. Because that wasn't real yet."

But coming home three months after his accident didn't alleviate the depression. Instead, it heightened his anxiety and added a new component—vulnerability. In a span of three months, Michael had, in essence, his sense of masculinity and his security in himself completely stripped away. He was in an unfamiliar situation; and far from feeling strong, independent, and powerful, he felt vulnerable and afraid: "No one," he remarked, "can be prepared for a permanent disability."

His reliance on dominant masculinity, then, started with his predisability past and continued during his recovery as a coping mechanism to deal with his fears. The hegemonic standard Michael strove most to achieve was that of independence. It was central to his sense of masculinity before and at the time of our interview. Indeed, it was so important that it frustrated him greatly when he needed assistance. Much like Jerry, he refused to ask for it:

> *I feel that I should be able to do everything for my-self and I don't like it. . . . I don't mind asking for things that I absolutely can't do, like hanging pictures, or moving furniture, or having my oil changed in my car; but there are things that I'm capable of doing in my chair, like jumping up one step. That I feel like I should be able to do, and I find it frustrating when I can't do that sometimes. . . . I don't like asking for [help I don't think I need]. It kind of makes me mad.*

When asked if needing assistance was "un-manly," Michael replied, "There's probably some of that in there." For both Michael and Jerry, the independence ideal often led to risk-taking behavior in order to prove to themselves that they were more than their social definition.

Yet, much like Robert, Michael had reformulated his view of sexuality. He said that his physical sexuality made him "feel the most masculine"—apparently another reliant response with a stereotypical emphasis on sexual performance. However, it was more complicated. Michael said that he no longer concentrated on pleasing himself, as he did when able-bodied, but that he now had a more partner-oriented view of sexuality. "I think that my compensation for my feeling of vulnerability is I've overcompensated by trying to please my partner and leave little room to allow my partner to please me. . . . Some of my greatest pleasure is exhausting my partner while having sex." Ironically, while he focused more on his partner's pleasure than ever before, he did so at his own expense; a sense of balancing the needs of both partners was missing.

Thus, sex served multiple purposes for Michael—it gave him and his partner pleasure; it reassured his fears and his feelings of vulnerability; and it reconfirmed his masculinity. His sexuality, then, reflected both reliance and reformulation.

While independence and sexuality were both extremely important to Scott, a thirty-four-year-

old rehabilitation engineer, he emphasized a third area for his sense of manhood—athletics. Scott served in the Peace Corps during his twenties, working in Central America. He described his life-style as "rigorous" and "into the whole sports thing," and used a mountain bike as his primary means of transportation and recreation. He was also an avid hockey player in his youth and spent his summers in softball leagues.

Scott acquired a polio-like virus when he was twenty-five years old that left him permanently paraplegic, a situation that he did not initially accept. In an aggressive attempt to regain his physical ability, and similar to Robert, Scott obsessively attacked his rehabilitation

> *. . . thinking, that's always what I've done with all the sports. If I wasn't good enough, I worked a little harder and I got better. So, I kept thinking my walking isn't very good now. If I push it, it will get better.*

But Scott's athletic drive led not to miraculous recovery, but overexertion. When ordered by his doctors to scale back his efforts, he realized he could not recover strictly through tenacity. At the time of our interview, he was ambivalent about his limitations. He clearly did not feel like a failure: "I think that if I wouldn't have made the effort, I always would have wondered, could I have made a difference?" Following the athlete's code of conduct, "always give 110 percent," Scott attacked his recovery. But when his efforts were not enough—when he did not "emerge victorious"—he accepted it as an athlete would. Yet, his limitations also frustrated him at times, and in different areas.

For example, though his physical capacity was not what it was, Scott maintained a need for athletic competition. He played wheelchair basketball and was the only wheelchair-participant in a city softball league. However, he did not return to hockey, the sport he loved as a youngster; in fact, he refused to even try the sled-based equivalent.

Here was Scott's frustration. His spirit of athleticism was still alive, but he lamented the fact that he could not compete exactly as before:

[I miss] the things that I had. I played hockey; that was my primary sport for so many years. Pretty much, I did all the sports. But, like, I never played basketball; never liked basketball before. Which is why I think I can play now. See, it would be like the equivalent to wheelchair hockey. Some friends of mine have talked to me about it, [but] I'm not really interested in that. Because it wouldn't be real hockey. And it would make me feel worse, rather that better.

In this respect, Scott had not completely come to terms with his limitations. He still wanted to be a "real" athlete, competing in the same sports, in the same ways, with the same rules, with others who shared his desire for competition. Wheelchair hockey, which he derogatorily referred to as "gimp hockey," represented the antithesis of this for him.

Scott's other responses added to this emphasis. What he most disliked about having a disability was "that I can't do the things that I want to be able to do," meaning he could not ride his bike or motorcycle, he could not play "real" hockey, and he was unable to live a freewheeling, spontaneous life-style. Rather, he had to plan ahead of time where he went and how he got there. The frustration caused by having to plan nearly every move was apparent in almost all of our interviews.

However, on the subject of independence, Scott said "I think I'm mostly independent," but complained that there were some situations where he could not meet his expectations and had to depend on his wife. Usually this was not a "major issue," but "there's still times when, yeah, I feel bad about it; or, you know it's the days where she doesn't feel like it, but she kind of has to. That's what bothers me the most, I guess." Thus, he reflected the general desire among men with disabilities not to be a burden of any kind on family members.

Much of the time, Scott accepted being "mostly independent." His reliance on the ideals of athleticism and independence played a significant part in his conception of masculinity and self. However, Scott learned, though to a limited

degree, to let go of some of his previous ideals and to accept a different, reformulated notion of independence and competition. Yet, he could not entirely do so. His emphasis on athletics and independence was still strong, and there were many times when athletics and acceptance conflicted.

However, one should stop short of a blanket assessment of men with disabilities who rely on hegemonic masculinity standards. "Always" is a dangerous word, and stating that "men who rely on hegemonic standards are *always* troubled" is a dangerous assumption. An apparent exceptional case among men who follow a reliant pattern came from Aaron, a forty-one-year-old paraplegic. Rather than experiencing inner turmoil and conflict, Aaron was one of the most upbeat individuals we interviewed. Aaron said that, before his 1976 accident, he was "on top of the world," with a successful business, a commitment to athletics that included basketball shoot-arounds with NBA prospects, and a wedding engagement. Indeed, from the time of his youth, Aaron relied on such hegemonic standards as sexuality, independence, athleticism, and occupational accomplishment.

For example, when asked what masculinity meant to him before his accident, Aaron said that it originally meant sexual conquest. As a teen, he viewed frequent sexual activity as a "rite of passage" into manhood.

Aaron said he had also enjoyed occupational success, and that this success was central to his definition of self, including being masculine. Working a variety of jobs ranging from assembly-line worker to white-collar professional, Aaron said, "I had been very fortunate to have good jobs, which were an important part of who I was and how I defined myself."

According to Aaron, much of his independence ideal came from his father. When his parents divorced, Aaron's father explained to him that, though he was only five, he would have to be "the man of the house." Aaron took this lesson to heart, and strived to fulfill this role both in terms of independence and providing for the family. "My image of manhood was that of a provider," he said, "one who was able to make a contribution to the financial stability of the family in addition to dealing with the problems and concerns that would come up."

His accident, a gunshot wound injuring his spinal cord, left him completely dependent. Predictably, Aaron could not immediately cope with this. "My whole self-image itself was real integrally tied up with the things I used to do," he said. "I found my desire for simple pleasures to be the greatest part of the pain I had to bear."

His pain increased when he left the hospital. His fiancee had left him, and within two years he lost "everything that was important to me"— his house, his business, his savings, most of his friends, and even, for a while, his hope.

However, much as with Robert, Aaron's resiliency eventually turned his life around. Just as he hit bottom, he began telling himself that "if you hold on long enough, if you don't quit, you'll get through it." Additionally, he attacked his therapy with the vengeance he had always devoted to athletics. "I'd never been confronted with a situation in my entire life before that I was not able to overcome by the efforts of my own merit," he said. "I took the same attitude toward this."

Further, he reasserted his sexuality. Though he then wore a colostomy bag, he resumed frequent sexual intercourse, taking the attitude that "this is who I was, and a woman was either going to have to accept me as I was, or she's got to leave me f—— alone."

However, he realized after those five years that his hard work would not be rewarded nor would he be miraculously healed. Figuring that "there's a whole lot of life that I need to live, and this wasn't the most efficient way to live it," he bought a new sport wheelchair, found a job, and became involved in wheelchair athletics. In this sense, a complex combination of all three patterns emerged in Aaron as reliance was mixed with reformulation and rejection.

Furthermore, his soul-searching led him to develop a sense of purpose in his life, and a reason for going on:

[During my recovery] I felt that I was left here to enrich the lives of as many people as I could before I left this earth, and it gave me a new purpose, a new vision, a new mission, new dreams.

Tenacity, the quest for independence, athletics, and sexual activity carried Aaron through his recovery. Many of these ideals, which had their source in his father's teachings, remained with him as he continued to be active in athletics (everything from basketball to softball to scuba diving), to assert his sexuality, and to aim for complete autonomy. To Aaron, independence, both physical and financial, was more than just a personal ideal; it was one that should be shared by all people with disabilities. As such, he aspired to be a role model for others:

The work that I am involved in is to help people gain control over their lives, and I think it's vitally important that I walk my talk. If . . . we hold ourselves out to be an organization that helps people gain control over their lives, I think it's vitally important for me as the CEO of that organization to live my life in a way that embodies everything that we say we're about.

Clearly, Aaron was not the same man he was before his disability. He said that his maturity and his experience with disability "made me stronger," and that manhood no longer simply meant independence and sexual conquest. Manhood also meant

. . . being responsible for one's actions; being considerate of another's feelings; being sensitive to individuals who are more vulnerable than yourself, to what their needs would be; standing up on behalf and fighting for those who cannot speak out for themselves, fight for themselves. It means being willing to take a position and be committed to a position, even when it's inconvenient or costly to take that point of view, and you do it only because of the principle involved.

This dovetailed significantly with his occupation, which was of great importance to him. But as alluded to above, Aaron's emphasis on occupation cannot be seen as mere reliance on the hegemonic conception of occupational achievement. It was more a reformulation of that ideal from self-achievement to facilitating the empowerment of others.

Nevertheless, Aaron's struggle to gain his current status, like the struggle of others who rely on hegemonic masculinity's standards, was immense. Constructing hegemonic masculinity from a subordinated position is almost always a Sisyphean task. One's ability to do so is undermined continuously by physical, social, and cultural weakness. "Understandably, in an effort to cope with this stress (balancing the demands for strength and the societal perception of weakness)," writes political scientist Harlan Hahn, "many disabled men have tended to identify personally and politically with the supposed strength of prevalent concepts of masculinity rather than with their disability" (1989: 3). To relinquish masculinity under these circumstances is to court gender annihilation, which is untenable to some men. Consequently, relying on hegemonic masculinity becomes more understandable (Connell 1990a: 471).

Rejection

Despite the difficulties it presents, hegemony, including that related to gender, is never complete (Janeway 1980, Scott 1985). For some of our informants, resistance took the form of creating alternative masculine identities and subcultures that provided them with a supportive environment. These men were reflected in the final pattern: rejection. Informants who followed this pattern did not so much share a common ideology or set of practices; rather, they believed that the dominant conception of masculinity was wrong, either in its individual emphases or as a practice. One of these men developed new standards of masculinity in place of the ones he had rejected. Another seemingly chose to deny masculinity's importance, although he was neither effeminate or androgynous. Instead, they both emphasized their status as "persons," under the motto of "people first." This philosophy reflected a key tenet of the Disability Rights Movement.

Alex, a twenty-three-year-old, first-year law student, survived an accident that left him an incomplete quadriplegic when he was fourteen. Before that time, he felt he was an outsider at his private school because he eschewed the superficial, athletically oriented, and materialistic atmosphere. Further, he said the timing of the accident, when many of his peers were defining their social roles, added to this outsider perspective, in that it made him unable to participate in the highly social, role-forming process. "I didn't learn about the traditional roles of sexuality, and whatever the rules are for such behavior in our society, until later," he said. "Because of my physical characteristics, I had to learn a different set of rules."

Alex described himself as a "nonconformist." This simple moniker seemed central to his conception of selfhood and masculinity. Alex, unlike men who primarily reformulate these tenets, rejected the attitudinal and behavioral prescriptions of hegemonic masculinity. He maintained that his standards were his own—not society's—and he scoffed at commonly held views of masculinity.

For example, Alex blamed the media for the idea that men must be strong and attractive, stating "The traditional conception is that everyone has to be Arnold Schwartzenegger . . . [which] probably lead[s] to some violence, unhappiness, and things like that if they [men] don't meet the standards."

As for the importance of virility and sexual prowess, Alex said "There is a part of me that, you know, has been conditioned and acculturated and knows those [dominant] values"; but he sarcastically laughed at the notion of a man's sexual prowess being reflected in "making her pass out," and summed up his feelings on the subject by adding, "You have to be willing to do things in a nontraditional way."

Alex's most profound rejection of a dominant ideal involved the importance of fathering, in its strictest sense of the man as impregnator:

There's no reason why we (his fiancee and himself) couldn't use artificial insemination or adoption.

Parenting doesn't necessarily involve being the male sire. It involves being a good parent. . . . Parenting doesn't mean that it's your physical child. It involves responsibility and an emotional role as well. I don't think the link between parenthood is the primary link with sexuality. Maybe in terms of evolutionary purposes, but not in terms of a relationship.

Thus, Alex rejected the procreation imperative encouraged in hegemonic masculinity. However, while Alex took pride at overtly rejecting prevailing masculinity as superficial and silly, even he relied on it at times. Alex said he needed to support himself financially and would not ever want to be an emotional or economic "burden" in a relationship. On one level, this is a common concern for most people, disabled or not. But on another level, Alex admitted that it tied in to his sense of masculinity:

If I was in a relationship and I wasn't working, and my spouse was, what could be the possible reasons for my not working? I could have just been fired. I could be laid off. Who knows what happened? I guess . . . that's definitely an element of masculinity, and I guess I am just as influenced by that as, oh, as I guess as other people, or as within my definition of masculinity. What do you know? I have been caught.

A different form of rejection was reflected in Leo, a fifty-eight-year-old polio survivor. Leo, who had striven for occupational achievement since his youth, seemed to value many hegemonic traits: independence, money-making ability, and recognition by peers. But he steadfastly denied masculinity's role in shaping his outlook.

Leo said the most important trait to him was his mental capacity and intelligence, since that allowed him to achieve his occupational goals. Yet he claimed this was not related to the prevailing standard. Rather, it tied into his ambitions from before his disability and his willingness to do most anything to achieve his goals.

Before we label him "a rejector," however, note that Leo was a believer in adaptive technology and personal assistance, and he did not see a

contradiction between using personal-care assistants and being independent. This seemed to be a reformulation, just as with Damon and Harold, but when we asked Leo about this relation to masculinity, he flatly denied any connection.

Leo explained his renunciation of masculinity by saying "It doesn't mean a great deal . . . it's not how I think [of things]." He said that many of the qualities on our list of hegemonic characteristics were important to him on an individual level but did not matter to his sense of manhood. Leo maintained that there were "external" and "internal" reasons for this.

The external factors Leo identified were the Women's and Disability Rights Movements. Both provided support and alternatives that allow a person with a disability the freedom to be a person, and not (to use Leo's words) a "strange bird." Indeed, Leo echoed the call of the Disability Rights Movement when he described himself as a "person first." In this way, his humanity took precedence and his gender and his disability became less significant.

Also, Leo identified his background as a contributing factor to his outlook. Since childhood, he held a group of friends that valued intellectual achievement over physical performance. In his youth, Leo said he was a member of a group "on the college route." He remained in academia.

Internally, his view of masculinity came from maturity. He had dealt with masculinity and related issues for almost sixty years and reached a point at which he was comfortable with his gender. According to him, his gender conceptions ranged across all three patterns. This was particularly evident in his sexuality. When younger, he relied on a culturally valued, genital sexuality and was concerned with his potency. He wanted to "be on top," despite the physical difficulties this presented him. At the time of our interview, he had a reformulated sexuality. The Women's Movement allowed him to remain sexually active without worrying about "being on top." He even rejected the idea (but not necessarily the physical condition) of potency, noting that it was "even a funny word—potent—that's power."

Further, his age allowed Leo to let go of many of the expectations he had for himself when younger. For instance, he used to overcompensate with great physical activity to prove his manhood and to be "a good daddy." But, he said, he gradually learned that such overcompensation was not necessary.

The practice of "letting go," as Leo and many of our other informants had done, was much like that described by essayist Leonard Kriegel (1991) who, in a series of autobiographical essays, discussed the metaphor of "falling into life" as a way of coping with a disability and masculinity. Kriegel described a common reaction to coping with disability; that is, attempting to "overcome" the results of polio, in his case, by building his upper-body strength through endless hours of exercise. In the end, he experienced premature arthritis in his shoulders and arms. The metaphor of giving up or letting go of behavioral expectations and gender practices as a way to gain greater strength and control over one's life was prevalent among the men who primarily rejected dominant masculinity. As Hahn notes, this requires a cognitive shift and a change in reference group as well as a source of social support:

> I think, ironically, that men with disabilities can acquire strength by acknowledging weakness. Instead of attempting to construct a fragile and ultimately phony identity only as males, they might have more to gain, and little to lose, both individually and collectively by forging a self-concept about the concept of disability. Certainly this approach requires the exposure of a vulnerability that has been a primary reason for the elaborate defense mechanisms that disabled men have commonly employed to protect themselves (1989:3).

Thus, men with disabilities who rejected or renounced masculinity did so as a process of deviance disavowal. They realized that it was societal conceptions of masculinity, rather than themselves, that were problematic. In doing so, they were able to create alternative gender practices.

SUMMARY AND CONCLUSION

The experiences of men with physical disabilities are important, because they illuminate both the insidious power and limitations of contemporary masculinity. These men have insider knowledge of what the subordinated know about both the gender and social order (Janeway 1980). Additionally, the gender practices of some of these men exemplify alternative visions of masculinity that are obscured but available to men in our culture. Finally, they allow us to elucidate a process of paramount importance: How men with physical disabilities find happiness, fulfillment, and a sense of self-worth in a culture that has, in essence, denied them the right to their own identity, including their own masculinity.

Based on our interviews, then, we believe that men with physical disabilities depend on at least three patterns in their adjustment to the double bind associated with the demands of hegemonic masculinity and the stigmatization of being disabled. While each of our informants used one pattern more than the others, none of them depended entirely on any one of the three.

To judge the patterns and practices associated with any form of masculinity, it is necessary to explore the implications for both the personal life of the individual and the effect on the reproduction of the societal gender order (Connell 1990a). Different patterns will challenge, comply, or actively support gendered arrangements.

The reliance pattern is reflected by an emphasis on control, independence, strength, and concern for appearances. Men who rely on dominant conceptions of masculinity are much more likely to internalize their feelings of inadequacy and seek to compensate or overcompensate for them. Because the problem is perceived to be located within oneself rather than within the social structure, this model does not challenge, but rather perpetuates, the current gender order.

A certain distancing from dominant ideals occurs in the reformulation pattern. But reformulation tends to be an independent project, and class-based resources play an important role. As such, it doesn't present a formidable challenge to the gender order. Connell (1990a: 474) argues that this response may even modernize patriarchy.

The rejection model, the least well represented in this article, offers the most hope for change. Linked closely to a sociopolitical approach that defines disability as a product of interactions between individuals and their environment, disability (and masculinity) is understood as socially constructed.

Members of the Disability Rights Movement, as a result, seek to reconstruct masculinity through a three-prong strategy. First, they focus on changing the frame of reference regarding who defines disability and masculinity, thereby changing the social-construction dynamics of both. Second, they endeavor to help people with disabilities be more self-referent when defining

their identities. To do that, a third component must be implemented: support structures, such as alternative subcultures, must exist. If the Disability Rights Movement is successful in elevating this struggle to the level of collective practice, it will challenge the legitimacy of the institutional arrangements of the current gender order.

In closing, there is much fruitful work to be done in the area of masculinity and disability. For instance, we should expect men with disabilities to respond differently to the demands associated with disability and masculinity due to sexual orientation, social class, age of onset of one's disability, race, and ethnicity. However, *how* and *why* gender identity varies for men with disabilities merits further study. We hope that this work serves as an impetus for others to take up these issues.

REFERENCES

Callahan, John. 1989. *Don't Worry, He Won't Get Far on Foot*. New York: Vintage Books.

Connell, R. W. 1991. "Live Fast and Die Young: The Construction of Masculinity among Young Working-Class Men on the Margin of the Labor Market." *The Australian and New Zealand Journal of Sociology*, Volume 27, Number 2, August, pp. 141–171.

———. 1990a. "A Whole New World: Remaking Masculinity in the Context of the Environmental Movement." *Gender & Society*, Volume 4, Number 4, December, pp. 452–478.

———. 1990b. "An Iron Man: The Body and Some Contradictions of Hegemonic Masculinity," In *Sport, Men, and the Gender Order*, Michael Messner and Donald Sabo, eds. Champaign, IL: Human Kinetics Publishers, Inc., pp. 83–96.

———. 1987. *Gender and Power: Society, the Person, and Sexual Politics*. Stanford, CA: Stanford University Press.

Denzin, Norman. 1989. *The Research Act: A Theoretical Introduction to Sociological Methods*. Englewood Cliffs, NJ: Prentice-Hall.

Emerson, Robert. 1988. "Introduction." In *Contemporary Field Research: A Collection of Readings*, Robert Emerson, ed. Prospect Heights, IL: Waveland Press, pp. 93–107.

Hahn, Harlan. 1989. "Masculinity and Disability." *Disability Studies Quarterly*, Volume 9, Number 3, pp. 1–3.

Janeway, Elizabeth. 1980. *Powers of the Weak*. New York: Alfred A. Knopf.

Katz, Jack. 1988. "A Theory of Qualitative Methodology: The Social System of Analytic Fieldwork." In *Contemporary Field Research: A Collection of Readings*, Robert Emerson, ed. Prospect Heights, IL: Waveland Press, pp. 127–148.

Kriegel, Leonard. 1991. *Falling into Life*. San Francisco: North Point Press.

Messner, Michael A. 1992. *Power at Play: Sports and the Problem of Masculinity*. Boston: Beacon Press.

Murphy, Robert F. 1990. *The Body Silent*. New York: W. W. Norton.

Scott, James C. 1985. *Weapons of the Weak: Everyday Forms of Peasant Resistance*. New Haven: Yale University Press.

West, Candace, and Don H. Zimmerman. 1987. "Doing Gender." *Gender and Society*, Volume 1, Number 2, June, pp. 125–151.

Zola, Irving Kenneth. 1982. *Missing Pieces: A Chronicle of Living with a Disability*. Philadelphia: Temple University Press.

PART SIX

MEN WITH WOMEN: INTIMACY AND POWER

Why do many men have problems establishing and maintaining intimate relationships with women? What different forms do male–female relational problems take within different socioeconomic groups? How do men's problems with intimacy and emotional expressivity relate to power inequities between the sexes? Are rape and domestic violence best conceptualized as isolated deviant acts by "sick" individuals, or are they the illogical consequences of male socialization? This complex web of male-female relationships, intimacy, and power is the topic of this section.

Lillian Rubin begins this section with a psychoanalytic interpretation of male–female relational problems. Early-developmental differences, rooted in the social organization of the nuclear family (especially the fact that it is women who care for infants), have set up fundamental emotional and sexual differences between men and women that create problems and conflicts for heterosexual couples. Clyde W. Franklin, in examining conflicts between black males and females, focuses more on how the larger socioeconomic structure of society places strains on black family life, and especially on black males' work and family roles. Whereas Rubin's and Franklin's articles tend to portray both males and females as being victimized by socially structured gender differences and problems with intimacy and communication, Jack W. Sattel asks some different questions. Male emotional and verbal inexpressivity, rather than being a "tragedy," might better be conceptualized as situational strategy that males utilize to retain control in their relationships with women. Intimacy and power are closely intertwined.

Men's anger and insecurities toward women surface in other ways. Wayne Ewing's examination of the dynamics of domestic violence, Jane Hood's exploration of adolescent gang rape, "Jack M.'s" confession of his own experience, and Tim Beneke's dissection of the ideology of rape show that violence against women is the illogical consequence of insecurity, anger, the need for control, the need to assert and demonstrate manliness—all within a social context that condones sexual violence. As sociologist Diana Russell has written:

Rape is not so much a deviant act as an over-conforming act. Rape may be understood as an extreme acting-out of qualities that are regarded as super masculine in this and

many other societies: aggression, force, power, strength, toughness, dominance, compet-
itiveness. To win, to be superior, to be successful, to conquer—all demonstrate masculinity
to those who subscribe to common cultural notions of masculinity, i.e., the masculine
mystique. *And it would be surprising if these notions of masculinity did not find expres-*
sion in men's sexual behavior. Indeed, sex may be the arena where these notions of mas-
culinity are most intensely played out, particularly by men who feel powerless in the rest
of their lives, and hence, whose masculinity is threatened by this sense of powerlessness.[1]

What links all the articles in this section is *not* a sense that males are inherently incapable of authentic emotional connections with women, or that men are "naturally"
batterers or rapists. The problems that men and women have relating to each other are
rooted in the socially structured system of gender difference and inequality. As feminists have long argued, the humanization of men is directly linked to the social empowerment of women. As long as men feel a need to control and subordinate women,
either overtly or subtly, their relationships with women will be impoverished. We hope
the essays in this section will provide a better context to the current discussions about
prescribing campus sexual conduct.

---

[1] Diana Russell, "Rape and the Masculine Mystique," paper presented to the American Sociological
Association, New York, 1973.

THE APPROACH–AVOIDANCE DANCE:
MEN, WOMEN, AND INTIMACY

LILLIAN B. RUBIN

For one human being to love another, that is perhaps the most difficult of all our tasks, the ultimate, the last test and proof, the work for which all other work is but preparation.
—Rainer Maria Rilke

Intimacy. We hunger for it, but we also fear it. We come close to a loved one, then we back off. A teacher I had once described this as the "go away a little closer" message. I call it the approach–avoidance dance.

The conventional wisdom says that women want intimacy, men resist it. And I have plenty of material that would *seem* to support that view. Whether in my research interviews, in my clinical hours, or in the ordinary course of my life, I hear the same story told repeatedly. "He doesn't talk to me," says a woman. "I don't know what she wants me to talk about," says a man. "I want to know what he's feeling," she tells me. "I'm not feeling anything," he insists. "Who can feel nothing?" she cries. "I can," he shouts. As the heat rises, so does the wall between them. Defensive and angry, they retreat—stalemated by their inability to understand each other.

Women complain to each other all the time about not being able to talk to their men about the things that matter most to them—about what they themselves are thinking and feeling, about what goes on in the hearts and minds of the men they're relating to. And men, less able to expose themselves and their conflicts—those within themselves or those with the women in their lives—either turn silent or take cover by holding women up to derision. It's one of the norms of male camaraderie to poke fun at women, to complain laughingly about the mystery of their minds, wonderingly about their ways. Even Freud did it when, in exasperation, he asked mockingly, "What do women want? Dear God, what do they want?"

But it's not a joke—not for the women, not for the men who like to pretend it is.

The whole goddamn business of what you're calling intimacy bugs the hell out of me. I never know what you women mean when you talk about it. Karen complains that I don't talk to her, but it's not talk she wants, it's some other damn thing, only I don't know what the hell it is. Feelings, she keeps asking for. So what am I supposed to do if I don't have any to give her or to talk about just because she decides it's time to talk about feelings? Tell me, will you: maybe we can get some peace around here.

The expression of such conflicts would seem to validate the common understandings that suggest that women want and need intimacy more than men do—that the issue belongs to women alone; that, if left to themselves, men would not suffer it. But things are not always what they seem. And I wonder: "If men would renounce intimacy, what is their stake in relationships with women?"

Some would say that men need women to tend to their daily needs—to prepare their meals, clean their houses, wash their clothes, rear their children—so that they can be free to attend to life's larger problems. And, given the traditional structure of roles in the family, it has certainly worked that way most of the time. But, if that were all men seek, why is it that, even when they're not relating to women, so much of their lives is spent in search of a relationship with another, so much agony experienced when it's not available?

These are difficult issues to talk about—even to think about—because the subject of intimacy isn't just complicated, it's slippery as well. Ask yourself: What is intimacy? What words come to mind, what thoughts?

It's an idea that excites our imagination, a word that seems larger than life to most of us. It lures us, beckoning us with a power we're unable to resist. And, just because it's so seductive, it frightens us as well—seeming sometimes to be some mysterious force from outside ourselves that, if we let it, could sweep us away.

But what is it we fear?

Asked what intimacy is, most of us—men and women—struggle to say something sensible, something that we can connect with the real experience of our lives. "Intimacy is knowing there's someone who cares about the children as much as you do." "Intimacy is a history of shared experience. It's sitting there having a cup of coffee together and watching the eleven o'clock news." "It's knowing you care about the same things." "It's knowing she'll always understand." "It's him sitting in the hospital for hours at a time when I was sick." "It's knowing he cares when I'm hurting." "It's standing by me when I was out of work." "It's seeing each other at our worst." "It's sitting across the breakfast table." "It's talking when you're in the bathroom." "It's knowing we'll begin and end each day together."

These seem the obvious things—the things we expect when we commit our lives to one another in a marriage, when we decide to have children together. And they're not to be dismissed as inconsequential. They make up the daily experience of our lives together, setting the tone for a relationship in important and powerful ways. It's sharing such commonplace, everyday events that determines the temper and the texture of life, that keeps us living together even when other aspects of the relationship seem less than perfect. Knowing someone is there, is constant, and can be counted on in just the ways these thoughts express provides the background of emotional security and stability we look for when we enter a marriage. Certainly a marriage and the people in it will be tested and judged quite differently in an unusual situation or in a crisis. But how often does life present us with circumstances and events that are so out of the range of ordinary experience?

These ways in which a relationship feels intimate on a daily basis are only one part of what we mean by intimacy, however—the part that's most obvious, the part that doesn't awaken our fears. At a lecture where I spoke of these issues recently, one man commented also, "Intimacy is putting aside the masks we wear in the rest of our lives." A murmur of assent ran through the audience of a hundred or so. Intuitively we say, "yes." Yet this is the very issue that also complicates our intimate relationships.

On the one hand, it's reassuring to be able to put away the public persona—to believe we can be loved for who we *really* are, that we can show our shadow side without fear, that our vulnerabilities will not be counted against us. "The most important thing is to feel I'm accepted just the way I am," people will say.

But there's another side. For, when we show ourselves thus without the masks, we also become anxious and fearful. "Is it possible that someone could love the *real* me?" we're likely to ask. Not the most promising question for the further development of intimacy, since it suggests that, whatever else another might do or feel, it's we who have trouble loving ourselves. Unfortunately, such misgivings are not usually experienced consciously. We're aware only that our discomfort has risen, that we feel a need to get away. For the person who has seen the "real me" is also the one who reflects back to us an image that's usually not wholly to our liking. We get angry at that, first at ourselves for not living up to our own expectations, then at the other, who becomes for us the mirror of our self-doubts—a displacement of hostility that serves intimacy poorly.

There's yet another level—one that's further below the surface of consciousness, therefore, one that's much more difficult for us to grasp, let alone to talk about. I'm referring to the differences in the ways in which women and men deal with their inner emotional lives—differences that create barriers between us that can be high indeed. It's here that we see how those early childhood experiences of separation and individuation—the psychological tasks that were required of us in order to separate from mother, to distinguish ourselves as autonomous persons, to internalize a firm sense of gender identity—take their toll on our intimate relationships.

Stop a woman in mid-sentence with the question, "What are you feeling right now?" and you might have to wait a bit while she reruns the mental tape to capture the moment just passed. But, more than likely, she'll be able to do it successfully. More than likely, she'll think for a while and come up with an answer.

The same is not true of a man. For him, a similar question usually will bring a sense of wonderment that one would even ask it, followed quickly by an uncomprehending and puzzled response. "What do you mean?" he'll ask. "I was just talking," he'll say.

I've seen it most clearly in the clinical setting where the task is to get to the feeling level—or, as one of my male patients said when he came into therapy, to "hook up the head and the gut." Repeatedly when therapy begins, I find myself having to teach a man how to monitor his internal states—how to attend to his thoughts and feelings, how to bring them into consciousness. In the early stages of our work, it's a common experience to say to a man, "How does that feel?," and to see a blank look come over his face. Over and over, I find myself listening as a man speaks with calm reason about a situation which I know must be fraught with pain. "How do you feel about that?" I'll ask. "I've just been telling you," he's likely to reply. "No," I'll say, "you've told me what happened, not how you *feel* about it." Frustrated, he might well respond, "You sound just like my wife."

It would be easy to write off such dialogues as the problems of men in therapy, of those who happen to be having some particular emotional difficulties. But it's not so, as any woman who has lived with a man will attest. Time and again women complain: "I can't get him to verbalize his feelings." "He talks, but it's always intellectualizing." "He's so closed off from what he's feeling, I don't know how he lives that way." "If there's one thing that will eventually ruin this marriage, it's the fact that he can't talk about what's going on inside him." "I have to work like hell to get anything out of him that resembles a feeling that's something besides anger. That I get plenty of—me and the kids, we all get his anger. Anything else is damn hard to come by with him." One woman talked eloquently about her husband's anguish over his inability to get problems in his work life resolved. When I asked how she knew about his pain, she answered:

> I pull for it, I pull hard, and sometimes I can get something from him. But it'll be late at night in the dark—you know, when we're in bed and I can't look at him while he's talking and he doesn't have to look at me. Otherwise, he's just defensive and puts on what I call his bear act, where he makes his warning, go-away faces, and he can't be reached or penetrated at all.

To a woman, the world men live in seems a lonely one—a world in which their fears of exposing their sadness and pain, their anxiety about allowing their vulnerability to show, even to a woman they love, is so deeply rooted inside them that, most often, they can only allow it to happen "late at night in the dark."

Yet, if we listen to what men say, we will hear their insistence that they *do* speak of what's inside them, *do* share their thoughts and feelings with the women they love. "I tell her, but she's never satisfied," they complain. "No matter how much I say, it's never enough," they grumble.

From both sides, the complaints have merit. The problem lies not in what men don't say, however, but in what's not there—in what, quite simply, happens so far out of consciousness that it's not within their reach. For men have integrated all too well the lessons of their childhood—the experiences that taught them to repress and deny their inner thoughts, wishes, needs, and fears; indeed, not even to notice them. It's real, therefore, that the kind of inner thoughts and feelings that are readily accessible to a woman generally are unavailable to a man. When he says, "I don't know what I'm feeling," he isn't necessarily being intransigent and withholding. More than likely, he speaks the truth.

Partly that's a result of the ways in which boys are trained to camouflage their feelings under cover of an exterior of calm, strength, and rationality. Fears are not manly. Fantasies are not rational. Emotions, above all, are not for the strong, the sane, the adult. Women suffer them, not men—women, who are more like children with what seems like their never-ending preoccupation with their emotional life. But the training takes so well because of their early childhood experience when, as very young boys, they had to shift their identification from mother to father and sever themselves from their earliest emotional connection. Put the two together and it does seem like suffering to men to have to experience that emotional side of themselves, to have to give it voice.

This is the single most dispiriting dilemma of relations between women and men. He complains, "She's so emotional, there's no point in talking to her." She protests, "It's him you can't talk to, he's always so darned rational." He says, "Even when I tell her nothing's the matter, she won't quit." She says, "How can I believe him when I can see with my own eyes that something's wrong?" He says, "Okay, so something's wrong! What good will it do to tell her?" She cries, "What are we married for? What do you need me for, just to wash your socks?"

These differences in the psychology of women and men are born of a complex interaction between society and the individual. At the broadest social level is the rending of thought and feeling that is such a fundamental part of Western thought. Thought, defined as the ultimate good, has been assigned to men; feeling, considered at best a problem, has fallen to women.

So firmly fixed have these ideas been that, until recently, few thought to question them. For they were built into the structure of psychological thought as if they spoke to an eternal, natural, and scientific truth. Thus, even such a great and innovative thinker as Carl Jung wrote, "The woman is increasingly aware that love alone can give her her full stature, just as the man begins to discern that spirit alone can endow his life with its highest meaning. Fundamentally, therefore, both seek a psychic relation one to the other, because love needs the spirit, and the spirit love, for their fulfillment."*

For a woman, "love"; for a man, spirit"—each expected to complete the other by bringing to the relationship the missing half. In German, the word that is translated here as spirit is *Geist*. But *The New Cassell's German Dictionary* shows that another primary meaning of *Geist* is "mind, intellect, intelligence, wit, imagination, sense of reason." And, given the context of these words, it seems reasonable that *Geist* for Jung referred to a man's highest essence—his mind. There's no ambiguity about a woman's calling, however. It's love.

Intuitively, women try to heal the split that these definitions of male and female have foisted upon us.

---

*Carl Gustav Jung, *Contributions to Analytical Psychology* (New York: Harcourt, Brace & Co., 1928), p. 185.

I can't stand that he's so damned unemotional and expects me to be the same. He lives in his head all the time, and he acts like anything that's emotional isn't worth dealing with.

Cognitively, even women often share the belief that the rational side, which seems to come so naturally to men, is the more mature, the more desirable.

I know I'm too emotional, and it causes problems between us. He can't stand it when I get emotional like that. It turns him right off.

Her husband agrees that she's "too emotional" and complains:

Sometimes she's like a child who's out to test her parents. I have to be careful when she's like that, not to let her rile me up because otherwise all hell would break loose. You just can't reason with her when she gets like that.

It's the rational-man-hysterical-woman script, played out again and again by two people whose emotional repertoire is so limited that they have few real options. As the interaction between them continues, she reaches for the strongest tools she has, the mode she's most comfortable and familiar with: She becomes progressively more emotional and expressive. He falls back on his best weapons: He becomes more rational, more determinedly reasonable. She cries for him to attend to her feelings, whatever they may be. He tells her coolly, with a kind of clenched-teeth reasonableness, that it's silly for her to feel that way, that she's just being emotional. And of course she is. But that dismissive word "just" is the last straw. She gets so upset that she does, in fact, seem hysterical. He gets so bewildered by the whole interaction that his only recourse is to build the wall of reason even higher. All of which makes things measurably worse for both of them.

The more I try to be cool and calm her the worse it gets. I swear, I can't figure her out. I'll keep trying to tell her not to get so excited, but there's nothing I can do. Anything I say just makes it worse. So then I try to keep quiet, but . . . wow, the explosion is like crazy, just nuts.

And by then it *is* a wild exchange that any outsider would agree was "just nuts." But it's not just her response that's off, it's his as well—their conflict resting in the fact that we equate the emotional with the nonrational.

This notion, shared by both women and men, is a product of the fact that they were born and reared in this culture. But there's also a difference between them in their capacity to apprehend the *logic* of emotions—a difference born in their early childhood experiences in the family, when boys had to repress so much of their emotional side and girls could permit theirs to flower. . . . It should be understood: Commitment itself is not a problem for a man; he's good at that. He can spend a lifetime living in the same family, working at the same job—even one he hates. And he's not without an inner emotional life. But when a relationship requires the sustained verbal expression of that inner life and the full range of feelings that accompany it, then it becomes burdensome for him. He can act out anger and frustration inside the family, it's true. But ask him to express his sadness, his fear, his dependency—all those feelings that would expose his vulnerability to himself or to another—and he's likely to close down as if under some compulsion to protect himself.

All requests for such intimacy are difficult for a man, but they become especially complex and troublesome in relations with women. It's another of those paradoxes. For, to the degree that it's possible for him to be emotionally open with anyone, it is with a woman—a tribute to the power of the childhood experience with mother. Yet it's that same early experience and his need to repress it that raises his ambivalence and generates his resistance.

He moves close, wanting to share some part of himself with her, trying to do so, perhaps even yearning to experience again the bliss of the infant's connection with a woman. She responds, woman style—wanting to touch him just a little more deeply, to know what he's thinking, feeling, fearing, wanting. And the fear closes in— the fear of finding himself again in the grip of a powerful woman, of allowing her admittance only to be betrayed and abandoned once again, of being overwhelmed by denied desires.

So he withdraws.

It's not in consciousness that all this goes on. He knows, of course, that he's distinctly uncomfortable when pressed by a woman for more intimacy in the relationship, but he doesn't know why. And, very often, his behavior doesn't please him any more than it pleases her. But he can't seem to help it.

BLACK MALE–BLACK FEMALE CONFLICT:
INDIVIDUALLY CAUSED AND CULTURALLY NURTURED

CLYDE W. FRANKLIN II

Who is to blame? Currently, there is no dearth of attention directed to Black male–Black female relationships. Books, magazine articles, academic journal articles, public forums, radio programs, television shows, and everyday conversations have been devoted to Black male–Black female relationships for several years. Despite the fact that the topic has been discussed over the past several decades by some authors (e.g., Frazier, 1939; Drake and Cayton, 1945; Grier and Cobb, 1968), Wallace's *Black Macho and the Myth of the Superwoman* has been the point of departure for many contemporary discussions of the topic since its publication in 1979.

Actually, Wallace's analysis was not so different in content from other analyses of Black male–Black female relationships (e.g., Drake and Cayton's analysis of "lower-class life" in *Black Metropolis*). But Wallace's analysis was "timely." Coming so soon on the heels of the Black movement in the late 1960s and early 1970s, and, at a time when many Black male-inspired gains for Blacks were disappearing rapidly, the book was explosive. Its theme, too, was provocative. Instead of repeating the rhetoric of the late 1960s and early 1970s that blamed conflictual relationships between Black men and Black women on White society, Wallace implied that the blame lay with Black males. In other words, the blame lay with those Black warriors who only recently had been perceived as the "saviors" of Black people in America. Wallace's lamenting theme is captured in a quote from her book: "While she stood by silently as he became a man, she assumed that he would finally glorify and dignify Black womanhood just as the White man has done for White women." Wallace goes on to say that this has not happened for Black women.

Wallace updates her attack on Black men in a later article entitled "A Black Feminist's Search for Sisterhood (1982:9). Her theme, as before, is that Black men are just as oppressive of Black women as White men. She states:

> *Whenever I raised the question of a Black woman's humanity in conversations with a Black man, I got a similar reaction. Black men, at least the ones I knew, seemed totally confounded when it came to treating Black women like people. . . . I discovered my voice and when brothers talked to me, I talked back. This had its hazards. Almost got my eye blackened several times. My social life was like guerilla warfare. Here was the logic behind our grandmother's old saying, "A nigga man ain't shit."*

Wallace, however, is not alone in placing the blame on Black men for deteriorating relations between Black men and Black women. Allen (1983:62), in a recent edition of *Essence* magazine, states:

From *Journal of Black Studies* 15 (2 December 1984): 139–154. Reprinted by permission.

Black women have a tendency to be male-defined, subjugating their own needs for the good of that fragile male ego. . . . The major contradiction is that we Black women, in our hearts, have a tendency to believe Black men need more support and understanding than we do. We bought the Black Revolutionary line that a woman's place was three paces behind the man. We didn't stomp Stokeley when he made the statement that the only position for a woman in the movement was prone.

Such attacks on Black men have been met with equally ferocious counterattacks by some Black authors (both Black men and Black women). A few months following the publication of Wallace's book, an entire issue of the *Black Scholar* was devoted to Black male–Black female relationships. Of the responses to Wallace by such scholars as Jones (1979), Karenga (1979), Staples (1979), and numerous others, Karenga's response is perhaps the most controversial and maybe the most volatile. Karenga launches a personal attack on Wallace suggesting that she is misguided and perhaps responding from personal hurt. Recognizing the complexity of Black male–Black female relationships, Karenga contends that much of it is due not to Black men but to the White power structure. Along similar lines, Moore (1980) has exhorted Black women to stop criticizing Black men and blame themselves for disintegrating bonds between Black men and Black women.

Staples, in his response to Wallace and others who would place the blame on Black men for disruptive relationships between Black men and Black women, points out that while sexism within the Black culture may be an emerging problem, most Black men do not have the institutionalized power to oppress Black women. He believes that the Black male's "condition" in society is what bothers Black males. Staples devotes much attention to the institutional decimation of Black men and suggests that this is the reason for Black male–Black female conflict. Noting the high mortality and suicide rates of Black men, the fact that a half a million Black men are in prison, one-third of urban Black men are saddled with drug problems and that 25% to 30% do not have steady employment, Staples implied that Black male–Black female conflict may be related to *choice*. This means that a shortage of Black men may limit the choices that Black women have in selecting partners. As Braithwaite (1981) puts it, the insufficient supply of Black men places Black women at a disadvantage by giving Black men the upper hand. In a specific relationship, for example, if a Black woman fails to comply with the Black man's wishes, the Black man has numerous other options, including not only other Black women but also women of other races.

In a more recent discussion of Black male–Black female relationships, Alvin Poussaint (1982:40) suggests that Black women "adopt a patient and creative approach in exploring and creating new dimensions of the Black male–Black female bond." Others, like Ronald Braithwaite, imply in their analyses of relationships between Black men and Black women that Black women's aggressiveness, thought to be a carryover from slavery, may be partly responsible for Black male–Black female conflict.

Succinctly, by and large, most Black male and Black female authors writing on the subject seem to agree that many Black male–Black female relationships today are destructive and potentially explosive. What they do not agree on, however, are the causes of the problems existing between Black men and Black women. As we have seen, some believe that Black men are the cause. Others contend that Black women contribute disproportionately to Black male–Black female conflict. Still others blame White racism solely, using basic assumptions that may be logically inadequate (see Franklin, 1980). Many specific reasons for the conflict often postulated include the notions that Black men are abusive toward Black women, that Black men are irresistibly attracted to White women (despite the fact that only approximately 120,000 Black men were married to White women in 1980), that too many Black men are homosexual, that Black women are too aggressive, that Black women don't support Black men—the list goes on. Few of these reasons, however, really explore the underlying cause of the conflict. Instead, they are descriptions of the conflict-behaviors that are indicators of the tension between Black men and Black women. But what is the cause of the behavior—the cause of the tension that so often disrupts harmony in Black male–Black female relationships?

Given the various approaches many Black authors have taken in analyzing Black male–Black female relationships, it is submitted that two major sources of Black male–Black female conflict can be identified: (1) the noncomplementarity of sex-role definitions internalized by Black males and Black females; and (2) structural barriers in the environments of Black males and Black females. Each source is explored separately below.

SOURCES OF CONFLICT BETWEEN BLACK MEN AND BLACK WOMEN

Sex-Role Noncomplementarity among Black Males and Black Females

Much Black male–Black female conflict stems directly from incompatible role enactments by Black males and Black females. Incompatible role enactments by Black men and Black women occur because they internalize sex-role definitions that are noncomplementary. For example, a Black woman in a particular conflictual relationship with a Black male may feel that her Black man is supposed to assume a dominant role, but she also may be inclined to exhibit behaviors that are opposed to his dominance and her subordinance. In the same relationship, the Black man may pay lip service to assuming a dominant role but may behave "passively" with respect to some aspects of masculinity and in a dominant manner with respect to other aspects.

One reason for role conflict between Black men and Black women is that many contemporary Black women internalize two conflicting

definitions of femininity, whereas many contemporary Black men internalize only a portion of the traditional definition of masculinity. Put simply, numerous Black women hold attitudes that are both highly masculine and highly feminine. On the other hand, their male counterparts develop traits that are highly consistent with certain aspects of society's definition of masculinity, but that are basically unrelated to other aspects of the definition. Thus, in a given relationship, one may find a Black woman who feels and behaves in ways that are both assertive and passive, dominant and subordinant, decisive and indecisive, and so on. Within that same relationship, a Black man may exhibit highly masculine behaviors, such as physical aggressiveness, sexual dominance, and even violence, but behave indifferently with respect to the masculine work ethic—assuming responsibility for family-related activities external to the home, being aggressive in the work place and the like.

The reason these incongruent attitudes and behaviors exist among Black men and Black women is that they have received contradictory messages during early socialization. It is common for Black women to have received two messages. One message states, "Because you will be a Black woman, it is imperative that you learn to take care of yourself because it is hard to find a Black man who will take care of you." A second message frequently received by young Black females that conflicts with the first message is "your ultimate achievement will occur when you have snared a Black man who will take care of you." In discussing early socialization experiences with countless young Black women in recent years, I have found that most of them agree that these two messages were given them by socialization agents and agencies such as child caretakers, relatives, peer group members, the Black church, and the media.

When internalized, these two messages often produce a Black woman who seems to reject aspects of the traditional female sex role in America such as passivity, emotional and economic dependence, and female subordinance while accepting other aspects of the role such as expressiveness, warmth, and nurturance. This is precisely why Black women seem to be more androgynous than White women. Black women's androgyny, though, may be more a function of necessity than anything else. It may be related to the scarcity of Black men who assume traditional masculine roles in male–female relationships.

Whatever the reason for Black women's androgynous orientations, because of such orientations Black women often find themselves in conflictual relationships with Black men or in no stable relationships at all. The scenario generally can be described as follows. Many Black women in early adulthood usually begin a search for a Black Prince Charming. However, because of the dearth of Black men who can be or are willing to be Prince Charmings for Black women, Black women frequently soon give up the search for such a Black man. They give up the search, settle for less, and "like" what they settle for even less. This statement is important because many Black women's eventual choices are destined to become constant reminders that the "female independence" message received during the early socialization process is the correct message. But, because Black women also have to deal with the second socialization message, many come to feel that they have failed in their roles as women. In an effort to correct their mistakes, Black women often choose to enact the aspect of their androgynous role that is decidedly aggressive and/or independent. They may decide either to "go it alone" or to prod their Black men into becoming Prince Charmings. The first alternative for Black women often results in self-doubt, lowered self-esteem, and, generally, unhappiness and dissatisfaction. After all, society nurtures the "find a man" message far beyond early socialization. The second message, unfortunately, produces little more than the first message because Black women in such situations usually end up in conflictual relationships with Black men, who also have undergone a rather complicated socializa-

tion process. Let us explore briefly the conflicting messages numerous Black men receive during early socialization.

One can find generally that Black men, too, have received two conflicting messages during early socialization. One message received by young Black males is "to become a man means that you must become dominant, aggressive, decisive, responsible, and in some instances, violent in social encounters with others." A second message received by young Black males that conflicts with the first is, "You are Black and you must not be too aggressive, too dominant, and so on, because the *man* will cut you down." Internalization of these two messages by some Black men (a substantial number) produces Black men who enact a portion of the traditional definition of masculinity but remain inactive with respect to other parts of traditional masculinity. Usually those aspects of traditional masculinity that can be enacted within the Black culture are the ones exhibited by these Black men. Other aspects of the sex role that require enactment external to the Black culture (e.g., aggressiveness in the work place) may be related to impassively by Black men. Unfortunately, these are aspects of the male sex role that must be enacted if a male is to be "productive" in American society.

Too many Black men fail to enact the more "productive" aspects of the male sex role. Instead, "being a man," for many Black males who internalize the mixed messages, becomes simply enacting sexual aggression, violence, sexism, and the like—all of which promote Black male–Black female conflict. In addition, contributing to the low visibility and low salience of "productive" masculine traits among Black men is the second socialization message, which provides a rationale for nonenactment of the role traits. Moreover, the "man will get you" message serves to attenuate Black men's motivations to enact more "positive" aspects of the traditional male sex role. We must keep in mind, however, that not all of the sources of Black male–Black female conflict are social-psychological. Some of the sources are structural, and in the next section these sources are discussed.

Structural Barriers Contributing to Black Male–Black Female Conflict

It is easy to place the blame for Black male–Black female conflict on "White society." Several Black authors have used this explanatory approach in recent years (e.g., Anderson and Mealy, 1979). They have suggested that Black male–Black female conflict is a function of America's capitalistic orientation and White society's long-time subjugation of Black people. Certainly historical conditions are important to understand when discussing the status of Black people today. Often, however, too much emphasis is placed on the historical subjugation of Black people as the source of Black male–Black female conflict today. Implicit in such an emphasis is the notion that independent variables existing at some point in the distant past cause a multiplicity of negative behaviors between Black males and Black females that can be capsulized as Black male–Black female conflict. A careful analysis of the contemporary environments of Black men and women today will show, instead, that factors responsible, in part, for Black male–Black female conflict are inextricably interwoven in those environments. In other words, an approach to the analysis of conflict between Black men and Black women today must be ahistorical. Past conditions influence Black male–Black female relationships only in the sense that vestiges of these conditions exist currently and are identifiable.

Our society today undoubtedly remains structured in such a manner that the vast majority of Black men encounter insurmountable barriers to the attainment of a "masculine" status as defined by most Americans (Black and White Americans). Black men still largely are locked within the Black culture (which has relatively limited resources), unable to compete successfully for societal rewards—the attainment of which defines American males as "men." Unquestionably, Black men's powerlessness in society's basic institutions such as the government and the economy contributes greatly to the pathological states of many Black men. The high mortality and suicide rates of young Black men, the high incarceration rates of Black men, the high incidence of drug addiction among Black men, and the high unemployment rate of Black men are all functions of societal barriers to Black male upward mobility. These barriers render millions of Black males socially impotent and/or socially dysfunctional. Moreover, as Staples has pointed out, such barriers also result in a scarcity of functional Black men, thereby limiting Black women's alternatives for mates.

While some may be tempted to argue for a psychological explanation of Black male social impotence, it is suggested here that any such argument is misguided unless accompanied by a recognition of the role of cultural nurturance factors. Cultural nurturance factors such as the rigid castelike social stratum of Blacks in America foster and maintain Black men's social impotence. The result is powerless Black men primed for conflictual relationships with Black women. If Black men in our society were not "American," perhaps cultural nurturance of Black people's status in our society could not be translated into cultural nurturance of Black male–Black female conflict. That Black men are Americanized, however, is seen in the outcome of the Black movement of the last decade.

The Black movement of the late 1960s and early 1970s produced little structural change in America. To be sure, a few Black men (and even fewer Black women) achieved a measure of upward mobility; however, the vast majority did not reap gains from the Black movement. What did happen, though, was that Black people did get a glimpse of the rewards that can be achieved in America through violence and/or aggression. White society did bend when confronted by the Black movement, but it did not break. In addition, the few upward mobility doors that were ajar during the height of the movement were quickly slammed shut when the movement began to wane in the middle and late 1970s. Black men today find themselves in a position similar to the one Black men were in prior to the movement. The only difference this time around is that Black men are equipped with the psychological armor of aggression and violence as well as with a distorted perception of a target—Black women, the ones who "stood silently by."

Wallace's statement that Black women "stood silently by" must not be taken lightly. Black women did this; in addition, they further internalized American definitions of masculinity and femininity. Previously, Black women held modified definitions of masculinity and femininity because the society's definition did not fit their everyday experiences. During the Black movement they were exhorted by Black men to assume a sex role that was more in line with the traditional "feminine" role White women assumed in male–female relationships. Although this may have been a noble (verbal) effort on the part of Black men to place Black women on pedestals, it was shortsighted and doomed to fail. Failure was imminent because even during the peak of the Black movement, societal resistance to structural changes that would benefit Black people was strong. The strength of this resistance dictated that change in Black people's status in America could come about only through the united efforts of both Black men and Black women.

Unfortunately, the seeds of division between Black men and Black women were sown during the Black movement. Black men bought the Moynihan report (1965) that indirectly blamed Black women for Black people's underclass status in America. In doing so, Black men convinced themselves that they could be "men" only if they adopted the White male's sex role. An examination of this role reveals that it is characterized by numerous contradictions. The traditional White masculine role requires men to assume protective, condescending, and generally patriarchal stances with respect to women. It also requires, ironically, that men display dominant, aggressive, and often violent behaviors toward women. Just as important, though, is that White masculine role

enactment can occur only, when there is full participation in masculinist American culture. Because Black men continue to face barriers to full participation in American society, the latter requirement for White male sex-role assumption continues to be met by only a few Black men. The result has been that many Black men have adopted only a part of the culture's definition of masculinity because they are thwarted in their efforts to participate fully in society. Structural barriers to Black male sex-role adoption, then, have produced a Black male who is primed for a conflictual relationship with Black women. In the next section, an exploration is presented of some possible solutions to Black male–Black female conflict that arise from the interactive relationship between the noncomplementarity of sex-role internalization by Black men and Black women and structural barriers to Black men's advancement in American society.

TOWARD SOLVING BLACK MALE–BLACK FEMALE CONFLICT

Given that societal conditions are extremely resistant to rapid changes, the key to attenuating conflict between Black men and Black women lies in altering three social psychological phenomena: (1) Black male and Black female socialization experiences; (2) Black male and Black female role-playing strategies; and (3) Black male and Black female personal communication mechanisms. I first propose some alterations in Black male and Black female socialization experiences. . . .

Black female socialization must undergo change if Black men and Black women are to enjoy harmonious relationships. Those agents and agencies responsible for socializing young Black females must return to emphasizing a monolithic message in young Black female socialization. This message can stress warmth, caring, and nurturance, but it must stress simultaneously self-sufficiency, assertiveness, and responsibility. The latter portion of this message requires that young Black females must be cautioned against sexual freedom at relatively early ages—not necessarily for moral reasons, but because sexual freedom for Black women seems to operate against Black women's self-sufficiency, assertiveness, and responsibility. It is important to point out here, however, that this type of socialization message must be imparted without the accompanying castigation of Black men. To say "a nigger man ain't shit" informs any young Black female that at least one-half of herself "ain't shit." Without a doubt this strategy teaches self-hate and sets the stage for future Black male–Black female conflict.

Young Black males, on the other hand, must be instructed in self-sufficiency, assertiveness, and responsibility without the accompanying warning opposed to these traits in Black males. Such warnings serve only to provide rationales for future failures. To be sure, Black men do (and will) encounter barriers to upward mobility because they are Black. But, as many Black men have shown, such barriers do not have to be unsurmountable. Of course it is recognized that innumerable Black men have been victims of American racist policies, but some, too, have been victims because they perceived only that external factors hindered their upward mobility and did not focus on some internal barriers that may have thwarted their mobility. The former factors are emphasized much too often in the contradictory socialization messages received by most young Black males.

Along with the above messages, young Black males must learn that the strong bonds that they establish with their mothers can be extended to their relationships with other Black women. If Black men perceive their mothers to he symbols of strength and perseverance, they must also be taught that most other Black women acquire these same qualities and have done so for generations. It must become just as "cool," in places like urban Black barbershops, to speak of Black women's strength and dignity as it is now to hear of Black women's thighs, breasts, and hips.

On an issue closely related to the above, few persons reading this article can deny that Black men's attempts to enact the White male sex role in America are laughable. Black men are relatively powerless in this country, and their attempts at domination, aggression, and the like, while sacrificing humanity, are ludicrous. This becomes apparent when it is understood that usually the only people being dominated and aggressed against by Black men are Black women (and other Black men). Moreover, unlike White males, Black males receive no societal rewards for their efforts; instead, the result is Black male–Black female disharmony. Black men must avoid the tendency to emulate the nauseatingly traditional male sex role because their experiences clearly show that such a role is counterproductive for Black people. Because the Black man's experiences are different, his role-playing strategies must be different and made to be more complementary with Black females' altered role-playing strategies. The Black females' role-playing strategies, as we have seen, are androgynous, emphasizing neither the inferiority nor the superiority of male or female sex roles.

On a final note, it is important for Black people in our society to alter their personal communication mechanisms. Black men and Black women interact with each other in diverse ways and in diverse situations, ranging from intimate to impersonal. Perhaps the most important element of this diverse communication pattern is empathy. For Black people in recent years, this is precisely the element that has undergone unnecessary transformation. As Blacks in America have accepted increasingly White society's definition of male–female relationships, Black men and Black women have begun to interact with each other less in terms of empathy. While Black women have retained empathy in their male–female relationships to a greater degree than Black men have, Black men have become increasingly nonexpressive and nonempathic in their male–female relationships. Nearly 60% of Black women (approximately 25,000) in a recent *Essence* survey cited nonexpressiveness as a problem in male–female relationships; 56% also pointed out that Black male nonempathy was a problem (Edwards, 1982). It seems, then, that as Black males have attempted to become "men" in America they have shed some of the important qualities of humanity. Some Black women, too, who have embraced the feminist perspective also have discarded altruism. The result of both phenomena, for Black people as a whole, has been to divide Black men and Black women further. Further movement away from empathic understanding in Black male–Black female relationships by both Black men and Black women undoubtedly will be disastrous for Black people in America.

REFERENCES

Allen B. 1983 "The Price for Giving It Up." *Essence* (February): 60–62, 118.

Anderson, S. E., and R. Mealy. 1979 "Who Originated the Crisis: A Historical Perspective." *Black Scholar* (May/June): 40–44.

Braithwaite, R. L. 1981 "Interpersonal Relations between Black Males and Black Females." In *Black Men*, L. E. Gary, ed., pp 83–97. Beverly Hills, Calif.: Sage.

Drake, S. C., and H. R. Cayton. 1945 *Black Metropolis*. New York: Harcourt.

Edwards, A. 1982 "Survey Results: How You're Feeling." *Essence* (December): 73–76.

Franklin, C. W., II. 1980 "White Racism As a Cause of Black Male–Black Female Conflict: A Critique." *Western Journal of Black Studies* 4 (1): 42–49.

Frazier, E. F. 1939 *The Negro Family in the United States*. Chicago: University of Chicago Press.

Grier, W. II., and P. M. Cobb. 1968 *Black Rage*. New York: Basic Books.

Jones, T. 1979 "The Need to Go beyond Stereotypes." *Black Scholar* (May/June): 48–49.

Karenga, M. R. 1979 "On Wallace's Myth: Wading through Troubled Waters." *Black Scholar* (May/June): 36–39.

Moore, W. F. 1980 "Black Women, Stop Criticizing Black Men—Blame Yourselves." *Ebony* (December): 128–130.

Moynihan, D. P. 1965 *The Negro Family: The Case for National Action*. Washington, D.C.: U.S. Department of Labor, Office of Planning and Research.

Poussaint, A. F. 1982 "What Every Black Woman Should Know about Black Men." *Ebony* (August): 36–40.

Staples, R. 1979 "The Myth of Black Macho: A Response to Angry Black Feminists." *Black Scholar* (March/April): 24–32.

Wallace, M. 1979 *Black Macho and the Myth of the Superwoman*. New York: Dial.

——— 1982 "A Black Feminist's Search for Sisterhood." In *All the Blacks Are Men, All the Women Are White, but Some of Us Are Brave*, G. T. Hull et al., eds. pp. 5–8. Old Westbury, N.Y.: Feminist Press.

THE INEXPRESSIVE MALE:
TRAGEDY OR SEXUAL POLITICS?

JACK W. SATTEL

In this brief essay, I am concerned with the phenomenon of "male inexpressiveness" as it has been conceptualized by Balswick and Peek (1971). In their conceptualization, male inexpressiveness is seen as a culturally produced temperament trait which is learned by boys as the major characteristic of their forthcoming adult masculinity. Such inexpressiveness is evidenced in two ways. First, adult male behavior which does not indicate affection, tenderness, or emotion is inexpressive behavior. Second, and somewhat differently, behavior which is not supportive of the affective expectations of one's wife is inexpressive behavior. It is the latter variety of inexpressiveness which occupies the major concern of Balswick and Peek. They suggest that the inability of the American male to unlearn inexpressiveness in order to relate effectively to a woman is highly dysfunctional to the emerging standards of the companionate, intimate American marriage. Ironically, Balswick and Peek see inexpressiveness in contexts outside the marriage relationship as functional insofar as in nonmarital situations the inexpressiveness of the male to females other than one's spouse works to prevent threats to the primacy of the marital bond, that is, it presumably functions to ward off infidelity. The authors further suggest two styles of adult inexpressiveness: the "cowboy—John Wayne" style of almost total inarticulateness and the more cool, detached style of the "playboy," who communicates only to exploit women sexually.

The article has proved to be an important one in forcing sociologists to rethink old conceptual stereotypes of masculinity and femininity. In part, it has helped to contribute to efforts to rescue for both sexes qualities and, potentials that previously were thought to belong to only one sex. On the other hand, it would be unfortunate if Balswick and Peek's conceptualization would enter the sociological literature as the last word on the dilemma of male inexpressiveness—unfortunate because, despite their real insight, I think they fundamentally misconstrue both the origin and the playing out of male inexpressiveness in our society.

In the note which follows, I would like to reconsider the phenomenon of male inexpressiveness, drawing upon my own and other men's experiences in consciousness-raising groups (especially as recounted in *Unbecoming Men: A Men's Consciousness-Raising Group Writes on Oppression and Themselves* (Bradley et al., 1971), as well as some of the literature which has appeared since Balswick and Peek first published their article.

BECOMING INEXPRESSIVE: SOCIALIZATION

The process of becoming inexpressive is cast by Balswick and Peek in the traditional vocabulary of the literature of socialization:

*Children, from the time they are born both explic-
itly and implicitly are taught how to be a man or
how to be a woman. While the girl is taught to act
"feminine," . . . the boy is taught to be a man. In
learning to be a man, the boy in American society
comes to value expressions of masculinity . . .
[such as] physical courage, toughness, competitiveness, and aggressiveness. (1971: 363–364)*

Balswick and Peek's discussion of this socialization process is marred in two ways. Theoretically, their discussion ignores the critique
of the socialization literature initially suggested
by Wrong (1961) in his analysis of sociology's
"oversocialized concept of man [sic]." Wrong,
using a largely Freudian vocabulary, argued that
it is incorrect to see the individual as something
"hollowed out" into which norms are simply
poured. Rather, "conformity" and "internalization" should always be conceptualized as
problematic. For example, if we consider inexpressiveness to be a character trait, as do Balswick and Peek, we should also be aware that the
normative control of that trait is never complete—being threatened constantly by both the
presumably more expressive demands of the id
and the excessive ("perfectionist") demands of
the "internalized norms" of the superego.
Wrong's point is well taken. While the norms of
our society may well call for all little boys to
grow up to be inexpressive, the inexpressiveness
of the adult male should never be regarded as
complete or total, as Balswick and Peek would
have it.

For them to have ignored this point is particularly crucial given their concern to rescue some
capacity of authentic expressiveness for the
male. Their suggestion that men simply "unlearn" their inexpressiveness through contact
with a woman (spouse) is unsatisfactory for two
reasons. First, it forfeits the possibility that men
can rescue themselves through enhanced self-
knowledge or contact with other men. Second, *it
would seem to make the task of rescuing men just
one more task of women.* That is, the wife is expected to restore to her husband that which was
initially taken from him in socialization.

A second problem with Balswick and Peek's
discussion of socialization and inexpressiveness
is that they ignore the peculiarly asymmetrical
patterns of socialization in our society which
make it much more dangerous for a boy to be
incompletely socialized than a girl. For example, much of the literature suggests that parents
and other adults exert greater social control to
insure that boys "grow up male" than that girls
"grow up female" (Parsons, 1951)—as can be
seen in the fact that greater stigma is attached
to the boy who is labeled a sissy than to the girl
who is known as a tomboy. Failure to even consider this asymmetry reveals, I think, the major
weakness of Balswick and Peek's conceptualization of male inexpressiveness. They have no
explanation of *why* male inexpressiveness exists
or *how* it came into being and is maintained
other than to say that "our culture demands it."
Thus, while we can agree that male inexpressiveness is a tragedy, their analysis does not help
us to change the social conditions which produce that tragedy.

INEXPRESSIVENESS AND POWER

To break this chain of reasoning, I would like to
postulate that, in itself, male inexpressiveness is
of no particular value in our culture. Rather, it is
an instrumental requisite for assuming adult
male roles of power.

Consider the following. To effectively wield
power, one must be able both to convince others
of the rightness of the decisions one makes and
to guard against one's own emotional involvement in the consequences of that decision; that
is, one has to show that decisions are reached rationally and efficiently. One must also be able to
close one's eyes to the potential pain one's decisions have for others and for oneself. The general who sends troops into battle must show that
his decision is calculated and certain; to effectively implement that decision—hence, to maintain his position of power to make future
decisions—the general must put on a face of im-
passive conviction.

I would argue, in a similar vein, that a little boy must become inexpressive not simply because our culture expects boys to be inexpressive *but because our culture expects little boys to grow up to become decision makers and wielders of power.*

From this example, I am suggesting that inexpressiveness is not just learned as an end in itself. Rather, it is learned as a means to be implemented later in men assuming and maintaining positions of power. More generally:

(A) INEXPRESSIVENESS in a role is determined by the corresponding power *(actual or potential) of that role.*

In light of this generalization, we might consider why so many sociologists tend to merge the universalistic–particularistic (rational) and the affective neutrality–affectivity (expressive) distinction in any discussion of real social behavior. In the case of the general, it would seem that the ability to give an inexpressive—that is, an affectively neutral—coloring to his decisions or positions contributes to the apparent rationality of those decisions or positions. Inexpressiveness validates the rightness of one's position. In fact, the social positions of highest power—not incidentally always occupied by men—demand veneers of both universalism and inexpressiveness of their incumbents, suggesting that at these levels *both* characteristics merge into a style of control. (Consider both Kennedy in the missile crisis and Nixon at Watergate. While otherwise quite dissimilar, in a crisis and challenge to their position, both men felt that "stonewalling" was the solution to the situation.)

From the above, it also follows logically the inexpressiveness might be more a characteristic of upper-class, powerful males than of men in the working classes. Many people—sociologists included—would probably object to such a deduction, saying the evidence is in the other direction, pointing at the Stanley Kowalski or Marty of literary fiction. I am not so sure. To continue with examples from fiction for a moment, the early autobiographical novels of, say, James Baldwin and Paul Goodman, dealing with lower- and working-class youth, consistently depicted "making it" as a not unusual tradeoff for one's sensitivity and expressiveness. More empirically, the recent work of Sennett and Cobb in their study of working-class life, *The Hidden Injuries of Class* (1972), suggests that upward mobility by working-class men was seen by them as entailing a certain phoniness or inauthentic relationship with one's *male* peers as well as a sacrifice of a meaningful expressive relationship with children and wife. The result of this for the men interviewed by Sennett and Cobb was often a choice to forego upward mobility and power because it involved becoming something one was not. It involved learning to dissemble inauthentic display of expressiveness toward higher-ups as well as involving the sacrifice of already close relationships with one's friends and family.

INEXPRESSIVENESS AND POWER AS SITUATIONAL VARIABLES

In their article, Balswick and Peek include a notion of inexpressiveness not just as a socially acquired temperament trait but also as a situational variable. Thus while they argue that all males are socialized into inexpressiveness, they also argue that "for many males . . . through progressively more serious involvements with women (such as going steady, being pinned, engagement, and the honeymoon period of marriage), [these males] begin to make some exceptions. That is, they may learn to be *situationally rather than totally inexpressive*" (1971, 365–366). As noted above, this is seen by Balswick and Peek as functional for men and for the marriage relation in two ways. It meets the wife's expectation of affective support for herself while usually being accompanied by continued inexpression toward women who are not one's spouse. Thus, in this sense, the situational unlearning of inexpressiveness enhances the marital relationship while guarding against extramarital relationships which would threaten the basic pairing of husband-wife.

There is, on the surface, a certain descriptive validity to Balswick and Peek's depiction, although, interestingly, they do not consider a latent function of such unlearning. To the extent that an ability to be expressive *in situ* with a woman leads to satisfactory and gratifying consequences in one case, it probably doesn't take long for the male to learn to be expressive with *any* woman—not just his spouse—as a mode of approaching that woman. Some men, for example, admit to this in my consciousness-raising group. This, in fact, is a way of "coming on" with a woman—a relaxation of the usual standards of inexpressiveness as a calculated move to establish a sexual relationship. Skill at dissembling in this situation may have less to do with handing a woman a "line" than with showing one's weaknesses and frailties as clues intended to be read by her as signs of authentic male interest. In many Latin cultures, which might be considered to epitomize traditional male supremist modes, the style of *machismo*, in fact, calls for the male to be dependent, nominally open, and very expressive to whichever woman he is currently trying to "make." The point of both these examples is to suggest that the *situational unlearning* of inexpressiveness need not lead to strengthening the marriage bond and, in fact, may be detrimental to it, since what works in one situation will probably be tried in others.

Following the argument developed in the previous section concerning the interplay between power and inexpressiveness, I would suggest a different conceptualization of the situational relevance of inexpressiveness:

> (B) EXPRESSIVENESS in a sexist culture empirically emerges as an effort on the part of the male to control a situation (once again, on his terms) and to maintain his position.

What I am suggesting is that in a society such as ours, which so permeates all social relationships with notions of power and exchange, even what may appear on the surface to be authentic can be an extension rather than a negation of (sexual) politics.

This is even more true of male inexpressive behavior in intimate male-female relationships. The following dialogue is drawn from Erica Jong's novel of upper-middle-class sexual etiquette, *Fear of Flying*. Consider the political use of male inexpressiveness:

SHE: "Why do you always have to do this to me? You make me feel so lonely."

HE: "That comes from you."

"What do you mean it comes from me? Tonight I wanted to be happy. It's Christmas Eve. Why do you turn on me? What did I do?"

Silence

"What did I do?"

He looks at her as if her not knowing were another injury. "Look, let's just go to sleep now. Let's just forget it."

"Forget what?"

He says nothing.

"Forget the fact that you turned on me? Forget the fact that you're punishing me for nothing? Forget the fact that I'm lonely and cold, that it's Christmas Eve and again you've ruined it for me? Is that what you want me to forget?"

"I won't discuss it."

"Discuss what?" "What won't you discuss?"

"Shut up! I won't have you screaming in the hotel."

"I don't give a fuck what you won't have me do. I'd like to be treated civilly. I'd like you to at least do me the courtesy of telling me why you're in such a funk. And don't look at me that way. . . ."

"What way?"

"As if my not being able to read your mind were my greatest sin. I *can't* read your mind. I *don't* know why you're so mad. I can't intuit your wish. If that's what you want in a wife you don't have it in me."

"I certainly don't."

"Then what is it? Please tell me."

"I shouldn't have to."

"Good God! Do you mean to tell me I'm expected to be a mind reader? Is that the kind of mothering you want?"

"If you had any empathy for me . . ."

"But I *do*. My God, you just don't give me a chance."

"You tune out. You don't listen."

"It was something in the movie wasn't it?"

"What in the movie?"

"The quiz again. Do you have to quiz me like some kind of criminal. Do you have to cross-examine me? . . . It was the funeral scene . . . The little boy looking at his dead mother. Something got you there. That was when you got depressed."

Silence

"Oh come on, Bennett, you're making me *furious*. Please tell me. Please."

(He gives the words singly like little gifts. Like hard little turds.) "What was it about the scene that got me?"

"Don't quiz me. Tell me!" (She puts her arms around him. He pulls away. She falls to the floor holding onto his pajama leg. It looks less like an embrace than a rescue scene, she sinking, he reluctantly allowing her to cling to his leg for support.)

"Get up!"

(Crying) "Only if you tell me."

(He jerks his leg away.) "I'm going to bed."
    (Jong, 1973: 108–109)

One wonders if this is what Balswick and Peek mean by a man "unlearning" his inexpressiveness. Less facetiously, this is clearly an example which indicates that inexpression on the part of the male is not just a matter of inarticulateness or even a deeply socialized inability to respond to the needs of others. The male here is *using* inexpression to guard his own position. To *not* say anything in this situation is to say something very important indeed: that the battle we are engaged in is to be fought by my rules and when I choose to fight. In general:

(C) Male INEXPRESSIVENESS empirically emerges as an intentional manipulation of a situation when threats to the male position occur.

INEXPRESSIVENESS AND MALE CULTURE

Balswick and Peek see inexpressiveness as a major quality of male–female interaction. I have tried to indicate about where they might be right in making such an attribution as well as some of the inadequacies of their conceptualization of the origins of that inexpressiveness. A clear gap in their conceptualization, however, is their lack of any consideration of the inexpressive male in interaction with other men. In fact, their conceptualization leads to two contradictory deductions. First, given the depth and thoroughness of socialization, we might deduce that the male is inexpressive with other men, as well as with women. Second, the male, who is only situationally inexpressive, can interact and express himself truly in situations with other men. This latter position finds support in the notions of male bonding developed by Lionel Tiger (1969). The former position is validated by some of the contributors to Pleck and Sawyer's recent reader on *Men and Masculinity* (1974; esp. Candell, Jourard, and Fasteau). In this section, I would like to raise some of the questions that bear on the problem of male-to-male inexpressiveness. (1) Is there a male subculture? Subcultural differences are usually identified as having ethnic, religious, occupational, etc., boundaries; gender is not usually considered to define subcultural differences. This is so even though gender repeatedly proves to be among the most statistically significant variables in most empirical research. Yet, if we think of a subculture as consisting of unique patterns of belief, value, technique, and language use, there would be a *prima facie* case for considering "male" and "female" definitive of true subcultures in almost all societies. (2) What is the origin of male and female subcultures? This question is probably the most inclusive of all the questions one can ask about gender and sex-role differences. It thrusts us into the very murky swamp of the origin of the family, patriarchy, sexism, etc. Sidestepping questions of the ultimate origin of male and female cultural differences, I would only suggest that a good case might be made for considering the persistence—if not the origin—of male and female subcultural differences as due to male efforts to maintain privilege and position *vis-à-vis* women. This is the point anthropologists have been quick to make about primitive societies. The ritual and magic of the males is a secret to be guarded against the women's eyes. Such magic is privy only to the men, and access to it in rites of passage finally determines who is man and who is only *other*. Similar processes are at work in our own society. Chodorow's distinction between "being" and "doing" (1971) is a way of talking about male and female subcultural differences that makes it clear that what men "do" defines not only their own activity but the activity ("being") of women as well. Benston's (1969) distinction between male production of exchange-value in the public sphere and female creation of use-value in the private sphere captures the same fundamental differential of power underlying what appears to be merely cultural. (3) Is male culture necessarily inexpressive? Many observers would say it is flatly wrong to assert that men are inexpressive when interacting with other men. Tiger (1969), for example, talks of the games (sport) men share as moments of intense and authentic communication and expression. In fact, for Tiger, sport derives from the even more intense solidarity of the prehistoric hunt—a solidarity that seems, in his scheme to be almost genetic in origin. I think Tiger, and others who would call our attention to this capacity for male expressiveness, are saying something important but partial. Perhaps the following example drawn from adult reminiscences of one's fourteenth year can make this clearer:

I take off at full speed not knowing whether I would reach it but knowing very clearly that this is my chance. My cap flies off my head . . . and a second later I one-hand it as cool as can be. . . . I hear the applause. . . . I hear voices congratulating my mother for having such a good athlete for a son. . . . Everybody on the team pounds my back as they come in from the field, letting me know that I've made it. (Candell in Pleck and Sawyer, 1974: 16)

This is a good picture of boys being drawn together in sport, of sharing almost total experience.

But is it? The same person continues in the next paragraph:

But I know enough not to blow my cool so all I do is mumble thanks under a slightly trembling upper lip which is fighting the rest of my face, the rest of being, from exploding with laughter and tears of joy. (Candell in Pleck and Sawyer, 1974: 19)

Why this silence? Again, I don't think it is just because our culture demands inexpression. I think here, as above, silence and inexpression are the ways men learn to *consolidate* power, to make the effort appear as effortless, to guard against showing the real limits of one's potential and power by making it *all* appear easy. Even among males alone, one maintains control over a situation by revealing only strategic proportions of oneself.

Further, in Marc Fasteau's very perceptive article "Why Men Aren't Talking" (Pleck and Sawyer, 1974), the observation is made that when men do talk, they talk of "large" problems—war, politics, art—but never of anything really personal. Even when men have equal credentials in achieved success, they tend not to make themselves vulnerable to each other, for to do so may be interpreted as a sign of weakness and an opportunity for the other to secure advantage. As Fasteau puts it, men talk, but they always do so for a *reason*—getting together for its own sake would be too frightening—and that reason often amounts to just another effort at establishing who *really* is best, stronger, smarter, or ultimately, more powerful.

INEXPRESSIVENESS AND THE SOCIOLOGY OF SEX ROLES

In the preceding sections, I have tried to change the grounds of an explanation of male inexpressiveness from one which holds that it is simply a cultural variable to one which sees it as a consequence of the political (power) position of the sexes in our society. I have not tried to deny that male inexpressiveness exists but only that it does so in different forms and for different reasons than Balswick and Peek suggest. I am making no claims for the analytic completeness of the ideas presented here.

A direct result of the feminist movement has been the effort on the part of sociologists concerned with family and sex-role-related behavior to discard or recast old concepts in the face of the feminist critique. One tendency of this "new sociology" has been an attempt to rescue attributes of positive human potential from the exclusive domain of one sex and, thus, to validate those potentials for all people. Although they do not say this explicitly, some such concern certainly underlies Balswick and Peek's effort. I think that this is social science at its best.

On the other hand, I am not convinced, as Balswick and Peek seem to be, that significant change in the male sex role will be made if we conceptualize the problem as one that involves individual males gradually unlearning their inexpressiveness with individual females. Balswick (1974) wrote an article based on the analysis developed with Peek entitled "Why Husbands Can't Say 'I Love You'" and printed it in a mass distribution women's magazine. Predictably, the article suggests *to the wife* some techniques she might develop for drawing her husband out of his inexpressive shell. I think that

kind of article—at this point in the struggle of women to define themselves—is facile and wrongheaded. Such advice burdens the wife with additional "emotional work" while simultaneously creating a new arena in which she can—and most likely will—fail.

Similarly, articles that speak to men about their need to become more expressive also miss the point if we are concerned about fundamental social change. Such arguments come fairly cheap. Witness the essentially honest but fatally narrow and class-bound analyses of Korda (1973) and Farrell (1974). Their arguments develop little more than strategies capable of salvaging a limited number of upper-class male heterosexual egos. The need I see and feel at this point is for arguments and strategies capable of moving the majority of men who are not privileged in that fashion. What such arguments would say—much less to whom they would be addressed—is a question I cannot now answer. But I know where my work lies. For if my argument is correct—and I believe it is—that male inexpressiveness is instrumental in maintaining positions of power and privilege for men, then male sociologists might well begin to search through their own experiences and the accumulated knowledge of the sociological literature for sensitizing models which might indicate how, and if, it would be possible to relinquish the power which has historically been ours.

REFERENCES

Balswick, Jack. 1974. "Why husbands can't say 'I love you.'" *Woman's Day*, April.

Balswick, Jack and Charles Peek. 1971. "The inexpressive male: a tragedy of American society." *The Family Coordinator*, 20: 363–368.

Benston, Margaret. 1969. "The political economy of women's liberation." *Monthly Review*, 21: 13–27.

Bradley, Mike. 1971. *Unbecoming Men: A Men's Consciousness Raising Group Writes on Oppression and Themselves.* New York: Times Change Press.

Chodorow, Nancy. 1971. "Being and doing: a cross-cultural examination of the socialization of males and females," pp. 259–291 In Gornick and Moran

(eds.), *Women in Sexist Society.* New York: New American Library.

Farrell, Warren. 1974. *The Liberated Man.* New York: Random House.

Jong, Erica. 1973. *Fear of Flying.* New York: New American Library.

Korda, Michael. 1973. *Male Chauvinism: How It Works.* New York: Random House.

Parsons, Talcott. 1951. *The Social System* (Chapter VI and VII). Glencoe, Illinois: Free Press.

Pleck, Joseph and Jack Sawyer. 1974. *Men and Masculinity.* Englewood Cliffs, New Jersey: Prentice-Hall.

Sennett, Richard and Jonathan Cobb. 1973. *The Hidden Injuries of Class.* New York: Random House.

Tiger, Lionel. 1971. *Men in Groups.* London: Granada Publishing.

Wrong, Dennis. 1961. "The oversocialized conception of man in modern sociology." *American Sociological Review*, 26: 183–193.

THE CIVIC ADVOCACY OF VIOLENCE

WAYNE EWING

The ruling paradigm for male supremacy remains, to this hour, physical violence. This paradigm remains unchecked and untouched by change. Critically, the permissive environment for male violence against women is supported by a civic advocacy of violence as socially acceptable, appropriate and necessary. Physically abusive men, particularly men who batter their spouses, continue for the most part to be a protected population. And the sources which provide us with what we know of the batterer—largely clinical and treatment models—have themselves remained too isolated from sexual politics and from a social analysis of male cultures. Until the code of male violence is read, translated and undone, male batterers will not be largely affected by what we are coming to know about them.

PROFILING THE MALE BATTERER

I sometimes think that none of the literature will ever move our knowledge dramatically further than Erin Pizzey's observation that all batterers are either alcoholics or psychotics or psychopaths or just plain bullies. That is good common sense applied to the all too ordinary affair of men beating up women. I also think that the following observation, more often than not made rhetorically and politically, has a measure of significance that we can draw on. When the question is raised,

"Who is the male batterer?" the answer is sometimes given, "Every man!" Without pushing too quickly let me simply point out here that this observation is accurate. It is not simply an attention-getter. Attempts to profile the male batterer always wind up with a significant body of information which points to . . . every man.

I believe the most striking example of this is found in those studies which support the—in my estimation, accurate—view of male violence as a learned behavior. Depending on the study, 81% to 63% of the population of batterers researched have either experienced abuse as victims in the home of their childhood or have witnessed their fathers beat their mothers. While that is significant enough to support our forming knowledge that socialization into violence in the home perpetuates violence, and that individual men can be conditioned to domestic violence as normal, I do not believe we have spent enough time looking at the chilling fact that remains: from 19% to 37% of these populations have literally invented violence in an intimate relationship. It is clear that the experience as victim or observer of physical violence is not necessary to "produce" a violent, abusive man.

And so it is with any of the many categories of inquiry applied to populations of male batterers. I will tick some of these off here, and in each case refer to the batterers with whom I work in Denver. *Ethnic backgrounds*, for example, will

Reprinted from *M.,* Spring 1982.

Adapted from a paper delivered in the Women's Studies Division of the Western Social Science Association annual meeting, 1981, and part of a book-length manuscript in progress, *Violence Works/Stop Violence.*

closely parallel the ethnic makeup of the community in which the study is made. In intake interviews of men either volunteering or ordered by the Courts into the men's groups of our project in Denver, the statistics generated on ethnicity are the statistics available about our community in general. *Age* is not a major factor. While most physically abusive men are in their 20s or early 30s, batterers are also under 20 and over 50. The fact that slightly more than half the men we deal with in Denver are in their 20s is attributable to so many other possibilities, that the fact itself recedes in significance. *Education* is not a major determinant. While a majority of batterers may have a high-school education, the ones we know are equally balanced on either side by men with undergraduate, graduate and professional degrees and men with less than a high-school education. *Income* studies do not support the popular idea that battering men are low income earners. Over a third of the men studied in Denver have incomes of $15,000 and above; and regular employment is as much a feature of the batterer as is infrequent employment. The *onset and frequency of violence* within a relationship are not consistent indicators of the behavior profile of the male batterer. The only conclusion safely drawn from these inquiries is that the probability of maiming and permanently crippling injury for the victim rises with the increase of frequency, and that the period of contrition on the part of the batterer becomes briefer between episodes as frequency increases. *Substance abuse* may as easily accompany battering episodes as not. In Denver, it is involved in a little over a third, while in other populations studied, substance abuse may figure in as much as 80% of battering episodes. And of course the self-reported "*causes*" of violence from both victims and abusers runs from sex to in-laws to money to housework to children to employment and around and around and around. There is no real clue to the profile of the abusive male in these reported occasions for battering episodes. With respect to the *psychological makeup* of the abusive male, there is considerable consensus

that these men evidence low self-esteem, dependency needs, unfamiliarity with their emotions, fear of intimacy, poor communication skills and performance orientation. But what is intriguing about these observations is that they span all of these other indicators.

And so I end this brief review where I started. The abusive male—that is, the violent man of low self-esteem, high dependency need, slow on affect, fearful of intimacy, poor in communicating emotions, and oriented to performance—the abusive male is every man.

THE CYCLE OF VIOLENCE

How is it we know so little, then, about the male batterer? In part this is due to the fact that the movement begun by the female victims of male violence has not spawned a fervent desire to look at the abuser. The simple fact is that as massive as male domestic violence is, we know more about the victims than we do about the abusers. There are some very obvious realities at work here. If we are to serve, counsel, protect, renurture and heal victims, we must come to know them, to understand the cycle of violence in which they are terrorized and victimized. We need to elicit from them the motivation to break the cycle of violence. But if we are to intervene in the cycle of violence in society at large—which is after all, the sustainer of violence from men toward women—the batterer must be known as well. For every female victim who is freed from the cycle of violence without intervening in the actual behavior of the male abuser, we still have a battering male-at-large.

We do know that a particular characteristic of the cycle of male violence—the period of contrition—is critical to how the cycle repeats itself in relationships: the building up of tension and conflict; the episode of battering; the time of remorse; the idyllic time of reconciliation. And then the cycle begins again. What is going on in the time of remorse? How is it that this apparent recognition of violent behavior is insufficient to provoke change and to begin a cycle of nonviolent behaviors? It seems to me that remorse is a time-honored device, within male-dominant, sexist cultures, for "making things right" again. I refer of course to the Judeo-Christian model of "making things right"—as it was always stated until very recently in the texts of theology and of devotion—between "God and man." This whole pattern of remorse, guilt, repentance, newly invigorated belief, and forgiveness has had one of the most profound symbolic impacts on Western male consciousness.

When a man physically abuses a woman, it is a matter of course for him to fall back on this model. Things can be "made right," not by actual change, but by feeling awful, by confessing it, and by *believing* that the renewal of the relationship is then effected. That this is more hocus-pocus than authentically religious hardly matters. A crippling consequence of this major model for renewal and change—remorse followed by forgiveness-taken-for-granted—is an almost guaranteed start up of the previous behavior once again. The *non* resolution which we violent men rehearse by remorse and "resolve" is vacuous. It is the exercise of a mere accompaniment to violence. And particularly where our dependency on the female victim of our abuse is so strong, the simple telling of the "resolve" not to be violent again is seen as establishing how good we are in fact.

Actually, the interweaving of the violence and the remorse is so tight that the expression of remorse to the victim establishes how good we have been, and how good we are. The remorse is not even a future-oriented "resolve"; it is more an internalized benediction we give to the immediately preceding episode of battery. There is no shock of recognition here in the cycle of violence. It is not a matter of "Oh my god, did I do that?" It is a matter of *stating* "Oh my god, I couldn't have done that," implying that *I in fact did not do it*. The confession of remorse then only reinforces the self-perception that I did not do it. Remorse, in this model of "making things right" again, literally wipes the slate clean. Over and over again we violent men are puzzled as to

how it is our victims come to a place where they will not tolerate our violence and so report us or walk out on us. Can't they see that the violence no longer counts as real, because I said I was sorry?

Whatever clinical research reveals to us about the population of batterers, the fact of denial built into the cycle of violence itself veils from both us and the batterer the reality of the violence. Over and over again, abusive men will ask what the fuss is all about. They hold as a right and privilege the behavior of assault and battery against "their" women. Our groups in Denver are filled with men from all walks and circumstances of life to whom it has never occurred that battering is wrong. In other words, one reason we know so little about male batterers is that they only reluctantly come to *speak* of battering at all.

Another factor further veils this population from us. Male batterers continue to be deliberately protected in the careful construction of familial silence; in the denial of neighbors, friends, clergy, teachers and the like that battering can be "true" for John and Mary; in the failure of law enforcement to "preserve and protect" the victims of domestic violence; in the unwillingness of local and state governments to provide shelter for victims; or in the editorializing of the Eagle Forum that the safe house movement is an anti-male, lesbian conspiracy. Male violence has become the ordinary, the expected, the usual.

THE CIVIC ADVOCACY OF VIOLENCE

What remains is for us to deal with what very few of us want to confront: American life remains sexist and male supremacist in spite of the strides of the second wave of American feminism. Whether it be snide—"You've come a long way, baby"—or whether it be sophisticated—George Gilder's *Sexual Suicide*—the put down of women's quest for equality, dignity and freedom from male oppression is damn near total in the America of the 1980s. I contend that the ultimate put down is the continuing advocacy of violence against women, and that until we confront that advocacy with integrity and resolve, the revolution in men's consciousness and behavior cannot get underway.

I used to think that we simply tolerated and permitted male abusiveness in our society. I have now come to understand rather, that we *advocate* physical violence. Violence is presented as effective. Violence is taught as the normal, appropriate and necessary behavior of power and control.

We apparently have no meaningful response to violence. I am convinced that until the voices that say "No!" to male violence are more numerous than those that say "Yes?," we will not see change. Nor will we men who want to change our violent behaviors find the support necessary to change. And silence in the face of violence is heard as "Yes!"

Under the governing paradigm of violence as effective and normal, every man can find a place. The individual male who has not beaten a woman is still surrounded by a civic environment which claims that it *would* and *could* be appropriate for him to beat a woman. He is immersed in a civic advocacy of violence which therefore contends that should he have committed battery, it is normal; and should he have not committed battery, it is only that he has not *yet* committed battery, given the ordinary course of affairs. In sexual political terms, we men can simply be divided into pre-battery and post-battery phases of life.

The teaching of violence is so pervasive, so totally a part of male experience, that I think it best to acknowledge this teaching as a *civic*, rather than as a cultural or as a social phenomenon. Certainly there are social institutions which form pieces of the total advocacy of violence: marriage and family; ecclesiastical institutions; schools; economic and corporate institutions; government and political institutions. And there are cultural and sub-cultural variations on the theme and reality of violence, of course. I believe, however, that if we are to crack the code of violent male behavior, we must begin where the environment of advocacy

is total. Total civic advocacy is the setting for all the varieties of cultural adaptations from which violent men come.

For this total, pervasive advocacy of violence, I can find no better word than *civic*. The word has a noble ring to it, and calls up the manner in which the people of a nation, a society, a culture are schooled in basic citizenship. That's precisely what I want to call up. Civic responsibilities and civil affairs are what we come to expect as normal, proper and necessary. Violence, in male experience, *is* just such an expectation. Violence is *learned* within the environment of civic advocacy.

Demonstrating this is perhaps belaboring the obvious. But when we fail to belabor the obvious, the obvious continues to escape us and becomes even in its pervasiveness, part of an apparently innocent environment or backdrop. "Oh, say can you see. . . ." Our National Anthem can perhaps be thought of as simply romanticizing war, mayhem, bloodshed and violence. But more than that, reflection on the content of the song shows that we pride ourselves, civically, on the fortress mentality of siege, endurance and battle. The headier virtues of civic responsibility—freedom and justice—are come to only in the context of violence. "The rockets' red glare, the bombs bursting in air, are as ordinary to us as the school event, the sporting event, the civic sanction in which we conjure up hailing America "o'er the ramparts."

"I pledge allegiance. . . ." The flag of violence becomes the object of fidelity and devotion for American children even before they know the meaning of "allegiance." Yet feudal-like obeisance—the hand over the heart and devotional hush to the recitation—to the liege lords of violence is sanctioned as appropriate behavior quite calmly with this ritual.

We might assume of course that because this is ritual no one takes it seriously. That's precisely my point. We don't take it seriously at all. We just take it, live it, breathe it, feel awkward when we don't participate in the ritual, feel condemnatory when others around us don't participate in the ritual, and so on. The environment of civic advocacy of violence *is* ordinary, and not extra-ordinary.

THE EVERYDAY LANGUAGE OF VIOLENCE

Language is not innocent of meaning, intent and passion. Otherwise, there would be no communication between us at all. Yet words fall from our mouths—even in the civil illustrations above—as if there were no meaning, intent and passion involved. What I make of this is that the advocacy of violence is so pervasive, that the human spirit somehow, someway, mercifully inures itself to the environment. We are numbed and paralyzed by violence, and so continue to speak the language of violence as automatons.

I am not referring to the overt, up front renditions of violence we men use in describing battery and battering. "Giving it to the old woman" and "kicking the shit out of her" however, are phenomenologically on the same level of meaning, intention and passion as: assaulting a problem; conquering fear, nature, a woman; shooting down opinions; striking out at injustices; beating you to the punch; beating an idea to death; striking a blow for free enterprise, democracy; whomping up a meal; pounding home an idea; being under the gun to perform; "It strikes me that. . . ." You can make your own list of violent language. Listen to yourself. Listen to those around you. The meaning, intent and passion of violence are everywhere to be found in the ordinary language of ordinary experience.

Analyses which interweave the advocacy of male violence with "Super-Bowl Culture" have never been refuted. It is too obvious. Civic expectations—translated into professionalism, financial commitments, city planning for recreational space, the raising of male children for competitive sport, the corporate ethics of business ownership of athletic teams, profiteering on entertainment—all result in the monument of the National Football League, symbol and reality at once of the advocacy of violence. How piously the network television cameras turn

away from out-and-out riots on the fields and in the stands. But how expertly the technologies of the television medium replay, stop action, and replay and replay and replay "a clean hit." Like the feelies of George Orwell's 1984, giant screens in bar and home can go over and over the bone-crunching tackle, the quarterback sack, the mid-air hit—compared in slow motion to dance and ballet, sophisticating violence in aesthetic terms. We love it. We want it. We pay for it. And I don't mean the black market price or a Bronco season ticket or the inflated prices of the beer, automobile accessories and tires, shaving equipment and the like which put the violence on the screen. I mean the human toll, the broken women and children of our land, and we frightened men who beat them. And even if I were to claim that neither you nor I is affected by the civic advocacy of violence in commercialism and free enterprise, we would still have to note that the powers and scions of industry *believe*—to the tune of billions of dollars a year—that we are so affected.

Pornography is no more a needed release for prurient sexual energies than would be the continuation of temple prostitutes. But it is sanctioned, and the civic advocacy of violence through pornography is real. It is not on the decrease. Soft porn is no longer *Charlie's Angels* or the double entendres of a Johnny Carson-starlet interview; that's simply a matter of course. Soft porn is now *Playboy*, *Penthouse*, and *Oui*, where every month, right next to the chewing gum and razor blades at the corner grocery, air-sprayed photographs play into male masturbatory fantasies. Hard porn itself is becoming more "ordinary" every day; child porn and snuff films lead the race in capturing the male market for sex and violence. We love it. We want it. And we pay for it. Violence works.

Insofar as violence works, the male batterer is finally, and somewhat definitively, hidden from us. I would not denigrate or halt for a moment our struggle to know the male batterer through clinical research models. But I would call all who are interested in knowing him and in intervening in and ending the cycle of the violence of men against women, to the larger context of the civic advocacy of violence. There, I believe, is the complement of the analysis generated by profiling the male batterer.

Until the code of male violence is undone, male dominance and sexism will prevail. Until the commerce in violence against women ceases, and we finally create an environment in which violence is no longer acceptable or conceivable, male supremacy will remain a fact of life for all of us.

"LET'S GET A GIRL":
MALE BONDING RITUALS IN AMERICA

JANE C. HOOD

PROLOGUE

Wednesday, April 19, 1989: 10:05 P.M. "A 28 year old investment banker, jogging through Central Park, was attacked by a group of teenagers. They kicked and beat her, smashed her in the head with a pipe and raped her. The teenagers who were from East Harlem, were quickly arrested" (Terry 1989, p. 28).

Wednesday, March 1, 1989: c. 6:00 P.M. In Glen Ridge, New Jersey, five high-school football players sexually assaulted a 17-year-old mentally handicapped girl in a basement while eight other teenagers looked on (Foderado 1989). "No sexual intercourse took place, investigators said, but the girl was believed to have been forced to perform sexual acts with the boys and she was raped with several objects including a broomstick and a miniature baseball bat" . . . "The arrests were announced on May 24 by Essex County Prosecutor, Herbert H. Tate, Jr whose office took over the case last month when the son of Lieut. Richard Corcoran, a Glen Ridge officer, was identified as being present when the assault took place" (*New York Times* 1989).

For weeks following the April 19 assault of the Central Park jogger, newspapers around the nation carried stories about the backgrounds of the youths who had attacked her. Newspapers reported that the assailants had been rampaging through the park attacking victims at will, a prac-tice that some people called "wilding." Talk show participants debated whether the attack was racially motivated, and both black and white community leaders worried about how the publicity following the attack would affect race relations in the city. While sociologists discussed the socioeconomic roots of urban violence and clinicians described the psychic terror experienced by youths growing up in East Harlem, incumbent politicians urged "get tough" policies to "stamp out terrorism in the streets." Over a month after the attack, local New York City newspapers still carried headlines on the jogger's condition such as "Jogger Kisses Cardinal."

With the exception of some excellent articles in the *Village Voice* (1989) and op-ed articles by Susan Chace (1989) and Elizabeth Holtzman (1989), hardly any of this "media orgy" dealt with gender or the phenomenon of gang rape. However, by the time news of the Glen Ridge assault surfaced on May 24, at least part of the media spotlight had shifted to rape. On May 29, *New York Times* readers finally learned that 28 other rapes had been reported to New York City police during the week of April 16 and that nearly all of these were of black and Hispanic women (Terry 1989). Of all these assaults, only the rape of an upper-middle-class white jogger by a group of black youths had made the news.

This essay is a revised and expanded version of the full text of an article originally published in the *New York Times* under the title, "Why Our Society is Rape Prone" (Hood 1989). This version includes examples cut from the original text as well as references to the Glen Ridge case.

GANG RAPE AS A MALE BONDING RITUAL

Why did eight teenagers beat and rape a jogger in Central Park? Mostly missing from the analyses of "wilding," and lost among the suggestions for preventing similar tragedies, is one crucial issue: gender.

With the exception of prison assaults, gang rape is a crime committed almost exclusively by males against females. Yet few commentators have focused on gender and what it means to be raised male in America. Like the proverbial fish who cannot describe water, we Americans see everything *but* gender at work in the April 19 assault.

Given over 30 years of research on patterns of forcible rape, our myopia is hard to explain. In his classic 1959 study of 646 Philadelphia rapes, Menachem Amir (1971) described the prototype for the Central Park assault. Of 646 cases, 43% were pair or group rapes. Like the boys from Schomberg Plaza, the offenders were disproportionately very young (10 to 19). Amir also found that group rapes were much more likely than single-offender rapes to involve violence far beyond what would be necessary to restrain the victim. In an attempt to make sense of this pattern, several researchers (Amir 1971; Brownmiller 1975; Groth 1979; Sanday 1981; Herman 1984) reached a similar conclusion: In a society that equates masculinity with dominance and sex with violence, gang rape becomes one way for adolescents to prove their masculinity both to themselves and to each other.

Although other studies of sexual assault patterns do not find as high an incidence of pair and group rape as did Amir (Groth 1979, p. 110; Ageton 1983), when group rape does occur, the attack has a dual focus. Interaction among the assailants may take center stage as the men compete with each other in punishing, dominating, and humiliating the victim (Groth 1979, p. 118; Scully and Marolla 1985). In addition to being an outlet for rage and the need to dominate, gang rapes can also be a form of group recreation. The Schomburg Plaza boys said that they were "just having fun," and gang rapists interviewed by Scully and Marolla (1985, p. 260) described cruising an area "looking for girls" that they could pick up, drive to a deserted area, and then rape. Although not as well practiced in the art of gang rape as Scully and Marolla's informants, the teenagers rampaging through Central Park reportedly said, "Let's get a girl" shortly before they attacked the jogger (Chace 1989).

The attack on the investment banker was particularly brutal, but both it and the Glen Ridge assault have something in common with gang rapes of the sort portrayed in the film, "Saturday Night Fever." There, one boy lures a girl into the backseat of a car so that a whole group can have sex with her. An event that started as "sex" becomes rape as the boys begin to compete with each other, disregarding the girl's welfare or feelings. Similarly, in Glen Ridge, the girl appears to have gone willingly to the house with the boys before she was subjected to an hour of degradation at the hands of four boys while another urged them on and eight others watched (Foderaro 1989). Because victims may be reluctant to report this kind of assault to police or interviewers, Scully and Marolla (1985) think that these "date gang rapes" may be much more common than either police reports or the Uniform Crime Surveys indicate.

Both the Central Park and the Glen Ridge incidents also share some characteristics of "gang bangs" in fraternity houses and random violence against women on college campuses. These apparently diverse phenomena are connected, not by the severity of the crime and not by the characteristics of the victim, but rather by the common context of an adolescent male-bonding ritual in a rape-prone society.

In her research on gang rapes at the University of Pennsylvania, anthropologist Peggy Sanday has compiled vivid descriptions of gang rapes, which she suspects are a common practice on college campuses all over the United States (Sanday 1986, p. 99; 1988). They are, as are most gang rapes, planned in advance. The intended victim is plied with alcohol and/or pills until she can be dragged into a bedroom where she is then systematically raped by one boy after the other while the others look on. Afterward, the boys use the excuse that the girl was drunk and did not know what she was doing.

In comparing the fraternity members to the street gangs that Amir studied in the 1950s, Sanday argues that the two groups are similar in that both are peripheral to society. Whereas members of Amir's lower class Philadelphia street gangs may never escape their peripheral social and economic status, college males are temporarily peripheral "while they are learning skills they will eventually use to usurp their fathers' places in the corporate world" (Sanday 1986, p. 99).

Gang rape may be the most shocking male bonding ritual on college campuses, but it is not the only one that depends on objectifying women.

In an excellent article on the use of sexist jokes among fraternity men Peter Lyman (1987) describes an incident that took place at a sorority house. There a group of 45 fraternity men shoved their way into the dining room, encircled the women residents, and forced them to watch for 10 minutes while one "pledge" stroked a rubber phallus and another recited a speech on penis envy. After a resident adviser told the men to leave, the pranksters were surprised. After all (like the boys in Central Park), they were "just having fun," and the penis envy joke was a tradition. The women, however, argued that the raid had rape overtones and asked, "Why do you men always think about women in terms of violating them, in sexual imagery?" Why indeed?

RAPE-FREE VS. RAPE-PRONE SOCIETIES

The answer, I think, lies in understanding the difference between what University of Pennsylvania anthropologist Peggy Sanday calls "rape-prone" societies and those that are "rape-free." In a study of 95 band and tribal societies, Sanday (1981) found a high incidence of rape to be associated with militarism, interpersonal violence in general, an ideology of male toughness, and distant father–child relationships. Rape-free societies,

on the other hand, encourage female participation in the economy and political system and male involvement in child-rearing.

In rape-free societies men speak of women with respect. For example, a Minangakabau man in West Sumatra told Peggy Sanday:

Women are given more privileges because people think that women determine the continuation of the generations. Whether the next generation is good or bad depends upon women ... Women have more human feeling and they are more humanitarian. They think more about people's feelings and because of this they should be given rights to speak. (Sanday 1986, pp. 96–97)

In nonindustrial rape-free societies, women and men may have different roles, but the roles that women play are highly valued and help to shape the culture as a whole.

Despite recent moves toward gender equality, our society is still very much "rape-prone." In fact, the United States has the distinction of being among the most rape-prone of all modern societies (Scully and Marolla 1985). In surveys of U.S. and Canadian college students, for example, psychologist Neil Malamuth finds that one of three college men say that if they could get away with it, they would be at least "somewhat likely" to rape a woman (Malamuth 1981). Similarly, several recent surveys of high-school students find 40 to 50% of both boys and girls agreeing with such statements as, "If a girl goes to a guy's apartment after a date, it's OK for him to force her to have sex" (Hall, Howard, & Boezio 1986; Kikuchi 1989). Even jurors in rape trials studied by LaFree and Reskin (LaFree 1989, p. 219) found it hard to believe that an attractive man would rape a woman if he could have just as easily seduced her. As many authors point out, in rape-prone societies, rape is easily confused with "normal" sex.

In our own society, sex is so inextricably linked to violence that attempts to uncouple the two can fail in ways some of us may find hard to imagine. For example, after the release of *The Accused* (a film dramatizing the New Bedford pool hall gang rape), some middle-class male viewers were observed cheering at the harrowing gang rape scene (*The Nation*, 5-29-1989). Like the Schomburg Plaza boys, these movie goers had learned that masculinity means domination over others through sex and violence.

PREVENTION STRATEGIES

In a letter to the *New York Times*, John Gutfreund (1989), the jogger's employer, called for "an all-out national emergency effort to solve the problem of violence on urban streets." Others urged prosecuting the teenagers as adults and advocated long prison terms. Ridiculing the earlier version of this article, the *Richmond Times-Dispatch* called for "A little more jail time and a little less blame-society-first rationalizing."

Unfortunately, more lights in Central Park, more police on the streets, and more time in jail for convicted rapists will not do much to lower the overall incidence of rape. A man caught robbing a jewelry store is unlikely to use the defense that "it wasn't really a robbery." For rapists, however, the defense that "it wasn't really a rape" is commonplace (LaFree 1989; Scully and Marolla 1985). In spite of the creation of special Sexual Offense units in police departments and in spite of the adoption of "rape shield" laws that disallow questions concerning the victim's moral character, most rapes are never reported to the police and of those that are reported only a small proportion result in any jail time for offenders. Thus, in a study of 881 rapes reported to Indianapolis police in 1970, 1973, and 1975. LaFree found that only 12% resulted in convictions (LaFree 1989, p. 60). Because both male and female jurors believe that only certain kinds of men can rape and only certain kinds of women can be raped, rapes that do not fit the public's stereotype of "a real rape" are less likely to yield convictions.

As long as rapes of wives, girlfriends, hitchhikers, women in bars, and girls at fraternity parties are dismissed as "not really rape," doubling the jail time for the few men that are convicted will do little to reduce American women's one-out-of-three lifetime probability (Johnson 1980)

of sexual assault. If our society is to become less rape-prone, we must instead find ways of redefining gender relationships so that women become men's peers and boys can become men without controlling, dominating, and objectifying girls and women.

Therefore, if corporate leaders want to mount an effective national campaign to prevent assaults on women by bands of young men, they should target, not "criminals," but

- advertisements portraying women as sex objects
- sexual harassment in the work place
- resistance to paternity leave policies
- Rambo dolls and other violent games and toys
- gender inequality in the workplace.

For their part, community groups can do the following:

- Bring more fathers into daycare and kindergarten classrooms to show that "real men" are nurturing people.
- Support sex education programs that teach that rape is not sex but violence and that good sex takes place in the context of love and respect.
- Encourage co-ed sports at the elementary and middle school levels so that boys can learn that girls are not "the other," to be made fun of and put down.
- Learn the common "rape myths" ("You can tell a rapist by the way he looks." "Women enjoy being raped." "Good girls don't get raped.") and teach against them on all fronts.
- Protest the production and showing of "slasher" films that eroticize violence.

In his otherwise excellent May 2 column, Tom Wicker (*New York Times* 1989) described the Central Park rape as "a chance event that could have happened to anyone." In a way it was. On the other hand, when was the last time anyone has heard of a gang of teenage girls raping and beating a man in Central Park? To get to the roots of this particular brand of violence, we need to look beyond race and class to gender relations in America.

REFERENCES

Ageton, S. 1983. *Sexual Assault among Adolescents*. Lexington, MA: D. C. Heath.

Amir, M. 1971. *Patterns of Forcible Rape*. Chicago: University of Chicago Press.

Brownmiller, S. 1975. *Against Our Will: Men, Women and Rape*. New York: Simon and Schuster.

Chace, S. 1989. "Safety in the Park: In Women's Hands." *New York Times*, April 27.

Foderaro, L. 1989. "After a Sex Assault, a Town Worries Its Athletes Were too Often Forgiven." *New York Times*, June 12.

Groth, A. N. 1979. *Men Who Rape: The Psychology of the Offender*. New York: Plenum Press.

Gutfreund, J. 1989. "Letters to the Editor." *New York Times*, April 27.

Hall, E., J. Howard, and S. Boezio 1986. "Tolerance of Rape: A Sexist or Anti-Social Attitude?" *Psychology of Women Quarterly* 10: 101–118.

Herman, D. 1984. "The Rape Culture." Pp. 20–38 in *Women: A Feminist Perspective*, edited by J. Freeman. Palo Alto, CA: Mayfield.

Holtzman, E. 1989. "Rape: The Silence is Criminal." *New York Times*, May 5.

Hood, J. 1989. "Why Our Society is Rape-Prone." *New York Times*, May 16.

Johnson, A. G. 1980. "On the Prevalence of Rape in the United States." *Signs: Journal of Women in Culture and Society* 6: 136–146.

Kikuchi, J. 1989. Presentation on Rhode Island rape attitudes study at meetings of Association of Women in Psychology, Providence, R.I., March.

LaFree, G 1989. *Rape and Criminal Justice: The Social Construction of Sexual Assault*. Belmont, CA: Wadsworth.

Lyman, P. 1987. "The Fraternal Bond as a Joking Relationship." Pp. 148–164 in *Changing Men*, edited by M. Kimmel. Newbury Park, CA: Sage.

Malamuth, N. 1981. "Rape Proclivity among Males." *Journal of Social Issues* 37: 138–157.

New York Times 1989. "5 New Jersey Youths Held in Sexual Assault on Impaired Girl, 17." May 25.

Richmond Times-Dispatch 1989. "Blame Society First." May 19.

Sanday, P. R. 1981. "The Socio-Cultural Context of Rape: A Cross Cultural Study." *Journal of Social Issues* 37: 5–27.

———. 1986. "Rape and the Silencing of the Feminine." Pp. 84–101 in *Rape*, edited by S. Tomaselli and R. Porter. Oxford: Basil Blackwell.

———. 1988. Excerpts from Sanday's unpublished manuscript on sexual expression among college students read as part of discussant's comments at the Annual Meetings of the American Anthropological Association, Phoenix, AZ, November 19.

Scully, D., and J. Marolla 1985. "Riding the Bull at Gilley's": Convicted Rapists Describe the Rewards of Rape." *Social Problems* 32: 251–263.

Terry, D. 1989. "In Week of an Infamous Rape, 28 Other Victims Suffer." *New York Times*, May 29.

Village Voice 1989. "The Voices Not Heard: Black and Women Writers on the Central Park Rape." May 9.

MEN ON RAPE

TIM BENEKE

Rape may be America's fastest growing violent crime; no one can be certain because it is not clear whether more rapes are being committed or reported. It *is* clear that violence against women is widespread and fundamentally alters the meaning of life for women; that sexual violence is encouraged in a variety of ways in American culture; and that women are often blamed for rape.

Consider some statistics:

- In a random sample of 930 women, sociologist Diana Russell found that 44 percent had survived either rape or attempted rape. Rape was defined as sexual intercourse physically forced upon the woman, or coerced by threat of bodily harm, or forced upon the woman when she was helpless (asleep, for example). The survey included rape and attempted rape in marriage in its calculations. (Personal communication)
- In a September 1980 survey conducted by *Cosmopolitan* magazine to which over 106,000 women anonymously responded, 24 percent had been raped at least once. Of these, 51 percent had been raped by friends, 37 percent by strangers, 18 percent by relatives, and 3 percent by husbands. 10 percent of the women in the survey had been victims of incest. 75 percent of the women had been "bullied into making love." Writer Linda Wolfe, who reported on the survey, wrote in reference to such bullying: "Though such harassment stops short of rape, readers reported that it was nearly as distressing."

- An estimated 2–3 percent of all men who rape outside of marriage go to prison for their crimes.[1]
- The F.B.I. estimates that if current trends continue, one woman in four will be sexually assaulted in her lifetime.[2]
- An estimated 1.8 million women are battered by their spouses each year.[3] In extensive interviews with 430 battered women, clinical psychologist Lenore Walker, author of *The Battered Woman*, found that 59.9 percent had also been raped (defined as above) by their spouses. Given the difficulties many women had in admitting they had been raped, Walker estimates the figure may well be as high as 80 or 85 percent (Personal communication.) If 59.9 percent of the 1.8 million women battered each year are also raped, then a million women may be raped in marriage each year. And a significant number are raped in marriage without being battered.
- Between one in two and one in ten of all rapes are reported to the police.[4]
- Between 300,000 and 500,000 women are raped each year outside of marriage.[5]

What is often missed when people contemplate statistics on rape is the effect of the *threat* of sexual violence on women. I have asked women repeatedly, "How would your life be different if rape were suddenly to end?" (Men may learn a lot by asking this question of women to whom they are close.) The threat of rape is an assault upon the meaning of the world; it alters the feel of the human condition. Surely any attempt to comprehend the lives of women that fails to take issues of violence against women into account is misguided.

Through talking to women, I learned: *The threat of rape alters the meaning and feel of the night.* Observe how your body feels, how the night feels, when you're in fear. The constriction in your chest, the vigilance in your eyes, the rubber in your legs. What do the stars look like? How does the moon present itself? What is the difference between walking late at night in the dangerous part of a city and walking late at night in the country, or safe suburbs? When I try to imagine what the threat of rape must do to the night, I think of the stalked, adrenalated feeling I get walking late at night in parts of certain American cities. Only, I remind myself, it is a fear different from any I have known, a fear of being raped.

It is night half the time. If the threat of rape alters the meaning of the night, it must alter the meaning and pace of the day, one's relation to the passing and organization of time itself. For some women, the threat of rape at night turns their cars into armored tanks, their solitude into isolation. And what must the space inside a car or an apartment feel like if the space outside is menacing?

I was running late one night with a close woman friend through a path in the woods on the outskirts of a small university town. We had run several miles and were feeling a warm, energized serenity.

"How would you feel if you were alone?" I asked.

"Terrified!" she said instantly.

"Terrified that there might be a man out there?" I asked, pointing to the surrounding moonlit forest, which had suddenly been transformed into a source of terror.

"Yes."

Another woman said, "I know what I can't do and I've completely internalized what I can't do. I've built a viable life that basically involves never leaving my apartment at night unless I'm directly going some place to meet somebody. It's

unconsciously built into what it occurs to women to do." When one is raised without freedom, one may not recognize its absence.

The threat of rape alters the meaning and feel of nature. Everyone has felt the psychic nurturance of nature. Many women are being deprived of that nurturance, especially in wooded areas near cities. They are deprived either because they cannot experience nature in solitude because of threat, or because, when they do choose solitude in nature, they must cope with a certain subtle but nettlesome fear.

Women need more money because of rape and the threat of rape makes it harder for women to earn money. It's simple: if you don't feel safe walking at night, or riding public transportation, you need a car. And it is less practicable to live in cheaper, less secure, and thus more dangerous neighborhoods if the ordinary threat of violence that men experience, being mugged, say, is compounded by the threat of rape. By limiting mobility at night, the threat of rape limits where and when one is able to work, thus making it more difficult to earn money. An obvious bind: women need more money because of rape, and have fewer job opportunities because of it.

The threat of rape makes women more dependent on men (or other women). One woman said: "If there were no rape I wouldn't have to play games with men for their protection." The threat of rape falsifies, mystifies, and confuses relations between men and women. If there were no rape, women would simply not need men as much, wouldn't need them to go places with at night, to feel safe in their homes, for protection in nature.

The threat of rape makes solitude less possible for women. Solitude, drawing strength from being alone, is difficult if being alone means being afraid. To be afraid is to be in need, to experience a lack; the threat of rape creates a lack. Solitude requires relaxation; if you're afraid, you can't relax.

The threat of rape inhibits a woman's expressiveness. "If there were no rape," said one woman, "I could dress the way I wanted and walk the way I wanted and not feel self-conscious about the responses of men. I could be friendly to people. I wouldn't have to wish I was ugly. I wouldn't have to make myself small when I got on the bus. I wouldn't have to respond to verbal abuse from men by remaining silent. I could respond in kind."

If a woman's basic expressiveness is inhibited, her sexuality, creativity, and delight in life must surely be diminished.

The threat of rape inhibits the freedom of the eye. I know a married couple who live in Manhattan. They are both artists, both acutely sensitive and responsive to the visual world. When they walk separately in the city, he has more freedom to look than she does. She must control her eye movements lest they inadvertently meet the glare of some importunate man. What, who, and how she sees are restricted by the threat of rape.

The following exercise is recommended for men.

> *Walk down a city street. Pay a lot of attention to your clothing; make sure your pants are zipped, shirt tucked in, buttons done. Look straight ahead. Every time a man walks past you, avert your eyes and make your face expressionless. Most women learn to go through this act each time we leave our houses. It's a way to avoid at least some of the encounters we've all had with strange men who decided we looked available.[6]*

To relate aesthetically to the visual world involves a certain playfulness, spirit of spontaneous exploration. The tense vigilance that accompanies fear inhibits that spontaneity. The world is no longer yours to look at when you're afraid.

I am aware that all culture is, in part, restriction, that there are places in America where hardly anyone is safe (though men are safer than women virtually everywhere), that there are many ways to enjoy life, that some women may not be so restricted, that there exist havens, whether psychic, geographical, economic, or class. But they are *havens*, and as such, defined by threat.

Above all, I trust my experience: no woman could have lived the life I've lived the last few years. If suddenly I were restricted by the threat of rape, I would feel a deep, inexorable depression. And it's not just rape; it's harassment, battery, Peeping Toms, anonymous phone calls, exhibitionism, intrusive stares, fondlings—all contributing to an atmosphere of intimidation in women's lives. And I have only scratched the surface; it would take many carefully crafted short stories to begin to express what I have only hinted at in the last few pages. I have not even touched upon what it might mean for a woman to be sexually assaulted. Only women can speak to that. Nor have I suggested how the threat of rape affects marriage.

Rape and the threat of rape pervade the lives of women, as reflected in some popular images of our culture.

"SHE ASKED FOR IT"—
BLAMING THE VICTIM[7]

Many things may be happening when a man blames a woman for rape.

First, in all cases where a woman is said to have asked for it, her appearance and behavior are taken as a form of speech. "Actions speak louder than words" is a widely held belief; the woman's actions—her appearance may be taken as action—are given greater emphasis than her words; an interpretation alien to the woman's intentions is given to her actions. A logical extension of "she asked for it" is the idea that she wanted what happened to happen; if she wanted it to happen, she *deserved* for it to happen. Therefore, the man is not to be blamed. "She asked for it" can mean either that she was consenting to have sex and was not really raped, or that she was in fact raped but somehow she really deserved it. "If you ask for it, you deserve it," is a widely held notion. If I ask you to beat me up and you beat me up, I still don't deserve to be beaten up. So even if the notion that women asked to be raped had some basis in reality, which it doesn't, on its own terms it makes no sense.

Second, a mentality exists that says: a woman who assumes freedoms normally restricted to a man (like going out alone at night) and is raped is doing the same thing as a woman who goes out in the rain without an umbrella and catches a cold. Both are considered responsible for what happens to them. That men will rape is taken to be a legitimized given, part of nature, like rain or snow. The view reflects a massive abdication of responsibility for rape on the part of men. It is so much easier to think of rape as natural than to acknowledge one's part in it. So long as rape is regarded as natural, women will be blamed for rape.

A third point. The view that it is natural for men to rape is closely connected to the view of women as commodities. If a woman's body is regarded as a valued commodity by men, then of course, if you leave a valued commodity where it can be taken, it's just human nature for men to take it. If you left your stereo out on the sidewalk, you'd be asking for it to get stolen. Someone will just take it. (And how often men speak of rape as "going out and *taking* it.") If a woman walks the streets at night, she's leaving a valued commodity, her body, where it can be taken. So long as women are regarded as commodities, they will be blamed for rape.

Which brings us to a fourth point. "She asked for it" is inseparable from a more general "psychology of the dupe." If I use bad judgment and fail to read the small print in a contract and later get taken advantage of "screwed" (or "fucked over") then I deserve what I get; bad judgment makes me liable. Analogously, if a woman trusts a man and goes to his apartment, or accepts a ride hitchhiking, or goes out on a date and is raped, she's a dupe and deserves what she gets. "He didn't *really* rape her" goes the mentality— "he merely took advantage of her." And in America it's okay for people to take advantage of each other, even expected and praised. In fact, you're considered dumb and foolish if you don't take advantage of other people's bad judgment. And so, again, by treating them as dupes, rape will be blamed on women.

Fifth, if a woman who is raped is judged attractive by men, and particularly if she dresses to look attractive, then the mentality exists that she attacked him with her weapon so, of course, he counter-attacked with his. The preview to a popular movies states: "She was the victim of her own *provocative beauty*." Provocation: "There is a line which, if crossed, will *set me off* and I will lose control and no longer be responsible for my behavior. If you punch me in the nose then, of course, I will not be responsible for what happens: you will have provoked a fight. If you dress, talk, move, or act a certain way, you will have provoked me to rape. If your appearance *stuns* me, *strikes* me, *ravishes* me, *knocks me out*, etc., then I will not be held responsible for what happens; you will have asked for it." The notion that sexual feeling makes one helpless is part of a cultural abdication of responsibility for sexuality. So long as a woman's appearance is viewed as a weapon and sexual feeling is believed to make one helpless, women will be blamed for rape.

Sixth, I have suggested that men sometimes become obsessed with images of women, that images become a substitute for sexual feeling, that sexual feeling becomes externalized and out of control and is given an undifferentiated identity in the appearance of women's bodies. It is a process of projection in which one blurs one's own desire with her imagined, projected desire. If a woman's attractiveness is taken to signify one's own lust and a woman's lust, then when an "attractive" woman is raped, some men may think she wanted sex. Since they perceive their own lust in part projected onto the woman, they disbelieve women who've been raped. So long as men project their own sexual desires onto women, they will blame women for rape.

And seventh, what are we to make of the contention that women in dating situations say "no" initially to sexual overtures from men as a kind of pose, only to give in later, thus revealing their true intentions? And that men are thus confused and incredulous when women are raped because in their sexual experience women can't be believed? I doubt that this has much to do with men's perceptions of rape. I don't know to what extent women actually "say no and mean yes"; certainly it is a common theme in male folklore. I have spoken to a couple of women who went through periods when they wanted to be sexual but were afraid to be, and often rebuffed initial sexual advances only to give in later. One point is clear: the ambivalence women may feel about having sex is closely tied to the inability of men to fully accept them as sexual beings. Women have been traditionally punished for being openly and freely sexual; men are praised for it. And if many men think of sex as achievement of possession of a valued commodity, or aggressive degradation, then women have every reason to feel and act ambivalent.

These themes are illustrated in an interview I conducted with a 23 year old man who grew up in Pittsburgh and works as a file clerk in the financial district of San Francisco. Here's what he said:

"Where I work it's probably no different from any other major city in the U.S. The women dress up in high heels, and they wear a lot of makeup, and they just look really *hot* and really sexy, and how can somebody who has a healthy sex drive not feel lust for them when you see them? I feel lust for them, but I don't think I could find it in me to overpower someone and rape them. But I definitely get the feeling that I'd like to rape a girl. I don't know if the actual act of rape would be satisfying, but the *feeling* is satisfying.

"These women look so good, and they kiss ass of the men in the three-piece suits who are *big* in the corporation, and most of them relate to me like "Who are *you*? Who are *you* to even *look* at?" They're snobby and they condescend to me, and I resent it. It would take me a lot longer to get to first base than it would somebody with a three-piece suit who had money. And to me a lot of the men they go out with are superficial assholes who have no real feelings or substance, and are just trying to get ahead and make a lot of money. Another things that makes me resent these women is thinking, "How could

she want to hang out with somebody like that? What does that make her?"

"I'm a file clerk, which makes me feel like a nebbish, a nurd, like I'm not making it, I'm a failure. But I don't really believe I'm a failure because I know it's just a phase, and I'm just doing it for the money, just to make it through this phase. I catch myself feeling like a failure, but I realize that's ridiculous."

What Exactly Do You Go Through When You See These Sexy, Unavailable Women?

"Let's say I see a woman and she looks really pretty and really clean and sexy, and she's giving off very feminine, sexy vibes. I think, 'Wow, I would love to make love to her,' but I know she's not really interested. It's a tease. A lot of times a woman knows that she's looking really good and she'll use that and flaunt it, and it makes me feel like she's laughing at me and I feel *degraded.*

"I also feel dehumanized, because when I'm being teased I just turn off, I cease to be human. Because if I go with my human emotions I'm going to want to put my arms around her and kiss her, and to do that would be unacceptable. I don't like the feeling that I'm supposed to stand there and take it, and not be able to hug her or kiss her; so I just turn off my emotions. It's a feeling of humiliation, because the woman has forced me to turn off my feelings and react in a way that I really don't want to.

"If I were actually desperate enough to rape somebody, it would be from wanting the person, but it would be a very spiteful thing, just being able to say, 'I have power over you and I can do anything I want with you,' because really I feel that *they* have power over *me* just by their presence. Just the fact that they can come up to me and just melt me and make me feel like a dummy makes me want revenge. They have power over me so I want power over them. . . .

"Society says that you have to have a lot of sex with a lot of different women to be a real man. Well, what happens if you don't? Then what are you? Are you half a man? Are you still a boy? It's ridiculous. You see a whiskey ad with a guy and two women on his arm The implication is that real men don't have any trouble getting women."

How Does It Make You Feel toward Women to See All These Sexy Women in Media and Advertising Using Their Looks to Try to Get You to Buy Something?

"It makes me hate them. As a man you're taught that men are more powerful than women, and that men always have the upper hand, and that it's a man's society; but then you see all these women and it makes you think, 'Jesus Christ, if we have all the power how come all the beautiful women are telling us what to buy?' And to be honest, it just makes me hate beautiful women because they're using their power over me. I realize they're being used themselves, and they're doing it for money. In *Playboy* you see all these beautiful women who look so sexy and they'll be giving you all these looks like they want to have sex so bad; but then in reality you know that except for a few nymphomaniacs, they're doing it for the money; so I hate them for being used and for using their bodies in that way.

"In this society, if you ever sit down and realize how manipulated you really are it makes you pissed off—it makes you want to take control. And you've been manipulated by women, and they're a very easy target because they're out walking along the streets, so you can just grab one and say, 'Listen, you're going to do what I want you to do,' and it's an act of revenge against the way you've been manipulated.

"I know a girl who was walking down the street by her house, when this guy jumped her and beat her up and raped her, and she was black and blue and had to go to the hospital. That's beyond me. I can't understand how somebody could do that. If I were going to rape a girl, I wouldn't hurt her. I might *restrain* her, but I wouldn't *hurt* her. . . .

"The whole dating game between men and women also makes me feel degraded. I hate being put in the position of having to initiate a relationship. I've been taught that if you're not aggressive with a woman, then you've blown it. She's not going to jump on *you*, so *you've* got to jump on *her*. I've heard all kinds of stories where the woman says, 'No! No! No!' and they end up making great love. I get confused as hell if a woman pushes me away. Does it mean she's trying to be a nice girl and wants to put up a good appearance, or does it mean she doesn't want anything to do with you? You don't know. Probably a lot of men think that women don't feel like real women unless a man tries to force himself on her, unless she brings out the 'real man,' so to speak, and probably too much of it goes on. It goes on in my head that you're complimenting a woman by actually staring at her or by trying to get into her pants. Lately, I'm realizing that when I stare at women lustfully, they often feel more threatened than flattered."

NOTES

1. Such estimates recur in the rape literature. See *Sexual Assault* by Nancy Gager and Cathleen Schurr, Grosset & Dunlap, 1976, or *The Price of Coercive Sexuality* by Clark and Lewis, The Women's Press, 1977.
2. *Uniform Crime Reports*, 1980.
3. See *Behind Closed Doors* by Murray J. Strauss and Richard Gelles, Doubleday, 1979.
4. See Gager and Schurr (above) or virtually any book on the subject.
5. Again, see Gager and Schurr, or Carol V. Horos, *Rape*, Banbury Books, 1981.
6. From "Willamette Bridge" in *Body Politics* by Nancy Henley, Prentice-Hall, 1977, p. 144.
7. 1 would like to thank George Lakoff for this insight.

CONFESSIONS OF A DATE RAPIST

JACK M.

Readers are advised that the following article graphically describes and discusses the author's sexual assault of a woman. Our intent is not to reproduce the rape; rather to provide enough information to understand what happened and how, and to evaluate the extent to which the rapist now understands what he did and accepts responsibility for his actions.

Seven years ago I raped someone. I did not use a knife, a gun or a fist. I did not threaten her and she did not scream for help, but I had sex with a woman who did not consent—and that is rape.

I don't think of myself as a bad guy. I have a college degree in the arts from a prestigious school, and my parents, still married, are very supportive. I do not hate women or the world, or myself for that matter. My female friends here in New York, as well as many of my ex-girlfriends, think I am a bright, caring, understanding person. But none of that kept me from raping.

I did not understand that what I did was rape until about a year ago. What made me finally realize my crime was the recent surge in media coverage of the phenomenon of "date rape." The St. Johns University and Palm Beach rape cases, as well as other highly publicized scenarios where the alleged assaults were more ambiguous than a knife to the throat and a demand for sex, made me think about what date rape really is, as I relived that night.

I went to an upper West Side bar "scamming" with some of my friends. We had already been drinking

steadily and by the time we got there, we were still coherent, but basically numb.

Through the entire night, even though I was drinking, I remained in control of my body. The booze accentuated my confidence and made me feel invincible—immune to rejection. Tonight, whatever I wanted I was going to take, and nothing was going to stop me.

I met her at the bar. She was from England and had come to New York for a short time to tour with a theater company, I think. When I walked in I knew I wanted to bed this woman. I wanted to have sex that night and she looked like an inviting prospect.

This was a period of my life where I was "slutting" heavily. I would pick a woman up at a bar and sleep with her the same night. I started to think I was entitled to sex. After talking a woman up and buying her a few drinks, I would do everything I could to make her go to bed with me. Usually she was willing. Sometimes, however, it took a little more work to convince her.

I was often cruel to these women. If the sex was good, I might see them again, but I would quickly get bored, and after gaining their trust

---

This is an edited version of an article that appeared in *Manhattan Spirit*. Published courtesy of *Manhattan Spirit*, a division of News Communications, Inc.

and having them fully confide in me, I would abruptly blow them off. They would be shocked and hurt, and would call me in the middle of the night to cry and call me names and demand an explanation. I would tell them, "I don't have to give you an explanation. Good night"; or I would be brutally straightforward, saying, "I'm bored with you," "I don't like your body" or "You don't turn me on anymore."

She had only recently arrived and did not know much about the City. We talked for awhile and a mild seduction took place. I made her believe I was interested in what she was saying, and she thought I really cared about her. Our thighs rubbed together, my arm brushed against her breast.

I was getting to her.

We drank some more and I grew confident that I was not going home alone tonight. She was staying at a friend's place in midtown, and I assumed that when we left together, it meant she was going over to my place.

This is exactly the kind of assumption which often leads to a data rape. She had no idea that I wanted to sleep with her that night, but from my point of view, it was a given. Why else would I leave the bar? If I was not going to have sex with her, I would much rather drink more and try my hand at someone else. So it was understood on my part that we were going to sleep together. That understanding was not mutual. There was no understanding.

I asked her if she wanted to leave the bar, saying, "Do you want to take a walk?" I told her that I would take her back to the bar or to her friend's place. She believed me, and I was on the road to getting her to sleep over.

I have always had a secret agenda with women. I would do anything I could to seduce them. I would use empathy, understanding, humor, ever my deepest secrets to get them on my side. I would show that I was a "sensitive guy" and use that for the sole purpose of bedding them.

This time I used a woman's drunkenness and unfamiliarity with the City for my purposes.

Now that she was out of the bar, she had no friends to help her, no one to call, nowhere to go except where I wanted her to go.

We started walking and she asked, "Where are we going?" I said, "Just walking," all the time knowing that we were walking in the direction of my apartment.

We would stop sporadically and make out. During one heavy session I said to her, "Come back to my place." She refused. I said, "What do you mean, no? This is New York City. You don't leave a bar with a guy and not sleep with him. C'mon, this isn't England. This is the big city! This is how we do things."

She still refused, but I could tell I was influencing her with that ridiculous line. So we walked some more and made out some more, all the time getting closer and closer to my apartment. I used that "New York code of etiquette" line time and time again as I took her through unfamiliar streets.

We reached my apartment and I asked her if she wanted to come up. She said no, and I said, "Just come up for a little bit and then I'll take you back." That sat better with her and I congratulated myself for the brilliant sell.

To use language as I did is abusive and irresponsible. I took advantage of someone's innocence for my own ends. I was so confident that I could manipulate her that I did not understand where seduction ended and abusive behavior began.

Before I admitted to myself that I raped this woman, I would say, "She deserved it. If she was gullible enough to fall for that line, then I am not responsible for what happens." But I am responsible. I know I have a command of the language, and I can make some people do what I want by shaping my speech in a certain way and charging it with emotion.

We got up to my apartment and I began kissing her, but now she was not responding as she had on the street. I asked her, "What's the matter?" But she just stared blankly past me into the wall. I gave up on kissing her and began to touch her in ways that would appear lewd on the street. Still no response. I felt like I was fondling a rag doll.

Not that I cared. I did not need any response on her part to get what I wanted.

I tried to take her blouse off and she locked her arms to her sides. I was stronger than her, so I pulled and forced her arms until I got it off.

If the rape did not start when I verbally manipulated her, it was certainly starting now. Now I was forcing her to do something against her will. I was using my strength as well as unfamiliar surroundings to my advantage—and completely disregarding her signals to stop.

I eased her down on the bed and she moved like dead weight. She did not resist me, but she did not hop onto the bed in anticipation either. She just stared straight ahead and began grinding her teeth furiously.

Grinding her teeth and tensing her body were the only ways she could safely express her fear. Here was a girl in a dark apartment with a man she never met before who could easily kill her, in a city which I described to her as a moral vacuum. She did not cry, scream or fight. Only recently have I put myself in her place and realized the terror she must have felt. To me she was a source of sex and that was all. Getting the sex was a little more challenging than I was used to, but it was still a game.

I got the rest of her clothes off the same way I got her shirt off—I forced them off. There she was, naked on her back with her knees locked firmly together, staring at the ceiling and grinding her teeth. Not a word was spoken during this struggle. It was just me trying to get her legs apart and her trying to get them back together. . . .

The sex lasted about a minute or two, and when I was done, I had the familiar aftertaste of unsatisfying sex. My power, so active five minutes before, was spent. All of the manipulative force I'd used left me empty.

I did not want this woman sleeping in my bed. I also did not want to walk her home, but it was dark and she did not know the area. She sat up in bed and again said she wanted to leave. By now it was 4 a.m. and I could not let her go out alone, even if she did know how to get back. I still find it amazing that after raping her I could feel concerned about her safety.

"Just sleep over," I said reluctantly. "You can leave when it's light out."

She did sleep over, and she never stopped grinding her teeth through the entire night.

When we awoke the next morning, I insisted she wait and walk out with me, since I had to leave for work anyway. I guess I still wanted to be a nice guy. The last thing I said to her when we reached the street was, "You have to walk that way to get back to your friend's place."

I've talked to my male friends about this and there is a fair amount of denial. "I did something like that once, but I don't think it's rape. It isn't like you forced her to have sex with you."

But I did force her! What constitutes force? Do they require that I threaten her life? Do they require physical injury? If I were walking in a dangerous and unfamiliar neighborhood and a man twice my size walked up to me on a deserted street and said, "Give me your money," I would probably hand it over. The thoughts going through my head would be, "This guy could easily kill me. He did not threaten me, but merely demanded I give him something. I could run, but I would not know where to go for help. I may lose my money and feel violated, but it is better than having him kill me."

I do not remember her name but I think about her now. It hurts me to know that I damaged someone like that. Have I caused her to mistrust men, to be more confused about sex than she needs to be, to fear that she might have AIDS (I did not use a condom when I assaulted her), to hate New York?

Maybe she blamed herself for getting into that situation with me and allowing herself to be taken advantage of. Maybe she buried it deep in her subconscious for years until she could deny the pain no longer and had a nervous breakdown. I have an image of her in long-term therapy, my face conjuring up awful memories as she recounts the events of that night. I am responsible for her realization that a man can steal from you something that belongs to you, that you are supposed to be able to share with someone only when you desire to. It can be stolen from you as easily as someone might snatch a chain from around your neck.

I am aware that the power to rape is inside me. Now, when I meet a woman and see that she likes me, here's what I'm learning and wanting to do. I'm more cautious about making unwanted moves. I am learning to interact non-aggressively. I'm learning to talk *with* her, not *to* her, possibly about intimacy with her, but speaking and listening with genuine interest. If the interest is not there, I know something's wrong.

Most of all, I will not seduce. I will not try to pull desire out of her whether or not it is there.

Even if she initiates sexual contact, I want to proceed more slowly than before. I don't want to rely on body language or guesses or assumptions about what we *should* be doing. I want consent, without any coercion, if we're going to be intimate.

I never want to rape again. And until I understand more about my own power, I will do everything I can to make sure I do not express it as rape.

PART SEVEN

MEN WITH MEN: FRIENDSHIPS AND FEARS

What is the nature of men's relationships with other men? Do most men have close, intimate male friends, or do they simply bond together around shared activities and interests? How do competition, homophobia, and violence enter into men's relationships with each other?

Traditionally, in literature and in popular mythology, the Truly Great Friendships are those among men. In the late 1960s and early 1970s, the concept of civilization being a "fraternity of men" was criticized by feminists, who saw women as isolated and excluded from public life. In the mid-1970s, though, the men's liberation literature began to focus on the *quality* of men's relationships, and found them wanting. Men, we discovered, have "acquaintances," "activities buddies," but rarely true friends with whom they can intimately share their inner lives. Lillian Rubin and others argued that it is not that men do not want or need closeness with other men, it is just that they are so very threatened by the actuality of intimacy. Thus, when men organize their time together around work, watching a game, or playing cards, the structure of the activity mediates their time together, thus maintaining a "safe" level of emotional distance.

But why do men need emotional distance from each other? And what are the costs of maintaining emotionally shallow relationships with other men? What kinds of pressure does this place on women to be the primary "emotion workers" in men's lives? Most men, when asked who their best friend is, will name a woman, often their wife. (Few women, by the way, will name their husband—most will name another woman.) Men rarely feel comfortable with intimate self-disclosure with other men. Certainly an overemphasis on competition among males, from a very early age, is one factor that places a damper on intimate self-disclosure among men. Why would a man give away information that would make him vulnerable among his competitors in games, education, or the workplace? Another important barrier to male–male intimacy, as the article by Gregory Lehne points out, is homophobia. The fear of homosexuality—or of being thought to be homosexual by others—places severe limitations on the emotional, verbal, and physical interactions among men. Next, Peter M. Nardi discusses the contemporary political importance of friendship among gay men. Martin Simmons illustrates the ways that confronting racism together becomes a central element in cementing black men's friendships.

© Ebet Roberts 1993.

If men's power over women and other men (sexism and homophobia) are among the central elements in the construction of masculinities then we must also address the negative consequences of male–male intimacy. Chris O'Sullivan finds that collegiate groups that stress homosocial intimacy (fraternities and athletic teams) have higher incidence of sexual assault than other groups, and Greg Herek suggests that homophobia often has violent consequences for men perceived as gay.

HOMOPHOBIA AMONG MEN:
SUPPORTING AND DEFINING
THE MALE ROLE

GREGORY K. LEHNE

Homophobia is the irrational fear or intolerance of homosexuality. Although both men and women can be homophobic, homophobia is most often associated with the fear of male homosexuality. Homophobia is not currently classified as a "mental illness" (neither is homosexuality), although psychiatrists such as Dr. George Weinberg (1972) have stated, "I would never consider a patient healthy unless he had overcome his prejudice against homosexuality." Homophobia is the threat implicit in "*What are you, a fag?*" If male homosexuality were no more threatening than being left-handed, for example, homophobia would not exist. In many ways, and in all but extreme cases, homophobia is a socially determined prejudice much like sexism or racism, rather than a medically recognized phobia.

Homophobia, as I will show, does not exist in most cases as an isolated trait or prejudice; it is characteristic of individuals who are generally rigid and sexist. Homophobia, with its associated dynamic of fear of being labeled a homosexual, is an underlying *motivation* in maintaining the male sex role. I believe that it must be eliminated for fundamental changes to occur in male and female roles. To support this thesis, I will discuss first whether homophobia reflects an accurate perception and understanding of homosexuality or whether it is an irrational fear. Then I will examine the social aspects of homophobia and personal characteristics of people who are highly

homophobic. Finally, I will explore the social functions of homophobia in maintaining the male sex role, and its effects on society and the individual.

IS HOMOPHOBIA IRRATIONAL?

Homophobia is irrational because it generally embodies misconceptions and false stereotypes of male homosexuality. These belief systems, or prejudices, are rationalizations supporting homophobia, not causes of homophobia. Levitt and Klassen's 1973 Kinsey Institute study of 3,000 American adults found the following beliefs about homosexuality to be widespread: homosexuals are afraid of the opposite sex (56% of the sample believed this), homosexuals act like the opposite sex (69%), only certain occupations are appropriate for homosexuals, homosexuals molest children (71%), and homosexuality was unnatural.

First, let us consider the mistaken belief that homosexual men do not like women. Since relations with women (especially sexual) are considered one of the proving grounds of masculinity, homosexual men who do not treat women as sex objects are regarded as suspect and unmanly in our male-oriented culture. Research does not support the belief, however, that homosexual males are afraid of women. About 20% of men who consider themselves homosexuals have been married, or currently are married; about half of these gay men are fathers (Bell and Weinberg, 1978). Around 75% of homosexual males have engaged in heterosexual kissing and necking, and about 50% have participated in heterosexual intercourse in their youth, with a frequency and success rate highly similar to that of heterosexual males (Saghir and Robins, 1973). About 50% of the homosexual men in this comprehensive study reported to have at some time established a relationship with a woman, lasting more than one year and including sexual relations.

Although homosexual males were not adequately satisfied with their heterosexual experiences, they generally did not have negative reactions toward women or heterosexual activities. In studies measuring the change in the penis to various stimuli, it was found that homosexual men gave neutral (not negative) responses to pictures of female nudes (McConaghy, 1967; Freund, Langevin, Gibiri, and Zajac, 1973), pictures of mature vulva or breasts (Freund, Langevin, and Zajac, 1974), or auditory or written descriptions of heterosexual intercourse (Freund, Langevin, Chamberlayne, Deosoran, and Zajac, 1974). Heterosexual men, in comparison, were turned on by the pictures of female nudes, but revealed their homophobia through decreased penile volume in response to pictures of male nudes, or male homosexual activities (McConaghy, 1967; Turnbull and Brown, 1977). Thus, the evidence shows that homosexual males have no particular aversion to women or heterosexual intercourse, although heterosexual males often do have aversions to male nudes and homosexual activity.

Another popular stereotype is that homosexual men are similar to women, in appearance and/or psychological functioning. For example, Tavris (1977) reports that 70% of the *Psychology Today* readership believes that "homosexual men are not fully masculine." Studies reported by Freedman (1971) as well as Saghir and Robins (1973) suggest that only about 15% of male homosexuals appear effeminate. Effeminacy itself is highly stigmatized in the homosexual subculture. Weinberg and Williams (1974) estimate that not more than 20% of male homosexuals are suspected of being gay by the people they come in contact with, although Levitt and Klassen (1973) report that 37% of the American public believes that "it is easy to tell homosexuals by how they look."

Appearances aside, some studies indicate that homosexual men are psychologically sex typed similar to heterosexual men (e.g., Heilbrun and Thompson, 1977), whereas others find they are more androgynous or sex-role undifferentiated than heterosexuals (Spence and Helmreich, 1978). Homosexual men have not been found to be similar to women in their psychological functioning. Androgynous sex-role behavior, expressing a wider variety of interests and sensitivity than stereotypic male or female roles, is believed by many to represent a better level of psychological adjustment than more rigid sex-role-defined personalities (for example, see Kaplan and Bean, 1976). Several studies report that the psychological adjustment of homosexuals who have accepted their sexual orientation is superior in many cases to most heterosexual males in terms of openness and self-disclosure, self-actualization, lack of neurotic tendencies, and happiness or exuberance (Bell and Weinberg, 1978; Freedman, 1975; Weinberg and Williams, 1974).

Levitt and Klassen (1973) found that many people (the percentages given in parentheses below) stereotyped some professions as appropriate for homosexuals and others as inappropriate. For example, the "unmasculine" careers of artist (83%), beautician (70%), florist (86%), and musician (84%) were believed a appropriate for homosexual men. But the "masculine" careers of medical doctors (66%), government officials (66%), judges (76%), teachers (76%), and ministers (75%) were considered inappropriate for homosexuals.

Gallup in 1977 found a decrease since 1970 in public opinion seeking to deny homosexuals the right to be doctors (44%), teachers (65%), or ministers (54%). Notice that the professions that people would close to homosexuals are those characteristic bastions of either male power or social influence. In the real world of work, however, there is no evidence that homosexual men tend to avoid characteristically "masculine" or professional occupations. Ironically it may be true that heterosexual men avoid certain stereotyped "homosexual" occupations, resulting in a higher proportion of homosexuals in those fields.

Many studies of homosexual males have found that they tend to be disproportionately concentrated in higher status occupations, especially those requiring professional training (Saghir and Robins, 1973; Weinberg and Williams, 1974). A study in Germany suggests that homosexual males tend to be more upwardly mobile than comparable heterosexuals (Dannecker and Reiche, 1974). This carefully conducted study of a large group of homosexuals found that the social class of the families of homosexual men was representative of the general population, whereas the social status of the homosexual men themselves was higher than would be predicted from their family backgrounds, even when the mobility trends of the entire population were taken into account. This suggests that in spite of the prejudice that homosexuals . encounter in work, they are still highly successful in fields outside the low-status occupations that the general public seems to feel are appropriate for homosexuals.

Although the belief that homosexuals often molest children is widespread, I have been unable to locate any scientific research supporting it. A pedophile, an adult who seeks sex with young children, generally does not have sexual relationships with other adults and thus could not appropriately be considered either heterosexual or homosexual. Many of these individuals have sex with children of either gender. Pedophilia is a rare disturbance. Heterosexual rape, involving adolescents or adults, is much more common than homosexual rape, according to court records and sexual experience surveys. The fear that homosexuals molest children (or rape adolescents) is grossly exaggerated, and ultimately

is based on the confusion of pedophilia with homosexuality.

There is evidence supporting the effectiveness of gay people in positively dealing with children. Gay parents tend to provide a psychologically healthy environment for their own children, who are actually no more predisposed than the children of heterosexuals to become homosexuals themselves, or to exhibit signs of psychological disturbance (Bell, 1973; Kirkpatrick, Roy, and Smith, 1976). Dorothy Riddle (1978) has done a sensitive analysis of the positive ways in which gay people relate to children, and their effectiveness as role models fostering healthy psychological development in children. Public fears of the negative effects of gay people on children tend to be totally unfounded.

A final misconception relevant to homophobia is the idea that homosexuality is "unnatural." Evidence reviewed by Ford and Beach (1951) indicates that homosexual activities occur in the majority of species of animals. Some porpoises form lifelong, monogamous, homosexual relationships. Homosexual relations are common, and are important in establishing dominance, among monkeys and various canines. Lorenz (1974) has discussed homosexual coupling among geese and other birds, concluding that it is often very adaptive.

Homosexual activities are as common or "natural" in human society as in the animal world. In 49 of the 77 societies for which we have adequate anthropological data, homosexual activities are socially sanctioned; in some situations they are virtually compulsory (Churchill, 1967). In most of Europe and many other parts of the world, homosexual relations are legal. The "unnatural" rationalization supporting homophobia receives further disconfirmation from the experiences of the 37% of the American male population who Kinsey, Pomeroy, and Martin (1948) reported had homosexual experiences to orgasm after adolescence.

Robert Brannon characterizes contemporary scientific thinking about the "naturalness" of homosexuality in this way:

Every human society in the world today, from vast industrial nations to the smallest and simplest tribes in remote parts of the world, has some degree of homosexuality. Every society in the history of the Earth for which we have records, going back to the beginnings of recorded history, had some degree of homosexuality.

Some of these societies accepted homosexuality readily while others severely condemned it, but all human societies have been aware of it because homosexuality has always existed wherever human beings have existed.

The closest scientific analogy to homosexuality is probably the phenomenon of left-handedness, the origins and causes of which also remain unknown to science. Like homosexuality, left-handedness exists for a minority of people in every human society on record. There is no more objective reason to consider homosexuality unnatural than there is to consider left-handedness unnatural.

These facts about homosexuality suggest an interesting dilemma. Even if the stereotypes about homosexuality were accurate (I have tried to show that they are not), then why should homosexuality be threatening to males who presumably do not fit these stereotypes? If these stereotypes are not valid, then how and why are the rationalizations of homophobia maintained?

Since sexual orientation, unlike race or sex, is rarely known for certain in everyday interactions, it is relatively easy to maintain false stereotypes of the invisible minority of homosexuals. Men who appear to exhibit parts of the stereotypes are labeled homosexual, and the rest are presumed to be heterosexual. Thus, as long as most homosexuals conceal their sexual preference, homophobia is easily maintained, because heterosexuals are rarely aware of homosexuals who do not reflect their stereotypes of homosexuality.

Since stereotypes of homosexuals are not characteristic of most homosexuals, it is clear that these stereotypes are not learned from direct experiences with homosexuals. Homophobia is socially learned and transmitted. It precedes and encourages the development of stereotypes of homosexuals, in a world in which most homosexuals are not known. The presence of homophobia even among some homosexuals, whose experiences disconfirm stereotypes of homosexuality, suggests that homophobia must be derived from other sources. For homophobia to exist as a threat, it is necessary that the associated stereotypes of homosexuality be false; otherwise the taunt, *"What are you, a fag?,"* would be so patently untrue that it would not be threatening.

HOMOPHOBIA AND SOCIAL BELIEFS

Although there is no rational basis for the negative stereotypes of homosexuals, and thus homophobia, nevertheless homophobia is widespread. It is characteristic of entire societies as well as individuals. The bases for homophobic social attitudes are generally related to (1) religious beliefs that homosexuality is morally wrong, (2) scientific theories of homosexuality as an illness or deviance, and (3) social beliefs that homosexuality is damaging to society.

Religious prohibitions have sometimes been considered to be the source of homophobia (Symonds, 1896; Churchill, 1967; Weinberg, 1972; Weinberg and Williams, 1974). The United States, as a result of its Puritan heritage, is generally considered one of the most homophobic (and erotophobic) cultures in the world. Although some researchers (such as Irwin and Thompson, 1977) have shown a strong relationship between church attendance, religious beliefs, and antihomosexual attitudes, religion seems unlikely to be a causal factor in homophobia for most Americans.

Science seems to have replaced religion as a source of justification of homophobia for many people. However, there is no scientific evidence that homosexuality is a mental illness. In 1973 the American Psychiatric Association removed the classification of homosexuality from its official list of mental illnesses. The belief among many psychiatrists that homosexuality is a mental illness, in spite of the lack of scientific evidence, is probably a result of their uncritical acceptance of common stereotypes of homosexuals (see Fort, Steiner, and Conrad, 1971; Davidson and Wilson, 1973), and the important fact that they frequently overgeneralize from homosexuals who were possibly mentally ill, and sought treatment, to the entire homosexual population. Nevertheless, the psychologically untenable conceptualization of homosexuality per se as a mental illness, which can be "cured," is still believed by 62% of the American adult population, according to Levitt and Klassen (1973).

Certain psychological theories, such as Freud's, posit that although homosexuality is not an illness, it is nevertheless also not "normal." Freud viewed it as a form of arrested psychosexual development, related to aspects of the parent/child relationship. Psychoanalysts such as Bieber (Bieber *et al.*, 1962) have selectively analyzed cases of homosexuals from their clinical practice that they interpret as supporting Freud's theory. Bieber's conclusions have not been supported in other studies sampling a cross section of homosexuals (Saghir and Robins, 1973).

Freud further believed that homophobia, and also paranoia, is related to "latent homosexuality," which he thought to be present in nearly everyone, since he conceived of people being born ambisexual and later developing heterosexuality. Freud's belief in latent homosexuality has received general acceptance in our culture, both among heterosexuals and homosexuals. Latency, by definition, implies the existence of no behavioral evidence. Therefore if it is possible for anyone to be a latent homosexual, in spite of the absence of sexual activity, it becomes extremely difficult for a person to prove beyond a doubt that he is not a homosexual. Thus, the concept of latent homosexuality contributes in a major way to homophobia, for it allows the possibility that anyone might be a secret homosexual even though the person does not exhibit any of the stereotypes, or behaviors, or homosexuals.

Sociological studies of homosexuality provide another popular scientific justification of homophobia, as they tend to label homosexuality as deviant since it is practiced by only a small proportion of society. However, the term deviant has taken on moral connotations not in keeping with its scientific meaning of "not majority." (See Scarpitti and McFarlane, 1975, for further discussion of this point.) When Simmons (1965) asked a cross section of Americans to list the people who they considered deviant, the most common response was homosexuals (49%). The equation of deviance with bad or immoral, although it may be indicative of popular thinking, is not inherent in sound sociological research.

Another possible source of homophobia is the belief that homosexuality is damaging to society. An Opinion Research Center poll in 1966 showed that more than 67% of the people contracted viewed homosexuality as "detrimental to society." The Harris Survey has been asking large cross sections of American households whether they feel homosexuals (and other groups) do more harm than good for the country. In 1965 homosexuals were placed third (behind Communists and atheists), with 82% of the males and 58% of the females thinking they were primarily a danger to the country. In 1973 about 50% of the respondents still felt that homosexuals did more harm than good. Levitt and Klassen (1973) similarly found that 49% of their sample agreed that "homosexuality is a social corruption which can cause the downfall of a civilization." These studies do not make it clear, however, why homosexuality is perceived as a social menace, especially by men. Legislatures in 24 states have decriminalized sexual activities commonly engaged in by consenting homosexual adults, as recommended in the model penal code of the American Bar Association. Homosexuality is also legal in most other countries, including Canada, England, Germany, and France. Thus, there is not general official support or evidence, either here or abroad, for the misconception that homosexuality is damaging to society.

Two arguments have been frequently advanced against legalization of homosexuality, in states considering legal reform. Groups such as firemen and policemen have argued that if homosexuality is legalized, homosexuals will sexually corrupt" their fellow workers. (This is also a belief of 38% of Americans, according to Levitt and Klassen, 1973.) In reality, homosexual men have little interest in sexual relationships with unwilling heterosexual colleagues.

The most influential argument advanced against decriminalizing homosexuality is that it would allow homosexuals to "convert" or to molest children. We have discussed the distinction between pedophiles and homosexuals and the mistaken stereotype that homosexuals molest children. The children's issue is a red herring because in no state has legalization of sex acts between adults and children ever been proposed. Homosexuals are not seduced or converted into homosexuality. In a study by Lehne (1978) only 4% of the male homosexuals reported that they were somewhat seduced into their first homosexual act, and in not one case was force involved. By comparison, Sorensen (1973) reports that the first sexual experience of 6% of adolescent girls was heterosexual rape. Lehne's study also found that most of the homosexual men reported that they were aware of their sexual orientation (because of their sexual fantasies) about four to five years before their first homosexual experience. The notion that homosexuals, legally or illegally, will seduce, rape, or convert others into homosexuality is not supported by any substantial data. There seems to be no reason to believe that homosexuals act any less morally than most Americans of different sexual orientations, or that they in fact pose a threat to society.

HOMOPHOBIA AND THE INDIVIDUAL

Although homophobia is still widespread in American society, it is increasingly a fear of only a minority of people. Studies of homophobia in individuals suggest that it is not an isolated prejudice or fear; it is consistently related to traditional attitudes about sex roles and other social phenomena. This supports the conceptualization that homophobia functions as a motivation or threat in defining and maintaining the male role.

In an early study of homophobic attitudes, Smith (1971) found that college students who held negative attitudes toward homosexuals were significantly more status conscious, more authoritarian, and more sexually inflexible than individuals scoring low on homophobia. Later research refined Smith's methodology and analysis to show that homophobia is most closely related to traditional sex-role beliefs, and to general lack of support for equality between the sexes (see Morin and Garfinkle, 1978).

MacDonald (MacDonald, 1974, 1976; MacDonald, Huggins, Young, and Swanson, 1973; MacDonald and Games, 1974) developed effective scales of Attitudes toward Homosexuality and a Sex Role Survey. In research with several different adult populations, he demonstrated clear relationships between negative attitudes toward homosexuality and support for the double standard in sex-role behavior and conservative standards of sexual morality. Through the analysis of the semantic differential, he showed that homosexual males are devalued and viewed as less powerful due to their association with femininity, whereas lesbians are seen to be more powerful than heterosexual women because they are believed to be more masculine. Similar analyses were also reported by Storms (1978) and Shively, Rudolph, and DeCecco (1978). The public confusion between sexual orientation and sex role contributes to the devaluation of homosexuals, since they are believed to violate sex-role norms.

MacDonald's findings have been confirmed by numerous other researchers. Weinberger and Millham (1979) concluded that "homophobia is associated with valuing traditional gender distinctions," whereas Minnigerode (1976) found that nonfeminist and conservative sex attitudes were closely related to homophobia. These and other researchers found that people reacted more negatively to same-sex homosexuals, and in particular men were more negative toward male homosexuals than they were toward lesbians, and men overall were more negative in their homophobic attitudes than were women (Nutt and Sedlacek, 1974; Steffensmeier and Steffensmeier, 1974; Turnbull and Brown, 1977). Some researchers, including MacDonald, did not find such clear sex differences; Morin and Garfinkle (1978) have reviewed these studies and related the lack of findings of sex differences to the different methodologies that were used.

A constellation of traditional or sex-negative beliefs was found to be characteristic of homophobic individuals in several other studies. Morin and Wallace (1975, 1976) found that belief in a traditional family ideology was a slightly better predictor of homophobia than traditional beliefs about women; traditional religious beliefs and general sexual rigidity were also related. Negative beliefs about premarital and extramarital affairs were closely associated with homophobia in Nyberg and Alston's (1976–77) analysis of a representative sample of the American population. With a similar sample, Irwin and Thompson (1977) found traditional sex-role standards to be closely related to homophobia. Individuals with nontraditional sex-role behavior were less likely to hold negative attitudes toward homosexuality (Montgomery and Burgoon, 1977), whereas personal anxiety and guilt about sexual impulses were also characteristic of homophobic individuals (Berry and Marks, 1969; Millham, San Miguel, and Kellogg, 1976).

The general picture that emerges from this research is that individuals who are not comfortable with changes in sex roles and sexual behavior are most likely to be homophobic. Cross-cultural research has confirmed the relationship between high levels of sex-role stereotyping and antihomosexual attitudes among West Indians, Brazilians, and Canadians (Dunbar, Brown, and Amoroso, 1973a; Dunbar, Brown, and Vourinen, 1973b; Brown and Amoroso, 1975). Research with homosexuals has also shown that although they are not generally as homophobic as heterosexuals, those holding negative attitudes toward homosexuality are also likely to have traditional beliefs of sex-role

stereotyping. Those homosexuals with positive attitudes and self-concepts are more likely to support equality between the sexes and have positive views on feminism (May, 1974; Lumby, 1976; McDonald and Moore, 1978; Glenn, 1978). Thus, homophobia seems to be a dynamic in maintaining traditional sex-role distinctions, rather than an isolated belief or attitude.

The negative influence of homophobic attitudes on social behavior has been demonstrated in several clever research studies. Morin, Taylor, and Kielman (1975) showed that in an interview situation, men and women sit farther away from an interviewer wearing a "Gay and Proud" button than they do from the same nonidentified interviewer; this effect is strongest for men, who sit three times as far away from a male homosexual than a lesbian. On a task arranging stick figures, Wolfgang and Wolfgang (1971) found that homosexuals were placed farther away than were marijuana users, drug addicts, and the obese, and past homosexuals were viewed as even less desirable and less trustworthy than present homosexuals. Subjects, particularly men, in another experiment were found to be significantly less willing to personally interact with homosexuals than heterosexuals (Millham and Weinberger, 1977). San Miguel and Millham (1976) found that people with homophobic attitudes were significantly more aggressive toward homosexuals than heterosexuals, even when they lost money in a cooperation experiment as a result of their aggression. They were highly aggressive regardless of whether their interaction with the individual prior to labeling as a homosexual was positive, and they were most aggressive toward homosexuals perceived as otherwise similar to themselves. Clearly homophobia is not only reflected in attitudes, but influences social behavior, and thus can have a potent influence in maintaining conformity to conventional sex-role behavior.

The process of homosexual labeling also has strong influences on behavior. Men labeled as homosexuals were perceived as more feminine, emotional, submissive, unconventional, and weaker than when the same men were not labeled (Weissbach and Zagon, 1975). Karr (1978) found also that the male who identified another man as a homosexual was perceived as more masculine, sociable, and desirable, and that highly homophobic individuals would sit farther away from the labeled homosexual. Karr effectively demonstrates that one's status as a man can be improved in social situations merely by the act of labeling someone else as gay. Another study found that men who were (incorrectly) labeled as a homosexual became increasingly more stereotypically masculine in their behavior (Farina, 1972); thus, the stigmatization of homosexuals can be a powerful molder of social behavior and conformity to traditional sex roles.

This growing body of research clearly supports the conceptualization that homophobia among individuals is closely related to traditional beliefs about sex roles, rather than individual prejudices against homosexuals. Furthermore, it demonstrates that these homophobic attitudes devalue in thought and action anyone who deviates from traditional sex-role stereotypes, and that this devaluation is reflected in social behavior. Homophobia reduces the willingness of others to interact with a suspected or labeled homosexual, and it may support direct aggression against the labeled deviant. Clearly homophobia is a powerful motivation for maintaining traditional sex-role behavior. MacDonald's assertions (1974, 1976) that sex-role issues are crucial for gay liberation, and that people seeking changes in traditional sex roles must be prepared to also challenge homophobia, are strongly supported by these data.

HOMOPHOBIA AND THE MALE ROLE

The male role is predominantly maintained by men themselves. Men devalue homosexuality, then use this norm of homophobia to control other men in their male roles. Since any male could potentially (latently) be a homosexual, and since there are certain social sanctions that can be directed against homosexuals, the fear of being labeled a homosexual can be used to ensure that males maintain appropriate male behavior. Homophobia is only incidentally directed against actual homosexuals—its more common use is against the heterosexual male. This explains why homophobia is closely related to beliefs about sex-role rigidity, but not to personal experience with homosexuals or to any realistic assessment of homosexuality itself. Homophobia is a threat used by societies and individuals to enforce social conformity in the male role, and maintain social control. The taunt *"What are you, a fag?"* is used in many ways to encourage certain types of male behavior and to define the limits of "acceptable" masculinity.

Since homosexuals in general constitute an invisible minority that is indistinguishable from the 49% male majority in most ways except for sexual preference, any male can be accused of being a homosexual, or "latent" homosexual. Homosexuality, therefore, can be "the crime of those to whom no crime could be imputed." There is ample historical evidence for this use of homophobia from Roman times to the present. For example, even homosexual fantasies were made illegal in Germany in 1935, and Hitler sent more than 220,000 "homosexuals" to concentration camps (Lauritsen and Thorstad, 1974). It is probable that many of these men actually were not homosexuals. But since there was no satisfactory way for individuals to prove that they were not homosexuals (and for this offense in Germany, accusation was equivalent to conviction), imputed homosexuality was the easiest way to deal with undesirable individuals. Homosexuality was likewise an accusation during the American McCarthy hearings in the 1950s when evidence of Communism was lacking. The strong association of homophobia with authoritarianism means that the potential for this exploitation of homophobia is very real during times of stress and strong-arm governments. This is no accident, but is in fact an explanation for the maintenance of homophobia. When homosexuality is stigmatized, homophobia exists as a device of social control, directed specifically against men to maintain male behavior appropriate to the social situation.

Homophobia may also be used to enforce social stereotypes of appropriate sex-role behavior for women. In general men define and enforce women's roles, and men who do not participate in this process may be suspected of being homosexuals. The direct use of homophobia to maintain female roles is necessary only in extreme cases, since male power is pervasive. But it is sometimes alleged that women who do not defer to men, or who do not marry, or who advocate changes in women's roles, are lesbians. There are, of course, other factors besides homophobia that maintain sex roles in society. I am arguing not that the elimination of homophobia will bring about a change in sex roles, but that homophobia must be eliminated before a change in sex roles can be brought about.

THE PERSONAL PAIN OF HOMOPHOBIA

The pain that *heterosexual* males bear as a consequence of homophobia is so chronic and pervasive that they probably do not notice that they are in pain, or the possible source of their discomfort. Homophobia is especially damaging to their personal relationships. Homophobia encourages men to compete. Since competition is not a drive easily turned on and off at will, there is probably a tendency for homophobic men to compete with others in their personal lives as well as at work. Only certain types of relationships are possible between competitors. Love and close friendship are difficult to maintain in a competitive environment because to expose your weaknesses and admit your problems is to be less than a man, and gives your competitor an advantage.

When men realize the intensity of their bonds with other men, homosexuality can be very threatening, and might lead to a limiting of otherwise fulfilling relationships. On the basis of a suggestion from Lester Kirkendall, I've asked men to describe their relationships with their best male friends. Many offer descriptions

that are so filled with positive emotion and satisfaction that you might think they were talking about their spouses (and sortie will admit that they value their close male friendships more than their relationship with their wife, "although they're really different, not the same at all"). However, if I suggest that it sounds as if they are describing a person whom they love, these men become flustered. They hem and haw, and finally say, "Well, I don't think I would like to call it love, we're just best friends. I can relate to him in ways I can't with anyone else. But, I mean, we're not homosexuals or anything like that." Homosexual love, like heterosexual love, does not imply participation in sex, although many people associate love with sex. The social stigma of homosexual love denies these close relationships the validity of love in our society. This potential loss of love is a pain of homophobia that many men suffer because it delimits their relationships with other men.

Because men are unwilling to admit the presence of love in their male friendships, these relationships may be limited or kept in careful check. If male love is recognized, these men may be threatened because they may mistakenly believe this indicates they are homosexuals. Male friendships offer an excellent opportunity to explore ways in which individuals can relate as equals, the type of relationship that is increasingly demanded by liberated women. Most men have learned to relate to some other men as equals, but because they deny themselves the validity of these relationships they respond to equality with women out of fear, or frustration that they don't know how to deal with this "new" type of relationship. Loving male relationships are part of the experiences of many men that are rarely thought about or discussed because of homophobia. As a consequence, many men are unable to transfer what they have learned in these male relationships to their relationships with women. They may also deny to themselves the real importance of their relationships with other men. Male love is so pervasive that it is virtually invisible.

Homophobia also circumscribes and limits areas of male interest. Homophobic men do not participate in sissy, womanly, "homosexual" activities or interests. Maintenance of the male sex role as a result of homophobia is as limiting for men as female sex roles are for women. An appreciation of many aspects of life, although felt by most men at different times in their lives, cannot be genuinely and openly enjoyed by men who must defend their masculinity through compulsively male-stereotyped pursuits. Fear of being thought a homosexual thus keeps some men from pursuing areas of interest, or occupations, considered more appropriate for women or homosexuals.

The open expression of emotion and affection by men is limited by homophobia. Only athletes and women are allowed to touch and hug each other in our culture; athletes are allowed this only because presumably their masculinity is beyond doubt. But in growing up to become men in our culture, we learned that such contact with men was no longer permissible, that only homosexuals enjoy touching other men, or that touching is only a prelude to sex. In a similar way men learn to curb many of their emotions. They learn not to react emotionally to situations in which, although they may feel the emotion, it would be unmasculine to express it. Once men have learned not to express some of their emotions, they may find it difficult to react any other way, and may even stop feeling these emotions. Men are openly allowed to express anger and hostility, but not sensitivity and sympathy. The expression of more tender emotions among men is thought to be characteristic only of homosexuals.

Is a society without homophobia a fairy-tale, or will it become a reality? Only when men begin to make a serious attempt to deal with their prejudice against homosexuality can we look forward to living in a world that is not stratified by rigid sex-role distinctions.

REFERENCES

Alston, J. P. "Attitudes toward extramarital and homosexual relations." *Journal of the Scientific Study of Religion*, 1974, *13*, 479–481.

Bell, A. P. "Homosexualities: Their range and character," In J. K. Cole & R. Dienstbier (Eds.), *Nebraska Symposium on Motivation*, Vol. 21. Lincoln: University of Nebraska Press, 1973.

Bell, A. P., & M. Weinberg. *Homosexualities: A Study of Human Diversity*. New York: Simon & Schuster, 1978.

Berry, D. F., & F. Marks. "Antihomosexual prejudice as a function of attitudes toward own sexuality." *Proceedings of the 77th Annual Convention of the American Psychological Association*, 1969, *4*, 573–574.

Bieber, I. et al. *Homosexuality: A Psychoanalytic Study of Male Homosexuals*. New York: Basic Books, 1962.

Brown, M., & D. Amoroso. "Attitudes toward homosexuality among West Indian male and female college students." *Journal of Social Psychology*, 1975, *97*, 163–168.

Churchill, W. *Homosexual Behavior Among Males: A Cross-Cultural and Cross Species Investigation*. Englewood Cliffs, N.J.: Prentice-Hall, 1967.

Dannecker, M., & R. Reiche. *Ger gewoehnliche Homosexuelle*. Frankfurt am Main, Germany: S. Fischer, 1974.

Davidson, G., & T. Wilson. "Attitudes of behavior therapists toward homosexuality." *Behavior Therapy*. 1973, *4*(5), 686–696.

Dunbar, J., M. Brown, & D. Amoroso, "Some correlates of attitudes toward homosexuality." *Journal of Social Psychology*, 1973, *89*, 271–279. (a)

Dunbar, J., M. Brown, & S. Vourinen. "Attitudes toward homosexuality among Brazilian and Canadian college students." *Journal of Social Psychology*, 1973, *90*, 173–183. (b)

Farina, A. "Stigmas potent behavior molders." *Behavior Today*, 1972, *2*, 25.

Ford, C., & F. Beach. *Patterns of Sexual Behavior*, New York: Harper & Row, 1951.

Fort, J., C. Steiner, & F. Conrad. "Attitudes of mental health professionals toward homosexuality and its treatment." *Psychological Reports*, 1971, *29*, 347–350.

Freedman, M. *Homosexuality and Psychological Functioning*. Belmont, Ca.: Brooks/Cole, 1971.

Freedman, M. "Homosexuals may be healthier than straights." *Psychology Today*, 1975, *1*(10), 28–32.

Freund, K., R. Langevin, R. Chamberlayne, A. Deosoran, & Y. Zajac. "The phobic theory of male homosexuality." *Archives of General Psychiatry*, 1974, *31*, 495–499.

Freund, K., R. Langevin, S. Gibiri, & Y. Zajac. "Heterosexual aversion in homosexual males." *British Journal of Psychiatry*, 1973, *122*, 163–169.

Freund, K., R. Langevin, & Y. Zajac. "Heterosexual aversion in homosexual males: A second experiment." *British Journal of Psychiatry*, 1974, *125*, 177–180.

Gallup, G. "Gallup poll on gay rights: Approval with reservations." *San Francisco Chronicle*, July 18, 1977, 1, 18.

Gallup, G. "Gallup poll on the attitudes homosexuals face today." *San Francisco Chronicle*, July 20, 1977, 4.

Glenn, G. L. "Attitudes toward homosexuality and sex roles among homosexual men." Unpublished M. A. Thesis: Antioch University/Maryland, 1978.

Heilbrun, A. B., & N. L. Thompson. "Sex-role identity and male and female homosexuality." *Sex Roles*, 1977, *3*, 65–79.

Irwin, P., & N. L. Thompson. "Acceptance of the rights of homosexuals: A social profile." *Journal of Homosexuality*, 1977, *3*, 107–121.

Kaplan, A. G., & J. P. Bean (Eds.). *Beyond Sex Role Stereotypes: Readings toward a Psychology of Androgyny*. Boston: Little, Brown, 1976.

Karr, R. "Homosexual labeling and the male role." *Journal of Social Issues*, 1978, *34*(3), 73–84.

Kinsey, A., W. Pomeroy, & C. Martin. *Sexual Behavior in the Human Male*. Philadelphia: Saunders, 1948.

Kirkpatrick, M., R. Roy, & K. Smith. "A new look at lesbian mothers." *Human Behavior*, August 1976, 60–61.

Langevin, R., A. Stanford, & R. Block. "The effect of relaxation instructions on erotic arousal in homosexual and heterosexual males." *Behavior Therapy*, 1975, *6*, 453–458.

Lauritsen, J., & D. Thorstad. *The Early Homosexual Rights Movement* (1864–1935). New York: Times Change Press, 1974.

Lehne, G. "Gay male fantasies and realities." *Journal of Social Issues*, 1978, *34*(3), 28–37.

Levitt, E., & A. Klassen. "Public attitudes toward sexual behavior: The latest investigation of the Institute for Sex Research." Paper presented at the annual convention of the American Orthopsychiatric Association, 1973.

Levitt, E., & A. Klassen. "Public attitudes toward homosexuality: Part of the 1970 National Survey by the Institute for Sex Research." *Journal of Homosexuality*, 1974, *1*, 29–43.

Lorenz, K. Interviewed by R. Evans in *Psychology Today*, November 1974, 82–93.

Lumby, M. E. "Homophobia: The quest for a valid scale." *Journal of Homosexuality*, 1976, *2*, 39–47.

MacDonald, A. "The importance of sex role to gay liberation." *Homosexual Counselling Journal*, 1974, *1*, 169–180.

MacDonald, A. "Homophobia: Its roots and meanings." *Homosexual Counselling Journal*, 1976, *3*, 23–33.

MacDonald, A., & R. Games. "Some characteristics of those who hold positive and negative attitudes toward homosexuals." *Journal of Homosexuality*, 1974, *1*, 9–27.

MacDonald, A., J. Huggins, S. Young, & R. Swanson. "Attitudes toward homosexuality: Preservation of sex morality or the double standard?" *Journal of Counselling and Clinical Psychology*, 1973, *40*, 161. Extended report available from the author (1972).

May, E. P. "Counselors', psychologists', and homosexuals' philosophies of human nature and attitudes toward homosexual behavior." *Homosexual Counselling Journal*, 1974, *1*, 3–25.

McConaghy, N. "Penile volume changes to moving pictures of male and female nudes in heterosexual and homosexual males." *Behavior Research and Therapy*, 1967, *5*, 43–48.

McDonald, G., & R. Moore. "Sex-role self-concepts of homosexual men and their attitudes toward both women and male homosexuality." *Journal of Homosexuality*, 1978, *4*, 3–14.

Millham, J., C. San Miguel, & R. Kellogg. "A factor analytic conceptualization of attitudes toward male and female homosexuals." *Journal of Homosexuality*, 1976, *2*, 3–10.

Millham, J., & L. Weinberger. "Sexual preference, sex role appropriateness and restriction of social access." *Journal of Homosexuality*, 1972, *2*, 343–357.

Minnigerode, F. "Attitudes toward homosexuality: Feminist attitudes and social conservation." *Sex Roles*, 1976, *2*, 347–352.

Montgomery, C., & M. Burgoon. "An experimental study of the interactive effects of sex and androgyny on attitude change." *Communication Monographs*, 1977, *44*, 130–135.

Morin, S., & E. Garfinkle. "Male homophobia." *Journal of Social Issues*, 1978, *34*, 29–47.

Morin, S., K. Taylor, & S. Kielman. "Gay is beautiful at a distance." Paper presented at the meeting of the American Psychological Association, Chicago, August 1975.

Morin, S., & S. Wallace. "Religiosity, sexism, and attitudes toward homosexuality." Paper presented at the meeting of the California State Psychological Association, March 1975.

Morin, S., & S. Wallace. "Traditional values, sex-role stereotyping, and attitudes toward homosexuality." Paper presented at the meeting of the Western Psychological Association, Los Angeles, April 1976.

Nutt, R., & W. Sedlacek. "Freshman sexual attitudes and behaviors." *Journal of College Student Personnel*, 1974, *15*, 346–351.

Nyberg, K., & J. Alston. "Analysis of public attitudes toward homosexual behavior." *Journal of Homosexuality*, 1976–77, *2*, 99–107.

Riddle, D. "Relating to children: Gays as role models." *Journal of Social Issues*, 1978, *34*, 38–58.

Rooney, E., & D. Gibbons. "Social reactions to crimes without victims." *Social Problems*, 1966, *13*, 400–410.

Saghir, M., & E. Robins. *Male and Female Homosexuality: A Comprehensive Investigation*. Baltimore: Williams & Wilkins, 1973.

San Miguel, C., & J. Millham. "The role of cognitive and situational variables in aggression toward homosexuals." *Journal of Homosexuality*, 1976, *2*, 11–27.

Scarpitti, F., & P. McFarlane (Eds.). *Deviance: Action, Reaction, Interaction*. Reading, Mass.: Addison-Wesley, 1975.

Shively, M., J. Rudolph, & J. DeCecco. "The identification of the social sex-role stereotypes." *Journal of Homosexuality*, 1978, *3*, 225–234.

Simmons, J. "Public stereotypes of deviants." *Social Problems*, 1965, *13*, 223–232.

Smith, K. "Homophobia: A tentative personality profile." *Psychological Reports*, 1971, *29*, 1091–1094.

Sorensen, R. *Adolescent Sexuality in Contemporary America*. New York: World, 1973.

Spence, J., & R. Helmreich. *Masculinity & Femininity*. Austin, Tx.: University of Texas Press, 1978.

Steffensmeier, D., & R. Steffensmeier. "Sex differences in reactions to homosexuals: Research continuities and further developments." *The Journal of Sex Research*, 1974, *10*, 52–67.

Storms, M. "Attitudes toward homosexuality and femininity in men." *Journal of Homosexuality*, 1978, *3*, 257–263.

Symonds, J. *A Problem in Modern Ethics*, London: 1896.

Tavris, C. "Men and women report their views on masculinity." *Psychology Today*, January, 1977, 35.

Turnbull, D., & M. Brown. "Attitudes toward homosexuality and male and female reactions to homosexual slides." *Canadian Journal of Behavioural Science*, 1977, *9*, 68–80.

Weinberg, G. *Society and the Healthy Homosexual*. New York: Doubleday, 1972.

Weinberg, M., & C. Williams. *Male Homosexuals*. New York: Oxford University Press, 1974.

Weinberger, L., & J. Millham. "Attitudinal homophobia and support of traditional sex roles." *Journal of Homosexuality*, 1979, *4*, 237–246.

Weissbach, T., & G. Zagon. "The effect of deviant group membership upon impressions of personality." *Journal of Social Psychology*, 1975, *95*, 263–266.

Wolfgang, A., & J. Wolfgang. "Exploration of attitudes via physical interpersonal distance toward the obese, drug users, homosexuals, police and other marginal figures." *Journal of Clinical Psychology*, 1971, *27*, 510–512.

THE POLITICS OF
GAY MEN'S FRIENDSHIPS

PETER M. NARDI

Towards the end of Wendy Wasserstein's Pulitzer Prize-winning play, *The Heidi Chronicles*, a gay character, Peter Patrone, explains to Heidi why he has been so upset over all the funerals he has attended recently: "A person has so many close friends. And in our lives, our friends are our families" (Wasserstein, 1990: 238). In his collection of stories, *Buddies*, Ethan Mordden (1986: 175) observes: "What unites us, all of us, surely, is brotherhood, a sense that our friendships are historic, designed to hold Stonewall together. . . . It is friendship that sustained us, supported out survival." These statements succinctly summarize an important dimension about gay men's friendships: Not only are friends a form of family for gay men and lesbians, but gay friendships are also a powerful political force.

Mordden's notion of "friends is survival" has a political dimension that becomes all the more salient in contemporary society where the political, legal, religious, economic, and health concerns of gay people are routinely threatened by the social order. In part, gay friendship can be seen as a political statement, since at the core of the concept of friendship is the idea of "being oneself" in a cultural context that may not approve of that self. For many people, the need to belong with others in dissent and out of the mainstream is central to the maintenance of self and identity (Rubin, 1986). The friendships formed by a shared marginal identity, thus, take on powerful political dimensions as they organize around a stigmatized status to confront the dominant culture in solidarity. Jerome (1984: 698) believes that friendships have such economic and political implications, since friendship is best defined as "the cement which binds together people with interests to conserve."

Suttles(1970: 116) argues that

The very basic assumption friends must make about one another is that each is going beyond a mere presentation of self in compliance with "social dictates." Inevitably, this makes friendship a somewhat deviant relationship because the surest test of personal disclosure is a violation of the rules of public propriety.

Friendship, according to Suttles (1970), has its own internal order, albeit maintained by the cultural images and situational elements that structure the definitions of friendship. In friendship, people can depart from the routine and display a portion of the self not affected by social control. That is, friendships allow people to go beyond the basic structures of their cultural institutions into an involuntary and uncontrollable exposure of self—to deviate from public propriety (Suttles, 1970).

Little (1989) similarly argues that friendship is an escape from the rules and pieties of social life. It's about identity: who one is rather than one's roles and statuses. And the idealism of friendship "lies in its detachment from these [roles and statuses], its creative and spiritual transcendence, its fundamental skepticism as a platform from which to survey the givens of society and culture" (Little, 1989: 145). For gay men, these descriptions illustrate the political meaning friendship can have in their lives and their society.

The political dimension of friendship is summed up best by Little (1989; 154–155):

the larger formations of social life—kinship, the law, the economy—must be different where there is, in addition to solidarity and dutiful role-performance, a willingness and capacity for friendship's surprising one-to-one relations, and this difference may be enough to transform social and political life. . . . Perhaps, finally, it is true that progress in democracy depends on a new generation that will increasingly locate itself in identity-shaping, social, yet personally liberating, friendships.

The traditional, nuclear family has been the dominant model for political relations and has structured much of the legal and social norms of our culture. People have often been judged by their family ties and history. But as the family becomes transformed into other arrangements, so do the political and social institutions of society. For example, the emerging concept of "domestic partnerships" has affected a variety of organizations, including insurance companies, city governments, private industry, and religious institutions (Task Force on Family Diversity Final Report, 1988).

For many gay people, the "friends as family" model is a political statement, going beyond the practicality of developing a surrogate family in times of needed social support. It is also a way of refocusing the economic and political agenda to include nontraditional family structures composed of both romantic and nonromantic nonkin relationships.

In part, this has happened by framing the discussions in terms of gender roles. The women's movement and the emerging men's movement have highlighted the negative political implications of defining gender roles according to traditional cultural norms or limiting them to biological realities. The gay movement, in turn, has often been one source for redefining traditional gender roles and sexuality. So, for example, when gay men exhibit more disclosing and emotional interactions with other men, it demonstrates the limitations of male gender roles typically enacted among many heterosexual male friends. By calling attention to the impact of homophobia on heterosexual men's lives, gay men's friendships illustrate the potentiality for expressive intimacy among all men.

Thus, the assumptions that biology and/or socialization have inevitably constrained men from having the kinds of relationships and intimacies women often typically have can be called into question. This questioning of the dominant construction of gender roles is in itself a sociopolitical act with major implications on the legal, religious, and economic order.

White (1983:16) also sees how gay people's lives can lead to new modes of behavior in the society at large:

In the case of gays, our childlessness, our minimal responsibilities, the fact that our unions are not consecrated, even our very retreat into gay ghettos for protection and freedom: all of these objective conditions have fostered a style in which we may be exploring, even in spite of our conscious intentions, things as they will someday be for the heterosexual majority. In that world (as in the gay world already), love will be built on esteem rather than passion or convention, sex will be more playful or fantastic or artistic than marital—and friendship will be elevated into the supreme consolation for this continuing tragedy, human existence.

If, as White and others have argued, gay culture in the post-Stonewall, sexual liberation years of the 1970s was characterized by a continuous fluidity between what constituted a friend, a sexual partner, and a lover, then we need to acknowledge the AIDS decade of the 1980s as a source for restructuring of gay culture and the reorganization of sexuality and friendship. If indeed gay people (and men in particular) have focused attention on developing monogamous sexual partnerships, what then becomes the role of sexuality in the initiation and development of casual or close friendships? Clearly, gay culture is not a static phenomenon, unaffected by the larger social order. Certainly, as the moral order in the AIDS years encourages the re-establishment of more traditional relationships, the implications for the ways sexuality and friendships are organized similarly change.

Friends become more important as primary sources of social and emotional support when illness strikes; friendship becomes institutionally organized as "brunch buddies" dating services or "AIDS buddies" assistance groups; and self-help groups emerge centering on how to make and keep new friends without having "compulsive sex." While AIDS may have transformed some of the meanings and role of friendships in gay men's lives from the politicalization of sexuality and friendship during the post-Stonewall 1970s, the newer meanings of gay friendships, in turn, may be having some effect on the culture's definitions of friendships.

Interestingly, the mythical images of friendships were historically more male-dominated: bravery, loyalty, duty, and heroism (see Sapadin, 1988). This explained why women were typically assumed incapable of having true friendships. But today, the images of true friendship are often expressed in terms of women's traits: intimacy, trust, caring, and nurturing, thereby excluding the more traditional men from true friendship. However, gay men appear to be at the forefront of establishing the possibility of men overcoming their male socialization stereotypes and restructuring their friendships in terms of the more contemporary (i.e., "female") attributes of emotional intimacy.

To do this at a wider cultural level involves major sociopolitical shifts in how men's roles are structured and organized. Friendships between men in terms of intimacy and emotional support inevitably introduce questions about homosexu-

ality. As Rubin (1985: 103) found in her interviews with men: "The association of friendship with homosexuality is so common among men." For women, there is a much longer history of close connections with other women, so that the separation of the emotional from the erotic is more easily made.

Lehne (1989) has argued that homophobia has limited the discussion of loving male relationships and has led to the denial by men of the real importance of their friendships with other men. In addition, "the open expression of emotion and affection by men is limited by homophobia. . . . The expression of more tender emotions among men is thought to be characteristic only of homosexuals" (Lehne, 1989: 426). So men are raised in a culture with a mixed message: strive for healthy, emotionally intimate friendships, but if you appear to intimate with another man you might be negatively labelled homosexual.

This certainly wasn't always the case. As a good illustration of the social construction of masculinity, friendship, and sexuality, one need only look to the changing definitions and concepts surrounding same-sex friendship during the nineteenth century (see Rotundo, 1989; Smith-Rosenberg, 1975). Romantic friendships could be erotic but not sexual, since sex was linked to reproduction. Because reproduction was not possible between two women or two men, the close relationship was not interpreted as being a sexual one:

> *Until the 1880s, most romantic friendships were thought to be devoid of sexual content. Thus a woman or man could write of affectionate desire for a loved one of the same gender without causing an eyebrow to be raised (D'Emilio and Freedman, 988: 121).*

However, as same-sex relationships became medicalized and stigmatized in the late 19th century, "the labels 'congenital inversion' and 'perversion' were applied not only to male sexual acts, but to sexual or romantic unions between women, as well as those between men"

(D'Emilio and Freedman, 1988: 122). Thus, the twentieth century is an anomaly in its promotion of female equality, the encouragement of male-female friendships, and its suspicion of intense emotional friendships between men (Richards, 1987). Yet, in Ancient Greece and the medieval days of chivalry, comradeship, virtue, patriotism, and heroism were all associated with close male friendship. Manly love, as it was often called, was a central part of the definition of manliness (Richards, 1987).

It is through the contemporary gay, women's, and men's movements that these twentieth century constructions of gender are being questioned. And at the core is the association of close male friendships with negative images of homosexuality. Thus, how gay men structure their emotional lives and friendships can affect the social and emotional lives of all men and women. This is the political power and potential of gay friendships.

REFERENCES

D'Emilio, John and Freedman, Estelle. (1988). *Intimate Matters: A History of Sexuality in America.* New York: Harper & Row.

Jerome, Dorothy. (1984). Good company: The sociological implications of friendship. *Sociological Review*, 32(4), 696–718.

Lehne, Gregory. (1989 [1980]). Homophobia among men: Supporting and defining the male role. In M. Kimmel and M. Messner (Eds.), *Men's Lives* (pp. 416–429). New York: Macmillan.

Little, Graham. (1989). Freud, friendship, and politics. In R. Porter and S. Tomaselli (Eds.), *The Dialectics of Friendship* (pp. 143–158). London: Routledge.

Mordden, Ethan. (1986). *Buddies*. New York: St. Martin's Press.

Richards, Jeffrey. (1987). "Passing the love of women": Manly love and Victorian society. In J. A. Mangan and J. Walvin (Eds.), *Manliness and Morality: Middle-Class Masculinity in Britain and America (1800–1940)* (pp. 92–122). Manchester, England: Manchester University Press.

Rotundo, Anthony. (1989). Romantic friendships: Male intimacy and middle-class youth in the northern United States, 1800–1900. *Journal of Social History*, 23(1), 1–25.

Rubin, Lillian. (1985). *Just Friends: The Role of Friendship in Our Lives*. New York: Harper & Row.

Sapadin, Linda. (1988). Friendship and gender: Perspectives of professional men and women. *Journal of Social and Personal Relationships*, 5(4), 387–403.

Smith-Rosenberg, Carroll. (1975). The female world of love and ritual: Relations between women in nineteenth-century America. *Signs*, 1(1): 1–29.

Suttles, Gerald. (1970). Friendship as a social institution. In G. McCall, M. McCall, N. Denzin, G. Suttles, and S. Kurth, *Social Relationships* (pp. 95–135). Chicago: Aldine.

Task Force on Family Diversity. (1988). *Strengthening Families: A Model for Community Action*. City of Los Angeles.

Wasserstein, Wendy. (1990) *The Heidi Chronicles*. San Diego: Harcourt, Brace, Jovanovich.

White, Edmund. (1983). Paradise found: Gay men have discovered that there is friendship after sex. *Mother Jones*, June, 10–16.

PSYCHOLOGICAL HETEROSEXISM AND ANTI-GAY VIOLENCE:

THE SOCIAL PSYCHOLOGY OF BIGOTRY AND BASHING

GREGORY M. HEREK

Roughly two thirds of Americans[1] condemn homosexuality or homosexual behavior as morally wrong or a sin; this pattern has not changed significantly since the late 1970s.[2] According to Gallup polls (Colasanto, 1989), only a plurality of Americans felt in 1989 that homosexual relations between consenting adults should be legal (47% versus 36% who say they should not be legal). Many heterosexual Americans also reject gay people at the personal level. In 1987 a Roper poll found that 25% of the respondents to a national survey would strongly object to working around people who are homosexual, and another 27% would prefer not to do so; only 45% "wouldn't mind." In a 1985 *Los Angeles Times* poll, 35% of the respondents reported that they felt discomfort around either gay men (6%) or lesbians (11%) or both (18%); 50% reported that they did *not* feel *un*comfortable around gay people.

Despite this evidence for widespread condemnation and avoidance of lesbians and gay men, other data indicate that heterosexual Americans are increasingly reluctant to condone discrimination on the basis of sexual orientation (e.g., Colasanto, 1989; Schneider & Lewis, 1984; see Rayside & Bowler, 1988, for evidence of a similar trend in Canada). Roper surveys found that the proportion of Americans agreeing that "homosexuals should be guaranteed equal treatment under the law in jobs and housing" rose from 60% in 1977 to 66% in 1985, while the pro-

portion supporting legalized discrimination declined from 28% to 22%. Similarly, the proportion of American adults surveyed by the Gallup organization who say that homosexual men and women should have equal rights in terms of job opportunities increased from 56% in 1977 to 59% in 1982 and to 71% in 1989; the proportion opposing such rights declined from 33% to 28% to 18%, respectively (Colasanto, 1989).

Respondents sometimes show more willingness to discriminate when asked about specific occupations, but a steady trend toward supporting gay rights still is evident. In Gallup polls (Colasanto, 1989), the proportion stating that gay people should be hired as doctors increased from 44% in 1977 to 56% in 1989; similar increases were observed for hiring them as salespersons (from 68% to 79%), members of the armed forces (51% to 60%), clergy (36% to 44%), and elementary schoolteachers (27% to 42%). For all of these occupations, the long-term trend appears to be toward increased public opposition to discrimination on the basis of sexual orientation.

CULTURAL AND PSYCHOLOGICAL HETEROSEXISM

I define *heterosexism* as an ideological system that denies, denigrates, and stigmatizes any nonheterosexual form of behavior, identity, relationship, or community. Cultural heterosexism, like institutional racism and sexism, is manifested in societal customs and institutions. Through cultural heterosexism, homosexuality is rendered invisible and, when it becomes visible, is condemned by society. The poll data cited above make it clear that, although cultural heterosexism is pervasive in society, Americans display considerable variability in their individual attitudes toward lesbians and gay men. This observation reveals the inadequacy of an analysis of heterosexism that is restricted to its cultural manifestations.

In this article, I discuss *psychological heterosexism*—the manifestation of heterosexism in individuals' attitudes[3] and actions—and its role in violence against lesbians and gay men. In particular, I consider how psychological and situational factors affect the attitudes and behaviors of heterosexual individuals. The article is based on the assumptions that (a) psychological heterosexism and anti-gay violence are often functional for the person who manifests them; (b) the principal function served by these attitudes and actions differs for each person, depending upon her or his psychological needs; and (c) the translation of individual needs into anti-gay attitudes and behaviors involves a complex interaction of deep-seated personality characteristics, salient aspects of the immediate situation, and cultural definitions of sexuality and gender. In short; no single explanation of psychological heterosexism applies to all people.[4]

In the next section of the article, I discuss heterosexism as an attitude or prejudice and consider how it can serve different psychological functions for different people. Following that, I apply a similar analysis to overt acts of anti-gay behavior.

The Psychological Functions of Heterosexism

Why do some heterosexuals feel strongly hostile toward gay people while others are tolerant or accepting in their attitudes? In my own empirical research (Herek, 1984, 1987), I have tried to answer this question by using a perspective that earlier researchers applied to Whites' attitudes toward Blacks and Americans' attitudes toward Russians (e.g., McClintock, 1958; Smith, Bruner, & White, 1956.) This perspective is called the *functional approach* to attitudes. Its central assumption is that people hold and express particular attitudes because they get some sort of psychological benefit from doing so. In other words, attitudes and opinions serve psychological functions for the person who holds them. According to the functional approach, two people can have very different motivations for expressing what appears to be the same attitude. Or they can express opposing opinions for essentially the same reason. Further, an individual's attitudes are more likely to change when they stop being functional or actually become dysfunctional.

Using this perspective, I analyzed essays about homosexuality written by 205 heterosexual college students (Herek, 1987) and found three principal psychological functions underlying the students' attitudes. I labeled the first of these the *experiential* function.[5] Attitudes serving an experiential function assisted the students in making sense of their previous interactions with gay people. Those who had experienced pleasant interactions with a gay man or lesbian generalized from that experience and accepted gay people in general. For example, one woman wrote:

[I have generally positive attitudes because] I have come to know some of these people and find them no different from any other people. This has not always been the case. In junior high and high school I didn't condemn so to speak but I held strong opinions against them. This was an attitude formed without any knowledge of homosexuality or homosexuals. When I first came to [college] I still had some of the same attitudes. Little did I know that the guy in the next room was gay. We became good friends and did things together all the time. Eventually he told me and it was then that I realized that homosexuals only differ in sexual preference.

Others reported negative attitudes resulting from their unpleasant experiences with gay men or lesbians. Another woman wrote:

> *Personally, I don't like most male homosexuals. I once worked under one and worked with some and they were everything homosexuals are stereotyped to be—someone once said "male homosexuals have all the bad qualities of women" (shrewishness, pettiness, etc.)—and unfortunately, for the men I worked with this statement applied.*

Whether favorable or unfavorable, experiential attitudes help an individual to make sense of past experiences and fit them into a larger worldview, one that is organized primarily in terms of her or his own self-interest.

Because only about 30% of American adults know an openly gay person,[6] most heterosexuals' attitudes are not based on actual experiences with gay people. The attitudes of some of the remaining 70% probably serve an *anticipatory* function. Like the experiential function, the anticipatory function helps an individual to understand the world and to develop strategies for maximizing rewards and minimizing negative experiences. Unlike the experiential function, however, the anticipatory function is not based on past experiences with lesbians and gay men. Rather, it is based on the anticipation of future interactions with them.

For most of the 70% of Americans who do not personally know lesbians or gay men, however, homosexuality and gay people are primarily symbols. Whereas attitudes toward people with whom one has direct experience function primarily to organize and make sense of those experiences, attitudes toward symbols serve a different kind of function. Such attitudes help people to increase their self-esteem by expressing important aspects of themselves—by declaring (to themselves and to others) what sort of people they are. Affirming who one *is* often is accomplished by distancing oneself from or even attacking people who represent the sort of person one is *not* (or does not want to be).

Many respondents in my study wrote essays that appeared to serve this type of function. Some essays, for example, manifested what I call a *social identity* function:[7]

> *I have generally positive attitudes toward homosexuals because I don't think sexual preferences are a basis of judgment of someone's character or personality. Sexual preferences are a personal matter, and as long as a homosexual doesn't offend anyone or force his temptations on someone who is unwilling, there is no reason to condemn him/her. Homosexual tendencies aren't a deficit in someone's upbringing. I have these attitudes because of my own upbringing to be open-minded and non-stereotypical or non-judgmental.*

An example of negative social identity attitudes:

> *[I have generally negative attitudes because] in the Bible it clearly states that homosexuality is a* sin. *I believe that no one can be a Christian if he/she is a homosexual. I believe the Bible is correct, and I follow its beliefs word for word. I am a Christian.*

The opinions expressed in these essays appeared to help the authors to increase their feelings of self-esteem in two ways. Consequently, I divided the social identity function into two interrelated components. The first of these is the *value-expressive* function. Attitudes serving a value-expressive function enable people to affirm their belief in and adherence to important values that are closely related to their self-concepts. In one of the latter essays printed above, for example, the author expressed her personal philosophy of "live and let live." For her, being gay represented a personal issue; her values dictated that people should not be condemned for what they do in their personal lives so long as they do not force themselves on unwilling others. Expressing her views about gay people allowed her to express her personal values about individual liberties, which were fundamental to her perception of herself as an open-minded person.

Although the last essay above conveyed a considerably different message, it also manifested a value-expressive function. Through it, the writer expressed her need to perceive herself in terms of her religious faith. In her view, opposing homosexuality was an integral part of being a good Christian, which was of central importance to feeling good about herself. It was not homosexuality per se that was important; homosexuality was a symbol for all that is immoral and contrary to her religious views. If her religion were to define left-handedness as it now defines homosexuality, she would probably express comparable hostility toward left-handed people.

The second component of the social identity function is *social expression*. With this function, expressing an attitude strengthens one's sense of belonging to a particular group and helps an individual to gain acceptance, approval, or love from other people whom she or lie considers important (e.g., peers, family, neighbors). When social-expressive attitudes are hostile, gay people are perceived as the epitome of outsiders; denigrating them solidifies one's own status as an insider, one who belongs to the group. When social-expressive attitudes are positive, lesbians and gay men are regarded favorably by one's group or are members of that group. In either case, the approval that is won through expressing these attitudes increases the individual's own self-esteem, which is of central importance to her or him. Sometimes social support for attitudes is experienced directly, as when others tell us that they agree with our opinions or approve of our actions, that they accept us and like us. At other times, the support is indirect or imagined, as when we experience satisfaction because we feel that others would approve of us if they knew what we were saying or doing. The writers in these two essays most likely experienced both kinds of reinforcement for their attitudes. Their friends and family probably directly supported one's open-mindedness and the other's religiosity. At the same time, expressing their views probably helped them to feel kinship with larger social groupings (namely, open-minded people and good Christians).

I observed one other attitude function that also treats lesbians and gay men as symbols: the *ego-defensive* function. Defensive attitudes lower a person's anxiety resulting from her or his unconscious psychological conflicts, such as those surrounding sexuality or gender. This function is summarized in the notion that heterosexuals who express anti-gay prejudice do so out of fear that they themselves are latent homosexuals. This explanation for anti-gay prejudice has become widespread in recent years. Although it is used more often than is appropriate, it does fit some people for whom lesbians or gay men symbolize unacceptable parts of themselves (e.g., "effeminacy" for some men, "masculinity" for some women). Expressing anti-gay hostility represents an unconscious strategy through which they can avoid an internal conflict by externalizing it—projecting it onto a suitable symbol apart from themselves. By rejecting (or even attacking) gay people, the defensive individual can deny that unacceptable aspect of him- or herself while also symbolically attacking it. Defensive attitudes are often expressed in strong feelings of disgust toward homosexuality or in perceptions of danger from gay people of one's own gender. For example, one woman wrote:

> *[I have generally negative attitudes] because I feel homosexuality is not a normal lifestyle. I do, however, feel more comfortable with a male homosexual than with a lesbian. Male homosexuals may have a different lifestyle but they are not physically dangerous to me as a woman, and I feel casual friendships between myself and male homosexuals are less tense. Lesbianism, however, is disgusting to me.*

Another essay with defensive themes hinted strongly at some of the author's struggles with his own sexuality. Denying that anyone is truly homosexual, he expressed the unrealistic belief that society encourages young people to become gay:

> *I don't believe such tendencies come about because of a person's true feelings. Our society keeps telling everyone that it's okay to be a les or fag, and that there's nothing wrong with it. Many guys and girls who have never had sexual relations with the opposite sex think they're "different" right away and they turn gay because everyone says it's okay anyway. I don't think anyone should hold the passive view that "if they don't bother me, let them*

be" because they are ruining this country's morals in a very disguised fashion. I feel people with these tendencies aren't that abnormal—they've just been taken in by society's view that it's okay. Let's give these people help so they can enjoy life to its fullest like everyone else.

The value-expressive, social-expressive, and ego-defensive functions share a common characteristic: With all of them, anti-gay prejudice helps people to define who they are by directing hostility toward gay people as a symbol of what they are not. With the value-expressive function, a heterosexual's attitudes help to define the world according to principles of good and evil, right and wrong; by opposing the embodiment of evil (gay people), the individual affirms her or his own morality and virtue. With the social-expressive function, one's attitudes help to designate who is in the in-group and who is in the out-group; by denigrating outsiders (lesbians and gay men), the individual affirms her or his own status as an insider. With the defensive function, attitudes toward gay people help to affirm and "own" the good or acceptable parts of the self while denying the bad or unacceptable parts. Unacceptable feelings (such as homoerotic desires, "feminine" tendencies for men, or "masculine" tendencies for women) are projected onto gay people, who are then disliked. In this way, individuals can symbolically (and often unconsciously) prove to themselves that those unacceptable feelings are not their own.

Here then is a nexus between psychological and cultural heterosexism: *Psychological heterosexism can serve these functions only when an individual's psychological needs converge with the culture's ideology.* Anti-gay prejudice can be value expressive only when an individual's self-concept is closely tied to values that also have become socially defined as antithetical to homosexuality. It can be social expressive only insofar as an individual strongly needs to be accepted by members of a social group that rejects gay people or homosexuality. It can be defensive only when lesbians and gay men are culturally defined in a way that links them to an individual's own psychological conflicts.

The functions discussed here are summarized in Table 9.1, from which it can be seen that the benefits received from attitudes toward lesbians and gay men are contingent upon either of two principal sources. One source is gay people themselves. With attitudes serving an experiential function, lesbians and gay men have been the source of pleasant or unpleasant experiences in the past. Holding and expressing attitudes consistent with that earlier experience allows an individual to exert some control over future experiences, either by avoiding what has been unpleasant or by seeking out what has been pleasant. With the anticipatory function, the individual has not had direct interactions with lesbians or gay men in the past but expects to have them in the future and expects gay people to be the source of either benefit or detriment; the attitude helps the individual to prepare for those anticipated interactions. Because these attitudes involve an evaluation or appraisal of gay men and lesbians as a group in terms of whether they have been or will be a source of reward or punishment, I refer to them as the *evaluative* attitude functions (Herek, 1986b).[8]

With the social identity (value-expressive and social-expressive) and defensive functions, in contrast, the source of benefit is not contingent upon the actions or characteristics of lesbians and gay men but upon what happens when the individual expresses her or his attitudes. Lesbians and gay men serve as symbols of personal values, group membership, or unconscious conflicts. They are a means to an end: Expressing a particular attitude toward them helps the individual to affirm her or his self-concept in terms of important values, to feel accepted by significant others, or to reduce anxieties. Consequently, I refer to them as the *expressive* functions.

Distinguishing between the evaluative and expressive functions is useful because it suggests different strategies for reducing prejudice. Prejudice that serves one of the evaluative functions can best be reduced through direct experiences with lesbians and gay men. Prejudice that serves an expressive function can be reduced through addressing the individual's identity needs, affil-

TABLE 1   The Psychological Functions of Heterosexism

NAME OF FUNCTION	DESCRIPTION	BENEFIT TO INDIVIDUAL
Evaluative functions		
Experiential	Generalizes from past experiences with specific lesbians or gay men to create a coherent image of gay people in relation to one's own interests.	Makes sense of past experiences and uses them to guide behavior.
Anticipatory	Anticipates benefits or punishments expected to be received directly from lesbians or gay men.	In absence of direct experience with gay men or lesbians, plans future behavior so as to maximize rewards and minimize punishments.
Expressive functions		
Social identity:		
Value-expressive	Lesbians or gay men symbolize an important value conflict.	Increases self-esteem by affirming individual's view of self as a person who adheres to particular values.
Social-expressive	Lesbians or gay men symbolize the in-group or out-group.	Increases self-esteem by winning approval of others whose opinion is valued; increases sense of group solidarity.
Defensive:	Lesbians or gay men symbolize unacceptable part of the self.	Reduces anxiety associated with a psychological conflict by denying and externalizing the unacceptable aspect of self and then attacking it.

NOTE: With the evaluative functions, benefit is contingent upon direct experiences with lesbians and gay men. With the expressive functions, benefit is contingent upon the consequences of expressing the attitude.

iation needs, or unconscious conflicts. Some implications of this distinction for reducing psychological heterosexism are discussed more fully in the final section of this chapter.

THE PSYCHOLOGICAL FUNCTIONS OF ANTI-GAY VIOLENCE

In the discussion so far, psychological heterosexism has been examined as an attitude—that is, something "in the heads" of individuals. But what about behaviors such as actively discriminating against gay people or physically attacking them? When a teenage boy participates in a gang attack against a gay man on the street, for example, do his actions serve psychological functions

for him in the same way that heterosexist attitudes do? In this section, I consider how the functional approach can be applied to hate crimes against lesbians and gay men.

Violence Serving Evaluative Functions

Some anti-gay crimes may serve an experiential function by enabling the attacker to make sense of his or her past negative interactions with a particular lesbian or gay man. Although discussions of anti-gay violence usually focus on the victim's status as a representative of the lesbian or gay male community, it should be recognized that gay people are not immune from attacks based on personal dislike or vengeance. They can be targeted by an individual with whom they have previously had an argument or disagreement unrelated to their sexual orientation. Or a perpetrator may have had a negative experience with someone who is gay and then attacked another gay person (e.g., a friend of the first individual) as a proxy. From the viewpoint of the victim, the attack may well be experienced as a hate crime regardless of the assailant's actual motives. But from the perpetrator's perspective, the attack was directed at a specific individual rather than all gay women and men.

Other violent attacks against gay people may be based on an anticipatory function. For example, the perpetrator perceives gay people to be vulnerable and unlikely to resist and consequently targets them for robbery (Harry, 1982). The assailant's primary motivation in this case is the desire for personal gain with minimal risk (*actuarial* crimes). The victim and the larger community are likely to experience this as a hate crime, especially if anti-gay epithets are uttered by the assailant. But the perpetrator might well have been responding more to situational cues than to personal prejudice—for example, an unexpected opportunity to rob an easy target.

Violence Serving an Expressive Function

Value-expressive Violence. Value-expressive violence provides a way for perpetrators to express important values that are the basis for their self-concepts. The value-expressive motivation was illustrated in an interview conducted by journalist Michael Collins with members of a Los Angeles gang called the Blue Boys. At one point in Collins's interview, the gang's leader justified their actions in value-expressive terms. Characterizing homosexuality as a serious societal problem, he stated that the gang members would not "sit back and watch the poisoning of America." He further portrayed the group members as upholding important values when he compared their violent assaults on gay men to "the work of Batman or some other masked avenger." His comments are consistent with the rhetoric of hate groups such as the Ku Klux Klan, which regularly appeal to moral authority (see Segrest & Zeskind, 1989). Value-based justifications for anti-gay violence often derive from societal norms surrounding the institution of gender. Although disengaged from the conventional moral order, perpetrators may develop rationalizations that designate gay people as worthy of punishment and that allow attackers to see themselves as "rendering gender justice and reaffirming the natural order of gender-appropriate behavior."

Social-expressive Violence. Membership in a social group often is a central component of one's identity. By clearly differentiating and then attacking an out-group, anti-gay violence can help in-group members to feel more positive about their group and, consequently, about themselves as well. For example, Weissman interviewed several young men who had thrown eggs and oranges at gay men at a gay bar in Greenwich Village. They generally described the incident as a practical joke, but it appears also to have strengthened their sense of group solidarity. The informal leader explained, "Peer pressure has a lot to do with it. Sometimes you're forced into doing some-thing to prove yourself to others." Another group member described his feelings after the incident: "Relief. A kind of high. There was also a strong, close feeling that we were all in something together."

Social-expressive motivations also were apparent among the Blue Boys. They had a clearly formed in-group, signified by their "uniform" of blue baseball jackets, their blue bats, and their framed "Statement of Principals," which they claimed to have signed in blood. Additionally, the Blue Boys' leader also seemed to seek recognition and acceptance from a larger audience; he fantasized that people who read about the group's exploits would cheer them on, much the way that baseball fans cheer a home run.

Perpetrators of anti-gay sexual assaults also may be motivated by needs to maintain status and affiliation with their peers. From a series of interviews with perpetrators of male–male rapes, for example, Groth and Burgess (1980, p. 808) concluded, "Some offenders feel pressured to participate in gang rape to maintain status and membership with their peers. . . . [A]cceptance and recognition by one's peers becomes a dynamic in group rape, and mutual participation in the assault serves to strengthen and confirm the social bond among the assailants."

Ego-defensive Violence. Anti-gay assaults can provide a means for young males to affirm their heterosexuality or masculinity by attacking someone who symbolizes an unacceptable aspect of their own personalities (e.g., homoerotic feelings or tendencies toward effeminacy). This process may be partly conscious, as evidenced in comments by the Blue Boys (in Chapter 12). Their leader repeatedly affirmed that they were "*real* men" who were "out there fucking chicks every night" and explained that they "chose the blue baseball bats because it's the color of the boy. The man is one gender. He is not female. It is male. There is no confusion. Blue is the color of men, and that's the color that men use to defeat the anti-male, which is the queer."

The Blue Boys appeared to use their anti-gay beatings as a way of establishing their own manhood. Their brutal assaults on men whom they perceived as the antithesis of masculinity may have been an attempt to deny any trace of femininity in themselves.

The ego-defensive motivations of anti-gay attacks probably often are hidden from the perpetrators themselves. A dramatic example can be found in the brutal murder of Robert Hillsborough by a gang of young men in San Francisco in the summer of 1977 (Shilts, 1982). One of the men convicted of the murder, 19-year-old John Cordova, stabbed Hillsborough 15 times while shouting "Faggot, faggot." What makes this story a possible example of defensive attitudes is the interesting fact that Cordova was sexually attracted to men but he could not admit it to himself. He had an occasional sexual relationship with a male construction contractor, who said that Cordova often initiated sexual encounters

but "never wanted to act like he knew what he was doin'" during them (Shilts, 1982, p. 168). Cordova would always wake up as if he were in a daze, insisting he had no idea what had happened the night before. When he stabbed Hillsborough over and over, Cordova may have been unconsciously attacking and striking out at his own homosexual desires.

Ego-defensive motives also can underlie sexual assaults in which the perpetrator apparently wished to punish the victim as a way of dealing with his own unresolved and conflictual sexual interests. Groth and Burgess (1980, p. 808) quoted an assailant who had assaulted a young hustler after having sex with him:

> *After I came, I dragged him out of the car and punched him out and called him a punk. I told him I was going to kill him. Then I threw his clothes out of the car and took off. I was angry at him. I don't know why. At what I was doing, I guess, is what I was really angry at.*

Groth and Burgess (1980) speculated that assailants in male–male rape who are conflicted about their own homosexual attraction may see the victim as a temptation and may subsequently use rape in an attempt to punish him for arousing them.

Violence with Multiple Motivations

In many anti-gay assaults, the perpetrators act from several motives simultaneously. Multiple motivations seem especially likely in street assaults by young male perpetrators. Such assailants are at an age when establishing their adult identity, including their manhood, is of considerable importance (Erikson, 1963). Many of them strongly embrace what the culture has defined as "masculine" characteristics, while rejecting "feminine" characteristics (Horwitz & White, 1987). Identity formation is both a personal and a social process; it must be done for oneself, for one's peers, and for the larger society. Consequently, gay men and lesbians may serve simultaneously as multiple symbols for young male gangs. They may represent (a) unacceptable feelings or tendencies experienced privately by each gang member (for example, deviations from heterosexuality or culturally prescribed gender roles), (b) the out-group, and (c) what society has defined as evil. At the same time, such attacks may be based in part on past experiences with gay people. The perpetrator, for example, may have had an unpleasant interaction with an individual who incidentally was gay and may seek vengeance by attacking a proxy for that individual. Consequently, gang attacks may simultaneously serve experiential, ego-defensive, social-expressive, and value-expressive functions for the perpetrators.

Other perpetrators also are likely to have multiple motives for their anti-gay attacks. Police officers, for example, work to uphold societal values in an institution where the sense of the in-group is strong and where masculinity traditionally has been revered (Niederhoffer, 1967). Some have interacted with gay people only when attesting them. Especially for young policemen, who may still be solidifying their adult identities, anti-gay violence may serve psychological functions quite similar to those previously discussed for street gangs. Similarly, parents who assault their lesbian daughters or gay sons may have multiple motivations: They may be trying to banish unacceptable feelings from a child whom they consider to be an extension of their own identity (an ego-defensive function), while fulfilling their culturally defined parental role of imparting society's values to their children (a value-expressive function) and while seeking to protect the integrity of their family from what they perceive as outside, perhaps alien influences (a social-expressive function). The assault also may result in part from the parent's feelings of anger and frustration that have built up toward the child during a long series of unpleasant interactions (an experiential function).

Situational Influences on Anti-Gay Violence

From the examples in this section, it should be clear that the primary cause of anti-gay violence is not always the attacker's own personal prejudice against lesbians and gay men. Although anti-gay (or, for that matter, progay) actions may reflect an individual's deeply felt attitudes and beliefs, this is not always the case. A heterosexual person's behaviors toward lesbians and gay men may be more a product of immediate circumstances than of her or his strong dislikes (or likes) for lesbians and gay men. In this sense, I agree with Ehrlich's observation that the term *hate crime* can be misleading if it implies that the attacker's motivation always is intense personal hatred for the victim's group. Acts of anti-gay violence need not always be driven primarily by psychological heterosexism (although it is likely to be present to some extent in all anti-gay hate crimes). Instead, such crimes can serve a variety of social and psychological functions for those who commit them. Rather than acting from their own bigotry, for example, some perpetrators of violence against lesbians and gay men may be responding primarily to peer pressure or other situational factors. This was illustrated in the comments of a young man interviewed by Weissman: "We were trying to be tough to each other. It was like a game of chicken—someone dared you to do something and there was just no backing down."

This observation points to another reason for distinguishing between psychological and cultural heterosexism. Whereas psychological heterosexism may not always be the principal reason for an anti-gay attack (e.g., a gang might well have selected another type of "outsider" as a suitable victim), the importance of cultural heterosexism cannot be underestimated. For it is cultural heterosexism that defines gay people as suitable targets that can be "used" for meeting a variety of psychological needs. And anti-gay attacks, regardless of the perpetrator's motivation, reinforce cultural heterosexism. Thus, when a teenage gang member attacks a gay man on the street, it is a hate crime *not* because hate necessarily was the attacker's primary motive (it may or may not have been) but because the attack expresses cultural hostility, condemnation, and disgust toward gay people and because it has the effect of terrorizing the individual victim as well as the entire lesbian and gay community. The attack in effect punishes the gay person for daring to be visible.

In summary, although cultural heterosexism is the principal determinant of anti-gay hate crimes as a cultural phenomenon, additional factors must be considered to explain why a particular person commits a specific act of anti-gay violence. Among these are the individual's past experiences with the victim (if any), her or his psychological needs and personality characteristics, and the demands created by the immediate situation (e.g., peer pressures).

STRATEGIES FOR CHANGE

The functional approach is important not only because it explains the motivations for individuals' attitudes and actions but also because it suggests a strategy for combating anti-gay prejudice and violence, namely, by making them dysfunctional. This involves determining what psychological functions are served by a person's feelings or behaviors and then intervening in either of two ways: preventing the individual's anti-gay attitudes or actions from fulfilling that psychological need or helping her or him to meet the same need in another, less destructive way.

Consider, for example, someone whose anti-gay attitudes result from a value-expressive need to perceive herself as a religious person. Attempts to reduce her prejudice by eliminating the role played by religious values in her self-concept is not likely to succeed. It might be possible, however, to disentangle her condemnation of gay people from her moral beliefs so that she can continue to express her religious values but without attacking lesbians and gay men. This might be accomplished by presenting her with alternative, noncondemnatory theological perspectives on homosexuality by religious leaders whom she respects. She also might be influenced by juxtaposing her religious values against equally important but contradictory values. If she places a high value on patriotism, for example, she might be influenced by arguments that

appeal to justice and liberty. A third source of change might be her realization that a person whom she loves (e.g., a close friend or relative) is gay. This might create a conflict between her moral condemnation of homosexuality as a symbol and her feelings for the flesh-and-blood individual whom she has always considered to be a good person and whom she now knows to be gay (see Herek, 1984, 1986b, 1987, 1991, for further discussion).

This approach requires that institutions and society, as well as individuals, be targeted for change. Individual anti-gay attitudes and actions will become dysfunctional when they are no longer supported by religious and political institutions, when they are not reinforced by social norms, and when they are not integral to society's images of sexuality and gender. Even more broadly, anti-gay prejudice and violence will become much less functional when the majority of heterosexual Americans stop perceiving homosexuality in symbolic terms and instead associate it with their close friends and loved ones who are lesbian or gay.

Coming out to heterosexuals is perhaps the most powerful strategy that lesbians and gay men have for overcoming psychological heterosexism and anti-gay violence. Empirical research with other minority groups has shown that intergroup contact often reduces prejudice in the majority group when the contact meets several conditions: When it makes shared goals salient, when intergroup cooperation is encouraged, when the contact is ongoing and intimate rather than brief and superficial, when representatives of the groups are of equal status, and when they share important values (Allport, 1954; Amir, 1976). These conditions occur most often when lesbians and gay men disclose their sexual orientation to their relatives, friends, neighbors, and coworkers. When heterosexuals learn that someone about whom they care is gay, formerly functional prejudice can quickly become dysfunctional. The untruth in stereotypes becomes obvious, social norms are perceived to have changed, and traditional moral values concerning sexuality are juxtaposed against the values of caring for a loved one. Thus having a friend, coworker, or family member who is openly gay can eventually change a prejudiced person's perception of homosexuality from an emotionally charged, value-laden symbolic construct to a mere demographic characteristic, like hair color or political party affiliation.

Coming out, however, is difficult and possibly dangerous. It requires making public an aspect of oneself that society perceives as more appropriately kept private. It can mean being defined exclusively in terms of sexuality by strangers, friends, and family. It also can mean being newly perceived as possessing some sort of disability or handicap, an inability to be what one should be as man or woman. In the worst situations, it can mean being completely rejected or even physically attacked by those to whom one has come out. Many gay people remain in the closet because they fear these negative interpersonal consequences as well as discrimination and stigmatization. Additionally, continually having to overcome invisibility is itself a frustrating experience; allowing others to assume that one is heterosexual often is the path of least resistance.

The challenge, therefore, is for all people who abhor heterosexism to do whatever they can to remove these barriers, to create a social climate in which coming out is safer and easier. This requires a comprehensive approach in which we all confront heterosexism in both its cultural and its psychological manifestations. As a first step, we must confront hate crimes against lesbians and gay men and other minority groups; we must clearly establish that these crimes are unacceptable and punish the perpetrators. We also must work to change the individual attitudes that give rise to such attacks and that tolerate them. And we must change the institutions that perpetuate prejudice by keeping lesbians and gay men invisible and punishing them when they come out.

Our culture already has witnessed the beginnings of a transformation as more and more lesbians and gay men have come out to those around them and as they have challenged heterosexism in its many forms—both psychological and cultural. Prejudice and violence work to prevent this transformation; they threaten to set back the clock by making gay people invisible once again. It is up to each of us to confront prejudice, to challenge violence, and to fight invisibility.

NOTES

1. Following popular usage, the word *American* is used in this chapter to describe residents of the United States of America.
2. For example, see polls by ABC (August, 1987), the *Los Angeles Times* (August, 1987), Roper (September, 1985), Yankelovich (March, 1978), and Gallup (November, 1978). When not otherwise indicated, the national survey data described in this chapter were obtained through the Roper Center, University of Connecticut at Storrs. I am grateful to Professor Bliss Siman of Baruch College, City University of New York, for her assistance in securing these data.
3. In this chapter, the term *attitude* is used to refer to an individual's evaluative stance toward a particular group of persons or objects. Such an evaluation might be described with terms such as *good-bad*, *like-dislike*, or *favorable-unfavorable*. The term *opinion* is

used interchangeably with *attitude*. An attitude or opinion can be expressed privately (to oneself) or publicly (through speaking, writing, or some other observable behavior).
4. In this chapter, I purposely avoid the term *homophobia*, which has often been used to describe such attitudes (Herek, 1984; Smith, 1971; Weinberg, 1972). Any single word is necessarily limited in its ability to characterize a phenomenon that encompasses issues of morality, legality, discrimination, civil liberties, violence, and personal discomfort. *Homophobia* is particularly ill-suited to this purpose, however, for three reasons. First, it is linguistically awkward; its literal meaning is something like "fear of sameness." Second, anti-gay prejudice is not truly a phobia; it is not necessarily based on fear; nor is it inevitably irrational or dysfunctional for individuals who manifest it (Fyfe,

1983; Herek, 1986a; Nungesser, 1983; Shields & Harriman, 1984). Third, using homophobia can easily mislead us into thinking of anti-gay prejudice in exclusively individual terms, as a form of mental illness rather than as a pattern of thought and behavior that can actually be adaptive in a prejudiced society.

5. In my earlier papers (Herek, 1986b, 1987), I used the term *experiential-schematic*. This somewhat cumbersome term has been shortened for the current chapter.

6. For example, 29% of the respondents to a 1986 *Newsweek*/Gallup poll indicated they knew a gay person. In a 1983 *Los Angeles Times* poll, the figure was 30%.

7. In my earlier papers (Herek, 1986b, 1987), I used the term *social expressive*. For greater clarity, I have substituted the term *social identity* in this chapter.

8. The term *instrumental* also might be used to describe these functions, in that they are based on the attitude object's instrumental value to the person holding the attitude. All attitudes can be considered instrumental, however, to the extent that they provide some sort of psychological benefit to the holder. I think that understanding this dual usage of *instrumental* helps to resolve Ehrlich's disagreement with Harry over whether violence is instrumental or symbolic. Harry uses the term in the more specific sense of benefits derived directly from the victim (e.g., valuables obtained through robbery); his usage matches the evaluative functions described here. Ehrlich's use of *instrumental* refers to the actor's need for some general benefit from the violence; this usage includes both evaluative and expressive violence and matches the more general concept of *function* as used in this chapter.

REFERENCES

Allport, G. (1954). *The nature of prejudice*. New York: Addison-Wesley.

Amir, Y. (1976). The role of intergroup contact in change of prejudice and intergroup relations. In P. Katz (Ed.), *Towards the elimination of racism* (pp. 245–308). New York: Pergamon.

Colasanto, D. (1989, October 25). Gay rights support has grown since 1982, Gallup poll finds. *San Francisco Chronicle*, p. A21.

Erikson, E. H. (1963). *Childhood and society* (2nd ed.). New York: Norton.

Fyfe, B. (1983). "Homophobia" or homosexual bias reconsidered. *Archives of Sexual Behavior*, *12*, 549–554.

Groth, A. N., & Burgess, A. W. (1980). Male rape: Offenders and victims. *American Journal of Psychiatry*, *137*(7), 806–810.

Harry, J. (1982). Derivative deviance: The cases of extortion, fag-bashing, and shakedown of gay men. *Criminology*, *19*, 251–261.

Herek, G. M. (1984). "Beyond homophobia:" A social psychological perspective on attitudes toward lesbians and gay men. *Journal of Homosexuality*, *10*(1/2), 1–21.

Herek, G. M. (1986a). The social psychology of homophobia: Toward a practical theory. *NYU Review of Law & Social Change*, *14*(4), 923–934.

Herek, G. M. (1986b). The instrumentality of attitudes: Toward a neofunctional theory. *Journal of Social Issues*, *42*(2), 99–114.

Herek, G. M. (1987). Can functions be measured? A new perspective on the functional approach to attitudes. *Social Psychology Quarterly*, *50*, 285–303.

Herek, G. M. (1991). Stigma, prejudice, and violence against lesbians and gay men. In J. Gonsiorek & J. Weinrich (Eds.), *Homosexuality: Research implications for public policy* (pp. 60–80). Newbury Park, CA: Sage.

Horwitz, A. V., & White, H. R. (1987). Gender role orientations and styles of pathology among adolescents. *Journal of Health and Social Behavior*, *28*, 158–170.

McClintock, C. (1958). Personality syndromes and attitude change. *Journal of Personality*, *26*, 479–492.

Niederhoffer, A. (1967). *Behind the shield: The police in urban society*. Garden City, NY: Doubleday.

Nungesser, L. G. (1983). *Homosexual acts, actors, and identities*. New York: Praeger.

Rayside, D., & Bowler, S. (1988). Public opinion and gay rights. *Canadian Review of Sociology and Anthropology*, *25*, 649–660.

Schneider, W., & Lewis, I. A. (1984, February). The straight story on homosexuality and gay rights. *Public Opinion*, pp. 16–20, 59–60.

Segrest, M., & Zeskind, L. (1989). *Quarantines and death: The Far Right's homophobic agenda.* (Available from the Center for Democratic Renewal, P.O. Box 50469, Atlanta, GA 30302)

Shields, S. A., & Harriman, R. E. (1984). Fear of male homosexuality: Cardiac responses of low and high homonegative males. *Journal of Homosexuality, 10*(1/2), 53–67.

Shilts, R. (1982). *The mayor of Castro Street: The life and times of Harvey Milk.* New York: St. Martin's.

Smith, K. T. (1971). Homophobia: A tentative personality profile. *Psychological Reports, 29,* 1091–1094.

Smith, M. B., Bruner, J. S., & White, R. W. (1956). *Opinions and personality.* New York: John Wiley.

Weinberg, G. (1972). *Society and the healthy homosexual.* New York: St. Martin's.

FRATERNITIES AND THE RAPE CULTURE

CHRIS O'SULLIVAN

When I took a teaching position at Bucknell University in 1989, there was a move afoot among the faculty to get rid of the fraternities on campus. I joined and found myself somewhat in the forefront of the movement to sever our ties with them. The faculty voted to abolish the fraternities, but the fraternity alumni threatened to withdraw financial support, and, even more upsetting to Bucknell, the fraternity alumni corporations threatened to board up their houses on campus and leave them to deteriorate. In the end, the university decided to keep the fraternities and get rid of me. I was certainly more expendable: fraternities have great wealth and influence. At many universities, most trustees are fraternity men, and the wealthiest alumni are loyal to their fraternities.

By the fall of 1991, fraternity rush had been pushed back to sophomore year, and I was collecting unemployment. None of the fraternity houses was closed. In fact, the university spent a half million dollars to renovate a fraternity house that had been trashed by its members when it was shut down because of a possible gang rape a few years before.

My opposition to fraternities derives from my professional experience as a social psychologist, from my research and the research of others, from studying the social psychology of groups, and, as a faculty member at several universities, from observing the impact of membership on my students. It does not come from any negative personal experience with fraternities, although fraternity loyalists insist it must.

A number of social psychological processes occur in groups that promote mistreatment of outsiders and poor decision-making processes. Combined with male socialization in our society and the connotations of masculinity in our culture, fraternal cultures at schools and colleges breed a propensity to abuse women sexually, along a continuum of behaviors. I came to this conclusion by studying gang rape on campus, which led me to study fraternities and athletic teams. The analysis applies to both, since both are "fraternal cultures."

Social cognitive processes in groups are modes of thinking to which we are susceptible because they arise from the way the human mind works. I'll note three such processes that are underpinnings of misogyny and abuse.

- The "outgroup homogeneity effect," the belief that all members of the outgroup (defined as not one's own group) are alike. Independents think that all Greeks are alike. Members of one sorority feel that their membership is diverse, but that members of another sorority all fit one stereotype.
- The natural sense of "ingroup superiority." In one experiment, participants were given false feedback that they were either "dot overesti-

mators" or "dot underestimators." The underestimators attributed negative characteristics to overestimators and positive characteristics to themselves, and vice versa. Of course, the categories were meaningless and the trait inferences groundless, nor were the assignments of individuals to groups based on their actual performance.

- "Groupthink," a faulty decision-making process of groups, particularly elite groups. The concept was coined by Irving Janis at Yale, and the primary example was the decision to execute the Bay of Pigs invasion of Cuba. Janis delineated the reasons that groups head down the path to a really stupid decision, including an inflated belief in the group's righteousness, accompanied by an exaggerated belief in the ineptitude and unworthiness of the opposition. Dissent within the group is squelched by the isolation of critics and self-censorship of doubt.

These cognitive processes give group members a sense of invulnerability and entitlement, as well as a disdain for nonmembers that makes it easier to victimize them.

In addition, people are often more aggressive in groups than they would be individually. Strong identification with a group replaces individual ethics with group ethics. This process can lead people to behave more honorably as a group member than as an individual, but more commonly the result is the opposite. Group identification, along with alcohol, excitement, noise, anonymity, "de-individuation" (loss of a sense of self), and even darkness, has often been found to promote heedless aggression.

Socialization and social roles also contribute to group sexual aggression by men. Male friendships involve elements of competition and camaraderie. Sex as a competitive arena necessarily results in exploiting girls and women, because the motive is to "score," to impress one's male friends rather than to relate to the female. Drinking is another common arena for competition, as is risk-taking. Throughout childhood, boys' friendship groups provide support in violating adult and societal notions of propriety.

A boy's prestige with his group may be based on the degree to which he takes risks in breaking rules (although for most groups there is a boundary beyond which risky troublemaking earns disapproval of the group). Self-esteem for boys and young men typically comes from their reputation for success in these areas, as judged by their male peers. In our society, the perception of males by females counts for little, except insofar as female attention enhances their reputation among other males.

The definition of masculinity in our culture includes independence (from relationships), lack of sentimentality, sexual success (which usually means access to numbers of different women, but can also mean getting women to do things they don't want to), physical toughness, and worldly success, measured in dollars or achievements. Each of these elements of constructed masculinity has implications for a male's relationships with women. The requirement that a man be physically tough means tuning out his own pain, which also weakens his capacity for empathy. Attachment to a woman can threaten the image of independence and produce accusations that a man is "dominated" or "pussy-whipped" by his mother, girlfriend, or wife. A man's need to "score" and to push women into sexual acts that earn masculinity credits objectifies women. "Scoring" is enhanced by getting women to perform sex acts that the men consider demeaning. Thus, fellatio earns more points than intercourse, and anal intercourse more than vaginal intercourse. Of course, a woman who would do such things is not worthy of respect and must not be treated as a serious person or real girlfriend.

When I began to study group sexual assault on campus, I found that the majority of gang rapes were perpetrated by fraternity men. Athletes were also overrepresented, but interestingly only those who played team sports such as basketball, football, lacrosse, or rugby. I have isolated a number of reasons for this concentration of gang rapists among fraternity men and team athletes.

In part, this correlation has to do with *opportunity*. The perpetrators typically share housing in an all-male residence reserved for the group. They have privacy from men not in the group, from women, and from authority figures. They have bedrooms and social areas that are their exclusive territory or turf. This group residency is one reason that these men are more likely than other college men to engage in sex collectively with only one woman, but it doesn't touch on the question of why they would *want* to.

Second, these are men who have chosen to spend their college years living in a single-sex residence, or at least taking their meals and socializing in an all-male group. Men who don't like to live around women, who have difficulty accepting women as equals and relating to them, may be more likely than other men to choose to join a fraternity; thus, men Mary Koss calls "hidden rapists" may self-select for fraternity life. This explanation is less applicable to athletes. Other research has shown, however, that both athletes and fraternity men are also more likely to commit acquaintance rape *individually* than other college men. That is, the values and ways of relating to women that they learn in these all-male groups foster sexual aggression. Furthermore, women, for a variety of reasons, place greater trust in men who are members of high-prestige groups.

In addition to the common experiences of growing up male in our culture and being a member of a male friendship group, there are several practices often indulged in by these groups that may explain why fraternity men and athletes who play team sports may be more likely to be sexually aggressive, and especially to engage in group sexual assaults.

During fraternity "pledging," there are many rites that serve both to objectify women and, perhaps more importantly, to alienate men from their own sexuality. Many high-school and college athletic teams have initiation rituals that are similar. The quasi-sexual, or homosexual, nature of these rituals is striking. Nudity is often involved, along with heavy drinking, to allow men to suffer the humiliations they must endure. One common example from fraternities and teams around the U.S. and Canada is a race in which pledges have to run across a room holding a grape, ice cube, or marshmallow between the cheeks of their buttocks and then drop it into a box. The last guy has to eat the first guy's grape. Wood paddles are an accoutrement of fraternity life. In one fraternity, the initiates kneel in a row for the final initiation ceremony; the president walks down the row, putting his penis in each man's mouth. There are many other examples of this kind of ritual.

In addition to the physical exposure and contact involved in the all-male contests of humiliation, some rituals involve humiliation of pledges in front of women. One example is the "elephant walk," in which men form a public procession with their pants pockets pulled inside out to form an elephant's ears and their penises hanging out for the trunk; another rite is performing naked jumping jacks in front of a sorority house.

Still other practices involve sexual humiliation of women: in one such pledging ritual, the men surrounded sorority women at the dinner table in their sorority; one man read a lecture on Freud while another masturbated a dildo. Additionally, there is the sexual exploitation category of behavior, such as having sex with a teenager as a pledging requirement.

Many common practices of fraternity men after pledging can promote sexual aggression. These include videotaping, photographing, or merely observing through peepholes or windows a brother having sex with a woman. Most fraternity houses have collections of pornographic magazines and videos. Sexual contests are common among fraternity men. At the most benign, the contest may simply be "notch" contests over who has sex with the greatest number of women. A step up in victimizing and objectifying women, as well as alienating men from their own sexuality, are pig contests, also called "hog contests," in which a man wins by having sex with the woman the group considers most unattractive. There is a lively verbal component to the sexual competitions, including "date reports" given in locker rooms or at fraternity meals, in which the men compete in telling the most disgusting and/or funny sexual encounter (often considered the same), encouraging the men to mock their romantic relations. Fraternity logs and newsletters, laced with scatological and obscene humor, repeat these stories and add mocking tales of brothers' sexual failures and successes.

All of these practices make sexuality dirty, exploitative, and public, rather than intimate, cooperative, and private. Men who resist this "take" on sexual relations between men and women may be ostracized by the group, or they may be left alone and excluded from full acceptance. I heard a story of a man who found a woman friend drunk, unconscious, and naked in the hall of his fraternity. He took her into his room for the night and escorted her home in the morning. His modestly gallant behavior caused a major rift in the fraternity. Some of his brothers were furious because he didn't "share" her with them.

It is a contradictory goal to establish organizations that discriminate on the basis of sex and then expect the members to consider those who are excluded as equal, full human beings. A basic, although counterintuitive, tenet of social psychology, well documented through extensive research, is that not only do attitudes guide our behavior, but also, quite powerfully, our behavior influences our attitudes. Specifically, discrimination produces prejudice.

While I know that people cling to membership associations that allow them to be "one of the guys," I hope that the social evolution of our society will make belonging to a fraternity a source of shame rather than of pride. Fraternities encourage behavior in young men that falls along a continuum of sexual violence. I believe that abolishing college fraternities will be an important step in healing a rape culture.

THE TRUTH ABOUT MALE FRIENDSHIPS

MARTIN SIMMONS

If a dude buys me a drink, drops the winning two points through the hoop or comes stepping out with a fine woman, I might say, "My man! Slap me five!" Twenty or 30 minutes later, I might lay another "my man" on someone else. It's not that the term "my man" used in these contexts doesn't mean anything. It's just that it doesn't mean anything much. It's transitory, and has more to do with the style and stance that Black men adopt with each other during brief encounters than with the real substance of their relationships.

But when I say "My *main* man," I'm talking about my stone ace boon coon. My running cut buddy. My partner. Number One. Him and me against the world. And that's different. It is not temporary or transitory. It's been long-term, and frankly, I hope it will be forever. Or at least until one of us is dropped into a hole in the ground.

For Black men in this society, the world is a hostile, dangerous place—a jungle. It is uncompromising territory where a man is either the hunter or the hunted; he either seizes the power or loses it; he either rises to the never-ending tests of his manhood or falls a victim. Since Black men's relationship to power and sense of manhood has always been challenged in this land, we must always be on the move, always wary, always careful, always thinking and always on guard. We must walk that fine line between paranoia and prudence. It helps if we have a main man to walk it with. In fact, I think it's critical.

Without that main partner who helps you keep sight of the line, you can easily fall prey to the hunter. Without that main man to walk with, relate to, bounce thoughts off, you can easily lose sight of the real meaning of power and manhood. To walk alone means that it is always necessary to present a "front," an image, a projection of bravado that ensures protection.

Every Black man knows such bravado is sometimes a must. In public he knows he is supposed to be a bad dude. He is expected to brag and strut and lie. To do otherwise is to be considered less than a man. But in his private moments, those honest times when he faces only himself, he is—regardless of his true strength—likely to be haunted by insecurities, fears, doubts and an overwhelming sense of powerlessness. He can lie to the world, but never to the image in the mirror.

Of course, most men travel through life in some sort of partnership with women. It is relatively easy for a man to find a woman to whom he can relate. It seems to me, though, that if he is a thinking man, he knows the areas of his psyche that he can and cannot allow a woman access to. He can rarely let her know that he can or wants to be violent, that he is sometimes so angry with a world that would cheat him of his manhood that he often wants to kill or explode,

Reprinted from *Essence*, November 1981: 134, 137, 139–140.

because he knows that her response would be maternal and protective. She would want him to suppress those feelings lest they bring him harm. Furthermore, if they've been to bed a couple of times, he knows that he has a claim on her feelings, and he knows the things that she could be sympathetic to. He can therefore let her see that he is gentle, tender or sometimes even afraid.

But just let him go bopping down to the corner talking about how gentle or tender he is. Or let him try to tell the guys over a beer that he doesn't control his woman, that he doesn't sock it to her because he can't or doesn't want to. He'd be laughed out of the bar, and branded a punk, a chump, a fool—maybe even a faggot. In front of the boys, he'd better have made it with every woman he has ever said he wanted. He'd better be rough, tough, don't take no stuff. Out in the jungle, he'd better be a lion.

It's hard. It ain't funny. The image of the rootin'-tootin', six-shooting' Black man willing to fight and die because someone stepped in front of him in the supermarket line, thereby challenging his manhood, takes a lot of energy to keep up. At some point he *must* relax—totally, completely and absolutely.

So a man is lucky to find another man in whose presence he does not have to brag and strut and lie. Extremely lucky to find a cut buddy, an ace, a main man to fall back on. I've been that lucky. I have a main man.

Any man who has roamed the jungle alone—and I have—knows that the slightest hill can be as steep and slippery as Mt. Everest in January. But I also know that a good friend is another set of hands to help you make the climb. My ace not only has his own pick and climbing boots but has an extra set for me. He's got my back, and if necessary, I can get a lift on his shoulders. If I slip, I know he'll grab me. If I fall, he'll catch me. All he expects is that I do the same for him.

This is not to say that women don't often give such support to men. But I know the truth is that whatever the relationship a man has with a woman, rarely will he tell her everything, or be too weak in her presence, because he knows that

she, like everyone else, ultimately expects him to be a lion. Besides, other men expect a man to exercise control over a woman, and to reveal weakness to her means relinquishing a measure of control. Most important, however, a man knows that women do not have to move through the jungle in quite the same way he does. Though as Black people we are up against the same forces, those forces strike men and women in entirely different ways—with entirely different results.

Black men do not become cut buddies unless they have in common a basic and instinctive understanding of each other's psychological and emotional needs, as well as the forces they must confront, and share a willingness to meet those needs and forces. This instinctive understanding is built on shared experiences, which is why so many main-man partnerships go back to grade school or high school or the military. Although my partner and I spent our youths in widely separated places and environments, we are both struggling artists, we both know that it is the loneliest business in the world.

More important, my partner and I know the common forces that we as Black men are up against as we move to forge our definitions of what it means to be men. We know that no one—not friends, not family, not the wife who may want you to get a nine to five and a steady income—no one, except your main man, believes in your worth as a writer until it is demonstrated by some commercial standard of success; your name on a book jacket, your byline appearing 40 times.

Try to build a dream or realize a vision and the world won't buy in until the elevator reaches the fifth floor. But your main man buys in at the basement. He believes in you because he knows you. He believes in you because to believe in you is to believe in himself and the power of every Black man to make his dream come true, his own way in the world.

Since meeting seven years ago, my main man and I have faced crises together, fought battles side by side and back to back, cruised the jungle as twin panthers each looking out for predators who would endanger us.

For a Black man in particular, to roam the jungle alone—without the backup of a main man—is to be without perspective or protection. It means being afraid, and feeling that you are the only one who knows fear. It means thinking that no one else thinks like you do, and wondering if you should trust your own thoughts. It means not knowing that other men are sometimes gentle, sometimes weak, sometimes crazy—just as you sometimes are. It means you have no positive way to measure manhood or maleness, so what gets played out in behavior are false and often negative definitions of maleness: brutality, cold-bloodedness, hardheartedness. In short, being a "bad dude," being the kind of man you think you're supposed to be, which, in a very real way, can mean being insane.

But with a main man, an ace, you have not only another set of hands but another set of eyes—eyes that see you and accept you as you are and reflect what he is, too. My main man came of age at about the same time I did. We see the same world, which means we can reinforce each other's position in it. We share the same attitude toward life in all important respects. We walk in the same direction and we walk side by side. We understand each other, advise each other and keep each other on track. Together we are more than when we are apart, because our strengths are complementary and our weaknesses compensatory.

I can confide in my ace, share secrets and real feelings and never fear that he'll think I'm a fool, or a clown or a coward—or anything less than a man. As I said before, I know I'm lucky because so much of what being a man is supposed to mean has to do with being a "strong, silent type" who keeps his emotions in check and his feelings locked away. Deep emotional friendships among men are not usually encouraged. I know, too, that truly trusting relationships between any two people are not common because trust, faith and honesty with another person have somehow become equated with weakness.

As for me, I know that having this running buddy has made me stronger. I respect the brother, I trust the brother. I love the brother. He is my other ear, eye and mind. His opinions matter as much to me as my own. They take on equal weight, they get equal consideration. In this jungle of a world, he halves my burdens and doubles my joys.

Unfortunately, there are women who feel threatened by the relationship my partner and I have. Though they may have girlfriends, they somehow don't grasp the need for men to run together or hand together. The fact is, men need the company of each other as much as women need the company of other women or men need the company of women. Men need to shoot the breeze, talk shit, chase women and run the jungle together. More to the point, Black men need to reaffirm their worth in this place that is constantly denying that worth—and such affirmation can only come from other Black men.

When I tell my partner that during a job interview, the white boy sitting behind the desk said that my resume would threaten most of the white males already in the company and that therefore he wouldn't hire me, I know that my main man understood the insidiousness of that in a way that my woman never could. What Black men ultimately understand with each other is that we "are all in this together." Women provide sympathy. Most men, I think, neither need or want sympathy from other men. What they need and get in good male relationships is *empathy*. Black men's thoughts and conversations are colored by the fact that society treats them always as political entities. Black men who come together, therefore, have a "you and me against the world" attitude. It seems to me that women are more insular and home-centered, and their concerns tend to be for those things they label "security" and "stability." Their attitude when they are with their men is "you and me I fixed you a hot meal. Don't worry about the world tonight."

A woman who truly loved me and had my interests at heart would understand that her view of the world and the world's view of her are un-like those of the man in her life. She would real-ize that in many ways there can be no empathetic understanding between us. She would, therefore, not try to come between me and my main man. She would understand the differences between my relationship with her and with my partner, and recognize that both are equally important and equally necessary. And, if she could be hon-est with herself, she would know that both are limited: neither she nor he can be my whole world.

My cut buddy, although he will give me a blunt and honest opinion of the woman I'm deal-ing with, would not attempt to come between her and me because he knows she fulfills needs he can't. He knows that what I seek, what he seeks and what most men seek from women is the ful-fillment of relatively mundane, though ab-solutely critical, needs: sex, physical warmth and touching, love, care for their health, home and children.

I think that men who cannot or have not es-tablished deep friendships with other men—men who have no main man or say that their best friends are their wives or their women—are men without strong psychological support, without another worldly male view, without a truly em-pathetic understanding of the social and politi-cal forces at work in the jungle, so they are often too paranoid, prudent or alone to challenge the world.

"Him and me against the world" may sound like a serious phrase for a serious world, but it's not always so heavy. There are times when I'm hanging with my ace and the world is light-weight. We can talk and laugh and joke and run a smooth, sweet double-game on any and every-body. Fortunately, we are as different physically as we are alike spiritually. This physical differ-ence means that women who are attracted or at-tractive to me are seldom attracted or attractive to him and vice versa. Therefore, we never have to fight over women.

Which is not to say that we don't compete. Like most men, we are both very competitive—and we both play to win. We just confine our competition to the game board or to those situa-tions in which competition will benefit both of us by sharpening and honing our skills, our per-spective and our ability to do battle with the world at large.

When we do compete, the winner gloats and crows and laughs in the loser's face. God knows, we're both poor winners. But we aren't poor losers because, win or lose against each other, I know in the final go-down that I can count on him. My main man. My running partner. My ace. Me and him against the world.

PART EIGHT

MALE SEXUALITIES

How do many men learn to desire women? What are men thinking about when they are sexual with women? Are gay men more sexually promiscuous than straight men? Are gay men more obsessed with demonstrating their masculinity than straight men, or are they likely to be more "effeminate?" Recent research indicates that there are no simple answers to these questions. What is increasingly clear though is that men's sexuality, whether homosexual, bisexual, or heterosexual, is experienced as an experience of their gender.

Since there is no anticipatory socialization for homosexuality and bisexuality, future straight and gay men receive the same socialization as boys. As a result, sexuality as a gender enactment is often a similar internal experience for all men. Early socialization teaches us—through masturbation, locker-room conversations, sex-ed classes and conversations with parents, and the tidbits that boys will pick up from various media—that sex is private, pleasurable, guilt provoking, exciting, and phallocentric, and that orgasm is the goal toward which sexual experience is oriented.

The articles in this section explore how male sexualities express issues of masculinity. Robert Staples explains how the norms of masculinity are expressed in somewhat different ways among black heterosexual males. Jeffrey Fracher and Michael Kimmel argue that men discuss their sexual experiences—both their "successes" and their "failures"—in terms of gender, not pleasure. A man experiencing, for instance, premature ejaculation would be more likely to complain that he wasn't "enough of a man" than that he was unable to feel enough pleasure.

Articles by Edward Donnerstein and David Linz, and by Harry Brod explore some of the controversial political implications of pornography as a source of both straight and gay men's sexual information. Next, M. Rochlin's questionnaire challenges us to question the normative elements of heterosexuality. In a similar vein, Gary Kinsman argues that we can begin to understand the present lives of gay men only by constructing a "history of heterosexuality." In the past, what we call "homosexual behavior" has always existed, but social definitions and meanings surrounding sexual expression have shifted dramatically—most recently in response to the gay liberation movement. Finally, articles by Tomas Almaguer and by Susan Cochran and Vickie Mays explore the meanings of homosexuality among Chicano and black men, respectively.

HARD ISSUES AND SOFT SPOTS:
COUNSELING MEN ABOUT SEXUALITY

JEFFREY FRACHER
MICHAEL S. KIMMEL[1]

Nothing shows more clearly the extent to which modern society has atomized itself than the isolation in sexual ignorance which exists among us. . . . Many cultures, the most primitive and the most complex, have entertained sexual fears of an irrational sort, but probably our culture is unique in strictly isolating the individual in the fears that society has devised.

—Lionel Trilling[2]

Sam[3] is a 28–year-old white, single factory worker. He lives alone in a two-family home which he owns, and attends night school at a community college. The third of six sons in a blue-collar, Eastern European Catholic family, Sam is a conscientious, hardworking, and responsible man with very traditional values. He describes himself as a sexual late-bloomer, having begun dating only after graduation from an all-male Catholic high school. Although strong and handsome, he has always lacked confidence with women, and describes himself as male peer oriented, actively involved in sports, and spending much of his leisure time with "the boys."

Prior to his first sexual intercourse, two years ago at age 26, Sam had fabricated stories to tell his friends so as not to appear inadequate. He felt a great deal of shame and embarrassment that his public presentation of his sexual exploits had no basis in reality. His limited sexual knowledge caused him great anxiety and difficulty, especially since the woman with whom he was involved had had previous sexual encounters. Upon completion of intercourse, she reported that "he came too fast" (i.e., less than one minute, or after several thrusts), a statement that, he reported, "hit me between the eyes." His second attempt at intercourse was no more successful, in spite of his use of a condom to reduce sensation, and he subsequently broke off this relationship because of the shame and embarrassment about his sexual incompetence, and the fear that word would leak out to his friends. He subsequently developed a secondary pattern of sexual avoidance, and when he first came to treatment, indicating that he was "not a real man because I can't satisfy a woman," he had not had sex for two years, and was reluctant to resume dating until his premature ejaculation was vastly improved.

Joe is a 34-year-old C.P.A. who has been married for three years. The youngest of five children and the only male in a middle-class Irish-American family, Joe feels his father had high expectations from him, and exhibited only neutrality or criticism. Joe was without a male role model who conveyed that it was OK to fail. In fact, he portrayed men as strong, competent, without feelings, and without problems or failings, and believes he can never live up to the image his father had for him. Consequently, Joe is terrified that failure to please a woman sexually may result in criticism that will challenge his masculinity; he will not be a "real man." Anticipating this criticism from his wife, his sexual interest is reduced.

When first seen in therapy, Joe evidenced a total lack of sexual interest in his wife, but a high degree of sexual interest involving sexual fantasies, pornography, and masturbation. He said "lust is an obsession with me," indicating a high sex drive when sex is anonymous and though he felt sexually inadequate with his wife, he felt sexually potent with women he devalues, such as prostitutes. He could not understand his almost total lack of sexual interest in his wife.

Bill is a 52–year-old engineer, who has been married for 25 years. From a white, middle-class Protestant background, he has one grown child, and initially came to treatment upon referral from a urologist. He had seen numerous physicians after experiencing erectile dysfunction three years ago, and has actively sought a physical explanation for it.

Bill's wife, Ann was quite vocal about her disappointment in his failure to perform sexually. Bill had always been the sexual initiator, and Ann had come to expect that he should be in charge. Both believed that the only "real sex" is intercourse with an erect penis. Ann frequently commented that she felt "emotionally empty" without intercourse, thereby adding to his sense of inadequacy. The loss of his capacity for erection, Bill told the therapist, meant that he had lost his masculinity, and he worried openly about displeasing Ann and her possibly leaving him.

His fear of lost masculinity spilled over into his job performance, and he became depressed and withdrew from social activities. Bill was unaware that as an older man, he required more direct penile stimulation for an erection, since he had never required it in the past, and was unable to ask for it from Ann. He felt that a "real man never has to ask his wife for anything sexually," and should be able to perform without her help. The pattern of erectile dysfunction was part of a broader pattern of inability to tolerate failure,

and he had begun to lose self-confidence since his masculinity was almost entirely predicated upon erectile functioning. "Nothing else matters," he confided, if his masculinity (evidenced by a functional erection) was not present. Everything was suddenly on the line—his self-worth, his marriage, and his career—if he proved unable to correct his problem.

Sam, Joe, and Bill manifest the three most common sexual complaints of men seeking therapy. But underlying premature ejaculation, inhibited sexual desire, and erectile dysfunction is a common thread, binding these and other sexual problems together. Each fears that his sexual problem damages his sense of masculinity, making him less of a "real man." In a sense, we might say that all three men "suffer" from masculinity.

This chapter will explore how gender becomes one of the key organizing principles of male sexuality, informing and structuring men's sexual experiences. It will discuss how both gender and sexuality are socially constructed, and how therapeutic strategies to help men deal with sexual problems can raise issues of gender identity. This is especially important, of course, since so many therapeutic interventions rely on a diagnostic model that is simultaneously overly individualistic (in that it locates the source of the problem entirely within the individual) and transhistorical (in that it assumes that all cultures exhibit similar patterns at all times). The chapter combines a comparative and historical understanding of how both gender and sexuality are socially constructed with a psychoanalytic understanding of the transformative possibilities contained within the therapeutic relationship. This combination will lead us to discuss both social and therapeutic interventions that might facilitate healthier sexual expression for men.

THE SOCIAL CONSTRUCTION OF SEXUALITY AND MASCULINITY

Sexuality is socially constructed, a learned set of both behaviors and cognitive interpretations of those behaviors. Sexuality is less the product of biological drives than of a socialization process, and this socialization process is specific to any culture at any particular time. This means that "social roles are not vehicles for the expression of sexual impulse but that sexuality becomes a vehicle for expressing the needs of social roles" (Gagnon and Simon, 1973:45). *That* we are sexual is determined by a biological imperative toward reproduction, but *how* we are sexual—where, when, how often, with whom, and why—has to do with cultural learning, with meanings transmitted in a cultural setting. Sexuality varies from culture to culture; it changes in any one culture over time; it changes over the course of each of our lives. Sexual beings are made and not born; we make ourselves into sexual beings within a cultural framework. Although it may appear counterintuitive, this perspective suggests that the elusive quality commonly called "desire" is actually a relatively unimportant part of sexual conduct. As Gagnon and Simon argue (1973: 103), "the availability of sexual partners, their ages, their incomes, their point in the economic process, their time commitments . . . shape their sexual careers far more than the minor influence of sexual desire." Sexuality is learned in roughly the same way as anything else is learned in our culture. As Gagnon writes (1977: 2):

> *In any given society, at any given moment, people become sexual in the same way as they become everything else. Without much reflection, they pick up directions from their social environment. They acquire and assemble meanings, skills and values from the people around them. Their critical choices are often made by going along and drifting. People learn when they are quite young a few of the things that they are expected to be, and continue slowly to accumulate a belief in who they are and ought to be through the rest of childhood, adolescence, and adulthood. Sexual conduct is learned in the same ways and through the same processes; it is acquired and assembled in human interaction, judged and performed in specific cultural and historical worlds.*

If sexuality is socially constructed, perhaps the most significant element of the construction, the

foundation on which we construct our sexuality, is gender. For men, the notion of masculinity, the cultural definition of manhood, serves as the primary building block of sexuality. It is through our understanding of masculinity that we construct a sexuality, and it is through our sexualities that we confirm the successful construction of our gender identity. Gender informs sexuality; sexuality confirms gender. Thus, men have a lot at stake when they confront a sexual problem: they risk their self-image as men.

Like sexuality, gender in general, and masculinity in particular is socially constructed; that is, what we understand to be masculine varies from culture to culture, over historical time within any one culture, and over the course of any one person's life within any culture. What we consider masculine or feminine in our culture is the result of neither some biological imperative nor some religious requirement, but a socially organized mode of behavior. What is masculine is not set in stone, but historically fluid. The pioneering research on gender by anthropologist Margaret Mead (1935) and others has specified how widely the cultural requirements of masculinity—what it takes to be a "real man" in any particular culture—vary. And these gender categories also shift in any one culture over time. Who would suggest, for example, that what was prescribed among upper class Frenchmen in the eighteenth century—rare silk stockings and red patent-leather high heels, prolific amounts of perfume and facial powder, powdered wigs and very long hair, and a rather precious preoccupation with love poems, dainty furniture, and roses—resembles our contemporary version of masculinity?

The assertion of the social construction of sexuality and gender leads naturally to two related questions. First, we need to specify precisely the dimensions of masculinity within contemporary American culture. How is masculinity organized as a normative set of behaviors and attitudes? Second, we need to specify precisely the ways in which this socially constructed gender identity informs male sexual development. How is masculinity expressed through sexuality?

Brannon's (Brannon and David, 1976: 12) summary of the normative structure of contemporary American masculinity is relevant here. Masculinity requires the avoidance and repudiation of all behaviors that are even remotely associated with femininity ("no sissy stuff"); this requires a ceaseless patrolling of one's boundaries and an incessant surveillance of one's performances to ensure that one is sufficiently male. Men must be "Big Wheels," since success and status are key determinants of masculinity, and be "Sturdy Oaks," exuding a manly air of self-confidence, toughness, and self-reliance, as well as reliability. Men must "Give 'em Hell," presenting an aura of aggression and daring, an attitude of constantly "going for it."

The normative organization of masculinity has been verified empirically (cf. Thompson and Pleck, 1986) and has obviously important implications for male sexuality. In a sense, sexuality is the location of the enactment of masculinity; sexuality allows the expression of masculinity. Male sexual socialization informs men that sexuality is the proving ground of adequate gender identity, and provides the script that men will adopt, with individual modification, as the foundation for sexual activity.

In a sense, when we examine the normative sexuality that is constructed . from the typical organization of masculinity, it is not so much sexual problems that are of interest, but the problematization of "normal" sexuality, understanding perhaps the pathological elements within normal sexual functioning. This allows us to bridge the chasm between men who experience sexual dysfunction and those who, ostensibly, do not, and explore how men array themselves along a continuum of sexual expressions. Because masculinity provides the basic framework of sexual organization, and because masculinity requires adherence to certain rules that may retard or constrain emotional expression, we might fruitfully explore how even "normal" male sexuality evidences specific pathological symp-

toms, so that men who present exaggerated versions of these symptoms in therapy may better perceive their problems in a larger, sociological context of gender relations in contemporary society.[4]

The social construction of male sexuality raises a crucial theoretical issue. In the past, both social science research and clinical practice were informed by a model of discrete dichotomies. Categories for analysis implied a dualistic world view in which a phenomenon was classified as either X or Y. Thus, one was either male or female, heterosexual or homosexual, normal or pathological. Since the pioneering studies of Alfred Kinsey and his associates (cf. Kinsey et al., 1948, 1953), however, this traditional model of mutually exclusive dichotomous variables has given way to a model of a continuum of behaviors along which individuals array themselves. The continuum model allows individuals to reposition themselves at different moments in the life course, and it allows the researcher or clinician a point of entry into a relationship with the behaviors being discussed. The people we study and the people we counsel are less some curious "other" and more a variation on a set of behaviors that we, ourselves, embody as well. The articulation of the continuum model also requires that the level of analysis of any behavior include a social analysis of the context for behavior and the social construction of definitions of normality. It thus permits a truly *social* psychology.

THE MALE SEXUAL SCRIPT

Male sexual socialization teaches young men that sex is secret, morally wrong, and pleasurable, the association of sexual pleasure with feelings of guilt and shame is articulated early in the young boy's development, and reinforced throughout the life course by family, school, religion, and media images of sexuality. Young males are instructed, in locker rooms and playgrounds, to detach their emotions from sexual expression. In early masturbatory experience, the logic of detachment accommodates the twin demands of sexual pleasuring and guilt and shame. Later, detachment serves the "healthy" heterosexual male by permitting delay of orgasm in order to please his sexual partner, and serves the "healthy" homosexual male by permitting numerous sexual partners without cluttering up the scene with unpleasant emotional connection. (We will return to an exploration of the similarities between heterosexual and homosexual male sexuality below.)

Detachment requires a self-objectification, a distancing from one's self, and the development of a "secret sexual self" that performs sexual acts according to culturally derived scripts (Gagnon and Simon, 1973: 64). That men use the language of work as metaphors for sexual conduct—"getting the job done," "performing well," "achieving orgasm"—illustrates more than a passing interest in turning everything into a job whose performance can be evaluated; it reinforces detachment so that the body becomes a sexual machine, a performer instead of an authentic actor. The penis is transformed from an organ of sexual pleasure into a "tool," an instrument by which the performance is carried out, a thing, separate from the self. Many men report that they have conversations with their penises, and often cajole, plead with, or demand that they become and remain erect without orgasmic release. The penis can become the man's enemy, ready to engage in the most shameful conspiracy possible: performance failure. Is it any wonder that "performance anxiety" is a normative experience for male sexual behavior?

Men's earliest forays into sexuality, especially masturbation, are the first location of sexual anxiety. Masturbation teaches young men that sexuality is about the detachment of emotions from sex, that sex is important in itself. Second, men learn that sex is something covert, to be hidden; that is, men learn to privatize sexual experience, without skills to share the experience. And masturbation also teaches men that sexuality is phallocentric that the penis is the center of the sexual universe. Finally, the tools of masturbation, es-

pecially sexual fantasy, teach men to objectify the self, to separate the self from the body, to focus on parts of bodies and not whole beings, often to speak of oneself in the third person.

Adolescent sexual socialization reinforces these behavioral demands that govern male sexuality. Passivity is absolutely forbidden, and the young male must attempt to escalate the sexual element at all times. To do otherwise is to avoid "giving 'em hell" and expose potential feminine behaviors. This constant pressure for escalation derives from the phallocentric component to male sexuality—"it only counts if I put it in" a student told one of the authors. Since normative heterosexuality assigns to men the role of "doer" and to women the role of "gatekeeper," determining the level of sexual experience appropriate to any specific situation, this relentless pressure to escalate prevents either the male or the female from experiencing the sexual pleasure of any point along the continuum. No sooner does he "arrive" at a particular sexual experience—touching her breast, for example, than he begins strategizing the ways in which he can escalate, go further. To do less would expose him as less than manly. The female instantly must determine the limits of the encounter and devise the logistics that will prevent escalation if those limits have been reached. Since both male and female maintain a persistent orientation to the future (how to escalate and how to prevent escalation) neither can experience the pleasure of the points en route to full sexual intercourse. In fact, what men learn is that intercourse is the appropriate end-point of any sexual encounter, and that only intercourse "counts" in the tabulation of sexual encounters.

Since the focus is entirely phallocentric and intercourse is the goal to be achieved in adolescent sexual encounters, the stakes regarding sexual performance are extremely high, and consequently so is the anxiety about performance failure. Big wheels and sturdy oaks do not experience sexual dysfunction.

This continuum of male sexual dysfunction—ranging from what we might call the "normatively operative dysfunctional" to the cases of extreme distress of men who present themselves for therapeutic intervention—is reinforced in adult heterosexual relations as well. How do men maintain the sexual distancing and objectification that they perceive are required for healthy functioning? American comedian Woody Allen described, in his nightclub routines, a rather typical male strategy. After describing himself as "a stud," Allen comments:

While making love, in an effort [pause] to prolong [pause] the moment of ecstasy, I think of baseball players. All right, now you know. So the two of us are making love violently, and she's digging it, so I figure I better start thinking of baseball players pretty quickly. So I figure it's one out, and the Giants are up. Mays lines a single to right. He takes second on a wild pitch. Now she's digging her nails into my neck. I decide to pinch-hit for McCovey. [pause for laughter] Alou pops out. Haller singles, Mays takes third. Now I've got a first and third situation. Two outs and the Giants are behind by one run. I don't know whether to squeeze or to steal. [pause for laughter] She's been in the shower for ten minutes already. [pause] I can't tell you anymore, this is too personal. [pause] The Giants won.[5]

Readers may be struck by several themes—the imputation of violence, how her pleasure leads to his decision to think of baseball players, the requirement of victory in the baseball game, and the sexual innuendo contained within the baseball language—but the text provides a startlingly honest revelation of male sexual distancing. Here is a device that is so successful at delaying ejaculation that the narrator is rendered utterly unaware of his partner. "She's been in the shower for ten minutes already," Allen remarks, as if he's just noticed.

Much of peer sexual socialization consists of the conveying of these strategic actions that the male can perform to make himself a more adequate sexual partner. Men are often told to think of sports, work, or some other nonsexual event, or to repeat multiplication tables or mathematical formulas in order to keep themselves from premature ejaculation. It's as if sexual adequacy could be measured by time elapsed between penetration and orgasm, and the sexual experience itself is transformed into an endurance test in which pleasure, if present at all, is almost accidental.

The contemporary male sexual script—the normative construction of sexuality—provides a continuum along which men array themselves for the script's enactment. The script contains dicta for sexual distancing, objectification, phallocentrism, and a pressure to become and remain erect without ejaculation for as long as possible, all of which serve as indicators of masculinity as well as sexual potency. Adequate sexual functioning is seen as the proof of masculinity, so sexual problems will inevitably damage male gender identity. This is what makes treatment of sexual disorders a treatment of gender identity issues.

Although this chapter has concentrated on sexual disorders for heterosexual men, this is neither for analytic reasons nor from a sense of how these problems might manifest differently for gay men. Quite the contrary, in fact. Since gender identity is the key variable in understanding sexual behaviors, we would argue that heterosexual and homosexual men have more in common in regard to their sexuality than they evidence differences. This is especially true since 1969, when the Stonewall riots in New York, and the subsequent emergence of the Gay Liberation Movement, led to the possibility for gay men to recover and repair their "damaged" sense of masculinity. Earlier gay men had been seen as "failed men," but the emergence of the gay male "clone" particularly has dispelled that notion. In the nation's gay ghettos, gay men often enact a hypermasculine ethic, complete with its attendant sexual scripting of distancing, phallocentrism, objectification, and separation of emotion from physical sensation. Another reason that heterosexual and homosexual men exhibit similar gender-based sexual behaviors is that all boys are subject to an anticipatory socialization toward heterosexuality, regardless of their eventual sexual preference. There is no anticipatory socialization toward homosexuality in this culture, so male gender socialization will be enacted with both male and female sexual partners. Finally, we have not focused on gay men as a specific group because to do so would require the marginalization of gay men as a group separate from the normative script of male sexuality. Both gay and straight men are men first, and both have "male sex."

THERAPEUTIC INTERVENTIONS

Our analysis of the social context of men's sexual problems makes it essential that therapeutic strategies remain aware of a context larger than simple symptom remission. Treatment must also challenge the myths, assumptions, and expectations that create the dysfunctional context for male sexual behavior (cf. Kaplan, 1974, 1983; LoPiccolo and LoPiccolo 1978; Tollison and Adams, 1979).

Men seeking treatment for sexual difficulties will most often present with a symptom such as erectile failure, premature ejaculation, or inhibited desire. However, the *response* to this symptom, such as anxiety, depression, or low self-esteem, is usually what brings the man into treatment, and this response derives from the man's relationship to an ideal vision of masculinity. The construction of this masculine ideal, therefore, needs to be addressed, since it often creates the imperative command—to be in a constant state of potential sexual arousal, to achieve and maintain perfectly potent erections on command, and to delay ejaculation for a long time—which results in the performance anxiety that creates the symptom in the first place.

Sex therapy exercises, such as those developed by Willam Masters and Virginia Johnson and others, are usually effective only when the social context of gender ideals has also been addressed. This is accomplished by exploring and challenging the myths of male sexuality, modeling by the therapist of a different version of masculinity, giving permission to the patient to fail,

and self-disclosure by the therapist of the doubts, fears of inadequacy, and other anxieties that all men experience. These will significantly reduce the isolation that the patient may experience, the fear that he is the only man who experiences such sexually linked problems. These methods may be used to reorient men's assumptions about what constitutes masculinity, even though the therapist will be unable to change the entire social edifice that has been constructed on these gender assumptions. Both the cognitive as well as the physical script must be addressed in treating sexual dysfunction; the cognitive script is perhaps the more important.

Recall these specific examples we drew from case materials. Sam's sexual performance was charged with anxiety and shame regarding both female partners and male peers. He was adamant that no one know he was seeking therapy, and went to great lengths to assure that confidentiality be preserved. He revealed significant embarrassment and shame with the therapist in early sessions, which subsided once the condition was normalized by the therapist.

Sam had grown up with exaggerated expectations of male sexual performance—that men must perform sexually on cue and never experience any sexual difficulty—that were consistent with the social milieu in which he was raised. He held women on a pedestal, and he believed that a man must please a woman or risk losing her. The stakes were thus quite high. Sam was also terrified of appearing "unmanly" with women, which resulted in a high degree of performance anxiety, which, in turn, prompted the premature ejaculation. The cycle of anxiety and failure finally brought Sam to treatment. Finally, Sam was detached from his own sexuality, his own body both sexually and emotionally. His objectification of his penis made it impossible for him to monitor impending ejaculation, and he was therefore unable to moderate the intensity of sensation prior to the point of ejaculatory inevitability. This common pattern among men who experience premature ejaculation suggests that such a response comes not from hypersensitivity but rather an atrophied sensitivity, based on objectification of the phallus.

Sam's treatment consisted of permission to experience this problem from another man, and the attempt by the therapist to normalize the situation and reframe it as a problem any man might encounter. The problem was redefined as a sign of virility rather than an indication of its absence; Sam came to understand his sexual drive as quite high, which led to high levels of excitement that he had not yet learned to control. The therapist presented suggestions to control ejaculation that helped him moderate the intensity of arousal in order to better control his ejaculation. The important work, however, challenged the myths and cognitive script that Sam maintained regarding his sexuality. The attention given to his sexual performance, what he demanded of himself and what he believed women demanded of him, helped him reorient his sexuality into a less performance-oriented style.

Joe, the 34-year-old C.P.A. experienced low sexual desire with his wife though he masturbated regularly. Masturbatory fantasies involving images of women wanting him, finding him highly desirable, populated his fantasy world. When his self-esteem was low, as when he lost his job, for example, his sexual fantasies increased markedly. These fantasies of prowess with devalued women restored, he felt, his worth as a man. Interest in pornography included a script in which women were passive and men in control, very unlike the situation he perceives with his wife. He complained that he is caught in a vicious cycle, since without sexual interest in his wife he's not a "real man," and if he's not a "real man" then he has no sexual desire for her. He suggested that if he could only master a masculine challenge that was not sexual, such as finding another job or another competitive situation, he believed his sexual interest in his wife would increase. He felt he needed the mastery of a masculine challenge to confirm his sense of self as a man, which would then find further conformation in the sexual arena. This adds an empirical confirmation of Gagnon and Simon's argument (1973) that genital sexuality contains many nonsexual motives, including the desire for achievement, power, and peer approval. Joe came to therapy with a great deal of shame at having to be there, and was especially ashamed at having to tell another man about his failures as a man. He was greatly relieved by the therapist's understanding, self-disclosure, and nonjudgmental stance, which enhanced the therapist's credibility and Joe's commitment to treatment.

One cognitive script that Joe challenged in counseling was his embrace of the "madonna/whore" ideology. In this formulation, any woman worth having (the madonna—mother or wife) was perceived as both asexual and as sexually rejecting of him, since his failures rendered him less of a real man. A "whore," on the other hand, would be both sexually available and interested in him, so she is consequently devalued and avoided. He could be sexual with her because the stakes are so low. This reinforces the cultural equation between sexual pleasure and cultural guilt and shame, since Joe would want to be sexual only with those who would not want to be sexual with him. This common motif in male sexual socialization frequently emerges in descriptions of "good girls" and "bad girls" in high school.

Joe's therapy included individual short-term counseling with the goal of helping him see the relationship between his self-esteem and his inhibited sexual desire. Traditional masculine definitions of success were the sole basis for Joe's self-esteem, and these were challenged in the context of a supportive therapeutic environment. The failure of childhood male role models was contrasted with new role models that provide permission to fail and helped Joe view sexuality as noncompetitive and nonachievement-oriented activity. Joe began to experience a return of sexual desire for his wife, as he became less phallocentric and more able to see sex as a vehicle for expressing intimacy and caring rather than a performance for an objectified self and other.

Bill, the 52-year-old married engineer presented with erectile failure, which is part of a larger pattern of intolerance of failure in himself. The failure of his penis to function properly symbolized to him the ultimate collapse of his manhood. Not surprisingly, he had searched for physiological etiologies before seeking psychological counseling, having been referred by a urologist. It is estimated that less than 50% of all men who present themselves for penile implant surgery have a physiological basis for their problem; if so, the percentage of all men who experience erectile disorders whose etiology is physiological is less than 5%. Yet the pressure to salvage a sense of masculinity that might be damaged by a psychological problem leads thousands of men to request surgical prosthesis every year (cf. for example, Tiefer, 1986).

Bill and his wife, Ann, confronted in therapy the myths of male sexuality that they embraced, including such dicta as "a real man always wants sex," "the only real sex is intercourse," and "the man must always be in charge of sex." (cf. Zilbergeld, 1978). The therapist gave Bill permission to fail by telling him that all men at some time experience erectile dysfunction. Further, Bill was counseled that the real problem is not the erectile failure, but his reaction to this event. Exercises were assigned in which Bill obtained an erection through manual stimulation and then purposely lost the erection to desensitize himself to his terrible fear of failure. This helped him overcome the "what if" fear of losing the erection. Bill was counseled to "slow down" his sexual activity, and to focus on the sensations rather than the physical response, both of which were designed to further remove the performance aspects from his sexual activity. Finally, the therapist helped Bill and Ann redefine the notion of masculinity by stating that "a real man is strong enough to take risks, eschew stereotypes, to ask for what he needs sexually from a partner, and, most of all, to tolerate failure."

As Bill and Ann's cognitive script changed, his ability to function sexually improved. Though Bill still does not get full erections on a consistent basis, this fact is no loner catastrophic for him. He and Ann now have a broader script

both physically and cognitively, which allows them to have other sexual play and the shared intimacy that it provides.

As one can see from these case studies, several themes run consistently through therapeutic strategies in counseling men about sexual problems, and many of these themes also relate directly to issues of social analysis as well as clinical practice. For example, the therapeutic environment must be experienced as supportive, and care must be taken so that the therapist not appear too threatening or too "successful" to the patient. The gender of the therapist with the male patient will raise different issues at this point. A male therapist can empathize with the patient, and greatly reduce his sense of isolation, whereas a female therapist can provide positive experience with a woman that may translate to nontherapeutic situations.

Second, the presenting symptom should be "normalized," that is it should be cast within the wider frame of male socialization to sexuality. It is not so much that the patient is "bad, "'wrong," or "abnormal," but that he has experienced some of the contradictory demands of masculinity in ways that have become dysfunctional for his sexual experiences. It is often crucial to help the patient realize that he is not the only man who experiences these problems, and that these problems are only problems seen from within a certain construct of masculinity.

In this way, the therapist can help the patient to dissociate sexuality from his sense of masculinity, to break the facile identification between sexual performance and masculinity. Masculinity can be confirmed by more than erectile capacity, constant sexual interest, and a long duration of intercourse; in fact, as we have argued, normal male sexuality often requires the dissociation of emotional intimacy and connectedness for adequate sexual functioning. Raising the level of analysis from the treatment of individual symptoms to a social construction of gender and sexuality does not mean abandoning the treatment of the presenting symptoms, but rather retaining their embeddedness in the social context from which they emerge. Counseling men about sexuality involves, along with individualized treatment, the redefinition of what it means to be a man in contemporary American society. Therapeutic treatments pitched at both the social and the individual levels can help men become more expressive lovers and friends and fathers, as well as more "functional" sexual partners. That a man's most important sexual organ is his mind is as true today as ever.

NOTES

l. This paper represents a full collaboration, and our names appear in alphabetical order for convenience. Critical reactions from John Gagnon, Murray Scher, and Mark Stevens have been very helpful.
2. Lionel Trilling, *The Liberal Imagination*. New York: Alfred Knopf, 1954.
3. The names of the individual patients have been changed.
4. To assert a pathological element to what is culturally defined as "normal" is a contentious argument. But such an argument derives logically from assertions about the social construction of gender and sexuality. Perhaps an analogy would prove helpful. One might also argue that given the cultural definition of femininity in our culture, especially the normative prescriptions for how women are supposed to look to be most attractive, *all* women manifest a problematic relationship to food. Even the most "normal" woman, having been socialized in a culture stressing unnatural thinness, will experience some pathological symptoms around eating. This assertion will surely shed a very different light on the treatment of women presenting eating disorders, such as bulimia or anorexia nervosa. Instead of treating them in their *difference* from other women, by contextualizing their symptoms within the larger frame of the construction of femininity in American culture, they can be seen as *exaggerating* an already culturally prescribed problematic relationship to eating. This position has the additional benefit, as it would in the treatment of male sexual disorders, of resisting the temptation to "blame the victim" for her/his acting out an exaggerated version of a traditional script.
5. Woody Allen, *The Nightclub Years*, United Artists Records, 1971. Permission requested.

REFERENCES

Brannon, Robert and Deborah David (1976). *The Forty-Nine Percent Majority*. Reading, MA: Addison-Wesley.

Gagnon, John (1977). *Human Sexualities*. Chicago: Scott, Foresman.

Gagnon, John and William Simon (1973). *Sexual Conduct*. Chicago: Aldine.

Kaplan, Helen Singer (1974). *The New Sex Therapy*. New York: Brunner-Mazel.

Kaplan, Helen Singer (1983). *The Evaluation of Sexual Disorders*. New York: Brunner-Mazel.

Kimmel, Michael, ed. (1987). *Changing Men: New Directions in Research on Men and Masculinity*. Beverly Hills, CA: Sage Publications.

Kinsey, Alfred C., Wardell Pomeroy, and C. Martin (1948). *Sexual Behavior in the Human Male*. Chicago: Saunders.

Kinsey, Alfred C. and Paul Gebhard (1953). *Sexual Behavior in the Human Female*. Chicago: Saunders.

LoPiccolo, J. and L. LoPiccolo (1978). *Handbook of Sex Therapy*. New York: Plenum Press.

Mead, Margaret (1935). *Sex and Temperament in Three Primitive Societies*. New York: William Morrow.

Thompson, Edward and Joseph Pleck (1986). "The Structure of Male Role Norms." *American Behavioral Scientist* 29(5), May–June.

Tiefer, Leonore (1986). "In Pursuit of the Perfect Penis: the Medicalization of Male Sexuality." *American Behavioral Scientist* 29(5).

Tollison, C. D. and H. Adams (1979). *Sexual Disorders: Treatment, Theory, and Research*. New York: Gardner Press.

Wagner, Gorm and Richard Green (1984). *Impotence: Physiological, Psychological, Surgical Diagnosis and Treatment*. New York: Plenum.

Zilbergeld, Bernard (1978). *Male Sexuality*. New York: Simon and Schuster.

STEREOTYPES OF BLACK MALE SEXUALITY:
THE FACTS BEHIND THE MYTHS

ROBERT STAPLES

It is difficult to think of a more controversial role in American society than that of the black male. He is a visible figure on the American scene, yet the least understood and studied of all sex–race groups in the United States. His cultural image is typically one of several types: the sexual superstud, the athlete, and the rapacious criminal. That is how he is perceived in the public consciousness, interpreted in the media and ultimately how he comes to see and internalize his own role. Rarely are we exposed to his more prosaic role as worker, husband, father and American citizen.

The following essay focuses on the stereotypical roles of black male heterosexuality, not to reinforce them, but to penetrate the superficial images of black men as macho, hypersexual, violent and exploitative. Obviously, there must be some explanation for the dominance of black men in the nations' negative statistics on rape, out-of-wedlock births, and premarital sexual activity. This is an effort to explore the reality behind the image.

BLACK MANHOOD

As a starting point, I see the black male as being in conflict with the normative definition of masculinity. This is a status which few, if any, black males have been able to achieve. Masculinity, as defined in this culture, has always implied a cer-

tain autonomy and mastery of one's environment. It can be said that not many white American males have attained this ideal either. Yet, white males did achieve a dominance in the nuclear family. Even that semblance of control was largely to be denied black men. During slavery he could receive the respect and esteem of his wife, children and kinsmen, but he had no formal legal authority over his wife or filial rights from his children. There are numerous and documented instances of the slave-owning class's attempts to undermine his respect and esteem in the eyes of his family.[1]

Beginning with the fact that slave men and women were equally subjugated to the capricious authority of the slaveholder, the African male saw his masculinity challenged by the rape of his woman, sale of his children, the rations issued in the name of the woman and children bearing her name. While those practices may have presaged the beginning of a healthier sexual egalitarianism than was possible for whites, they also provoked contradictions and dilemmas for black men in American society. It led to the black male's self-devaluation as a man and set the stage for internecine conflict within the black community.

A person's sex role identity is crucial to their values, life-style and personality. The black man has always had to confront the contradiction between the normative expectations attached to being male in this society and the proscriptions on his behavior and achievement of goals. He is subjected to societal opprobrium for failing to live up to the standards of manhood on the one hand and for being super macho on the other. It is a classical case of "damned if you do and damned if you don't." In the past there was the assertion that black men were effeminate because they were raised in households with only a female parent or one with a weak father figure. Presently, they are being attacked in literature, in plays, and at conferences as having succumbed to the male chauvinist ideal.

Although the sexual stereotypes apply equally to black men and women, it is the black male who has suffered the worst because of white notions of his hypersexuality. Between 1884 and 1900 more than 2,500 black men were lynched, the majority of whom were accused of sexual interest in white women. Black men, it was said, had a larger penis, a greater sexual capacity and an insatiable sexual appetite. These stereotypes depicted black men as primitive sexual beasts, without the white male's love for home and family.[2] These stereotypes persist in the American consciousness.

It is in the area of black sexual behavior, and black male sexuality in particular, that folk beliefs are abundant but empirical facts few. Yet public policy, sex education and therapeutic programs to deal with the sex-related problems of black people cannot be developed to fit their peculiar needs until we know the nature and dynamics of black sexual behavior. Thus, it is incumbent upon researchers to throw some light on an area enmeshed in undocumented myths and stereotypes.

SEXUALITY OF THE MALE ADOLESCENT

The Kinsey data, cited by Bell,[3] reveal that black males acquire their knowledge about condoms at a later age than white males. The white male learns about sexual intercourse at a later age than black males. Because of poorer nutrition, the black male reaches puberty at a later age than his white male counterpart. A critical distinction between black and white males was the tendency of the more sexually repressed white male to substitute masturbation, fellatio and fantasy for direct sexual intercourse. Masturbation, for instance, was more likely to be the occasion of the first ejaculation for the white male while intercourse was for the black male. A larger percentage of white males reported being sexually aroused by being bitten during sexual activity, seeing a member of the opposite sex in a social situation, seeing themselves nude in the mirror or looking at another man's erect penis, hearing dirty jokes, reading sadomasochistic literature and viewing sexy pictures. Conversely, black males tended to engage in premarital intercourse at earlier ages, to have intercourse and to reach orgasm more frequently. As Bell notes in his analysis of these data, the black male's overabundance of sexuality is a myth. The sexuality of black and white men just tends to take different forms and neither group has any more self-control or moral heroism than the other.

Among young black American males, sexual activity begins at an earlier age, is more frequent and involves more partners. Apparently white males are more likely to confine their associations in the adolescent years with other men. Larson and his associates found that black male adolescents were twice as likely to be romantically involved with women than white males.[4] The kind of rigid gender segregation found in white culture is largely absent from black society. For example, blacks are less likely to be associated with all male clubs, organizations or colleges.

The sexual code of young black males is a permissive one. They do not, for example, divide black women into "good" (suitable for marriage) and "bad" (ineligible for marriage) categories. In the lower income groups, sexual activity is often a measure of masculinity. Thus, there is a greater orientation toward premarital sexual experimentation. In a study of premarital sexual standards among blacks and whites in the 1960s, Ira Reiss found that the sexual permissiveness of white males could be affected by a number of social forces (e.g., religion), but the black male was influenced by none of them.[5] Leanor Johnson and this author found that few black male adolescents were aware of the increased risk of teenage pregnancy, but there was an almost unanimous wish not to impregnate their sexual partner. Another survey of black male high school students reported their group believed that a male respects his partner when he uses a condom.[6]

POVERTY AND THE BLACK FATHER

The period of adolescence, with its social, psychological and physical changes (particularly sex-role identity and sexuality), is the most problematic of the life cycle stages. The prolongation of adolescence in complex technological society and the earlier onset of puberty have served to compound the problem. While adolescents receive various messages to abandon childlike behavior, they are systematically excluded from adult activity such as family planning. This exclusion is justified not only by their incomplete social and emotional maturity, but by their lack of marketable skills which are necessary to command meaningful status-granting jobs. Unskilled adolescents are further disadvantaged if they are members of a minority racial group in a racially stratified society.

Parenthood at this stage of the life cycle is most undesirable. Yet, recent upsurges in teenage pregnancy and parenthood have occurred, specifically among females younger than 14. Approximately 52% of all children born to black women in 1982 were conceived out-of-wedlock. Among black women under age 20, about 75% of all births were out-of-wedlock compared with only 25% of births to young white women.[7] Although the rate of white out-of-wedlock pregnancy is increasing and that of non-whites decreasing, black unwed parenthood remains higher than that of whites.

Because life and family support systems of black males are severely handicapped by the effects of poverty and discrimination, the conse-quences of becoming a father in adolescence are more serious for the minority parent. Many family planning agencies offer counseling to the unwed mother, while the father is usually involved only superficially or punitively—as when efforts are made to establish legal paternity as a means for assessing financial responsibility. This omission, however, is not unique to black males. It is, perhaps, the single fact of inadequate economic provision which has resulted in the social agencies' premature conclusion that unwed fathers are unwilling to contribute to the future of their child and the support of the mother. Furthermore, sociological theory purports that slavery broke the black man's sense of family responsibility. Thus, it is assumed that black women do not expect nor demand that black men support them in raising their children.

FAMILY PLANNING

Recent evidence, however, suggests that the matrifocality of present theory and social services is myopic. Studies have demonstrated that most unwed fathers are willing to face their feelings and responsibilities.[8] The findings suggest that unmarried black males do not consider family planning a domain of the female, but rather a joint responsibility to be shared by both parents.[9]

Throughout the world one of the most important variables affecting birth rates is the male attitude toward family planning and the genesis of this attitude. Too often we are accustomed to thinking of reproduction as primarily a female responsibility. Since women are the main bearers and main rearers of children in our society, we tend to believe that they should be primarily concerned with planning the size of a family and developing those techniques of contraception consistent with family's earning power, their own health and happiness and the psychological well-being of their children.

However, in a male-dominated world it is women who are given the burden of having and raising children, while it is often men who determine what the magnitude of that burden should be. Unfortunately, the male's wishes in regard to the size of his family are not contingent on the effect of childbearing on the female partner, but are often shaped by his own psychological and status concerns.

Within many societies there is an inseparable link between men's self-image and their ability to have sexual relations with women and the subsequent birth of children from those sexual acts. For example, in Spanish-speaking cultures this masculine norm is embedded in the concept of "machismo." "Machismo," derived from the Latin word "masculus," literally means the ability to produce sperm and thus sire—abilities which define the status of a man in society. In male-dominated society other issues involved in reproduction are subordinated to the male's desire to affirm his virility, which in turn confirms his fulfillment of the masculine role. The research literature tells us that the male virility cult is strongest in countries and among groups where the need for family planning is greatest.

Thus, we find that in underdeveloped countries—and among low-income ethnic groups in industrialized societies, including much of the black population in the U.S.—men are resistant to anything but natural controls on the number of children they have. Studies show that males who strongly believe that their masculine status is associated with their virility do not communicate very well with their wives on the subject of family planning. As a result the wives are less effective in limiting their families to the number of children they desire.

SEXUAL AGGRESSION

Sexual attacks against women are pervasive and sharply increasing in this country. The typical rapist is a black male and his victim is most often a black female. However, the most severe penalties for rape are reserved for black males accused of raping white women. Although 50% of those convicted for rape in the South were white males, over 90% of those executed for this crime in that region were black. Most of their alleged victims were white. No white male has ever been executed for raping a black woman.[10]

As is probably true of white females, the incidence of rape of black women is underreported. Lander reported that an eight-year-old girl has a good chance of being exposed to rape and violence if she is a member of the black underclass.[11] While widespread incidents of this kind are rooted in the sexist socialization of all men in society, it is pronounced among black men who have other symbols of traditional masculinity blocked to them. Various explanations have been put forth to explain why black men seem to adopt the attitudes of the majority group toward black women. Poussaint believes that because white men have historically raped black women with impunity, many black males believe they can do the same.[12]

Sexual violence is also rooted in the dynamics of the black dating game. The majority of black rape victims know their attacker—a friend, relative, or neighbor. Many of the rapes occur after a date and are what Amir describes as misfired attempts at seduction.[13] A typical pattern is for the black male to seek sexual compliance from his date, encounter resistance which he thinks is feigned, and proceed to forcibly obtain his sexual gratification from her. Large numbers of black men believe sexual relations to be their "right" after a certain amount of dating.

Rape, however, is not regarded as the act of a sexually starved male but rather as an aggressive act toward females. Students of the subject suggest that it is a long-delayed reaction against authority and powerlessness. In the case of black men, it is asserted that they grow up feeling emasculated and powerless before reaching manhood. They often encounter women as authority figures and teachers or as the head of their household. These men consequently act out their feelings of powerlessness against black women in the form of sexual aggression. Hence, rape by black men should be viewed as both an aggressive and political act because it occurs in the context of racial discrimination which denies most black men a satisfying manhood.

Manhood in American society is closely tied to the acquisition of wealth. Men of wealth are rarely required to rape women because they can gain sexual access through other means. A female employee who submits to the sexual demands of a male employer in order to advance in her job is as much an unwilling partner in this situation as is the rape victim. The rewards for her sexual compliance are normatively sanctioned, whereas the rapist does not often have the resources to induce such sexual compliance. Moreover, the concept of women as sexual property is at the root of rape. This concept is peculiar to capitalistic, western societies rather than African nations (where the incidence of rape is much lower). For black men, rape is often an act of aggression against women because the kinds of status men can acquire through success in a job is not available to them.

RECOMMENDATIONS

To address the salient issues in black male sexuality, I offer the following recommendations:

1. An educational program for black men must be designed to sensitize them to the need for their responsibility for, and participation in, family planning. This program will best be conducted by other men who can convey the fact that virility is not in and of itself the measure of masculinity. Also, it should be emphasized that the use of contraception—or obtaining a vasectomy—does not diminish a male's virility.

2. An over-all sex education program for both sexes should begin as early as kindergarten, before the male peer group can begin to reinforce attitudes of male dominance. Sex education courses should stress more than the physiological aspects in its course content. Males should be taught about the responsibility of men in sex relations and procreation. Forms of male contraception should be taught along with female measures of birth control.

3. The lack of alternative forms of role fulfillment available to many men, especially in industrialized societies, must be addressed. In cases of unemployment and underemployment, the male often resorts to the virility cult because it is the only outlet he has for a positive self-image and prestige within his peer group. Thus, we must provide those conditions whereby men can find meaningful employment.

4. Lines of communication must be opened between men and women. A supplement to the educational program for men should be seminars and workshops involving both men and women. Hopefully, this will lead to the kind of dialog between men and women that will sensitize each of them to the feelings of the other.

NOTES

1. Robert Staples, *The Black Family: Essays and Studies*. (Belmont, CA: Wadsworth, 1978.)

2. Robert Staples, *Black Masculinity*, (San Francisco: The Black Scholar Press, 1982.)

3. Alan P. Bell, "Black Sexuality: Fact and Fancy" in R. Staples. ed., *The Black Family: Essays and Studies*, pp. 77–80.

4. David Larson, et al., "Social Factors in the Frequency of Romantic Involvement Among Adolescents." *Adolescence* 11: 7–12, 1976.

5. Ira Reiss, *The Social Context of Premarital Sexual Permissiveness*. (New York: Holt, Rinehart and Winston, 1968.)

6. Leanor Johnson and Robert Staples, "Minority Youth and Family Planning: A Pilot Project." *The Family Coordinator* 28: 534–543, 1978.

7. U.S. Bureau of the Census, *Fertility of American Women*. (Washington, D.C. U.S. Government Printing Office, 1984.)

8. Lisa Connolly, "Boy Fathers." *Human Behavior* 45: 40–43, 1978.

9. B. D. Misra, "Correlates of Males' Attitudes Toward Family Planning" in D. Bogue, ed., *Sociological Contributions to Family Planning Research*. (Chicago: Univ. of Chicago Press, 1967), pp. 161–167.

10. William J. Bowers, *Executions in America*. (Lexington Books, 1974).

11. Joyce Lander, *Tomorrow's Tomorrow: The Black Woman*. (Garden City, New York: Doubleday, 1971.)

12. Alvin Poussaint, *Why Blacks Kill Blacks*. (New York: Emerson-Hall, 1972.)

13. Menachim Amir, "Sociocultural Factors in Forcible Rape" in L. Gross, ed., *Sexual Behavior*. (New York: Spectrum Publications, 1974), pp. 1–12.

MASS MEDIA SEXUAL VIOLENCE
AND MALE VIEWERS:
CURRENT THEORY AND RESEARCH

EDWARD DONNERSTEIN
DANIEL LINZ

The influence of pornography on male viewers has been a topic of concern for behavioral scientists for many years, as well as a recent volatile political and legal question. Often research on pornography and its effects on behavior or attitudes are concerned with sexual explicitness. But it is not an issue of sexual explicitness; rather, it is an issue of violence against women and the role of women in "pornography" that is of concern to us here. Research over the last decade has demonstrated that sexual images per se do not facilitate aggressive behavior, change rape-related attitudes, or influence other forms of antisocial behaviors or perceptions. It is the violent images in pornography that account for the various research effects. This will become clearer as the research on the effects of sexual violence in the media is discussed. It is for these and other reasons that the terms *aggressive pornography* and *sexually violent mass media images* are preferred. We will occasionally use the term *pornography* in this article for communication and convenience.

In this chapter we will examine both the research on aggressive pornography and the research that examines nonpornographic media images of violence against women—the major focus of recent research and the material that provokes negative reactions. Our final section will examine the research on nonviolent pornography. We will also refer to various ways in which this research has been applied to the current political debate on pornography and offer suggestions to mitigate the negative effects from exposure to certain forms of pornography and sexually violent mass media.

RESEARCH ON THE EFFECTS OF AGGRESSIVE PORNOGRAPHY

Aggressive pornography, as used here, refers to X-rated images of sexual coercion in which force is used or implied against a woman in order to obtain certain sexual acts, as in scenes of rape and other forms of sexual assault. One unique feature of these images is their reliance upon "positive victim outcomes," in which rape and other sexual assaults are depicted as pleasurable, sexually arousing, and beneficial to the female victim. In contrast to other forms of media violence in which victims suffer, die, and do not enjoy their victimization, aggressive pornography paints a rosy picture of aggression. The myths regarding violence against women are central to the various influences this material has

Reprinted from *American Behavioral Scientist*, 29(5), May/June 1986. © 1986 by Sage Publications. Reprinted by permission.

Authors' Note: This research was partially funded by National Science Foundation Grant BNS-8216772 to the first author and Steven Penrod.

upon the viewer. This does not imply that there are not images of suffering, mutilation, and death—there are. The large majority of images, however, show violence against women as justified, positive, and sexually liberating. Even these more "realistic" images, however, can influence certain viewers under specific conditions. We will address this research later.

There is some evidence that these images increased through the 1970s (Malamuth & Spinner, 1980). However, more recent content analysis suggests that the increase has abated in the 1980s (Scott, 1985). The Presidential Commission on Obscenity and Pornography of 1970 did not examine the influence of aggressive pornography, mainly because of its low frequency. This is important to note, as it highlights differences between the commission and the position outlined in this chapter. The major difference is not in the findings but in the type of material being examined. (The Commission on Obscenity and Pornography was interested only in sexually explicit media images.)

In many aggressive pornographic depictions, as noted, the victim is portrayed as secretly desiring the assault and as eventually deriving sexual pleasure from it (Donnerstein & Berkowitz, 1982; Malamuth, Heim, & Feshbach, 1980). From a cognitive perspective, such information suggest to the viewer that even if a woman seems repelled by a pursuer, eventually she will respond favorably to forceful advances, aggression, and overpowering by a male assailant (Brownmiller, 1975). The victim's pleasure could further heighten the aggressor's. Viewers might then come to think, at least for a short while, that their own sexual aggression would also be profitable, thus reducing restraints or inhibitions against aggression (Bandura, 1977). These views diminish the moral reprehensibility of any witnessed assault on a woman and, indeed, suggest that the sexual attack may have a highly desirable outcome for both victim and aggressor. Men having such beliefs might therefore be more likely to attack a woman after they see a sup-

posedly "pleasurable" rape. Furthermore, as there is a substantial aggressive component in the sexual assault, it could be argued that the favorable outcome lowers the observers restraints against aggression toward women. Empirical research in the last few years, which is examined below, as well as such cases as the New Bedford rape, in which onlookers are reported to have cheered the rape of a woman by several men, suggests that the above concerns may be warranted.

AGGRESSIVE PORNOGRAPHY AND SEXUAL AROUSAL

Although it was once believed that only rapists show sexual arousal to depictions of rape and other forms of aggression against women (Abel, Barlow, Blanchard, & Guild, 1977), research by Malamuth and his colleagues (Malamuth, 1981b, 1984; Malamuth & Check, 1983; Malamuth & Donnerstein, 1982; Malamuth, Haber, & Feshbach, 1980; Malamuth, Heim, & Feshbach, 1980) indicates that a nonrapist population will show evidence of increased sexual arousal to media-presented images of rape. This increased arousal primarily occurs when the female victim shows signs of pleasure and arousal, the theme most commonly presented in aggressive pornography. In addition, male subjects who indicate that there is some likelihood that they themselves would rape display increased sexual arousal to all forms of rape depictions, similar to the reactions of known rapists (Malamuth, 1981a, 1981b; Malamuth & Donnerstein, 1982). Researchers have suggested that this sexual arousal measure serves as an objective index of a proclivity to rape. Using this index, an individual whose sexual arousal to rape themes was found to be similar to or greater than his arousal to nonaggressive depictions would be considered to have an inclination to rape (Abel et al., 1977; Malamuth, 1981a; Malamuth & Donnerstein, 1982).

AGGRESSIVE PORNOGRAPHY AND ATTITUDES TOWARD RAPE

There are now considerable data indicating that exposure to aggressive pornography may alter the observer's perception of rape and the rape victim. For example, exposure to a sexually explicit rape scene in which the victim shows a "positive" reaction tends to produce a lessened sensitivity to rape (Malamuth & Check, 1983), increased acceptance of rape myths and interpersonal violence against women (Malamuth & Check, 1981), and increases in the self-reported possibility of raping (Malamuth, 1981a). This self-reported possibility of committing rape is highly correlated with (a) sexual arousal to rape stimuli, (b) aggressive behavior and a desire to hurt women, and (c) a belief that rape would be a sexually arousing experience for the rapist (see Malamuth, 1981a; Malamuth & Donnerstein, 1982). Exposure to aggressive pornography may also lead to self-generated rape fantasies (Malamuth, 1981b).

AGGRESSIVE PORNOGRAPHY AND AGGRESSION AGAINST WOMEN

Recent research (Donnerstein, 1980a, 1980b, 1983, 1984; Donnerstein & Berkowitz, 1982) has found that exposure to aggressive pornography increases aggression against women in a laboratory context. The same exposure does not seem to influence aggression against other men. This increased aggression is most pronounced when the aggression is seen as positive for the victim and occurs for both angered and nonangered individuals.

Although this research suggests that aggressive pornography can influence the male viewer, the relative contribution of the sexual and the aggressive components of the material remains unclear. Is it the sexual nature of the material or the messages about violence that are crucial? This is an extremely important question. In many discussions of this research the fact that the mater-

ial is aggressive is forgotten and it is assumed that the effects occur owing to the sexual nature of the material. As we noted earlier the sexual nature of the material is not the major issue. Recent empirical studies shed some light on this issue.

THE INFLUENCE OF NONPORNOGRAPHIC DEPICTIONS OF VIOLENCE AGAINST WOMEN

It has been alleged that images of violence against women have increased not only in pornographic materials but also in more readily accessible mass media materials ("War Against Pornography," 1985). Scenes of rape and violence have appeared in daytime TV soap operas and R-rated movies shown on cable television. These images are sometimes accompanied by the theme, common in aggressive pornography, that women enjoy or benefit from sexual violence. For example, several episodes of the daytime drama *General Hospital* were devoted to a rape of one of the well known female characters by an equally popular male character. At first the victim was humiliated; later the two characters were married. A similar theme was expressed in the popular-film, *The Getaway*. In this film, described by Malamuth and Check (1981):

> Violence against women is carried out both by the hero and the antagonist. The hero, played by Steve McQueen, is portrayed in a very "macho" image. At one point, he slaps his wife several times causing her to cry from the pain. The wife, played by Ali McGraw, is portrayed as deserving this beating. As well, the antagonist in the movie kidnaps a woman (Sally Struthers) and her husband. He rapes the woman but the assault is portrayed in a manner such that the woman is depicted as a willing participant. She becomes the antagonist's girlfriend and they both taunt her husband until he commits suicide. The woman then willingly continues with the assailant and at one point frantically searches for him. (p. 439)

In a field experiment, Malamuth and Check (1981a) attempted to determine whether or not the depiction of sexual violence contained in *The Getaway* and in another film with similar content influenced the viewers' perceptions of attitudes toward women. A total of 271 male and female students participated in a study that they were led to believe focused on movie ratings. One group watched, on two different evenings, *The Getaway* and *Swept Away* (which also shows women as victims of aggression within erotic contexts). A group of control subjects watched neutral, feature-length movies. These movies were viewed in campus theaters as part of the Campus Film Program. The results of a "Sexual Attitudes Survey," conducted several days after the screenings, indicated that viewing the sexually aggressive films significantly increased male but not female acceptance of interpersonal violence and tended to increase rape myth acceptance. These effects occurred not with X-rated materials but with more "prime-time" materials.

A recent study by Donnerstein and Berkowitz (1985) sought to examine more systematically the relative contributions of aggressive and sexual components of aggressive pornography. In a series of studies, male subjects were shown one of four different films: (1) the standard aggressive pornography used in studies discussed earlier, (2) an X-rated film that contained no forms of aggression or coercion and was rated by subjects to be as sexual as the first; (3) a film that contained scenes of aggression against a woman but without any sexual content and was considered less sexual and also less arousing (physiologically) than were the previous two films; and (4) a neutral film. Although the aggressive pornographic film led to the highest aggression against women, the aggression-only film produced more aggressive behavior than did the sex-only film. In fact, the sex-only film produced no different results than did the neutral film. Subjects were also examined for their attitudes about rape and their willingness to say they might commit a rape. The most callous attitudes and the highest percentage indicating some likelihood to rape were found in the aggression-only

conditions; the X-rated sex-only film was the lowest.

This research suggests that violence against women need not occur in pornographic or sexually explicit context in order for the depictions to have an impact on both attitudes and behavior. Angered individuals became more aggressive toward a female target after exposure to films judged not to be sexually arousing but that depict a woman as a victim of aggression. This supports the claim by Malamuth and Check (1983) that sexual violence against women need not be portrayed in a pornographic fashion for greater acceptance of interpersonal violence and rape myths.

In the Malamuth and Check study the victim's reaction to sexual violence was always, in the end, a positive one. Presumably the individual viewer of nonsexually explicit rape depictions with a positive outcome comes to accept the view that aggression against women is permissible because women enjoy sexual violence. In the studies by Donnerstein and Berkowitz, however, several other processes may have been at work. Exposure to nonpornographic aggression against women resulted in the highest levels of aggressive behavior when subjects were first angered by a female confederate of the experimenter or when the victim of aggression in the film and the female confederate were linked by the same name. Presumably, subjects did not come to perceive violence as acceptable because victims enjoy violence from this material. Instead, the cue value or association of women with the characters in the film (Berkowitz, 1974) and the possibility that the pain cues stimulated aggression in angry individuals might better account for the findings. When the individual is placed in a situation in which cues associated with aggressive responses are salient (for example, a situation involving a female victim) or one in which he is predisposed to aggression because he is angered, he will be more likely to respond aggressively both because of the stimulus-response connection previously built up through exposure to the films and/or because the pain and suffering of the victim reinforce already established aggressive tendencies.

An important element in the effects of exposure to aggressive pornography is violence against women. Because much commercially available media contain such images, researchers have begun to examine the impact of more popular film depictions of violence against women. Of particular interest have been R-rated "slasher" films, which combine graphic and brutal violence against women within a sexual context. These types of materials do not fit the general definition of pornography, but we believe their impact is stronger.

THE EFFECTS OF EXPOSURE TO R-RATED SEXUALIZED VIOLENCE

In a recent address before the International Conference on Film Classification and Regulation, Lord Harlech of the British Film Board noted the increase in R-rated sexually violent films and their "eroticizing" and "glorification" of rape and other forms of sexual violence. According to Harlech:

Everyone knows that murder is wrong, but a strange myth has grown up, and been seized on by filmmakers, that rape is really not so bad, that it may even be a form of liberation for the victim, who may be acting out what she secretly desires— and perhaps needs—with no harm done. . . . Filmmakers in recent years have used rape as an exciting and titillating spectacle in pornographic films, which are always designed to appeal to men.

As depictions of sex and violence become increasingly graphic, especially in feature-length movies shown in theaters, officials at the National Institute of Mental Health are becoming concerned:

Films had to be made more and more powerful in their arousal effects. Initially, strong excitatory reactions [may grow] weak or vanish entirely with repeated exposure to stimuli of a certain kind. This is known as "habituation." The possibility of habituation to sex and violence has significant social consequences. For one, it makes pointless the search for stronger and stronger arousers. But more important is its potential impact on real life behavior. If people become inured to violence from seeing much of it, they may be less likely to respond to real violence.

This loss of sensitivity to real violence after repeated exposure to films with sex and violence, or "the dilemma of the detached bystander in the presence of violence," is currently a concern of our research program. Although initial exposure to a violent rape scene may act to create anxiety and inhibitions about such behavior, researchers have suggested that repeated exposure to such material could counter these effects. The effects of long-term exposure to R-rated sexually violent mass media portrayals are the major focus of our ongoing research program investigating how massive exposure to commercially released violent and sexually violent films influence (1) viewer perceptions of violence, (2) judgments about rape and rape victims, (3) general physiological desensitization to violence, and (4) aggressive behavior.

This research presents a new approach to the study of mass media violence. First, unlike many previous studies in which individuals may have seen only 10–30 minutes of material, the current studies examine 10 hours of exposure. Second, we are able to monitor the process of subject's desensitization over a longer period of time than in previous experiments. Third, we examine perceptual and judgmental changes regarding violence, particularly violence against women.

In the program's first study, Linz, Donnerstein, and Penrod (1984) monitored desensitization of males to filmed violence against women to determine whether this desensitization "spilled over" into other kinds of decision making about victims. Male subjects watched nearly 10 hours (five commercially released feature-length films, one a day for five days) of R-rated or X-rated fare—either R-rated sexually violent films such as *Tool Box Murders, Vice Squad, I Spit on Your Grave, Texas Chainsaw Massacre*; X-rated movies that depicted sexual assault; or X-rated movies that depicted only consensual sex (nonviolent). The

R-rated films were much more explicit with regard to violence than they were with regard to sexual content. After each movie the men completed a mood questionnaire and evaluated the films on several dimensions. The films were counterbalanced so that comparisons could be made of the same films being shown on the first and last day of viewing. Before participation in the study subjects were screened for levels of hostility, and only those with low hostility scores were included to help guard against the possibility of an overly hostile individual imitating the filmed violence during the week of the films. This is also theoretically important because it suggests that any effects we found would occur with a normal population. (It has been suggested by critics of media violence research that only those who are already predisposed toward violence are influenced by exposure to media violence. In this study, those individuals have been eliminated.) After the week of viewing the men watched yet another film. This time, however, they saw a videotaped reenactment of an actual rape trial. After the trial they were asked to render judgments about how responsible the victim was for her own rape and how much injury she had suffered.

Most interesting were the results from the men who had watched the R-rated films such as *Texas Chainsaw Massacre* or *Maniac*. Initially, after the first day of viewing, the men rated themselves significantly above the norm for depression, anxiety, and annoyance on a mood adjective checklist. After each subsequent day of viewing, these scores dropped until, on the fourth day of viewing, the males' levels of anxiety, depression, and annoyance were indistinguishable from baseline norms.

What happened to the viewers as they watched more and more violence? We believe they were becoming desensitized to violence, particularly against women, which entailed more than a simple lowering of arousal to the movie violence. The men actually began to perceive the films differently as time went on. On Day 1, for example, on the average, the men estimated that they had seen four "offensive scenes." By the fifth day,

however, subjects reported only half as many offensive scenes (even though exactly the same movies, but in reverse order, were shown). Likewise, their ratings of the violence within the films receded from Day 1 to Day 5. By the last day the men rated the movies less graphic and less gory and estimated fewer violent scenes than they did on the first day of viewing. Most startling, by the last day of viewing graphic violence against women the men were rating the material as significantly less debasing and degrading to women, more humorous, and more enjoyable, and they claimed a greater willingness to see this type of film again. This change in perception due to repeated exposure was particularly evident in comparisons of reactions to two specific films—*I Spit on Your Grave* and *Vice Squad*. Both films contain sexual assault; however, rape is portrayed more graphically in *I Spit on Your Grave* and more ambiguously in *Vice Squad*. Men who were exposed first to *Vice Squad* and then to *I Spit on Your Grave* gave nearly identical ratings of sexual violence. However, subjects who had seen the more graphic movie first saw much less sexual violence (rape) in the more ambiguous film.

The subjects' evaluations of a rape victim after viewing a reenacted rape trial were also affected by the constant exposure to brutality against women. The victim of rape was rated as more worthless and her injury as significantly less severe by those exposed to filmed violence when compared to a control group of men who saw only the rape trial and did not view films. Desensitization to filmed violence on the last day was also significantly correlated with assignment of greater blame to the victim of her own rape. (These types of effects were not observed for subjects who were exposed to sexually explicit but nonviolent films.)

MITIGATING THE EFFECTS OF EXPOSURE TO SEXUAL VIOLENCE

This research strongly suggests a potential harmful effect from exposure to certain forms of aggressive pornography and other forms of sexualized violence. There is now, however, some evidence that these negative changes in attitudes and perceptions regarding rape and violence against women not only can be eliminated but can be positively changed. Malamuth and Check (1983) found that if male subjects who had participated in such an experiment were later administered a carefully constructed debriefing, they actually would be less accepting of certain rape myths than were control subjects exposed to depictions of intercourse (without a debriefing). Donnerstein and Berkowitz (1981) showed that not only are the negative effects of previous exposure eliminated, but even up to four months later, debriefed subjects have more "sensitive" attitudes toward rape than do control subjects. These debriefings consisted of (1) cautioning subjects that the portrayal of the rape they had been exposed to is completely fictitious in nature, (2) educating subjects about the violent nature of rape, (3) pointing out to subjects that rape is illegal and punishable by imprisonment, and (4) dispelling the many rape myths that are perpetrated in the portrayal (e.g., in the majority of rapes, the victim is promiscuous or has a bad reputation, or that many women have an unconscious desire to be raped).

Surveys of the effectiveness of debriefings for male subjects with R-rated sexual violence have yielded similar positive results. Subjects who participated in the week-long film exposure study that was followed by a certain type of debriefing changed their attitudes in a positive direction. The debriefings emphasized the fallacious nature of movie portrayals that suggests that women deserve to be physically violated and emphasized that processes of desensitization may have occurred because of long-term exposure to violence. The results indicated an immediate effect for debriefing, with subjects scoring lower on rape myth acceptance after participation than they scored before participation in the film viewing sessions. These effects remained, for the most part, six weeks later. The effectiveness of the debriefing for the subjects who participated in two later experiments (one involving

two weeks of exposure to R-rated violent films) indicated that even after seven months, subjects' attitudes about sexual violence showed significant positive change compared to the preparticipation levels.

This research suggests that if the callous attitudes about rape and violence presented in aggressive pornography and other media representations of violence against women are learned, they can likewise be "unlearned." Furthermore, if effective debriefings eliminate these negative effects, it would seem possible to develop effective "prebriefings" that would also counter the impact of such materials. Such programs could become part of sex education curricula for young males. Given the easy access and availability of many forms of sexual violence to young males today, such programs would go a long way toward countering the impact of such images.

THE IMPACT OF NONAGGRESSIVE PORNOGRAPHY

An examination of early research and reports in the area of nonaggressive pornography would have suggested that effects of exposure to erotica were, if anything, nonharmful. For instance:

> It is concluded that pornography is an innocuous stimulus which leads quickly to satiation and that the public concern over it is misplaced. (Howard, Liptzin, and Reifler, 1973, p. 133)

> Results . . . fail to support the position that viewing erotic films produces harmful social consequences. (Mann, Sidman, & Starr, 197, p. 113)

> If a case is to be made against "pornography" in 1970, it will have to be made on grounds other than demonstrated effects of a damaging personal or social nature. (President's Commission on Obscenity and Pornography, 1970, p. 139)

A number of criticisms of these findings, however (such as Cline, 1974; Dienstbier, 1977; Wills, 1977), led to reexamination of the issue of exposure to pornography and subsequent aggressive behavior. Some—for example, Cline

(1974)—saw major methodological and interpretive problems with the Pornography Commission report; others (for example, Liebert & Schwartzberg, 1977) believed that the observations were premature. Certainly the relationship between exposure to pornography and subsequent aggressive behavior was more complex than first believed. For the most part, recent research has shown that exposure to nonaggressive pornography can have one of two effects.

A number of studies in which individuals have been predisposed to aggression and were later exposed to nonaggressive pornography have revealed increases in aggressive behavior (such as Baron & Bell, 1977; Donnerstein, Donnerstein, & Evans, 1975; Malamuth, Feshbach, & Jaffe, 1977; Meyer, 1972; Zillmann, 1971, 1979). Such findings have been interpreted in terms of a general arousal model, which states that under conditions in which aggression is a dominant response, any source of emotional arousal will tend to increase aggressive behavior in disinhibited subjects (for example, Bandura, 1977; Donnerstein, 1983). A second group of studies (Baron, 1977; Baron & Bell, 1973; Donnerstein et al., 1975; Frodi, 1977; Zillmann & Sapolsk 1917) reports the opposite-that exposure to pornography of a nonaggressive nature can actually reduce subsequent aggressive behavior.

These results appear contradictory, but recent research (Baron, 1977; Donnerstein, 1983; Donnerstein et al., 1975; Zillmann, 1979) has begun to reconcile seeming inconsistencies. It is now believed that as pornographic stimuli become more arousing, they give rise to increases in aggression. At a low level of arousal, however, the stimuli distract individuals, and attention is directed away from previous anger. Acting in an aggressive manner toward a target is incompatible with the pleasant feelings associated with low-level arousal (see Baron, 1977; Donnerstein, 1983). There is also evidence that individuals who find the materials "displeasing or pornographic" will also increase their aggression after exposure, whereas those who have more positive reactions to the material will not increase their aggression even to highly arousing materials (Zillmann, 1979).

The research noted above was primarily concerned with same-sex aggression. The influence of nonaggressive pornography on aggression against women tends to produce mixed effects. Donnerstein and Barrett (1978) and Donnerstein and Hallam (1978) found that nonaggressive pornography had no effect on subsequent aggression unless constraints against aggressing were reduced. This was accomplished by both angering male subjects by women and giving subjects multiple chances to aggress. Donnerstein (1983) tried to reduce aggressive inhibitions through the use of an aggressive model but found no increase in aggression after exposure to an X-rated nonviolent film. It seems, therefore, that nonaggressive sexual material does not lead to aggression against women except under specific conditions (for example when inhibitions against aggression are lowered deliberately by the experimenter).

Almost without exception, studies reporting the effects of nonviolent pornography have relied on short-term exposure; most subjects have been exposed to only a few minutes of pornographic material. More recently, Zillman and Bryant (1982, 1984) demonstrated that long-term exposure (4 hours and 48 minutes over a six-week period) to pornography that does not contain overt aggressiveness may cause male and female subjects to (1) become more tolerant of bizarre and violent forms of pornography, (2) become less supportive of statements about sexual equality, and (3) become more lenient in assigning punishment to a rapist whose crime is described in a newspaper account. Furthermore, extensive exposure to the nonaggressive pornography significantly increased males' sexual callousness toward women. This latter finding was evidenced by increased acceptance of statements such as "A man should find them, fool them, fuck them, and forget them," "A women doesn't mean 'no' until she slaps you," and "If they are old enough to bleed, they are old enough to butcher." Zillman and others (such as Berkowitz, 1984) have offered several possible explanations for this effect, suggesting that certain viewer attitudes are strengthened through long-term exposure to nonviolent pornographic material.

A common scenario of the material used in the Zillman research is that women are sexually insatiable by nature. Even though the films shown do not feature the infliction of pain or suffering, women are portrayed as extremely permissive and promiscuous, willing to accommodate any male sexual urge. Short-term exposure to this view of women (characteristic of early studies of nonviolent pornography) may not be sufficient to engender changes in viewers' attitudes congruent with these portrayals. However, attitudinal changes might be expected under conditions of long-term exposure. Continued exposure to the idea that women will do practically anything sexually may prime or encourage other thoughts regarding female promiscuity (Berkowitz, 1984). This increase in the availability of thoughts about female promiscuity or the ease with which viewers can imagine instances in which a female has been sexually insatiable may lead viewers to inflate their estimates of how willingly and frequently women engage in sexual behavior. The availability of thoughts about female insatiability may also affect judgments about sexual behavior such as rape, bestiality, and sadomasochistic sex. Further, these ideas may endure. Zillman and Bryant (1982), for example, found that male subjects still had a propensity to trivialize rape three weeks after exposure to nonviolent pornography. It is important to point out, however, that in these studies long-term exposure did not increase aggressive behavior but in fact decreased subsequent aggression.

Unfortunately, the role that images of female promiscuity and insatiability play in fostering callous perceptions of women can only be speculated upon at this point because no research has systematically manipulated film content in an experiment designed to facilitate or inhibit viewer cognitions. One cannot rule out the possibility, for example, that simple exposure to many sexually explicit depictions (regardless of their "insatiability" theme) accounts for the attitudinal changes found in their study. Sexual explicitness and themes of insatiability are experimentally confounded in this work.

Another emerging concern among political activists about pornography is its alleged tendency to degrade women (Dworkin, 1985; MacKinnon, 1985). This concern has been expressed recently in the form of municipal ordinances against pornography originally drafted by Catherine MacKinnon and Andrea Dworkin that have been introduced in a variety of communities, including Minneapolis and Indianapolis. One central feature of these ordinances is that pornography is the graphic "sexually explicit subordination of women" that also includes "women presented in scenarios of degradation, injury, abasement, torture, shown as filthy or inferior, bleeding, bruised, or hurt in a context that makes these conditions sexual" (City County general ordinance No. 35, City of Indianapolis, 1984). These ordinances have engendered a great deal of controversy, as some individuals have maintained that they are a broad form of censorship. A critique of these ordinances can be found in a number of publications (for example, Burstyn, 1985; Russ, 1985).

The framers of the ordinance suggest that after viewing such material, "a general pattern of discriminatory attitudes and behavior, both violent and nonviolent, that has the capacity to stimulate various negative reactions against women will be found" (Defendants' memorandum, U.S. District Court for the Southern District of Indiana, Indianapolis Division, 1984, p. 8). Experimental evidence is clear with respect to the effects of pornography showing injury, torture, bleeding, bruised, or hurt women in sexual contexts. What has not been investigated is the effect of material showing women in scenarios of degradation, as inferior and abased.

No research has separated the effect of sexual explicitness from degradation, as was done with aggressive pornography, to determine whether the two interact to foster negative evaluations of women. Nearly all experiments conducted to date have confounded sexual explicitness with the presentation of women as a subordinate, objectified class. Only one investigation (Donnerstein, 1984) has attempted to disentangle sexual explicitness and violence. The results of this short-term exposure investigation, discussed above, revealed that although the combination of sexual explicitness and violence against a woman (the violent pornographic condition) resulted in the highest levels of subsequent aggression against a female target, the nonexplicit depiction that showed only violence resulted in aggression levels nearly as high and attitudes that were more callous than those that resulted from the combined exposure. The implication of this research is that long-term exposure to material that may not be explicitly sexual but that depicts women in scenes of degradation and subordination may have a negative impact on viewer attitudes. This is one area in which research is still needed.

CONCLUSION

Does pornography influence behaviors and attitudes toward women? The answer is difficult and centers on the definition of pornography. There is no evidence for any "harm"-related effects from sexually explicit materials. But research may support potential harmful effects from aggressive materials. Aggressive images are the issue, not sexual images. The message about violence and the sexualized nature of violence is crucial. Although these messages may be part of some forms of pornography, they are also pervasive media messages in general, from prime-time TV to popular films. Men in our society have callous attitudes about rape. But where do these attitudes come from? Are the media, and in particular pornography, the cause? We would be reluctant to place the blame on the media. If anything, the media act to reinforce already existing attitudes and values regarding women and violence. They do contribute, but are only part of the problem.

As social scientists we have devoted a great deal of time to searching for causes of violence against women. Perhaps it is time to look for ways to reduce this violence. This chapter has noted several studies that report techniques to mitigate the influence of exposure to sexual violence in the media, which involves changing attitudes about violence. The issue of pornography and its relationship to violence will continue for years, perhaps without any definitive answers. We may never know if there is any real causal influence. We do know, however, that rape and other forms of violence against women are pervasive. How we change this situation is of crucial importance, and our efforts need to be directed to this end.

REFERENCES

Abel, G., Barlow, D., Blanchard, E., & Guild, D. (1977). The components of rapists' sexual arousal. *Archives of General Psychiatry, 34*, 395–403, 895–903.

Bandura, A. (1977). *Social learning theory*. Englewood Cliffs, NJ: Prentice-Hall.

Baron, R. A. (1977). *Human aggression*. New York: Plenum.

Baron, R. A. (1984). The control of human aggression: A strategy based on incompatible responses. In R. Green & E. Donnerstein (Eds.), *Aggression: Theoretical and empirical reviews* (Vol. 2). New York: Academic Press.

Baron, R. A., & Bell, P. A. (1977). Sexual arousal and aggression by males: Effects of type of erotic stimuli and prior provocation. *Journal of Personality and Social Psychology, 35*, 79–87.

Berkowitz, L. (1974). Some determinants of impulsive aggression: Role of mediated associations with reinforcements for aggression. *Psychological Review, 81*, 165-179.

Berkowitz, L. (1984). Some effects of thoughts on anti- and prosocial influences of media events: A cognitive-neoassociation analysis. *Psychological Bulletin, 95*, 410–427.

Brownmiller, S. (1975). *Against our will: Men, women and rape*. New York: Simon & Schuster.

Burstyn, V. (1985). *Women against censorship*. Manchester, NH: Salem House.

Burt, M. R. (1980). Cultural myths and supports for rape. *Journal of Personality and Social Psychology*, 38, 217–230.

Check, J. V. P., & Malamuth, N. (1983). Violent pornography, feminism, and social learning theory. *Aggressive Behavior*, 9, 106–107.

Check, J. V. P., & Malamuth, N. (in press). Can participation in pornography experiments have positive effects? *Journal of Sex Research*.

Cline, V. B. (Ed.). (1974). *Where do you draw the line?* Salt Lake City: Brigham Young University Press.

Dienstbier, R. A. (1977). Sex and violence: Can research have it both ways? *Journal of Communication*, 27, 176–188.

Donnerstein, E., & Berkowitz, L. (1985). *Role of aggressive and sexual images in violent pornography*. Manuscript submitted for publication.

Donnerstein, E. (1980a). Pornography and violence against women. *Annals of the New York Academy of Sciences*, 347, 277–288.

Donnerstein, E. (1980b). Aggressive-erotica and violence against women. *Journal of Personality and Social Psychology,* 39, 269-277.

Donnerstein, E. (1983). Erotica and human aggression. In R. Geen & E. Donnerstein (Eds.). *Aggression: Theoretical and empirical reviews*. New York: Academic Press.

Donnerstein, E. (1984). Pornography: Its effect on violence against women. In N. Malamuth & E. Donnerstein (Eds.) *Pornography and sexual aggression*. Orlando, FL: Academic Press.

Donnerstein, E., & Barrett, G. (1978). The effects of erotic stimuli on male aggression toward females. *Journal of Personality and Social Psychology*, 36, 180–188.

Donnerstein, E., & Berkowitz, L. (1982). Victim reactions in aggressive-erotic films as a factor in violence against women. *Journal of Personality and Social Psychology*, 41, 710–724.

Donnerstein, E., & Hallam, J. (1978). Facilitating effects of erotica on aggression against women. *Journal of Personality and Social Psychology*, 36, 1270–1277.

Donnerstein, E., & Linz, D. (1984, January). Sexual violence in the media, a warning. *Psychology Today*, pp. 14–15.

Donnerstein, E., Donnerstein, M., & Evans, R. (1975). Erotic stimuli and aggression: Facilitation or inhibition. *Journal of Personality and Social Psychology*, 32, 237–244.

Dworkin, A. (1985). Against the male flood: Censorship, pornography, and equality. *Harvard Women's Law Journal*, 8.

Frodi, A. (1977). Sexual arousal, situational restrictiveness, and aggressive behavior. *Journal of Research in Personality*, 11, 48–58.

Howard, J. L., Liptzin, M. B., & Reifler, C. B. (1973). Is pornography a problem? *Journal of Social Issues*, 29, 133–145.

Liebert, R. M. & Schwartzberg, N. S. (1977). Effects of mass media. *Annual Review of Psychology*, 28, 141–173.

Liuz, D., Donnerstein, E., & Penrod, S. (1984). The effects of long-term exposure to filmed violence against women. *Journal of Communication*, 34, 130–147.

MacKinnon, C. A. (1985). Pornography, civil rights, and speech. *Harvard Civil Rights-Civil Liberty Law Review*, 20(1).

Malamuth, N. (1981a). Rape proclivity among males. *Journal of Social Issues*, 37, 138–157.

Malamuth, N. (1981b). Rape fantasies as a function of exposure to violent-sexual stimuli. *Archives of Sexual Behavior*, 10, 33–47.

Malamuth, N. (1984). Aggression against women: Cultural, and individual causes. In N. Malamuth & F. Donnerstein (Eds.) *Pornography and sexual aggression*. Orlando, FL: Academic Press.

Malamuth N., Feshbach, S., & Jaffe, Y. (1977). Sexual arousal and aggression: Recent experiments and theoretical issues. *Journal of Social Issues*, 33, 110–133.

Malamuth, N. M., & Spinner, B. (1980). A longitudinal content analysis of sexual violence in the best-selling erotic magazines. *Journal of Sex Research*, 16(3), 116–237.

Malamuth, N., & Check, J. V. P. (1981). The effects of mass media exposure on acceptance of violence against women: A field experiment. *Journal of Research in Personality*, 15, 436–446.

Malamuth, N., & Check, J. V. P. (1983). Sexual arousal to rape depictions: Individual differences. *Journal of Abnormal Psychology*, 92, 55–67.

Malamuth, N., & Donnerstein, E. (1982). The effects of aggressive pornographic mass media stimuli. In L. Berkowitz (Ed.), *Advances in experimental social psychology (vol. 15)*. New York: Academic Press.

Malamuth, N., & Donnerstein, E. (Eds.), (1983). *Pornography and sexual aggression.* New York: Academic Press.

Malamuth, N., Haber, S., & Feshbach, S. (1980). The sexual responsiveness of college students to rape depictions: Inhibitory and disinhibitory effects. *Journal of Research in Personality, 14,* 399–408.

Mann, J., Sidman, J., & Starr, S. (1971). Effects of erotic films on sexual behavior of married couples. In *Technical Report of the Commission on Obscenity and Pornography (vol. 8).* Washington, DC: Government Printing Office.

Meyer, T. (1972). The effects of viewing justified and unjustified real film violence on aggressive behavior. *Journal of Personality and Social Psychology, 23,* 21–29.

President's Commission on Obscenity and Pornography (vol. 8). Washington, DC: Government Printing Office.

Russ, J. (1985). *Magic mommas, trembling sisters, puritans and perverts.* New York: Crossing.

Scott, J. (1985). *Sexual violence in* Playboy *magazine: Longitudinal analysis.* Paper presented at the meeting of the American Society of Criminology.

The war against pornography. (1985, March 18). *Newsweek,* pp. 58–62, 65–67.

Wills, G. (1977, November). Measuring the impact of erotica. *Psychology Today,* pp. 30–34.

Zillman, D. (1971). Excitation transfer in communication-mediated aggressive behavior. *Journal of Experimental Social Psychology, 7,* 419–433.

Zillman, D. (1979). *Hostility and aggression.* Hillsdale, NJ: Erlbaum.

Zillman, D. (1984). *Victimization of women through pornography.* Proposal to the National Science Foundation.

Zillman, D., & Bryant, J. (1982). Pornography, sexual callousness, and the trivialization of rape. *Journal of Communication, 32,* 10–21.

Zillman, D., & Bryant, J. (1984). Effects of massive exposure to pornography. In N. Malamuth & E. Donnerstein (Eds.), *Pornography and sexual aggression.* New York: Academic Press.

Zillman, D., & Sapolsky, B. S. (1977). What mediates the effect of mild erotica on annoyance and hostile behavior in males? *Journal of Personality and Social Psychology, 35,* 587–596.

PORNOGRAPHY AND THE ALIENATION
OF MALE SEXUALITY

HARRY BROD

This paper is intended as a contribution to an ongoing discussion. It aims to augment, not refute or replace, what numerous commentators have said about pornography's role in the social construction of sexuality. I have several principal aims in this paper. My primary focus is to examine pornography's model of male sexuality. Furthermore, in the discussion of pornography's role in the social construction of sexuality, I wish to place more emphasis than is common on the social construction of pornography. As I hope to show, these are related questions. One reason I focus on the image of male sexuality in pornography is that I believe this aspect of the topic has been relatively neglected. In making this my topic here, I do not mean to suggest that this is the most essential part of the picture. Indeed, I am clear it is not. It seems clear enough to me that the main focus of discussion about the effects of pornography is and should be the harmful effects of pornography on women, its principal victims. Yet, there is much of significance which needs to be said about pornography's representation, or perhaps I should more accurately say misrepresentation, of male sexuality. My focus shall be on what is usually conceived of as "normal" male, sexuality, which for my purposes I take to be consensual, non-violent

heterosexuality, as these terms are conventionally understood. I am aware of analyses which argue that this statement assumes distinctions which are at least highly problematic, if not outright false, which argue that this "normal" sexuality is itself coercive, both as compulsory heterosexuality and as containing implicit or explicit coercion and violence. My purpose is not to take issue with these analyses, but simply to present an analysis of neglected aspects of the links between mainstream male sexuality and pornography. I would argue that the aspect of the relation between male sexuality and pornography usually discussed, pornography's incitement to greater extremes of violence against women, presupposes such a connection with the more accepted mainstream. Without such a link, pornography's messages would be rejected by rather than assimilated into male culture. My intention is to supply this usually missing link.

My analysis proceeds from both feminist and Marxist theory. These are often taken to be theories which speak from the point of view of the oppressed, in advocacy for their interests. That they indeed are, but they are also more than that. For each claims not simply to speak for the oppressed in a partisan way, but also to speak a truth about the social whole, a truth perhaps spoken in the

From *Social Theory and Practice*, Vol. 14, No. 3, Fall 1988, pp. 265–284. Reprinted with permission of the publisher and the author.

An earlier version of this paper was presented at the Philosophers for Social Responsibility National Workshop on Pornography, Eastern Division Meetings of the American Philosophical Association, New York, December 1987. I am grateful to members of the audience, and to Roger Gottlieb, Lenore Langsdorf, Maria Papacostaki, and Ricky Sherover-Marcuse for helpful comments.

name of the oppressed, but a truth objectively valid for the whole. That is to say, Marxism is a theory which analyzes the ruling class as well as the proletariat, and feminism is a theory which analyzes men as well as women. It is not simply that Marxism is concerned with class, and feminism with gender, both being united by common concerns having to do with power. Just as Marxism understands class as power, rather than simply understanding class differences as differences of income, lifestyle, or opportunities, so the distinctive contribution of feminism is its understanding of gender as power, rather than simply as sex role differentiation. Neither class nor gender should be reified into being understood as fixed entities, which then differentially distribute power and its rewards. Rather, they are categories continually constituted in ongoing contestations over power. The violence endemic to both systems cannot be understood as externalized manifestations of some natural inner biological or psychological drives existing prior to the social - order, but must be seen as emerging in and from the relations of power which constitute social structures. Just as capitalist exploitation is caused not by capitalists' excess greed but rather by the structural imperatives under which capitalism functions, so men's violence is not the manifestation of some inner male essence, but rather evidence of the bitterness and depth of the struggles through which genders are forged.[1]

For my purposes here, to identify this as a socialist feminist analysis is not, in the first instance, to proclaim allegiance to any particular set of doctrinal propositions, though I am confident that those I subscribe to would be included in any roundup of the usual suspects, but rather to articulate a methodological commitment to make questions of power central to questions of gender, and to understand gendered power in relation to economic power, and as historically, materially structured.[2] If one can understand the most intimate aspects of the lives of the dominant group in these terms, areas which would usually be taken to be the farthest afield from where one might expect these categories to be

applicable, then I believe one has gone a long way toward validating claims of the power of socialist feminist theory to comprehend the totality of our social world. This is my intention here. I consider the analysis of male sexuality I shall be presenting part of a wider socialist feminist analysis of patriarchal capitalist masculinity, an analysis I have begun to develop elsewhere.[3]

As shall be abundantly clear, I do not take a "sexual liberationist" perspective on pornography. I am aware that many individuals, particularly various sexual minorities, make this claim on pornography's behalf. I do not minimize nor negate their personal experiences. In the context of our society's severe sexual repressiveness, pornography may indeed have a liberating function for certain individuals. But I do not believe an attitude of approval for pornography follows from this. Numerous drugs and devices which have greatly helped individual women have also been medical and social catastrophes—the one does not negate the other.

I shall be claiming that pornography has a negative impact on men's own sexuality. This is a claim that an aspect of an oppressive system, patriarchy, operates, at least in part, to the disadvantage of the group it privileges, men. This claim does not deny that the overall effect of the system is to operate in men's advantage, nor does it deny that the same aspect of the system under consideration, that is, male sexuality and pornography under patriarchy, might not also contribute to the expansion and maintenance of male power even as it also works to men's disadvantage. Indeed, I shall be arguing precisely for such complementarity. I am simply highlighting one of the "contradictions" in the system. My reasons for doing so are in the first instance simply analytic: to, as I said, bring to the fore relatively neglected aspects of the issue. Further, I also have political motivations for emphasizing this perspective. I view raising consciousness of the prices of male power as part of a strategy through which one could at least potentially mobilize men against pornography's destructive effects on both women and men.

It will aid the following discussion if I ask readers to call to mind a classic text in which it is argued that, among many other things, a system of domination also damages the dominant group, and prevents them from realizing their full humanity. The argument is that the dominant group is "alienated" in specific and identifiable ways. The text I have in mind is Marx's "Economic and Philosophic Manuscripts of 1844." Just as capitalists as well as workers are alienated under capitalism according to Marxist theory (in a certain restricted sense, even more so), so men, I shall argue, and in particular male modes of sexuality, are also alienated under patriarchy. In the interests of keeping this paper a manageable length, I shall here assume rather than articulate a working familiarity with Marx's concept of alienation, the process whereby one becomes a stranger to oneself and one's own powers come to be powers over and against one. Since later in the paper I make use of some of Marx's more economistic concepts, I should however simply note that I see more continuity than rupture between Marx's earlier, more philosophical writings and his later, more economic ones.[4] While much of this paper presents an analysis of men's consciousness, I should make clear that while alienation may register in one's consciousness (as I argue it does), I follow Marx in viewing alienation not primarily as a psychological state dependent on the individual's sensibilities or consciousness but as a condition inevitably caused by living within a system of alienation. I should also note that I consider what follows an appropriation, not a systematic interpretation, of some of Marx's concepts.

Alienated pornographic male sexuality can be understood as having two dimensions, what I call the objectification of the body and the loss of subjectivity. I shall consider each in greater detail, describing various aspects of pornographic male sexuality under each heading in a way which I hope brings out how they may be conceptualized in Marx's terms. Rather than then redoing the analysis in Marx's terms, I shall then simply cite Marx briefly to indicate the contours of such a translation.

1. OBJECTIFICATION OF THE BODY

In terms of both its manifest image of and its effects on male sexuality, that is, in both intrinsic and consequentialist terms, pornography restricts male sensuality in favor of a genital, performance oriented male sexuality. Men become sexual acrobats endowed with oversized and overused organs which are, as the chapter title of a fine book on male sexuality describes, "The Fantasy Model of Sex: Two Feet Long, Hard as Steel, and Can Go All Night."[5] To speak non-euphemistically, using penile performance as an index of male strength and potency directly contradicts biological facts. There is no muscle tissue in the penis. Its erection when aroused results simply from increased blood flow to the area. All social mythology aside, the male erection is physiologically nothing more than localized high blood pressure. Yet this particular form of hypertension has attained mythic significance. Not only does this focusing of sexual attention on one organ increase male performance anxieties, but it also desensitizes other areas of the body from becoming what might otherwise be sources of pleasure. A colleague once told me that her favorite line in a lecture on male sexuality I used to give in a course I regularly taught was my declaration that the basic male sex organ is not the penis, but the skin.

The predominant image of women in pornography presents women as always sexually ready, willing, able, and eager. The necessary corollary to pornography's myth of female perpetual availability is its myth of male perpetual readiness. Just as the former fuels male misogyny when real-life women fail to perform to pornographic standards, so do men's failures to similarly perform fuel male insecurities. Furthermore, I would argue that this diminishes pleasure. Relating to one's body as a performance machine produces a split consciousness wherein part of one's attention is watching the machine, looking for flaws in its performance, even while one is supposedly immersed in the midst of sensual pleasure. This produces a self-distancing self-consciousness which mechanizes sex and reduces pleasure. (This is a problem perpetuated by numerous sexual self-help manuals, which treat sex as a matter of individual technique for fine-tuning the machine rather than as human interaction. I would add that men's sexual partners are also affected by this, as they can often intuit when they are being subjected to rote manipulation.)

2. LOSS OF SUBJECTIVITY

In the terms of discourse of what it understands to be "free" sex, pornographic sex comes "free" of the demands of emotional intimacy or commitment. It is commonly said as a generalization that women tend to connect sex with emotional intimacy more than men do. Without romantically blurring female sexuality into soft focus, if what is meant is how each gender consciously thinks or speaks of sex, I think this view is fair enough. But I find it takes what men say about sex, that it doesn't mean as much or the same thing to them, too much at face value. I would argue that men do feel similar needs for intimacy, but are trained to deny them, and are encouraged further to see physical affection and intimacy primarily if not exclusively in sexual terms. This leads to the familiar syndrome wherein, as one man put it:

> Although what most men want is physical affection, what they end up thinking they want is to be laid by a Playboy bunny.[6]

This puts a strain on male sexuality. Looking to sex to fulfill what are really non-sexual needs, men end up disappointed and frustrated. Sometimes they feel an unfilled void, and blame it on their or their partner's inadequate sexual performance. At other times they feel a discomfiting urgency or neediness to their sexuality, leading in some cases to what are increasingly recognized as sexual addiction disorders (therapists are here not talking about the traditional "perversions,"

but behaviors such as what is coming to be called a "Don Juan Syndrome," an obsessive pursuit of sexual "conquests"). A confession that sex is vastly overrated often lies beneath male sexual bravado. I would argue that sex seems overrated because men look to sex for the fulfillment of nonsexual emotional needs, a quest doomed to failure. Part of the reason for this failure is the priority of quantity over quality of sex which comes with sexuality's commodification. As human needs become subservient to market desires, the ground is laid for an increasing multiplication of desires to be exploited and filled by marketable commodities.[7]

For the most part the female in pornography is not one the man has yet to "conquer," but one already presented to him for the "taking." The female is primarily there as sex object, not sexual subject. Or, if she is not completely objectified, since men do want to be desired themselves, hers is at least a subjugated subjectivity. But one needs another independent subject, not an object or a captured subjectivity, if one either wants one's own prowess validated, or if one simply desires human interaction. Men functioning in the pornographic mode of male sexuality, in which men dominate women, are denied satisfaction of these human desires.[8] Denied recognition in the sexual interaction itself, they look to gain this recognition in wider social recognition of their "conquest."

To the pornographic mind, then, women become trophies awarded to the victor. For women to serve this purpose of achieving male social validation, a woman "conquered" by one must be a woman deemed desirable by others. Hence pornography both produces and reproduces uniform standards of female beauty. Male desires and tastes must be channeled into a single mode, with allowance for minor variations which obscure the fundamentally monolithic nature of the mold. Men's own subjectivity becomes masked to them, as historically and culturally specific and varying standards of beauty are made to appear natural and given. The ease with which men reach quick agreement on what makes a woman "attractive," evidenced in such things as the "1–10" rating scale of male banter and the reports of a computer programs success in predicting which of the contestants would be crowned "Miss America," demonstrates how deeply such standards have been internalized, and consequently the extent to which men are dominated by desires not authentically their own.

Lest anyone think that the analysis above is simply a philosopher's ruminations, too far removed from the actual experiences of most men, let me just offer one recent instantiation, from among many known to me, and even more, I am sure, I do not know. The following is from the *New York Times Magazine*'s "About Men" weekly column. In an article titled "Couch Dancing," the author describes his reactions to being taken to a place, a sort of cocktail bar, where women "clad only in the skimpiest of bikini underpants" would "dance" for a small group of men for a few minutes for about 25 or 30 dollars, men who "sat immobile, drinks in hand, glassy-eyed, tapping their feet to the disco music that throbbed through the room."

Men are supposed to like this kind of thing, and there is a quite natural part of each of us that does. But there is another part of us—of me, at least— that is not grateful for the traditional male sexual programming, not proud of the results. By a certain age, most modern men have been so surfeited with images of unattainably beautiful women in preposterous contexts that we risk losing the capacity to respond to the ordinarily beautiful women we love in our bedrooms. There have been too many times when I have guiltily resorted to impersonal fantasy because the genuine love I felt for a woman wasn't enough to convert feeling into performance. And in those sorry, secret moments, I have resented deeply my lifelong indoctrination into the esthetic of the centerfold.[9]

3. ALIENATION AND CRISIS

I believe that all of the above can be translated without great difficulty into a conceptual framework paralleling Marx's analysis of the alien-

ation experienced by capitalists. The essential points are captured in two sentences from Marx's manuscripts:

> 1. All *the physical and intellectual senses have been replaced by the simple alienation of* all *these senses; the sense of* having.[10]
> 2. *The wealthy man is at the same time one who* needs *a complex of human manifestations of life, and whose own self-realization exists as an inner necessity, a need.*[11]

Both sentences speak to a loss of human interaction and self-realization. The first articulates how desires for conquest and control prevent input from the world. The second presents an alternative conception wherein wealth is measured by abilities for self-expression, rather than possession. Here Marx expresses his conceptualization of the state of alienation as a loss of sensuous fulfillment, poorly replaced by a pride of possession, and a lack of self-consciousness and hence actualization of one's own real desires and abilities. One could recast the preceding analysis of pornographic male sexuality through these categories. In Marx's own analysis, these are more properly conceived of as the results of alienation, rather than the process of alienation itself. This process is at its basis a process of inversion, a reversal of the subject-object relationship, in which one's active powers become estranged from one, and return to dominate one as an external force. It is this aspect which I believe is most useful in understanding the alienation of male sexuality of which pornography is part and parcel. How is it that men's power turns against them, so that pornography, in and by which men dominate women, comes to dominate men themselves?

To answer this question I shall find it useful to have recourse to two other concepts central to Marxism, the concept of "crisis" in the system and the concept of "imperialism."[12] Marx's conception of the economic crisis of capitalism is often misunderstood as a prophecy of a cataclysmic doomsday scenario for the death of capitalism. Under this interpretation, some look for a single event, perhaps like a stock market crash, to precipitate capitalism's demise. But such events are for Marx at most triggering events, particular crises, which can shake the system, if at all, only because of the far more important underlying structural general crisis of capitalism. This general crisis is increasingly capitalism's ordinary state, not an extraordinary occurrence. It is manifest in the ongoing fiscal crisis of the state as well as recurring crises of legitimacy, and results from basic contradictory tensions within capitalism. One way of expressing these tensions is to see them as a conflict between the classic laissez-faire capitalist market mode, wherein capitalists are free to run their own affairs as individuals, and the increasing inability of the capitalist class to run an increasingly complex system without centralized management. The result of this tension is that the state increasingly becomes a managerial committee for the capitalist class, and is increasingly called upon to perform functions previously left to individuals. As entrepreneurial and laissez-faire capitalism give way to corporate capitalism and the welfare state, the power of capitalism becomes increasingly depersonalized, increasingly reft from the hands of individual capitalists and collectivized, so that capitalists themselves come more and more under the domination of impersonal market forces no longer under their direct control.

To move now to the relevance of the above, there is currently a good deal of talk about a perceived crisis of masculinity, in which men are said to be confused by contradictory imperatives given them in the wake of the women's movement. Though the male ego feels uniquely beleaguered today, in fact such talk regularly surfaces in our culture—the 1890's in the United States, for example, was another period in which the air was full of a "crisis of masculinity" caused by the rise of the "New Woman" and other factors.[13] Now, I wish to put forward the hypothesis that these particular "crises" of masculinity are but surface manifestations of a much deeper and broader phenomenon which I call the "general

crisis of patriarchy," paralleling Marx's general crisis of capitalism. Taking a very broad view, this crisis results from the increasing depersonalization of patriarchal power which occurs with the development of patriarchy from its pre-capitalist phase, where power really was often directly exercised by individual patriarchs, to its late capitalist phase where men collectively exercise power over women, but are themselves as individuals increasingly under the domination of those same patriarchal powers.[14] I would stress that the sense of there being a "crisis" of masculinity arises not from the decrease or increase in patriarchal power as such. Patriarchal imperatives for men to retain power over women remain in force throughout. But there is a shift in the mode of that power's exercise, and the sense of crisis results from the simultaneous promulgation throughout society of two conflicting modes of patriarchal power, the earlier more personal form and the later more institutional form. The crisis results from the incompatibility of the two conflicting ideals of masculinity embraced by the different forms of patriarchy, the increasing conflicts between behavioral and attitudinal norms in the political/economic and the personal/familial spheres.

4. FROM PATRIARCHY TO FRATRIARCHY

To engage for a moment in even broader speculation than that which I have so far permitted myself, I believe that much of the culture, law, and philosophy of the nineteenth century in particular can be reinterpreted as marking a decisive turn in this transition. I believe the passing of personal patriarchal power and its transformation into institutional patriarchal power in this period of the interrelated consolidation of corporate capitalism is evidenced in such phenomena as the rise of what one scholar has termed "judicial patriarchy," the new social regulation of masculinity through the courts and social welfare agencies, which through new support laws, poor laws, desertion laws and other changes transformed what were previously personal obligations into legal duties, as well as in the "Death of God" phenomenon and its aftermath.[15] That is to say, I believe the loss of the personal exercise of patriarchal power and its diffusion through the institutions of society is strongly implicated in the death of God the Father and the secularization of culture in the nineteenth century, as well as the modern and postmodern problem of grounding authority and values.

I would like to tentatively and preliminarily propose a new concept to reflect this shift in the nature of patriarchy caused by the deindividualization and collectivization of male power. Rather than speak simply of advanced capitalist patriarchy, the rule of the *fathers*, I suggest we speak of fratriarchy, the rule of the *brothers*. For the moment, I propose this concept more as a metaphor than as a sharply defined analytical tool, much as the concept of patriarchy was used when first popularized. I believe this concept better captures what I would argue is one of the key issues in conceptualizing contemporary masculinities, the disjunction between the facts of public male power and the feelings of individual male powerlessness. As opposed to the patriarch, who embodied many levels and kinds of authority in his single person, the brothers stand in uneasy relationships with each other, engaged in sibling rivalry while trying to keep the power of the family of man as a whole intact. I note that one of the consequences of the shift from patriarchy to fratriarchy is that some people become nostalgic for the authority of the benevolent patriarch, who if he was doing his job right at least prevented one of the great dangers of fratriarchy, fratricide, the brothers' killing each other. Furthermore, fratriarchy is an intragenerational concept, whereas patriarchy is intergenerational. Patriarchy, as a father-to-son transmission of authority, more directly inculcates traditional historically grounded authority, whereas the dimension of temporal continuity is rendered more problematic in fratriarchy's brother-to-brother relationships. I believe this helps capture the problematic nature of modern historical consciousness as it emerged from the

nineteenth century, what I would argue is the most significant single philosophical theme of that century. If taken in Freudian directions, the concept of fratriarchy also speaks to the brothers' collusion to repress awareness of the violence which lies at the foundations of society.

To return to the present discussion, the debate over whether pornography reflects men's power or powerlessness, as taken up recently by Alan Soble in his book *Pornography: Marxism, Feminism, and the Future of Sexuality*, can be resolved if one makes a distinction such as I have proposed between personal and institutional male power. Soble cites men's use of pornographic fantasy as compensation for their powerlessness in the real world to argue that "pornography is therefore not so much an expression of male power as it is an expression of their lack of power."[16] In contrast, I would argue that by differentiating levels of power one should more accurately say that pornography is both an expression of men's public power and an expression of their lack of personal power. The argument of this paper is that pornography's image of male sexuality works to the detriment of men personally even as its image of female sexuality enhances the powers of patriarchy. It expresses the power of alienated sexuality, or, as one could equally well say, the alienated power of sexuality.

With this understanding, one can reconcile the two dominant but otherwise irreconcilable images of the straight male consumer of pornography: on the one hand the powerful rapist, using pornography to consummate his sexual violence, and on the other hand the shy recluse, using it to consummate his masturbatory fantasies. Both images have their degree of validity, and I believe it is a distinctive virtue of the analysis presented here that one can understand not only the merits of each depiction, but their interconnection.

5. EMBODIMENT AND EROTICA

In the more reductionist and determinist strains of Marxism, pornography as ideology would be relegated to the superstructure of capitalism. I would like to suggest another conceptualization: that pornography is not part of patriarchal capitalism's superstructure, but part of its infrastructure. Its commodification of the body and interpersonal relationships paves the way for the ever more penetrating ingression of capitalist market relations into the deepest reaches of the individual's psychological makeup. The feminist slogan that "The Personal is Political" emerges at a particular historical moment, and should be understood not simply as an imperative declaration that what has previously been seen solely as personal should now be viewed politically, but also as a response to the real increasing politicization of personal life.

This aspect can be illuminated through the Marxist concept of imperialism. The classical Marxist analysis of imperialism argues that it is primarily motivated by two factors: exploitation of natural resources and extension of the market. In this vein, pornography should be understood as imperialism of the body. The greater public proliferation of pornography, from the "soft-core" pornography of much commercial advertising to the greater availability of "hard-core" pornography, proclaims the greater colonization of the body by the market.[17] The increasing use of the male body as a sex symbol in contemporary culture is evidence of advanced capitalism's increasing use of new styles of masculinity to promote images of men as consumers as well as producers.[18] Today's debates over the "real" meaning of masculinity can be understood in large part as a struggle between those espousing the "new man" style of masculinity more suited to advanced corporate, consumerist patriarchal capitalism and those who wish to return to an idealized version of "traditional" masculinity suited to a more production-oriented, entrepreneurial patriarchal capitalism.[19]

In a more theoretical context, one can see that part of the reason the pornography debate has been so divisive, placing on different sides of the question people who usually find themselves allies, is that discussions between civil libertarians and feminists have often been at cross purposes. Here one can begin to relate political theory not to political practice, but to metaphysical theory. The classical civil liberties perspective on the issue remains deeply embedded in a male theoretical discourse on the meaning of sexuality. The connection between the domination of nature and the domination of women has been argued from many Marxist and feminist points of view.[20] The pivot of this connection is the masculine overlay of the mind-body dualism onto the male-female dichotomy. Within this framework, morality par excellence consists in the masculinized mind restraining the feminized body, with sexual desires seen as the crucial test for these powers of restraint. From this point of view, the question of the morality of pornography is primarily the quantitative question of how much sexual display is allowed, with full civil libertarians opting to uphold the extreme end of this continuum, arguing that no sexual expression should be repressed. But the crucial question, for at least the very important strain of feminist theory which rejects these dualisms which frame the debate for the malestream mainstream, is not *how much* sexuality is displayed but rather *how* sexuality is displayed. These theories speak not of mind-body dualism, but of mind/body wholism, where the body is seen not as the limitation or barrier for the expression of the free moral self, but rather as the most immediate and intimate vehicle for the expression of that self. The question of sexual morality here is not that of restraining or releasing sexual desires as they are forced on the spiritual self by the temptations of the body, but that of constructing spirited and liberating sexual relationships with and through one's own and others' bodies. Here sexual freedom is not the classical liberal freedom *from* external restraint, but the more radical freedom *to* construct authentically expressive sexualities.

I have argued throughout this paper that pornography is a vehicle for the imposition of socially constructed sexuality, not a means for the expression of autonomously self-determined sexuality. (I would add that in contrasting imposed and authentic sexualities I am not endorsing a sexual essentialism, but simply carving out a space for more personal freedom.) Pornography is inherently about commercialized sex, about the eroticization of power and the power of eroticization. One can look to the term's etymology for confirmation of this point. It comes from the classical Greek "*pornographos*, meaning 'writing (sketching) of harlots,'" sometimes women captured in war.[21] Any distinction between pornography and erotica remains problematic, and cannot be drawn with absolute precision. Yet 1 believe some such distinction can and must be made. I would place the two terms not in absolute opposition, but at two ends of a continuum, with gray areas of necessity remaining between them. The gradations along the continuum are marked not by the explicitness of the portrayal of sexuality or the body, nor by the assertiveness vs. passivity of persons, nor by any categorization of sexual acts or activities, but by the extent to which autonomous personhood is attributed to the person or persons portrayed. Erotica portrays sexual subjects, manifesting their personhood in and through their bodies. Pornography depicts sex objects, persons reduced to their bodies. While the erotic nude presents the more pristine sexual body before the social persona is adopted through donning one's clothing, the pornographic nude portrays a body whose clothing has been more or less forcibly removed, where the absence of that clothing remains the most forceful presence in the image. Society's objectification remains present, indeed emphasized, in pornography, in a way in which it does not in erotica. Erotica, as sexual art, expresses a self, whereas pornography, as sexual commodity, markets one. The latter "works" because the operation it performs on women's bodies resonates with the "pornographizing" the male gaze does to women in other areas of society.[22] These distinctions remain problematic, to say the least, in their application, and disagreement in particular cases will no doubt remain. Much more work needs to be done before one would with any reasonable confidence distinguish authentic from imposed, per-

sonal from commercial, sexuality. Yet I believe this is the crucial question, and I believe these concepts correctly indicate the proper categories of analysis. Assuming a full definition of freedom as including autonomy and self-determination, pornography is therefore incompatible with real freedom.

6. CONCLUSIONS

It has often been noted that while socialist feminism is currently a major component of the array of feminisms one finds in academic feminism and women's studies, it is far less influential on the playing fields of practical politics.[23] While an analysis of male sexuality may seem an unlikely source to further socialist feminism's practical political agenda, I hope this paper's demonstration of the interconnections between intimate personal experiences and large-scale historical and social structures, especially in what may have initially seemed unlikely places, may serve as a useful methodological model for other investigations.

In one sense, this paper hopes to further the development of socialist feminist theory via a return to Hegel, especially the Hegel of the *Phenomenology*. Not only is Hegel's master-servant dialectic the *sine qua non* for the use of the concept of alienation in this paper, but the inspiration for a mode of analysis, which is true to the experimental consciousness of social actors while at the same time delimiting that consciousness by showing its partiality and placing it in a broader context, is rooted in Hegel's *Phenomenology*. It is not a coincidence that the major wave of socialist feminist theory and practice in the late 60's and early 70's coincided with a wave of Marxist interest in Hegel, and that current signs of a new feminist interest in Hegel coincide with signs of the resurgence of radical politics in the United States.[24] Analogous to the conception of socialist feminism I articulated in the Introduction to this paper, my conception of Hegelianism defines Hegelianism as method rather than doctrine.[25] In some sense, contemporary Marxism and feminism can already be said to be rooted in Hegel, in the case of Marxism through Marx himself, and in the case of feminism through Beauvoir's *The Second Sex*. A more explicitly Hegelian influenced socialist feminism would embody a theory and practice emphasizing the following themes: the dialectic between individual consciousness and social structure, a thoroughly historical epistemology a non-dualistic metaphysics, an understanding of gender, class, and other differences as being constituted through interaction rather than consisting of isolated "roles," the priority of political over moralistic or economistic theory, a probing of the relations between state power and cultural hegemony, a program for reaching unity through difference rather than through sameness, a tolerance of if not preference for ambiguity and contradiction, and an orientation toward process over end product.[26]

l would like to conclude with some remarks on the practical import of this analysis. First of all, if the analysis of the relationship between pornography and consumerism and the argument about pornography leading to violence are correct, then a different conceptualization of the debate over the ethics of the feminist anti-pornography movement emerges. If one accepts, as I do, the idea that this movement is not against sex, but against sexual abuse, then the campaign against pornography is essentially not a call for censorship but a consumer campaign for product safety. The proper context for the debate over its practices is then not issues of free speech or civil liberties, but issues of business ethics. Or rather, this is the conclusion I reach remaining focused on pornography and male sexuality. But we should remember the broader context I alluded to at the beginning of this paper, the question of pornography's effects on women. In that con-text, women are not the consumers of pornography, but the consumed. Rather than invoking the consumer movement, perhaps we should then look to environmental protection as a model.[27] Following this line of reasoning, one could in principle then perhaps develop under the tort law of product liability an argument to accomplish much of the regulation of sexually explicit material some are now trying to achieve through legislative means, perhaps developing a new definition of "safe" sexual material.

Finally, for most of us most of our daily practice as academics consists of teaching rather than writing or reading in our fields. If one accepts the analysis I have presented, a central if not primary concern for us should therefore be how to integrate this analysis into our classrooms. I close by suggesting that we use this analysis and others like it from the emerging field of men's studies to demonstrate to the men in our classes the direct relevance of feminist analysis to their own lives, at the most intimate and personal levels, and that we look for ways to demonstrate to men that feminism can be personally empowering and liberating for them without glossing over, and in fact emphasizing, the corresponding truth that this will also require the surrender of male privilege.[28]

NOTES

1. I am indebted for this formulation to Tim Carrigan, Bob Connell, and John Lee, "Toward a New Sociology of Masculinity," in Harry Brod, ed., *The Making of Masculinities: The New Men's Studies* (Boston: Allen & Unwin, 1987).

2. For the *locus classicus* of the redefinition of Marxism as method rather than doctrine, see Georg Lukács, *History and Class Consciousness: Studies in Marxist Dialectics*, trans. Rodney Livingstone (Cambridge, MA: MIT Press, 1972).

3. See my Introduction to Brod, T*he Making of Masculinities*. For other recent books by men I consider to be engaged in essentially the same or a kindred project, see Jeff Hearn, *The Gender of Oppression: Men, Masculinity, and the Critique of Marxism* (New York: St. Martin's Press, 1987) and R. W. Connell, *Gender*

and Power (Stanford, CA: Stanford University Press, 1987), particularly the concept of "hegemonic masculinity," also used in Carrigan, Connell, and Lee, "Toward A New Sociology of Masculinity." Needless to say, none of this work would be conceivable without the pioneering work of many women in women's studies.

4. For book-length treatments of Marx's concept of alienation, see István Mészéros, *Marx's Theory of Alienation* (New York: Harper & Row, 1972), and Bertell Ollman, *Alienation: Marx's Conception of Man in Capitalist Society* (Cambridge: Cambridge University Press, 1971).

5. Bernie Zilbergeld, *Male Sexuality: A Guide to Sexual Fulfillment* (Boston: Little, Brown and Company, 1978).

6. Michael Betzold, "How Pornography Shackles Men and Oppresses Women," in *For Men Against Sexism: A Book of Readings*, ed. Jon Snodgrass (Albion, CA: Times Change Press, 1977), p. 46.

7. I am grateful to Lenore Langsdorf and Paula Rothenberg for independently suggesting to me how this point would fit into my analysis.

8. See Jessica Benjamin, "The Bonds of Love: Rational Violence and Erotic Domination," *Feminist Studies* 6 (1980): 144–74.

9. Keith McWalter, "Couch Dancing," *New York Times Magazine*, December 6, 1987, p. l38.

10. Karl Marx, "Economic and Philosophic Manuscripts: Third Manuscript," in *Early Writings*, ed. and trans. T. B. Bottomore (New York: McGraw-Hill, 1964), pp. 159–60.

11. Marx., pp. l64–65.

12. An earlier version of portions of the following argument appears in my article "Eros Thanatized: Pornography and Male Sexuality" with a "1988 Postscript," forthcoming in Michael Kimmel, ed., *Men Confronting Pornography* (New York: Crown, 1989). The article originally appeared (without the postscript) in *Humanities in Society* 7 (1984) pp. 47–63.

13. See the essays by myself and Michael Kimmel in Brod, *The Making of Masculinities*.

14. Compare Carol Brown on the shift from private to public patriarchy: "Mothers, Fathers, and Children: From Private to Public Patriarchy" in Lydia Sargent, ed., *Women and Revolution* (Boston: South End Press, 1981).

15. According to Martha May in her paper "'An Obligation on Every Man': Masculine Breadwinning and the Law in Nineteenth Century New York," pre-

sented at the American Historical Association, Chicago, Illinois, 1987, from which I learned of these changes, the term "judicial patriarchy" is taken from historian Michael Grossberg *Governing the Hearth: Law and the Family in Nineteenth Century America* (Chapel Hill: University of North Carolina Press, 1985) and "Crossing Boundaries: Nineteenth Century Domestic Relations Law and the Merger of Family and Legal History," *American Bar Foundation Research Journal* (1985): 799–847.

16. Alan Soble, *Pornography: Marxism, Feminism, and the Future of Sexuality* (New Haven: Yale University Press, 1986), p. 82. I agree with much of Soble's analysis of male sexuality in capitalism, and note the similarities between much of what he says about "dismemberment" and consumerism and my analysis here. (See p. 141 of this volume.)

17. See John D'Emilio and Estelle B. Freedman, *Intimate Matters: A History of Sexuality in America* (New York: Harper & Row, 1988).

18. See Barbara Ehrenreich, *The Hearts of Men: American Dreams and the Flight from Commitment* (New York: Anchor-Doubleday, 1983); and Wolfgang Fritz Haug, *Critique of Commodity Aesthetics: Appearance, Sexuality, and Advertising in Capitalist Society*, trans. Robert Bock (Minneapolis: University of Minnesota Press, 1986).

19. See my "Work Clothes and Leisure Suits: The Class Basis and Bias of the Men's Movement," in *Changing Men* 11 (1983) 10–12 and 38–40.

20. This features prominently in the work of the Frankfurt school as well as contemporary ecofeminist theorists.

21. Rosemarie Tong, "Feminism, Pornography and Censorship," *Social Theory and Practice* 8 (1982): 1–17.

22. I learned to use "pornographize" as a verb in this way from Timothy Beneke's "Introduction" to his *Men on Rape* (New York: St. Martin's Press, 1982).

23. See the series of ten articles on "Socialist-Feminism Today" in *Socialist Review* 73–79 (1984–1985).

24. For the most recent feminist re-examinations of Hegel, see Heidi M. Raven, "Has Hegel Anything to Say to Feminists?", *The Owl of Minerva* 19 (1988) 149–68. Patricia Jagentowicz Mills, *Women, Nature, and Psyche* (New Haven: Yale University Press, 1987); and Susan M. Easton, "Hegel and Feminism," in David Lamb, ed., *Hegel and Modern Philosophy* (London: Croom Helm, 1987). Hegel enters contemporary radical legal thought primarily through the

Critical Legal Studies movement. Especially relevant here is the work of Drucilla Cornell, for example, "Taking Hegel Seriously: Reflections on Beyond Objectivism and Relativism," *Cardozo Law Review* 7 (1985): 139; "Convention and Critique," *Cardozo Law Review* 7 (1986): 679; "Two Lectures on the Normative Dimensions of Community in the Law," *Tennessee Law Review* 54 (1987); 327; "Toward a Modern/Postmodern Reconstruction of Ethics," *University of Pennsylvania Law Review* 133 (1985): 291. See also papers from the Conference on "Hegel and Legal Theory," March 1988 at the Cardozo Law School of Yeshiva University, New York City, forthcoming in a special issue of the *Cardozo Law Review*. For signs of radical resurgence in the United States, I would cite such phenomena as the Jackson candidacy and the 1988 National Student Convention. In a recent issue of *The Nation* (actually, the current issue as I write this) Jefferson Morley writes: "The most fundamental idea shared by popular movements East and West is the principle of 'civil society.'" Jefferson Morley, "On 'Civil Society,'" *The Nation*, May 7, 1988, p. 630.

25. I believe this is true to Hegel's own conception of Hegelianism, for Hegel put the Logic at the core of his system, and at the center of the Logic stands the transfiguration and transvaluation of form and content.

26. Much of the feminist critique of the philosophical mainstream echoes earlier critiques of the mainstream made in the name of "process thought." See *Feminism and Process Thought: The Harvard Divinity School/Claremont Center for Process Studies Symposium Papers*, ed. Sheila Greeve Davaney (Lewiston, NY: Edwin Mellen Press, 1981).

27. I am indebted to John Stoltenberg for this point.

28. I attempt to further articulate this perspective in *A Mensch Among Men: Explorations in Jewish Masculinity* (The Crossing Press, 1988) and "Scholarly Studies of Men: The Field Is an Essential Complement to Women's Studies" in *Against the Tide: Pro-Feminist Men in the United States 1776–1990, A Documentary History*, eds. Michael S. Kimmel and Thomas E. Mosmiller (Beacon Press, 1992). See also generally the academic journal *masculinities* and the organizational newsletter *brother* published by the National Organization for Men Against Sexism (54 Mint St., Suite 300, San Francisco, CA 94103) and the magazine *Changing Men* (306 North Brooks St., Madison, WI 53715).

THE HETEROSEXUAL QUESTIONNAIRE

M. ROCHLIN

1. What do you think caused your heterosexuality?

2. When and how did you decide you were a heterosexual?

3. Is it possible that your heterosexuality is just a phase you may grow out of?

4. Is it possible that your heterosexuality stems from a neurotic fear of others of the same sex?

5. If you have never slept with a person of the same sex, is it possible that all you need is a good Gay lover?

6. Do your parents know that you are straight? Do your friends and/or roommate(s) know? How did they react?

7. Why do you insist on flaunting your heterosexuality? Can't you just be who you are and keep it quiet?

8. Why do heterosexuals place so much emphasis on sex?

9. Why do heterosexuals feel compelled to seduce others into their lifestyle?

10. A disproportionate majority of child molesters are heterosexual. Do you consider it safe to expose children to heterosexual teachers?

11. Just what do men and women *do* in bed together? How can they truly know how to please each other, being so anatomically different?

12. With all the societal support marriage receives, the divorce rate is spiraling. Why are there so few stable relationships among heterosexuals?

13. Statistics show that lesbians have the lowest incidence of sexually transmitted diseases. Is it really safe for a woman to maintain a heterosexual lifestyle and run the risk of disease and pregnancy?

14. How can you become a whole person if you limit yourself to compulsive, exclusive heterosexuality?

15. Considering the menace of overpopulation, how could the human race survive if everyone were heterosexual?

16. Could you trust a heterosexual therapist to be objective? Don't you feel s/he might be inclined to influence you in the direction of her/his own leanings?

17. There seem to be very few happy heterosexuals. Techniques have been developed that might enable you to change if you really want to. Have you considered trying aversion therapy?

18. Would you want your child to be heterosexual, knowing the problems that s/he would face?

MEN LOVING MEN:
THE CHALLENGE OF GAY LIBERATION

GARY KINSMAN

The limits of "acceptable" masculinity are in part defined by comments like "What are you, a fag?"[1] As boys and men we have heard such expressions and the words "queer," "faggot," and "sissy" all our lives. These words encourage certain types of male behavior and serve to define, regulate, and limit our lives, whether we consider ourselves straight or gay. Depending on who is speaking and who is listening, they incite fear or hatred.

Even among many heterosexual men who have been influenced by feminism, the taboo against loving the same sex remains unchallenged. Lines like "I may be anti-sexist, but I am certainly not gay" can still be heard. These men may be questioning some aspects of male privilege, but in attempting to remake masculinity they have not questioned the institution of heterosexuality.[2] As a result their challenge to male privilege is partial and inadequate.

Gay men have often found much support in the "men's movement" or in groups of men against sexism. At the same time we have also seen our concerns as gay men marginalized and pushed aside and have often felt like outsiders. Joe Interrante expresses some of the reservations of gay men about the "men's movement" and its literature:

> As a gay man . . . I had suspicions about the heterocentrist bias of this work. It told me that my gayness existed "in addition to" my masculinity, whereas I found that it colored my entire experience of manhood. I distrusted a literature which claimed that gay men were just like heterosexual men except for what they did in bed.[3]

The literature of the men's movement has tended to produce an image of men that is white, middle-class, and heterosexual. As Ned Lyttleton has pointed out, "an analysis of masculinity that does not deal with the contradictions of power imbalances that exist between men themselves will be limited and biased, and its limits and biases will be concealed under the blanket of shared male privilege."[4] A series of masculinities becomes subsumed under one form of masculinity that becomes "masculinity." As a result, socially organized power relations among and between men based on sexuality, race, class, or age have been neglected. These power relations are major dividing lines between men that have to be addressed if progressive organizing among men is to encompass the needs and experiences of all men. The men's movement has reached a turning point.[5] It has to choose whether it is simply a movement for men's rights—defending men's rights to be human too—or whether it will deepen the challenge to an interlocked web of oppression: sexism, heterosexism, racism, and class exploitation. We have to choose between a vision of a world in which men are more sensitive and human but are still "real" men at the top of the social order, and a radically new vision

Reprinted from *Beyond Patriarchy: Essays by Men on Pleasure, Power, and Change*, Michael Kaufman, ed. Toronto: Oxford University Press, 1987.

that entails the transformation of masculinity and sexuality and the challenging of other forms of domination.

In developing this radical vision—radical in the sense of getting to the roots of the problem—the politics of gay liberation and the politics of lesbian feminism are important. So too are the experiences of those of us who have been made into outsiders, people labeled "faggot," "queer," or "dyke" who have reclaimed these stigmatized labels as ways of naming experiences of the world and as weapons of resistance to heterosexual hegemony. The struggle against the institutionalized social norm of heterosexuality opens up the door to other kinds of social and personal change.

GAY LIBERATION VERSUS HETEROSEXUAL PRIVILEGE

In our society heterosexuality as an institutionalized norm has become an important means of social regulation, enforced by laws, police practices, family and social policies, schools, and the mass media. In its historical development heterosexuality is tied up with the institution of masculinity, which gives social and cultural meaning to biological male anatomy, associating it with masculinity, aggressiveness, and an "active" sexuality. "Real" men are intrinsically heterosexual; gay men, therefore, are not real men.

While gay men share with straight men the privilege of being in a dominant position in relation to women, we are at the same time in a subordinate position in the institution of heterosexuality. As a result, gay men's lives and experiences are not the same as those of heterosexual men. For instance, while we share with straight men the economic benefits of being men in a patriarchal society, we do not participate as regularly in the everyday interpersonal subordination of women in the realms of sexuality and violence. Although, like other men, we have more social opportunities, we are not accepted as open gays in corporate boardrooms or in many jobs, sports, and professions. We can still be labeled

"national security risks" and sick, deviant, or abnormal. Consequently, gay men experience a rupture between the presumably universal categories of heterosexual experience and their own particular experience of the world, a rupture that denies many of our experiences; for gay men exist in social situations that allow us to see aspects of life, desire, sexuality, and love that cannot be seen by heterosexual men.[6]

Gay men have had to question the institution of masculinity—which associates masculinity with heterosexuality—in our daily lives. We have experimented with and developed new ways of organizing our sexual lives and our love and support relations, of receiving and giving pleasure. Heterosexual men interested in seriously transforming the fabric of their lives have to stop seeing gay liberation as simply a separate issue for some men that has nothing to say to them. They should begin to ask what the experience of gay men can bring into view for them. As we break the silence and move beyond liberal tolerance toward gays and lesbians, we can begin to see how "queer baiting" and the social taboo against pleasure, sex, and love between men serves to keep all men in line, defining what proper masculinity is for us. Gay liberation suggests that heterosexuality is not the only natural form of sexuality but has instead been socially and culturally made the "normal" sexual practice and identity. As the Kinsey Institute studies suggested, the actual flux of human desire cannot be easily captured in rigid sexual categories. Many men who define themselves as straight have had sexual experiences with other men.[7] This has demonstrated the contradictions that can exist between our actual experiences and desires and the rigid social categories that are used to divide normal from deviant and that imply that any participation in homosexual activity automatically defines one as a homosexual.

Breaking the silence surrounding homosexuality requires challenging heterosexism and heterosexual privilege. Lesbian-feminist Charlotte Bunch once explained to heterosexual women that the best way to find out what heterosexual privilege is all about is to go about for a few days as an open lesbian:

> *What makes heterosexuality work is heterosexual privilege—and if you don't have a sense of what privilege is, I suggest that you go home and announce to everybody that you know—a roommate, your family, the people you work with—everywhere that you go—that you're a queer. Try being a queer for a week.*[8]

This statement could also be applied to the situation of straight men, and any heterosexual man can easily imagine the discomfort, ridicule, and fear he might experience, how his "coming out" would disrupt "normal" relations at work and with his family. Such experiences are the substance of gay oppression that make our lives different from those of straight men. Gay men in this heterosexist society are labeled with many terms of abuse. Young boys hurl the labels "queer," "fag," or "cocksucker" at each other before they know what the words mean. As we grow up we are denied images of men loving men and any models for our lives outside heterosexuality. In the United States, the age of consent varies from state to state, usually from sixteen to eighteen, although in some states all homosexual acts remain technically illegal. Under Canadian and British law males under twenty-one are denied the right to have sexual relations with other boys and men. Many members of the medical and psychiatric professions still practice psychological and social terrorism against us by trying to adjust us to fit the norm. We are excluded as open lesbians and gay men from most activities and institutions. When the mass media does cover us they use stereotypes or other means to show us to be sick, immoral, indecent, as some sort of social problem or social menace, or they trivialize us as silly and frivolous.[9] The police continue to raid our bookstores and seize our magazines. In 1983–6, the media fostered fear and hatred against gay men by associating all gay men with AIDS. Such media stories shift and mold public opinion against us. On city streets we are often violently attacked by gangs of "queerbashers." Most countries deny lesbians and gay men the basic civil and human rights, leaving us open to arbitrary firings and evictions.

A variety of sexual laws are used to regulate and control gay men's sexual and community lives. Police in many cities have a policy of systematically entrapping and harassing gays. In recent years hundreds of men across North America have been arrested and often entrapped by the police in washrooms and parks. These campaigns—especially in small towns and cities—and the associated media attention have torn apart the lives of these men, many of whom define themselves as heterosexual and are married with families.

In fact, the society in which we have all grown up is so profoundly heterosexist that even many gays have internalized the social hatred against us in forms of "self-oppression."[10] This fear keeps many of us isolated and silent, hiding our sexuality. One of the first steps in combating this self-oppression is to reject this denial of our love and sexuality by affirming our existence and pride publicly. Assertions that "gay is good" and affirmations of gay pride are the beginning of our resistance to heterosexual hegemony on the individual and social levels.

THE HISTORY OF SEXUALITY

In addressing the matter of gay and lesbian oppression, we have to ask where this oppression has come from. How did heterosexuality come to be the dominant social relation? How did homosexuality come to be seen as a perverse outcast form of sexuality? If we can answer those questions, we can begin to see how we could break down the institution of heterosexuality and its control over our lives.

As a result of numerous cross-cultural and historical studies that have demonstrated that there is no natural or normal sexuality, we can no longer see sex as simply natural or biologically given. Our biological, erotic, and sexual capabilities are only the precondition for the organization of the social and cultural forms of meaning and activity that compose human sexuality. Our biological capabilities are transformed and mediated culturally, producing sexuality as a social need and relation. As Gayle Rubin explained, each social system has its own "sex/gender system" which

> is the set of arrangements by which a society transforms biological sexuality into products of human activity, and in which these transformed sexual needs are satisfied.[11]

Recent historical studies have challenged the assumed natural categories of heterosexuality and homosexuality themselves.[12] Gay, lesbian, and feminist historians have expanded our understanding of sexual meaning and identity, contesting the dominant ways in which sexuality has been discussed and viewed in our society.[13] The dominant perspective for looking at sexuality is what has been called the "repression hypothesis," which assumes that there is a natural sexuality that is repressed to maintain social and moral order. Many leftists argue that sexuality is repressed by the ruling class—to maintain class society because of capitalism's need for the family and a docile work force. This interpretation was popularized in the writings and activities of Wilhelm Reich,[14] who called for the end of sexual repression through the liberation of natural sexuality, which was for him completely heterosexual. Variations of this repression theory, and its corresponding call for the liberation of natural sexuality, have inspired sexual liberationist politics, including much of the gay liberation movement, which sees homosexuality as a natural sexuality that simply needs to be released from social repression.

The experience by women of the male sexual (i.e., heterosexual) revolution of the sixties and seventies has led much of the feminist movement to a more complex understanding of sexuality than simple theories of sexual repression. Feminism has exposed the contradictions in a sexual revolution that increased women's ability to seek sexual satisfaction but only within male-dominated heterosexual relations. Feminism has also begun to explore how sexuality and social power are bound together and how sexuality has been socially organized in male-dominated forms in this society.[15] This view of sex opens up new possibilities for sexual politics—our sexual lives are no longer seen as divorced from human and social activity but as the results of human praxis (the unity of thought and activity). Sexual relations are therefore changeable and are themselves the site of personal and social struggles. We can then begin to question the natural appearance of such sexual categories as heterosexual and homosexual and to make visible the human activity that is involved in the making of sexuality. This opens up a struggle, not for the liberation of some inherent sexuality that just has to be freed from the bonds of capitalism or repressive laws, but for a much broader challenge to the ways our sexual lives are defined, regulated, and controlled. It opens up questions about the very making and remaking of sex, desire, and pleasure.

Enter the Homosexual

The historical emergence of the "homosexual" required a number of social preconditions, which can be summarized as three interrelated social processes: first, the rise of capitalist social relations, which created the necessary social spaces for the emergence of homosexual cultures;[16] second, the regime of sexuality that categorized and labeled homosexuality and sexual "deviations"; and third, the activities, cultural production, and resistance to the oppression of men in these same-sex desire-based cultures.

The rise of capitalism in Europe between the fifteenth and nineteenth centuries separated the rural household economy from the new industrial economy and undermined the interdependent different-sex household economy. The working class was made, and made itself, in the context of this industrialization, urbanization, and commercialization. This separation of "work" from the household and the development of wage labor meant that it became possible for more men in the cities to live outside the family, earning a wage and living as boarders. Later they would be able to eat at restaurants or taverns and rent their own accommodation. This created the opportunities for some men to start organizing what would become, through a process of development and struggle, the beginnings of a homosexual culture, from the eighteenth century on.[17]

A regime of sexuality has emerged as part of a series of social struggles over the last two centuries. The transition from feudalism to capitalism in the western countries meant a transition in the way kinship and sexual and class relations were organized. The new ruling class was no longer able to understand itself or organize its social life simply through the old feudal ties of blood or lineage.[18] New forms of family and state formation led to new forms of self-understanding, class consciousness, and notions of moral and social order. Sexuality emerged as an autonomous sphere separate from household production. A proper, respectable sexual and gender identity became an essential feature of the class unity of the bourgeoisie. This process is linked to the emergence of the ideology of individual identity. The regime of sexual definitions was first applied to the bodies of the bourgeoisie itself through its educational and medical systems and through the sexological knowledge that was generated by the new professional groups of doctors and psychiatrists and that served to draw a boundary between bourgeois respectability and the "bestial" sexual practices of the outcast poor and "lower orders." These norms of sex and gender definition helped organize the relations of the bourgeois family and its sexual morality.

Later these same norms of sexual identity and morality were used against the urban working class and poor, who were considered a threat to social order by middle-class and state agencies. The working class both resisted this enforcement of social norms and at the same time adopted them as its own. The male-dominated "respectable" sections of the working class developed their own norms of family and sexual life that incorporated the socially dominant norms of masculinity, femininity, and reproductive heterosexuality. The uneven and at times contradictory development of sexual identity in different classes, genders, races, and nationalities is a subject that remains to be more fully explored.

In the big cities sexuality becomes an object to be studied and a terrain for the expanding male-dominated fields of medicine, psychiatry, and sexology. Various forms of sexual behavior were categorized, classified, and ranked, with heterosexuality on the top and homosexuality and lesbianism near the bottom. The norm and the perversions were defined, separating normal and abnormal behavior. In this context sex in the ruling discourses became the truth of our being.[19]

The heterosexual man was no longer simply carrying out the types of activities he had to carry out in the sexual divisions of labor, or the activities that would lead to the reproduction of the species; rather he had become someone with a particular erotic, sexual, and gender identity that linked his masculinity to an exclusively heterosexual way of life. The heterosexual and the homosexual emerged in relation to each other as part of the same historical and social process of struggle and negotiation.

Men who engaged in sexual relations with other men in this emerging regime of sexuality (and who were affected by the ideology of individualism) began to organize their lives around their sexuality and to see themselves as separate and different from other men. They fought against campaigns by religious fundamentalists and the police who wished to curtail their activities.[20] In the last century, the emergence of sexology, increased police regulation of sexual behavior, and the passing of laws against sexual offenses combined with the development of these same-sex desire-based cultures to make the new social experience and social category of homosexuality.

The term homosexual itself was not devised until 1869, when Károly Mária Benkert, a Hungarian, coined the term in an appeal to the government to keep its laws out of peoples lives.[21] The category of homosexuality was originally elaborated by some homosexuals themselves, mostly professional men it seems, in order to name their "difference" and in order to protect themselves from police and legal prohibitions. The word was taken up by the various agencies of social regulation from the medical profession to the police and courts. Homosexuality was defined as an abnormality, a sickness, and a symptom of degeneracy. The efforts of medical and legal experts

> were chiefly concerned with whether the disgusting breed of perverts could be physically identified for courts and whether they should be held legally responsible for their acts.[22]

An early Canadian reference—in 1898—to same-sex "perversion" among men by a Dr. Ezra Stafford (which refers to the work of Krafft-Ebing, one of the grandfathers of sexology) linked sex between men with prostitution in a theory of degeneracy. Stafford wrote that these things "may lead to the tragedy of our species."[23] This connection between homosexuality and prostitution as stigmatized social and sexual practices continued even to England's Wolfenden report of 1957, which linked these topics, and it continues to this day, in, for example, the use by the Canadian police of bawdy-house legislation, originally intended to deal with houses of female prostitutes, against gay men.

Simultaneously the needs of capitalism for a skilled labor force and a continuing supply of wage-laborers led to an emphasis on the heterosexual nuclear family. The rise of modern militarism and the scramble for colonies by the western powers led to demands for a larger and healthier supply of cannon fodder at the beginning of the twentieth century. An intensification of military discipline resulted in stiff prohibitions against homosexuality, which was seen as subversive of discipline and hierarchy in the armed forces. As a result, reproductive heterosexuality was reinforced for men, and motherhood further institutionalized for women.[24]

The category of the male homosexual emerged in sexology as an "invert" and was associated with some form of effeminacy and "gender inversion." A relation between gender dysfunction and abnormal sexuality was established:

> As defined by the ancient civil or canonical codes, sodomy was a category of forbidden acts. . . . The nineteenth century homosexual became a personage, a past, a case history, and a childhood, in addition to being a type of life, a life form, and a morphology, with an indiscreet anatomy and possibly a mysterious physiology. Nothing that went into his total composition was unaffected by his sexuality. . . . Homosexuality appeared as one of the forms of sexuality when it was transposed from the practice of sodomy onto a kind of interior androgyny, a hermaphrodism of the soul. The sodomite had been a temporary aberration; the homosexual was now a species.[25]

The categorization of "perverse" sexual types also provided a basis for resistance. Sexual categorization, as Foucault puts it,

> also made possible the formation of a "reverse" discourse: homosexuality began to speak on its own behalf, to demand that its legitimacy or "naturality" be acknowledged, often in the same vocabulary, using the same categories by which it was radically disqualified.[26]

Homosexuals themselves used this category to name their experiences, to articulate their differences and cultures, moving this category in a more progressive direction. There has been a century-long struggle over the meaning of homosexuality that has involved sexologists, the police, lawyers, psychiatrists, and homosexuals, a struggle that continues today. The regime of sexuality and the specification of different sexual categories in an attempt to buttress the emerging norm of heterosexuality have unwittingly also provided the basis for homosexual experiences, identities, and cultures. Through these experiences a series of new social and sexual needs, human capacities, and pleasures have been created among a group of men. This homosexual experience, along with the slightly later emergence of a distinct lesbian experience,[27] and the feminist movement have created the basis for contemporary challenges to the hegemony of heterosexuality.

Enter Gay Liberation and the Gay Community

Recent social changes in the western capitalist countries have put in question the patriarchal, gender, and sexual relations established during the last century. A prolonged crisis in sexual and gender relations and in the meaning of sexuality has occurred. The feminist and gay liberation movements, for example, have challenged the relegation of sexual relations and particularly "deviant" forms of sexuality to the socially defined private realm, subverting the public/private categories that have been used to regulate our sexual lives. The development of contraceptive and reproductive technologies has made it more and more possible to separate heterosexual pleasure and procreation, although the struggle continues about who will have access to, and control over, this technology. The expansion of consumer markets and advertising in the post-war period has led to an increasing drawing of sexuality and sexual images into the marketplace and the public realm.[28] This increasing public visibility of sexual images and sexual cultures has led to objections from those who would wish to reprivatize sexuality, in particular its "deviant" strains. And feminists have challenged the patriarchal values that are visible in much advertising and heterosexual male pornography.

The social ferment of the sixties—particularly the civil rights, black power, and feminist movements—combined with earlier forms of homosexual activism and the expansion of the gay commercial scene and culture to produce the gay liberation movement, which erupted in 1969 in the Stonewall Riot in New York City.[29] The movement developed a new, positive identity that has served as a basis for our resistance to heterosexual hegemony. The movement's most sig-

nificant achievements were its contesting of the psychiatric definition of homosexuality as a mental illness and its creation of a culture and community that have transformed the lives of hundreds of thousands of men and women. As usual in a patriarchal society, many more opportunities have opened up for men than for women.

In a challenge to the "universality" of heterosexuality, gays have affirmed that gay is just as good as straight, calling on lesbians and gay men to affirm themselves and their sexualities. This has challenged the gender and social policies of the state, suggesting that sexual activity does not have to be solely for reproduction, but can also be for play, pleasure, love, and support, and questioning the very right of the state to regulate people's sexual lives. We have affirmed our right to sexual self-determination and control over our own bodies and sexuality and have affirmed this right for others as well.

The growth of a visible gay community and the emergence of gay streets and commercial areas in many big cities have led to a reaction from the police, conservative political parties, and the new right. These groups fear the breakdown of "traditional" sexual and family relations, which they associate with social and moral order, and see the challenge that gay liberation presents to heterosexual hegemony as a threat to the ways in which their lives and institutions are organized. They want lesbians and gay men out of public view and back in the closets, threatening our very existence as a public community.

In a sense the gay ghetto is both a playground and a potential concentration camp. While it provides people a place to meet and to explore and develop aspects of their lives and sexuality, it can also separate people from the rest of the population in a much larger closet that can be isolated and contained. The ghetto can tend to obscure the experiences gay men share with other men in their society. Locking people into the new categorization of gays as minority group or community may weaken the critique of sex and gender relations in society as a whole. As Altman explains, the "ethnic homosexual" has emerged, "the widespread recognition of a distinct cultural category which appears to be pressing for the same sort of 'equality,' in Western society as do ethnic minorities."[30] However, lesbians and gay men are not born into a minority group, but like heterosexuals assume a sexual identity through social and psychological processes.[31] Gays and lesbians are not only a minority group but also an oppressed and denied sexuality. The position that gays are simply a new minority group can deflect our challenges to the dominant way of life.

In challenging heterosexuality as the social norm gays have brought into question aspects of the institutions of masculinity and male privilege. Over the last decade images of gay men have shifted from the effeminacy of the "gender invert" to the new macho and clone looks that have dominated the gay men's community. This imagery challenges the previous stereotypes of homosexuals that associated our sexuality with gender nonconformity and has asserted that we can be both homosexual and "masculine" at the same time.[32] In defining ourselves as masculine we have had to make use of and transform the existing images of straight masculinity we find around us. These new images challenge heterosexual norms that associate "deviant" gender stereotypes with sexual "deviancy," for instance effeminacy with male homosexuality, but at the same time also tend to create new standards and stereotypes of what gay men are supposed to be like. These images and styles themselves continue to be imprisoned within the polarities of gender dichotomy. While gay men often believe we have freed ourselves from the social organization of gender, what we have actually done is exchange "gender inversion" for a situation where homosexuality can be organized through "normal" gender identification. This assertion of masculinized imagery can to some extent lead us away from the critique of the institution of masculinity and its effects in our lives and persuade us that gender is no longer a problem for gay men.

It is ironic that some forms of resistance to past ways in which we were stigmatized can serve to accommodate us to aspects of the existing order of things. It is in this context that some of the challenges to masculinity and gender norms by straight men fighting against sexism will also be valuable to gay men. To be successful, gay liberation must challenge not only the institutionalization of heterosexuality as a social norm but also the institution of masculinity.

GAY LIBERATION AND THE RULING REGIME OF SEX

Gay liberation has emerged from the contradictions within the ruling system of sexual regulation and definition. It is fundamentally a struggle to transform the norms and definitions of sexual regulation. Gay liberation strives for the recognition of homosexuality as socially equal to the dominant social institution of heterosexuality. Yet as Weeks suggests,

> *the strategic aim of the gay liberation movement must be not simply the validation of the rights of a minority within a heterosexual majority but the challenge to all the rigid categorizations of sexuality. . . . The struggle for sexual self-determination is a struggle in the end for control over our bodies. To establish this control we must escape from those ideologies and categorizations which imprison us within the existing order.*[33]

The struggle to transform our sexual norms and to end the control of the institution of heterosexuality over our lives holds out the possibility of beginning to disengage us from the ruling regime of sex and gender. As Foucault suggested, movements that have been called sexual liberation movements, including gay liberation, are

> *movements that start with sexuality, with the apparatus of sexuality in the midst of which they are caught and which make it function to the limit; but, at the same time, they are in motion relative to it, disengaging themselves and surmounting them.*[34]

The struggle for gay liberation can be seen as a process of transformation. The assertion that gay is just as good as straight—which lies at the heart of gay liberation—is formally within the present regime of sexual categorization, for it still separates gay from straight as rigid categories and assigns value to sexuality, thus mirroring the limitations of the current sexual regime. However, the gay liberation movement operates both within *and* against this regime of sexual regulation. In asserting equal value for homosexuality and lesbianism, it begins to turn the ruling practices of sexual hierarchy on their head. Resistance begins within the present regime of sexual definitions, but it begins to shift the sexual boundaries that they have defined, opening up the possibility of transcending their limitations. By naming our specific experiences of the world, gay liberation provides the basis for a social and political struggle that can transform, defy, cut across, and break down the ruling regime of sex and gender.

The gay and lesbian communities, like other oppressed social groups, oscillate between resistance and accommodation to oppression. This is a struggle on two closely interrelated fronts. First, the gay community itself needs to strengthen cultures of resistance by building on sexual and cultural traditions that question gender norms and the relegation of erotic life to the state-defined private sphere. This will involve challenging the internalization and reproduction of sexism, racism, ageism, and class divisions within the gay community, as well as building alliances with other social groups fighting these forms of domination. Secondly, it requires a struggle outside the gay and lesbian communities for the defense of a community under attack by the police, government, and media. A key part of this strategy would be campaigning for new social policies that uproot heterosexuality as *the* social norm.

OPENING UP EROTIC CHOICES FOR EVERYONE

In developing a radical perspective we need to draw on the insights of lesbian feminism about the social power of heterosexuality and also on the historical perspectives provided by the new critical gay history, which reveals the social and historical process of the organization of heterosexual hegemony and the present system of sexual regulation more generally. These understandings create the basis for alliances between feminists, lesbians, gay liberationists, anti-sexist men, and other groups against the institution of heterosexuality, which lies at the root of the social oppression of women, lesbians, and gays. This alliance would contest the hegemony of heterosexuality in the legal system, state policies, in forms of family organization, and in the churches, unions, and other social bodies. The struggle would be for women, gays, and others to gain control over our bodies and sexuality and to begin to define our own eroticism and sexuality. A fundamental aspect of such an approach would be the elaboration and exploration of the experiences and visions of those of us living outside institutionalized heterosexuality.

Proposals for new and different ways of living (including collective and nonsexist ways of rearing children) are particularly vital since the new right and moral conservative in their various incarnations are taking advantage of people's fears about changes in family organization and sexual mores to campaign in support of patriarchal and heterosexist social norms. The defense of a male-dominated heterosexuality is not only central to the policies of the new right and moral conservatives regarding feminism and gay liberation, but is a central theme of their racial and class politics as well.[35] The progressive movement's failure to deal with people's real fears, concerns, and hopes regarding sexual and gender politics is an important reason why right-wing groups are able to gain support. Feminism, gay liberation, and all progressive movements will have to articulate a vision that will allow us to move forward beyond the confines of institutionalized heterosexuality.

Gay liberation enables heterosexual men who question heterosexism to contribute to this new social vision. The issues raised by gay liberation must be addressed by all men interested in fundamental change because heterosexism limits and restricts the lives of all men. This challenge will only be effective, however, if heterosexual privilege is challenged in daily life and in social institutions. This could help begin the long struggle to disentangle heterosexual desire from the confines of institutionalized masculinity and heterosexuality. Together we could begin to redefine and remake masculinity and sexuality. If sexuality is socially produced, then heterosexuality itself can be transformed and redefined and its pleasures and desires separated from the social relations of power and domination. Gay liberation can allow all men to challenge gender and sexual norms and redefine gender and sex for ourselves in alliance with feminism; it can allow all men to explore and create different forms of sexual pleasures in our lives. This redefining of masculinity and sexuality will also help destroy the anxieties and insecurities of many straight men who try so hard to be "real men." But the success of this undertaking depends on the ability to develop alternative visions and experiences that will help all people understand how their lives could be organized without heterosexuality as the institutionalized social norm. Such a goal is a radically transformed society in which everyone will be able to gain control of his or her own body, desires, and life.

ACKNOWLEDGMENTS

Special thanks to Ned Lyttleton, Brian Conway, and Bob Gardner for comments on this paper. For more general comments on matters that pertain to topics addressed in this paper I am indebted to Varda Burstyn, Philip Corrigan, Bert Hansen, Michael Kaufman, Ian Lumsden, Dorothy E. Smith, George Smith, Mariana Valverde, and Lorna Weir.

NOTES

1. See G. K. Lehne, "Homophobia Among Men," in Deborah David and Robert Brannon, *The Forty-Nine Percent Majority* (Reading, Mass: Addison-Wesley, 1976), 78.

2. On the notion of institutionalized heterosexuality see Charlotte Bunch, "Not For Lesbians Only," Quest 11, no. 2 (Fall 1975), also see Adrienne Rich, "Compulsory Heterosexuality And Lesbian Existence," in Snitow, Stansell and Thompson, eds., *Powers of Desire: The Politics of Sexuality* (New York: Monthly Review Press, 1983): 177–205.

3. Joe Interrante, "Dancing Along the Precipice: The Men's Movement in the '80s," *Radical America* 15, no. 5 (September–October 1981): 54.

4. Ned Lyttleton, "Men's Liberation, Men Against Sexism and Major Dividing Lines," *Resources for Feminist Research* 12, no. 4 (December/January 1983/1984): 33. Several discussions with Ned Lyttleton were very useful in clarifying my ideas in this section and throughout this paper.

5. Interrante, *op cit.*, 54.

6. For further elaboration see my *The Regulation of Desire* (Montreal: Black Rose, 1986).

7. See Kinsey, Pomeroy, and Martin, *Sexual Behavior in the Human Male* (Philadelphia: W. B. Saunders, 1948) and Mary McIntosh, "The Homosexual Role," in Plummer, ed., *The Making Of The Modern Homosexual* (London: Hutchinson, 1981), 38–43.

8. Bunch, "Not For Lesbians Only."

9. See Frank Pearce, "How to be Immoral and Ill, Pathetic and Dangerous all at the same time: Mass Media and the Homosexual," in Cohen and Young, eds., *The Manufacture of News: Deviance, Social Problems and the Mass Media* (London: Constable, 1973), 284–301.

10. See Andrew Hodges and David Hutter. *With Downcast Gays, Aspects of Homosexual Self-Oppression* (Toronto: Pink Triangle Press, 1977).

11. Gayle Rubin, "The Traffic In Women: Notes on the Political Economy of Sex," in Reiter, eds., *Towards An Anthropology Of Women* (New York: Monthly Review Press, 1975), 159. I prefer the use of sex and gender relations to sex/gender system since the notion of system tends to conflate questions of sexuality and gender and suggests that sex/gender relations are a separate system from other social relations rather than an integral aspect of them.

12. See Joe Interrante, "From Homosexual to Gay to?: Recent Work in Gay History," in *Radical America* 15, no. 6 (November–December 1981): Martha

Vicinus, "Sexuality and Power: A Review of Current Work in the History of Sexuality," *Feminist Studies* 8, no. 1 (Spring 1982): 133–56; and Robert A. Padgug, "Sexual Matters: On Conceptualizing Sexuality In History," *Radical History Review*, "Sexuality in History" Issue, no. 20 (Spring/Summer 1979): 3–23.

13. See for instance Michel Foucault, *The History Of Sexuality* (New York: Vintage, 1980), vol. 1, *An Introduction*; Jeffrey Weeks, *Sex, Politics and Society: The Regulation of Sexuality since 1800* (London: Hutchinson, 1981); and Jonathan Ned Katz, *Gay/Lesbian Almanac* (New York: Harper and Row, 1983). For recent feminist explorations of sexuality see Snitow, Stansell and Thompson, *Powers of Desire* (New York: Monthly Review, 1983); Carol Vance, ed., *Pleasure and Danger, Exploring Female Sexuality* (Boston: Routledge and Kegan Paul, 1984); Rosalind Coward, *Female Desire, Women's Sexuality Today* (London: Routledge and Kegan Paul, 1984); and Mariana Valverde, *Sex, Power and Pleasure* (Toronto: Women's Press, 1985).

14. See Wilhelm Reich, *The Sexual Revolution* (New York: Straus and Giroux, 1974) and *Sex-Pol. Essays, 1929–1934* (New York: Vintage, 1972).

15. Unfortunately, over the last few years some anti-pornography feminists have suggested that sexuality is only a realm of danger for women, obscuring how it can also be a realm of pleasure. Some anti-porn feminists have been used by state agencies in attempts to clamp down on sexually explicit material including sexual material for gay men and lesbians. See Vance, *Pleasure and Danger*; Varda Burstyn, ed., *Women Against Censorship* (Vancouver and Toronto: Douglas and McIntyre, 1985); and Varda Burstyn, "Anatomy of a Moral Panic" and Gary Kinsman, "The Porn Debate," *Fuse 3*, no. 1 (Summer 1984).

16. On this see the work of John D'Emilio, for instances his "Capitalism and Gay Identity," in Snitow, Stansell and Thompson, eds., *Powers of Desire*, 100–13, and his *Sexual Politics, Sexual Communities* (Chicago: University of Chicago Press, 1983).

17. See Randolph Trumbach, "London's Sodomites: Homosexual Behaviour and Western Culture in the 18th Century," *Journal of Social History*, Fall 1977, 1–33; Mary McIntosh, "The Homosexual Role," in Plummer, ed., *The Making of The Modern Homosexual*; Alan Bray, *Homosexuality in Renaissance England* (London: Gay Men's Press, 1982); and Jeffrey Weeks, *Sex, Politics and Society*.

18. See Foucault, *The History of Sexuality*, vol. 1 and Kinsman, *The Regulation of Desire*.

19. This idea comes from the work of Foucault.

20. See Bray, *Homosexuality in Renaissance England* for the activities of the Society for the Reformation of Morals, which campaigned against same-sex desire-based networks in the early eighteenth century.

21. John Lauritsen and David Thorstad, *The Early Homosexual Rights Movement* (New York: Times Change Press, 1974), 6.

22. Arno Karlen, *Sexuality and Homosexuality* (New York: W. W. Norton, 1971), 185.

23. Ezra Hurlburt Stafford, "Perversion," the *Canadian Journal of Medicine and Surgery* 3, no. 4 (April 1898).

24. On this see Anna Davin, "Imperialism and Motherhood," *History Workshop*, no. 5 (Spring 1978).

25 Foucault, *op. cit.*, 43.

26. *Ibid.*, 101.

27. See Lillian Faderman, *Surpassing The Love Of Men* (New York: William Morrow, 1981); Christina Simmons, "Companionate Marriage and the Lesbian Threat," in Frontiers 4, no. 3 (Fall 1979); Martha Vicinus, "Sexuality and Power": and Ann Ferguson, "Patriarchy, Sexual Identity, and the Sexual Revolution," *Signs* 7, no. 1 (Fall 1981): 158–72.

28. See Gary Kinsman, "Porn/Censor Wars And The Battlefields of Sex," in *Issues of Censorship* (Toronto: A Space, 1985), 31–9.

29. See John D'Emilio, *Sexual Politics, Sexual Communities*.

30. Dennis Altman, "What Changed in the Seventies?," in Gay Left Collective, eds., *Homosexuality, Power and Politics* (London: Allison and Busby, 1980), 61.

31. One prejudice that is embodied in sexual legislation and social policies is the myth that lesbians and gay men are a special threat to young people and that gay men are "child molesters." Most studies show, on the contrary, that more than 90 percent of sexual assaults on young people are committed by heterosexual men and often within the family or home. Breines and Gordon state that, "approximately 92 percent of the victims are female and 97 percent of the assailants are males." See Wini Breines and Linda Gordon, "The New Scholarship on Family Violence," *Signs* 8, no. 3 (Spring 1983); 522. Also see Elizabeth Wilson, *What Is To Be Done About Violence Against Women* (London: Penguin, 1983), particularly 117–34. We have to eliminate special age restrictions on the right to par-

ticipate in consensual lesbian and gay sex so that lesbian and gay young people can express their desires and instead challenge the principal source of violence against children and young people—the patriarchal family and straight-identified men. We have to propose changes in family relations and schooling and alternative social policies that would allow young people to take more control over their own lives, to get support in fighting unwanted sexual attention *and* to be able to participate in consensual sexual activity.

32. See John Marshall, "Pansies, Perverts and Macho Men: Changing Conceptions of Male Homosexuality" and Greg Blachford, "Male Dominance In The Gay World," in Plummer, ed., *The Making of The Modern Homosexual*; and also Seymour Kleinberg's article elsewhere in this volume for a different approach.

33. Jeffrey Weeks, "Capitalism and the Organization of Sex," Gay Left Collective, eds., *Homosexuality, Power and Politics* 19–20.

34. Michel Foucault, "Power and Sex," *Telos*, no. 32 (Summer 1977): 152–61.

35. See Allen Hunter, "In the Wings, New Right Ideology and Organization," *Radical America* 15, no. 1–2 (Spring 1981): 127–38.

CHICANO MEN:
A CARTOGRAPHY OF HOMOSEXUAL IDENTITY AND BEHAVIOR

TOMÁS ALMAGUER

The sexual behavior and sexual identity of Chicano male homosexuals is prinicipally shaped by two distinct sexual systems, each of which attaches different significance and meaning to homosexuality. Both the European-American and Mexican/Latin-American systems have their own unique ensemble of sexual meanings, categories for sexual actors, and scripts that circumscribe sexual behavior. Each system also maps the human body in different ways by placing different values on homosexual erotic zones. The primary socialization of Chicanos into Mexican/Latin-American cultural norms, combined with their simultaneous socialization into the dominant European-American culture, largely structures how they negotiate sexual identity questions and confer meaning to homosexual behavior during adolescence and adulthood. Chicano men who embrace a "gay" identity (based on the European-American sexual system) must reconcile this sexual identity with their primary socialization into a Latino culture that does not recognize such a construction: there is no cultural equivalent to the modern "gay man" in the Mexican/Latin-American sexual system.

How does socialization into these different sexual systems shape the crystallization of their sexual identities and the meaning they give to their homosexuality? Why does only a segment of homosexually active Chicano men identify as "gay"? Do these men primarily consider themselves *Chicano* gay men (who retain primary emphasis on their ethnicity) or *gay* Chicanos (who place primary emphasis on their sexual preference)? How do Chicano homosexuals structure their sexual conduct, especially the sexual roles and relationships into which they enter? Are they structured along lines of power/dominance firmly rooted in a patriarchal Mexican culture that privileges men over women and the masculine over the feminine? Or do they reflect the ostensibly more egalitarian sexual norms and practices of the European-American sexual system? These are among the numerous questions that this paper problematizes and explores.

We know little about how Chicano men negotiate and contest a modern gay identity with aspects of Chicano culture drawing upon more Mexican/Latin-American configurations of sexual meaning. Unlike the rich literature on the Chicana/Latina lesbian experience, there is a paucity of writings on Chicano gay men.[1] There does not exist any scholarly literature on this topic other than one unpublished study addressing this issue as a secondary concern (Carrillo and Maiorana). The extant literature consists primarily of semi-autobiographical, literary texts by authors such as John Rechy, Arturo Islas, and

An edited version of the original article appeared in *differences: A Journal of Feminist Cultural Studies* 3:2(1991), pp. 75–100. Reprinted with permission. I gratefully acknowledge the valuable comments on an earlier version of this article by Jackie Goldsby, David Halperin, Teresa de Lauretis, Bob Blauner, Carla Trujillo, Patricia Zavella, Velia Garcia, and Ramón Gutiérrez.

Richard Rodriguez.[2] Unlike the writings on Chicana lesbianism, however, these works fail to discuss directly the cultural dissonance that Chicano homosexual men confront in reconciling their primary socialization into Chicano family life with the sexual norms of the dominant culture. They offer little to our understanding of how these men negotiate the different way these cultural systems stigmatize homosexuality and how they incorporate these messages into their adult sexual practices.

In the absence of such discussion or more direct ethnographic research to draw upon, we must turn elsewhere for insights into the lives of Chicano male homosexuals. One source of such knowledge is the perceptive anthropological research on homosexuality in Mexico and Latin America, which has direct relevance for our understanding of how Chicano men structure and culturally interpret their homosexual experiences. The other, ironically, is the writings of Chicana lesbians who have openly discussed intimate aspects of their sexual behavior and reflected upon sexual identity issues. How they have framed these complex sexual issues has major import for our understanding of Chicano male homosexuality. Thus, the first section of this paper examines certain features of the Mexican/Latin-American sexual system which offer clues to the ensemble of cultural meanings that Chicano homosexuals give to their sexual practices. The second section examines the autobiographical writings of Chicana lesbian writer Cherríe Moraga. I rely upon her candid discussion of her sexual development as ethnographic evidence for further problematizing the Chicano homosexual experience in the United States.

THE CARTOGRAPHY OF DESIRE IN THE MEXICAN/LATIN-AMERICAN SEXUAL SYSTEM

American anthropologists have recently turned their attention to the complex meaning of homosexuality in Mexico and elsewhere in Latin America. Ethnographic research by Joseph M. Carrier, Roger N. Lancaster, Richard Parker, Barry D. Adam, and Clark L. Taylor has documented the inapplicability of Western European and North American categories of sexual meaning in the Latin American context. Since the Mexican/Chicano population in the U.S. shares basic features of these Latin cultural patterns, it is instructive to examine this sexual system closely and to explore its impact on the sexuality of homosexual Chicano men and women.

The rules that define and stigmatize homosexuality in Mexican culture operate under a logic and a discursive practice different from those of the bourgeois sexual system that shaped the emergence of contemporary gay/lesbian identity in the U.S. Each sexual system confers meaning to homosexuality by giving different weight to the two fundamental features of human sexuality that Freud delineated in the *Three Essays on the Theory of Sexuality*: sexual object choice and sexual aim. The structured meaning of homosexuality in the European-American context rests on the sexual object-choice one makes—i.e., the biological sex of the person toward whom sexual activity is directed. The Mexican/Latin-American sexual system, on the other hand, confers meaning to homosexual practices according to sexual aim—i.e., the act one wants to perform with another person (of either biological sex).

The contemporary bourgeois sexual system in the U.S. divides the sexual landscape according to discrete sexual categories and personages defined in terms of sexual preference or object choice: same sex (homosexual), opposite sex (heterosexual), or both (bisexual). Historically, this formulation has carried with it a blanket condemnation of all same-sex behavior. Because it is non-procreative and at odds with a rigid, compulsory heterosexual norm, homosexuality traditionally has been seen as either 1) a sinful transgression against the word of God, 2) a congenital disorder wracking the body, or 3) a psychological pathology gripping the mind. In underscoring object choice as the crucial factor in defining sexuality in the U.S., anthropologist

Roger Lancaster argues that "homosexual desire itself, without any qualifications, stigmatizes one as a homosexual" (116). This stigmatization places the modern gay man at the bottom of the homosexual sexual hierarchy. According to Lancaster, "the object-choice of the homosexual emarginates him from male power, except insofar as he can serve as a negative example and . . . is positioned outside the operational rules of normative (hetero)sexuality" (123–24).

Unlike the European-American system, the Mexican/Latin-American sexual system is based on a configuration of gender/sex/power that is articulated along the active/passive axis and organized through the scripted sexual role one plays.[3] It highlights sexual aim—the act one wants to perform with the person toward whom sexual activity is directed—and gives only secondary importance to the person's gender or biological sex. According to Lancaster, "it renders certain organs and roles 'active,' other body passages and roles 'passive,' and assigns honor/ shame and status/stigma accordingly" (123). It is the mapping of the body into differentiated erotic zones and the unequal, gender-coded statuses accorded sexual actors that structure homosexual meaning in Latin culture. In the Mexican/Latin-American context there is no cultural equivalent to the modern gay man. Instead of discrete sexual personages differentiated according to sexual preference, we have categories of people defined in terms of the role they play in the homosexual act. The Latin homosexual world is divided into *activos* and *pasivos* (as in Mexico and Brazil) and *machistas* and *cochóns* (in Nicaragua).

Although stigma accompanies homosexual practices in Latin culture, it does not equally adhere to both partners. It is primarily the anal-passive individual (the *cochón* or *pasivo*) who is stigmatized for playing the subservient, feminine role. His partner (the *activo* or *machista*) typically "is not stigmatized at all and, moreover, no clear category exists in the popular language to classify him. For all intents and purposes, he is just a normal . . . male" (Lancaster 113). In fact,

Lancaster argues that the active party in a homosexual drama often gains status among his peers in precisely the same way that one derives status from seducing many women (113). This cultural construction confers an inordinate amount of meaning to the anal orifice and to anal penetration. This is in sharp contrast to the way homosexuality is viewed in the U.S., where the oral orifice structures the meaning of homosexuality in the popular imagination. In this regard, Lancaster suggests the lexicon of male insult in each context clearly reflects this basic difference in cultural meaning associated with oral/anal sites (111). The most common derisive term used to refer to homosexuals in the U.S. is "cocksucker." Conversely, most Latin American epithets for homosexuals convey the stigma associated with their being anally penetrated.

Consider for a moment the meaning associated with the passive homosexual in Nicaragua, the *cochón*. The term is derived from the word *colchón* or mattress, implying that one gets on top of another as one would a mattress, and thereby symbolically affirms the former's superior masculine power and male status over the other, who is feminized and indeed objectified (Lancaster 112). *Cochón* carries with it a distinct configuration of power, delineated along gender lines that are symbolically affirmed through the sexual role one plays in the homosexual act. Consequently, the meaning of homosexuality in Latin culture is fraught with elements of power/dominance that are not intrinsically accorded homosexual practices in the U.S. It is anal passivity alone that is stigmatized and that defines the subordinate status of homosexuals in Latin culture. The stigma conferred to the passive role is fundamentally inscribed in gender-coded terms.

> *"To give" (*dar*) is to be masculine, "to receive" (*recibir, aceptar, tomar*) is to be feminine. This holds as the ideal in all spheres of transactions between and within genders. It is symbolized by the popular interpretation of the male sexual organ as active in intercourse and the female sexual organ (or male anus) as passive. (Lancaster 114)*

This equation makes homosexuals such as the *pasivo* and *cochón* into feminized men; biological males, but not truly men. In Nicaragua, for example, homosexual behavior renders "one man a machista and the other a cochón. The machista's honor and the cochón's shame are opposite sides of the same coin" (Lancaster 114).

MALE HOMOSEXUAL IDENTITY AND BEHAVIOR IN MEXICO

Some of the most insightful ethnographic research on homosexuality in Mexico has been conducted by anthropologist J. M. Carrier. Like other Latin American specialists exploring this issue, Carrier argues that homosexuality is construed very differently in the U.S. and in Mexico. In the U.S., even one adult homosexual act or acknowledgment of homosexual desire may threaten a man's gender identity and throw open to question his sexual identity as well. In sharp contrast, a Mexican man's masculine gender and heterosexual identity are not threatened by a homosexual act as long as he plays the inserter's role. Only the male who plays the passive sexual role and exhibits feminine gender characteristics is considered to be truly homosexual and is, therefore, stigmatized. This "bisexual" option, an exemption from stigma for the "masculine" homosexual, can be seen as part of the ensemble of gender privileges and sexual prerogatives accorded Mexican men. Thus it is primarily the passive, effeminate homosexual man who becomes the object of derision and societal contempt in Mexico.

The terms used to refer to homosexual Mexican men are generally coded with gendered meaning drawn from the inferior position of women in patriarchal Mexican society. The most benign of these contemptuous terms is *maricón*, a label that highlights the non-conforming gender attributes of the (feminine) homosexual man. Its semantic equivalent in the U.S. is "sissy" or "fairy" (Carrier, "Cultural Factors" 123–24). Terms such as *joto* or *puto*, on the other hand, speak to the passive sexual role taken by these

men rather than merely their gender attributes. They are infinitely more derogatory and vulgar in that they underscore the sexually non-conforming nature of their passive/receptive position in the homosexual act. The invective associated with all these appellations speaks to the way effeminate homosexual men are viewed as having betrayed the Mexican man's prescribed gender and sexual role. Moreover, it may be noted that the Spanish feminine word *puta* refers to a female prostitute while its male form *puto* refers to a passive homosexual, not a male prostitute. It is significant that the cultural equation made between the feminine, anal-receptive homosexual man and the most culturally-stigmatized female in Mexican society (the whore) share a common semantic base.[4]

Carrier's research suggests that homosexuality in Mexico is rigidly circumscribed by the prominent role the family plays in structuring homosexual activity. Whereas in the U.S., at least among most European-Americans, the role of the family as a regulator of the lives of gay men and lesbians has progressively declined, in Mexico the family remains a crucial institution that defines both gender and sexual relations between men and women. The Mexican family remains a bastion of patriarchal privilege for men and a major impediment to women's autonomy outside the private world of the home.

The constraints of family life often prevent homosexual Mexican men from securing unrestricted freedom to stay out late at night, to move out of their family's home before marriage, or to take an apartment with a male lover. Thus their opportunities to make homosexual contacts in other than anonymous locations, such as the balconies of movie theaters or certain parks, are severely constrained (Carrier, "Family Attitudes" 368). This situation creates an atmosphere of social interdiction which may explain why homosexuality in Mexico is typically shrouded in silence. The concealment, suppression, or prevention of any open acknowledgment of homosexual activity underscores the stringency of cultural dictates surrounding gender and sexual norms within Mexican family life. Unlike the generally more egalitarian, permissive family life of white middle-class gay men and lesbians in the U.S., the Mexican family appears to play a far more important and restrictive role in structuring homosexual behavior among Mexican men ("Family Attitudes" 373).

Given these constraints and the particular meanings attached to homosexuality in Mexican culture, same-sex behavior in Mexico typically unfolds in the context of an age-stratified hierarchy that grants privileges to older, more masculine men. It is very significant that in instances where two masculine, active men enter into a homosexual encounter, the rules that structure gender-coded homosexual relations continue to operate with full force. In these exchanges one of the men—typically he who is defined as being more masculine or powerful—assumes the active, inserter role while the other man is pressed into the passive, anal-receptive role. Moreover, men who may eventually adopt both active and passive features of homosexual behavior typically do not engage in such reciprocal relations with the same person. Instead, they generally only play the active role with one person (who is always viewed as being the more feminine) and are sexually passive with those they deem more masculine than themselves ("Cultural Factors" 120–21).

In sum, it appears that the major difference between bisexually-active men in Mexico and bisexual males in the U.S. is that the former are not stigmatized because they exclusively play the active, masculine, inserter role. Unlike in the North American context, "one drop of homosexuality" does not, ipso facto, make a Mexican male a *joto* or a *maricón*. As Carrier's research clearly documents, none of the active inserter participants in homosexual encounters ever considers himself a "homosexual" or to be "gay" ("Mexican Male" 83). What may be called the "bisexual escape hatch" functions to insure that the tenuous masculinity of Mexican men is not compromised through the homosexual act; they remain men, *hombres*, even though they participate in this

sexual behavior. Moreover, the Mexican sexual system actually militates against the construction of discernable, discrete "bisexual" or "gay" sexual identities because these identities are shaped by and draw upon a different sexual system and foreign discursive practices. One does not, in other words, become "gay" or "lesbian" identified in Mexico because its sexual system precludes such an identity formation in the first place. These "bourgeois" sexual categories are simply not relevant or germane to the way gender and sexual meanings are conferred in Mexican society.

IMPLICATIONS FOR CHICANO GAY MEN IN THE U.S.

The emergence of the modern gay identity in the U.S. and its recent appearance in Mexico have implications for Chicano men that have not been fully explored. What is apparent, however, is that Chicanos, as well as other racial minorities, do not negotiate the acceptance of a gay identity in exactly the same way white American men do. The ambivalence of Chicanos vis-à-vis a gay sexual identity and their attendant uneasiness with white gay/lesbian culture do not necessarily reflect a denial of homosexuality. Rather, I would argue, the slow pace at which this identity formation has taken root among Chicanos is attributable to cultural and structural factors which differentiate the experiences of the white and non-white populations in the U.S.

Aside from the crucial differences discussed above in the way homosexuality is culturally constructed in the Mexican/Latin-American and European- or Anglo-American sexual systems, a number of other structural factors also militate against the emergence of a modern gay identity among Chicano men. In this regard, the progressive loosening of familial constraints among white, middle-class homosexual men and women at the end of the nineteenth century, and its acceleration in the post-World War II period, structurally positioned the white gay and lesbian population to redefine their primary self-identity in terms of their homosexuality. The shift from a family-based economy to a fully developed wage labor system at the end of the nineteenth century dramatically freed European-American men and women from the previously confining social and economic world of the family. It allowed both white men and the white "new woman" of the period to transgress the stifling gender roles that previously bound them to a compulsory heterosexual norm.[5] Extricating the nuclear family from its traditional role as a primary unit of production enabled homosexually inclined individuals to forge a new sexual identity and to develop a culture and community that were not previously possible. Moreover, the tremendous urban migration ignited (or precipitated) by World War II accelerated this process by drawing thousands of homosexuals into urban settings where the possibilities for same-sex intimacy were greater.

It is very apparent, however, that the gay identity and communities that emerged were overwhelmingly white, middle class, and male-centered. Leading figures of the first homophile organizations in the U.S., such as the Mattachine Society, and key individuals shaping the newly emergent gay culture were primarily drawn from this segment of the homosexual population. Moreover, the new communities founded in the post-war period were largely populated by white men who had the resources and talents needed to create "gilded" gay ghettos. This fact has given the contemporary gay community—despite its undeniable diversity—a largely white, middle class, and male form. In other words, the unique class and racial advantages of white gay men provided the foundation upon which they could boldly carve out the new gay identity. Their collective position in the social structure empowered them with the skills and talents needed to create new gay institutions, communities, and a unique sexual subculture.

Despite the intense hostility that, as gay men, they faced during that period, nevertheless, as white gay men, they were in the best position to risk the social ostracism that this process engendered. They were *relatively* better situated

than other homosexuals to endure the hazards unleashed by their transgression of gender conventions and traditional heterosexual norms. The diminished importance of ethnic identity among these individuals, due principally to the homogenizing and integrating impact of the dominant racial categories which defined them foremost as white, undoubtedly also facilitated the emergence of gay identity among them. As members of the privileged racial group—and thus no longer viewing themselves primarily as Irish, Italian, Jewish, Catholic, etc.—these middle-class men and women arguably no longer depended solely on their respective cultural groups and families as a line of defense against the dominant group. Although they may have continued to experience intense cultural dissonance leaving behind their ethnicity and their traditional family-based roles, they were now in a position to dare to make such a move.

Chicanos, on the other hand, have never occupied the social space where a gay or lesbian identity can readily become a primary basis of self-identity. This is due, in part, to their structural position at the subordinate ends of both the class and racial hierarchies, and in a context where ethnicity remains a primary basis of group identity and survival. Moreover, Chicano family life requires allegiance to patriarchal gender relations and to a system of sexual meanings that directly militate against the emergence of this alternative basis of self-identity. Furthermore, factors such as gender, geographical settlement, age, nativity, language usage, and degree of cultural assimilation further prevent, or at least complicate, the acceptance of a gay or lesbian identity by Chicanos or Chicanas respectively. They are not as free as individuals situated elsewhere in the social structure to redefine their sexual identity in ways that contravene the imperatives of minority family life and its traditional gender expectations. How they come to define their sexual identities as gay, straight, bisexual or, in Mexican/Latin-American terms, as an *activo*, *pasivo*, or *macho marica*, therefore, is not a straightforward or unmediated process. Unfortunately, there are no published studies to date exploring this identity formation process.

However, one unpublished study on homosexual Latino/Chicano men was conducted by Hector Carrillo and Horacio Maiorana in the spring of 1989. As part of their ongoing work on AIDS within the San Francisco Bay Area Latino community, these researchers develop a typology capturing the different points in a continuum differentiating the sexual identity of these men. Their preliminary typology is useful in that it delineates the way homosexual Chicanos/Latinos integrate elements of both the North American and Mexican sexual systems into their sexual behavior.

The first two categories of individuals, according to Carrillo and Maiorana, are: 1) Working class Latino men who have adopted an effeminate gender persona and usually play the passive role in homosexual encounters (many of them are drag queens who frequent the Latino gay bars in the Mission District of San Francisco); and 2) Latino men who consider themselves heterosexual or bisexual, but who furtively have sex with other men. They are also primarily working class and often frequent Latino gay bars in search of discrete sexual encounters. They tend to retain a strong Latino or Chicano ethnic identity and structure their sexuality according to the Mexican sexual system. Although Carrillo and Maiorana do not discuss the issue, it seems likely that these men would primarily seek out other Latino men, rather than European-Americans, as potential partners in their culturally-circumscribed homosexual behavior.

I would also suggest from personal observations that these two categories of individuals occasionally enter into sexual relationships with middle class Latinos and European-American men. In so doing, these working class Latino men often become the object of the middle class Latino's or the white man's colonial desires. In one expression of this class-coded lust, the effeminate *pasivo* becomes the boyish, feminized object of the middle class man's colonial desire. In another, the masculine Mexican/Chicano *activo* becomes the embodiment of a potent ethnic masculinity that titillates the middle class man who thus enters into a passive sexual role.

Unlike the first two categories of homosexually active Latino men, the other three have integrated several features of the North American sexual system into their sexual behavior. They are more likely to be assimilated into the dominant European-American culture of the U.S. and to come from middle class backgrounds. They include 3) Latino men who openly consider themselves gay and participate in the emergent gay Latino subculture in the Mission district; 4) Latino men who consider themselves gay but do not participate in the Latino gay subculture, preferring to maintain a primary identity as Latino and only secondarily a gay one; and, finally, 5) Latino men who are fully assimilated into the white San Francisco gay male community in the Castro District and retain only a marginal Latino identity.

In contrast to the former two categories, Latino men in the latter three categories are more likely to seek European-American sexual partners and exhibit greater difficulty in reconciling their Latino cultural backgrounds with their gay lifestyle. In my impressionistic observations, these men do not exclusively engage in homosexual behavior that is hierarchically differentiated along the gender-coded lines of the Mexican sexual system. They are more likely to integrate both active and passive sexual roles into their sexuality and to enter into relationships in which the more egalitarian norms of the North American sexual system prevail. We know very little, however, about the actual sexual conduct of these individuals. Research has not yet been conducted on how these men express their sexual desires, how they negotiate their masculinity in light of their homosexuality, and, more generally, how they integrate aspects of the two sexual system into their everyday sexual conduct.

In the absence of such knowledge, we may seek clues about the social world of Chicano gay men in the perceptive writings of Chicana lesbians. Being the first to shatter the silence on the homosexual experience of the Chicano population, they have candidly documented the perplexing issues Chicanos confront in negotiating the conflicting gender and sexual messages imparted by the coexisting Chicano and European-American cultures. The way in which Chicana lesbians have framed these problems, I believe, is bound to have major significance for the way Chicano men reconcile their homosexual behavior and gay sexual identity within a Chicano cultural context. More than any other lesbian writer's, the extraordinary work of Cherríe Moraga articulates a lucid and complex analysis of the predicament that the middle class Chicana lesbian and Chicano gay man face in this society. A brief examination of her autobiographical writings offers important insights into the complexities and contradictions that may characterize the experience of homosexuality for all Chicanos and Chicanas in the U.S.

CHERRÍE MORAGA AND CHICANA LESBIANISM

An essential point of departure in assessing Cherríe Moraga's work is an appreciation of the way Chicano family life severely constrains the Chicana's ability to define her life outside of its stifling gender and sexual prescriptions. As a number of Chicana feminist scholars have clearly documented, Chicano family life remains rigidly structured along patriarchal lines that privilege men over women and children.[6] Any violation of these norms is undertaken at great personal risk because Chicanos draw upon the family to resist racism and the ravages of class inequality. Chicano men and women are drawn together in the face of these onslaughts and are closely bound into a family structure that exaggerates unequal gender roles and suppresses sexual non-conformity.[7] Therefore, any deviation from the sacred link binding husband, wife, and child not only threatens the very existence of *la familia* but also potentially undermines the

mainstay of resistance to Anglo racism and class exploitation. "The family, then, becomes all the more ardently protected by oppressed people and the sanctity of this institution is infused like blood into the veins of the Chicano. At all costs, la familia must be preserved," writes Moraga. Thus, "we fight back . . . with our families—with our women pregnant, and our men as indispensable heads. We believe the more severely we protect the sex roles within the family, the stronger we will be as a unit in opposition to the anglo threat" (*Loving* 110).

These cultural prescriptions do not, however, curb the sexually non-conforming behavior of certain Chicanos. As in the case of Mexican homosexual men in Mexico, there exists a modicum of freedom for the Chicano homosexual who retains a masculine gender identity while secretly engaging in the active homosexual role. Moraga has perceptively noted that the Latin cultural norm inflects the sexual behavior of homosexual Chicanos: "Male homosexuality has always been a 'tolerated' aspect of Mexican/Chicano society, as long as it remains 'fringe'. . . . But lesbianism, in any form, and male homosexuality which openly avows both the sexual and the emotional elements of the bond, challenge the very foundation of la familia" (111). The openly effeminate Chicano gay man's rejection of heterosexuality is typically seen as a fundamental betrayal of Chicano patriarchal cultural norms. He is viewed as having turned his back on the male role that privileges Chicano men and entitles them to sexual access to women, minors, and even other men. Those who reject these male prerogatives are viewed as non-men, as the cultural equivalents of women. Moraga astutely assesses the situation as one in which "the 'faggot' is the object of Chicano/Mexicano's contempt because he is consciously choosing a role his culture tells him to despise. That of a woman" (111).

The constraints that Chicano family life imposed on Moraga herself are candidly discussed in her provocative autobiographical essays "La Guera" and "A Long Line of Vendidas" in *Lov-*

ing in the War Years. In recounting her childhood in Southern California, Moraga describes how she was routinely required to make her brother's bed, iron his shirts, lend him money, and even serve him cold drinks when his friends came to visit their home. The privileged position of men in the Chicano family places women in a secondary, subordinate status. She resentfully acknowledges that "to this day in my mother's home, my brother and father are waited on, including by me" (90). Chicano men have always thought of themselves as superior to Chicanas, she asserts in unambiguous terms: "I have never met any kind of Latino who . . . did not subscribe to the basic belief that men are better" (101). The insidiousness of the patriarchal ideology permeating Chicano family life even shapes the way a mother defines her relationships with her children: "The daughter must constantly earn the mother's love, prove her fidelity to her. The son—he gets her love for free" (102).

Moraga realized early in life that she would find it virtually impossible to attain any meaningful autonomy in that cultural context. It was only in the Anglo world that freedom from oppressive gender and sexual strictures was remotely possible. In order to secure this latitude, she made a necessary choice: to embrace the white world and reject crucial aspects of her Chicana upbringing. In painfully honest terms, she states:

> *I gradually became anglocized because I thought it was the only option available to me toward gaining autonomy as a person without being sexually stigmatized. . . . I instinctively made choices which I thought would allow me greater freedom of movement in the future. This meant resisting sex roles as much as I could safely manage and that was far easier in an anglo context than in a Chicano one. (99)*

Born to a Chicana mother and an Anglo father, Moraga discovered that being fair-complexioned facilitated her integration into the Anglo social world and contributed immensely to her academic achievement. "My mother's desire to pro-

tect her children from poverty and illiteracy" led to their being "anglocized," she writes; "the more effectively we could pass in the white world, the better guaranteed our future" (51). Consequently her life in Southern California during the 1950s and 1960s is described as one in which she "identified with and aspired toward white values" (58). In the process, she "rode the wave of that Southern California privilege as far as conscience would let me" (58).

The price initially exacted by anglicization was estrangement from family and a partial loss of the nurturing and love she found therein. In reflecting on this experience, Moraga acknowledges that "I have had to confront that much of what I value about being Chicana, about my family, has been subverted by anglo culture and my cooperation with it. . . . I realized the major reason for my total alienation from and fear of my classmates was rooted in class and culture" (54). She poignantly concedes that, in the process, "I had disavowed the language I knew best—ignored the words and rhythms that were closest to me. The sounds of my mother and aunts gossiping—half in English, half in Spanish—while drinking cerveza in the kitchen" (55). What she gained, on the other hand, was the greater autonomy that her middle class white classmates had in defining their emergent sexuality and in circumventing burdensome gender prescriptions. Her movement into the white world, however, was viewed by Chicanos as a great betrayal. By gaining control of her life, Moraga became one of a "long line of vendidas," traitors or "sellouts," as self-determined women are seen in the sexist cultural fantasy of patriarchal Chicano society. This is the accusation that "hangs above the heads and beats in the hearts of most Chicanas, seeking to develop our own autonomous sense of ourselves, particularly our sexuality" (103).

Patriarchal Chicano culture, with its deep roots in "the institution of heterosexuality," requires Chicanas to commit themselves to Chicano men and subordinate to them their own sexual desires. "[The Chicano] too, like any other man," Moraga writes, "wants to be able to determine how, when, and with whom his women—mother, wife, and daughter—are sexual" (110–11). But "the Chicana's sexual commitment to the Chicano male [is taken as] proof of her fidelity to her people" (105). "It is no wonder," she adds, that most "Chicanas often divorce ourselves from conscious recognition of our own sexuality" (119). In order to claim the identity of a Chicana lesbian, Moraga had to take "a radical stand in direct contradiction to, and in violation of, the women [sic] I was raised to be" (117); and yet she also drew upon themes and images of her Mexican Catholic background. Of its impact on her sexuality Moraga writes:

> I always knew that I felt the greatest emotional ties with women, but suddenly I was beginning to consciously identify those feeling as sexual. The more potent my dreams and fantasies became and the more I sensed my own exploding sexual power, the more I retreated from my body's messages and into the region of religion. By giving definition and meaning to my desires, religion became the discipline to control my sexuality. Sexual fantasy and rebellion became "impure thoughts" and "sinful acts." (119)

These "contrary feelings," which initially surfaced around the age of twelve, unleashed feelings of guilt and moral transgression. She found it impossible to leave behind the Catholic Church's prohibitions regarding homosexuality, and religious themes found their way into how she initially came to define herself as a sexual subject—in a devil-like form. "I wrote poems describing myself as a centaur: half-animal/half-human, hairy-rumped and cloven-hoofed, como el diablo. The images emerged from a deeply Mexican and Catholic place" (124).

As her earliest sexual feelings were laden with religious images, so too were they shaped by images of herself in a male-like form. This is understandable in light of the fact that only men in Chicano culture are granted sexual subjectivity. Consequently, Moraga instinctively gravitated toward a butch persona and assumed a male-like stance toward other women.

> In the effort to avoid embodying la chingada, I became the chingón. In the effort not to feel fucked, I became the fucker, even with women. . . . The fact of the matter was that all those power struggles of "having" and "being had" were played out in my own bedroom. And in my psyche, they held a particular Mexican twist. (126)

In a candid and courageously outspoken conversation with lesbian activist Amber Hollibaugh, Moraga recounts that

> . . . what turned me on sexually, at a very early age, had to do with the fantasy of capture, taking a woman, and my identification was with the man. . . . The truth is, I do have some real gut-level misgivings about my sexual connection with capture. It might feel very sexy to imagine "taking" a woman, but it has sometimes occurred at the expense of my feeling, sexually, like I can surrender myself to a woman; that is, always needing to be the one in control, calling the shots. It's a very butch trip and I feel like this can keep me private and protected and can prevent me from fully being able to express myself. (Moraga and Hollibaugh 396)

Moraga's adult lesbian sexuality defined itself along the traditional butch/femme lines characteristic of lesbian relationships in the postwar period.[8] It is likely that such an identity formation was also largely an expression of the highly gender-coded sexuality imparted through Chicano family life. In order to define herself as an autonomous sexual subject, she embraced a butch, or more masculine, gender persona, and crystallized a sexual desire for feminine, or femme, lovers.

THE FINAL FRONTIER: UNMASKING THE CHICANO GAY MAN

Moraga's experience is certainly only one expression of the diverse ways in which Chicana lesbians come to define their sense of gender and experience their homosexuality. But her odyssey reflects and articulates the tortuous and painful path traveled by working class Chicanas (and Chicanos) who embrace the middle class Anglo world and its sexual system in order to secure, ironically, the "right to passion expressed in our own cultural tongue and movements" (136). It is apparent from her powerful autobiographical writings, however, how much her adult sexuality was also inevitably shaped by the gender and sexual messages imparted through the Chicano family.

How this complex process of integrating, reconciling, and contesting various features of both Anglo and Chicano cultural life are experienced by Chicano gay men, has yet to be fully explored. Moraga's incisive and extraordinarily frank autobiographical account raises numerous questions about the parallels in the homosexual development of Chicana lesbians and Chicano gay men. How, for example, do Chicano male homosexuals internalize and reconcile the gender-specific prescriptions of Chicano culture? How does this primary socialization impact on the way they define their gender personas and sexual identities? How does socialization into a patriarchal gender system that privileges men over women and the masculine over the feminine structure intimate aspects of their sexual behavior? Do most Chicano gay men invariably organize aspects of their sexuality along the hierarchical lines of dominance/subordination that circumscribe gender roles and relationships in Chicano culture? My impression is that many Chicano gay men share the Chicano heterosexual man's underlying disdain for women and all

that is feminine. Although it has not been documented empirically, it is likely that Chicano gay men incorporate and contest crucial features of the Mexican/Latin-American sexual system into their intimate sexual behavior. Despite having accepted a "modern" sexual identity, they are not immune to the hierarchical, gender-coded system of sexual meanings that is part and parcel of this discursive practice.

Until we can answer these questions through ethnographic research on the lives of Chicano gay men, we must continue to develop the type of feminist critique of Chicano male culture that is so powerfully articulated in the work of lesbian authors such as Cherríe Moraga. We are fortunate that courageous voices such as hers have irretrievably shattered the silence on the homosexual experience within the Mexican American community. Her work, and that of other Chicana lesbians, has laid a challenge before Chicano gay men to lift the lid on their homosexual experiences and to leave the closeted space they have been relegated to in Chicano culture. The task confronting us, therefore, is to begin interpreting and redefining what it means to be both Chicano and gay in a cultural setting that has traditionally viewed these categories as a contradiction in terms. This is an area of scholarly research that can no longer be left outside the purview of Chicano Studies, Gay and Lesbian Studies, or even more traditional lines of sociological inquiry.

NOTES

1. See, for example, the writings by Chicana and Latina lesbians in Ramos; Alarcón, Castillo, and Moraga; Moraga and Anzaldúa, and Anzaldúa. See also the following studies on Latinas: Arguelles and Rich; Espin; and Hidalgo and Hidalgo-Christensen.
2. See Bruce-Novoa's interesting discussion of homosexuality as a theme in the Chicano novel.
3. There is a rich literature documenting the ways in which our sexuality is largely structured through sexual scripts that are culturally defined and individually internalized. See, for example, Gagnon and Simon; Simon and Gagnon; and Plummer. What is being referred to here as the Mexican/Latin-American sexual system is part of the circum-Mediterranean construction of gender and sexual meaning. In this regard, see the introduction and essays in Gilmore. For further discussion of this theme in the Mexican context, see Alonso and Koreck. Their essay, which uses many of the many sources as the present essay, explores male homosexual practices in Mexico in relation to AIDS.
4. In "Birth of the Queen," Trumback has perceptively documented that many of the contemporary terms used to refer to homosexual men in Western Europe and the United States (such as queen, punk, gay,

faggot, and fairy) also were at one time the slang term for prostitutes (137). See also Alonso and Koreck, 111–113.

5. For a broad overview of the development of a gay and lesbian identity and community in the United States, see D'Emilio; D'Emilio and Freedman; and Katz. A number of articles in the important anthology edited by Duberman, Vicinus, and Chauncey document the white middle class–centered nature of gay/lesbian identity construction and community formation.

6. Some of the very best research in Chicano studies has been conducted by Chicana feminists who have explored the intersection of class, race, and gender in Chicanas' lives. Some recent examples of this impressive scholarship include Zavella; Segura; Pesquera; and Baca-Zinn.

7. This solidarity is captured in the early Chicano movement poster fittingly entitled "La Familia." It consists of three figures in a symbolic pose: a Mexican woman, with a child in her arms, is embraced by a Mexican man, who is centrally positioned in the portrait and a head taller. This poster symbolized the patriarchal, male-centered privileging of the heterosexual, nuclear family in Chicano resistance against white racism. For a provocative discussion of these themes in the Chicano movement, see Gutiérrez.

8. For an interesting discussion of the butch/femme formulation among working-class white women at the time, see Davis and Kennedy; and Nestle.

REFERENCES

Adam, Barry D. "Homosexuality without a Gay World: Pasivos y Activos en Nicaragua." *Out/Look* 1.4 (1989): 74–82.

Alarcón, Norma. "Chicana's Feminist Literature: A Re-vision Through Malintzin/or Malintzin: Putting Flesh Back on the Object." Moraga and Anzaldúa 182–90.

Alarcón, Norma, Ana Castillo, and Cherríe Moraga, eds. *Third Woman: The Sexuality of Latinas.* Berkeley: Third Woman, 1989.

Alonso, Ana Maria, and Maria Theresa Koreck. "Silences: 'Hispanics,' AIDS, and Sexual Practices." *differences: A Journal of Feminist Cultural Studies* 1.1 (1989): 101–24.

Anzaldúa, Gloria. *Borderlands/La Frontera: The New Mestiza.* San Francisco: Spinsters, 1987.

Arguelles, Lourdes, and B. Ruby Rich. "Homosexuality, Homophobia, and Revolution: Notes Toward an Understanding of the Cuban Lesbian and Gay Male Experience, Part 1." *Signs: Journal of Woman in Culture and Society* 9 (1984): 683–99.

———. "Homosexuality, Homophobia, and Revolution: Notes Toward an Understanding of the Cuban Lesbian and Gay Male Experience, Part 2." *Signs: Journal of Women in Culture and Society* 11 (1985): 120–36.

Baca-Zinn, Maxine. "Chicano Men and Masculinity." *The Journal of Ethnic Studies* 10.2 (1982): 29–44.

———. "Familism Among Chicanos: A Theoretical Review." *Humboldt Journal of Social Relations* 10.1 (1982–83): 224–38.

Blackwood, Evelyn, ed. *The Many Faces of Homosexuality: Anthropological Approaches to Homosexual Behavior.* New York: Harrington Park, 1989.

Bruce-Novoa, Juan. "Homosexuality and the Chicano Novel." *Confluencia: Revista Hispanica de Cultura y Literatura* 2.1 (1986): 69–77.

Carrier, Joseph M. "Cultural Factors Affecting Urban Mexican Male Homosexual Behavior." *The Archives of Sexual Behavior: An Interdisciplinary Research Journal* 5.2 (1976): 103–24.

———. "Family Attitudes and Mexican Male Homosexuality." *Urban Life: A Journal of Ethnographic Research* 5.3 (1976): 359–76.

———. "Gay Liberation and Coming Out in Mexico." Herdt 225–53.

———. "Mexican Male Bisexuality." *Bisexualities: Theory and Research.* Ed. F. Klein and T. Wolf. New York: Haworth, 1985. 75–85.

Carrillo, Hector, and Horacio Maiorana. "AIDS Prevention Among Gay Latinos in San Francisco: From Behavior Change to Social Change." Unpublished ms., 1989.

Davis, Madeline, and Elizabeth Lapovsky Kennedy. "Oral History and the Study of Sexuality in the Lesbian Community: Buffalo, New York, 1940–1960." Duberman 426–40.

D'Emilio, John. "Capitalism and Gay Identity." Snitow, Stansell, and Thompson 100–13.

———. *Sexual Politics, Sexual Communities: The Making of a Homosexual Minority in the United*

States, 1940–1970. Chicago: U of Chicago P, 1983.

D'Emilio, John, and Estelle B. Freedman. *Intimate Matters: A History of Sexuality in America*. New York: Harper, 1988.

Duberman, Martin Bauml, Martha Vicinus, and George Chauncey Jr., eds. *Hidden from History: Reclaiming the Gay and Lesbian Past*. New York: NAL, 1989.

Espin, Oliva M. "Cultural and Historical Influences on Sexuality in Hispanic/Latin Women: Implications for Psychotherapy." *Pleasure and Danger: Exploring Female Sexuality*. Ed. Carol Vance. London: Routledge, 1984, 149–63.

———. "Issues of Identity in the Psychology of Latina Lesbians." *Lesbian Psychologies*. Ed. Boston Lesbian Psychologies Collective. Urbana: U of Illinois P, 1987. 35–55.

Freud, Sigmund. *Three Essays on the Theory of Sexuality*. 1905. *The Standard Edition of the Complete Psychological Works of Sigmund Freud*. Trans. and ed. James Strachey. Vol. 7. London: Hogarth, 1953. 123–243.

Gagnon, John H., and William Simon. *Sexual Conduct: The Social Sources of Human Sexuality*. Chicago: Aldine, 1973.

Gilmore, David D., ed. *Honor and Shame and the Unity of the Mediterranean*. No. 22, Washington: American Anthropological Association, 1987.

Goldwert, Marvin. "Mexican Machismo: The Flight from Femininity." *Psychoanalytic Review* 72.1 (1985): 161–69.

Gutiérrez, Ramón. "Community, Patriarchy, and Individualism: The Politics of Chicano History and the Dream of Equality." Forthcoming in *American Quarterly*.

Herdt, Gilbert, ed. *Gay and Lesbian Youth*. New York: Haworth, 1989.

Hidalgo, Hilda, and Elia Hidalgo-Christensen. "The Puerto Rican Lesbian and the Puerto Rican Community." *Journal of Homosexuality* 2 (1976–77): 109–21.

———. "The Puerto Rican Cultural Response to Female Homosexuality." *The Puerto Rican Woman*. Ed. Edna Acosta-Belen. New York: Praeger, 1979. 110–23.

Islas, Arturo. *Immigrant Souls*. New York: Morrow, 1990.

———. *The Rain God: A Desert Tale*. Palo Alto, CA: Alexandrian, 1984.

Katz, Jonathan Ned. *Gay/Lesbian Almanac: A New Documentary*. New York: Harper, 1983.

Lancaster, Roger N. "Subject Honor and Object Shame: The Construction of Male Homosexuality and Stigma in Nicaragua." *Ethnology* 27.2 (1987): 111–25.

Martin, Robert K. "Knights-Errant and Gothic Seducers: The Representation of Male Friendship in Mid-Nineteenth Century America." Duberman 169–82.

Moraga, Cherríe. *Loving in the War Years: Lo que nunca pasó por sus labios*. Boston: South End, 1983.

Moraga, Cherríe, and Gloria Anzaldúa, eds. *This Bridge Called My Back: Writings by Radical Women of Color*. Watertown, MA: Persephone, 1981.

Moraga, Cherríe, and Amber Hollibaugh. "What We're Rollin Around in Bed With: Sexual Silences in Feminism." Snitow, Stansell, and Thompson 394–405.

Nestle, Joan. "Butch-Fem Relationships: Sexual Courage in the 1950s." *Heresies* 12 (1981): 21–24.

Newton, Esther. "The Mythic Mannish Lesbian: Radcliffe Hall and the New Woman." Duberman 281–93.

Parker, Richard. "Youth Identity, and Homosexuality: The Changing Shape of Sexual Life in Contemporary Brazil." Herdt 269–89.

———. "Masculinity, Femininity, and Homosexuality: On the Anthropological Interpretation of Sexual Meanings in Brazil." Blackwood 155–64.

Paz, Octavio. *Labyrinth of Solitude: Life and Thought in Mexico*. New York: Grove, 1961.

Pesquera, Beatriz M. "Work and Family: A Comparative Analysis of Professional, Clerical and Blue-Collar Chicana Workers." PhD diss. U of California, Berkeley, 1985.

Plummer, Kenneth. "Symbolic Interaction and Sexual Conduct: An Emergent Perspective." *Human Sexual Relations*. Ed. Mike Brake. New York: Pantheon, 1982. 223–44.

Ramos, Juanita, ed. *Compañeras: Latina Lesbians*. New York: Latina Lesbian History Project, 1987.

Rechy. John. *City of Night*. New York: Grove, 1963.

———. *Numbers*. New York: Grove, 1967.

———. *Rushes*. New York: Grove, 1979.

———. *The Sexual Outlaw*. New York: Grove, 1977.

Rodriguez, Richard. *Hunger of Memory: The Education of Richard Rodriguez, An Autobiography*. Boston: Godine, 1982.

————. "Late Victorians: San Francisco, AIDS, and the Homosexual Stereotype." *Harper's Magazine* Oct. 1990: 57–66.

Rupp, Leila J. "Imagine in My Surprise: Woman's Relationships in Mid-Twentieth Century America." Duberman 395–410.

Segura, Denise. "Chicana and Mexican Immigrant Women in the Labor Market: A Study of Occupational Mobility and Stratification." PhD diss. U of California, Berkeley, 1986.

————. "Chicana and Mexican Immigrant Women at Work: The Impact of Class, Race, and Gender on Occupational Mobility." *Gender and Society* 3.1 (1989): 37–52.

————. "The Interplay of Familism and Patriarchy on Employment Among Chicana and Mexican Women." *Renato Rosaldo Lecture Series* 5 (1989): 35–53.

Simon, William, and John H. Gagnon. "Sexual Scripts: Permanence and Change." *Archives of Sexual Behavior* 15.2 (1986): 97–120.

Smith-Rosenberg, Carroll. "Discourses of Sexuality and Subjectivity: The New Woman, 1870–1936." Duberman 264–80.

Snitow, Ann, Christine Stansell, and Sharon Thompson, eds. *Powers of Desire: The Politics of Sexuality*. New York: Monthly Review, 1983.

Taylor, Clark L. "Mexican Male Homosexual Interaction in Public Contexts." Blackwood 117–36.

Trumbach, Randolph. "The Birth of the Queen: Sodomy and the Emergence of Gender Equality in Modern Culture, 1660–1750." Duberman 129–40.

Zavella, Patricia. *Women's Work and Chicano Families: Cannery Workers of the Santa Clara Valley*. Ithaca: Cornell UP, 1987.

SOCIOCULTURAL FACETS OF THE BLACK GAY MALE EXPERIENCE

SUSAN D. COCHRAN
VICKIE M. MAYS

This article reviews the literature on Black gay and bisexual men. It reports on the development of a Black gay identity, the integration of Black gay men into the Black heterosexual world, some of their sexual practices, behavior that places them at risk for AIDS and alcoholism, and their social networks. The authors caution that the experiences of Black gay men cannot be interpreted in terms of a white gay male standard.

Prior to the appearance of AIDS in this country, studies on the sexual preferences and behaviors of gay men generally ignored the specific experiences of Black men (Bell, Weinberg, and Hammersmith, 1981). With the press of the AIDS epidemic to develop baseline information on men's intimate behaviors, this tendency rarely to study Black gay men, or do so in the same manner as White gay men, persists. While many researchers may recognize the importance of possible cultural differences, their approach has been to assume that Black gay men would be more like White gay men than Black heterosexuals. Questionnaires, sampling procedures, and topics of focus have been more consistent with White gay men's experiences (see Becker and

Joseph, 1988, for a comprehensive review of behavior change studies). This proclivity has resulted in an emergence of comparisons between Black and White men using White gay standards of behavior that may be obscuring our understanding of important psychosocial determinants of sexual behaviors in Black gay men. Given the differences that have been observed in family structure and sexual patterns between Black and White heterosexuals, there is no empirical basis upon which to assume that Black gay men's experience of homosexuality would perfectly mimic that of Whites (Bell, Weinberg, and Hammersmith, 1981). Indeed, very little is known empirically about the lives of Black gay men (Mays and Cochran, 1987), though there are

An abridged version of the article "Epidemiologic and Sociocultural Factors in the Transmission of HIV Infection in Black Gay and Bisexual Men" printed in *A Sourcebook of Gay/Lesbian Health Care* (M. Shernoff and W. A. Scott, eds.) Washington, D.C.: National Gay and Lesbian Health Foundation, 2nd ed. Copyright 1988 by the National Gay and Lesbian Health Foundation. Reprinted by permission.

some indications, discussed below, that they are more likely to engage in activities that place them at greater risk for HIV infection.

In the absence of any data we need to proceed cautiously with assumptions that imply anything other than [that] same-sex *activities* of Black gay men resemble those of White gay men. This caution is particularly true for AIDS studies that purport to study psychosocial behavior. Studies of this type report not only on behavior but also attempt to describe motivations and circumstances that led to the behavior. In the absence of a set of questions or framework incorporating important cultural, ethnic, and economic realities of Black gay men, interpretations emanating from a White gay male standard may be misleading.

DEVELOPMENT OF A
BLACK GAY IDENTITY

In recent years, researchers (Spanier and Glick, 1980; Staples, 1981; Guttentag and Secord, 1983) have noted differences between Whites and Blacks in their intimate heterosexual relationships. Differential sociocultural factors presumably influence the development and specific structure of sexual behavior within Black heterosexual relationships. These factors include the unavailability of same ethnic group partners, fewer social and financial resources, residential immobility, and lack of employment opportunities. Many of these same conditions may surround the formation, maintenance and functioning of Black gay male relationships.

Popular writings in past years by Black gay men describe the difficulty in finding other Black gay men for potential partners, the lack of a visible Black gay community, an absence of role models, and the dearth of Black gay male social or professional organizations (Soares, 1979; Beame, 1983). While gay bars, gay baths and public places existed where White gay men gathered, some of these were off limits to Black gay men either due to actual or perceived racism within the White gay community or the danger of passing through White neighborhoods in order to participate in gay community activities. Thus, expectations that the experiences of Black gay men are identical to those of White gay men seem unwarranted.

In examining differences between Blacks and Whites in the emergence of a homosexual orientation, Bell, Weinberg, and Hammersmith (1981) found that, for the White males, pre-adult sexual feelings appeared to be very important. In contrast, among Black males, childhood and adolescent sexual activities, rather than feelings, were stronger predictors of the development of adult homosexual sexual orientation. Thus Blacks started to act at an earlier age on their sexual inclinations than Whites did (Bell, Weinberg, and Hammersmith, 1981). This would be consistent with Black-White differences in the onset of heterosexual sexual activity if socioeconomic status is not statistically controlled for (Wyatt, personal communication).

The typical conceptualization of sexual orientation is that individuals are located in terms of their sexual feelings and behaviors on a bipolar dimension where one extreme is heterosexuality, the other is homosexuality, and lying somewhere in between is bisexuality (Bell and Weinberg, 1978). This definition does not include ethnicity or culture as an interactive factor influencing the expression of sexual behavior or sexual orientation. For example, Smith (1986) makes a distinction between Black gays and gay Blacks complicating the demarcation between homosexuality and bisexuality:

> *Gay Blacks are people who identify first as being gay and who usually live outside the closet in predominantly white gay communities. I would estimate that they amount to roughly ten percent of all Black homosexuals. Black gays, on the other hand, view our racial heritage as primary and frequently live "bisexual front lives" within Black neighborhoods. (p. 226)*

These two groups are probably quite different in both social activities and sexual behaviors. The

Black gay man, strongly identified with Afro-American culture, will often look and behave much like the Black heterosexual man except in his sexual behavior. The extent to which his same-sex partners are integrated into his family and social environment may be a function of his class status (Soares, 1979). It has long been noted by Blacks that there are differences, both in values and behaviors, between middle-class and working-class Blacks. There is no reason to assume that within the Black gay community such diversity would not persist. While Smith (1986) has described the Black gay community in only two dimensions we would be remiss if we stopped here. There is a growing population of Black gays who have forged an identity acknowledging both statuses:

> At times I cried just remembering how it is to be both Black and gay during these truly difficult times. But here we are, still proud and living, with a culture all our own. (Sylvester, p. 11, 1986)

We know less about the behavior of Black men who identify as bisexual and least about those black men who engage in same-sex sexual behavior but identify as exclusively heterosexual. When the factor of social class is added the distinction between homosexuality and heterosexuality may become even more blurred. Among lower socioeconomic Black men, those engaged in same-sex sexual activities, regardless of their sexual object choices, may appear on the surface no different from Black heterosexuals. If the support systems of Black gay men are like those of Black lesbians (Cochran and Mays, 1986), fewer economic resources result in a greater reliance on a Black social network (both gay and heterosexual) for tangible and emotional support, a strong tendency to live in predominantly ethnic neighborhoods, and the maintenance of emotionally and economically close family ties.

This extensive integration into the Black heterosexual world may not only be a function of fewer economic resources, but also of ethnic identification. The culture of gay life, generally perceived to be White, may not be synonymous with the norms of Black culture. Choices of how to dress, what language to use, where to live, and whom to have as friends are all affected by culture. The White gay community, while diverse, has developed norms concerning language, social behavior, and other demarcations (Warren, 1974) that may not mesh well with certain subgroups of Black gays. For example, in the past there has been a heavy emphasis in the gay White community (except among the middle-aged, middle-class closeted gay men) on socializing in public places—bars, beaches, and resorts (Warren, 1974). In contrast, the Black gay community places greater emphasis on home entertainment that is private and not public, perhaps as a holdover from the days when discrimination in many public places was common. This pattern of socializing would facilitate the development of a distinct Black gay culture (Soares, 1979).

It is perhaps this difference in socializing that has frustrated health educators attempting to do AIDS education through the social network in gay bars. Generally, they have found that they do not reach a significant number of Black men using this technique. An understanding of the Black gay community makes salient that risk reduction strategies should focus on "risk behaviors" and *not* "risk groups." Emphasizing risk reduction strategies that rely on group membership requires a social and personal identification by Black men that for many may not be relevant.

SEXUAL BEHAVIOR

Bell and Weinberg, in a 1978 study comparing sexual activities of White and Black gay men, found that Blacks were more likely to report having engaged in anal sex, both passively and actively, than White gay men. In terms of our current knowledge of AIDS, this appears to be one of the highest risk factors for contracting the HIV virus (Friedland and Klein, 1987).

A second aspect of Black gay men's sexuality is that they may be more bisexual in their behaviors than White gay men. Evidence for this comes again from Bell and Weinberg (1978) who reported that Black gay men were significantly more likely to have engaged in heterosexual coitus (22 percent) in the previous twelve months than White gay men (14 percent). This seems to be borne out nationally by the AIDS statistics. Among male homosexual/bisexual AIDS patients, Black men are more likely than White men to be classified as bisexual (30 percent versus 13 percent) rather than homosexual (70 percent versus 87 percent). Due to the intense homophobia in the Black community and the factors we discussed above, men may be more likely to remain secretive regarding their homosexual activities (Mays and Cochran, 1987). This may provide a mode of transmission of the AIDS virus outside of an already identified high risk group.

There are several other differences between Black and White gay men noted in the Kinsey Institute data that have implications for contracting the HIV virus. Looking at sexual behavior both pre- and post-Stonewall, Black gay men, in comparison to White gay men, were more likely to be sexually active across ethnic boundaries and less likely to report that their sexual partners were strangers (Gebhard and Johnson, 1979; Bell and Weinberg, 1978). Sexual practices post-Stonewall underwent profound change in the gay community. Black gay men were a part of that change (Gebhard and Johnson, 1979; Bell and Weinberg, 1978). However, these differences in meeting partners or choice of partners remain. They are apparently less malleable to change than specific risk-related sexual behaviors.

While the 1978 Bell and Weinberg study was conducted on a small sample in the San Francisco area, it is suggestive of the need for further research to assess the prevalence of risk behaviors and strategies most effective for decreasing risk. Indeed, a recent report of ethnically based differences in syphilis incidence rates (Landrum, Beck-Sague, and Kraus, 1988) suggests Black gay men are less likely than White gay men to be practicing "safer sex." Sexual behavior has multiple determinants and it is important that variables such as culture, ethnic identification, and class be incorporated into health education programs designed to promote sexual behavior change by Black men.

INTRAVENOUS DRUG USE

IV drug use is more common in the Black community (Gary and Berry, 1985), which may explain the higher than expected prevalence of Blacks in the co-categories of IV drug user and homosexual/bisexual male. HIV infection is endemic among IV drug users in the urbanized Northeast who themselves are most likely to be Black (Ginzburg, MacDonald, and Glass, 1987). Ethnic differences exist between the percentage of homosexual/bisexual men with AIDS who are also IV drug users; for White gay and bisexual men with AIDS, 9 percent have histories of IV drug use, while for Blacks the figure is 16 percent. Black gays and bisexual men who do not use IV drugs may also be at increased risk because they are more likely than Whites to be sexual partners of Black men who are IV drugs users. In the Bell and Weinberg study (1978), 22 percent of White men had never had sex with a Black man, whereas for Black respondents, only 2 percent had never had sex with a White man.

ALCOHOL AS A COFACTOR

Recently, alcohol use has been implicated as a cofactor facilitating the occurrence of high risk sexual behavior among gay men (Stall et al., 1986). In predicting alcohol use among Black gay and bisexual men, one might expect that normative use patterns will be influenced by what is common behavior in both the Black community and gay community.

Norms for alcohol use in the Black community reflect a polarization of attitudes, shaped on the one hand by traditional religious fundamentalism and rural southern heritage and on the other by a focus on socializing in environments where drinking is common, such as bars, nightclubs, and home parties (Herd, 1986). This latter norm is more prevalent in urban Black communities. Blacks and Whites vary in small ways in their drinking patterns, although Blacks are more likely to suffer negative consequences, including alcohol-related mortality and morbidity, from their drinking than are Whites. Current rates of mortality due to liver cirrhosis indicates that rates are 10 times higher in Black men aged 25–34 as compared to White males. While drinking is found across all socioeconomic groups of Blacks, health and social problems associated with drinking have been found more often in low income urban Blacks (Lex, 1987). Similarly, for this group it was found that Black males 30–59 were most likely to use alcohol to face the stress of everyday life situations. This is the group most affected by HIV infection.

Within the gay male community, alcohol abuse is a serious problem (Icard and Traunstein, 1987). This may result from both the sociocultural stress of discrimination and the tendency for gay-oriented establishments to be drinking establishments as well. Thus, gay men frequently socialize in environments where alcohol consumption is normative.

Black gay and bisexual men, depending upon their relative identification with the Black or gay community, would be expected to demonstrate behavior consistent with these norms. For some, this might mean a high level of abstinence apart from social drinking consistent with other Black Americans; for others, alcohol consumption might more closely resemble that of White gay men with concomitantly higher rates of alcohol dependency.

CROSSING TRADITIONAL RISK GROUPS' BOUNDARIES

Early AIDS epidemiologic tracking programs conceptualize the disease as a result of the gay lifestyle (Mays, 1988). Indeed, now discarded names for different manifestations of the illness included Gay-related Immunodeficiency Disease and Gay cancer. This focus on discrete risk factors continues to the present, although the additional populations of IV drug abusers, hemo-

philiacs, persons born in Haiti and Central Africa, and recipients of blood transfusions after 1978 have been added to the list. For Whites, this approach is highly successfully, describing the presumed HIV transmission vector in 94 percent of cases; for native-born Blacks, the percentage of cases accurately labeled by a single risk factor (including the combination of IV drug use and male homosexual sexual contact) drops to 88 percent (Cochran, 1987). This underscores the reality that sociocultural factors varying across ethnic groups strongly influence individuals' behavior, and by this their risk of contracting HIV.

For Black gay and bisexual men, the reliance on highly specified risk groups (or factors) ignores the fundamental nature of their behavioral location in society. The multiplicity of their identities may indirectly increase their risk for HIV infection by exposing them to more diverse populations (Grob, 1983).

First, as Blacks, they are behaviorally closer to two epicenters of the AIDS epidemic. IV drug use and foreign-born Blacks (primarily those from Haiti and Central Africa where HIV infection is more common). Social and behavioral segregation by ethnic status is still a reality of the American experience and Black gay and bisexual men suffer, like other Blacks, from pervasive racism. As we noted above, if their social support systems are similar to what we know of Black lesbians (Cochran and Mays, 1986), extensive integration into the Black heterosexual community is common. Behaviorally, this may include both IV drug use and heterosexual activity with HIV infected individuals. Thus Black gay and bisexual men are at increased risk for HIV infection simply by virtue of being Black.

Second, as men who have sex with other men, Black gay and bisexual men are often members of the broader gay community in which ethnicity probably reflects the general U.S. population (84 percent White). Black gay and bisexual men may have relatively open sexual access to White men, although racism in the community may preclude other forms of socializing (Icard, 1985). Data from the Bell and Weinberg study (1978) suggests several interesting differences, as well as similarities, between White and Black gay men. Blacks reported equivalent numbers of sexual partners, both lifetime (median = 100–249 partners) and in the previous 12 months (median = 20–50), as Whites. Although they were significantly less likely than White gay men to engage in anonymous sexual contacts (51 percent versus 79 percent of partners), more than two-thirds reported that more than half their sexual partners were White men. In contrast, none of the White respondents reported that more than half their partners were Black. It should be kept in mind, however, that a greater percentage of the White sample (14 percent) was recruited at bath houses than the Black sample (2 percent). Nevertheless, at least sexually, Black gay men appear to be well integrated into the gay community. Therefore, Black gay and bisexual men are also at higher risk for HIV infection because they are behaviorally close to another epicenter of the AIDS epidemic: the gay male community.

Third, as a social grouping unto itself, the Black gay and bisexual male community may be more diverse than the White gay community (Icard, 1985). Some men identify more closely with the Black community than the gay community (Black gay men); others find their primary emotional affinity with the gay community and not the Black community (gay Black men). To the extent that this diversity of identity is reflected in behavioral diversity as well, HIV transmission may be greatly facilitated (Denning, 1987).

Thus Black gay and bisexual men are individuals often located behaviorally at the crossroads of HIV transmission. Their multiple social identities make it more likely that the practicing of high risk behavior, whether sexual or needle-sharing, will occur in the presence of HIV.

PERCEPTIONS OF RISK

There may be a reluctance among Black gay and bisexual men to engage in risk reduction behaviors because of the perception by some members of the Black community that AIDS is a "gay White disease," or a disease of intravenous drug users (Mays and Cochran, 1987). In addition, many risk reduction programs are located within outreach programs of primarily White gay organizations. These organizations often fail to attract extensive participation by Black gay men.

Research findings suggest that the personal perception of being at risk is most often influenced by accurate knowledge of one's actual risk and personal experiences with the AIDS epidemic (McKusick, Horstman, and Coates, 1985). There may be a variety of reasons why Black gay and bisexual men do not see themselves as at risk. These include the notion of relative risk and a lack of ethnically credible sources for encouraging risk perceptions (Mays and Cochran, 1988). Relative risk refers to the importance of AIDS in context with other social realities. For example, poverty, with its own attendant survival risks, may outweigh the fear of AIDS in a teenager's decision to engage in male prostitution. Economic privilege, more common in the White gay community, assists in permitting White gay men to focus their energies and concerns on the AIDS epidemic. For Black gay men of lesser economic privilege other pressing realities of life may, to some extent, diffuse such concerns. Credible sources relate to the issues that we have presented here of ethnic identification. Black gay men who are emotionally and behavioral distant from the White community may tend to discount media messages from White sources.

REFERENCES

Centers for Disease Control, Acquired Immunodeficiency Syndrome (AIDS) Weekly Surveillance Report, United States AIDS Activity, Center for Infectious Diseases, April 4, 1988.

Bakeman, R., J. Lumb, R. E. Jackson, and P. N. Whitley 1987. "The Incidence of AIDS among Blacks and Hispanics." *Journal of the National Medical Association* 79: 921–928.

Beame, T. 1983. "Racism from a Black Perspective." In *Black Men/White Men: A Gay Anthology*. M. J. Smith ed. San Francisco: Gay Sunshine Press.

Becker, M. H. and J. G. Joseph. 1988. "AIDS and Behavioral Change to Reduce Risk: A Review." *American Journal of Public Health* 78: 394–410.

Bell, A. P. and M. S. Weinberg. 1978. *Homosexualities: A Study of Diversity among Men and Women*. New York: Simon & Schuster.

Bell, A. P., M. S. Weinberg, and S. K. Hammersmith. 1981. *Sexual Preference: Its Development in Men and Women*. Bloomington: Indiana University Press.

Bureau of the Census. 1983. "General Population Characteristics, 1980." U.S. Department of Commerce: U.S. Government Printing Office.

Centers for Disease Control. 1987. "Human Immunodeficiency Virus Infection in the United States: A Review of Current Knowledge." *Morbidity and Mortality Weekly* 36 (Suppl. no. S-6): 1–48.

Cochran, S. D. 1987. "Numbers That Obscure the Truth: Bias in Data Presentation." Paper presented at the meetings of the American Psychological Association, New York, August.

Cochran, S. D. and V. M. Mays. 1986. "Sources of Support among Black Lesbians." Paper presented at the meetings of the American Psychological Association, Washington, D.C., August.

Cochran, S. D., V. M. Mays, and V. Roberts. 1988. "Ethnic Minorities and AIDS." In *Nursing Care of Patients with AIDS/ARC*, A. Lewis ed., pp. 17–24. Maryland: Aspen Publishers.

Denning, P. J. 1987. "Computer Models of AIDS Epidemiology." *American Scientist* 75: 347–351.

Friedland, G. H. and R. S. Klein. 1987. "Transmission of the Human Immunodeficiency Virus." *New England Journal of Medicine* 317: 1125–1135.

Friedman, S. R., J. L. Sotheran, A. Abdul-Quader, B. J. Primm, D. C. Des Jarlais, P. Kleinman, C. Mauge, D. S. Goldsmith, W. El-Sadr, and R. Maslansky. 1987. "The AIDS Epidemic among Blacks and Hispanics." *The Milbank Quarterly* 65, Suppl. 2.

Gary, L. E. and G. L. Berry. 1985. "Predicting Attitudes toward Substance Use in a Black Community: Implications for Prevention." *Community Mental Health Journal* 21: 112–118.

Gebhard, P. H. and A. B. Johnson. 1979. *The Kinsey Data: Marginal Tabulations of the 1938–1963 Interviews Conducted by the Institute for Sex Research*. Philadelphia: W. B. Saunders Co.

Ginzburg, H. M., M. G. MacDonald, and J. W. Glass. 1987. "AIDS, HTLV-III Diseases, Minorities and Intravenous Drug Abuse." *Advances in Alcohol and Substance Abuse* 6: 7–21.

Gottlieb, M. S., H. M. Schanker, P. Fan, A. Saxon, J. D. Weisman, and I. Posalki. 1981. "Pneumocystic Pneumonia—Los Angeles." *Morbidity and Mortality Weekly Report* 30: 250–252.

Grob, G. N. 1983. "Diseases and Environment in American History." In *Handbook of Health, Health Care, and the Health Professions*, D. Mechanic, ed., pp. 3–23. New York: Free Press.

Guttentag, M. and P. F. Secord. 1983. *Too Many Women: The Sex Ratio Question*. Beverly Hills, Calif.: Sage Publications.

Herd, D. 1986. "A Review of Drinking Patterns and Alcohol Problems among U.S. Blacks." In *Report of the Secretary's Task Force on Black and Minority Health*: Volume 7, M. Heckler ed. USDHHS.

Icard, L. 1985. "Black Gay Men and Conflicting Social Identities: Sexual Orientation versus Racial Identity." *Journal of Social Work and Human Sexuality* 4: 83–93.

Icard, L., and D. M. Traunstein. 1987. "Black, Gay, Alcoholic Men: Their Character and Treatment." *Social Casework* 68: 267–272.

Landrum, S., C. Beck-Sague, and S. Kraus. 1988. "Racial Trends in Syphilis among Men with Same-Sex Partners in Atlanta, Georgia." *American Journal of Public Health* 78: 66–67.

Lex, B. W. 1987. "Review of Alcohol Problems in Ethnic Minority Groups." *Journal of Consulting and Clinical Psychology* 55 (3): 293–300.

Macdonald, D. I. 1986. "Coolfont Report: A PHS Plan for the Prevention and Control of AIDS and the AIDS Virus." *Public Health Reports* 101: 341–348.

Mays, V. M. 1988. "The Epidemiology of AIDS in U.S. Blacks: Some Problems and Projections." Unpublished manuscript.

Mays, V. M. and S. D. Cochran. 1987. "Acquired Immunodeficiency Syndrome and Black Americans: Special Psychosocial Issues." *Public Health Reports* 102: 224–231.

——— "Issues in the Perception of AIDS Risk and Risk Reduction Activities by Black and Hispanic Women." *American Psychologist* 1988; 43: 11.

McKusick, L., W. Horstman, and T. J. Coates. 1985. "AIDS and Sexual Behavior Reported by Gay Men in San Francisco." *American Journal of Public Health* 75: 493–496.

Morgan, W. M. and J. W. Curran. 1986. "Acquired Immunodeficiency Syndrome: Current and Future Trends." *Public Health Reports* 101: 459–465.

Samuel, M. and W. Winkelstein. 1987. "Prevalence of Human Immunodeficiency Virus in Ethnic Minority Homosexual/Bisexual Men." *Journal of the American Medical Association* 257: 1901 (letter).

Smith, M. C. 1986. "By the Year 2000." *In the Life: A Black Gay Anthology*, J. Beam ed. Boston: Alyson Publications.

Soares, J. V. 1979. "Black and Gay." In *Gay Men: The Sociology of Male Homosexuality*, M. P. Levine, ed. New York: Harper & Row Publishers.

Spanier, G. B. and P. C. Glick. 1980. "Mate Selection Differentials between Whites and Blacks in the United States." *Social Forces* 58: 707–725.

Stall, R. S., L. McKusick, J. Wiley, T. J. Coates, and D. G. Ostrow. 1986. "Alcohol and Drug Use during Sexual Activity and Compliance with Safe Sex Guidelines for AIDS: The AIDS Behavioral Research Project." *Health Education Quarterly* 13: 359–371.

Staples, R. 1981. *The Changing World of Black Singles*. Connecticut: Greenwood Press.

Sylvester. 1986. Foreword. In *In the Life: A Black Gay Anthology*, J. Beam ed. Boston: Alyson Publications.

Warren, C. A. B. 1974. *Identity and Community Formation in the Gay World*. New York: John Wiley & Sons.

PART NINE

MEN IN FAMILIES

Are men still taking their responsibilities as family breadwinners seriously? Are today's men sharing more of the family housework and childcare than those in previous generations? The answers to these questions are complex, and often depend on which men we are talking about and what we mean when we say "family."

Many male workers long ago won a "family wage," and with it made an unwritten pact to share that wage with a wife and children. But today, as Barbara Ehrenreich argued in her influential book, *The Hearts of Men*, increasing numbers of men are revolting against this traditional responsibility to share their wages, thus contributing to the rapidly growing impoverishment of women and children. Ehrenreich may be correct, at least with respect to the specific category of men who were labeled "yuppies" in the 1980s. But if we are looking at the growing impoverishment of women and children among poor, working class, and minority families, the causes have more to do with dramatic shifts in the structure of the economy—including skyrocketing unemployment among young black males—than they do with male irresponsibility. Increasing numbers of men have no wage to share with a family.

But how about the New Dual-Career Family? Can we look to this emerging family type as a model of egalitarianism? Hochschild's research indicates that the growth of the two-career family has not significantly altered the division of labor in the household. Women still, she argues, work a "second shift" when they return home from their paid-work job.

One of the most significant issues of the 1990s is fatherhood. Are men becoming more nurturing and caring fathers, developing skills, like the men in Hollywood films such as *Three Men and a Baby*, or is fatherhood more an unrealizable dream than a reality? Ralph LaRossa challenges commonsense assumptions about changes in fatherhood by suggesting that men have not changed all that drastically in their parenting behaviors. Brian Miller discusses the lives of gay fathers, illustrating the need to expand the definition of what we think of as "the family," while the articles by Scott Coltrane and by John and Julia McAdoo explore the meaning of fatherhood and family among Chicano and black men, respectively.

THE SECOND SHIFT:
EMPLOYED WOMEN ARE PUTTING IN ANOTHER DAY OF WORK AT HOME

ARLIE HOCHSCHILD

Every American household bears the footprints of economic and cultural trends that originate far outside its walls. A rise in inflation eroding the earning power of the male wage, an expanding service sector opening up jobs for women, and the inroads made by women into many professions—all these changes do not simply go on around the American family. They occur *within* a marriage or living-together arrangement and transform it. Problems between couples, problems that seem "unique" or "marital," are often the individual ripples of powerful economic and cultural shock waves. Quarrels between husbands and wives in households across the nation result mainly from a friction between faster-changing women and slower-changing men.

The exodus of women from the home to the workplace has not been accompanied by a new view of marriage and work that would make this transition smooth. Most workplaces have remained inflexible in the face of the changing needs of workers with families, and most men have yet to really adapt to the changes in women. I call the strain caused by the disparity between the change in women and the absence of change elsewhere the "stalled revolution."

If women begin to do less at home because they have less time, if men do little more, and if the work of raising children and tending a home requires roughly the same effort, then the questions of who does what at home and of what "needs doing" become a source of deep tension in a marriage.

Over the past 30 years in the United States, more and more women have begun to work outside the home, and more have divorced. While some commentators conclude that women's work *causes* divorce, my research into changes in the American family suggests something else. Since all the wives in the families I studied (over an eight-year period) worked outside the home, the fact that they worked did not account for why some marriages were happy and others were not. What *did* contribute to happiness was the husband's willingness to do the work at home. Whether they were traditional or more egalitarian in their relationship, couples were happier when the men did a sizable share of housework and child care.

In one study of 600 couples filing for divorce, researcher George Levinger found that the second most common reason women cited for wanting to divorce—after "mental cruelty"—was their husbands' "neglect of home or children." Women mentioned this reason more often than financial problems, physical abuse, drinking, or infidelity.

A happy marriage is supported by a couple's being economically secure, by their enjoying a supportive community, and by their having compatible needs and values. But these days it may also depend on a shared appreciation of the work it takes to nurture others. As the role of the homemaker is being abandoned by many women, the homemaker's work has been continually devalued and passed on to low-paid housekeepers, babysitters, or day-care workers. Long devalued by men, the contribution of cooking, cleaning, and care-giving is now being devalued as mere drudgery by many women, too.

In the era of the stalled revolution, one way to make housework and child care more valued is for men to share in that work. Many working mothers are already doing all they can at home. Now it's time for men to make the move.

If more mothers of young children are working at full-time jobs outside the home, and if most couples can't afford household help, who's doing the work at home? Adding together the time it takes to do a paid job and to do housework and child care and using estimates from major studies on time use done in the 1960s and 1970s, I found that women worked roughly 15 more hours each week than men. Over a year, they worked an extra month of 24-hour days. Over a dozen years, it was an extra year of 24-hour days. Most women without children spend much more time than men on housework. Women with children devote more time to both housework and child care. Just as there is a wage gap between men and women in the workplace, there is a "leisure gap" between them at home. Most women work one shift at the office or factory and a "second shift" at home.

In my research, I interviewed and observed 52 couples over an eight-year period as they cooked dinner, shopped, bathed their children, and in general struggled to find enough time to make their complex lives work. The women I interviewed seemed to be far more deeply torn between the demands of work and family than were their husbands. They talked more about the abiding conflict between work and family. They felt the second shift was *their* issue, and most of their husbands agreed. When I telephoned one husband to arrange an interview with him, explaining that I wanted to ask him how he managed work and family life, he replied genially, "Oh, this will *really* interest my *wife*."

Men who shared the load at home seemed just as pressed for time as their wives, and as torn between the demands of career and small children. But of the men I surveyed, the majority did not share the load at home. Some refused outright. Others refused more passively, often offering a loving shoulder to lean on, or an understanding ear, as their working wife faced the conflict they both saw as hers. At first it seemed to me that the problem of the second shift *was* hers. But I came to realize that those husbands who helped very little at home were often just as deeply affected as their wives—through the resentment their wives felt toward them and through their own need to steel themselves against that resentment.

A clear example of this phenomenon is Evan Holt, a warehouse furniture salesman who did very little housework and played with his four-year-old son, Joey, only at his convenience. His wife, Nancy, did the second shift, but she resented it keenly and half-consciously expressed her frustration and rage by losing interest in sex and becoming overly absorbed in Joey.

Even when husbands happily shared the work, their wives *felt* more responsible for home and children. More women than men kept track of doctor's appointments and arranged for kids' playmates to come over. More mothers than fathers worried about a child's Halloween costume or a birthday present for a school friend. They were more likely to think about their children while at work and to check in by phone with the babysitter.

Partly because of this, more women felt torn between two kinds of urgency, between the need to soothe a child's fear of being left at day-care and the need to show the boss she's "serious" at work. Twenty percent of the men in my study shared housework equally. Seventy percent did a substantial amount (less than half of it, but more than a third), and 10 percent did less than a third. But even when couples more equitably share the work at home, women do two thirds of the daily jobs at home, such as cooking and cleaning—jobs that fix them into a rigid routine. Most women cook dinner, for instance, while men change the oil in the family car. But, as one mother pointed out, dinner needs to be prepared every evening around six o'clock, whereas the car oil needs to be changed every six months, with no particular deadline. Women do more child care than men, and men repair more household appliances. A child needs to be tended to daily, whereas the repair of household appliances can often wait, said the men, "until I have time." Men thus have more control over when they make their contributions than women do. They may be very busy with family chores, but, like the executive who tells his secretary to "hold my calls," the man has more control over his time.

Another reason why women may feel under more strain than men is that women more often do two things at once—for example, write checks and return phone calls, vacuum and keep an eye on a three-year-old, fold laundry and think out the shopping list. Men more often will either cook dinner *or* watch the kids. Women more often do both at the same time.

Beyond doing more at home, women also devote proportionately more of their time at home to housework than men and proportionately less of it to child care. Of all the time men spend working at home, a growing amount of it goes to child care. Since most parents prefer to tend to their children than to clean house, men do more of what they'd rather do. More men than women take their children on "fun" outings to the park, the zoo, the movies. Women spend more time on maintenance, such as feeding and bathing children—enjoyable activities, to be sure, but often less leisurely or "special" than going to the zoo. Men also do fewer of the most undesirable household chores, such as scrubbing the toilet.

As a result, women tend to talk more intensely about being overtired, sick, and emo-

tionally drained. Many women interviewed were fixated on the topic of sleep. They talked about how much they could "get by on": six and a half, seven, seven and a half, less, more. They talked about who they knew who needed more or less. Some apologized for how much sleep they needed—"I'm afraid I need eight hours of sleep"—as if eight was "too much." They talked about how to avoid fully waking up when a child called them at night, and how to get back to sleep. These women talked about sleep the way a hungry person talks about food.

If, all in all, the two-job family is suffering from a speedup of work and family life, working mothers are its primary victims. It is ironic, then, that often it falls to women to be the time-and-motion experts of family life. As I observed families inside their homes, I noticed it was often the mother who rushed children, saying, "Hurry up! It's time to go," "Finish your cereal now," "You can do that later," or "Let's go!" When a bath needed to be crammed into a slot between 7:45 and 8:00, it was often the mother who called out, "Let's see who can take their bath the quickest!" Often a younger child would rush out, scurrying to be first in bed, while the older and wiser one stalled, resistant, sometimes resentful: "Mother is always rushing us." Sadly, women are more often the lightning rods for family tensions aroused by this speedup of work and family life. They are the villains in a process in which they are also the primary victims. More than the longer hours and the lack of sleep, this is the saddest cost to women of their extra month of work each year.

Raising children in a nuclear family is still the overwhelming preference of most people. Yet in the face of new problems for this family model we have not created an adequate support system so that the nuclear family can do its job well in the era of the two-career couple. Corporations have done little to accommodate the needs of working parents, and the government has done little to prod them.

The Reagan and Bush administrations say they are "pro-family" but confuse being pro-family with being against women's work outside the home. During a time when more than 70 percent of wives and mothers work outside the home (the rate is still climbing), the Reagan administration's Panel on the Family offered as its pro-family policy only a package of measures against crime, drugs, and welfare. In the name of protecting the family, the Republicans proposed to legitimize school prayer and eliminate family-planning services. They did nothing to help parents integrate work and family life. We have to ask, when marriages continue to end because of the strains of this life, is it pro-family or anti-family to make life in two-job families so very hard? As working parents become an interest group, a voting block, and a swing vote in elections, the issue of policies to ease life in two-job families is likely to become a serious political issue in years ahead.

We really need, as sociologist Frank Furstenberg has suggested, a Marshall Plan for the family. After World War II we saw that it was in our best interests to aid the war-torn nations of Europe. Now—it seems obvious in an era of growing concern over drugs, crime, and family instability—it is in our best interests to aid the overworked two-job families right here at home. We should look to other nations for a model of what could be done. In Sweden, for example, upon the birth of a child every working couple is entitled to 12 months of paid parental leave— nine months at 90 percent of the worker's salary, plus an additional three months at about three hundred dollars a month. The mother and father are free to divide this year off between them as they wish. Working parents of a child under eight have the opportunity to work no more than six hours a day, at six hours' pay. Parental insurance offers parents money for work time lost while visiting a child's school or caring for a sick child. That's a true pro-family policy.

A pro-family policy in the United States could give tax breaks to companies that encourage job sharing, part-time work, flex time, and family leave for new parents. By implementing comparable worth policies we could increase pay

scales for "women's" jobs. Another key element of a pro-family policy would be instituting fewer-hour, more flexible options—called "family phases"—for all regular jobs filled by parents of young children.

Day-care centers could be made more warm and creative through generous public and private funding. If the best form of day-care comes from the attention of elderly neighbors, students, or grandparents, these people could be paid to care for children through social programs.

In these ways, the American government would create a safer environment for the two-job family. If the government encouraged corporations to consider the long-range interests of workers and their families, they would save on long-range costs caused by absenteeism, turnover, juvenile delinquency, mental illness, and welfare support for single mothers.

These are real pro-family reforms. If they seem utopian today, we should remember that in the past the eight-hour day, the abolition of child labor, and the vote for women seemed utopian, too. Among top-rated employers listed in *The 100 Best Companies to Work for in America* are many offering country-club memberships, first-class air travel, and million-dollar fitness centers. But only a handful offer job sharing, flex time, or part-time work. Not one provides on-site day-care, and only three offer child-care deductions: Control Data, Polaroid, and Honeywell. In his book *Megatrends*, John Naisbitt reports that 83 percent of corporate executives believed that more men feel the need to share the responsibilities of parenting; yet only 9 percent of corporations offer paternity leave.

Public strategies are linked to private ones. Economic and cultural trends bear on family relations in ways it would be useful for all of us to understand. The happiest two-job marriages I saw during my research were ones in which men and women shared the housework and parenting. What couples called good communication often meant that they were good at saying thanks to one another for small aspects of taking care of the family. Making it to the school play, helping a child read, cooking dinner in good spirits, remembering the grocery list, taking responsibility for cleaning up the bedrooms—these were the silver and gold of the marital exchange. Until now, couples committed to an equal sharing of housework and child care have been rare. But, if we as a culture come to see the urgent need of meeting the new problems posed by the second shift, and if society and government begin to shape new policies that allow working parents more flexibility, then we will be making some progress toward happier times at home and work. And as the young learn by example, many more women and men will be able to enjoy the pleasure that arises when family life is family life, and not a second shift.

ARTICLE 50

FATHERHOOD AND SOCIAL CHANGE

RALPH LAROSSA

The consensus of opinion in American society is that something has happened to American fathers. Long considered minor players in the affairs of their children, today's fathers often are depicted as major parental figures, people who are expected to—people who presumably want to—*be there* when their kids need them. "Unlike their own fathers or grandfathers," many are prone to say.

But, despite all the attention that the so-called "new fathers" have been receiving lately, only a few scholars have systematically conceptualized the changing father hypothesis, and no one to date has marshalled the historical evidence needed to adequately test the hypothesis (Demos, 1982; Hanson & Bozett, 1985; Hanson & Bozett, 1987; Lamb, 1987; Lewis, 1986; Lewis & O'Brien, 1987; McKee & O'Brien, 1982; Pleck, 1987; Rotundo, 1985).

Given that there is not much evidence to support the hypothesis, (a) how do we account for the fact that many, if not most, adults in America believe that fatherhood has changed, and (b) what are the consequences—for men, for women, for families—resulting from the apparent disparity between beliefs and actuality? The purpose of this article is to answer these two questions.

THE ASYNCHRONY BETWEEN THE CULTURE AND CONDUCT OF FATHERHOOD

The institution of fatherhood includes two related but still distinct elements. There is the *culture of fatherhood* (specifically the shared norms, values, and beliefs surrounding men's parenting), and there is the *conduct of fatherhood* (what fathers do, their paternal behaviors). The distinction between culture and conduct is worth noting because although it is often assumed that the culture and conduct of a society are in sync, the fact is that many times the two are not synchronized at all. Some people make a habit of deliberately operating outside the rules, and others do wrong because they do not know any better (e.g., my 4-year-old son). And in a rapidly changing society like ours, countervailing forces can result in changes in culture but not in conduct, and vice-versa.

The distinction between culture and conduct is especially relevant when trying to assess whether fatherhood has changed because the available evidence on the history of fatherhood suggests that the *culture of fatherhood has changed more rapidly than the conduct.* For example, E. Anthony Rotundo (1985) argues that since 1970 a new style of American fatherhood has emerged, namely "Androgynous Fatherhood." In the androgynous scheme,

> *A good father is an active participant in the details of day-to-day child care. He involves himself in a more expressive and intimate way with his children, and he plays a larger part in the socialization process that his male forebears had long since abandoned to their wives. (p. 17)*

Rotundo (1985) is describing not what fathers lately have been doing but what some people would *like* fathers to *begin* doing. Later on he says that the new style is primarily a middle-class phenomenon and that "even within the upper-middle-class . . . there are probably far more men who still practice the traditional style of fathering than the new style." He also surmises that "there are more *women* who *advocate* 'Androgynous Fatherhood' than there are *men* who *practice* it" (p. 20). Similarly, Joseph Pleck (1987) writes about the history of fatherhood in the United States and contends that there have been three phases through which modern fatherhood has passed. From the early 19th to mid-20th centuries there was the father as distant breadwinner. Then, from 1940 to 1965 there was the father as sex role model. Finally, since around 1966 there has emerged the father as nurturer. Pleck's "new[est] father," like Rotundo's "androgynous father" is an involved father. He is also, however, more imagined than real. As Pleck acknowledges from the beginning, his analysis is a history of the "dominant *images* [italics added] of fatherhood" (p. 84).

Rotundo and Pleck are clear about the fact that they are focusing on the culture of fatherhood, and they are careful about drawing inferences about the conduct of fatherhood from their data. Others, however, have not been as careful. John Mogey, for example, back in 1957, appears to have mistaken cultural for behavioral changes when, in talking about the emerging role of men in the family, he asserts that the "newer" father's "behavior is best described as participation, the reintegration of fathers into the conspicuous consumption as well as the child rearing styles of family life" (Mogey, as cited in Lewis, 1986, p. 6). Ten years later, Margaret Mead (1967), too, extolled the arrival of the new father:

We are evolving a new style of fatherhood, in which young fathers share very fully with mothers in the care of babies and little children. In this respect American men differ very much from their own grandfathers and are coming to resemble much more closely men in primitive societies. (p. 36)

And recently there appeared in my Sunday newspaper the comment that "[Modern men] know more about the importance of parenting. They're aware of the role and of how they are doing it. Fifty years ago, fathers didn't think much about what kind of job they were doing" (Harte, 1987, p. 4G).

Neither Mogey nor Mead nor the newspaper presented any evidence to support their views. One can only guess that they were reporting what they assumed—perhaps hoped—was true generally (i.e., true not only for small "pockets" of fathers here and there), for, as was mentioned before, no one to date has carried out the kind of historical study needed to test the changing father hypothesis. If, however, the professional and lay public took seriously the thesis that fathers have changed and if others writing for professional and popular publications have echoed a similar theme, then one can easily understand how the notion that today's fathers are "new" could become implanted in people's minds. Indeed, there is a good chance that this is exactly what has happened. That is to say, Rotundo (1985) and Pleck (1987) probably are correct: there has been a shift in the culture of fatherhood—the way fathers and mothers think and feel about men as parents. But what separates a lot of fathers and mothers from Rotundo and Pleck is that, on some level of consciousness, the fathers and mothers also believe (incorrectly) that there has been a proportionate shift in the conduct of fatherhood.

I say on "some" level of consciousness because, "on another" level of consciousness, today's fathers and mothers *do* know that the conduct of fatherhood has not kept pace with the culture. And I include the word "proportionate" because, while some researchers have argued that there have been changes in paternal behavior since the turn of the century, no scholar has argued that these changes have occurred at the same rate as the ideological shifts that apparently have taken place. These two points are crucial to understanding the consequences of the asynchrony between culture and conduct, and they will soon be discussed in more detail. But first another question: If the behavior of fathers did not alter the ideology of fatherhood, then what did?

The answer is that the culture of fatherhood changed primarily in response to the shifts in the conduct of motherhood. In the wake of declines in the birth rate and increases in the percentage of mothers in the labor force, the culture of motherhood changed, such that it is now more socially acceptable for women to combine motherhood with employment outside the home (Margolis, 1984). The more it became apparent that today's mothers were less involved with their children, on a day-to-day basis, than were their own mothers or grandmothers, the more important it became to ask the question: Who's minding the kids? Not appreciating the extent to which substitute parents (day-care centers, etc.) have picked up the slack for mothers, many people (scholars as well as the lay public) assumed that fathers must be doing a whole lot more than before and changed their beliefs to conform to this assumption. In other words, mother-child interaction was erroneously used as a "template" to measure father-child interaction (Day & Mackey, 1986).

Generally speaking, culture follows conduct rather than vice-versa (Stokes & Hewitt, 1976). Thus, the fact that the culture of fatherhood has changed more rapidly than the conduct of fatherhood would seem to represent an exception to the rule. However, it may not be an exception at all. What may be happening is that culture *is* following conduct, but not in a way we normally think it does. Given the importance that American society places on mothers as parents, it is conceivable that the conduct of motherhood has had a "cross-fertilizing" effect on the culture of fatherhood. There is also the possibility that the conduct of fatherhood is affecting the culture of fatherhood, but as a stabilizer rather than a destabilizer. As noted, research suggests that androgynous fatherhood as an ideal has failed to become widespread. One reason for this may be that the conduct of fatherhood is arresting whatever "modernizing" effect the conduct of motherhood is having. Put differently, the conduct of fatherhood and the conduct of motherhood may, on a societal level, be exerting contradictory influences on the culture of fatherhood.

THE CONDUCT OF FATHERHOOD VERSUS THE CONDUCT OF MOTHERHOOD

Contending that the conduct of fatherhood has changed very little over the course of the 20th century flies in the face of what many of us see every day: dads pushing strollers, changing diapers, playing in the park with their kids. Also, what about the men who publicly proclaim that they have made a conscientious effort to be more involved with their children than their own fathers were with them?

What cannot be forgotten is that appearances and proclamations (both to others and ourselves) can be deceiving; everything hinges on how we conceptualize and measure parental conduct. Michael Lamb (1987) notes that scholars generally have been ambiguous about what they mean by parental "involvement," with the result that it is difficult to compare one study with the next, and he maintains that if we ever hope to determine whether or not fathers have changed, we must arrive at a definition that is both conceptually clear and comprehensive. The definition which he thinks should be used is one that separates parental involvement into three components: engagement, accessibility, and responsibility. *Engagement* is time spent in one-on-one interaction with a child (whether feeding, helping with homework, or playing catch in the backyard). *Accessibility* is a less intense degree of interaction and is the kind of involvement whereby the parent is doing one thing (cooking, watching television) but is ready or available to do another (respond to the child, if the need arises). *Responsibility* has to do with who is accountable for the child's welfare and care. Responsibility includes things like making sure that the child has clothes to wear and keeping track of when the child has to go to the pediatrician.

Reviewing studies that allow comparisons to be made between contemporary fathers' involvement with children and contemporary mothers' involvement with children, Lamb (1987) estimates that in two-parent families in which mothers are unemployed, fathers spend about one fifth to one quarter as much time as mothers do in an engagement status and about a third as much time as mothers do just being accessible to their children. In two-parent families with employed mothers, fathers spend about 33% as much time as mothers do in an engagement status and 65% as much time being accessible. As far as responsibility is concerned, mothers appear to carry over 90% of the load, regardless of whether they are employed or not. Lamb also notes that observational and survey data indicate that the behavioral styles of fathers and mothers differ. Mother–child interaction is dominated by caretaking whereas father–child interaction is dominated by play.

> Mothers actually play with their children more than fathers do but, as a proportion of the total amount of child–parent interaction, play is a much more prominent component of father–child interaction, whereas caretaking is more salient with mothers. (p. 10)

In looking for trends, Lamb relies on one of the few studies which allows historical comparisons to be made—a 1975 national survey that was repeated in 1981 (Juster, 1985). No data apparently were collected on parents' accessibility or responsibility levels, but between 1975 and 1981, among men and women aged 18 to 44, there was a 26% increase in fathers' engagement levels and a 7% increase in mothers'. Despite these shifts, paternal engagement was only about one third that of mothers, increasing from 29% in 1975 to 34% in 1981 (Lamb, 1987).

While there is nothing intrinsically wrong with talking about percentage changes, one should be careful about relying on them and them alone. If, for example, one examines the tables from which Lamb drew his conclusions (Juster, 1985), one finds that the number of hours per week that the fathers spent in child care was 2.29 hours in 1975, compared to 2.88 hours in 1981, which is an increase of about 35 minutes per week or 5 minutes per day. The mothers in the sample, on the other hand, spent 7.96 hours per week in child care in 1975, compared to 8.54 hours per week in child care in 1981, which also is an increase of about 35 minutes per week or 5 minutes per day. Thus, in absolute terms, fathers and mothers increased their child care by the same amount.

Bear in mind also that we are still talking about only *one* component of parental involvement, namely engagement. The two national surveys provide little, if any, information about changes in the accessibility and responsibility levels of fathers and mothers. Perhaps I am being overly cautious, but I cannot help but feel that until we gather historical data which would allow us to compare all three components of fatherhood, we should temper our excitement about surveys which suggest changes in the conduct of fatherhood over time. (For a tightly reasoned alternative viewpoint, see Pleck, 1985.)

Comparisons over time are difficult to make not only because so few scholars have chosen to study the history of fatherhood, but also because the studies carried out over the years to measure family trends provide scant information about fatherhood, per se. For instance, during a recent visit to the Library of Congress, I examined the Robert and Helen Lynd archival collection which I had hoped would include copies of the interview schedules from their two Middletown studies. It had occurred to me that if I could review the raw data from the studies, then I could perhaps plot paternal involvement trends from 1924 to 1935 to 1978, the times of the first, second, and third data collections in the Middletown series (Lynd & Lynd, 1929, 1937, Caplow, Bahr, Chadwick, Hill, & Williamson, 1982). Unfortunately, only four sample interviews from the earlier studies were in the archive. The rest apparently were destroyed. It is a shame that the Middletown data were not saved because the most recent book in the series presents a table which shows an increase in the weekly hours that fathers spent with their children between 1924 and 1987 (Caplow et al., 1982). There is no indication whether this represents an increase in engagement or accessibility or both. Had I been able to look at the interviews themselves, however, I might have been able to discern subtle variations.

What about the dads who are seen interacting with their kids in public (see Mackey & Day, 1979)? A thoughtful answer to this question also must address how we conceptualize and measure paternal involvement. Does the paternal engagement level of fathers in public square with the paternal engagement level of fathers in private, or are we getting an inflated view of fatherhood from public displays? If we took the time to scrutinize the behavior of fathers and mothers in public would we find that, upon closer examination, the division of child care is still fairly traditional. When a family with small children goes out to eat, for example, who in the family—mom or dad—is more accessible to the children; that is to say, whose dinner is more likely to be interrupted by the constant demands to "put ketchup on my hamburger, pour my soda, cut my meat?" And how can one look at a family in public and measure who is responsible for the children? How do we know, for instance, who decides whether the kids need clothes; indeed, how do we know who is familiar with the kids' sizes, color preferences, and tolerance levels for trying on clothes? The same applies to studies of paternal involvement in laboratory settings (see Parke, 1981). What can a study of father–child interaction in, say, a hospital nursery tell us about father–child interaction in general? The fact that fathers are making their presence known in maternity wards certainly is not sufficient to suggest that the overall conduct of fathers has changed in any significant way. Finally, the fact that fathers can be seen in public with their children may not be as important as the question, How much time do fathers spend *alone* with their children? One recent study found that mothers of young children spent an average of

44.45 hours per week in total child-interaction time (which goes beyond engagement), while fathers spent an average of 29.48 hours per week, a 1.5 to 1 difference. If one looked, however, at time spent alone with children, one discovered that 19.56 hours of mothers' child-interaction time, compared with 5.48 hours of fathers' child-interaction, was solo time, a 3.6 to 1 difference. Moreover, while fathers' total interaction time was positively affected by the number of hours their wives worked, fathers' solo time was not affected at all (Barnett & Baruch, 1987).

As for the public proclamations, almost all the books and articles which tout the arrival of "new" fatherhood are written not by a cross-section of the population but by upper-middle class professionals. Kort and Friedland's (1986) edited book, for instance, has 57 men writing about their pregnancy, birth, and child-rearing experiences. But who are these men? For the most part, they are novelists, educators, sculptors, real estate investors, radio commentators, newspaper editors, publishers, physicians, performers, psychologists, social workers, and attorneys. Not exactly a representative sample. As Rotundo (1985) notes, androgynous fatherhood as an ideal has caught the attention of the upper-middle class more than any other group, but that even in this group, words seem to speak louder than actions.

While the perception of fathers in public and the Kort and Friedland (1986) book may not accurately represent what fathers in general are *doing*, they can most certainly have an effect of what people *think* fathers are doing and should be doing. Which brings us back to the question, What are the consequences that have resulted from the apparent disparity between beliefs and actuality?

THE CONSEQUENCES OF ASYNCHRONOUS SOCIAL CHANGE

Thirty years ago, E. E. LeMasters (1957) made the point that parenthood (and not marriage, as many believe) is the real "romantic complex" in our society, and that even middle-class couples, who do more than most to plan for children, are caught unprepared for the responsibilities of parenthood. Later on, he and John DeFrain (1983) traced America's tendency to romanticize parenthood to a number of popular folk beliefs or myths, some of which are: raising children is always fun, children are forever sweet and cute, children will invariably turn out well if they have "good" parents, and having children will never disrupt but in fact will always improve marital communication and adjustment. Needless to say, anyone who is a parent probably remembers only too vividly the point at which these folk beliefs began to crumble in her/his mind.

The idea that fathers have radically changed— that they now are intimately involved in raising their children—qualifies also as a folk belief, and it too is having an impact on our lives and that of our children. On the positive side, people are saying that at least we have made a start. Sure, men are not as involved with their children as some of us would like them to be, but, so the argument goes, the fact that we are talking about change represents a step in the right direction. (Folk beliefs, in other words, are not necessarily negative. The myth that children are always fun, for example, does have the positive effect of making children more valued than they would be if we believed the opposite: that they are always a nuisance.) But what about the negative side of the myth of the changing father? Is there a negative side? My objective is to focus here on this question because up to now scholars and the media have tended to overlook the often unintentional but still very real negative consequences that have accompanied asynchronous change in the social institution of fatherhood.

I am not saying that professionals have been oblivious to the potentially negative consequences of "androgynization" on men's lives, for one could point to several articles and chapters which have addressed this issue (e.g., Benokraitis, 1985; Berger, 1979; Lamb, Pleck, & Levine, 1987; Lutwin & Siperstein, 1985; Pleck, 1979; Scanzoni, 1979). Rather, the point being

made is that scholars and the media, for the most part, have overlooked the difficulties associated with a *specific* social change, namely the asynchronous change in the social institution of fatherhood.

The Technically Present but Functionally Absent Father

The distinction between engagement and accessibility outlined by Lamb (1987) is similar to the distinction between *primary time* and *secondary time* in our study of the transition to parenthood (LaRossa & LaRossa, 1981). The social organization of a family with children, especially young children, parallels the social organization of a hospital in that both are *continuous coverage social systems* (Zerubavel, 1979). Both are set up to provide direct care to someone (be it children or patients) on a round-the-clock or continuous basis. And both the family and the hospital, in order to give caregivers a break every now and then, will operate according to some formal or informal schedule, such that some person or persons will be "primarily" involved with the children or patients (on duty) while others will be "secondarily" involved (on call or accessible).

Like Lamb, we also found that the fathers' levels of engagement, accessibility, and responsibility were only a fraction of the mothers', and that fathers tended to spend a greater part of their caregiving time playing with their children. Moreover, we found that the kinds of play that fathers were likely to be involved in were the kinds of activities that could be carried out at a secondary (semi-involved) level of attention, which is to say that it was not unusual for fathers to be primarily involved in watching television or doing household chores while only secondarily playing with their children.

When asked why they wanted to be with their children, the fathers often would answer along the lines that a father has to "put in some time with his kids" (LaRossa, 1983, p. 585). Like prisoners who "do time" in prison many fathers see themselves as "doing time" with their children. If, on some level of consciousness, fathers have internalized the idea that they should be more involved with their children, but on another level of consciousness they do not find the idea all that attractive, one would expect the emergence of a hybrid style: the technically present but functionally absent father (cf. Feldman & Feldman, 1975, cited in Pleck, 1983).

The technically present but functionally absent father manifests himself in a variety of ways. One father in our study prided himself on the fact that he and his wife cared for their new baby on an alternating basis, with him "covering" the mornings and his wife "covering" the afternoons. "We could change roles in a night," he said; "it wouldn't affect us." But when this father was asked to describe a typical morning spent alone with his infant son, he gave the distinct impression that he saw fatherhood as a *job* and that while he was "there" in body, he was someplace else in spirit.

> *I have the baby to be in charge of, [which has] really been no problem for me at all. But that's because we worked out a schedule where he sleeps a pretty good amount of that time. . . . I generally sort of have to be with him in the sense of paying attention to his crying or dirty diapers or something like that for anywhere between 30 to 45 minutes, sometimes an hour, depending. But usually I can have two hours of my own to count on each morning to do my own work, so it's no problem. That's just the breaks that go with it.*

Another example: Recently, there appeared an advertisement for one of those minitelevisions, the kind you can carry around in your pocket. Besides promoting the television as an electronic marvel, the man who was doing the selling also lauded how his mini-TV had changed his life: "Now when I go to my son's track meets, I can keep up with other ball games" (Kaplan, 1987, p. 32a). The question is: Is this father going to the track meets to see his son race, or is he going simply to get "credit" from his son for being in the stands? One more ex-

ample: A newspaper story about a father jogging around Golden State Park in San Francisco who is so immersed in his running that he fails to notice his 3-year-old daughter—whom he apparently had brought with him—crying "Daddy, Daddy" along the side of the running track. When he finally notices her, he stops only long enough to tell his daughter that it is not his job to watch her, but her job to watch for him (Gustatis, 1982).

What will be the impact of the mixed messages that these children—and perhaps countless others—are getting from their fathers? Research capable of measuring and assessing the complexity of these encounters is needed to adequately answer this question (Pleck, 1983).

Marital Conflict in Childbearing and Child-Rearing Families

Because our study was longitudinal, we were able to trace changes over time; and we found that from the third, to the sixth, to the ninth month postpartum, couples became more traditional, with fathers doing proportionately less child care (LaRossa & LaRossa, 1981). It was this traditionalization process that provided us with a close-up view of what happens when the bubble bursts; that is, what happens when the romanticized vision of dad's involvement starts to break down.

One father, first interviewed around the third month after his daughter's birth, wanted to communicate that he was not going to be an absentee father like some of his friends were:

> *I've got a good friend of mine, he's the ultimate male chauvinist pig. He will not change a diaper. . . . [But] I share in changing the diapers, and rocking the baby, and in doing those kinds of things. . . . I love babies.*

During the sixth month interview, however, it was revealed that he indeed had become very much the absentee father. In fact, almost every evening since the first interview he had left the house after dinner to play basketball, or participate in an amateur theater group, or sing in the local choir.

Since what he was doing contradicted what he said he would do, he was asked by his wife to "account" for his behavior. *Accounts* are demanded of social actors whose behavior is thought to be out of line. By submitting an account, which in common parlance generally takes the form of an excuse or justification, and having it honored or accepted by the offended party, a person who stands accused can manage to create or salvage a favorable impression (Scott & Lyman, 1968). Because the wife did not honor the accounts that her husband offered, the father was put in the position of either admitting he was wrong (i.e., apologizing) or coming up with more accounts. He chose the latter, and in due course offered no fewer than 20 different explanations for his conduct, to include "I help out more than most husbands do" and "I'm not good at taking care of the baby." At one dramatic point during the second interview, the husband and wife got into a verbal argument over how much of the husband's contribution to child care was "fact" and how much was "fancy." (He, with his head: "I *know* I was [around a lot]." She with her heart: "[To me] it just doesn't *feel* like he was.")

This couple illustrates what may be happening in many homes as a result of the asynchrony between the culture and conduct of fatherhood. In the past, when (as best we can tell) both the culture and conduct of fatherhood were more or less traditional, fathers may not have been asked to account for their low paternal involvement. If the culture said that fathers should not be involved with their children and if fathers were not involved with their children, then fathers were perceived as doing what they should be doing. No need for an explanation. Today, however, the culture and conduct of fatherhood appear to be out of sync. The culture has moved toward (not to) androgyny much more rapidly than the conduct. On some level of consciousness, fathers and mothers believe that the behavior of fathers will measure up to the myth. Usually, this is early in the parental game, before or just after the birth of the first child. In time, however, reality sets in, and on another level of consciousness it becomes apparent that mom is doing more than planned because dad is doing less than planned. The wife challenges the legitimacy of the (more unequal than she had foreseen) division of child care, demanding an explanation from her husband, which may or may not be offered, and if offered may or may not be honored, and so on.

In short, one would expect more conflict in marriage today centered around the legitimacy of the division of child care than, say, 40 years ago because of the shift in the culture of fatherhood that has occurred during this time. Some may say, "Great, with more conflict there will be needed change." And their point is valid. But what must be kept in mind is that conflict also can escalate and destroy. Given that at least one recent study has reported that the most likely conflict to lead a couple to blows is conflict over children (Straus, Gelles, & Steinmetz, 1980), family researchers and practitioners would be well advised to pay attention to the possibility that violence during the transition to parenthood may be one negative consequence of asynchronous social change.

Fathers and Guilt

Several years ago, Garry Trudeau (1985), who writes *Doonesbury*, captured to a tee the asynchrony between the culture and conduct of fatherhood when he depicted a journalist-father sitting at his home computer and working on an autobiographical column on "The New Fatherhood" for the Sunday section of the newspaper. "My editor feels there's a lot of interest in the current, more involved generation of fathers," the journalist tells his wife who has just come in the room. "He asked me to keep an account of my experiences." Trudeau's punch line is that when Super Dad is asked by his wife to watch his son because she has to go to a meeting, he says no because if he did, he would not meet his deadline. In the next day's *Doonesbury*, Trudeau fired another volley at the new breed of fathers.

Now the son is standing behind his computer-bound father and ostensibly is asking for his father's attention. But again Super Dad is too busy pecking away at his fatherhood diary to even look up: "Not now, son. Daddy's busy" (March 24 & 25).

Trudeau's cartoons, copies of which sit on my wall in both my office and my den, are a reminder to me not to be so caught up in writing about what it means to be a father (thus contributing to the culture of fatherhood) that I fail to *be* a father. The fact, however, that I took the time to cut the cartoons out of the newspaper (and make not one but two copies) and the fact that Trudeau, who is himself a father, penned the cartoons in the first place is indicative of a feeling that many men today experience, namely ambivalence over their performance as fathers.

To feel "ambivalent" about something is to feel alternately good and bad about it. The plethora of autobiographical books and articles written by fathers in the past few years conveys the impression that men do feel and, perhaps most importantly, should feel good about their performance as fathers. A lot of men do seem to be proud of their performance, what with all the references to "new" fatherhood and the like. At the same time, however, men are being almost constantly told—and can see for themselves, if they look close enough—that their behavior does not square with the ideal, which means that they are being reminded on a regular basis that they are *failing* as fathers. Failing not when compared with their own fathers or grandfathers perhaps, but failing when compared with the image of fatherhood which has become part of our culture and which they, on some level of consciousness, believe in.

This is not to suggest that in the past men were totally at ease with their performance as fathers, that they had no doubts about whether they were acting "correctly." For one thing, such an assertion would belie the fact that role playing is, to a large degree, improvisational, that in everyday life (vs. the theater) scripts almost always are ill defined and open to a variety of in-terpretations (Blumer, 1969). Perhaps more importantly, asserting that men in the past were totally at ease with their performance as fathers would ignore the fact that, contrary to what many think, some of our fathers and grandfathers were ambivalent about the kind of job they were doing. In a study just begun on the history of fatherhood in America, I have come across several cases of men in the early 1900s expressing concern over the quality of their paternal involvement. In 1925, for example, one father wrote to a psychologist to ask whether he was *too involved* with his 2-year-old son. Apparently, he had taught the boy both the alphabet and how to count, and he now wondered whether he had forced his son to learn too much too soon (LaRossa, 1988).

So, what *is* the difference between then and now? I would say it is a difference in degree, not kind. I would hypothesize that, given the asynchrony between the culture and conduct of fatherhood, the number of fathers who feel ambivalent and, to a certain extent, guilty about their performance as fathers has increased over the past three generations. I would also hypothesize that, given it is the middle class which has been primarily responsible for the changes in the culture of fatherhood, it is the middle class fathers who are likely to feel the most ambivalent and suffer from the most guilt.

There is a certain amount of irony in the proposition that middle-class men are the ones who are the most likely to experience ambivalence and guilt, in that middle-class men are also the ones who seem to be trying the hardest to act according to the emerging ideal. As noted, the testimonials from the so-called androgynous fathers almost invariably are written by middle-class professionals. But it is precisely because these middle-class professionals are trying to conform to the higher standards that one would expect that they would experience the most ambivalence and guilt. Like athletes training for the Olympics, androgynous-striving fathers often are consumed with how they are doing as fathers and how they can do better. For example:

Should I play golf today, or should I spend more time playing with Scott and Julie? Should I stay late in the office to catch up or should I leave early to go home and have dinner with the children? There is an endless supply of these dilemmas each day. (Belsky, 1986, p. 64)

Some may argue that the parental anxiety that men are beginning to experience is all for the better, that they now may start feeling bad enough about their performance to really change. This argument does have merit. Yes, one positive outcome of asynchronous social change is that ultimately men may become not only more involved with their children but also more sensitive to what it is like to be a mother. After all, for a long time women have worried about *their* performance as parents. It should not be forgotten, however, that the guilt which many women experience as mothers (and which has been the subject of numerous novels, plays, and films) has not always been healthy for mothers—or families. In sum, when it comes to parenthood, today it would appear that both men and women can be victims as well as beneficiaries of society's ideals.

CONCLUSION

Fatherhood is different today than it was in prior times but, for the most part, the changes that have occurred are centered in the culture rather than in the conduct of fatherhood. Whatever changes have taken place in the behavior of fathers, on the basis of what we know now, seem to be minimal at best. Also, the behavioral changes have largely occurred within a single group—the middle class.

The consequences of the asynchrony between the (comparatively speaking) "modern" culture of fatherhood and the "less modern" or "traditional" conduct of fatherhood are (a) the emergence of the technically present but functionally absent father, (b) an increase in marital conflict in childbearing and child-rearing families, and (c) a greater number of fathers, especially in the middle class, who feel ambivalent and guilty about their performance as fathers.

A number of recommendations seem to be in order. First, more people need to be made aware of the fact that the division of child care in America has not significantly changed, that—despite the beliefs that fathers are a lot more involved with their children—mothers remain, far and away, the primary child caregivers. The reason for publicizing this fact is that if our beliefs represent what we want (i.e., more involved fathers) and we mistakenly assume that what we want is what we have, our complacency will only serve to perpetuate the culture-conduct disjunction. Thus, scholars and representatives of the media must commit themselves to presenting a balanced picture of "new fatherhood."

Second, and in line with the above, men must be held responsible for their actions. In our study of the transition to parenthood, we found that the language that couples use to account for men's lack of involvement in infant care does not simply reflect the division of infant care, it constructs that division of infant care. In other words, the accounts employed by new parents to excuse and justify men's paternal role distance serves as a social lubricant in the traditionalization process (LaRossa & LaRossa, 1981). Thus, when men say things like "I'm not good at taking care of the baby" or "I can't be with Junior now, I have to go to the office, go to the store, go to sleep, mow the lawn, pay the bills, and so forth" the question must be raised, are these reasons genuine (i.e., involving insurmountable role conflicts) or are they nothing more than rationalizations used by men to do one thing (not be with their children) but believe another ("I like to be with my children")? If they are rationalizations, then they should not be honored. Not honoring rationalizations "delegitimates" actions and, in the process, puts the burden of responsibility for the actions squarely on the person who is carrying out the actions. Only when men are forced to seriously examine their commitment to fatherhood (vs. their commitment to their jobs and avocations) can we hope to bring about the kinds of changes that will be required to alter the division of child care in this country (LaRossa, 1983).

What kinds of changes are we talking about? Technically present but functionally absent fathers are products of the society in which we live. So also, the traditionalization process during the transition to parenthood and the conflict and guilt it apparently engenders cannot be divorced from the sociohistorical reality surrounding us and of which we are a part. All of which means that if we hope to alter the way men relate to their children, we cannot be satisfied with individualistic solutions which see "the problem" as a private therapeutic matter best solved through consciousness raising groups and the like. Rather, we must approach it as a public issue and be prepared to alter the institutional fabric of American society (cf. Mills, 1959). For example, the man-as-breadwinner model of fatherhood, a model which emerged in the 19th and early 20th centuries and which portrays fathers primarily as breadwinners whose wages make family consumption and security possible, remains dominant today (Pleck, 1987). This model creates structural barriers to men's involvement with their children, in that it legitimates inflexible and highly demanding job schedules which, in turn, increase the conflict between market work and family work (Pleck, 1985). More flex-time jobs would help to relieve this conflict. So would greater tolerance, on the part of employers, of extended paternity leaves (Levine, 1976). I am not suggesting that the only reason that men are not as involved with their children is that their jobs keep them from getting involved. The fact that many women also contend with inflexible and highly demanding job schedules and still are relatively involved with their children would counter such an assertion. Rather, the point is that the level of achievement in market work expected of men in America generally is higher than the level of achievement in market work expected of women and that this socio-historical reality must be entered into any equation which attempts to explain why fathers are not more involved.

When we will begin to see significant changes in the conduct of fatherhood is hard to say. The past generally provides the data to help predict the future. But, as the historian John Demos (1982) once noted, "Fatherhood has a very long history, but virtually no historians" (p. 425). Hence, our ability to make informed predictions about the future of fatherhood is severely limited. Hopefully, as more empirical research—historical and otherwise—on fatherhood is carried out, we will be in a better position to not only see what is coming but to deal with what is at hand.

REFERENCES

Barnett, R. C., & Baruch, G. K. (1987). Determinants of fathers' participation in family work. *Journal of Marriage and the Family, 49*, 29–40.

Belsky, M. R. (1986). Scott's and Julie's Daddy. In C. Kort & R. Friedland (Eds.), *The father's book: Shared experiences* (pp. 63–65). Boston: G. K. Hall.

Benokraitis, N. (1985). Fathers in the dual-earner family. In S. M. H. Hanson & F. W. Bozett (Eds.), *Dimensions of fatherhood* (pp. 243–268). Beverly Hills. CA: Sage Publications.

Berger, M. (1979). Men's new family roles—Some implications for therapists. *Family Coordinator, 28*, 636–646.

Blumer, H. (1969). *Symbolic interactionism: Perspective and method.* Englewood Cliffs, NJ: Prentice Hall.

Caplow, T. with Bahr, H. M., Chadwick, B. A., Hill, R., & Williamson, M. H. (1982). *Middletown families: Fifty years of change and continuity.* Minneapolis: University of Minnesota Press.

Day, R. D., & Mackey, W. C. (1986). The role image of the American father: An examination of a media myth. *Journal of Comparative Family Studies, 17*, 371–388.

Demos, J. (1982). The changing faces of fatherhood: A new exploration in American family history. In S. H. Cath, A. R. Gurwitt, & J. M. Ross (Eds.), *Fa-*

ther and child: Developmental and clinical perspectives (pp. 425–445). Boston: Little, Brown.

Gustatis, R. (1982, August l5). Children sit idle while parents pursue leisure. *Atlanta Journal and Constitution*, pp. 1D, 4D.

Hanson, S. M. H., & Bozett, F. W. (1985). *Dimensions of fatherhood*. Beverly Hills, CA: Sage Publications.

Hanson, S. M. H., & Bozett, F. W. (1987). Fatherhood: A review and resources. *Family Relations, 36,* 333–340.

Harte, S. (1987, June 21). Fathers and sons. Narrowing the generation gap: Atlanta dads reflect a more personal style of parenting. *Atlanta Journal and Constitution*, pp. 4G, 6G.

Juster, F. T. (1985). A note on recent changes in time use. In F. T. Juster & F. P. Stafford (Eds.), *Time, goods, and well-being* (pp. 313–332). Ann Arbor. MI: Institute for Social Research.

Kaplan, D. (1987, Early Summer). The great $39.00 2" TV catch. *DAK Industries Inc.*, p. 32A.

Kort C., & Friedland, R. (Eds.). (1986). *The father's book: Shared experiences*. Boston: G. K. Hall.

Lamb, M. E. (1987). Introduction: The emergent American father. In M. E. Lamb (Ed.), *The father's role: Cross-cultural perspectives* (pp. 3–25). Hillsdale, NJ: Lawrence Erlbaum.

Lamb, M. E., Pleck, J. H., & Levine, J. A. (1987). Effects of increased paternal involvement on fathers and mothers. In C. Lewis & M. O'Brien (Eds.), *Reassessing fatherhood: New observations on fathers and the modern family* (pp. 109–125). Beverly Hills, CA: Sage Publications.

LaRossa, R. (1983). The transition to parenthood and the social reality of time. *Journal of Marriage and the Family, 45,* 579–589.

LaRossa, R. (1986, November). *Toward a social history of fatherhood in America*. Paper presented at the Theory Construction and Research Methodology Workshop, Annual Meeting of National Council of Family Relations, Philadelphia, PA.

LaRossa, R., & LaRossa, M. M. (1981). *Transition to parenthood: How infants change families*. Beverly Hills, CA: Sage Publications.

LeMasters, E. E. (1957). Parenthood as crisis. *Marriage and Family Living, 19,* 352–355.

LeMasters, E. E., & DeFrain, J. (1983). *Parents in contemporary America: A sympathetic view* (4th ed.) Homewood, IL: Dorsey.

Levine, J. A. (1976). *Who will raise the children?* New York: Bantam.

Lewis, C. (1986). *Becoming a father*. Milton Keynes, England: Open University Press.

Lewis, C., & O'Brien, M. (1987). *Reassessing fatherhood: New observations on fathers and the modern family*. Beverly Hills, CA: Sage Publications.

Lutwin, D. R., & Siperstein, G. N. (1985). Househusband fathers. In S. M. H. Hanson & F. W. Bozett (Eds.), *Dimensions of fatherhood* (pp. 269–287). Beverly Hills, CA: Sage Publications.

Lynd, R. S., & Lynd, H. M. (1927). *Middletown: A study in American culture*. New York: Harcourt & Brace.

Lynd, R. S., & Lynd, H. M. (1937). *Middletown in transition: A study of cultural conflicts*. New York: Harcourt & Brace.

Mackey W. C., & Day, R. D. (1979). Some indicators of fathering behaviors in the United States: A crosscultural examination of adult male-child interaction. *Journal of Marriage and the Family, 41,* 287–297.

Margolis, M. L. (1984). *Mothers and such: Views of American women and why they changed*. Berkeley: University of California Press.

McKee, L., & O'Brien, M. (Eds.). (1982). *The father figure*. London: Tavistock.

Mead, M. (1967). Margaret Mead answers: How do middle-class American men compare with men in other cultures you have studied? *Redbook, 129,* 36.

Mills, C. W. (1959). *The sociological imagination*. New York: Oxford University Press.

Parke, R. D. (1981). *Fathers*. Cambridge, MA: Harvard University Press.

Pleck, J. H. (1979). Men's family work: Three perspectives and some data. *Family Coordinator, 28,* 481–488.

Pleck, J. H. (1983). Husbands' paid work and family roles: Current research issues. In H. Z. Lopata & J. H. Pleck (Eds.), *Research in the interweave of social roles. Vol 3. Families and jobs* (pp. 251–333). Greenwich, CT: JAI Press.

Pleck, J. H. (1985). *Working wives/Working husbands*. Beverly Hills, CA: Sage Publications.

Pleck, J. H. (1987). American fathering in historical perspective. In M. S. Kimmel (Ed.), *Changing men: New directions in research on men and masculinity* (pp. 83–97). Beverly Hills, CA: Sage Publications.

Rotundo, E. A. (1985). American fatherhood: A historical perspective. *American Behavioral Scientist, 29,* 7–25.

Scanzoni, J. (1979). Strategies for changing male family roles: Research and practice implications. *Family Coordinator*, *28*, 435–442.

Scott, M. B., & Lyman, S. M. (1968). Accounts. *American Sociological Review*, *33*, 46–62.

Stokes, R., & Hewitt, J. P. (1976). Aligning actions. *American Sociological Review*, *41*, 838–849.

Straus, M., Gelles, R. J., & Steinmetz, S. K. (1980).

Behind closed doors: Violence in the American family. New York: Anchor/Doubleday.

Trudeau, G. B. (1985, March 24 & March 25). *Doonesbury*. United Press Syndicate.

Zerubavel, E. (1979). *Patterns of time in hospital life: A sociological perspective*. Chicago: University of Chicago Press.

LIFE-STYLES OF GAY HUSBANDS AND FATHERS

BRIAN MILLER

The words "gay husband" and "gay father" are often regarded as contradictions in terms. This notion is hinted at in Anita Bryant's widely quoted non sequitur, "Homosexuals recruit because they cannot reproduce." Researchers estimate, however, that in America there are six million gay husbands and fathers (Bozett, 1987; Schulenberg, 1985). Why do these men marry and have children? How do they organize their lives? What are their difficulties and joys as a consequence of their behavior?

To address these questions, 50 gay husbands and fathers were contacted in 1976 by means of multiple-source chain-referral samples. At first interview, 24 of the men were living with their wives; three years later at the second interview, only three had intact marriages. Approximately two-thirds of the respondents have been followed to the present and all of them are now separated (Humphreys and Miller, 1980a). To show the modal developments in gay husbands' and fathers' life-styles, the data are organized along a four-point continuum: Covert Behavior, Marginal Involvement, Transformed Participation, and Open Endorsement.

COVERT BEHAVIOR

Early in adult life, gay husbands and fathers tend to regard their homosexual feelings as nothing more than genital urges. They are reluctant to refer to either themselves or their behavior as gay: "I hate labels" is a common response to questions about sexual orientation. These men have unstable self-concepts—one day thinking they are homosexual and another day thinking they are not. Their reluctance to label their same-sex activity as homosexual is not because they hate labels per se; indeed they strive to present themselves to others under a heterosexual label. Rather, they dislike a label that calls attention to behaviors they would prefer to forget.

Premarital homosexual experiences are often explained away with "It's only a phase" or "God, was I drunk last night!" These men report such activities prior to marriage as arranging heterosexual double-date situations in which they would perform coitus in the back seat of the car, for example, while fantasizing about the male in the front seat. Others report collaborating with a buddy to share a female prostitute. These ostensibly heterosexual acts allowed the men to buttress their sense of heterosexuality while gratifying homosexual urges. During the premarital period, respondents discounted gay life-styles and romanticized heterosexual family living as the only way to achieve the stable home life, loyal companionship, and fatherhood they desired.

These men married in good faith, thinking they could overcome their gay desires; they did not believe they were deceiving their spouses. In fact, most men broached the issue of their homosexual feelings to their wives before mar-

Revised and updated from an article in *Gay Men: The Sociology of Male Homosexuality* by Martin P. Levine. New York: Harper & Row, 1979.

riage, but the information was usually conveyed in an oblique manner and downplayed as inconsequential. This kept their future wives from thinking that they might be marrying homosexuals. Wives' denials of their husbands' homosexuality were further facilitated by the fact that half the women, at their nuptials, were pregnant by the men they were marrying.

In the early years of marriage, high libido provided husbands with easy erections for coitus. Respondents report, however, that this situation tended to deteriorate shortly after the birth of the first child. Increasingly, they found themselves fantasizing about gay erotica during coitus.

Marriage engulfs the men in a heterosexual role, making them marginal to the gay world. Their social isolation from others who share their sexual interests burdens them with "I'm-the-only-one-in-the-world" feelings. These men, realizing their behavior is inconsistent with their heterosexual reputation, try to reduce their anxiety and guilt by compartmentalizing gay and nongay worlds. One respondent said: "I never walk in the door without an airtight excuse of where I've been." Some men avoid the strain of remembering stories by intimidating the wife into silence: "She knows better than to question my whereabouts. I tell her, 'I get home when I get home; no questions asked.'" In these respects, respondents have parallels to their adulterous heterosexual counterparts (Libby and Whitehurst, 1977).

Extramarital sex for respondents usually consists of clandestine, impersonal encounters in parks, tearooms, or highway rest stops, with hitchhikers or male hustlers. (Regarding this, single gays sometimes comment, "Married gays give the rest of us a bad name.") Occasionally, furtiveness itself becomes eroticized, making the men sexually dysfunctional in calmer contexts. Recreational, gay scenes such as dances, parties, and gay organizations are not used by respondents, primarily because they dread discovery and subsequent marital dissolution. Many are further limited by fears that their jobs would be threatened, by lack of geographical access to gay institutions, or by religious scruples. In fact, these men are largely unaware of gay social events in their communities and have little idea of how to participate in them. They tend to be ideologically ambivalent about the gay world, sometimes thinking of it as exotic, and other times condemning it as "superficial, unstable, full of blackmail and violence." Given their exposure to only the impersonal homosexual underground, and not to loving gay relationships, their negative perception is somewhat justified. As long as they remain marginal to the gay world, the likelihood of their participation in safe, fulfilling gay relationships remains minimal (Miller and Humphreys, 1980).

Some men regard their homosexual desires not as an orientation, but as a compulsion: "I don't want to do these things, but I'm driven to do them." Other accounts that explain away their homosexual behavior, emphasize its nonseriousness, and minimize its consequences include (1) "I might be okay if my wife learned to give good blow jobs." (2) "I only go out for it when I'm drunk or depressed." (3) "I go to the truck-stop and meet someone. We're just a couple of horny married guys relieving ourselves. That's not sex. [It] doesn't threaten my marriage like adultery would." (4) "Sex with men is a minor aspect of my life that I refuse to let outweigh more important things."

The respondent who gave this last account also presented conflicting evidence. He spent time, effort, and anxiety in rearranging his schedule to accommodate sex, spending money on his car and fuel to search for willing men, constructing intricate stories to fool work associates and family, and buying his wife penance gifts. He also experienced near misses with police and gay bashers. Still, he viewed all this as only a "minor aspect" of his life.

Another rationalization is "I'm not really homosexual since I don't care if it's a man, woman or dog that's licking my cock. All I want is a hole." Further questioning, however, made clear that this respondent was not looking for just any available orifice. He stated that it was equally important that he persuade the most attractive man available to fellate him.

Another account is the "Eichmann dodge." Men may claim, like Eichmann, that they are the victims of other men's desire, inadvertently caught up and swept along by the events, thereby absolving themselves of responsibility. Men stating this rationalization, however, are often skilled at seducing others into making the first move. Some gay husbands and fathers claim that they limit themselves to one special "friendship" and that no one else of their sex could excite them. If they think of homosexuality at all, they conceive it as promiscuous behavior done by degenerates, not by people like themselves who are loyal and who look conventional.

These accounts help respondents deny homosexuality while practicing it. They find it difficult to simultaneously see themselves as worthwhile persons and as homosexuals, and to reconcile their masculine self-image with the popular image of gays as effeminate. The most they can acknowledge is that they get together with other men to ejaculate and that they fantasize about men during sex with their wives. In spite of their rationalizations, however, these men report considerable anxiety and guilt about maintaining their compartmentalized double lives.

Respondents are reluctant to rate their marriages as "happy," typically referring to them as "duties." The ambivalence is expressed by one who said: "My wife is a good person, but it's funny, I can't live with this marriage and I can't live without it." Respondents report conflict with wives who object to the disproportionate time these men spend away from home, neglecting parental responsibilities. The men view alternatives to marriage as limited, not seeing life in the gay world as a viable option. They find it difficult to talk about their children and express guilt that their work and sex schedules do not allow them to spend as much time with their children as they would like. Nevertheless, most of the men report that their children are the main rea-

son for remaining married: "In this horrible marriage, [the children] are the consolation prize."

MARGINAL INVOLVEMENT

Respondents at this point on the continuum engage in homosexual behavior and have a gay self-identity. However, these men are marginal to the gay community since they have heterosexual public identities, and are often living with their wives. Still, they are much more comfortable with their homoerotic desires than are those in the Covert Behavior group and are more disclosing about their sexual orientation to other gays.

Compared with men in the previous group, Marginally Involved respondents have an expanded repertoire of sexual outlets. They sometimes compile telephone-number lists of sex partners and have limited involvement with small networks of gay friends. The men maintain secrecy by using post office boxes or separate office phones for gay-related business. Fake identities and names may be constructed to prevent identification by sexual partners. Employing male "masseurs" or maintaining a separate apartment for gay sex provide other relatively safe outlets. Consequently, these men are less likely to encounter police entrapment or gay bashers. Gay bars are somewhat inaccessible since they often start too late, and the men cannot regularly find excuses for extended absences from home. Some men resort to lunch-hour or presupper "quickies" at the baths.

In spite of these measures, respondents report many facade-shattering incidents with heterosexuals. Such difficulties include being caught on the street with a gay friend whose presence cannot be explained, blurting out praise about an event, then remembering it was attended with a gay friend, not one's wife, and transferring body lice or a venereal disease from a hustler to the wife, an especially dangerous occurrence in this time of AIDS (Pearson, 1986). Many respondents, however, continue to deny wives' knowledge about their homosexuality: "I don't think my wife really knows. She's only mentioned it a couple of times, and only when she was too drunk to know what she was saying."

Men who travel as part of their business or who have loosely structured working hours enjoy relative freedom. For them, absences and sexual incidents may be more easily covered. A minority of men, specifically those in artistic and academic fields, are able to mix their heterosexual and homosexual worlds. Their circle is that of the relatively wealthy and tolerant in which the epithet "perversion" is replaced by the more neutral "eccentricity," and variant behavior is accepted as long as the man is discreet and does not "rub the wife's nose in it." Several respondents socialize openly with similarly situated men or with gay sex partners whom wives and others ostensibly know as merely work assistants or friends of the family.

Because Marginally Involved respondents are "out" to some audiences and not to others, they sometimes resemble, as one man said, "a crazy quilt of contradictions." This is emphasized by playing word games with questioners or with those who try to penetrate their defenses. Playing the role of the eccentric and giving mixed messages provide a smokescreen for their emotional whereabouts from both gays and nongays.

This adjustment, however, is tenuous and respondents are often ambivalent about maintaining their marriages. They fantasize about life as a gay single, and entertain ideas of divorce. The guilt these respondents experience is sometimes reflected in what might be called Santa Claus behavior. They shower their children—and sometimes their wives—with expensive gifts to counteract feelings that they have done a terrible thing to their family by being homosexual: "It's the least I can do for having ruined their chance to grow up in a normal home." Using credit cards to manage guilt has many of these men in serious debt and laboring as workaholics.

Like men in the first category, these men regret that performing their breadwinner, husband, and homosexual roles leaves little time for the father role. Nevertheless, they are reluctant to

leave their marriages, fearing permanent separation from their children. They also fear community stigma, ambivalently regard the gay world, and are unwilling to endure the decreased standard of living necessitated by divorce.

Over time, it becomes increasingly difficult for these men to reconcile their discordant identities as husband and as homosexual. Although some are able to routinize compartmentalization, others find sustaining the necessary maneuvers for secrecy to be not worth it. Conspiracies of silence and denial within the families become strained, if not transparent. Respondents tend to seek closure by communicating, directly and indirectly, their orientational needs to wives and by becoming more explicit in their methods of making gay contacts. Others are exposed by vice arrests or by being victimized by men they solicit. Most wives are surprised by the direct confrontation. Respondents are surprised that their wives are surprised since respondents may have thought their wives already knew, and tacitly accepted it. Initially wives often react with disbelief, revulsion, and anger: "I feel betrayed." This frequently gives way to a feeling of couple solidarity, that "we can conquer the problem together." When this is the adaptation, respondents do not come out of the closet so much as take their wives into the closet with them.

Couples try a variety of techniques to shore up the marriages. Respondents may seek therapy to "cure" their homosexuality. Some men generously offer wives the freedom to experience extramarital affairs, too, although it appears this is done mostly to relieve respondents' guilt since they know that wives are unlikely to take them up on the offer. When wives do not put the offer to the test, respondents further console their guilt by interpreting this as evidence that the wives are "frigid" or low in "sex drive," although data from the wives dispute this characterization (Hays and Samuels, 1988).

Some couples try instituting new sexual arrangements: a *ménage à trois*, or the husband is allowed out one night a week with gay friends. In the former interaction, wives tend to report feeling "used" and, in the latter, men tend to report feeling they are on a "leash."

Sexual conflicts spill into other domestic areas. Tardiness or missed appointments lead to wives' suspicions and accusations and general marital discord. One man calls this compromise period "white-knuckle heterosexuality." By negotiating groundrules that reinstate partial denial and by intellectualizing the situation, some couples maintain for years the compromise period. This uneasy truce ends if groundrules are repeatedly violated and when the wife realizes (1) that her husband finds men sexier than herself, (2) that he is unalterably gay, (3) that her primary place as object of permanent affection is challenged, and (4) that she has alternatives and can cope without the marriage. Wives gradually come to resent romanceless marriages with men who would rather make love to another man, and the homosexual husbands come to resent, as one man said, being "stifled in a nuptial closet."

Couples who remain married after disclosure tend not to have rejected divorce, but rather have an indefinite postponement of it: "After the children leave home." "After the finances are in order." Other considerations that keep the couples together include religious beliefs, family pressure, wives' dependence, and the perceived nonviability of the gay world.

In most cases, the immediate impetus for ending the marriage is the husband's establishment of a love relationship with another man. As such relationships intensify, men begin to reconstruct the gay world as favorable for effecting companionship and social stability. It is usually wives, however, who take action to terminate the marriages. Painful as this experience is, it somewhat eases the men's guilt for causing marital dissolution.

TRANSFORMED PARTICIPATION

Respondents who reach this point on the continuum engage in homosexual behavior and have self-identities—and to a limited extent, public identities—that reflect acceptance of their behavior. These men generally have come out as gay and left their wives.

Acculturation into the gay world involves three areas of concern for respondents: (1) disadvantage of advanced age and late arrival on the scene, (2) the necessity of learning new gay social definitions and skills, and (3) the need to reconcile prior fantasies to the realities of the gay world. Once respondents no longer live with wives and children, they begin to increase their contacts with the gay world and their marginality to it decreases. They may now subscribe to gay publications, join gay religious congregations, and go to gay social and political clubs and private gay parties. They experience a rapid expansion of gay consciousness and skills and take steps to form close friendships with others of their sexual orientation.

Moving out of the closet, these men report a stabilization of self-concept and a greater sense of psychological well-being. Their attitudes toward homoerotic behavior become more relaxed and better integrated into their everyday lives. Most experience a change in body image, exemplified by improved physical fitness and increased care with their appearance. Many report the elimination of nervous and psychosomatic disorders such as ulcers, excessive fatigue, and back aches, as well as substance abuse.

These respondents' sexual orientation tends to be known by significant others with two exceptions: their employers and children. Secrecy sometimes exists with employers since respondents believe the legal system does not protect their interests should they be dismissed for being gay (Levine, 1981).

Relatively little openness about homosexuality also exists with these respondents' children. Typically, only older children (if any) are told, and it is not considered a topic for general discussion. There is fear that, if the man's gayness becomes known in the community, his employer might find out or his ex-wife might become irked and deny him child visits. Successful legal appeal for gay people in such matters is difficult, a situation these men perceive as legally sanctioned blackmail.

In line with this, most respondents, rather than living with their children, have visiting schedules with them. They do not have the financial resources either to persuade their ex-wives to relinquish the children or to hire care for them while devoting time to their own careers.

Men who are able to terminate marriages without their spouse's discovering their homosexuality avoid this problem. However, fear of subsequent exposure and loss of children through a new court order remains and prompts some men to stay partially closeted even after marital dissolution. In spite of these fears, the degree of passing and compartmentalization of gay and nongay worlds is much less for men at this point on the continuum than for those who are Covert and Marginal.

OPEN ENDORSEMENT

Respondents who reach this point on the continuum not only engage in homosexual behavior and have a self-identity reflective of the behavior but also openly champion the gay community. Although they come from the full range of economic backgrounds, they tend to have high social and occupational resources. Some have tolerant employers; some are full-time gay activists; others are self-employed, often in businesses with largely gay clienteles.

Proud of their newfound identity, these men organize their world, to a great extent, around gay cultures. Much of their leisure, if not occupation, is spent in gay-related pursuits. They have experienced unhappy marriages and divorce, the struggle of achieving a gay identity, and now feel they have arrived at a satisfactory adjustment. These men, consequently, distinguish themselves in ideology from respondents in other categories. For example, what the others refer to as "discretion," men in this category call "duplicity" and "sneaking around." Moreover, what closeted men see as "flaunting," openly gay respondents call "being forthright" and "upfront."

Respondents' efforts in constructing this new life are helped not only by having a gay love relationship, but by the Gay Liberation Movement (Humphreys and Miller, 1980b). Parallel processes are at work whereby the building of a personal gay identity is facilitated by the larger cultural context of increasing gay pride and diversification of gay institutions and heritage (Adam, 1987; Harry and DeVall, 1978; Murray, 1979). Still, coming out is not easy or automatic. This is partly due to the fact that there is no necessary conjunction among sexual behavior fantasy, self-identity, and object of affectional attachment. Although there is a strain toward consistency for most people among these components of sexuality, this is not invariably so. The ways these components change over time and the combinations in which they link with each other are multiple (Miller 1983; Simon and Gagnon, 1969).

Men who reach the Open Endorsement point often have fears that their father and ex-husband statuses could distance them from single gays. Sometimes respondents fear that single gays, similar to nongays, regard them with confusion, curiosity, or pity. Integrating gay and father roles requires patience, since it is often difficult for respondents to find a lover who accepts him and his children as a "package deal," and the gay father may feel he has not enough time and energy to attend to both children and a lover. Selecting a lover who is also a gay father is a common solution to this situation.

Most respondents who have custody of their children did not experience court custody battles but gained custody because the mother did not want the children or because the children, being allowed to choose, chose to live with their fathers. Respondents who live with their children are more likely to have a close circle of gay friends as their main social outlet, rather than participating primarily in gay commercial establishments (McWhirter and Mattison, 1984).

Men at this point on the continuum have told their children about their homosexuality. They report children's reaction to be more positive than expected and, when there is a negative reaction, it generally dissipates over time (Miller, 1979). Children's negative reactions centered more on the parent's divorce and subsequent household changes than on the father's homosexuality per se. Daughters tend to be more accepting of their father's homosexuality than sons, although most children feel their father's honesty brings them closer together. Children report few instances of neighborhood homophobia directed against them, possibly because the children try to disclose only to people they know will react favorably. There is no indication that the children of gay fathers are disproportionately homosexual themselves although, of the children who turned out to be gay, there were more lesbian daughters than gay sons. Wives and relatives sometimes worry that gay men's children will be molested by him or his gay friends. Evidence from this study supports earlier research findings that indicate such fears are unwarranted (Bozett, 1987).

DISCUSSION

The general tendency is for the Covert Behavior respondents to move toward Open Endorsement. There are several caveats, however, about this movement. For example, the continuum should not be construed as reifying transient states into types. Additionally, movement out of marriage into an openly gay identity is not unilateral. There are many negotiations back and forth, in and out of the closet. There is not a finite number of stages; not everyone becomes publicly gay and not everyone passes through every step. Few respondents move easily or accidentally through the process. Rather," each level is achieved by a painful search, negotiating with both oneself and the larger world.

The event most responsible for initiating movement along the continuum and reconstructing gay fathers' perceptions of the gay community is the experience of falling in love with another man. By contrast, factors hindering movement along the continuum include inability to perceive the gay world as a viable alternative as well as perceived lack of support from other gays, economic difficulty, family pressure, poor health, wives' dependence, homophobia in respondents or community, and moral/religious scruples.

This study has several findings. Gayness and traditional marital relationships are perceived by the respondents as discordant compared to relationships established when they move into the gay world. Although respondents perceive gayness as incompatible with traditional marriage, they perceive gayness as compatible with fathering. Highly compartmentalized life-styles and deceit sometimes repress open marital conflict, but unresolved tension characterizes respondents' marriages. In contrast, men who leave their spouses and enter the gay world report gay relationships to be more harmonious than marital relationships. They also report fathering to be more salient once having left their marriages. Men who come out perceive less discrimination from family, friends, and co-workers than those who are closeted anticipate. Wives tend to be upset by their husbands' revelations, but respondents are typically surprised by the positive reactions of their children and their parents.

Future prospects for gay fathers hinge largely on the success of the gay liberation movement. If these men can politicize their status, if they can see their difficulties stemming from social injustice and society's homophobic conditioning rather than personal inadequacy, and if they can redefine themselves, not as deviants, but as an oppressed minority, self-acceptance is improved. This helps lift their depression and externalize anger—anger about prejudice and about wasting their precious early years in the closet. Further, it minimizes their guilt and eases adjustment into the gay community (Miller, 1987).

As the gay liberation movement makes alternatives for fathering available within the gay community, fewer gays are likely to become involved in heterosexual marriages and divorce. Adoption, surrogate parenting, and alternative fertilization are some of the new ways single gays can now experience fatherhood (Miller, 1988). If current trends continue, there will be a proliferation of family life-styles so that parenthood becomes available to all regardless of sexual orientation.

REFERENCES

Adam, B. (1987). *The rise of a gay and lesbian movement*. Boston: Hall.

Bozett, F. W. (1987). *Gay and lesbian parents*. New York: Praeger.

Harry, J. & DeVall, W. (1978). *The social organization of gay males*. New York: Praeger.

Hays, D. & Samuels, A. (1988). Heterosexual women's perceptions of their marriages to bisexual or homosexual men. In F. W. Bozett (Ed.), *Homosexuality in the family*. New York: Haworth.

Humphreys, L. & Miller, B. (1980a). Keeping in touch: Maintaining contact with stigmatized respondents. In W. Shaffir, R. Stebbins & A. Turowetz (Eds.), *Field work experience: Qualitative approaches in social research*. New York: St. Martin's.

Humphreys, L. & Miller, B. (1980b). Identities in the emerging gay culture. In J. Marmor (Ed.), *Homosexual behavior: A modern reappraisal*. New York: Basic.

Levine, M. (1981). Employment discrimination against gay men. In P. Stein (Ed.), *Single life*. New York: St. Martin's.

Libby, R. & Whitehurst, R. (1977). *Marriage and alternatives*. Glenview, IL: Scott, Foresman.

McWhirter, D. & Mattison, A. (1984). *The male couple*. Englewood Cliffs, NJ: Prentice-Hall.

Miller, B. (1979). Gay fathers and their children. *Family Coordinator* 28: 544–552.

Miller, B. (1983). Foreword. In M. W. Ross (Ed.), *The married homosexual man*. London: Routledge & Kegan Paul.

Miller, B. (1987). Counseling gay husbands and fathers. In F. W. Bozett (Ed.), *Gay and lesbian parents*. New York: Praeger.

Miller, B. (1988). Preface. In F. W. Bozett (Ed.), *Homosexuality in the family*. New York: Haworth.

Miller, B. & Humphreys, L. (1980). Lifestyles and violence: Homosexual victims of assault and murder. *Qualitative Sociology* 3: 169–185.

Murray, S. (1979). The institutional elaboration of a quasi-ethnic community. *International Review of Modern Sociology* 9: 165–177.

Pearson, C. (1986). *Good-by, I love you*. New York: Random House.

Schulenberg, J. (1985). *Gay parenting*. New York: Doubleday.

Simon, W. & Gagnon, J. (1969). On psychosexual development. In D. Goslin (Ed.), *Handbook of socialization theory and research*. New York: Rand McNally.

STABILITY AND CHANGE
IN CHICANO MEN'S FAMILY LIVES

SCOTT COLTRANE

One of the most popular pejorative American slang terms to emerge in the 1980s was "macho," used to describe men prone to combative posturing, relentless sexual conquest, and other compulsive displays of masculinity. Macho men continually guard against imputations of being soft or feminine and thus tend to avoid domestic tasks and family activities that are considered "women's work." Macho comes from the Spanish *machismo*, and although the behaviors associated with it are clearly not limited to one ethnic group, Latino men are often stereotyped as especially prone toward macho displays.[1] This chapter uses in-depth interviews with twenty Chicano couples to explore how paid work and family work are divided. As in other contemporary American households, divisions of labor in these Chicano families were far from balanced or egalitarian, and husbands tended to enjoy special privileges simply because they were men. Nevertheless, many couples were allocating household chores without reference to gender, and few of the Chicano men exhibited stereotypical macho behavior.

Chicanos, or Mexican-Americans, are often portrayed as living in poor farm-worker families composed of macho men, subservient women, and plentiful children. Yet these stereotypes have been changing, as diverse groups of people with Mexican and Latin-American heritage are responding to the same sorts of social and economic pressures faced by families of other ethnic backgrounds. For example, most Chicano families in the United States now live in urban centers or their suburbs rather than in traditional rural farming areas, and their patterns of marital interaction appear to be about as egalitarian as those of other American families. What's more, Chicanos will no longer be a numerical minority in the near future. Because of higher-than-average birth rates and continued inmigration, by the year 2015 Chicano children will outnumber Anglos in many southwest states, including California, Texas, Arizona, and New Mexico.[2]

When family researchers study white couples, they typically focus on middle-class suburban households, usually highlighting their strengths. Studies of ethnic minority families, in contrast, have tended to focus on the problems of poor or working-class households living in

This article is based on a study of Dual-Earner Chicano Couples conducted in 1990–1992 by Scott Coltrane with research assistance from Elsa Valdez and Hilda Cortez. Partial funding was provided by the Academic Senate of the University of California, Riverside, and the UCR Minority Student Research Internship Program. Included herein are analyses of unpublished interview excerpts along with selected passages from three published sources: (1) Coltrane, *Family Man: Fatherhood, Housework, and Gender Equity* (New York: Oxford University Press, 1994); (2) Coltrane and Valdez, "Reluctant Compliance: Work/Family Role Allocation in Dual-Earner Chicano Families," in Jane C. Hood (ed.), *Men, Work, and Family* (Newbury Park, CA: Sage, 1994); and (3) Valdez and Coltrane, "Work, Family, and the Chicana: Power, Perception and Equity," in Judith Frankel (ed.), *Employed Mothers and the Family Context* (New York: Springer, 1993).

inner-city or rural settings. Because most research on Latino families in the United States has not controlled for social class, wife's employment status, or recency of immigration, a narrow and stereotyped view of these families as patriarchal and culturally backward has persisted. In addition, large-scale studies of "Hispanics" have failed to distinguish between divergent groups of people with Mexican, Central American, South American, Cuban, Puerto Rican, Spanish, or Portuguese ancestry. In contrast, contemporary scholars are beginning to look at some of the positive aspects of minority families and to focus on the economic and institutional factors that influence men's lives within these families.[3]

In 1990 and 1991, Elsa Valdez and I interviewed a group of twenty middle-class Chicano couples with young children living in Southern California. We were primarily interested in finding out if they were facing the same sorts of pressures experienced by other families, so we selected only families in which both the husband and the wife were employed outside the home— the most typical pattern among young parents in the United States today. We wanted to see who did what in these families and find out how they talked about the personal and financial pushes and pulls associated with raising a family. We interviewed wives and husbands separately in their homes, asking them a variety of questions about housework, child care, and their jobs. Elsewhere, we describe details of their time use and task performance, but here I analyze the couples' talk about work, family, and gender, exploring how feelings of entitlement and obligation are shaped by patterns of paid and unpaid labor.[4]

When we asked husbands and wives to sort sixty-four common household tasks according to who most often performed them, we found that wives in most families were responsible for housecleaning, clothes care, meal preparation, and clean-up, whereas husbands were primarily responsible for home maintenance and repair. Most routine child care was also performed by wives, though most husbands reported that they

made substantial contributions to parenting. Wives saw the mundane daily housework as an ever-present burden that they had to shoulder themselves or delegate to someone else. While many wives did not expect the current division of labor to change, they did acknowledge that it was unbalanced. The men, although acknowledging that things weren't exactly fair, tended to minimize the asymmetry by seeing many of the short repetitive tasks associated with housekeeping as shared activities. Although there was tremendous diversity among the couples we talked to, we observed a general pattern of disagreement over how much family work the other spouse performed.

The sociologist Jesse Bernard provides us with a useful way to understand why this might be. Bernard suggested that every marital union contains two marriages—"his" and "hers."[5] We discovered from our interviews and observations that most of the husbands and wives were, indeed, living in separate marriages or separate worlds. Her world centered around keeping track of the countless details of housework and child care even though she was employed. His world centered around his work and his leisure activities so that he avoided noticing or anticipating the details of running a home. Husbands "helped out" when wives gave them tasks to do, and because they almost always complied with requests for help, most tended to assume that they were sharing the household labor. Because much of the work the women did was unseen or taken for granted by the men, they tended to underestimate their wives contributions and escaped the full range of tensions and strains associated with family work.

Because wives remained in control of setting schedules, generating lists for domestic chores, and worrying about the children, they perceived their husbands as contributing relatively little. A frequent comment from wives was that their husbands "just didn't see" the domestic details, and that the men would not often take responsibility for anticipating and planning for what needed to be done. Although many of the men we interviewed maintained their favored position within the family by "not seeing" various aspects of domestic life and leaving the details and planning to their wives, other couples were in the process of ongoing negotiations and, as described below, were successful at redefining some household chores as shared endeavors.

Concerning their paid work, the families we interviewed reported that both husbands and wives had jobs because of financial necessity. The men made comments like, "we were pretty much forced into it," or "we didn't really have any choice." Although most of the husbands and wives were employed full-time, only a few accepted the wife as an equal provider or true breadwinner. Using the type of job, employment schedule, and earnings of each spouse, along with their attitudes toward providing, I categorized the couples into main-provider families and co-provider families.[6] Main-provider couples considered the husband's job to be primary and the wife's job to be secondary. Co-provider couples in contrast, tended to accept the wife's job as permanent, and some even treated the wife's job as equally important to her husband's. Accepting the wife as an equal provider, or considering the husband to have failed as a provider, significantly shaped the couples' divisions of household labor.

MAIN-PROVIDER FAMILIES

In just under half of the families we interviewed, the men earned substantially more money than their wives and were assumed to be "natural" breadwinners, whereas the women were assumed to be innately better equipped to deal with home and children. Wives in all of these main-provider families were employed, but the wife's job was often considered temporary, and her income was treated as "extra" money and earmarked for special purposes.[7] One main-provider husband said, "I would prefer that my wife did not have to work, and could stay at home with my daughter, but finances just don't permit that." Another commented that his wife made just about enough to cover the costs of child care, suggesting that the children were still her primary responsibility, and that any wages she earned should first be allocated to cover "her" tasks.

The main-provider couples included many wives who were employed part-time, and some who worked in lower-status full-time jobs with wages much lower than their husband's. These women took pride in their homemaker role and readily accepted responsibility for managing the household, although they occasionally asked for help. One part-time bookkeeper married to a recent law-school graduate described their division of labor by saying, "It's a given that I take care of children and housework, but when I am real tired, he steps in willingly." Main-provider husbands typically remained in a helper role: in this case, the law clerk told his wife, "Just tell me what to do and I'll do it." He said that if he came home and she was gone, he might clean house, but that if she was home, he would "let her do it." This reflects a typical division of labor in which the wife acts as household manager and the husband occasionally serves as her helper.[8]

This lawyer-to-be talked about early negotiations between he and his wife that seemed to set the tone for current smoldering arguments about housework:

> When we were first married, I would do something and she wouldn't like the way that I did it. So I would say, "OK, then, you do it, and I won't do it again." That was like in our first few years of marriage when we were first getting used to each other, but now she doesn't discourage me so much. She knows that if she does, she's going to wind up doing it herself.

His resistance and her reluctance to press for change reflect an unbalanced economy of gratitude.[9] When he occasionally contributed to housework or child care, she was indebted to him. She complimented him for being willing to step in when she asked for help, but privately lamented the fact that she had to negotiate for each small contribution. Firmly entrenched in the main-provider role and somewhat oblivious to the daily rituals of housework and child care, he felt justified in needing prodding and encouragement. When she did ask him for help, she was careful to thank him for dressing the children or for giving her a ten-minute break from them. While these patterns of domestic labor and inequities in the exchange of gratitude were long-standing, tension lurked just below the surface for this couple. He commented, "My wife gets uptight with me for agreeing to help out my mom, when she feels she can't even ask me to go to the store for her."

Another main-provider couple reflected a similar pattern of labor allocation, but claimed that the arrangement was fair to them both. The woman, a part-time teacher's aide, acknowledged that she loved being a wife and mother and "naturally" took charge of managing the household. She commented, "I have the say so on the running of the house, and I also decide on the children's activities." Although she had a college degree, she described her current part-time job as "ideal" for her. She was able to work twenty hours per week at a neighborhood school and was home by the time her own children returned home from their school. While she earned only $6,000 per year, she justified the low salary because the job fit so well with "the family's schedule." Her husband's administrative job allowed them to live comfortably since he earned almost $50,000 annually.

This secondary-provider wife said that they divided household tasks in a conventional manner: She did most all of the cleaning, cooking, clothes-care, and child-care tasks, while he did the yard work, home repairs, and finances. Her major complaints were that her husband didn't notice things, that she had to nag him, and that he created more housework for her. "The worst part about the housework and child care is the amount of nagging I have to do to get him to help. Also, for example, say I just cleaned the house; he will leave the newspaper scattered all over the place or he will leave wet towels on the bathroom floor."

When asked whether there had been any negotiation over who would do what chores, the husband responded, "I don't think a set decision was made, it was a necessity." His wife's response was similar, "It just evolved that way, we never really talked about it." His provider role was taken for granted, but occasionally she voiced some muted resentment. For example, she commented that it upset her when he told her that she should not be working because their youngest child was only five years old. As an afterthought, she mentioned that she was sometimes bothered by the fact that she had not advanced her career, or worked overtime, since that would have interfered with "the family's" schedule.

In general, wives of main-providers not only performed virtually all housework and child care, but both spouses accepted this as "natural" or "normal." Main provider husbands assumed that financial support was their "job" or their "duty." When one man was asked about how it felt to make more money than his wife, he responded by saying: "It's my job, I wouldn't feel right if I didn't make more money. . . . Anyway that I look at it, I have to keep up my salary, or I'm not doing my job. If it costs $40,000 to live nowadays and I'm not in a $40,000-a-year job, then I'm not gonna be happy."

This same husband, a head mechanic who worked between 50 and 60 hours per week, also showed how main-provider husbands sometimes felt threatened when women begin asserting themselves in previously all-male occupational enclaves:

As long as women mind their own business, no problem with me. . . . There's nothing wrong with them being in the job, but they shouldn't try to do more than that. Like, if you get a secretary that's nosy and wants to run the company, hey, well, we tell her where to stick it. . . . When you can't do my job, don't tell me how to do it.

The mechanic's wife, also a part-time teacher's aide, subtly resisted by "spending as little time on housework as I can get away with." Nevertheless, she still considered it her sole duty to cook, and only when her husband was away at

National Guard training sessions did she feel she could "slack off" by not placing "regular meals" on the family's table each night.

THE PROVIDER ROLE AND FAILED ASPIRATIONS

Wives performed most of the household labor in main-provider couples, but if main-provider husbands had failed career aspirations, more domestic work was shared. What appeared to tip the economy of gratitude away from automatic male privilege was the wife's sense that the husband had not fulfilled his occupational potential. For example, one main-provider husband graduated from a four-year college and completed two years of post-graduate study without finishing his Master's Thesis. At the time of the interview, he was making about $30,000 a year as a self-employed house painter, and his wife was making less than half that amount as a full-time secretary. His comments show how her evaluation of his failed or postponed career aspirations led to more bargaining over his participation in routine housework:

She reminds me that I'm not doing what we both think I should be doing, and sometimes that's a discouragement. I might have worked a lot of hours, and I'll come home tired, for example, and she'll say, "You've gotta clean the house," and I'll say, "Damn I'm tired, I'd like to get a little rest in," but she says "you're only doing this because it's been your choice." She tends to not have sympathy for me in my work because it was more my choice than hers.

He acknowledged that he should be doing something more "worthwhile," and hoped that he would not be painting houses for more than another year. Still, as long as he stayed in his current job, considered beneath him by both of them, she would not allow him to use fatigue from employment as a way to get out of doing housework:

I worked about 60 hours a week the last couple of weeks. I worked yesterday [Saturday], and today—

if it had been my choice—I would have drank beer and watched TV. But since she had a baby shower to go to, I babysitted my nephews. And since we had you coming, she kind of laid out the program: "You've gotta clean the floors, and wash the dishes and do the carpets. So get to it buddy!" [Laughs.]

This main-provider husband capitulated to his wife's demands, but she still had to set tasks for him and remind him to perform them. In responding to her "program," he used the strategy of claimed incompetence that other main-provider husbands also used. While he admitted that he was proficient at the "janitorial stuff," he was careful to point out that he was incapable of dusting or doing the laundry:

It's amazing what you can do when you have little time and you just get in and do it. And I'm good at that. I'm good at the big cleaning, I'm good at the janitorial stuff. I can do the carpet, do the floors, do all that stuff. But I'm no good on the details. She wants all the details just right, so she handles dusting, the laundry, and stuff like that. . . . You know, like I would have everything come out one color.

By re-categorizing some of the housework as "big cleaning," this husband rendered it accountable as men's work. He drew the line at laundry and dusting, but he had transformed some household tasks, like vacuuming and mopping, into work appropriate for men to do. He was complying, albeit reluctantly, to many of his wife's requests because they agreed that he had not fulfilled "his" job as sole provider. He still yearned to be the "real" breadwinner and shared his hope that getting a better paying job would mean that he could ignore the housework:

Sharing the house stuff is usually just a necessity. If, as we would hope in the future, she didn't have to work outside the home, then I think I would be comfortable doing less of it. Then she would be the primary house-care person and I would be the primary financial-resource person. I think roles would change then, and I would be comfortable with her doing more of the dishes and more of the cleaning, and I think she would too. In that sense,

I think traditional relationships—if traditional means the guy working and the woman staying home—is a good thing. I wouldn't mind getting a taste of it myself!

A similar failed aspirations pattern was found in another main-provider household, in spite of the fact that the husband had a college degree and a job as an elementary-school teacher. While his wife earned less than a sixth of what he did, she was working on an advanced degree and co-ordinated a nonprofit community program. In this family, unlike most of the others, the husband performed more housework than he did child care, though both he and his wife agreed that she did more of both. Nevertheless, he performed these household chores reluctantly and only in response to prodding from his wife: "Housework is mostly her responsibility. I like to come home and kick back. Sometimes she has to complain before I do anything around the house. You know when she hits the wall, then I start doing things."

This main-provider husband talked about how his real love was art, and how he had failed to pursue his dream of being a graphic artist. The blocked occupational achievement in his case was not that he didn't make good money in a respected professional job, but that he was not fulfilling his "true" potential. His failed career goals increased her willingness to make demands on him, influenced their division of household labor, and helped shape feelings of entitlement between them: "I have talents that she doesn't have. I guess that's one of my strongest strengths, that I'm an artist. But she's very disappointed in me that I have not done enough of it . . ."

Another main-provider husband held a job as a telephone lineman, and his wife ran a family day-care center out of their home, which earned her less than a third of what he made. She talked about her regrets that he didn't do something "more important" for a living, and he talked about her frequent reminders that he was "too smart for what I'm doing." Like the other failed-

aspirations husbands, he made significant contributions to domestic chores, but his resentment showed when he talked about "the wife" holding a job far from home:

What I didn't like about it was that I used to get home before the wife, because she had to commute, and I'd have to pop something to eat. Most of the time it was just whatever I happened to find in the fridge. Then I'd have to go pick up the kids immediately from the babysitter, and sometimes I had evening things to do, so what I didn't like was that I had to figure out a way to schedule baby watch or baby sitting.

Even when main-provider husbands began to assume responsibility for domestic work in response to "necessity" or "nagging," they seemed to cling to the idea that these were still "her" chores. Coincidentally, most of the secondary-provider wives reported that they received little help unless they "constantly" reminded their husbands. What generally kept secondary-provider wives from resenting their husband's resistance was their own acceptance of the homemaker role and their recognition of his superior financial contributions. When performance of the male-provider role was deemed to be lacking in some way—i.e., failed aspirations or low occupational prestige—wives' resentment appeared closer to the surface, and they were more persistent in demanding help from their husbands.

AMBIVALENT CO-PROVIDERS

Over half of the couples we interviewed were classified as co-providers. The husbands and wives in these families had more equal earnings and placed a higher value the wife's employment than those in main-provider families, but there was considerable variation in terms of their willingness to accept the woman as a full and equal provider. Five of the twelve husbands in the co-provider group were ambivalent about sharing the provider role and were also reluctant to share most household tasks. Compared to their wives, ambivalent co-provider husbands usually held jobs that were roughly equivalent in terms of occupational prestige and worked about the same number of hours per week, but because of gender bias in the labor market, the men earned significantly more than their wives. Compared to main-provider husbands, they considered their wives' jobs to be relatively permanent and important, but they continued to use their own job commitments as justification for doing little at home. Ambivalent co-provider husbands' family obligations rarely intruded into their work lives, whereas their wives' family obligations frequently interfered with their paid work. Such asymmetrically permeable work/family boundaries are common in single-earner and main-provider families, but must be supported with subtle ideologies and elaborate justifications when husbands and wives hold similar occupational positions.[10]

Ambivalent co-provider husbands remained in a helper role at home, perceiving their wives to be more involved parents and assuming that housework was also primarily their wives' responsibility. The men used their jobs to justify their absence from home, but most also lamented not being able to spend more time with their families. For instance, one husband who worked full time as a city planner was married to a woman who worked an equal number of hours as an office manager. In talking about the time he put in at his job, he commented, "I wish I had more time to spend with my children, and to spend with my wife too, of course, but it's a fact of life that I have to work." His wife, in contrast, indicated that her paid job, which she had held for fourteen years, did not prohibit her from adequately caring for her three children, or taking care of "her" household chores. Ambivalent co-provider husbands did not perform significantly more housework and child care than main-provider husbands, and generally did fewer household chores than main-provider husbands with failed career aspirations.

Not surprisingly, ambivalent co-provider husbands tended to be satisfied with their current divisions of labor, even though they usually admitted that things were "not quite fair." One junior-high-school teacher married to a bilingual-education program coordinator described his reactions to their division of family labor:

> To be honest, I'm totally satisfied. When I had a first-period conference, I was a little more flexible; I'd help her more with changing 'em, you know, getting them ready for school, since I didn't have to be at school right away. Then I had to switch because they had some situation out at fifth-period conference, so that now she does it a little bit more than I do, and I don't help out with the kids as much in the morning because I have to be there an hour earlier.

This ambivalent co-provider clearly saw himself as "helping" his wife with the children, yet made light of her contributions by saying she does "a little bit more than I do." He went on to reveal how his wife did not enjoy similar special privileges due to her employment, since she had to pick up the children from day care every day, as well as taking them to school in the mornings:

> She gets out a little later than I do, because she's an administrator but I have other things outside. I also work out, I run, and that sort of gives me a time away, to do that before they all come here. I have community meetings in the evenings sometimes, too. So, I mean, it might not be totally fair—maybe 60/40—but I'm thoroughly happy with the way things are.

While he was "thoroughly happy" with the current arrangements, she thought that it was decidedly unfair. She said, "I don't like the fact that it's taken for granted that I'm available. When he goes out he just assumes I'm available, but when I go out I have to consult with him to make sure he is available." For her, child care was a given; for him, it was optional. He commented, "If I don't have something else to do, then I'll take the kids."

Ambivalent co-provider husbands also tended to talk about regretting that their family involvements limited their careers or personal activities. For instance the school teacher discussed above lamented that he could not do what he used to before he had children:

Having children keeps me away from thinking a lot about my work. You know, it used to be, before we had kids, I could have my mind geared to work—you know how ideas just pop in, you really get into it. But with kids it doesn't get as—you know, you can't switch. It gets more difficult, it makes it hard to get into it. I don't have that freedom of mind, you know, and it takes away from aspects of my work, like doing a little bit more reading or research that I would like to do. Or my own activities, I mean, I still run, but not as much as I used to. I used to play basketball, I used to coach, this and that . . .

Other ambivalent co-provider husbands talked about the impact of children on their careers and personal lives with less bitterness and more appreciation for establishing a relationship with their children. Encouraged by their wives to alter their priorities, some reinterpreted the relative importance of career and family commitments:

I like the way things are going. Let's put it this way. I mean, it's just that once you become a parent, it's a never-ending thing. I coach my kid for example, this past week we had four games. . . . I just think that by having a family that your life becomes so involved after awhile with your own kids, that it's very difficult. I coached at the varsity level for one year, but I had to give it up. I would leave in the morning when they were asleep, and I would get out of coaches' meetings at ten or eleven at night. My wife said to me, "think about your priorities, man; you leave when the kids are asleep, come back when they are asleep." So I decided to change that act. So I gave it up for one year, and I was home all the time. Now I am going to coach again, but it's at lower levels, and I'll be home every day. I have to make adjustments for my family. Your attitude changes, it's not me that counts anymore.

Whereas family labor was not shared equally in this ambivalent co-provider couple, the husband, at his wife's urging, was beginning to ac-

cept and appreciate that his children were more important than his job. He was evaluating his attachment to his children on his wife's terms, but he was agreeing with her, and he had begun to take more responsibility for them.

Many of these husbands talked about struggles over wanting to spend more time on their careers, and most did not relinquish the assumption that the home was the wife's domain. For example, some ambivalent co-provider couples attempted to alleviate stress on the wife by hiring outside help. In response to a question about whether their division of labor was fair, a self-employed male attorney said, "Do you mean fair like equal? It's probably not equal, so probably it wouldn't be fair, but that's why we have a housekeeper." His wife, a social worker earning only ten percent less than he, said that the household was still her responsibility, but that she now had fewer tasks to do: "When I did not have help, I tended to do everything, but with a housekeeper, I don't have to do so much." She went on to talk about how she wished he would do more with their five- and eight-year-old children, but speculated that he probably would as they grew older.

Another couple paid a live-in babysitter/housekeeper to watch their three children during the day while he worked full-time in construction and she worked full-time as a psychiatric social worker. While she labeled the outside help as "essential," she noted that her husband contributed more to the mess than he did to its cleanup. He saw himself as an involved father because he played with his children, and she acknowledged this, but she also complained that he competed with them in games as if he were a child himself. His participation in routine household labor was considered optional, as evidenced by his comment, "I like to cook once in a while."

CO-PROVIDERS

In contrast, about a third of the couples we interviewed fully accepted the wife's long-term employment, considered her career to be just as important as his, and were in various stages of redefining household labor as men's work. Like the ambivalent couples discussed above, full co-provider spouses worked about the same number of hours as each other, but on the whole, these couples worked more total hours than their more ambivalent counterparts, though their annual incomes were a bit lower. According to both husbands and wives, the sharing of housework and child care was substantially greater for full co-providers than for ambivalent co-providers, and also much more balanced than for main-providers.

Like ambivalent co-providers, husbands in full co-provider families discussed conflicts between work and family and sometimes alluded to the ways that their occupational advancement was limited by their commitments to their children. One husband and wife spent the same number of hours on the job, earned approximately the same amount of money, and were employed as engineering technicians for the same employer. When we asked him how his family involvement had affected his job performance, he responded by saying, "It should, OK, because I really need to spend a lot more time learning my work, and I haven't really put in the time I need to advance in the profession. I would like to spend, I mean I *would* spend, more time if I didn't have kids. I'd like to be able to play with the computer or read books more often." Although he talked about conflicts between job and family, he also emphasized that lost work time was not really a sacrifice because he valued time with his children so highly. He did not use his job as an excuse to get out of doing child care or housework, and he seemed to value his wife's career at least as much as his own:

I think her job is probably more important than mine because she's been at that kind of work a lot longer than I have. And at the level she is—it's awkward the way it is, because I get paid just a little bit more than she does, I have a higher position. But she definitely knows the work a lot more, she's been doing the same type of work for about nine years already, and I've only been doing this type of engineering work for about two-and-a-half

years, so she knows a lot more. We both have to work, that's for sure.

Recognition of their roughly equivalent professional status and the need for two equal providers affected this couple's division of parenting and housework. The husband indicated that he did more child care and housework than his wife, and she gave him much credit for his efforts, but in her interview, she indicated that he still did less than half. She described her husband's relationship with their seven-year-old son as "very caring," and noted that he assists the boy with homework more than she does. She also said that her husband did most of the heavy cleaning and scrubbing, but also commented that he doesn't clean toilets and doesn't always notice when things get dirty. The husband described their allocation of housework by saying, "Maybe she does less than I do, but some of the things she does, I just will not do. I will not dust all the little things in the house. That's one of my least favorite things, but I'm more likely to do the mopping and vacuuming." This husband's comments also revealed some ongoing tension about whose housework standards should be maintained. He said, "she has high standards for cleanliness that you would have to be home to maintain. Mind tend to acknowledge that you don't always get to this stuff because you have other things to do. I think I have a better acceptance that one priority hurts something else in the background."

While this couple generally agreed about how to raise their son, standards for child care were also subject to debate. He saw himself as doing more with his son than his wife, as reflected in comments such as "I tend to think of myself as the more involved parent, and I think other people have noticed that, too." While she had only positive things to say about his parenting, he offered both praise and criticism of her parenting:

She can be very playful. She makes up fun games. She doesn't always put enough into the educational part of it, though, like exploring or reading. . . . She cherishes tune-up time [job-related study or preparation], and sometimes I feel she should be using that time to spend with him. Like at the beach, I'll play with him, but she'll be more likely to be under the umbrella reading.

Like many of the other husbands, he went on to say that he thought their division of labor was unfair. Unlike the others, however, he indicated that he thought their current arrangements favored *her* needs, not his:

I think I do more housework. It's probably not fair, because I do more of the dirtier tasks. . . . Also, at this point, our solution tends to favor her free time more than my free time. I think that has more to do with our personal backgrounds. She has more personal friends to do things with, so she has more outside things to do whereas I say I'm not doing anything.

In this family, comparable occupational status and earnings, coupled with a relatively egalitarian ideology, led to substantial sharing of both child care and housework. While the husband tended to take more credit for his involvement than his wife gave him, we can see a difference between their talk and that of some of the families discussed above. Other husbands sometimes complained about their wife's high standards, but they also treated housework, and even parenting, as primarily *her* duty. They usually resented being nagged to do more around the house and failed to move out of a helper role. Rarely did such men consider it *their* duty to anticipate, schedule, and take care of family and household needs. In this co-provider household, in contrast, the gendered allocation of responsibility for child care and housework was not assumed. Because of this, negotiations over housework and parenting were more frequent than in the other families. Since they both held expectations that each would fulfill both provider and caretaker roles, resentments came from both spouses—not just from the wife.

Our interviews suggest that it might be easier for couples to share both provider and homemaker roles when, like the family above, the wife's earnings and occupational prestige equal or exceed those of her husband. For instance, in one of the couples reporting the most sharing of child care and housework, the wife earned $36,000 annually as the executive director of a non-profit community organization and a consultant, and her husband earned $30,000 as a self-employed general contractor. This couple started off their marriage with fairly conventional gender-role expectations and an unbalanced division of labor. While the husband's ideology had changed somewhat, he still talked like most of the main-provider husbands:

As far the household is concerned, I divide a house into two categories: one is the interior and the other is the exterior. For the interior, my wife pushes me to deal with that. The exterior, I'm left to it myself. So, what I'm basically saying is that generally speaking, a woman does not deal with the exterior. The woman's main concern is with the interior, although there is a lot of deviation.

In this family, an egalitarian belief system did not precede the sharing of household labor. The wife was still responsible for setting the "interior" household agenda and had to remind her husband to help with housework and child care. When asked whether he and his wife had arguments about housework, this husband laughed and said, "All the time, doesn't everybody?"

What differentiated this couple from most others, is that she made more money than he did and had no qualms about demanding help from him. While he had not yet accepted the idea that interior chores were equally his, he reluctantly performed them. She ranked his contributions to child care to be equal to hers, and rated his contributions to housework only slightly below her own. While not eagerly rushing to do the cooking, cleaning, or laundry, he complied with occasional reminders and according to his wife, was "a better cleaner" than she was.

His sharing stemmed, in part, from her higher earnings and their mutual willingness to reduce his "outside chores" by hiring outside help. Unlike the more ambivalent co-providers who hired housekeepers to do "her" chores, this couple hired a gardener to work on the yard so they could both spend more time focusing on the children and the house. Rather than complaining about their division of labor, he talked about how he has come to appreciate his situation:

> Ever since I've known my wife, she's made more money than I have. Initially—as a man—I resented it. I went through a lot of head trips about it. But as time developed, I appreciated it. Now I respect it. The way I figure it is, I'd rather have her sharing the money with me than sharing it with someone else. She has her full-time job and then she has her part-time job as a consultant. The gardener I'm paying $75 per week, and I'm paying someone else $25 per week to make my lunch, so I'm enjoying it! It's self-interest.

The power dynamic in this family, coupled with their willingness to pay for outside help to reduce his chores, and the flexibility of his self-employed work schedule, led to substantial sharing of cooking, cleaning, and child care. Because she was making more money and working more hours than he was, he could not emulate other husbands in claiming priority for his provider activities.

A similar dynamic was evident in other co-provider couples with comparable earnings and career commitments. One male IRS officer married to a school teacher now made more money than his wife, but talked about his feelings when she was the more successful provider:

> It doesn't bother me when she makes more money than me. I don't think it has anything to do with being a man. I don't have any hangups about it, I mean, I don't equate those things with manhood. It takes a pretty simple mind to think that way. First of all, she doesn't feel superior when she has made more money.

The woman in this couple commented that her husband was "better" at housework than she was, but that she still had to nag him to do it. Although only two wives in our sample of Chicano families earned more than their husbands, the reversal of symbolic provider status seemed to raise expectations for increased family work

from husbands. The husbands who made less than their wives performed significantly more of the housework and child care than the other husbands.

Even when wives' earnings did not exceed the husbands', some co-providers shared the homemaker role. A male college-admissions recruiter and his executive-secretary wife shared substantial housework and child care according to mutual ratings. He made $29,000 per year working a 50 hour week, while she made $22,000 working a 40 hour week. She was willing to give him more credit than he was willing to claim for child care, reflecting her sincere appreciation for his parenting efforts, which were greater than those of other fathers she knew. He placed a high value on her mothering and seemed to downplay the possibility that they should be considered equal parents. Like most of the men in this study, the college-recruiter husband was reluctant to perform house-cleaning chores. Like many co-providers, however, he managed to redefine some routine household chores as a shared responsibility. For instance, when we asked him what he liked least about housework, he laughingly replied, "Probably those damn toilets, man, and the showers, the bathrooms, gotta scrub 'em, argghh! I wish I didn't have to do any of that, you know the vacuuming and all that. But it's just a fact of life."

Even though he did more than most husbands, he acknowledged that he did less than his wife, and admitted that he sometimes tried to use his job to get out of doing more around the house. But whereas other wives often allowed husbands to use their jobs as excuses for doing less family work, or assumed that their husbands were incapable of performing certain chores like cooking or laundry, the pattern in this family resembled that of the failed-aspirations couples. In other words, the wife did not assume that housework was "her" job, did not accept her husband's job demands as justification for his doing less housework, and sometimes challenged his interpretation of how much his job required of him. She also got her husband to assume more responsibility by refraining from performing certain tasks. He commented:

> *Sometimes she just refuses to do something. . . . An example would be the ironing, you know, I never used to do the ironing, hated it. Now it's just something that happens. You need something ironed, you better iron it or you're not gonna have it in the morning. So, I think, you know, that kinda just evolved. I mean, she just gradually quit doing it so everybody just had to do their own. My son irons his own clothes, I iron my own clothes, my daughter irons her own clothes, the only one that doesn't iron is the baby, and next year she'll probably start.*

The sociologist Jane Hood, whose path-breaking family research highlighted the importance of provider role definition to marital power, describes this strategy as "going on strike," and suggests that it is most effective when husbands feel the specific task *must* be done.[11] Since appearing neat and well-dressed was a priority for this husband, when his wife stopped ironing his clothes, he started doing it himself. Because he felt it was important for his children to be "presentable" in public, he also began to remind them to iron their own clothes before going visiting or attending church.

While many co-provider couples reported that sharing housework was contingent upon ongoing bargaining and negotiation, others focused on how it evolved "naturally." One co-provider husband, director of a housing agency, reported that he and his wife didn't negotiate; "we pretty much do what needs to be done." His wife, an executive secretary, confirmed his description, and echoed the ad-hoc arrangements of many of the role-sharing couples: "We have not had to negotiate. We both have our specialties. He is great with dishes, I like to clean bathrooms. He does most of the laundry. It has worked out that we each do what we like best."

Although sharing tasks sometimes increases conflict, when both spouses assume that household tasks are a shared responsibility, negotiation can also become less necessary or contentious. For example, a co-provider husband who worked

as a mail carrier commented, "I get home early and start dinner, make sure the kids do their homework, feed the dogs, stuff like that." He and his wife, an executive secretary, agreed that they rarely talk about housework. She said, "When I went back to work we agreed that we both needed to share, and so we just do it." While she still reminded him to perform chores according to her standards or on her schedule, she summed up her appreciation by commenting, "at least he does it without complaining." Lack of complaint was a common feature of co-provider families. Whereas many main-provider husbands complained of having to do "her" chores, the co-providers rarely talked about harboring resentments. Main-provider husbands typically lamented not having the services of a stay-at-home wife, but co-provider husbands almost never made such comparisons.

SUMMARY AND DISCUSSION

For these dual-earner Chicano couples, we found conventional masculine privilege as well as considerable sharing in several domains. First, as in previous studies of ethnic minority families, wives were employed a substantial number of hours and made significant contributions to the household income. Second, like some who have studied Chicano families, we found that couples described their decision-making to be relatively fair and equal.[12] Third, fathers in these families were more involved in child rearing than their own fathers had been, and many were rated as sharing a majority of child care tasks. Finally, while no husband performed fully half of the housework, a few made substantial contributions in this area as well.

One of the power dynamics that appeared to undergird the household division of labor in these families was the relative earning power of each spouse, though this was modified by factors such as occupational prestige, provider role status, and personal preference. In just under half of the families, the wife earned less than a third of the family income, and in all of these families the husband performed little of the routine housework or child care. In two families, wives earned more than their husbands, and these two households reported sharing more domestic labor than others. Among the other couples who shared housework and child care, there was a preponderance of relatively balanced incomes. In the two families with large financial contributions from wives, but little household help from husbands, couples hired housekeepers to reduce the wives' household workload.

While relative income appeared to make a significant difference in marital power, we observed no simple or straightforward exchange of market resources for domestic services. Other factors like failed career aspirations or occupational status influenced marital dynamics and helped explain why some wives were willing to push a little harder for change in the division of household labor. In almost every case, husbands reluctantly responded to requests for help from wives. Only when wives explicitly took the initiative to shift some of the housework burden to husbands did the men begin to assume significant responsibility for the day-to-day operation of the household. Even when they began to share the housework and child care, men tended to do some of the less onerous tasks like playing with the children or washing the dinner dishes. When we compared these men to their own fathers, or their wives' fathers, however, we could see that they were sharing more domestic chores than the generation that preceded them.

Acceptance of wives as co-providers and wives' delegation of a portion of the homemaker role to husbands were especially important to creating more equal divisions of household labor in these families. If wives made lists for their husbands or offered them frequent reminders, they were more successful than if they waited for husbands to take the initiative. Remaining responsible for managing the home and children was cause for resentment on the part of many wives, however. Sometimes wives were effective in getting husbands to perform certain chores, like ironing, by stopping doing it altogether. For

other wives, sharing evolved more "naturally," as both spouses agreed to share tasks or performed the chores that they preferred.

Economies of gratitude continually shifted as the ideology, career attachments, and feelings of entitlement of each spouse changed over time. For some main-provider families, this meant that wives were grateful for husbands' "permission" to hold a job, or that wives worked harder at home because they felt guilty for making their husbands do any of the housework. Main-provider husbands usually let their job commitments limit their family work, whereas their wives took time off from work to care for a sick child or to attend a parent-teacher conference.

Even in families where co-provider wives had advanced degrees and earned high incomes, some wives' work/family boundaries were more permeable than their husbands', like the program director married to a teacher who was a "perpetual" graduate student and attended "endless" community meetings. While she was employed more hours than he, and made about the same amount of money, she had to "schedule him" to watch the children if she wanted to leave the house alone. His stature as a "community leader" provided him with subterranean leverage in the unspoken struggle over taking responsibility for the house and children. His "gender ideology," if measured with conventional survey questions, would undoubtedly have been characterized as "egalitarian," because he spoke in broad platitudes about women's equality and was washing the dishes when we arrived for the interviews. He insisted on finishing the dishes as he answered my questions, but in the other room, his wife confided to Elsa in incredulous tones, "He *never* does that!"

In other ambivalent co-provider families, husbands gained unspoken advantage because they had more prestigious jobs than their wives, and earned more money. While these highly educated attorneys and administrators talked about how they respected their wives' careers, and expressed interest in spending more time with their children, their actions showed that they did not fully assume responsibility for sharing the home-maker or parenting role. To solve the dilemma of too little time and too many chores, two of these families hired housekeepers. Wives were grateful for this strategy, though it did not alter inequities in the distribution of housework and child care, nor in the allocation of worry.

In other families, the economy of gratitude departed dramatically from conventional notions of husband as economic provider and wife as nurturing homemaker. When wives' earnings approached or exceeded their husbands', economies of gratitude shifted toward more equal expectations, with husbands beginning to assume that they must do more around the house. Even in these families, husbands rarely began doing more chores without prodding from wives, but they usually did them "without complaining." Similarly, when wives with economic leverage began expecting more from their husbands, they were usually successful in getting them to do more.

Another type of leverage that was important, even in main-provider households, was the existence of failed aspirations. If wives expected husbands to "make more" of themselves, pursue "more important" careers, or follow "dream" occupational goals, then wives were able to get husbands to do more around the house. This perception of failed aspirations, if held by both spouses, served as a reminder that husbands had no excuse for not helping out at home. In these families, wives were not at all reluctant to demand assistance with domestic chores, and husbands were rarely able to use their jobs as excuses for getting out of housework.

The economies of gratitude in these families were not equally balanced, but many exhibited divisions of household labor that contradicted cultural stereotypes of macho men and male-dominated families. Particularly salient in these families was the lack of fit between their own class position and that of their parents. Most of the parents were Mexican immigrants with little education and low occupational mobility. The couples we interviewed, in contrast, were well-ed-ucated and relatively secure in middle-class occupations. The couples could have compared themselves to their parents, evaluating themselves to be egalitarian and financially successful. While some did just that, most compared themselves to their Anglo and Chicano friends and coworkers, many of whom shared as much or more than they did. Implicitly comparing their earnings, occupational commitments, and perceived aptitudes, husbands and wives negotiated new patterns of work/family boundaries and developed novel justifications for their emerging arrangements. These were not created anew, but emerged out of the popular culture in which they found themselves. Judith Stacey labels such developments the making of the "postmodern family," because they signal "the contested, ambivalent, and undecided character of contemporary gender and kinship arrangements."[13] Our findings confirm that families are an important site of new struggles over the meaning of gender and the rights and obligations of men and women in each other and over each other's labor.

One of the most provocative findings from our study has to do with the class position of Chicano husbands and wives who shared household labor: white-collar, working-class families shared more than upper-middle-class professionals. Contrary to findings from nationwide surveys predicting that higher levels of education for either husbands or wives will be associated with more sharing, the most highly educated of our well-educated sample of Chicano couples shared only moderate amounts of child care and little housework.[14] Contrary to other predictions, neither was it the working-class women in this study who achieved the most balanced divisions of labor.[15] It was the middle occupational group of women, the executive secretaries, clerks, technicians, teachers, and mid-level administrators who extracted the most help from husbands. The men in these families were similarly in the middle in terms of occupational status for this sample—administrative assistants, a builder, a mail carrier, a technician—and in the middle in terms of income. What this means is that the highest status wives—the program coordinators, nurses, social workers, and office managers—were not able to, or chose not to, transform their salaries or occupational status into more participation from husbands. This was probably because their husbands had even higher incomes and more prestigious occupations than they did. The lawyers, program directors, ranking bureaucrats, and "community leaders" parlayed their status into extra leisure at home, either by paying for housekeepers or ignoring the housework. Finally, Chicana wives at the lowest end of the occupational structure fared least well. The teacher's aides, entry-level secretaries, day-care providers, and part-time employees did the bulk of the work at home whether they were married to mechanics or lawyers. When wives made less than a third of what their husbands did, they were only able to get husbands to do a little more if the men were working at jobs considered "below" them—a telephone lineman, a painter, an elementary-school teacher.

Only Chicano couples were included in this study, but results are similar to findings from previous interviews with Anglo couples.[16] My interpretation is that the major processes shaping divisions of labor in middle-class Chicano couples are approximately the same as those shaping divisions of labor in other middle-class couples. This is not to say that ethnicity did not make a difference to the Chicano couples we interviewed. They grew up in recently immigrating working-class families, watched their parents work long hours for minimal wages, and understood firsthand the toll that various forms of

racial discrimination can take. Probably because of some of these experiences, and their own more recent ones, our informants looked at job security, fertility decisions, and the division of household labor somewhat differently than their Anglo counterparts. In some cases, this can give Chicano husbands in working-class or professional jobs license to ignore more of the housework, and might temper the anger of some working-class or professional Chicanas who are still called on to do most of the domestic chores. If these findings are generalizable, however, it is those in between the blue-collar working-class and the upper-middle-class professionals that might be more likely to share housework and child-care.

Assessing whether these findings apply to other dual-earner Chicano couples will require the use of larger, more representative samples. If the limited sharing observed here represents a trend—however slow or reluctant—it could have far-reaching consequences. More and more Chicana mothers are remaining full-time members of the paid labor force. With the "postindustrial" expansion of the service and information sectors of the economy, Chicanos and Chicanas will be increasingly likely to enter white-collar middle-class occupations. As more Chicano families fit the occupational profile of those we studied, we may see more assumption of housework and child care by Chicano men. Regardless of the specific changes that the economy will undergo, we can expect Chicano men and women, like their Anglo counterparts, to continue to negotiate for change in their work and family roles.

NOTES

1. For a discussion of how the term machismo can also reflect positive attributes of respect, loyalty, responsibility and generosity, see Alfredo Mirandé, "Chicano Fathers: Traditional Perceptions and Current Realities," pp. 93–106, in *Fatherhood Today*, P. Bronstein and C. Cowan, eds. (New York: Wiley, 1988).
2. For reviews of literature on Latin-American families and projections on their future proportionate rep-

resentation in the population, see Randall Collins and Scott Coltrane, *Sociology of Marriage and the Family* (Chicago: Nelson Hall, 1994); William A. Vega, "Hispanic Families in the 1980s," *Journal of Marriage and the Family* 52(1990): 1015–1024; and Norma Williams, *The Mexican-American Family* (New York: General Hall, 1990).
3. Maxinne Baca Zinn, "Family, Feminism, and Race

in America," *Gender & Society* 4(1990): 68–82; Mirandé, "Chicano Fathers"; Vega, "Hispanic Families"; and Williams, *The Mexican-American Family*.

4. See Coltrane, *Family Man: Fatherhood, Housework, and Gender Equity* (New York: Oxford University Press, 1994); Coltrane and Valdez, "Reluctant Compliance: Work/Family Role Allocation in Dual-Earner Chicano Families," in *Men, Work, and Family*, Jane C. Hood, ed. (Newbury Park, CA: Sage, 1994) and Valdez and Coltrane, "Work, Family, and the Chicana: Power, Perception and Equity," in *Employed Mothers and the Family Context*, Judith Frankel, ed. (New York: Springer, 1993). I thank Hilda Cortez, a summer research intern at the University of California, for help in transcribing some of the interviews and for providing insight into some of the issues faced by these families.

5. Jessie Bernard, *The Future of Marriage* (New York: World, 1972).

6. See Jane Hood, 1986. "The Provider Role: Its Meaning and Measurement." *Journal of Marriage and the Family* 48: 349–359.

7. Hood, "The Provider Role."

8. See Coltrane, "Household Labor and the Routine Production of Gender." *Social Problems* 36: 473–490.

9. I am indebted to Arlie Hochschild, who first used this term in *The Second Shift* (New York: Viking, 1987). See also Karen Pyke and Scott Coltrane, "Entitlement, Obligation, and Gratitude in Remarriage: Toward a Gendered Understanding of Household Labor Allocation."

10. I am indebted to Joseph Pleck for his conceptualization of "asymmetrically permeable" work/family boundaries ("The Work-Family Role System." *Social Problems* 24: 417–427).

11. Jane Hood, *Becoming a Two-Job Family*, p. 131.

12. See, for example, V. Cromwell and R. Cromwell, 1978. "Perceived Dominance in Decision Making and Conflict Resolution among Anglo, Black, and Chicano Couples." *Journal of Marriage and the Family* 40: 749–760; G. Hawkes and M. Taylor, 1975. "Power Structure in Mexican and Mexican-American Farm Labor Families." *Journal of Marriage and the Family* 37: 807–81; L. Ybarra, 1982. "When Wives Work: The Impact on the Chicano Family." *Journal of Marriage and the Family* 44: 169–178.

13. Judith Stacey, 1990. *Brave New Families*. New York: Basic Books, p. 17.

14. See, for instance, Donna H. Berardo, Constance Shehan, and Gerald R. Leslie, "A Residue of Tradition: Jobs, Careers, and Spouses' Time in Housework." *Journal of Marriage and the Family* 49(1987): 381–390; Catherine E. Ross, "The Division of Labor at Home." *Social Forces* 65(1987): 816–833.

15. Patricia Zavella. 1987. *Women's Work and Chicano Families*. Ithaca, NY: Cornell University Press; Stacey, *Brave New Families*.

16. See, for example, Hochschild, *Second Shift*; Hood, *Two-Job Family*; Coltrane, *Family Man*.

THE AFRICAN-AMERICAN FATHER'S ROLES WITHIN THE FAMILY

JOHN LEWIS McADOO
JULIA B. McADOO

The study of the father's roles in the family is a relatively new phenomenon. In the past, the father's main contributions were assumed to be those of provider, protector, disciplinarian, and representative of the family to the wider community. This paper focuses on some of the contributions African-American scholars have made to the understanding of the father's role in the family.

The African-American father always seems to be either absent in family studies or dominated by the mother in mainstream literature. Even when he was observed to respond in the same way as white fathers, his behavior was interpreted negatively and sometimes even pejoratively (J. McAdoo 1988a, 1988b, 1990).

In reviewing the literature on fathers' participation in the family, the contributions of African-American scholars have been virtually ignored. This omission has led some scholars to feel that the disciplines of family studies, developmental psychology, and family sociology are ethnocentrically biased.

Several African-American researchers (H. McAdoo 1988; J. McAdoo 1988a, 1988b, 1991; Gary et al. 1983; Hill 1981; and Billingsley 1968) have reviewed the social science literature and noted that the following traits are crucial in any analysis and definition of African-American family strength and stability.

1. Economic sufficiency: stable employment, adequate income, property ownership, and a strong work orientation
2. Religiosity: positive ethical values and a positive religious orientation
3. Future orientation or achievement orientation: educational attainment, educational expectations and aspirations
4. Flexibility of family roles: the presence of a leader in a family, ability to deal with crisis in a positive manner, good communication patterns, and consistent rules
5. Strong kinship bonds: a high degree of commitment, appreciation, mutual obligations, helping networks and exchanges, and spending time together
6. Positive friendship relationships: reciprocal sharing and reaching out and support in times of crisis
7. A realistic attitude toward work: an ability to compartmentalize negative racial stereotypes, an ability to get along with others, and balancing work and family time

THEORETICAL PERSPECTIVES

Mainstream researchers on family life development have offered several theories to explain the functioning of African-American families in American society. The major theories include the

John L. McAdoo and Julia B. McAdoo, "The African-American Father's Roles within the Family," in R. Majors and J. Gordon, eds., *The American Black Male* (Chicago: Nelson-Hall, 1993). Reprinted with permission.

cultural deprivation theory, matriarchy theory, conflict theory, domestic colonialism theory, exchange theory, Black nationalism theory, and ecological theory.

African-American researchers sometimes adopted these theories, sometimes criticized the various theories, and sometimes modified the theories to control for weaknesses in their explanatory power.

Weaknesses of some of the major theories have been identified by African-American writers: cultural deprivation/deficiency (Peters 1988; White and Parham 1990), Black matriarchy (Staples 1978; White and Parham 1990); conflict, historical materialism, and domestic colonialism (Staples 1978); exchange theory, and ecological systems (Peters 1988).

Billingsley (1968) reacted to the negative evaluations of African Americans as pathological or culturally deprived by Eurocentric researchers and clearly presented the notion that the African-American family was a viable system. Peters (1988) provided an excellent critique of the research approaches and conceptual frameworks used in studying parenting roles in African-American families. She discussed the descriptive, comparative deficit and ecological approaches to studying the African-American family. From the comparative deficit perspective, families who experienced the ravages of enslavement lack the cultural background to fulfill the various family roles expected of those living in Western society. This cultural deprivation has led to a number of social psychological problems in the adjustment of African-American men in the performance of their provider, nurturer, and protective roles in the family.

Other theories seem to involve a value judgment of cultural deprivation that hinders objective observation in the real world. Peters suggested that these theories do not adequately take into account the demands, the extreme pressures, and the social constraints placed on African-American fathers.

White and Parham's (1990) analysis of the deprivation /deficiency theoretical models provided some further explanations of Peters's comparative deficit model. They feel that theorists from the deprivation/deficiency school assumed that the effects of years of racism and discrimination had deprived most African Americans of the strength to develop a healthy self-esteem (Kardner and Ovessey 1951) as well as legitimate family structures (Moynihan 1965). They noted that this model led to the concept of cultural deprivation that has been used to differentiate African Americans from others in the society. Cultural deprivation theory assumed that, due to inadequate exposure to European-American values, norms, customs, and life-styles, African Americans were culturally deprived and required cultural enrichment to be accepted by the dominant society.

While White and Parham suggested that white middle-class culture established the norms of society, their analysis of the Black matriarchy model as a variant of the deprivation/deficiency model may be of more interest here because it provides some of the social theorist's assumptions about the roles of African-American men in the family. Staples (1978) noted that matriarchy was seen as a pathological form of family life where the wife dominated the family members. The proponents of the matriarchy hypothesis suggest that the African-American male lacks the masculine role behaviors characterized by logical thinking, willingness to take responsibility for others, assertiveness, managerial skills, achievement orientation, and occupational mastery (White and Parham 1990).

The African-American female became the matriarch, from this point of view, because American society was unwilling to permit the African-American male to assume the legal, psychological, and social positions necessary to become a dominant force within his family. The African-American female was also seen, from this perspective, as unwilling to share the power she gained by default even in situations where the male was present and willing to take family responsibility. An analysis of mainstream and African-American empirical studies by the National Research Council (1989) testing this hypothesis found no evidence to support the theory of the Black matriarch. In a review of studies of power and decision making, the African American husband was found to share equally with his wife (J. McAdoo 1986, 1988b).

Staples (1978), while agreeing with much of Peters's analysis, noted that African-American researchers could utilize a Black nationalist orientation. He suggested that pan-Africanism has become a dominant conceptual model among African-American researchers in studying African-American families. Among the many tenets of this approach is that people of African descent have a common culture as well as a common history of racist oppression that has culminated in a shared destiny. An important ingredient of this model is its focus on the comparative study of African and African-American culture. Staples (1976) found some difficulties with this model. First, Africa has a diversity of cultures, cultural values, languages, and behavioral patterns. Another problem is the difficulty in translating cultural forms from Africa to the African-American experience. Staples felt that those who use this model tend to emphasize the study of cultural forms rather than political and economic analysis. The major weakness of this approach is that it focuses on cultural subjugation rather than the political and economic oppression that he feels affects African Americans. A basic assumption of this perspective is that a cultural group never loses its cultural heritage; it simply fuses it into another form.

In sociological research, the conflict theory provides some support for understanding the universal experiences of people of African descent, but Staples does not demonstrate its utility in understanding current research approaches. Instead, he sketchily presents two related approaches, domestic colonialism and historical materialism. Domestic colonialism seems to be a variant on the Marxist theme that all societies were divided into two groups—the oppressors and the oppressed. Domestic colonialist societies were divided along racial lines into groups of superior and inferior status. Do-

mestic colonialism defines the rules governing the relationships between European Americans, the exploiters and African Americans, the exploited (Staples 1978).

Historical materialism suggests that the economic influences on African American family life may play an important part in the destabilization and breakup of many families. From this perspective, the father's role in the family is heavily influenced by outside sources that control his access to economic resources and limit his capacity to fulfill the provider role. Those who see some utility in this approach point to racial economic disparities, segregated housing and schooling patterns, high unemployment and incarceration rates, and the predominance of African Americans in the underclass (Glasgow 1980).

Choice and exchange theory also has been suggested as a conceptual framework to understand the context in which the African-American male makes choices and participates within the family processes (J. McAdoo 1990). This theory shows how African American fathers make choices in the operations of their roles within the family. Fathers will choose negative roles or refuse to play some roles within the family when access to economic and social resources is perceived by them to be unavailable. The theoretical propositions were expanded to take into account the economic, political, residential, and educational barriers to the father's ability to carry out important roles within the family and the community. The assumption of this theory is that these can operate as barriers that limit the father's choices and options in his exchanges within the family.

Ecological theory presents family roles and functioning from an Afrocentric perspective. This perspective allows us to predict alternative outcomes to the racial barriers to employment, experiences of social isolation on the job and in the mainstream community, and the development of roles that African-American men play in their families. Ecological theory allows us to describe and explain the many roles fathers may play in their families. It allows us to test the assumptions of female dominance in the home and the lack of father involvement in the family. It helps us to better understand the historical, societal, political, and social influences on the roles African-American fathers play in the family. Peters (1988) sees the ecological framework as a move to understand African-American family functioning in a less ethnocentrically biased manner.

The assumption of ecological theory is that fathers may play a variety of roles in the family and community that can lead to positive family outcomes. Fathers may use a variety of coping strategies to control negative outside influences in the performance of their nurturing, support, disciplining, provider, and other family roles. Ecological theory allows us to explore the differential choices that working-, middle-, and upper-class fathers use to develop stability and positive growth in African American family life. The theory allows us to explore the positive and negative father roles and their effects within the family.

THE PROVIDER ROLE

In American society, a man is defined by his ability to provide for his family. Ecological theory allows us to understand how structural dissonance at the societal level may have profound influences on ethnic minority communities. As Duster (1988) has shown, at the structural level the extraordinarily high and sustained unemployment rates among African-American adults and youth are the results of such converging factors as moving of capital to foreign soil, from cities to suburbs, and from northern cities to selected areas of the Sun Belt. He also pointed to the decline in manufacturing and the increase in the advanced service sector occupations in major cities, where the majority of African Americans live, and the changing patterns of immigration that produce competition for scarce jobs.

Malveaux (1989) noted that finding and keeping a job is synonymous with being accepted into society for many Americans. This ability to provide for self and family has a great deal of impact on how a man perceives himself in a variety of family roles. From an ecological perspective, it might be suggested that an African-American man's ability to successfully fulfill the provider role depends upon other community systems over which he has little control. Several writers (J. McAdoo 1990; Gibbs 1988; Billingsley 1968) have discussed the historical, political, and social barriers that influence his ability to perform that role.

In an analysis of the work force participation of African-American youth, Malveaux suggested that the labor force may be a hostile place for them. These youths appear to suffer from the same employment and economic barriers faced by their fathers, grandfathers, and great-grandfathers before them. Wilson (1987) reviewed the national labor statistics for 1954–87 and found the unemployment rate for African Americans sixteen and over to be twice the national average during that period. He also provided empirical evidence that employed African-American males earned 57 percent of the wages earned by their European-American counterparts with the same experience and job classifications. African-American males experience a glass-ceiling effect when it comes to occupational and economic opportunities.

Gibbs (1988) eloquently discussed the educational and other structural barriers that influence the African-American male in participating in provider and community roles. Leshore (1981) noted that African-American males have been coerced by public social agencies and ignored by the private service sector.

Very few studies have been found that evaluated the family's ability to cope when, because of racial prejudice or severe economic depression, the father was unable adequately to fulfill the provider role. There needs to be some understanding of the father's reactions to sharing this role with his wife and sometimes his children. The role of the extended family (H. McAdoo 1988) in providing some support to the provider role could add another level to our understanding of the utilization of family resources. Provider role stress has been the major focus of our research efforts.

African-American men may experience stress related to their inability to fulfill their provider role in the family. Bowman (in press) found a link between unemployment and family estrangement in a national study of African-American fathers. His summary of the literature on the impact of massive deindustrialization in the urban communities noted that the loss of jobs and employment opportunities creates vulnerabilities in some fathers' personal lives and leads to a succession of provider role strains within some families. He discussed the impact of joblessness and job search discouragement, which can intensify provider role strain and lead to vulnerability to drugs, crime, family estrangement, and other psychological problems.

Bowman suggested that we need to evaluate existing research to determine how the harmful psychological and social effects of provider role strain might be reversed by extended family networks, religious orientation, and reality-based attributional patterns. We might begin by studying how some fathers are able to successfully reduce their provider role strain, maintain a positive feeling of self-esteem, and continue positive family relationships in spite of adversity.

Structural factors within society have both a direct and an indirect effect on how the provider's role is handled by fathers. J. McAdoo's (1988a) research with economically sufficient men in their role as providers found no significant differences across ethnic groups and races in the way they carried out that function. They were able to provide the necessary social and economic resources for their wives and children. Cazenave (1979), in a study of fifty-four mailmen, found that the greater their economic security, the more active these fathers became in their child-rearing functions.

DECISION-MAKING ROLES

African-American family decision making has been described from a resource and choice exchange perspective (J. McAdoo 1991). This perspective suggests that the father's role in the family depends upon how he and his spouse perceive the resources that each brings. Fathers who bring in the greater resources make the greater decisions from this perspective. Blood and Wolfe (1969), utilizing resource theory, suggested from the responses of spouses that African-American families were mother-dominated because mothers made all the decisions. This led many mainstream researchers to conclude that the structure of the decision-making process was different for African Americans than for European Americans. A reanalysis of the original Blood and Wolfe data revealed that the responses of African and European Americans were similar. Both groups reported they shared equally in family decision making with their spouses.

Our review of the African-American research on this issue provides support for a more ecological approach to studying the decision-making process within the family. This approach would allow us to consider the responses of both husband and wife before we reach conclusions about who was the dominant decision maker in the family. Fathers across a number of studies reported that they shared equally with their wives the major decision making in child rearing, important purchases, health care, transportation, and employment of either spouse (TenHouten 1970; Mack 1978; Grey-Little 1982; Hammond and Enoch 1976; Willie and Greenblatt 1978). Mack (1978) suggested that socioeconomic status may make a difference in the decision role African-American men perceive themselves as playing in the family. However, Jackson (1974), TenHouten (1970), Hammond and Enoch (1976), and Willie and Greenblatt (1978) reported few if any social class differences in the fathers' responses.

Jackson (1974), in a study of working- and middle-class fathers, noted that both groups reported being involved equally in the family decision making regarding disciplining children, grocery shopping, insurance, selection of a physician, and residential location. Middle-class fathers reported being more significantly ($p < .05$) involved than working-class fathers in shopping, vacationing, engaging in family recreation or commercial recreation, visiting relatives jointly, or engaging in other activities. She found that employed fathers were more likely to report attending church, shopping, vacationing, family and commercial recreation, and other activities with their spouses. They also reported visiting relatives with their spouses.

The Jackson study explored a wider range of father role behaviors than is usually found in the literature. While one may criticize the smallness of her sample size, her findings do suggest that African-American fathers play a variety of important roles within the family. Our summary of the decision-making literature found African-American fathers' responses to be similar across social classes to that of fathers of other ethnic groups. Future research on fathers who experience severe role strain as the result of unemployment or racial discrimination on the job is needed to clarify the impact on their psychological well-being and their decision-making capacity in the family. We need to examine the impact of extended family and community resources on family functioning related to family power relationships. Again, we need to evaluate differential responses across social economic statuses and to evaluate both positive and negative responses.

CHILD-REARING ROLES

Mainstream researchers have debated the issue of the roles fathers play within the family related to child-rearing activity. Most of these studies have been theoretical, with little recognition given to the context in which the fathers relate to their children. There has been little systematic attempt to evaluate father-child relationships across age levels or in other than family systems. Research is needed to evaluate these relationships in church, school, and other settings as well as the family.

Cazenave (1979), in a study of fathering roles across two generations, noted that middle-income fathers reported being involved in child-

care activities more than their fathers. These fathers reported being very actively involved in baby-sitting, changing baby diapers, and playing with their children. They reported that they were spending more time with their children and punishing them less often than their fathers punished them.

One (H. McAdoo 1988) observational study of African-American fathers noted that these economically sufficient fathers were warm and loving toward their children. While they perceived themselves to be strict, expecting their children to obey right away and not allowing any display of temper or bad behavior, their verbal and nonverbal interactions with their children were observed as nurturant. These fathers would interrupt the interview process to answer their children's questions. When they reprimanded their children, they would provide explanations regarding the unacceptable behavior and sometimes express their expectations about future child behaviors.

There is a need for more observational studies of fathers and their children in a variety of age and system contexts. An ecological approach would allow us to study fathers who are experiencing severe role strains and fathers who have been able to cope successfully with external threats to their personal and family systems. We would begin to develop normative adjustment patterns of reactions to external and internal pressures or role strains in terms of fathers' relationships with their children. This would lead to the possibility of discovering natural mediating factors in both role strains and child development. For example, in our research we found that nurturant fathers had little direct influence on the high self-esteem of their children. We also found that the father's nurturance of the mother led her to provide the support the children needed to feel good about themselves, their fathers, mothers, siblings, peers, and teachers.

Many young African-American fathers have been observed positively interacting with their young sons and daughters. Some fathers were unemployed; others were underemployed. However, their employment status did not seem to interfere with their ability to show love and affection to their children. Fathers have been observed working together on household chores with their teenagers in Washington, D.C., Los Angeles, Detroit, and other places by this researcher. However, public and private funds have not been made available to systematically study these occurrences. Funds have been more forthcoming to study the most problematic families, and there has been a proliferation of studies outlining the effects of disrupted families. An ecological perspective would allow researchers to describe, explain, and predict the effects of differing fathering roles and attitudes on child and adolescent development.

FAMILY AND MARITAL INFLUENCES

Many researchers seem to study the father's roles from a static linear perspective. The roles do not seem to change over time, and the father alone seems to be responsible for how those roles are played out in the family. An ecological perspective allows us to see that all family members are responsible for the family organizational climate, decision making, nurturance, and protection of the family. In all families, fathers play both positive and negative roles; however, little research has been found on the way the family develops rules that both regulate behaviors and provide support for positive development. What are the internal and external ingredients that allow for stability and positive change in the father's roles in the family?

It has been pointed out that the African-American father's nurturance of his wife leads to a positive self-evaluation in their children (H. McAdoo 1988). However, the literature on the subject seems to focus more on marital disruptions than on the way husbands and wives work cooperatively together in the mutual development of satisfactory marital roles. Future research should explore more fully the impact of the above ingredients on marital well-being and satisfaction with the family.

THE FUTURE

From an ecological perspective, our historical presence and the unity and integration of the patrilineal and matrilineal (Sudarkasa 1988) heritage within a capitalist society have led to changes and conflicts within our community and with the larger society to which we belong. The African-American community needs to return to the visions developed in the pre-enslavement era, and sustained during the enslavement period, to develop the kinds of institutions that will provide nurturance for positive growth for everyone in the community. Future visionaries may need to consider how we can maintain our values, namely, collective community responsibility, within a changing world economic community. How do we answer the question, What kind of world view should the African-American community develop that will lead to survival, growth, and positive relationships with communities that are not African American?

African-American fathers, mothers, and communities, if they are to have a future, must see how their problems relate to those of the larger world community. Our communities have been allowed to suffer from high crime rates, unemployment, homelessness, deadly diseases, and the movement of economic institutions out of our communities in much the same manner as what seems to be happening in third-world countries. We need to see the relationship between the flow of economic resources out the African-American community, which is sometimes described as one of the ten wealthiest countries in the world, and the inability of members of this community to find gainful employment, obtain meaningful education for their young, or receive competent protective and social services.

Finally, the survival of fathers'/husbands' roles within the family will depend upon the collective wisdom and courage of the African-American community to reject the divisive strategies represented by the terms "endangered species," "feminization of poverty," and "Black underclasses." The strategies have been fomented by other ethnic groups to blame the victims and force the victims to blame themselves. We must learn the lessons of our civil rights leaders and shun the retreatism of the 1980s and the me-isms of some of our current leaders. We must return to the basic understanding that in unity there is strength.

The future should bring a more balanced evaluation of the roles African-American men play in their families. There needs to be a shift from the focus on the most problematic families so as to study fathers in all socioeconomic groups. Future studies should focus more on what internal and external resources help fathers to help build successful families. Racial prejudices and racism have been a part of the experience of African Americans since they arrived on America's shores. There is no indication that things are going to be any different in the immediate future, and socioeconomic conditions may be getting worse for some families. However, some African-American men and women have been able to survive, and this again will be no different in the future.

CONCLUDING COMMENTS

The debate about family relationships in some African-American professional circles seems to be around the wrong issues. It should not focus on whether we will survive—we will—but rather on what can be done to help more African-American men, women and their families to survive, thrive, and provide positive nurturance, motivation, and support to their children and community. The discussion should not center around whether or not we have an underclass—not because the term relates to something real for us and many more European-American ethnics, but because it is a counterproductive, divisive discussion. It does not help us focus on what should be done to help African-American fathers who are in the lower socioeconomic stratum of our societies find ways to support and nurture their families.

Some of these so-called scholars need to spend a little less time in labeling and placing blame when family and community relationships are deteriorating and spend more time finding positive solutions for positive role functioning in families. Less research emphasis should be placed on evaluating African-American families from a European-American middle-class perspective, and more emphasis should be placed on developing a multicultural perspective (White and Parham 1990). We need to foster understanding of positive multiclass perspectives in trying to understand African-American father's roles and other ethnic group fathers' roles.

Arguments that the male is an endangered species have offered us little new or helpful information since the period of African-American enslavement in this country. African-American men have always been vulnerable in this society. The many chapters in this volume offer conclusive evidence that too many African-American men experience high arrest and incarceration rates, drop out of school at a high rate, and experience violence and deaths related to crime in their community. Some African-American men also experience significant and prolonged unemployment, and some are forced to rely on the drug trade for their economic survival when they and their family members are denied meaningful employment. The simple truth is that they have survived and they will survive and thrive as long as the African-American family and community survives. Professional literature might be better served by our collectively developing mechanisms for helping men in problematic economic, psychological, and social situations to become part of an economically stable family.

Fathers in African-American families seemed from the studies reported in this paper to perform their roles in the family about as well as their non-African-American counterparts within different social classes. The major causes for the diminution of these roles are related to stress around the father's ability to provide for his family. This ability is related to his educational and economic opportunities as well as his ability to handle and overcome racial prejudice and racism. While these are not fully within their control, many of these fathers throughout the postenslavement experience have found ways to mitigate the negative consequences of occupational and educational discrimination on the positive roles they play within their family and community.

Future analysts of the father's role within the family may need to evaluate some of the internal and external influences that help him to remain a provider, nurturer, motivator, stimulator, and protector of his wife and children. Learning what role the wife plays in this interaction is vitally important to the understanding of successfully coping fathers. As Bowman and Sanders (1988) suggested, provider role strain is a complex component of the equation and could lead to severe problems related to the psychological well-being of unmarried fathers. However, we suggest that in families where both spouses are working to provide economic support to the family, these strains may be reduced. American society is moving to a dual provider perspective, since it is becoming increasingly difficult for families to survive on one income. Dual role perspectives allow for a lessening of the pressure on the male to be the sole provider.

The survival of positive fathering/husbanding roles in the family may depend on how well African Americans are able to provide or obtain from outside resources the kinds of community services that may enhance the development of families in trouble. Role development in these fathers may depend upon how well we come together as a community to develop and utilize our political and economic clout so as to influence the broader American community to provide greater employment opportunities, including the ownership of major corporations, heading major franchises in the private service sector, and receiving equal wages for the same employment.

Father role development will depend even more on our ability to educate our children about the ingredients of positive family functioning and to provide community control and support for families who are in trouble. There is a need to develop strategies for educating children of all ethnic groups in our society about the rich heritage of African-American culture shared by the men in these communities. Father roles need to be seen from a perspective that takes in the community values for such roles. Finally, we will be able to provide more realistic family-role assessment when we are able to understand how differential spiritual values influence a father's ability to perform these roles. A more balanced approach to the evaluation of the influences on the different roles an African-American father plays in his family and community may lead to a realistic reassessment of the same influences on the European-American father's role and position in his family and community.

REFERENCES

American Council on Education. 1988. *One-Third of a Nation*. Washington, DC: ACE, Commission on Minority Participation in Education and American Life.

Billingsley, A. 1968. *Black Families in White America*. Englewood Cliffs, NJ: Prentice-Hall.

Blood, R. O., and D. M. Wolfe. 1969. "Negro-White Differences in Blue-Collar Marriages." *Social Forces* 48: 59–64.

Bowman, P. J. 1991. "Post-Industrial Displacement and Family Role Strains: Challenges to the Black Family. In P. Voydanof and L. C. Majka (eds.), *Families and Economic Distress*. Newbury Park, CA: Sage.

Bowman, P. J., and R. Sanders. 1988. "Black Fathers Across the Life Cycle: Providers Role Strain and Psychological Well-Being." Paper presented at the 12th Empirical Conference on Black Psychology, Ann Arbor, MI.

Cazenave, N. 1979. "Middle Income Black Fathers: An Analysis of the Provider Role." *Family Coordinator* 28(4): 583–93.

Connor, M. E. 1986. "Some Parenting Attitudes of Young Black Fathers." In R. A. Lewis and M. B. Sussman (eds.), *Men's Changing Roles in the Family*. New York: Hayworth Press.

Duster, T. 1988. "Social Implications of the New Underclass." *Black scholar* 19: 2–9.

Gary, L. E. 1981. "A Social Profile." In L. E. Gary (ed.), *Black Men*. Beverly Hills, CA: Sage.

———. 1986. "Family Life Events, Depression, and Black Men." In R. A. Lewis and M. B. Sussman (eds.), *Men's Changing Roles in the Family*. New York: Hayworth Press.

Gary, L. E.; L. Beaty; G. Berry; and M. D. Price. 1983. Stable Black Families: Final Report. Washington, DC: Howard University, Institute for Urban Affairs and Research.

Gibbs, J. T., ed. 1988. *Young, Black and Male in America: An Endangered Species*. Dover, MA: Auburn House.

Glasgow, D. 1980. *The Black Underclass: Poverty, Unemployment, and Entrapment of Ghetto Youth*. New York: Vintage Books.

Grey-Little, B. 1982. "Marital Quality and Power Processes among Black Couples." *Journal of Marriage and the Family* 44: 633–45.

Hammond, J., and J. R. Enoch. 1976. "Conjugal Power Relations among Black Working-Class Families." *Journal of Black Studies* 7(1): 107–33.

Hill, R. 1981. *The Strengths of Black Families*. New York: Emerson-Hall.

Jackson, J. J. 1974. "Ordinary Black Husbands: The truly Hidden Men." *Journal of Social and Behavioral Science* 20: 19–27.

Jaynes, G. D., and R. M. Williams, Jr., eds. 1989. *A Common Destiny: Blacks and American Society*. Washington, DC: National Academy Press.

Kardner, A., and L. Ovessey. 1951. *The Mark of Oppression*. New York: Norton.

Leshore, B. 1981. "Social Services and Black Men." In L. Gary (ed.), *Black Men*. Beverly Hills, CA: Sage.

Mack, D. 1978. "The Power Relationship in Black and White Families." In R. Staples (ed.), *The Black Family: Essays and Studies*. Belmont, CA: Wadsworth.

Malveaux, J. 1989. "Transitions: The Black Adolescent and the Labor Market." In R. E. Jones (ed.), *Black Adolescents*. Berkeley, CA: Cobb and Henry.

McAdoo, H. P. 1988. "Transgenerational Patterns of Upward Mobility in African-American Families." In H. P. McAdoo (ed.), *Black Families*. Newbury Park, CA: Sage.

McAdoo, J. L. 1986a. "Black Fathers' Relationships with Their Preschool Children and the Children's Ethnic Identity. In R. A. Lewis and R. E. Salt (eds.), *Men in Families*. Newbury Park, CA: Sage.

———. 1986b. "A Black Perspective on the Father's Role in Child Development." In R. A. Lewis and M. B. Sussman (eds.), *Men's Changing Roles in the Family*. New York: Hayworth Press.

———. 1988a. "Changing Perspectives on the Role of the Black Father." In P. Bronstein and C. P. Cowan (eds.), *Fatherhood Today: Men's Changing Role in the Family*. New York: Wiley.

———. 1988b. "The Roles of Black fathers in the Socialization of Black Children." In H. P. McAdoo (ed.), *Black Families*. Newbury Park, CA: Sage.

———. 1990. "Understanding African-American Teen Fathers." In P. E. Leone (ed.), *Understanding Troubled and Troubling Youth*. Newbury Park, CA: Sage.

———. 1991. "Urban African-American Youth: Problems and Solutions." In R. Lang (ed.), *Contemporary Urban America: Problems, Issues and Alternatives*. Boston: University Press of America.

Middleton, R., and S. Putney. 1960. "Dominance in Decisions in the Family: Race and Class Differences." In C. V. Willie (ed.), *The Family Life of Black People*. Columbus, OH: Merrill.

Moynihan, D. 1965. *The Negro Family: The Case for National Action*. Washington, DC: U.S. Department of Labor, Office of Planning Research.

Peters, M. F. 1988. "Parenting in Black Families with Young Children: A Historical Perspective." In H. P. McAdoo (ed.), *Black Families*. Newbury Park, CA: Sage.

Staples, R. 1976. *Introduction to Black Sociology*. New York: McGraw-Hill.

———. 1978. "The Black Family Revisited." In R. Staples (ed.), *The Black Family: Essays and Studies*. Belmont, CA: Wadsworth.

Sudarkasa, N. 1988. "Interpreting the African American Heritage in Afro-American Family Organization." In H. P. McAdoo (ed.), *Black Families*. Newbury Park, CA: Sage.

TenHousten, W. D. 1970. "The Black Family: Myth and Reality." *Psychiatry* 23: 145–73.

White, J. L., and T. A. Parham. 1990. *The Psychology of Blacks: An African-American Perspective*. Englewood Cliffs, NJ: Prentice-Hall.

Willie, C. V., and S. Greenblatt, 1978. "Four Classic Studies of Power Relationships in Black Families: A Review and Look to the Future. *Journal of Marriage and the Family* 40(4): 691–96.

Wilson, W. J. 1987. *The Truly Disadvantaged: The Inner City, the Under Class, and Public Policy*. Chicago: University of Chicago Press.

PART TEN

MEN AND THE FUTURE

Q: Why did you decide to record again?

A: Because *this* housewife would like to have a career for a bit! On October 9, I'll be 40, and Sean will be 5 and I can afford to say "Daddy does something else as well." He's not accustomed to it—in five years I hardly picked up a guitar. Last Christmas our neighbors showed him "Yellow Submarine" and he came running in, saying, "Daddy, you were singing . . . Were you a Beatle?" I said, "Well—yes, right."

—John Lennon, interview for *Newsweek*, 1980

Are men changing? If so, in what directions? Can men change even more? In what ways should men be different? We posed many of these questions at the beginning of our exploration of men's lives, and we return to them here, in the book's last section, to examine the directions men have taken to enlarge their roles, to expand the meaning of masculinity, to change the rules.

The articles in this section address the possibility of expanding the definitions of masculinity open to men, so that men may become more responsive to women and to other men. The "Statement of Principles" of the National Organization for Men Against Sexism (NOMAS) provides a political platform, while the essay by Michael Kimmel provides a growing list of men's names linked to current struggles for gender equality that gives a context for taking a political position—and also a sense of increasing urgency. Michael Schwalbe examines the mythopoetic men's movement most often associated with Robert Bly and his best-selling *Iron John* to see if it offers a vision of social change for the future. And, finally, black feminist author bell hooks adds her voice of hope for an alliance between women and men in this last decade of the twentieth century.

We began this book with a description of men's confusion. Men's confusion often makes men anxious, and some have said that men are experiencing a "crisis of masculinity." This confusion or "crisis" is beautifully captured by the Chinese character for the word "crisis," which is a combination of the characters for the words "danger" and "opportunity." If masculinity is in crisis, if men are confused, it is both dangerous and an exciting opportunity.

The danger is a danger of retreat. Confusion is often a frightening experience; one feels unsettled, problems are unresolved, and identity is off-center. Some people, when they are confused, will retreat to older, familiar ideas—ideas that may have once been appropriate but now are only safe anachronisms that will offer temporary solace from the confusion. Some men are therefore seeking a resolution to their confusion by the vigorous reassertion of traditional masculinity.

But many of us can recognize the opportunity that is presented by confusion. Feeling unsettled, restless, and anxious, confusion pushes us to wrestle with difficult issues, confront contradictory feelings and ideas, and challenge the ways in which our experiences do not fit with the traditional rules and expectations we have inherited from the past. Confusion opens the opportunity to change, to push beyond the traditional norms of masculinity. And with change comes the possibility to become more loving and caring fathers, more emotionally responsive lovers, and more reliable and compassionate friends, and to live longer and healthier lives. It is toward these changes that we hope this work has contributed.

CLARENCE, WILLIAM, IRON MIKE, TAILHOOK, SENATOR PACKWOOD, MAGIC . . . AND US

MICHAEL S. KIMMEL

The 1990s may be remembered as the decade in which the United States took a crash course on male sexuality. From the national teach-in on sexual harassment that emerged from Clarence Thomas's confirmation hearings, to accusations about sexual harassment against Senator Robert Packwood; from the U.S. Navy Tailhook scandal to Magic Johnson's revelations that he is infected with the HIV virus; from William Kennedy Smith and Mike Tyson's date rape trials to the trials of lacrosse players at St. John's University and Glen Ridge, New Jersey high-school athletes—we've had a steady discussion about male sexuality, a sexuality that is more about predatory conquest than pleasure and connection.

And there's no end in sight—which explains the title of this essay. In the immediate aftermath of the Clarence Thomas confirmation hearings, the media claimed, as if with one voice, that the hearings would have a "chilling effect" on American women—that women would be far less likely to come forward and report incidents of sexual harassment for fear that they would be treated in the same shameful way as was Anita Hill by the Senate Judiciary Committee. Have the media ever been more wrong?

Since then, we've had less of a "chilling effect" and more of a national thaw as women have come forward in record numbers to report cases of sexual harassment and date and acquaintance rape. "Every woman has her Clarence Thomas," commented one woman, sadly surveying the workplace over the past two decades. In an op-ed essay in the *New York Times*, novelist Mary Lee Settle commented that Anita Hill had, "by her heroic stance, given not only me but thousands of women who have been silenced by shame the courage and the need to speak out about what we have tried for so long to bury and forget."

Currently, corporations, state and local governments, universities, and law firms are scrambling to implement procedures to handle sexual harassment. Most seem motivated more out of fear of lawsuits than out of general concern for women's experiences; thus, they are more interested in adjudicating harassment *after the fact* than in developing mechanisms to prevent it. In the same way, colleges and universities are developing strategies to handle the remarkable rise in date and acquaintance rape, although only a few are developing programs on prevention.

With more women coming forward now than ever before, many men have reacted defensively; "Men on Trial" has been the common headline linking Smith and Thomas in the media. But it's not *men* on trial here, it's *masculinity*, or, rather,

Note: My thinking on these issues has benefitted enormously from collaborative work with Michael Kaufman and Martin Levine. The material in the sections on sexual harassment and AIDS draws from that collaborative work, and I am grateful to them for their insights and support.

a definition of masculinity that leads to certain behaviors that we now see as problematic and often physically threatening. Under prevailing definitions, men have and are the politically incorrect sex.

But why have these issues emerged now? And why, in particular, are issues like sexual harassment and date rape the issues we're facing? And, since it is certain that we will continue to face these issues for the rest of the decade, how can we understand these changes, and, most importantly, what can we do about it? How can we change the meanings of masculinity so that sexual harassment and date rape will disappear from our workplaces and our relationships?

THE SOCIAL CONSTRUCTION OF MALE SEXUALITY

To speak of transforming masculinity is to begin with the way men are sexual in our culture. As social scientists now understand, sexuality is less a product of biological urges and more about the meanings that we attach to those urges, meanings that vary dramatically across cultures, over time, and among a variety of social groups within any particular culture. Sexual beings are made, not born. John Gagnon, a well-known theoretician of this approach, argues in *Human Sexualities* that

> People learn when they are quite young a few of the things that they are expected to be, and continue slowly to accumulate a belief in who they are and ought to be through the rest of childhood, adolescence, and adulthood. Sexual conduct is learned in the same ways and through the same processes; it is acquired and assembled in human interaction, judged and performed in specific cultural and historical worlds.

And the major item in that assemblage, the chief building block in the social construction of sexuality, is gender. We experience our sexual selves through a gendered prism. And the meanings of sex to women and men are very, very different. There really are a "his" and "hers" when it

comes to sex. Just one example: think about the difference in the way we view a man or a woman who has a lot of different partners: the difference, say, between a stud and a slut.

The rules of masculinity and femininity are strictly enforced. And difference equals power. The difference between male and female sexuality reproduces men's power over women, and, simultaneously, the power of some men over other men, especially of the dominant, hegemonic form of manhood—white, straight, middle class—over marginal masculinities. Those who dare to cross over—women who are sexually adventurous and men who are sexually passive—risk being seen as *gender*, not sexual, nonconformists. We all know how homophobia links gender nonconformity to homosexuality. The stakes are high if you don't play along.

Sexual behavior confirms manhood. It makes men feel manly. Robert Brannon has identified the four traditional rules of American manhood: (1) No Sissy Stuff: men can never do anything that even remotely suggests femininity. Manhood is a relentless repudiation and devaluation of the feminine; (2) Be a Big Wheel: manhood is measured by power, wealth, and success. Whoever has the most toys when he dies, wins; (3) Be a Sturdy Oak: manhood depends on emotional reserve. Dependability in a crisis requires that men not reveal their feelings; and (4) Give 'em Hell: exude an aura of manly daring and aggression. Go for it. Take risks.

These four rules lead to a sexuality built around accumulating partners (scoring), emotional distance, and risk taking. In locker rooms and playgrounds across the country, men are taught that the goal of every encounter with women is to score. Men are supposed to be ever ready for sex, constantly seeking sex, and constantly seeking to escalate every encounter so that intercourse will result since, as one of my students once noted, "It doesn't count unless you put it in."

The emotional distancing of the Sturdy Oak is considered necessary for adequate male sexual functioning, but it leads to some strange behaviors. For example, to keep from ejaculating "too soon," men may devise a fascinating array of distractions, such as counting, doing multiplication tables in their heads, or thinking about sports.

Risk taking is a centerpiece of male sexuality. Sex is about adventure, excitement, danger. Taking chances. Responsibility is a word that seldom turns up is male sexual discourse. And this, of course, has serious medical side effects: STDs, the possibility of impregnation, and AIDS—currently the most gendered disease in American history.

To rein in this constructed male "appetite," women have been assigned the role of asexual gatekeeper; women decide, metaphorically and literally, who enters the desired garden of earthly delights, and who doesn't. Women's sexual agency, women's sense of entitlement to desire, is drowned out by the incessant humming of male desire, propelling him ever forward. A man's job is to wear down her resistance. (One fraternity at a college I was lecturing at last year offered seminars to pledges on dating etiquette, which appropriated the business-advice book, *Getting to Yes*.) Sometimes that hum can be so loud that it drowns out the actual voice of the real live woman that he's with. Men suffer from socialized deafness, a hearing impairment that strikes only when women say no.

WHO ARE THE REAL SEXUAL REVOLUTIONARIES?

Of course, a lot has changed along the frontiers of the sexual landscape in the past two decades. We've had a sexual revolution, after all. But as the dust is settling from the sexual revolution, what emerges in unmistakably finer detail is that it's been women, not men, who are our era's real sexual pioneers. Of course, we men like to think that the sexual revolution, with its promises of more access, to more partners, with less emotional commitment, was tailor-made for male sexuality's fullest flowering. But, in fact, it's been women's sexuality that's changed in the

past two decades, not men's. Women now feel capable, even *entitled*, to sexual pleasure. They have learned to say yes to their own desires, claiming their own sexual agency.

And men? We're still dancing the same tired dance of the sexual conquistadors. Look, for a minute, at that new late-night game show "Studs." Here are the results of the sexual revolution in media miniature. The men and women all date one another, and from implicit innuendo to explicit guffaws, one assumes that every couple has gone to bed. What's not news is that the men are joking about it; what *is* news is that the women are equally capable of it.

Now some might argue that this simply confirms that women can have "male" sex, that male sexuality was victorious because we've convinced women to be more like us. But, then, why are so many men wilting in the face of desiring women? Why are sex therapists offices crammed with men who complain not of premature ejaculation (the most common sexual problem twenty years ago—a sexual problem that involves being a bit overeager) but of what therapists euphemistically call "inhibited desire"—that is, men who don't want to have sex now that all these women are able to claim their sexual rights.

DATE RAPE AND SEXUAL PREDATION, AGGRESSION AND ENTITLEMENT

As women have claimed the right to say yes, they've also begun to assert their right to say no. Women are now demanding that men be more sexually responsible and are holding men accountable for their sexual behaviors. It is women who have changed the rules of sexual conduct. What used to be (and, in many places, still is) called male sexual etiquette—forcing a woman to have sex when she says no, conniving, coercing, pushing, ignoring her efforts to get you to stop, getting her so drunk that she loses the ability (or consciousness) that one needs to consent—is now defined as date rape.

In one recent study, by psychologist Mary Koss at the University of Arizona, 45 percent of all college women said that they had had some form of sexual contact against their will. A full 25 percent had been pressed or forced to have sexual intercourse against their will. And Patricia Bowman, who went home with William Kennedy Smith from Au Bar in Palm Beach, Florida, knows all about those statistics. She testified that when she told Smith that she'd called her friends and she was going to call the police, he responded "You shouldn't have done that. Nobody's going to believe you." And, indeed, the jury didn't. I did.

I also believed that the testimony of three other women who claimed they were sexually assaulted by Smith should have been allowed in the trial. Such testimony would have established a pattern not of criminal assault, but of Smith's obvious belief in sexual *entitlement*; that he was entitled to press his sexual needs on women, despite their resistance, because he didn't particularly care what they felt about it.

And Desiree Washington knows all about men who don't listen when a woman says no. Mike Tyson's aggressive masculinity in the boxing ring was sadly translated into a vicious misogyny with his ex-wife Robin Givens, and a predatory sexuality as evidenced by his behavior with Desiree Washington. Tyson's "grandiose sense of entitlement, fueled by the insecurities and emotions of adolescence," as writer Joyce Carol Oates put it, led to a behavior with women that was as out of control as his homosocial behavior inside the ring.

Tyson's case underscores our particular fascination with athletes, and the facile equation of athletes with sexual aggression. From the St. Johns University lacrosse team, to Glen Ridge, New Jersey high-school athletes, to dozens of athletic teams and individual players at campuses across the nation, we're getting the message that our young male athletes, trained for fearless aggression on the field, are translating that to a predatory sexual aggression in relationships with women. Columnist Robert Lipsyte calls it the "varsity syndrome"—"winner take all, winning at any cost, violence as a tool, aggression as a mark of masculinity." The very qualities we seek

in our athletes are exactly the qualities we do not want in young men today—disrespect for others, lack of compassion, inability to listen, disregard for process in achieving the end goal. Our task is to make it clear that what we want from our athletes when they are on the playing field is *not* the same as what we want from them when they are playing the field.

I think, though, that athletes only serve to illustrate a deeper problem: the problem of men in groups. Most athletes play on teams, and so much of their social life and much of a player's public persona is constructed through association with his teammates. Another homosocial preserve, fraternities, are the site of most of the gang rapes on college campuses, according to psychologist Chris O'Sullivan, who has been studying gang rape for several years. At scores of campus and corporate workshops over the past five years, women share a complaint that, while individual men may appear sympathetic when they are alone with a woman, they suddenly turn into macho louts, capable of the vilest misogynistic statements, when they are in groups of men. The members of the U.S. Navy Tailhook Association are, quite possibly, decent, law-abiding family men when they are alone or with their families. But put them together at a convention, and they seem to have become a marauding gang of hypermasculine thugs who should be prosecuted for felonious assault, not merely slapped on their collective wrists.

What is it about groups that seems to bring out the worst in men? I think it is because the animating condition for most American men is a deeply rooted fear of other men—a fear that other men will see us as less than manly. The fear of humiliation, of losing in a competitive ranking among men, of being dominated by other men—these are the fears that keep men in tow, that reinforce traditional definitions of masculinity as a false definition of safety. Homophobia—which I understand as more than the fear of homosexual men: it's the fear of other men—keeps men acting like men, keeps men exaggerating their adherence to traditional norms, so that no other men will get the idea that we might really be that-most dreaded person: the sissy.

Men's fear of being judged a failure in the eyes of other men leads to a certain homosocial element within the heterosexual encounter: men often will use their sexual conquest as a form of currency to gain status among other men. Such homosocial competition contributes to the strange hearing impairment that men experience in many sexual encounters, a socialized deafness that leads us to hear "no" as meaning "yes," to escalate the encounter, to always go for it, to score. And this is occurring just at the moment when women are, themselves, learning to say yes to their own sexualities, to say yes to their own desires for sexual pleasure. Instead of our so-cialized deafness, we need to become what Langston Hughes called "articulate listeners": we need to trust women when they tell us what they want and when they want it, and what they don't want as well. If we listen when women say no, then they will feel more trusting and open to saying yes when they feel that. And we need to listen to our own inner voices, our own desires and needs—not the voices that are about com-pulsively proving something that cannot be proved, but the voices that are about connection with another and the desires and passions that may happen between two equals.

Escalating a sexual encounter beyond what a woman may want is date rape, not sex; it is one of the most important issues we will face in the 1990s. It is transforming the sexual landscape as earlier sexual behaviors are being reevaluated in light of new ideas about sexual politics. We have to explore the meaning of the word consent, ex-plore our own understandings, and make sure that these definitions are in accord with women's definitions.

FROM THE BEDROOM TO THE BOARDROOM

Just as women have been claiming the right to say yes and demanding the right to say no (and have it listened to and respected) in the sexual arena, they've also transformed the public arena, the workplace. As with sexuality, the real revo-lution in the past thirty years has been women's dramatic entry into the labor force in unprece-dented numbers. Almost half the labor force is female. I often demonstrate this point to my classes by asking the women who intend to have careers to raise their hands. All do. Then I ask them to keep their hands raised if their mothers have had a career outside the home for more than ten years. Half put their hands down. Then I ask them to keep their hands raised if their grand-mothers had a career for ten years. Virtually no hands remain raised. In three generations, they can visibly see the difference in women's work-ing lives. Women are in the work force to stay, and men had better get used to having them around.

That means that the cozy boy's club—another homosocial arena—has been penetrated by women. And this, just when that arena is more suffused with doubt and anxieties than ever be-fore. We are, after all, a downwardly mobile cul-ture. Most Americans are less successful than their parents were at the same age. It now takes two incomes to provide the same standard of liv-ing that one income provided about a generation ago. And most of us in the middle class cannot afford to buy the houses in which we were brought up. Since men derive their identity in the public sphere, and the primary public arena where masculinity is demonstrated is the work-place, this is an important issue. There are fewer and fewer big wheels (and many of those big wheels are in jail); more and more men will feel as though they haven't made the grade, will feel damaged, injured, powerless, will need to demon-strate their masculinity all over again. Suddenly, men's fears of humiliation and domination are out in the open, and there's a convenient target at which to vent those anxieties.

And now, here come women into the work-place in unprecedented numbers. It now seems virtually impossible that a man will go through his entire working life without having a woman colleague, coworker, or boss. Just when men's economic breadwinner status is threatened, women appear on the scene as easy targets for men's anger. Thus, sexual harassment in the workplace is a distorted effort to put women back in their place, to remind women that they are not equal to men in the workplace, that they are, still, just women, even if they are in the workplace.

It seems to me that this is the context in which to explore the meaning of sexual harassment in our society. The Clarence Thomas confirmation hearings afford men a rare opportunity to do some serious soul searching. What is sexual harassment about? And why should men help put an end to it?

One thing that sexual harassment is usually *not* about, although you couldn't convince the Senate Judiciary Committee of this, is a matter of one person telling the truth and the other person lying. Sexual harassment cases are difficult and confusing precisely because there are often a multiplicity of truths. "His" truth might be what appear to him as an innocent indication of sexual interest or harmless joking with the "boys in the office" (even if those "boys" happen to include women workers). "Her" truth is that those seemingly innocent remarks cause stress, anxiety about promotion, firing, and sexual pressure.

Judge Thomas asserted during the course of his testimony that "At no time did I become aware, either directly or indirectly, that she felt I had said or done anything to change the cordial nature of our relationship." And there is no reason to assume that he would have been aware of it. But that doesn't mean his words or actions did not have the effect that Professor Hill states, but only that she was successful in concealing the resulting trauma from him—a concealment that women have carefully developed over the years in the workplace.

Why should this surprise us? Women and men often experience the same event differently. Men experience their behavior from the perspective of those who have power; women from the perspective of those upon whom that power is exercised.

If an employer asks an employee for a date and she declines, perhaps he has forgotten about it by the time he gets to the parking lot. No big deal, he says to himself. You ask someone out and she says no. You forget about it. In fact, re-pairing a wounded male ego often *requires* that you forget about it. But the female employee? She's now frozen, partly with fear. What if I said yes? Would I have gotten promoted? Would he have expected more than a date? Will I now get fired? Will someone else get promoted over me? What should I do? And so, she will do what millions of women do in that situation: she calls her friends, who counsel her to let the matter rest and get on with her work. And she remembers, for a long long time. Who, therefore, is likely to have a better memory: those in power or those against whom that power is deployed?

This is precisely the divergence in experience that characterizes the controversies spinning around Senator Bob Packwood. Long a public supporter of women's causes, it appears that Senator Packwood also chased numerous women around office desks, clumsily trying to have affairs with them. He claims, now, that alcoholism caused this behavior, and that he doesn't remember. It's a good thing that the women remember. They almost always do.

Sexual harassment is particularly volatile because it often fuses two levels of power: the power of employers over employees and the power of men over women. Thus, what may be said or intended as a man to a woman is also experienced in the context of superior and subordinate, or vice versa. Sexual harassment in the workplace results from men using their public position to demand or extract social relationships. It is the confusion of public and private, bringing together two arenas of men's power over women. Not only are men in positions of power in the workplace, but we are socialized to be the sexual initiators and to see sexual prowess as a confirmation of masculinity.

Sexual harassment is also a way to remind women that they are not yet equals in the workplace, that they really don't belong there.

Harassment is most frequent in those occupations and workplaces where women are new and in the minority, like surgeons, firefighters, and investment bankers. "Men see women as invading a masculine environment," says Louise Fitzgerald, a University of Illinois psychologist. "These are guys whose sexual harassment has nothing whatever to do with sex. They're trying to scare women off a male preserve."

When the power of men is augmented by the power of employer over employee, it is easy to understand how humiliating and debilitating sexual harassment can be, and how an individual woman would be frightened about seeking redress. The workplace is not a level playing field. Subordinates rarely have the resources to complain against managers, whatever the problem.

Some men were confused by Professor Hill's charges, others furious about sexual harassment because it feels like women are changing the rules. What used to be routine behavior for men in the workplace is now being called sexual harassment. "Clarence Thomas didn't do anything wrong, that any American male hasn't done," commented Dale Whitcomb, a 32-year-old machinist. How right he was. The fact that two-thirds of the men surveyed said they would be complimented if they were propositioned by a woman at work gives some idea of the vast gulf between women's and men's perceptions of workplace sexual conduct.

Although men surely do benefit from sexual harassment, I believe that we also have a stake in ending it. First, our ability to form positive and productive relationships with women colleagues in the workplace is undermined. So long as sexual harassment is a daily occurrence and women are afraid of their superiors in the workplace, innocent men's behaviors may be misinterpreted. Second, men's ability to develop social and sexual relationships that are both ethical and exciting is also compromised. If a male boss dates a subordinate, can he really trust that the reason she is with him is because she *wants* to be? Or will there always be a lingering doubt that she is there because she is afraid not to be, or because she seeks to please him because of his position?

Currently, law firms and corporations all over the country are scrambling to implement sexual harassment policies, to make sure that sexual harassment will be recognized and punished. But our challenge is greater than admonition and post-hoc counseling. Our challenge will be to prevent sexual harassment *before* it happens. And that means working with men. Men must come to see that female coworkers are not women who happen to be in the workplace (where, by this logic, they actually don't belong), but workers who happen to be women. And we'll need to change the meaning of success so that men don't look back at their work careers when they retire and wonder what it was all for, whether any of it was worth it. Again, we'll need to change the definition of masculinity, dislodging it from these misshapen public enactments, making masculinity the capacity to embrace others as equals because of an inner security and confidence that can last a lifetime. It is more important than ever to begin to listen to women—to listen with a compassion that understands women's and men's experiences as different, and an understanding that men, too, can benefit from the elimination of sexual harassment.

AIDS AS A MEN'S DISEASE

Surely, men will benefit from the eradication of AIDS. Although we are used to discussing AIDS as a disease of gay men and IV drug users, I think we need to see AIDS as a men's disease. Over 90 percent of all AIDS patients are men; AIDS is now the leading cause of death for men aged 33–45 nationwide. AIDS is American men's number-one health problem, and yet we rarely treat it as a men's issue. But AIDS is also the most gender-linked disease in American history. No other disease has ever attacked one gender so disproportionately, except those diseases, like hemophilia or uterine or prostate cancer, that are sex-linked (i.e., only men or only women are susceptible). AIDS *could* affect both men and women equally (and in Africa it seems to come closer to gender parity). But in the United States, AIDS patients are overwhelmingly men. (Let me be clear that in no way am I saying that one should not be compassionate for women AIDS patients. Of course, one must recognize that women are as likely to get AIDS from engaging in the same high-risk behaviors as men. But that's precisely my point. Women don't engage in those behaviors at rates anything like men.)

One is put at risk for AIDS by engaging in specific high-risk behaviors, activities that ignore potential health risks for more immediate pleasures. For example, sharing needles is both a defiant flaunting of health risks and an expression of community among IV drug users. And the capacity for high-risk sexual behaviors—unprotected anal intercourse with a large number of partners, the ability to take it, despite any potential pain—are also confirmations of masculinity.

And so is accumulation—of money, property, or sexual conquests. It's curious that one of the United States' most lionized heroes, Magic Johnson, doesn't seem particularly compassionate about the possibility of infecting the 2,500 women he reported that he slept with. Johnson told *Sports Illustrated* that, as a single man, he tried to "accommodate as many women as I could, most of them through unprotected sex." Accommodate? When he protested that his words were misunderstood, he told the *New York Times*, "I was a bachelor, and I lived a bachelor's life. And I'm paying the price for it. But you know, I respect women to the utmost." (I suppose that Wilt Chamberlain, who boasted in his autobiography that he slept with over 20,000 women, respected them almost ten times as much.)

As sociologists have long understood, stigmatized gender identity often leads to exaggerated forms of gender-specific behavior. Thus, those whose masculinity is least secure are precisely those most likely to enact behavioral codes and hold fast to traditional definitions of masculinity. In social science research, hypermasculinity as compensation for insecure gender identity has been used to explain the propensity

for homophobia, authoritarianism, racism, anti-Semitism, juvenile delinquency, and urban gangs.

Gay men and IV drug users—the two largest risk groups—can be seen in this light, although for different reasons. The traditional view of gay men is that they are not "real men." Most of the stereotypes revolve around effeminacy, weakness, passivity. But following the Stonewall riots of 1969, in which gay men fought back against a police raid on a gay bar in Greenwich Village, New York, and the subsequent birth of the Gay Liberation Movement, a new gay masculinity emerged in the major cities (see Kleinberg, in this volume). The "clone," as he was called, dressed in hypermasculine garb (flannel shirts, blue jeans, leather), had short hair (not at all androgynous) and a mustache; he was athletic, highly muscular. In short, the clone looked more like a "real man" than most straight men.

And the clones—who comprised roughly one-third of all gay men living in the major urban enclaves of the 1970s (see Kleinberg, in this volume)—enacted a hypermasculine sexuality in steamy back rooms, bars, and bathhouses where sex was plentiful, anonymous, and very hot. No unnecessary foreplay, romance, or postcoital awkwardness. Sex without attachment. One might even say that, given the norms of masculinity (that men are always seeking sex, ready for sex, wanting sex), gay men were the only men in America who were getting as much sex as they wanted. Predictably, high levels of sexual activity led to high levels of sexually transmitted diseases, such as gonorrhea, among the clones. But no one could have predicted AIDS.

Among IV drug users, we see a different pattern, but with some similar outcomes when seen from a gender perspective. The majority of IV drug users are African American and Latino, two groups for whom the traditional avenues of successful manhood are blocked by poverty and racism. More than half of the black men between 18 and 25 in our cities are unemployed, and one in four are in some way involved with the penal system (in jail, on probation, under arrest); you have an entire generation structurally prevented from demonstrating their manhood in that most traditional of ways: as breadwinners.

The drug culture offers an alternative. Dealing drugs can provide an income to support a family as well as the opportunity for manly risk and adventure. The community of drug users can confirm gender identity; the sharing of needles is a demonstration of that solidarity. And the ever-present risk of death by overdose take hyper-masculine bravado to its limits.

WHO ASKED FOR IT?

The victims of men's adherence to these norms of masculinity—AIDS patients, rape victims, victims of sexual harassment—did not become victims intentionally. They did not "ask for it," and they certainly do not deserve blame. That some women today are also sexual predators, going to swank bars or waiting outside athletes' locker rooms, or trying to score with male subordinates at work, doesn't make William Kennedy Smith, Mike Tyson, Magic Johnson, or Clarence Thomas any less predatory. When predatory animals threaten civil populations, we warn the population to stay indoors until the wild animals can be caught and recaged. When it's men on the prowl, women engage in a voluntary curfew, unless they want to risk being attacked.

And the men—the date rapists, the sexual harassers, the AIDS patients—are not "perverts" or "deviants" who have strayed from the norms of masculinity. They are, if anything, overconformists to destructive norms of male sexual behavior. Until we change the meaning of manhood, sexual risk taking and conquest will remain part of the rhetoric of masculinity. And we will scatter the victims, both women and men, along the wayside.

THE SEXUAL POLITICS OF SAFETY

What links the struggle against sexual harassment, date and acquaintance rape, and AIDS is that preventing all of them require that *safety* become the central term and organizing principle of men's relationships—with women, as well as with other men. The politics of safety may be the missing link in the transformation of men's lives, the capacity for change. Safety is more than the absence of danger—although that wouldn't be such a bad thing in itself. Safety is proactive, the creation of a space in which all people, women and men, gay and straight, and of all colors, can experience and express the fullness of their beings.

Think, for a moment, about how the politics of safety affects the three areas I have discussed in this essay. What is the best way to prevent AIDS—to use sterile needles for intravenous drug injections and to practice "safe sex." Sterile needles and safe sex share one basic characteristic: they both require that men act responsibly. This is not one of the cardinal rules of manhood. Safe-sex programs encourage men to have fewer partners, to avoid certain particularly dangerous practices, and to use condoms when having any sex that involves the exchange of bodily fluids. In short, safe-sex programs encourage men to stop having sex like men. To men, you see, "safe sex" is an oxymoron, one of those juxtapositions of terms that produce a nonsensical outcome. That which is sexy is not safe, that which is safe is not sexy. Sex is about danger, risk, excitement; safety is about comfort, softness, and security.

Seen this way, it is not surprising to find that, as some researchers have found, one-fourth of urban gay men report that they have not changed their unsafe sexual behaviors. What is, in fact, astonishing is that slightly more than three-fourths *have* changed and are now practicing safer sex.

What heterosexual men could learn from the gay community's response to AIDS is how to eroticize that responsibility—something that women have been trying to teach men for decades. Making safe sex into sexy sex has been one of the great transformations of male sexuality accomplished by the gay community. Straight men could also learn a thing or two about caring for one another through illness, supporting one another in grief, and maintaining resilience in the face of a devastating disease and the callous indifference of the larger society.

Safety is also the animating condition for women's expression of sexuality. While safety may be a turn-off for men—comfort, softness and security are the terms of postorgasmic detumescence, not sexual arousal—safety is a precondition for sexual agency for women. Only when women feel safe can they give their sexuality full expression. For men, hot sex leaves a warm afterglow; for women, warmth builds to heat, but warmth is not created by heat.

This perspective helps explain that curious finding in the sex research literature about the divergence of women's and men's sexualities as they age. We believe that men reach their sexual peak at around 18, and then go into steady, and later more precipitous, decline for the rest of their lives; while women hit their sexual stride closer to 30, with the years between 27 and 38 as their peak years. Typically, we understand these changes as having to do with differences in biology—hormonal changes find men feeling soft and cuddly just as women are getting all steamed up. But aging does not produce such changes in every culture, that is, biology doesn't seem to work the same way everywhere.

What biological explanations leave out is the way that men's and women's sexualities are related to each other, and the way that both are shaped by the institution of marriage. Marriage makes one's sexuality more predictable—the partner, the timing, the experience—and it places sex *always* in the context of the marriage relationship. Marriage makes sex safer. No wonder women find their sexuality heightening—they finally feel safe enough to allow their sexual desires to be expressed. And no wonder men's sexuality deflates—there's no danger, risk, or excitement left.

Safety is the precondition for women's sexual expression—only when a woman is absolutely certain, beyond the shadow of a doubt, that her no means no, can she ever say yes to her own sexual desires. So, if we men are going to have the sexual relationships with exciting, de-

siring women that we say we want, then we have to make the environment safe enough for women to express their desires. We have to make it absolutely certain to a woman that her no means no—no matter how urgently we feel the burning of our own desires.

To do this we will need to transform the definition of what it means to be a real man. But we have to work fast. AIDS is spreading rapidly, and date rape and sexual harassment are epidemic in the nation's colleges and workplaces. As AIDS spreads, as women speak up about these issues, there are more and more people who need our compassion and support. Yet compassion is in relatively short supply among American men, since it involves the capacity of taking the role of the other, of seeing ourselves in someone else's shoes—a quality that contradicts the manly independence we have so carefully cultivated.

Sexual democracy, just like political democracy, relies on a balance between rights and responsibilities, between the claims of the individual and the claims of the community. When one discusses one's sexual rights—that each person, every woman and man, has an equal right to pleasure—men understand immediately what you mean. Women often looked delighted and a little bit surprised. Add to the Bill of Sexual Rights a notion of responsibility—that each person treat sexual partners as if they had an integrity equal to your own—and it's the men who look puzzled. "Responsibility? What's that got to do with sex? I thought sex was about having fun."

Sure it is, but it's also political in the most intimate sense. Sexual democracy doesn't have to mean no sex. It means treating your partner as someone whose lust is equal to yours and also someone whose life is equally valuable. It's about enacting in daily life one's principles, claiming our rights to pleasure and making sure that our partners also feel safe enough to be able to fully claim theirs. This is what we demand for those who have come to America seeking refuge— safety—from political tyranny; could we ask any less for those who are now asking for protection and refuge from millennia of sexual tyranny?

MYTHOPOETIC MEN'S WORK AS A SEARCH FOR *COMMUNITAS*

MICHAEL SCHWALBE

In the late 1980s and early 1990s, the commercial media discovered the mythopoetic men's movement. Newspapers, magazines, and television reported that thousands of middle-aged, middle-class white men were retreating to rustic settings to share their feelings, to cry, hug, drum, dance, tell poems and fairy tales, and enact primitive rituals. The men were supposedly trying to get in touch with the inner "wildman" and other masculine archetypes as urged by movement leader Robert Bly, a famous poet and author of the 1991 bestseller *Iron John*.[1] Mythopoetic activity was covered because it was offbeat, and so, not surprisingly, most stories played up its odd trappings. The serious side of the movement— its implicit critique of men's lives in American society—was not examined.

While most observers thought mythopoetic activity was harmless and silly, others saw it as dangerous. Feminist critics accused Bly and the mythopoetic men of nefarious doings at their all-male retreats: whining about men's relatively minor psychological troubles while ignoring the much greater oppression of other groups, especially women; "modernizing" rather than truly changing masculinity; retreating from tough political realities into boyish play; unfairly blaming mothers and wives for men's troubles; and reproducing sexism by using fairy tales and rituals from patriarchal cultures. Critics thus saw the mythopoetic movement as part of an anti-feminist backlash, or as a New Age maneuver in the battle of the sexes.[2]

Much of the criticism of the movement was based on the same superficial stories fed to the public. More responsible critics at least read Bly's book, saw his 1990 PBS interview ("A Gathering of Men") with Bill Moyers, attended a retreat, or read other pieces of mythopoetic literature.[3] Even so, almost none of the criticism was based on firsthand knowledge of what the men involved in mythopoetic activity were thinking, feeling, and doing together. The men themselves either disappeared behind the inflated image of Bly, or critics presumed that there was no need to distinguish them from Bly. But while Bly was indeed the chief public figure of the movement and a main source of its philosophy, mythopoetic activity or, as the men themselves called it, "mythopoetic men's work," was much more than Robert Bly.

In the fall of 1990, before Bly's *Iron John* raised the visibility of the mythopoetic movement, I began a participant-observation study of a group of men, associated with a local men's center, who were engaged in mythopoetic activity. As a sociologist, I wanted to know how the men began doing "men's work" and how it was affecting them. I was especially interested in how it affected the meanings they gave to their identities as men. So from September 1990 to June 1993, I attended 128 meetings of various kinds; observed and participated in all manner of mythopoetic activities; attended events led by the movement's prominent teachers; read the movement's guiding literature; and interviewed 21 of the local men at length. The full account of my study appears elsewhere.[4]

Any sociologist who has studied a social movement from the inside will tell you that there is always more diversity within it than outsiders tend to see. This was true in the case of the mythopoetic men. As I was doing my research, people often asked me for a quick explanation of who the men were, what they were doing, and why—as if all the men were alike and one explanation would fit all. While there were commonalities of experience and outlook among the mythopoetic men, there were also significant differences. The men did not all experience the same troubles, want the same things, or think similarly about gender politics. It's important to recognize this diversity, since in writing about any group of people there is a tendency to make internal diversity disappear.

Two other points may aid understanding of the mythopoetic men. One is that, while they held Robert Bly in high esteem, they did not see him as an infallible guru. Most of the men knew that Bly could be obnoxious, that he tended to exaggerate, and that he liked to be the center of attention. It would be fair to say that the men saw him as wise, entertaining, charismatic, and challenging—but hardly without fault. Many of the men had equally high regard for other teachers in the mythopoetic movement, especially the Jungian psychologist James Hillman and the drummer/storyteller Michael Meade. Even so, the mythopoetic men were wary of leaders and did not want to be dependent on them. They believed that men could and should learn to do men's work on their own.

The second point is that many of the men rejected the label "movement" for what they were doing, since to them this implied central organization, the imposition of a doctrine, and political goals. It's true that mythopoetic activity was not centrally coordinated, overtly oriented to political goals, or restricted to those who swore allegiance to a particular set of beliefs. There was, however, an underlying philosophy (derived in large part from Jungian psychology), a "circuit-

riding" group of teachers, a body of inspirational literature, nationally circulated publications, and many similarities of practice among the mythopoetic men's groups that had sprung up around the country. So, to add all this up and call it a movement is a legitimate convenience.

Many of the men also shared certain goals, which they sought to achieve through mythopoetic work. As individuals they sought the therapeutic goals of self-acceptance, greater self-confidence, and better knowledge of themselves as emotional beings. As a group they sought to revalue "man" as a moral identity; that is, they collectively sought to define "man" as an identity that implied positive moral qualities. Identity work of this kind, which was partly a response to feminist criticism of men's behavior, was accomplished through talk at gatherings and through the movement's literature. Much of what the men sought to accomplish thus had to do with their feelings about themselves as men.

It's important to see, however, that mythopoetic men's work was not just about sharing feelings, as if the men knew what they were feeling and then met to talk about it. Things were not so simple. Often the work itself aroused feelings that surprised the men. And these feelings were not always pleasant. But even unpleasant feelings were resources for fashioning a special kind of collective experience. It was this experience, which the anthropologist Victor Turner calls *communitas*, that the men sought to create at their gatherings. This was a rare and seductive experience for men in a highly bureaucratized society such as ours.

COMMUNITY AND *COMMUNITAS*

Most of the mythopoetic men were between the ages of 35 and 60. Nearly all were white, self-identified as heterosexual, and college educated. Most had good jobs, owned homes, and helped maintain families. They were, by and large, successful in conventional, middle-class terms. Yet the men said that living out this conventional script had left them, at midlife, feeling empty and dissatisfied. They found that the external trappings of success were not spiritually fulfilling. What's more, many of the men felt isolated, cut off from other men, except for competitive contexts such as the workplace. Hence, many described mythopoetic activity as part of an effort to create a community where they could interact with other men in a supportive, noncompetitive way.

But it was not exactly community that these men created through mythopoetic work. Although they did sometimes establish serious friendships and networks of support, the men did not enter into relations of material dependence upon each other, live in close proximity to each other, work together, or interact on a daily basis. Usually, the men who met at gatherings and in support groups went home to their separate lives. Thus, strictly speaking, it was not a true community they created. What the mythopoetic men sought and tried to create at their gatherings was both more and less than community. It was *communitas*.

Victor Turner, an anthropologist who studied tribal rituals, describes *communitas* as both a shared feeling-state and a way of relating. To create *communitas*, people must relate to each other outside the constraints of formally defined roles and statuses. As Turner describes it:

> Essentially, communitas *is a relationship between concrete, historical, idiosyncratic individuals. These individuals are not segmentalized into roles and statuses but confront one another rather in the manner of Martin Buber's "I and Thou." Along with this direct, immediate, and total confirmation of human identities, there tends to go a model of society as a homogeneous, unstructured* communitas, *whose boundaries are ideally coterminous with those of the human species.*[5]

Communitas, as Turner says, can happen when the force of roles and statuses is suspended; that is, when individuals in a group feel themselves to be equals and there are no other significant differences to impede feelings of communality. Although the mythopoetic men did not use the

term *communitas*, they sought to relate to teach other in the way that Turner describes as characteristic of *communitas*. At gatherings they tried to engage each other in a way that was unmediated by the roles they played in their everyday work lives. The men tried to practice this kind of relating by talking about the feelings they had, which they believed arose out of their common experiences as men.

Turner distinguishes three types of *communitas*: normative, ideological, and spontaneous or existential. Of these, it is spontaneous or existential *communitas* that the mythopoetic men sought to create. Turner says that spontaneous *communitas* is "richly charged with affects, mainly pleasurable ones," that it "has something 'magical' about it," and that in it there is "the feeling of endless power."[6] He compares hippies and tribesmen in a passage that could also apply to the mythopoetic men:

> The kind of communitas *desired by tribesmen in their rites and by hippies in their "happenings" is not the pleasurable and effortless comradeship that can arise between friends, coworkers, or professional colleagues any day. What they seek is a transformative experience that goes to the root of each person's being and finds in that root something profoundly communal and shared.*[7]

There are several ways in which Turner's description of spontaneous *communitas* fits mythopoetic activity. First, the men sought personal growth through their experiences of "connection," as they called it, at mythopoetic gatherings. A connection was a feeling of emotional communion with another man or group of men. Such connections were made when a story, poem, dance, ritual, or psychodramatic enactment brought up strong feelings in one or more men, and this in turn induced emotional responses in others. In these moments the men learned about their own complexity as emotional beings. The changes they sought were greater awareness of their feelings, more clarity about them, and better ability to use those feelings constructively.

The mythopoetic men also presumed it was possible to establish deep emotional connections with each other because they were all, at root, men. This presumption grew out of the Jungian psychology that informed mythopoetic activity. The idea was that all men possessed the same set of masculine archetypes that predisposed them to think, feel, and act in similar ways.[8] In Jungian terms, these masculine archetypes are parts of the collective unconscious, to which we are all linked by our common humanity. Thus all men, simply by virtue of being male, were presumed to possess similar masculine energies and masculine ways of feeling. Mythopoetic activities were aimed at bringing out or tapping into these energies and feelings so that men could connect based on them and thereby mutually reinvigorate themselves.

Turner's references to pleasurable affects and mysterious feelings of power are echoed in how the mythopoetic men described their experiences. Mythopoetic activity was enjoyable, the men said, because "It's just being with men in a way that's very deep and powerful"; "There's a tremendous energy that grows out of men getting together and connecting emotionally"; and "It just feels great to be there connecting with other men in a noncompetitive way." And, indeed, the feelings were often intense. As one man said during a talking circle at the end of a weekend retreat, "I feel there's so much love in this room right now it hurts." Men also said that going back to their ordinary lives after a gathering meant "coming down from an emotional high." I, too, experienced this transition from the warm, open, supportive, emotionally charged atmosphere of a gathering to the relatively chilly atmosphere of a large research university.

The success of a gathering was measured by the intensity of the emotion it evoked and the connections thereby established. A less successful gathering was one where the emotional intensity was low and the men did not make strong connections. At a small two-day gathering, one man commented somewhat sadly, "We've had some good sharing, but only once did I feel much happening to me. That was when B. was talking. I felt tears welling up. So there's a deeper level we could get to." This was said at the beginning of the final talking circle, in hopes of prompting a more emotional discussion before the gathering was over. In addition to showing the desire for *communitas*, this statement also shows that it took effort to achieve. Spontaneous *communitas* did not happen spontaneously.

CREATING SPONTANEOUS *COMMUNITAS*

Mythopoetic men's work was in large part the conversation work required to create spontaneous *communitas*. I'll explain here how this work was done, through talk and other means. I should be understood that not all gatherings were aimed as intently at creating the same degree of spontaneous *communitas*. Some gatherings were more "heady," in that they were devoted to discussion of a topic, such as fathering or men's health or men's friendships. Often there were moments of *communitas* at these kinds of meetings; but it was at the retreats—those that had an explicit mythopoetic or "inner work" theme— where the greatest efforts were made to produce *communitas*. Talk, ritual, and drumming were the chief means for doing this.

Forms of Talk

At mythopoetic gatherings, men often made personal statements that revealed something shameful, tragic, or emotionally disturbing about their lives. Such statements might be made by each man in turn at the beginning of a retreat, as part of saying why he was there, what he was feeling, and what he hoped to accomplish at the retreat. Before any statements were made, the leader of the retreat or gathering would remind the men of the rules to follow in making statements: speak briefly, speak from the heart (i.e., focus on feelings), and speak to the other men—who were supposed to listen intently, make no judgments, and give no advice. The idea was that the statements should bring the unrehearsed truth up from a man's gut, since this would stir feelings in him and move other men to speak their "belly truth."

A great deal of feeling was stirred up as men talked about troubled relationships with fathers; being sexually abused as children; struggling to overcome addictions; repressed anger over past hurts and betrayals; grief and sadness over irreplaceable losses; efforts to be better fathers to their children. When men choked up, wept, shook with fear, or raged as they spoke it induced strong feelings in other men in the group. The sequence in which personal statements were made amplified this effect. Men would often begin their remarks by saying, "What that [the previous statement] brings up for me is . . . ," or "I really identify with what ——— said, because. . . ." The more disclosing, expressive, and moving a man's statement, the more likely it was to evoke from the other men heavy sighs, sympathetic "mmmms," or a loud chorus of "Ho!" (supposedly a Native American way of affirming that a man's statement has been heard and felt). If a statement seemed inauthentic or insufficiently revealing it might evoke little or no reaction. In this way the men reinforced a norm of making risky, revealing, and evocative statements.

Thus, the men were not only sharing feelings but, by virtue of how they talked, knitting those feelings together into a group mood. In this way they were also creating *communitas*. It is important, too, that the settings in which these statements were made were defined as "safe," meaning that, by agreement, the men were not there to compete with or judge each other, but to listen and provide support. Even so, there was an element of risk and a degree of anxiety associated with making personal statements, since the mythopoetic men, like most men in American society, were unused to sharing feelings of hurt and vulnerability with other men. This anxiety aided the achievement of *communitas* because it created a higher-than-usual level of emotional arousal to begin with. It also allowed the men immediately to identify with one another over being anxious. As Turner likewise noted: "Dan-

ger is one of the chief ingredients in the production of spontaneous *communitas*."[9]

In making personal statements and in their general conversation at gatherings, the men could not help but refer to people, events, and circumstances outside themselves that evoked the feelings they had. In doing this, the men were careful to add to their statements the disclaimer "for me," as in "For *me*, the Gulf War was very depressing." This disclaimer signified that the man speaking was talking about *his* feelings based on *his* perceptions of things, and he was making no presumptions about how other men should feel. The use of this disclaimer helped the men maintain the fellow-feeling they sought by avoiding arguments about what was true of the external world. The mythopoetic men wanted their feelings validated, not challenged. As long as each man spoke the truth from his heart, no one could say he was wrong.

Talk about fathers was another way the men achieved *communitas*. It worked because almost every man had a father to talk about, and those few who didn't could talk about not having fathers. So every man could participate. Father talk also worked because it brought up feelings of sadness and anger for many of the men, and thus created the necessary emotional charge. Because many of the men experienced their fathers as physically or emotionally absent, or in some way abusive, the men could identify with each other based on these common experiences. Father talk may have helped them to reach insights about their relationships to their fathers. But father talk went on to the extent it did because it was so useful for creating *communitas*.

Poems and fairy tales were also a staple part of mythopoetic activity.[10] Most of the time no commentary or discussion followed the reading or reciting of a poem. The men would just steep in the feelings the poem evoked. An especially stirring poem, like a moving personal statement, would elicit deep sighs, "mmmmm," "yeah," sometimes "Ho!", and, often, calls for the reader to "read it again!" And as with the personal statements, these responses, which were signs of shared feelings, served to turn the individual feelings into a collective mood, and thus helped to create *communitas*. When fairy tales were told, there usually was commentary and discussion in a form that also encouraged *communitas*.

When a story was told, the storyteller would usually instruct the men to look for an image that evoked strong feelings. That image, it was said, would be a man's "doorway into the story"—his way of discovering what the story could tell him about his life as a man. This is consistent with Turner's observation that the "concrete, personal, imagist mode of thinking is highly characteristic of those in love with existential [or spontaneous] *communitas*, with the direct relation between man and man, and man and nature. Abstractions appear as hostile to live contact."[11] In the case of the mythopoetics, the emphasis on specific images grew out of Jungian psychology, according to which the psyche was best explored by working with emotionally evocative images.

After a story or part of a story was told, men would talk about the images that struck them and the feelings these images evoked. In a large group of men many different images might be mentioned. Sometimes men reacted strongly to the same image. Talking about the stories in this way created more chances for men to express feelings and to find that they shared feelings and experiences with other men. This was in part how feelings of isolation were overcome and connections were made. Again, the stories may have helped the men to better understand their lives. But it was *how* the stories were talked about that helped the men to experience the good feelings and mysterious power of spontaneous *communitas*.

Ritual

Ritual is different from routine. Routine is the repetition of a behavioral pattern, like brushing one's teeth every night before bed. Ritual involves the symbolic enactment of values, beliefs, or feelings. It is a way of making external, visible, and public things that are normally internal,

invisible, and private. By doing this, members of a community create a shared reality, reaffirm their common embrace of certain beliefs and values, and thereby keep the community alive. Ritual can also be a way of acknowledging changes in community members or of actually inducing such changes. The mythopoetic men used ritual for the same purposes: to call up, express, and share their otherwise private feelings, and to make changes in themselves.

Not all gatherings were ritual gatherings, though most included some ritual elements. Those gatherings where an explicit attempt was made to create "ritual space" or "sacred space" usually began with a symbolic act of separation from the ordinary world. For example, sometimes men would dip their hands into a large bowl of water to symbolize a washing off of concerns and distractions linked to the outside world. Other times, at the outset of gatherings the "spirits of the four directions" (and sometimes of the earth and sky, too) would be invoked and asked to bring the men strength and wisdom. Still other times, the men would dance their way into the space where the meeting was to be held, while the men already inside drummed and chanted. The point was to perform some collective act to mark a boundary between outside life and the "ritual space."

The scene of a gathering also had to be properly set. Ritual gatherings were often held at rustic lodges, where various objects—candles, bird feathers, masks, antlers, strangely shaped driftwood, animal skulls—might be set up around the main meeting area. Sage was often burned (a practice called "smudging") to make the air pungent and to cleanse the ritual space for the action that was going to take place. Usually the leader or leaders of the gathering made sure these things were done. Again, the idea was to heighten the sense of separation from ordinary reality, to make the physical space where the gathering would take place seem special, and to draw the men together. This preparation was talked about in terms of "creating a container" that could safely hold the psychic energies about to be unleashed.

The separation from ordinary reality also helped the men let go of the concerns for status and power that influenced their interactions with other men in everyday life. In the ritual space, the men were supposed to be "present for each other" in a direct and immediate way, as equals, as "brothers," and not as inferiors and superiors. Defining the situation as one in which feelings and other psychic matters were the proper focus of attention and activity helped to create and sustain this sense of equality. Thus, the men seldom talked about their jobs, except to describe job-related troubles (and sometimes triumphs) in general terms. Too much talk about occupations would have introduced status concerns, which in turn would have corroded the sense of equality and brotherhood that fostered feelings of *communitas*.

Two examples can help show more concretely how the mythopoetic men used ritual to create *communitas*. One example is from a six-day gathering of about 120 men in a remote rural setting. At this gathering the men were divided into three clans: Trout, Ravens, and Lions. During the week each clan worked with a dance teacher to develop a dance of its own, a dance that would symbolize the spirit of the men in the clan. At the carnivale on the last night of the gathering, each clan was to share its dance with the rest of the men. One clan would drum while another danced and the third clan "witnessed."

The carnivale was held in a large, dimly lit lodge built of rough-cut logs. Many of the men wore the wildly decorated masks they had made earlier in the week. When their turn came, the 40 men in the Trout clan moved to the center of the room and formed a circle. The men stood for a few moments and then hunched down, extended their arms with their hands together in front of them, and began to dip and sway like fish swimming. Then half the men began moving to their right and half to their left, creating two flowing, interweaving circles. The Trout men also carried small stones, which they clicked together as they moved. About 30 men drummed as the Trout men danced. The rest of the men watched.

After a while the Trout men stopped and stood again, holding hands in a circle inside the larger circle of witnesses. They began a sweet and mournful African chant that they said was used to honor the passing away of loved ones. One by one, each of the Trout men moved to the center of their circle and put down the stones he was carrying. As he did so, he called out the name of a person or people whose passing he wished to honor. Another of the Trout men walked along the row of men standing in the outer ring and said, "We invite you to join us by putting a stone in the center of the circle to honor your dead." The drumming and chanting continued all the while.

At first a few, then more and more of the Raven and Lion men stepped outside to get stones. Each man as he returned went to the center of the circle, called the name of the dead he was honoring, put down a stone, and then stepped back. There was sadness in the men's voices as they spoke. This lent gravity to their acts and drew everyone into the ritual. By now all the men had picked up the chant and joined hands in one large circle. The sound filled the lodge. After about 20 minutes the chanting reached a lull—and then one man began to sing "Amazing Grace." Soon all the men joined in and again their voices rose in chorus and filled the lodge. When we finished singing we stood silent, looking at all the stones between us.

This example shows how a great deal of work went into creating spontaneous *communitas*. The dance was carefully choreographed and the stage was elaborately set (one could argue that the five days leading up to the carnivale were part of the stage setting). But later I talked to Trout men who said that they had planned the dance only up to the point of asking the other men to honor their dead. They were surprised by what happened after that, by how quickly and powerfully the other men were drawn in. No one had expected the surge of emotion and fellow-feeling that the ritual induced, especially when the men began to sing "Amazing Grace." Several men I talked to later cited this ritual as one of the most moving experiences they had had at a mythopoetic gathering.

Another example comes from a sweat-lodge ritual modeled on a traditional Native American practice.[12] In this case the lodge was tiny, consisting of a framework of saplings held together with twine upon which were draped several layers of old blankets and tarps. Before the frame was built, a fire pit was dug in the center of the spot on which the lodge stood. Although a lodge could be made bigger, here it was about ten feet in diameter and four feet high—big enough for a dozen men to squeeze in. From the outside it looked like a miniature domed stadium.

It was a drizzly 45-degree morning on the second day of a teacher-led weekend retreat. I was in the second group of 12 men who would go into the lodge together. This was the first "sweat" for all of us. The men in this group were almost giddy as we walked from the cabins to the shore of a small lake where the sweat lodge had been built. When we got there the men from the previous group had just finished.

The scene stopped us abruptly. Next to the lodge a large rock-rimmed fire was burning. A fierce, black-haired man with a beard stood by the fire, a five-foot staff in his hand. Some of the men who had just finished their sweat were standing waist-deep in the lake. Others were on shore hugging, their naked bodies still steaming in the cool air. Our moment of stunned silence ended when the leader of the retreat said to us, matter of factly, "Get undressed, stay quiet, keep your humility." We undressed and stashed our clothes under the nearby pine trees, out of the rain.

Before we entered the lodge, the teacher urged us to reflect on the specialness of the occasion and to approach it with seriousness. Upon entering the lodge through a small entry flap each man was to say, "all my relations," to remind himself of his connections to the earth, to his ancestors, and to the other men. Once we were inside, the teacher called for the fire tender to bring us fresh, red-hot rocks. As each rock was placed by shovel into the fire pit, we said in unison, "welcome Grandfather," again as sym-

bolic acknowledgment of our connection to the earth. The teacher then burned sage on the rocks to scent the air. When he poured water on the rocks, the lodge became a sauna. The space was tightly packed, lit only by the glow of the rocks, and very hot. We were to do three sessions of ten to fifteen minutes each. Because of the intensity of the heat, a few men could not do all three sessions.

During one of the sessions, the teacher urged us to call upon the spirits of our ancestors from whom we wanted blessings. In the cacophony of voices it was hard to make out what was being said. Some men were calling the names of people not present. A few were doing what sounded like a Native American Indian chant learned from the movies. The man next to me was gobbling like a turkey. At first this all struck me as ridiculous. I looked around the lodge for signs of similar bemusement in other men's faces. Surely they couldn't be taking this seriously. But those whose faces I could see appeared absorbed in the experience. Some men seemed oddly distant, as if they were engaged in a conversation going on elsewhere.

Although I was still put off by the bogus chanting and baffled by the gobbling, I, too, began to feel drawn in. I found myself wanting to suspend disbelief and find some meaning in the ritual, no matter how culturally foreign it was. In large part this was because the teacher and the other men seemed to be taking it seriously. I certainly didn't want to ruin the experience for them by showing any sign of cynicism. These were men who had taken my feelings seriously during the retreat. I felt I owed them the same consideration in the sweat lodge.

In both examples, a carefully crafted set of appearances made *communitas* likely to happen. The physical props, the words and actions of the ritual leaders, and the sincere words and actions of some men evoked real feelings in others and drew them in.[13] Because it seemed that there were genuine emotions at stake, it would have taken a hard heart to show any sign of cynicism during the Trout dance or the sweat lodge. To do so would have risked hurting other men's feelings and dimming the glow of *communitas*. It would also have cut the cynic himself off from the good feelings and mysterious power being generated by these occasions. Whether or not everyone really "believed" in what was happening didn't matter. Appearances made it seem so, and to achieve the *communitas* they desired, all the men needed to do was to act on these appearances.

Another dynamic was at work in the case of the sweat lodge. On the face of it, the idea of late twentieth-century white men enacting a Native American sweat lodge ritual was absurd. And for most of these men, the idea of squatting naked, haunch to haunch, with other men would have been—within an everyday frame of reference— embarrassing and threatening to their identities as heterosexuals. Thus, to avoid feeling ridiculous, threatened, or embarrassed, the men had to stay focused on the form of the ritual and show no sign of doubting its content or propriety. Because there was such a gap between their everyday frame of reference and the ritual, the men had to exaggerate their absorption in the ritual reality just to keep a grip on it. In so doing the men truly did create a common focus and, again, the appearance that a serious, collective spiritual activity was going on.

The sweat lodge example also illustrated how the creation of *communitas* was aided by literally stripping men of signs of their differences. In the sweat lodge, men were only men—as symbolized by their nakedness. As such they were also equals. When a small group of us spoke afterwards about the experience, one man said, "The closeness and physicality, and especially being naked, are what make it work. Everyone is just a man in there. You can't wear any merit badges."

Drumming

Next to Bly, the most widely recognized icon of the mythopoetic movement was the drum. Drumming was indeed an important part of mythopoetic activity. Some mythopoetic groups held gatherings just to drum, although the group I studied was more likely to mix drumming with other activities. Not all of the men drummed. A few didn't care for it; others preferred to use rattles or tambourines during drumming sessions. The most enthusiastic men had congas, African-styled djembes, or hand-held shaman's drums, though all manner of large and small folk drums appeared at gatherings. On one occasion a man used a five-gallon plastic pail turned upside down.

Why did the mythopoetic men drum? Some of the men in the local group said that they began drumming after a visit by Michael Meade, a prominent teacher in the mythopoetic movement, who was skilled at using drumming to accompany his telling of folk tales. This is what inspired one man I interviewed:

> *Bly came and told his Iron John story and that was my first introduction to using stories as a way of illuminating dilemmas or emotional situations in your life. Michael Meade came the following year in the spring and introduced some drumming at that weekend. I just loved the energy of that right away. It just really opened me up. After drumming I felt wonderful. I liked the feeling of it and felt a connection with the mythopoetic [movement] ever since then, more to the drumming than to anything else.*

But on only a few occasions did any of the local men use drumming as accompaniment to story telling. Most of the drumming was done in groups, which varied in size from six to forty. And while the men who were better drummers might lead the group into a complex rhythm, often something samba-like, the drumming was usually free-form, leaderless, and simple.

The appeal of this activity had little to with acquiring virtuosity at drumming. Rather, much of the appeal stemmed from the fact that the men could be bad drummers and still participate. It was, most importantly, another means to achieve *communitas*. Victor Turner notes that simple musical instruments are often used this way: "It is . . . fascinating to consider how expressions of *communitas* are culturally linked with simple wind instruments (flutes and harmonicas). Perhaps, in addition to their ready portability, it is their capacity to convey in music the quality of spontaneous human *communitas* that is responsible for this."[14] This was equally true of drums, which were also readily portable and required even less skill to play.

What the mythopoetic men say about their experiences drumming tells much about not only drumming, but about the communitas it helped create and about the mythopoetic experience in general. In another interview, a 48-year-old salesman spoke of drumming as both ordinary and special at the same time:

> You can kind of lose yourself in it. It's like any hobby—fishing or playing ball or whatever. There is something that happens. You go into an altered state almost, hearing that music. At this national meeting in Minnesota a month ago the common thing was the drums. You could hear the beating of that drum. At break people would drum and we would dance. So it's this common bond.

Put another way, drumming was an activity that gave men who were strangers a way to quickly feel comfortable and familiar with each other. Some of the mythopoetic men believed that men in general had a special facility for connecting with each other via nonverbal means. The way that men were able to quickly bond via drumming was seen as evidence of this.

Although the men were aware that drumming was not an activity limited to men, some clearly felt that it held a special appeal for them. Another man, a 33-year-old technical writer, said in an interview:

> Drumming does something—connects me with men in ways that I can't understand, in the same way I've observed women who have babies connecting with each other. There's something in it that I don't participate in emotionally. In the same way, the drumming—society with other men—is emotionally important to men in ways that women don't understand. They can't.

Some of the mythopoetic men's ideas about gender are exemplified by this statement. Many of

them believed that women, no matter how empathic they might be, could not know what it was like to be a man, just as men could not know what it was like to be a woman. Hence, men needed the understanding and support that could come only from other men just as women needed the same things from other women.

For other men, drumming was both a communal and, sometimes, a personal, spiritual experience. A 42-year-old therapist told me:

> There was one point where I was really deeply entranced just drumming and then all of a sudden I had this real powerful experience where I felt like I was on a hill, on some mountainside or some mountaintop, in some land far far away, in some time that was all time. And I was in the middle of my men, who were my brothers, who were all men. It was one of those powerful, mystical experiences where all of a sudden I felt planted in the community of men. And that changed my life, because I felt like I was a man among men in the community of men and we were drumming and the drum was in my bones and it was in my heartbeat and it was good.

This statement captures in spirit, tone, and rhythm the experience that many of the men found in drumming. Even if they didn't report such flights of imagination, others said that drumming provided a similar sense of communality, of connection—*communitas*.

My own experience corroborates this. I found that when I would pick up a beat and help sustain it without thinking, the sense of being part of the group was strong. It was as if the sound testified to the reality of the group, and the rhythm testified to our connection. By drumming in synch each man attached himself to the group and to the other men in it. The men valued this also because the attachment was created by physical action rather than by talk, and because it seemed to happen at a nonrational level. Drumming thus helped the men to do two other things that mythopoetic philosophy called for: getting out of their heads and into feeling their bodies, and by-passing the rational ego that kept a lid on the archetypal masculine energies the men sought to tap.

COMMUNITAS AND POLITICS

My point has been to show that much mythopoetic activity can be understood as a search for *communitas*. This experience was rare in these men's lives and precious on the occasions when it occurred. Sometimes the men talked about the activities at their gatherings as "inviting the sacred to happen." Particular forms of talk, the orchestration of ritual, and drumming were means to this end. Because *communitas* was so valuable to the men, there were also things they *avoided* doing to make *communitas* more likely to happen. One thing they avoided was serious talk about politics.

This is not to say that the men were apolitical. Most of the men I studied were well informed on social issues and supported progressive causes. They were also critical of the rapacious greed of big corporations, the duplicity and brutal militarism of Reagan and Bush, and the general oppressiveness of large bureaucracies. But there were two revealing ironies in the politics of the mythopoetic men. First, while they were critical of the behavior of corporations and government, they avoided saying that these institutions were run by men. Usually it was an unspecified, genderless "they" who were said to be responsible for destroying the environment or for turning all culture into mass marketable schlock. And second, while many of the men saw corporate power and greed as root problems in U.S. society, they were uninterested in collective action to address these problems. This is, as one might expect, because the white, middle-class mythopoetic men did not do so badly in reaping the material benefits of the economic system they occasionally criticized.

In other words, the men were selectively apolitical. They did not want to see that it was other *men* who were responsible for many of the social problems they witnessed and were sometimes affected by. To do so, and to talk about it, would have shattered the illusion of universal brotherhood among men that helped sustain feelings of *communitas*. Talk about power, politics, and inequality in the external world was incompatible with the search for *communitas*, because it would have led to arguments, or at least to intellectual discussions, rather than to warm emotional communion. When discussions at mythopoetic gatherings inadvertently turned political, disagreements surfaced and tensions arose; someone would usually say, "we're getting away from the important work here." Or, as one man said in trying to stop a conversation that was becoming an argument, "I think we're losing the power of the drums."

The mythopoetic men believed that engaging in political or sociological analysis would have led them away from their goals of self-acceptance, self-knowledge, emotional authenticity, and *communitas*. The men wanted to feel better about themselves as men, to learn about the feelings and psychic energies that churned within them, to live fuller and more authentic emotional lives, and to experience the pleasure and mysterious power of *communitas*. They did not want to compete over whose interpretation of social reality was correct. They wanted untroubled brotherhood in which their feelings were validated by other men, and in which their identities as men could be infused with new value.

Here can be seen both the power and limits of mythopoetic men's work. Through this work some men have begun to free themselves from the debilitating repression of emotion that was part of their socialization into traditional masculinity. Feminism provided the intellectual basis and political impetus for this critique of traditional masculinity, although the mythopoetics have difficulty appreciating this. Yet they deserve credit for developing a method that allows some men to explore and express more of the emotions that make them human. Mythopoetic men's work has also helped men to see how these emotions can be the basis for connections to men they might otherwise have feared, mistrusted, or felt compelled to compete with. And, to the extent that men begin to see that they don't have to live out traditional masculinity and can even cooperate to heal the damage it causes, mythopoetic men's work has progressive potential.

One problem is that the progressive potential of mythopoetic men's work is limited, because it leads men to think about gender and gender inequality in psychological or, at best, cultural terms. Mythopoetic men's work may open men to seeing things in themselves and help them make connections with each other, but it also blinds them to seeing important connections between themselves and society. For example, the mythopoetic men do not see that, in a male-supremacist society, there can be no innocent celebration of masculinity. In such a society the celebration of manhood and of masculinity—even if it is supposedly "deep" or "authentic" and thus a more fully human version of masculinity—reaffirms the lesser value of women, whether this is intended or not. The therapeutic focus of mythopoetic men's work—as done by a largely homogeneous group of middle-class white males—also blinds them to matters of class inequality and to the exploitation of work-ing-class people and people of color by the elite white *men* who run the economy.

Yet mythopoetic men's work is a form of resistance to domination. It's not just an entertaining form of group therapy or collective whining over imagined wounds, or retrograde male bonding. These middle-class white men, who are not the ruling elites, are responding to the alienation and isolation that stem from living in a capitalist society that encourages people to be greedy, selfish, and predatory. Their goal of trying to awaken the human sensibilities that have been benumbed by an exploitive economy is subversive. But to get to the root of the problem men will have to do more than take modest risks among themselves to try to heal their psyches. They will have to take big risks in trying to abolish the race, class, and gender hierarchies that damage us all. They will have to learn to create *communitas* in struggles for justice.

NOTES

1. Robert Bly, *Iron John: A Book About Men* (Reading, MA: Addison-Wesley, 1990).
2. See Kay Leigh Hagan, editor, *Women Respond to the Men's Movement* (San Francisco: HarperCollins, 1992); Kenneth Clatterbaugh, *Contemporary Perspectives on Masculinity* (Boulder, CO: Westview, 1990), pp. 85–103; Susan Faludi, *Backlash: The Undeclared War against American Women* (New York: Crown, 1991), pp. 304–312; R. W. Connell, "Drumming Up the Wrong Tree," *Tikkun* vol. 7, no. 1 (1992): 31–36; Sharon Doubiago, "Enemy of the Mother: A Feminist Response to the Men's Movement," *Ms.* March/April (1992): 82–85; Fred Pelka, "Robert Bly and Iron John," *On the Issues* Summer (1991): 17–19, 39; Diane Johnson, "Something for the Boys," *New York Review of Books* January 16 (1992): 13–17.
3. For a sampling of other writings in the mythopoetic genre, see Robert Moore and Douglas Gillette, *King, Warrior, Magician, Lover: Rediscovering the Archetypes of the Mature Masculine* (New York: HarperCollins, 1990); Wayne Liebman, *Tending the Fire: The Ritual Men's Group* (St. Paul, MN: Ally, 1991); Christopher Harding, editor, *Wingspan: Inside the Men's Movement* (New York: St. Martin's, 1992).
4. Michael Schwalbe, *Unlocking the Iron Cage: A Critical Appreciation of Mythopoetic Men's Work*. New York: Oxford University Press, forthcoming, 1995.
5. Victor Turner, *The Ritual Process* (Ithaca, NY: Cornell, 1969), pp. 94–165.
6. Ibid., p. 131–132.
7. Ibid., p. 139.
8. For an introduction to the basic concepts of Jungian psychology, see Calvin Hall and Vernon Nordby, *A Primer of Jungian Psychology* (New York: Penguin, 1973); or Frieda Fordham, *An Introduction to Jung's Psychology* (New York: Penguin, 1966). For more detail, see Edward C. Whitmont, *The Symbolic Quest* (Princeton, NJ: Princeton, 1991).
9. Turner, p. 154.
10. Many of the poems frequently read at mythopoetic gatherings are collected in Robert Bly, James Hillman, and Michael Meade (eds.), *The Rag and Bone Shop of the Heart* (New York: HarperCollins, 1992). Many of the fairy tales told at gatherings, including Bly's "Iron John," originally known as "Iron Hans," are taken from the Grimm brothers' collection.

11. Turner, p. 141.

12. A description of the sweat-lodge ritual can be found in Joseph Epes Brown (recorder and editor), *The Sacred Pipe: Black Elk's Account of the Seven Rites of the Oglala Sioux* (Norman, OK: Univ. of Oklahoma, 1953), pp. 31–43. This account was a source of inspiration for some of the mythopoetic men. See also William K. Powers, *Oglala Religion* (Lincoln, NE: Univ. of Nebraska, 1977).

13. Catherine Bell writes about how ritual "catches people up in its own terms" and provides a "resistant surface to casual disagreement." See Bell, *Ritual Theory, Ritual Practice* (New York: Oxford Univ. Press, 1992), pp. 214–215. Other observers have noted how the improvised rituals at mythopoetic gatherings had this power to draw the men in. See Richard Gilbert, "Revisiting the Psychology of Men: Robert Bly and the Mytho-Poetic Movement," *Journal of Humanistic Psychology* 32 (1992): 41–67.

14. Turner, p. 165.

MEN:
COMRADES IN STRUGGLE

BELL HOOKS

Feminism defined as a movement to end sexist oppression enables women and men, girls and boys, to participate equally in revolutionary struggle. So far, contemporary feminist movement has been primarily generated by the efforts of women—men have rarely participated. This lack of participation is not solely a consequence of anti-feminism. By making women's liberation synonymous with women gaining social equality with men, liberal feminists effectively created a situation in which they, not men, designated feminist movement "women's work." Even as they were attacking sex role divisions of labor, the institutionalized sexism which assigns unpaid, devalued, "dirty" work to women, they were assigning to women yet another sex role task: making feminist revolution. Women's liberationists called upon all women to join feminist movement but they did not continually stress that men should assume responsibility for actively struggling to end sexist oppression. Men, they argued, were all-powerful, misogynist oppressor—the enemy. Women were the oppressed—the victims. Such rhetoric reinforced sexist ideology by positing in an inverted form the notion of a basic conflict between the sexes, the implication being that the empowerment of women would necessarily be at the expense of men.

As with other issues, the insistence on a "woman only" feminist movement and a virulent anti-male stance reflected the race and class background of participants. Bourgeois white women, especially radical feminists, were envious and angry at privileged white men for denying them an equal share in class privilege. In part, feminism provided them with a public forum for the expression of their anger as well as a political platform they could use to call attention to issues of social equality, demand change, and promote specific reforms. They were not eager to call attention to the fact that men do not share a common social status; that patriarchy does not negate the existence of class and race privilege or exploitation; that all men do not benefit equally from sexism. They did not want to acknowledge that bourgeois white women, though often victimized by sexism, have more power and privilege, are less likely to be exploited or oppressed, than poor, uneducated, nonwhite males. At the time, many white women's liberationists did not care about the fate of oppressed groups of men. In keeping with the exercise of race and/or class privilege, they deemed the life experiences of these men unworthy of their attention, dismissed them, and simultaneously deflected attention away from their support of continued exploitation and oppression. Assertions like "all men are the enemy," "all men hate women" lumped all groups of men in one category, thereby suggesting that they share equally in all forms of male privilege. One of the first written statements which endeavored to make an anti-male stance a central feminist position was "The Redstocking Manifesto." Clause III of the manifesto reads:

We identify the agents of our oppression as men. Male supremacy is the oldest, most basic form of domination. All other forms of exploitation and oppression (racism, capitalism, imperialism, etc.) are extensions of male supremacy: men dominate women, a few men dominate the rest. All power situations throughout history have been male-dominated and male-oriented. Men have controlled all political, economic, and cultural institutions and backed up this control with physical force. They have used their power to keep women in an inferior position. All men receive economic, sexual, and psychological benefits from male supremacy. All men have oppressed women. (1970, p. 109)

Anti-male sentiments alienated many poor and working class women, particularly non-white women, from feminist movement. Their life experiences had shown them that they have more in common with men of their race and/or class group than bourgeois white women. They know the sufferings and hardships women face in their communities; they also know the sufferings and hardships men face and they have compassion for them. They have had the experience of struggling with them for a better life. This has been especially true for black women. Throughout our history in the United States, black women have shared equal responsibility in all struggles to resist racist oppression. Despite sexism, black women have continually contributed equally to anti-racist struggle, and frequently, before contemporary black liberation effort, black men recognized this contribution. There is a special tie binding people together who struggle collectively for liberation. Black women and men have been united by such ties. They have known the experience of political solidarity. It is the experience of shared resistance struggle that led black women to reject the anti-male stance of some feminist activists. This does not mean that

black women were not willing to acknowledge the reality of black male sexism. It does mean that many of us do not believe we will combat sexism or woman-hating by attacking black men or responding to them in kind.

Bourgeois white women cannot conceptualize the bonds that develop between women and men in liberation struggle and have not had as many positive experiences working with men politically. Patriarchal white male rule has usually devalued female political input. Despite the prevalence of sexism in black communities, the role black women play in social institutions, whether primary or secondary, is recognized by everyone as significant and valuable. In an interview with Claudia Tate (1983), black woman writer Maya Angelou explains her sense of the different role black and white women play in their communities:

Black women and white women are in strange positions in our separate communities. In the social gatherings of black people, black women have always been predominant. That is to say, in the church it's always Sister Hudson, Sister Thomas, and Sister Wetheringay who keep the church alive. In lay gatherings it's always Lottie who cooks, and Mary who's going to Bonita's where there is a good party going on. Also, black women are the nurturers of children in our community. White women are in a different position in their social institutions. White men, who are in effect their fathers, husbands, brothers, their sons, nephews, and uncles say to white women or imply in any case: "I don't really need you to run my institutions. I need you in certain places and in those places you must be kept—in the bedroom, in the kitchen, in the nursery, and on the pedestal." Black women have never been told this. . . .

Without the material input of black women, as participants and leaders, many male-dominated institutions in black communities would cease to exist; this is not the case in all white communities.

Many black women refused participation in feminist movement because they felt an anti-male stance was not a sound basis for action.

They were convinced that virulent expressions of these sentiments intensify sexism by adding to the antagonism which already exists between women and men. For years black women (and some black men) had been struggling to overcome the tensions and antagonisms between black females and males that is generated by internalized racism (i.e., when the white patriarchy suggests one group has caused the oppression of the other). Black women were saying to black men, "we are not one another's enemy," "we must resist the socialization that teaches us to hate ourselves and one another." This affirmation of bonding between black women and men was part of anti-racist struggle. It could have been a part of feminist struggle had white women's liberationists stressed the need for women and men to resist the sexist socialization that teaches us to hate and fear one another. They chose instead to emphasize hate, especially male woman-hating, suggesting that it could not be changed. Therefore no viable political solidarity could exist between women and men. Women of color, from various ethnic backgrounds, as well as women who were active in the gay movement, not only experienced the development of solidarity between women and men in resistance struggle, but recognized its value. They were not willing to devalue this bonding by allying themselves with anti-male bourgeois white women. Encouraging political bonding between women and men to radically resist sexist oppression would have called attention to the transformative potential of feminism. The anti-male stance was a reactionary perspective that made feminism appear to be a movement that would enable white women to usurp white male power, replacing white male supremacist rule with white female supremacist rule.

Within feminist organizations, the issue of female separatism was initially separated from the anti-male stance; it was only as the movement progressed that the two perspectives merged. Many all-female sex-segregated groups were formed because women recognized that separatist organizing could hasten female consciousness-raising, lay the groundwork for the development of solidarity between women, and generally advance the movement. It was believed that mixed groups would get bogged down by male power trips. Separatist groups were seen as a necessary strategy, not as a way to attack men. Ultimately, the purpose of such groups was integration with equality. The positive implications of separatist organizing were diminished when radical feminists, like Ti Grace Atkinson, proposed sexual separatism as an ultimate goal of feminist movement. Reactionary separatism is rooted in the conviction that male supremacy is an absolute aspect of our culture, that women have only two alternatives: accepting it or withdrawing from it to create subcultures. This position eliminates any need for revolutionary struggle and it is in no way a threat to the status quo. In the essay "Separate to Integrate," Barbara Leon (1975) stresses that male supremacists would rather feminist movement remain "separate and unequal." She gives the example of orchestra conductor Antonia Brico's efforts to shift from an all-women orchestra to a mixed orchestra, only to find she could not get support for the latter:

> *Antonia Brico's efforts were acceptable as long as she confined herself to proving that women were qualified musicians. She had no trouble finding 100 women who could play in an orchestra or getting financial backing for them to do so. But finding the backing for men and women to play together in a truly integrated orchestra proved to be impossible. Fighting for integration proved to be more a threat to male supremacy and, therefore, harder to achieve.*
>
> *The women's movement is at the same point now. We can take the easier way of accepting segregation, but that would mean losing the very goals for which the movement was formed. Reactionary separatism has been a way of halting the push of feminism. . . .*

During the course of contemporary feminist movement, reactionary separatism has led many women to abandon feminist struggle, yet it remains an accepted pattern for feminist organizing, e.g. autonomous women's groups within the peace movement. As a policy, it has helped to marginalize feminist struggle, to make it seem more a personal solution to individual problems, especially problems with men, than a political movement which aims to transform society as a whole. To return to an emphasis on feminism as revolutionary struggle, women can no longer allow feminism to be another arena for the continued expression of antagonism between the sexes. The time has come for women active in feminist movement to develop new strategies for including men in the struggle against sexism.

All men support and perpetuate sexism and sexist oppression in one form or another. It is crucial that feminist activists not get bogged down in intensifying our awareness of this fact to the extent that we do not stress the more unemphasized point which is that men can lead life affirming, meaningful lives without exploiting and oppressing women. Like women, men have been socialized to passively accept sexist ideology. While they need not blame themselves for accepting sexism, they must assume responsibility for eliminating it. It angers women activists who push separatism as a goal of feminist movement to hear emphasis placed on men being victimized by sexism; they cling to the "all men are the enemy" version of reality. Men are not exploited or oppressed by sexism, but there are ways in which they suffer as a result of it. This suffering should not be ignored. While it in no way diminishes the seriousness of male abuse and oppression of women, or negates male responsibility for exploitative actions, the pain men experience can serve as a catalyst calling attention to the need for change. Recognition of the painful consequences of sexism in their lives led some men to establish consciousness-raising groups to examine this. Paul Hornacek (1977) explains the purpose of these gatherings in his essay "Anti-Sexist Consciousness-Raising Groups for Men":

Men have reported a variety of different reasons for deciding to seek a C-R group, all of which have an underlying link to the feminist movement. Most are experiencing emotional pain as a result of their male sex role and are dissatisfied with it. Some have had confrontations with radical feminists in public or private encounters and have been repeatedly criticized for being sexist. Some come as a result of their commitment to social change and their recognition that sexism and patriarchy are elements of an intolerable social system that needs to be altered . . .

Men in the consciousness-raising groups Hornacek describes acknowledge that they benefit from patriarchy and yet are also hurt by it. Men's groups, like women's support groups, run the risk of overemphasizing personal change at the expense of political analysis and struggle.

Separatist ideology encourages women to ignore the negative impact of sexism on male personhood. It stresses polarization between the sexes. According to Joy Justice, separatists believe that there are "two basic perspectives" on the issue of naming the victims of sexism: "There is the perspective that men oppress women. And there is the perspective that people are people, and we are all hurt by rigid sex roles." Many separatists feel that the latter perspective is a sign of co-optation, representing women's refusal to confront the fact that men are the enemy—they insist on the primacy of the first perspective. Both perspectives accurately describe our predicament. Men *do* oppress women. People *are* hurt by rigid sex role patterns. These two realities co-exist. Male oppression of women cannot be excused by the recognition that there are ways men are hurt by rigid sex roles. Feminist activists should acknowledge that hurt—it exists. It does not erase or lessen male responsibility for supporting and perpetuating their power under patriarchy to exploit and oppress women in a manner far more grievous than the psychological stress or emotional pain caused by male conformity to rigid sex role patterns.

Women active in feminist movement have not wanted to focus in any way on male pain so as not to deflect attention away from the focus on male privilege. Separatist feminist rhetoric suggested that all men shared equally in male privilege, that all men reap positive benefits from sexism. Yet the poor or working class man has been socialized via sexist ideology to believe that there are privileges and powers he should possess solely because he is male often finds that few if any of these benefits are automatically bestowed him in life. More than any other male group in the United States, he is constantly concerned about the contradiction between the notion of masculinity he was taught and his inability to live up to that notion. He is usually "hurt," emotionally scarred because he does not have the privilege or power society has taught him "real men" should possess. Alienated, frustrated, pissed off, he may attack, abuse, and oppress an individual woman or women, but he is not reaping positive benefits from his support and perpetuation of sexist ideology. When he beats or rapes women, he is not exercising privilege or reaping positive rewards; he may feel satisfied in exercising the only form of domination allowed him. The ruling class male power structure that promotes his sexist abuse of women reaps the real material benefits and privileges from his actions. As long as he is attacking women and not sexism or capitalism, he helps to maintain a system that allows him few, if any, benefits or privileges. He is an oppressor. He is an enemy to women. He is also an enemy to himself. He is also oppressed. His abuse of women is not justifiable. Even though he has been socialized to act as he does, there are existing social movements that would enable him to struggle for self-recovery and liberation. By ignoring these movements, he chooses to remain both oppressor and oppressed. If feminist movement ignores his predicament, dismisses his hurt, or writes him off as just another male enemy, then we are passively condoning his actions.

The process by which men act as oppressors and are oppressed is particularly visible in black communities, where men are working class and poor. In her essay "Notes For Yet Another Paper on Black Feminism, or Will The Real Enemy Please Stand Up?," (1979) black feminist activist

Barbara Smith suggests that black women are unwilling to confront the problem of sexist oppression in black communities:

> By naming sexist oppression as a problem it would appear that we would have to identify as threatening a group we have heretofore assumed to be our allies—Black men. This seems to be one of the major stumbling blocks to beginning to analyze the sexual relationships/sexual politics of our lives. The phrase "men are not the enemy" dismisses feminism and the reality of patriarchy in one breath and also overlooks some major realities. If we cannot entertain the idea that some men are the enemy, especially white men and in a different sense Black men, too, then we will never be able to figure out all the reasons why, for example, we are beaten up every day, why we are sterilized against our wills, why we are being raped by our neighbors, why we are pregnant at age twelve, and why we are at home on welfare with more children than we can support or care for. Acknowledging the sexism of Black men does not mean that we become "manhaters" or necessarily eliminate them from our lives. What it does mean is that we must struggle for a different basis of interaction with them.

Women in black communities have been reluctant to publicly discuss sexist oppression, but they have always known it exists. We too have been socialized to accept sexist ideology and many black women feel that black male abuse of women is a reflection of frustrated masculinity—such thoughts lead them to see that abuse is understandable, even justified. The vast majority of black women think that just publicly stating that these men are the enemy or identifying them as oppressors would do little to change the situation; they fear it could simply lead to greater victimization. Naming oppressive realities, in and of itself, has not brought about the kinds of changes for oppressed groups that it can for more privileged groups, who command a different quality of attention. The public naming of sexism has generally not resulted in the institutionalized violence that characterized, for example, the response to black civil rights struggles. (Private naming, however, is often met with violent oppression.) Black women have not joined the feminist movement not because they cannot face the reality of sexist oppression; they face it daily. They do not join feminist movement because they do not see in feminist theory and practice, especially those writings made available to masses of people, potential solutions.

So far, feminist rhetoric identifying men as the enemy has had few positive implications. Had feminist activists called attention to the relationship between ruling class men and the vast majority of men, who are socialized to perpetuate and maintain sexism and sexist oppression even as they reap no life-affirming benefits, these men might have been motivated to examine the impact of sexism in their lives. Often feminist activists talk about male abuse of women as if it is an exercise of privilege rather than an expression of moral bankruptcy, insanity, and dehumanization. For example, in Barbara Smith's essay, she identifies white males as "the primary oppressor group in American society" and discusses the nature of their domination of others. At the end of the passage in which this statement is made she comments: "It is not just rich and powerful capitalists who inhibit and destroy life. Rapists, murderers, lynchers, and ordinary bigots do too and exercise very real and violent power because of this white male privilege." Implicit in this statement is the assumption that the act of committing violent crimes against women is either a gesture or an affirmation of privilege. Sexist ideology brainwashes men to believe that their violent abuse of women is beneficial when it is not. Yet feminist activists affirm this logic when we should be constantly naming these acts as expressions of perverted power relations, general lack of control over one's actions, emotional powerlessness, extreme irrationality, and in many cases, outright insanity. Passive male absorption of sexist ideology enables them to interpret this disturbed behavior positively. As long as men are brainwashed to equate violent abuse of women with privilege, they will have no understanding of the damage done to themselves, or the damage they do to others, and no motivation to change.

Individuals committed to feminist revolution must address ways that men can unlearn sexism. Women were never encouraged in contemporary feminist movement to point out to men their responsibility. Some feminist rhetoric "put down" women who related to men at all. Most women's liberationists were saying "women have nurtured, helped, and supported others for too long—now we must fend for ourselves." Having helped and supported men for centuries by acting in complicity with sexism, women were suddenly encouraged to withdraw their support when it came to the issue of "liberation." The insistence on a concentrated focus on individualism, on the primacy of self, deemed "liberatory" by women's liberationists, was not a visionary, radical concept of freedom. It did provide individual solutions for women, however. It was the same idea of independence perpetuated by the imperial patriarchal state which equates independence with narcissism and lack of concern with triumph over others. In this way, women active in feminist movement were simply inverting the dominant ideology of the culture—they were not attacking it. They were not presenting practical alternatives to the status quo. In fact, even the statement "men are the enemy" was basically an inversion of the male supremacist doctrine that "women are the enemy"— the old Adam and Eve version of reality.

In retrospect, it is evident that the emphasis on "man as enemy" deflected attention away from focus on improving relationships between women and men, ways for men and women to work together to unlearn sexism. Bourgeois women active in feminist movement exploited the notion of a natural polarization between the sexes to draw attention to equal rights effort. They had an enormous investment in depicting the male as enemy and the female as victim. They were the group of women who could dismiss their ties with men once they had an equal share in class privilege. They were ultimately more concerned with obtaining an equal share in class privilege than with the struggle to eliminate sexism and sexist oppression. Their insistence on separating from men heightened the sense that they, as women without men, needed equality of opportunity. Most women do not have the freedom to separate from men because of economic inter-dependence. The separatist notion that women could resist sexism by withdrawing from contact with men reflected a bourgeois class perspective. In Cathy McCandless' essay "Some Thoughts About Racism, Classism, and Separatism," she makes the point that separatism is in many ways a false issue because "in this capitalist economy, none of us are truly separate" (1979). However, she adds:

> Socially, it's another matter entirely. The richer you are, the less you generally have to acknowledge those you depend upon. Money can buy you a great deal of distance. Given enough of it, it is even possible never to lay eyes upon a man. It's a wonderful luxury, having control over who you lay eyes on, but let's face it: most women's daily survival still involves face-to-face contact with men whether they like it or not. It seems to me that for this reason alone, criticizing women who associate with men not only tends to be counterproductive, it borders on blaming the victim. Particularly if the women taking it upon themselves to set the standards are white and upper or middle class (as has often been the case in my experience) and those to whom they apply these rules are not.

Devaluing the real necessities of life that compel many women to remain in contact with men, as well as not respecting the desire of women to keep contact with men, created an unnecessary conflict of interest for those women who might have been very interested in feminism but felt they could not live up to the politically correct standards.

Feminist writings did not say enough about ways women could directly engage in feminist struggle in subtle, day-to-day contacts with men, although they have addressed crises. Feminism is politically relevant to the masses of women who daily interact with men both publicly and privately, if it addresses ways that interaction, which usually has negative components because sexism is so all-pervasive, can be changed. Women who have daily contact with men need useful strategies that will enable them to inte-

grate feminist movement into their daily life. By inadequately addressing or failing to address the difficult issues, contemporary feminist movement located itself on the periphery of society rather than at the center. Many women and men think feminism is happening, or happened, "out there." Television tells them the "liberated" woman is an exception, that she is primarily a careerist. Commercials like the one that shows a white career women shifting from work attire to flimsy clothing exposing flesh, singing all the while "I can bring home the bacon, fry it up in the pan, and never let you forget you're a man" reaffirm that her careerism will not prevent her from assuming the stereotyped sex object role assigned women in male supremacist society.

Often men who claim to support women's liberation do so because they believe they will benefit by no longer having to assume specific, rigid sex roles they find negative or restrictive. The role they are most willing and eager to change is that of economic provider. Commercials like the one described above assure men that women can be breadwinners or even "the" breadwinner, but still allow men to dominate them. Carol Hanisch's essay "Men's Liberation" (1975) explores the attempt by these men to exploit women's issues to their own advantage, particularly those issues related to work:

> Another major issue is the attempt by men to drop out of the work force and put their women to work supporting them. Men don't like their jobs, don't like the rat race, and don't like having a boss. That's what all the whining about being a "success symbol" or "success object" is really all about. Well, women don't like those things either, especially since they get paid 40% less than men for working, generally have more boring jobs, and rarely are even allowed to be "successful." But for women working is usually the only way to achieve some equality and power in the family, in their relationship with men, some independence. A man can quit work and pretty much still remain the master of the household, gaining for himself a lot of free time since the work he does doesn't come close to what his wife or lover does. In most cases, she's still doing more than her share of the house-

work in addition to wife work and her job. Instead of fighting to make his job better, to end the rat race, and to get rid of bosses, he sends his woman to work—not much different from the old practice of buying a substitute for the draft, or even pimping. And all in the name of breaking down "role stereotypes" or some such nonsense.

Such a "men's liberation movement" could only be formed in reaction to women's liberation in an attempt to make feminist movement serve the opportunistic interests of individual men. These men identified themselves as victims of sexism, working to liberate men. They identified rigid sex roles as the primary source of their victimization and though they wanted to change the notion of masculinity, they were not particularly concerned with their sexist exploitation and oppression of women. Narcissism and general self-pity characterized men's liberation groups. Kanisch concludes her essay with the statement:

Women don't want to pretend to be weak and passive. And we don't want phony, weak, passive acting men any more than we want phony supermen full of bravado and little else. What women want is for men to be honest. Women want men to be bold—boldly honest, aggressive in their human pursuits. Boldly passionate, sexual and sensual. And women want this for themselves. It's time men became boldly radical. Daring to go to the root of the own exploitation and seeing that it is not women or "sex roles" or "society" causing their unhappiness, but capitalists and capitalism. It's time men dare to name and fight these, their real exploiters.

Men who have dared to be honest about sexism and sexist oppression, who have chosen to assume responsibility for opposing and resisting it, often find themselves isolated. Their politics are disdained by antifeminist men and women, and are often ignored by women active in feminist movement. Writing about his efforts to publicly support feminism in a local newspaper in Santa Cruz, Morris Conerly explains:

Talking with a group of men, the subject of Women's Liberation inevitably comes up. A few laughs, snickers, angry mutterings, and denunci-

ations follow. There is a group consensus that men are in an embattled position and must close ranks against the assaults of misguided females. Without fail, someone will solicit me for my view, which is that I am 100% for Women's Liberation. That throws them for a loop and they start staring at me as if my eyebrows were crawling with lice.

They're thinking, "What kind of man is he?" I am a black man who understands that women are not my enemy. If I were a white man with a position of power; one could understand the reason for defending the status quo. Even then, the defense of a morally bankrupt doctrine that exploits and oppresses others would be inexcusable.

Conerly stresses that it was not easy for him to publicly support feminist movement, that it took time:

. . . Why did it take me some time? Because I was scared of the negative reaction I knew would come my way by supporting Women's Liberation. In my mind I could hear it from the brothers and sisters. "What kind of man are you?" "Who's wearing the pants?" "Why are you in that white shit?" And on and on. Sure enough, the attacks came as I had foreseen but by that time my belief was firm enough to withstand public scorn.

With growth there is pain . . . and that truism certainly applied in my case.

Men who actively struggle against sexism have a place in feminist movement. They are our comrades. Feminists have recognized and supported the work of men who take responsibility for sexist oppression—men's work with batterers, for example. Those women's liberationists who see no value in this participation must re-think and re-examine the process by which revolutionary struggle is advanced. Individual men tend to become involved in feminist movement because of the pain generated in relationships with women. Usually a woman friend or companion has called attention to their support of male supremacy. Jon Snodgrass introduces the book he edited, *For Men Against Sexism: A Book of Readings* (1977), by telling readers:

While there were aspects of women's liberation which appealed to men, on the whole my reaction was typical of men. I was threatened by the movement and responded with anger and ridicule. I believed that men and women were oppressed by capital, but not that women were oppressed by men. I argued that "men are oppressed too" and that it's workers who need liberation! I was unable to recognize a hierarchy of inequality between men and women (in the working class) not to attribute it to male domination. My blindness to patriarchy, I now think, was a function of my male privilege. As a member of the male gender case, I either ignored or suppressed women's liberation.

My full introduction to the women's movement came through a personal relationship. . . . As our relationship developed, I began to receive repeated criticism for being sexist. At first I responded, as part of the male backlash, with anger and denial. In time, however, I began to recognize the validity of the accusation, and eventually even to acknowledge the sexism in my denial of the accusations.

Snodgrass participated in the men's consciousness-raising groups and edited the book of readings in 1977. Towards the end of the 1970s, interest in male anti-sexist groups declined. Even though more men than ever before support the idea of social equality for women, like women they do not see this support as synonymous with efforts to end sexist oppression, with feminist movement that would radically transform society. Men who advocate feminism as a movement to end sexist oppression must become more vocal and public in their opposition to sexism and sexist oppression. Until men share equal responsibility for struggling to end sexism, feminist movement will reflect the very sexist contradictions we wish to eradicate.

Separatist ideology encourages us to believe that women alone can make feminist revolution—we cannot. Since men are the primary agents maintaining and supporting sexism and sexist oppression, they can only be successfully eradicated if men are compelled to assume responsibility for transforming their consciousness and the consciousness of society as a whole. After hundreds of years of anti-racist struggle, more than ever before non-white people are currently calling attention to the primary role white people must play in anti-racist struggle. The same is true of the struggle to eradicate sexism—men have a primary role to play. This does not mean that they are better equipped to lead feminist movement; it does mean that they should share equally in resistance struggle. In particular, men have a tremendous contribution to make to feminist struggle in the area of exposing, confronting, opposing, and transforming the sexism of their male peers. When men show a willingness to assume equal responsibility in feminist struggle, performing whatever tasks are necessary, women should affirm their revolutionary work by acknowledging them as comrades in struggle.

REFERENCES

Angelou, Maya. 1983. "Interview." In *Black Women Writers at Work*, edited by Claudia Tate. New York: Continuum Publishing.

Hanisch, Carol. 1975. "Men's Liberation," Pp. 60–63 in *Feminist Revolution*. New Paltz, NY: Redstockings.

Hornacek, Paul. 1977. "Anti-Sexist Consciousness Raising Groups for Men." In *A Book of Readings for Men Against Sexism*, edited by Jon Snodgrass. Albion: Times Change Press.

Leon, Barbara. 1975. "Separate to Integrate." Pp. 139–44 in *Feminist Revolution*. New Paltz, NY: Redstockings.

McCandless, Cathy. 1979. "Some Thoughts About Racism, Classism, and Separatism." Pp. 105–15 in *Top Ranking*, edited by Joan Gibbs and Sara Bennett. New York: February Third Press.

"Redstockings Manifesto." 1970. Page 109 in *Voices from Women's Liberation*, edited by Leslie B. Tanner. New York: Signet, NAL.

Smith, Barbara. 1979. "Notes for Yet Another Paper on Black Feminism, Or Will the Real Enemy Please Stand Up." *Conditions: Five* 2 (2): 123–27.

Snodgrass, Jon (ed.). 1977. *A Book of Readings for Men Against Sexism*. Albion: Times Change Press.

STATEMENT OF PRINCIPLES

THE NATIONAL ORGANIZATION FOR MEN AGAINST SEXISM

The National Organization For Men Against Sexism is an activist organization of men and women supporting positive changes for men. NOMAS advocates a perspective that is pro-feminist, gay-affirmative, and committed to justice on a broad range of social issues including race, class, age, religion, and physical abilities. We affirm that working to make this nation's ideals of equality substantive is the finest expression of what it means to be men.

We believe that the new opportunities becoming available to women and men will be beneficial to both. Men can live as happier and more fulfilled human beings by challenging the old-fashioned rules of masculinity that embody the assumption of male superiority.

Traditional masculinity includes many positive characteristics in which we take pride and find strength, but it also contains qualities that have limited and harmed us. We are deeply supportive of men who are struggling with the issues of traditional masculinity. As an organization for changing men, we care about men and are especially concerned with men's problems, as well as the difficult issues in most men's lives.

As an organization for changing men, we strongly support the continuing struggle of women for full equality. We applaud and support the insights and positive social changes that feminism has stimulated for both women and men. We oppose such injustices to women as economic and legal discrimination, rape, domestic violence, sexual harassment, and many others. Women and men can and do work together as allies to change the injustices that have so often made them see one another as enemies.

One of the strongest and deepest anxieties of most American men is their fear of homosexuality. This homophobia contributes directly to the many injustices experienced by gay, lesbian, and bisexual persons, and is a debilitating restriction for heterosexual men. We call for an end to all forms of discrimination based on sexual-affectional orientation, and for the creation of a gay-affirmative society.

We also acknowledge that many people are oppressed today because of their race, class, age, religion, and physical condition. We believe that such injustices are vitally connected to sexism, with its fundamental premise of unequal distribution of power.

Our goal is to change not just ourselves and other men, but also the institutions that create inequality. We welcome any person who agrees in substance with these principles to membership in the National Organization For Men Against Sexism.

CONTRIBUTORS

Tomás Almaguer is Associate Professor of American Studies at the University of California, Santa Cruz, and Associate Professor of Sociology and American Culture at the University of Michigan, Ann Arbor. His book, *Racial Fault Lines: The Historical Origins of White Supremacy*, will be published by University of California Press this fall.

Maxine Baca Zinn teaches in the Department of Sociology at Michigan State University. She has written widely in the area of family relations, Chicano studies, and gender studies, including (most recently) *Women of Color in U.S. Society* (with Bonnie Thorton Dill), *Diversity in Families* (with Stanley Eitzen, 1990), and *The Reshaping of America* (1989).

Tim Beneke is a freelance writer and editor living in the San Francisco Bay Area. He is the author of *Men on Rape* and the forthcoming *Sexism and the Pains of Manhood*.

Jessie Bernard, a Professor Emerita at Pennsylvania State University, has written and lectured widely on gender and family issues. Her influential writings include *The Female World*.

Peter R. Breggin is Executive Director of the Center for the Study of Psychiatry in Bethesda, Maryland, and a Contributing Editor to *Tikkun*.

Harry Brod is Associate Professor of Philosophy at University of Delaware. He is the editor of *The Making of Masculinities* (1987) and *A Mensch Among Men* (1989). He was the founding editor of *Men's Studies Review* and the Founding Chair of the National Men's Studies Association.

James Chin is a clinical psychologist at the Holliswood Hospital, a clinical research consultant to the New York State Office of Mental Health, and in private practice. His areas of specialization include the prevention and treatment of addictive disorders, behavioral medicine, and health psychology.

Susan D. Cochran currently teaches at California State University, Northridge.

Carol Cohn teaches at Bowdoin College. She is currently completing a book entitled *Deconstructing National Security Discourse and Reconstructing Security*.

David L. Collinson is in the Department of Management Sciences at the University of Manchester. His research focuses on the construction of masculinity in workplaces.

Scott Coltrane is Associate Professor of Sociology at the University of California, Riverside. His research on families, gender, and the changing role of fathers has appeared in various scholarly journals. He is co-author (with Randall Collins) of *Sociology of Mar-*

riage and the Family (1992), and the author of *Family Man: Fatherhood, Housework, and Gender Equity* (forthcoming).

Bob Connell is Professor of Sociology at University of California, Santa Cruz. His most recent works include *Gender and Power* (1987) and *Staking a Claim: Feminism, Bureaucracy and the State* (with Suzanne Franzway and Dianne Court).

Edward Donnerstein is Professor and Chair of the Communication Studies Program at University of California, Santa Barbara. His major research interest is in mass media violence and he has published widely in this area. His books include *The Question of Pornography* (with Dan Linz and Steve Penrod) and *Pornography and Sexual Aggression*.

Greg Drasler is an artist in New York City.

Wayne Ewing is Assistant Dean, Loretto Heights College, Denver, Colorado. He is the author of *Violence Works/Stop Violence*.

Jules Feiffer is a syndicated cartoonist and a regular contributor to *The Village Voice*.

Thomas Ficarrotto is a research associate with the Department of Psychiatry at the Langley Porter Psychiatric Institute at University of California, San Francisco. His areas of specialization include social psychology and health psychology. He writes on cross-cultural aspects of homophobia and sex differences in mortality and health behaviors.

Ben Fong-Torres is a journalist in the San Francisco Bay Area. His most recent book is *The Rice Room: Growing Up Chinese-American*.

Jeffrey Fracher is a psychotherapist who practices in Metuchen, New Jersey, specializing in the treatment of sexual disorders. He is adjunct Assistant Professor of Psychology at Rutgers University.

Clyde W. Franklin II is Professor of Sociology at the Ohio State University. His research focuses largely on black masculinity. His numerous publications include *The Changing Definition of Masculinity* and *Men and Society*.

Thomas J. Gerschick is Assistant Professor of Sociology at Illinois State University. His research focuses on identity, and marginalized and alternative masculinities.

Barry Glassner is Chairman of the Department of Sociology at the University of Southern California. He is the author of *Bodies* and *Career Crash*, among other books.

Jeffrey P. Hantover is a freelance writer and consultant living in New York City. He has published articles on photography, film, and social issues. He is presently working on a novel.

James Harrison is a clinical psychologist and codirector of Harrison Associates, a holistic psychological consultation center in New York City. He writes and produces videos on psychological issues, and produced a documentary about the psychologist Evelyn Hooker, which was nominated for an Academy Award.

Gregory M. Herek is Research Assistant Professor of Psychology at University of California, Davis. He has published widely on violence against lesbians and gay men.

Arlie Hochschild is Professor of Sociology at University of California, Berkeley. Her books include *The Managed Heart: Commercialization and Human Feeling* and *The Second Shift: Working Parents and the Revolution at Home*.

Jane C. Hood is Associate Professor of Sociology at the University of New Mexico. She has published widely on issues about violence, the family, and gender. She is Editor of *Men, Work, and Family* (1994).

bell hooks is a writer and lecturer who speaks on issues of race, class, and gender. She teaches at CUNY Graduate Center. Her books include *Ain't I a Woman*, *Feminist Theory*, and *Talking Back*. Her column, "Sisters of the Yam," appears monthly in *Z* magazine.

Michael Kaufman is the author or editor of several books on men and masculinity including *Cracking the Armor: Power, Pain, and the Lives of Men* (1993), *Theorizing Masculinities* (1994), and *Beyond Patriarchy* (1987). He lives in Toronto, Canada, and is active in efforts to end violence against women and in anti-sexist education for young men.

Michael S. Kimmel is Associate Professor of Sociology at State University of New York at Stony Brook. He is Editor of *Changing Men* (1987), *Men Confront Pornography* (1990), and (with Tom Mosmiller) *Against the Tide: Profeminist Men in the United States, 1776–1990* (1992). His new book, *Manhood: The American Quest*, will be published next year. He is the editor of *masculinities*, a scholarly journal, and also of a book series on men and masculinity at University of California Press. As National Spokesperson for the National Organization for Men Against Sexism (NOMAS), he lectures widely on gender issues.

Gary Kinsman is an activist in the gay liberation and socialist movements in Toronto and is a member of the collective that publishes *Rites*, a magazine for lesbian and gay liberation. He is the author of *The Regulation of Desire*.

Seymour Kleinberg is the author of *Alienated Affections: Being Gay in America* and teaches at the Brooklyn Center of Long Island University.

Barbara Kruger is a graphic artist in New York City.

Ralph LaRossa is Associate Professor of Sociology at Georgia State University. He has published widely on the topics of men, parenting, and families.

Gregory K. Lehne is Assistant Professor of Medical Psychology in the Department of Psychiatry and Behavioral Sciences at the Johns Hopkins School of Medicine.

Martin P. Levine was Associate Professor of Sociology at Florida Atlantic University and a Research Associate at Memorial Sloan Kettering Cancer Research Center. He published extensively on the sociology of AIDS, sexuality, and homosexuality. He died of AIDS in April, 1993.

Daniel Linz does research on the effects on males of exposure to various forms of media violence against women. He teaches in the Department of Psychology at University of California, Los Angeles Center for the Study of Women.

Peter Lyman is University Dean of Libraries at the University of Southern California. He is currently working on a study of how technical knowledge and hardware are "gendered," that is, founded in a masculine epistemology.

Jack M. is the pseudonym of a writer living in New York City.

Richard Majors is Assistant Professor of Psychology at the University of Wisconsin, Eau Claire. He is the cofounder and chairman of the National Council of African American Men. He is the coauthor of *Cool Pose: The Dilemma of Black Manhood* (1991) and *The American Black Male* (1993).

Manning Marable is Professor and Director of the Center for African American Studies at Columbia University.

Vickie M. Mays currently teaches at University of California, Los Angeles.

John Lewis McAdoo is Associate Professor of Social Work and Family Studies at Michigan State University.

Julia B. McAdoo is affiliated with the Department of Psychology at the University of Michigan.

Michael A. Messner is Associate Professor in the Department of Sociology and the Program for the Study of Women and Men in Society at the University of Southern California. He is co-editor (with Don Sabo) of *Sport, Men, and the Gender Order* (Human Kinetics, 1990), and the author of *Power at Play: Sports and the Problem of Masculinity* (Beacon, 1992), and (with Don Sabo) *Sex, Violence and Power in Sports: Rethinking Masculinity* (Crossing, 1994).

Adam Stephen Miller is a master's degree student in journalism at University of Michigan and an organizer of an Internet disability support group.

Brian Miller is a psychotherapist in West Hollywood, California. He writes a popular advice column for the gay community called "Out for Good." Besides gay husbands and fathers, he has researched victims of anti-gay violence.

Peter M. Nardi is Professor of Sociology at Pitzer College. He has published articles on AIDS, anti-gay crimes and violence, magic and magicians, and alcoholism and families. His books include *Men's Friendships* (1993) and *Growing Up Before Stonewall* (1994), with David Sanders and Judd Marmor. He has served as co-president of the Los Angeles chapter of the Gay and Lesbian Alliance Against Defamation.

Timothy Nonn is completing his Ph.D. at the Graduate Theological Union in Berkeley writing a dissertation on faith and masculinity among poor men. He has a background in community organizing among rural and urban poor and refugees. He has published several articles on religion, gender, and poverty.

Chris O'Sullivan is a social psychologist who has taught at Bucknell University. She is currently completing a book about fraternity culture.

Manuel Peña is Professor of Humanities at California State University, Fresno. He is an anthropologist with specializations in folklore and ethnomusicology. His research emphasizes class, gender, and ethnic aspects of culture and social organization.

Joseph H. Pleck is a Research Associate at the Wellesley College Center for Research on Women. He is the author of numerous articles and books about men and masculinity, including *The Myth of Masculinity* (1981), and *Working Wives/Working Husbands* (1985).

Brian Pronger is in the School of Physical and Health Education at the University of Toronto. He is the author of *The Arena of Masculinity: Sports, Homosexuality, and the Meaning of Sex* (1990).

Ebet Roberts is a photographer in New York City.

M. Rochlin is the creator of "The Heterosexual Questionnaire."

Richard Rodriguez is a well-known journalist and writer, whose books include *The Hunger of Memory*. He lives in San Francisco.

Lillian B. Rubin is a research associate at the Institute for the Study of Social Change at University of California, Berkeley, and a psychotherapist in private practice. Her books include *Intimate Strangers, Just Friends, Erotic Wars, Worlds of Pain*, and, most recently, *Families on the Fault Line*.

Don Sabo is Professor of Social Sciences at D'Youville College, Buffalo, New York. He writes and speaks widely about gender relations, particularly in relation to sport and health. He has, with Michael Messner, co-edited *Sport, Men and the Gender Order* and co-authored *Sex, Violence and Power in Sports: Rethinking Masculinity*.

Jack W. Sattel is in the Department of Sociology at Normandale Community College in South Bloomington, Minnesota. He was among the first researchers to investigate male inexpressivity.

Michael Schwalbe is Associate Professor of Sociology at North Carolina State University. He teaches courses in social theory, social psychology, and inequality, and is the author of *Unlocking the Iron Cage: Understanding the Mythopoetic Men's Movement* (Oxford University Press, 1995).

Martin Simmons was born and raised in Harlem, and he continues to reside in New York. He is a screenwriter, author, teacher, lecturer, and television producer. He is a former contributing editor to *Essence* magazine. His forthcoming novel is entitled *Blood at the Root*. He is a former member of the Harlem Writer's Guild and a founding member of New Renaissance Writers.

Sage Sohier has received photography fellowships from the Guggenheim Foundation and from the National Endowment for the Arts. Her photographs are in the collection of the Museum of Modern Art, New York.

Robert Staples is in the Department of Sociology at the University of California, San Francisco. He has written widely on black families and gender issues, including his book, *Black Masculinity*.

Gloria Steinem is a founding editor of *Ms.*, and the author of *Outrageous Acts and Everyday Rebellions* and *Revolution from Within*.

Barrie Thorne is Streisand Professor of Intimacy and Sexuality in the Program for the Study of Women and Men in Society and the Department of Sociology at the University of Southern California. She has written widely on feminist theory and gender issues, especially with respect to children. Her works include *Rethinking the Family* (with Marilyn Yalom) and *Gender Play: Girls and Boys in School*.

Christine L. Williams is Associate Professor of Sociology at University of Texas. Her books include *Gender Differences at Work* and *"Doing Women's Work": Men in Non-Traditional Occupations*. Her new book, *Still a Man's World*, is forthcoming.